SANPAKU™

Published by
ARCHAIA™

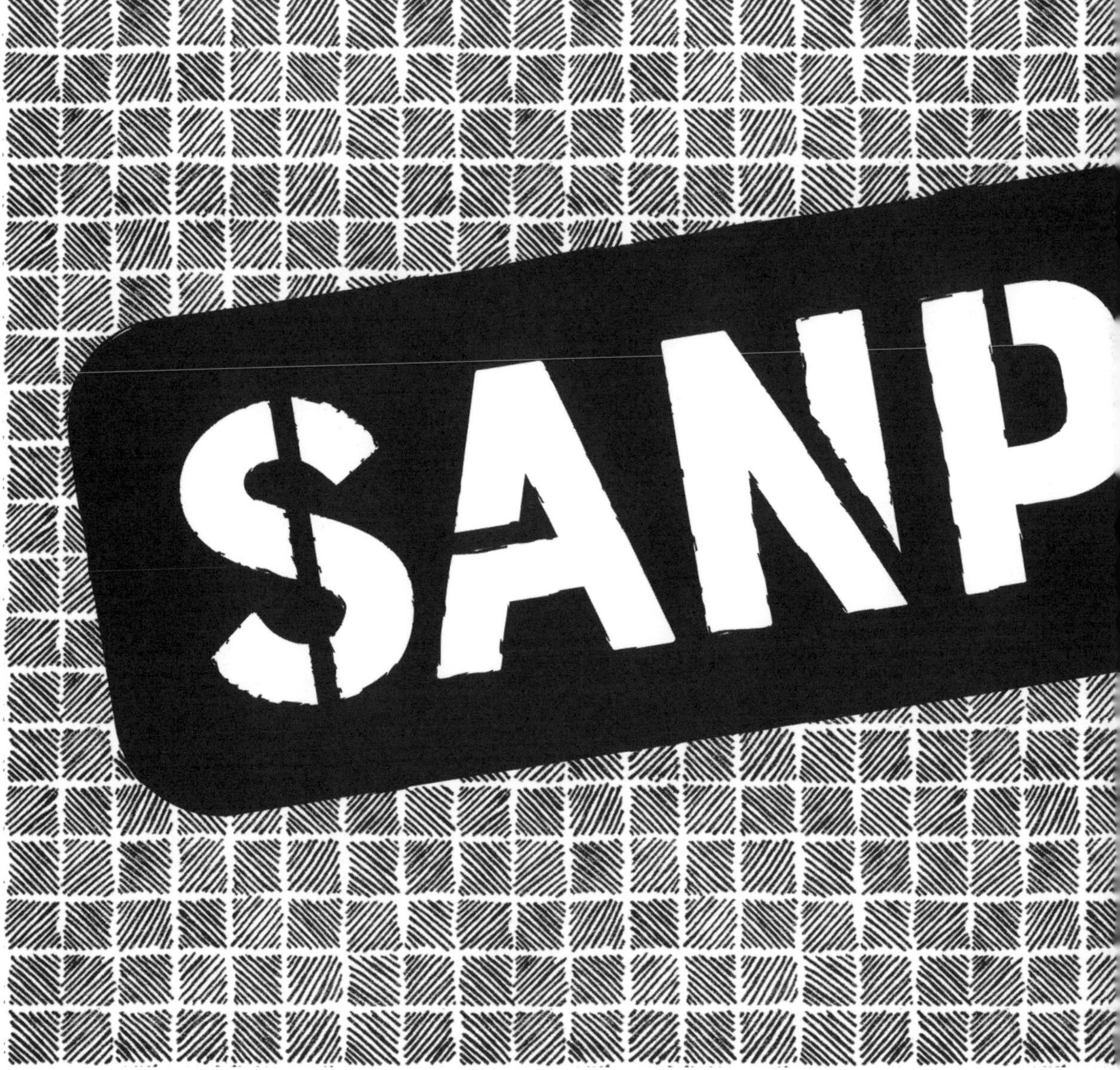
SAN

AKU™

KATE GAVINO

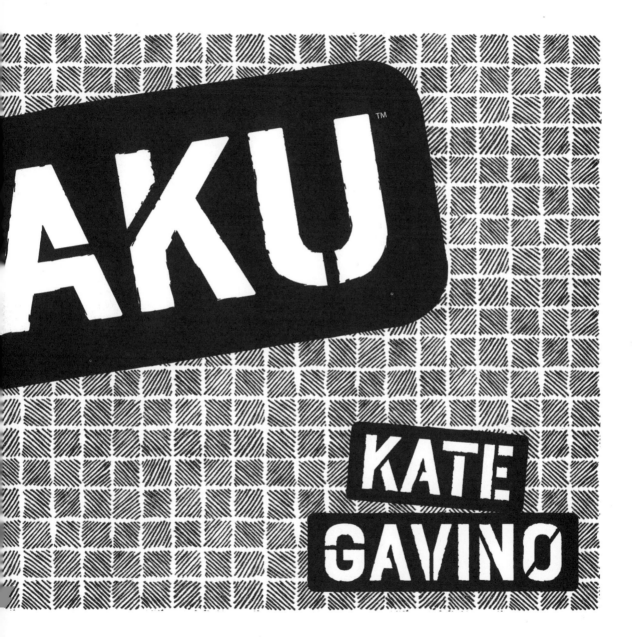

Designer **Jillian Crab**
Logo Designer **Michelle Ankley**
Assistant Editor **Sophie Philips-Roberts**
Editor **Sierra Hahn**

ROSS RICHIE CEO & Founder
MATT GAGNON Editor-in-Chief
FILIP SABLIK President of Publishing & Marketing
STEPHEN CHRISTY President of Development
LANCE KREITER VP of Licensing & Merchandising
PHIL BARBARO VP of Finance
ARUNE SINGH VP of Marketing
BRYCE CARLSON Managing Editor
SCOTT NEWMAN Production Design Manager
KATE HENNING Operations Manager
SPENCER SIMPSON Sales Manager
SIERRA HAHN Senior Editor
DAFNA PLEBAN Editor, Talent Development
SHANNON WATTERS Editor
ERIC HARBURN Editor
WHITNEY LEOPARD Editor
CAMERON CHITTOCK Editor
CHRIS ROSA Associate Editor
MATTHEW LEVINE Associate Editor
SOPHIE PHILIPS-ROBERTS Assistant Editor

GAVIN GRONENTHAL Assistant Editor
MICHAEL MOCCIO Assistant Editor
AMANDA LaFRANCO Executive Assistant
KATALINA HOLLAND Editorial Administrative Assistant
JILLIAN CRAB Design Coordinator
MICHELLE ANKLEY Design Coordinator
KARA LEOPARD Production Designer
MARIE KRUPINA Production Designer
GRACE PARK Production Design Assistant
CHELSEA ROBERTS Production Design Assistant
ELIZABETH LOUGHRIDGE Accounting Coordinator
STEPHANIE HOCUTT Social Media Coordinator
JOSÉ MEZA Event Coordinator
HOLLY AITCHISON Operations Coordinator
MEGAN CHRISTOPHER Operations Assistant
RODRIGO HERNANDEZ Mailroom Assistant
MORGAN PERRY Direct Market Representative
CAT O'GRADY Marketing Assistant
CORNELIA TZANA Publicity Assistant
LIZ ALMENDAREZ Accounting Administrative Assistant

SANPAKU, August 2018. Published by Archaia, a division of Boom Entertainment, Inc. Sanpaku is ™ & © 2018 Kathleen Gavino. All rights reserved. Archaia™ and the Archaia logo are trademarks of Boom Entertainment, Inc., registered in various countries and categories. All characters, events, and institutions depicted herein are fictional. Any similarity between any of the names, characters, persons, events, and/or institutions in this publication to actual names, characters, and persons, whether living or dead, events, and/or institutions is unintended and purely coincidental.

BOOM! Studios, 5670 Wilshire Boulevard, Suite 400, Los Angeles, CA 90036-5679. Printed in China. First Printing.

ISBN: 978-1-68415-210-0, eISBN: 978-1-64144-025-7

FOR
LOLA and LOLO

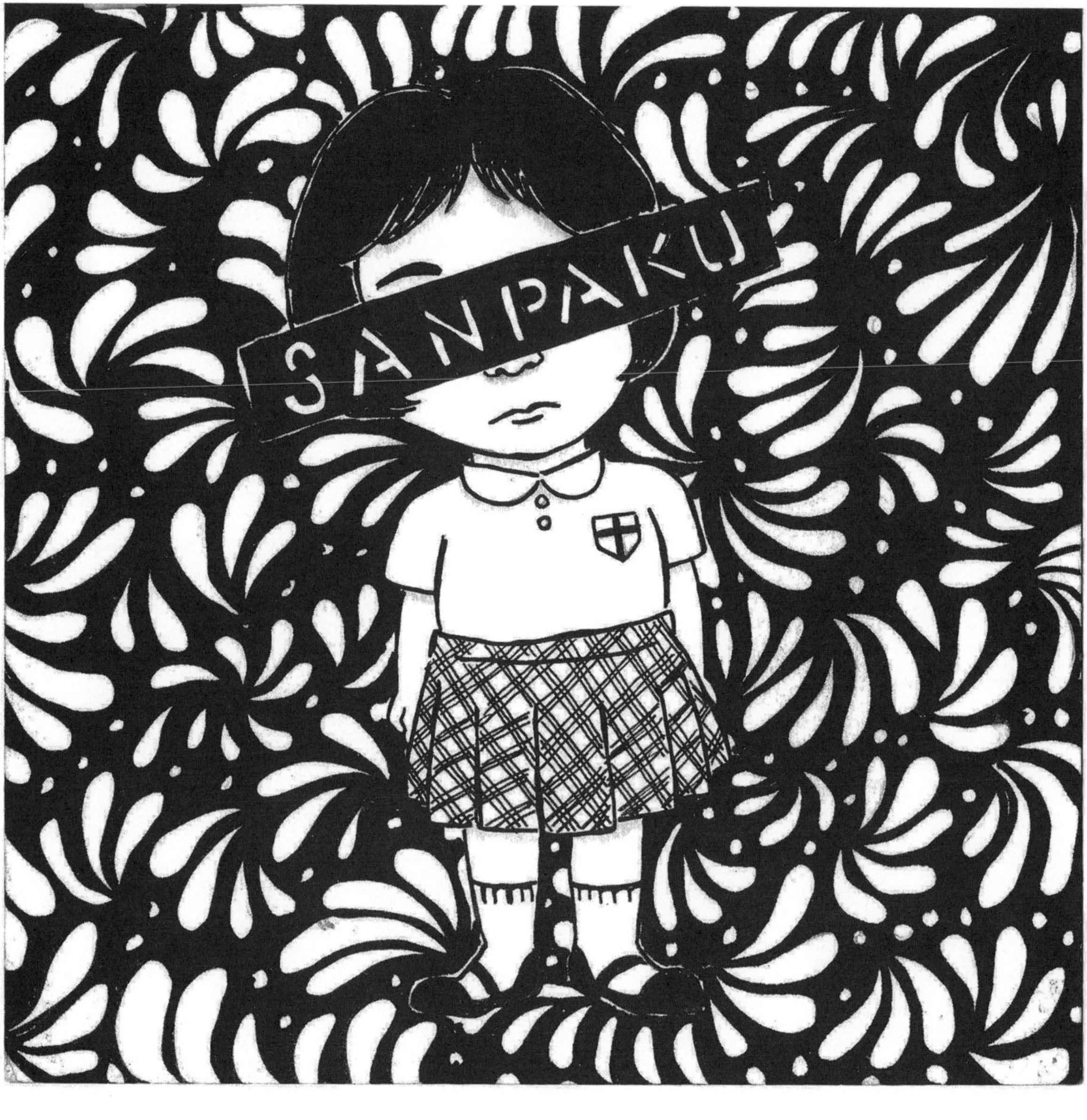
SANPAKU

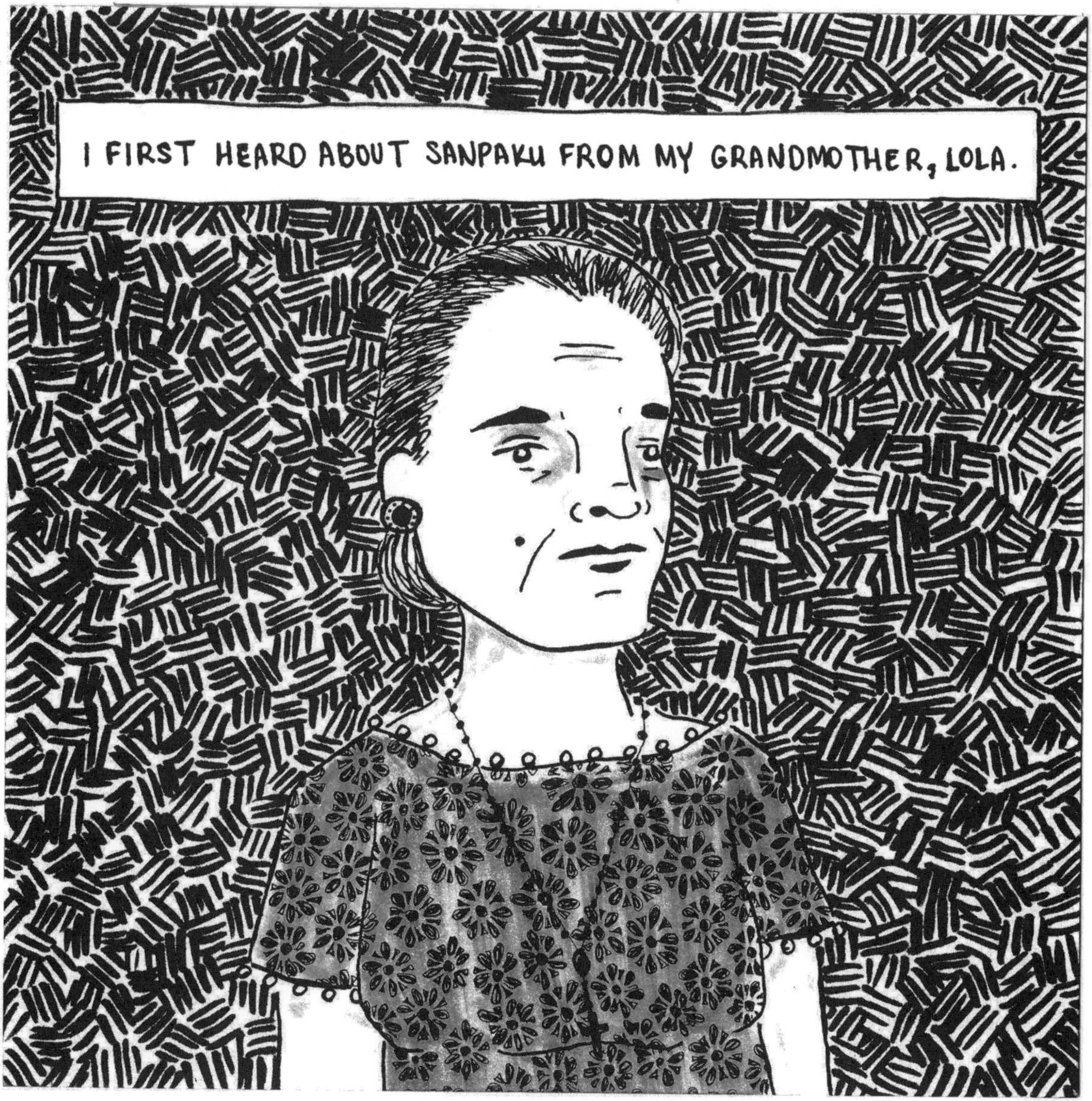
I FIRST HEARD ABOUT SANPAKU FROM MY GRANDMOTHER, LOLA.

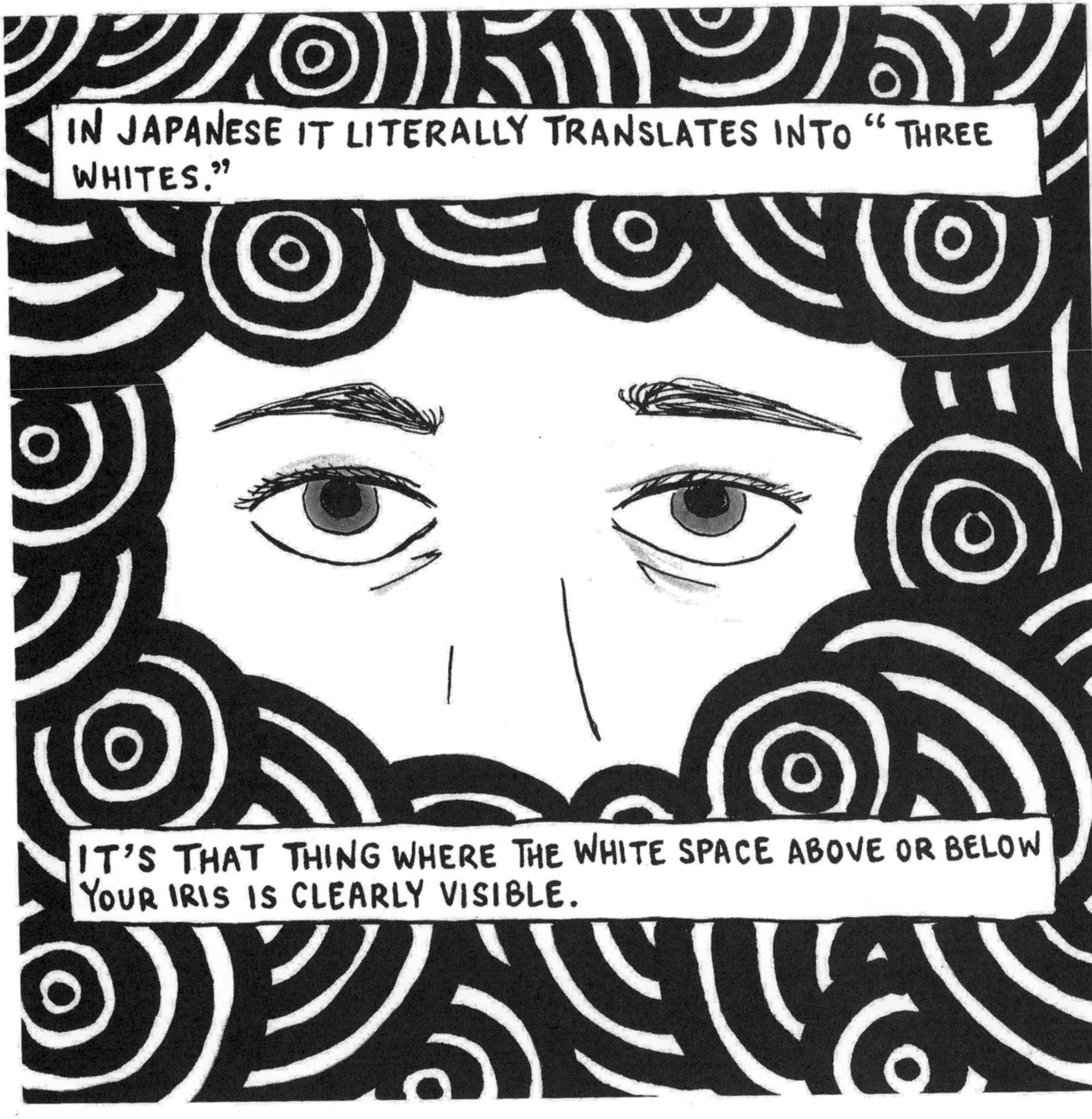
IN JAPANESE IT LITERALLY TRANSLATES INTO "THREE WHITES."
IT'S THAT THING WHERE THE WHITE SPACE ABOVE OR BELOW YOUR IRIS IS CLEARLY VISIBLE.

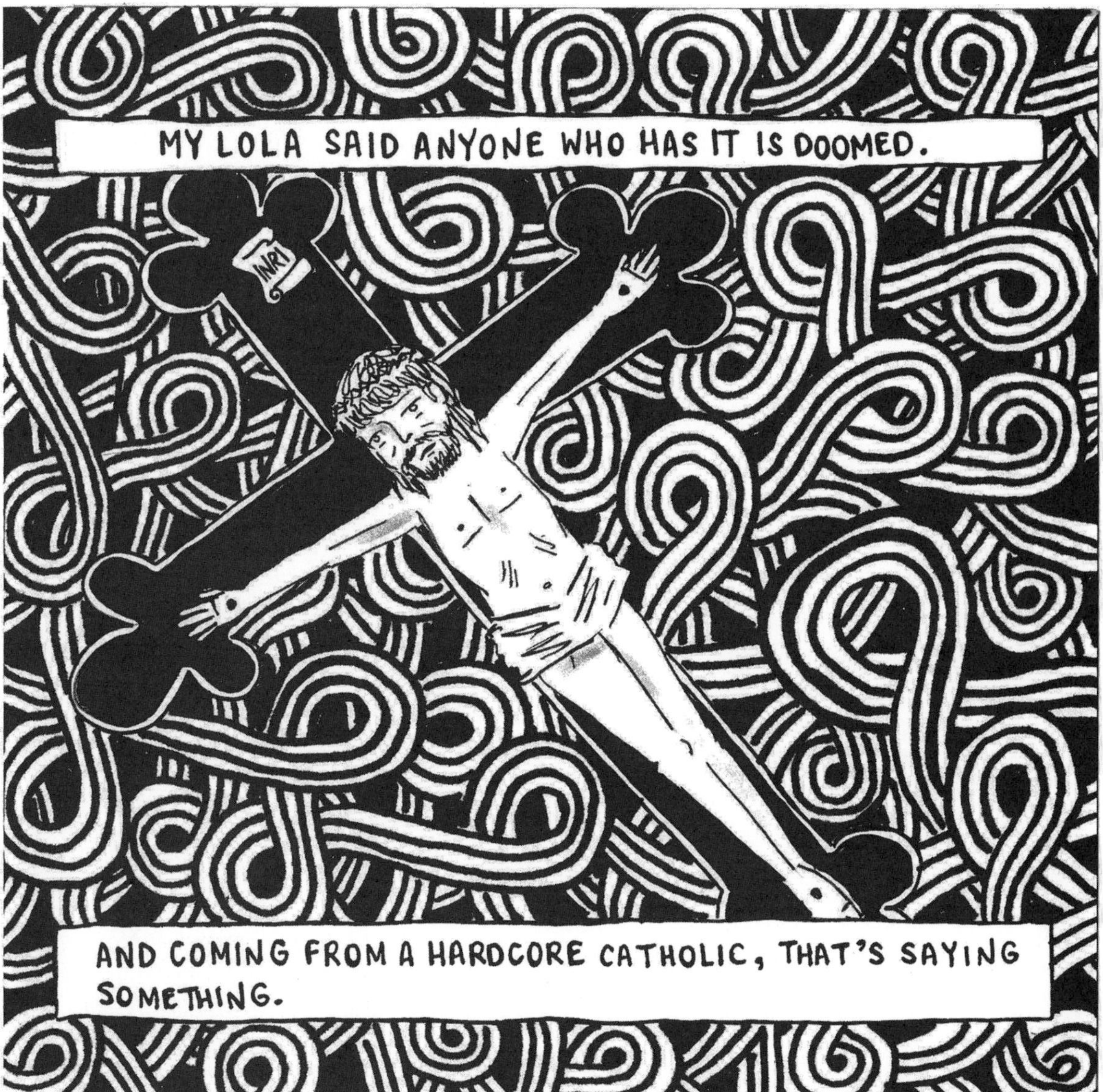
MY LOLA SAID ANYONE WHO HAS IT IS DOOMED.
INRI
AND COMING FROM A HARDCORE CATHOLIC, THAT'S SAYING SOMETHING.

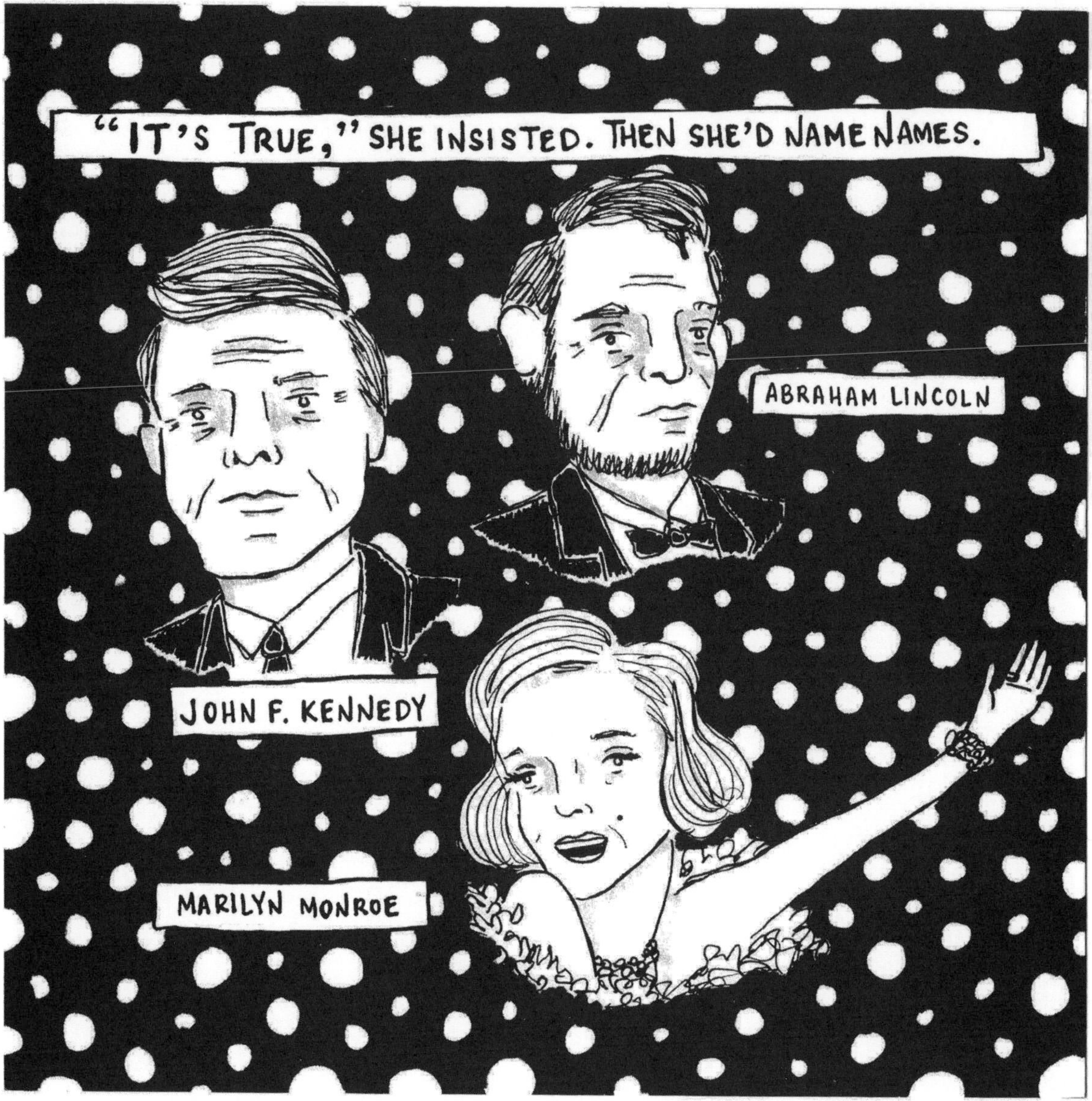
"IT'S TRUE," SHE INSISTED. THEN SHE'D NAME NAMES.
ABRAHAM LINCOLN
JOHN F. KENNEDY
MARILYN MONROE

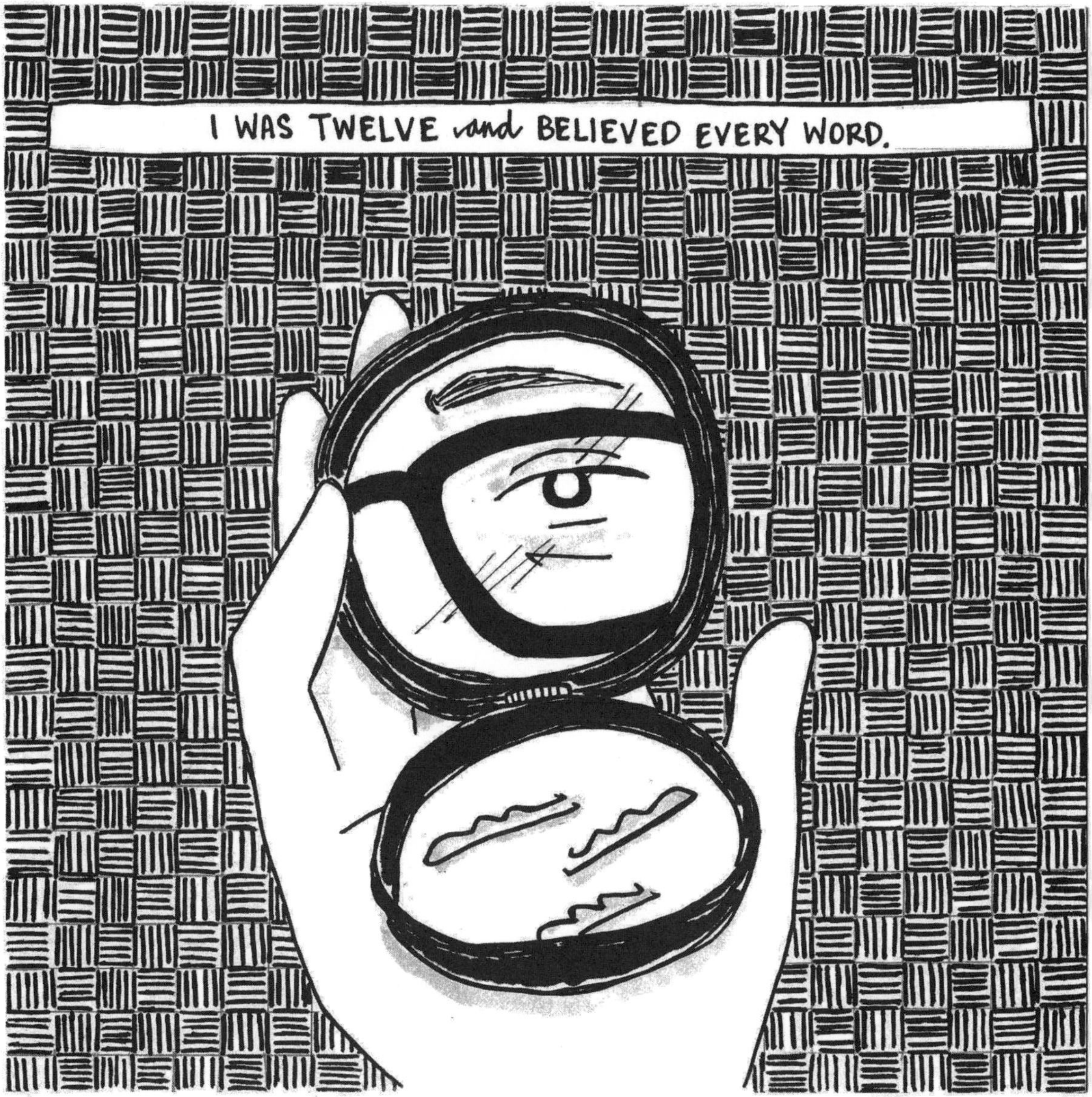
I WAS TWELVE and BELIEVED EVERY WORD.

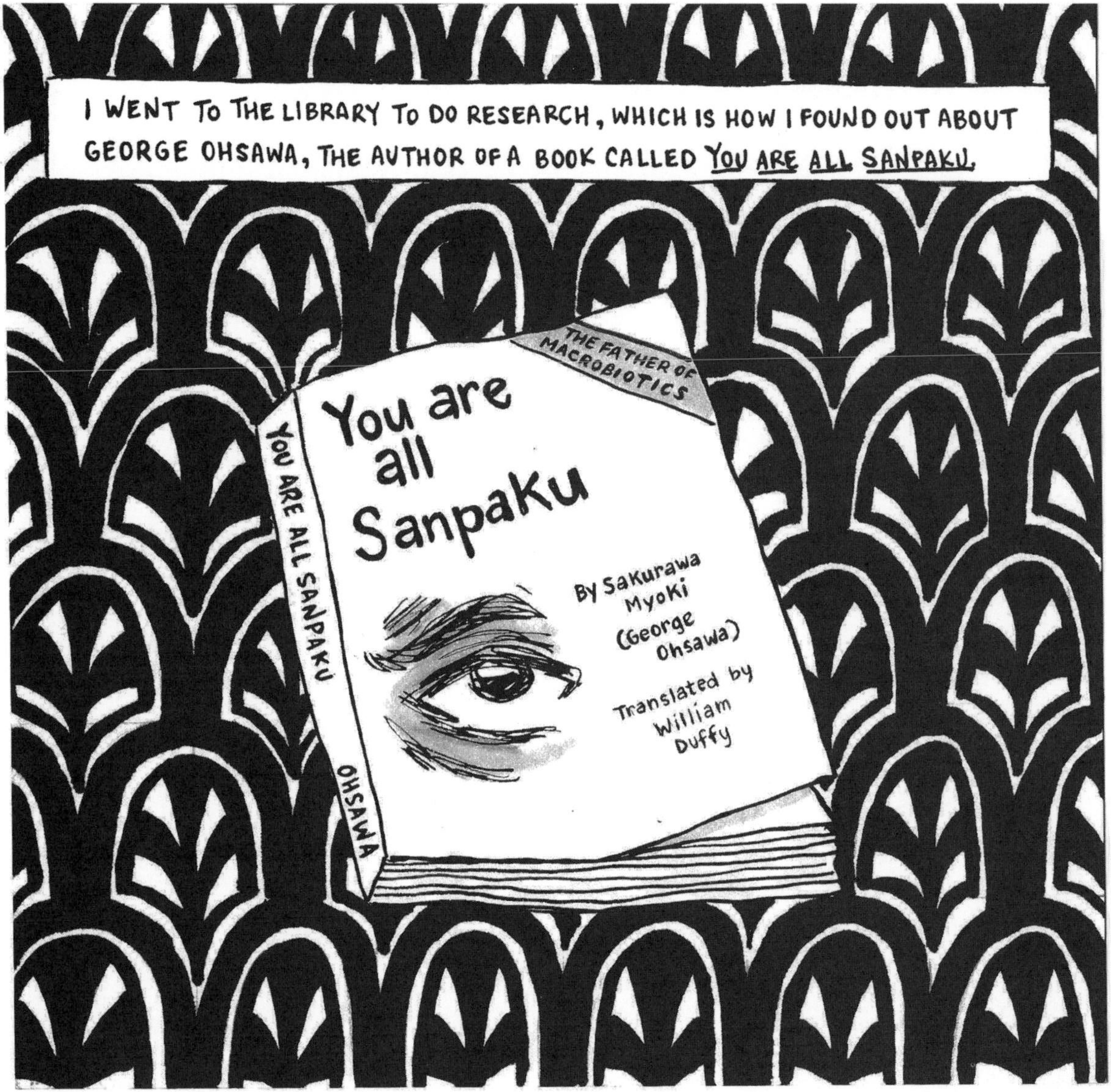
I WENT TO THE LIBRARY TO DO RESEARCH, WHICH IS HOW I FOUND OUT ABOUT GEORGE OHSAWA, THE AUTHOR OF A BOOK CALLED YOU ARE ALL SANPAKU.
THE FATHER OF MACROBIOTICS
You are all Sanpaku
YOU ARE ALL SANPAKU
OHSAWA
By Sakurawa Myoki (George Ohsawa)
Translated by William Duffy

OHSAWA MADE SANPAKU BIG, ALBEIT BRIEFLY, IN AMERICA IN THE 1970s.

FISH
OYSTERS
CLAMS
TROUT
DLE
MP
SNF
LOBST

HE BLAMED SANPAKU FOR THE WEST'S DECLINE, CLAIMING AMERICANS WERE OUT OF TUNE WITH THEIR BODIES and THUS THE UNIVERSE.

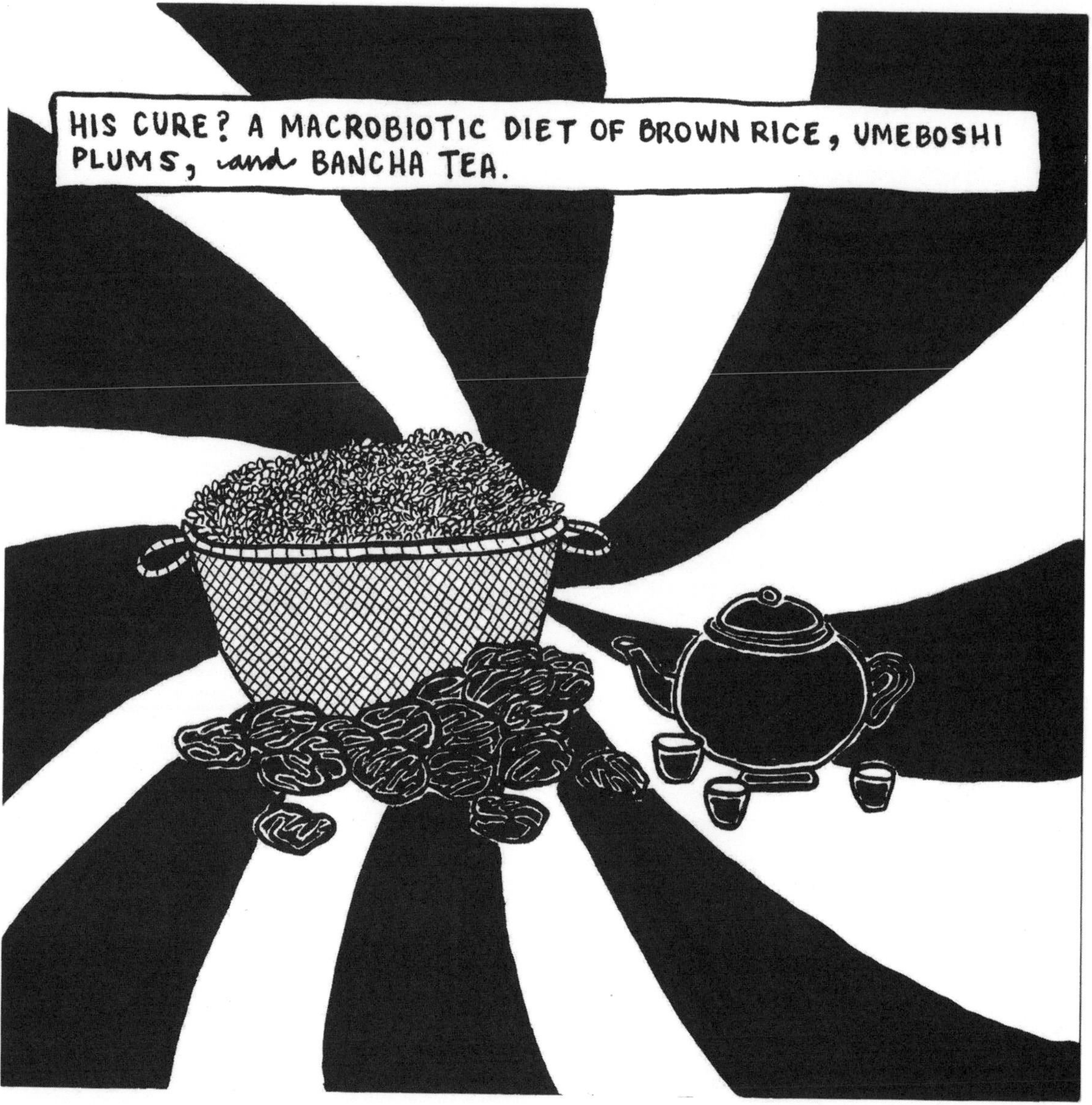
HIS CURE? A MACROBIOTIC DIET OF BROWN RICE, UMEBOSHI PLUMS, and BANCHA TEA.

OH, and YOU HAD TO CHEW YOUR FOOD AT LEAST FIFTY TIMES BEFORE SWALLOWING.
"CHEWING," GEORGE WROTE, "REMINDS ONE THAT THE TAKING IN OF NOURISHMENT IS A SACRED ACT."

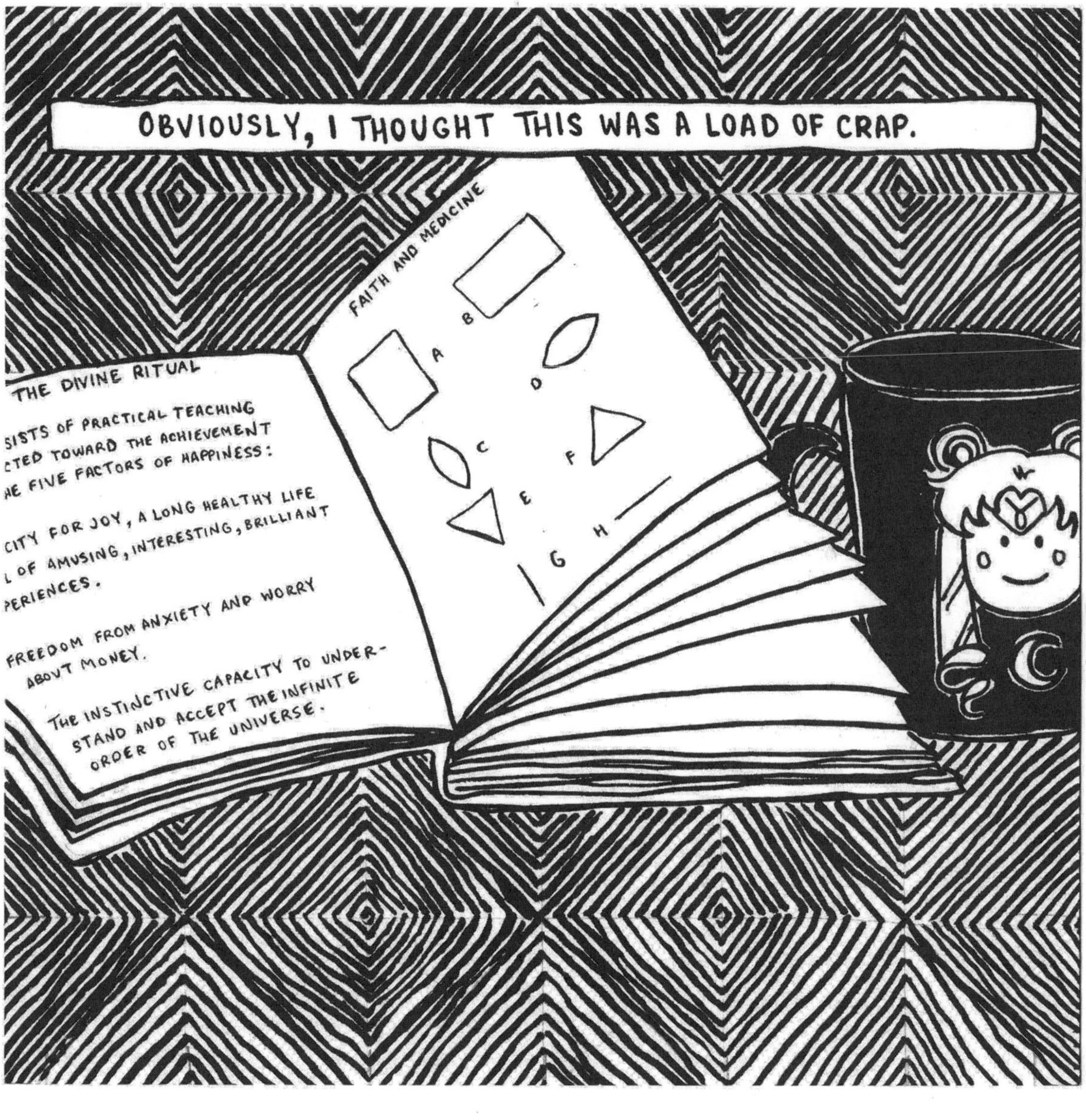
OBVIOUSLY, I THOUGHT THIS WAS A LOAD OF CRAP.
THE DIVINE RITUAL
SISTS OF PRACTICAL TEACHING
CTED TOWARD THE ACHIEVEMENT
HE FIVE FACTORS OF HAPPINESS:
CITY FOR JOY, A LONG HEALTHY LIFE
L OF AMUSING, INTERESTING, BRILLIANT
PERIENCES.
FREEDOM FROM ANXIETY AND WORRY
ABOUT MONEY.
THE INSTINCTIVE CAPACITY TO UNDER-
STAND AND ACCEPT THE INFINITE
ORDER OF THE UNIVERSE.
FAITH AND MEDICINE
A
B
C
D
E
F
G
H

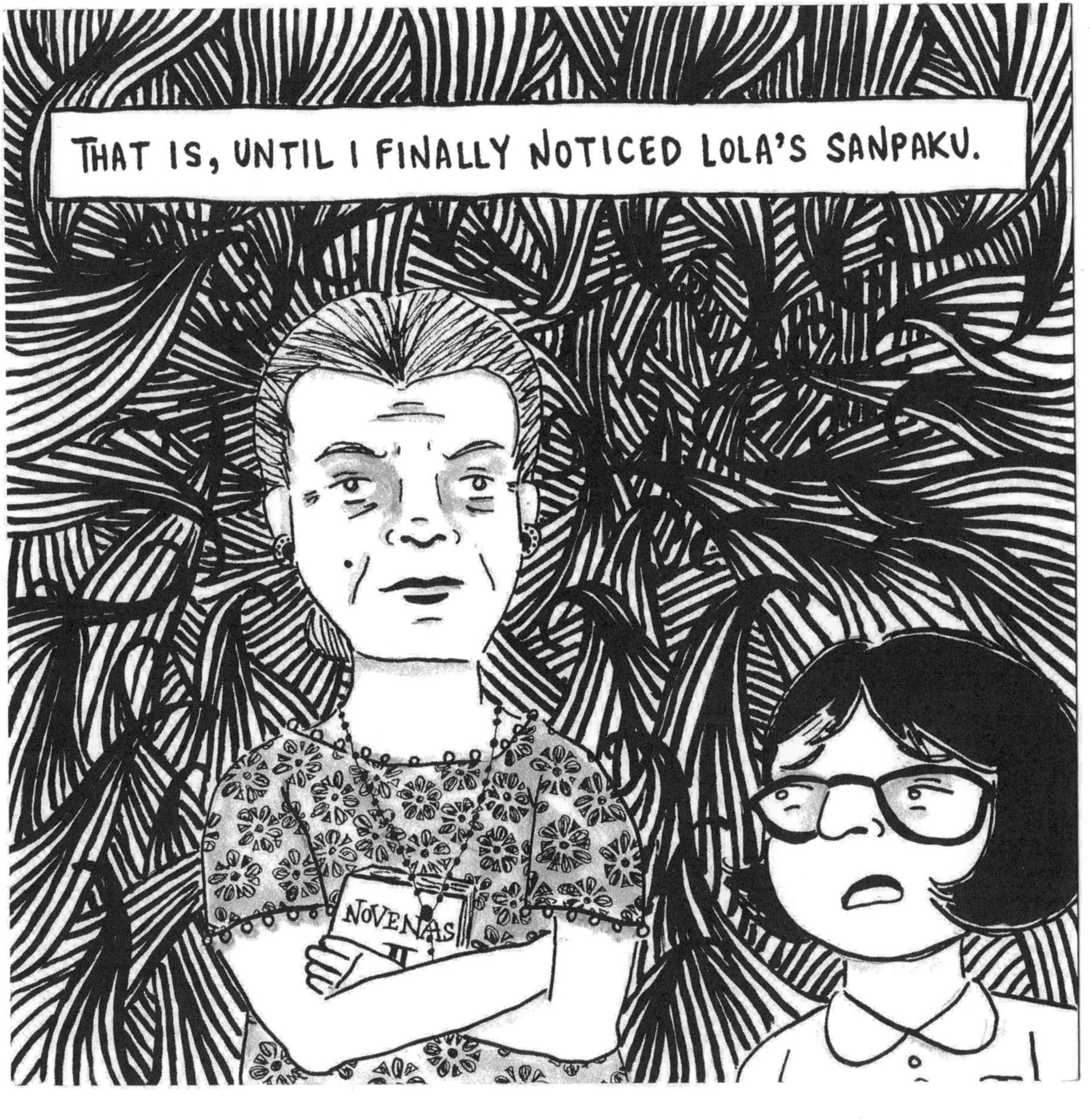
THAT IS, UNTIL I FINALLY NOTICED LOLA'S SANPAKU.
NOVENAS II

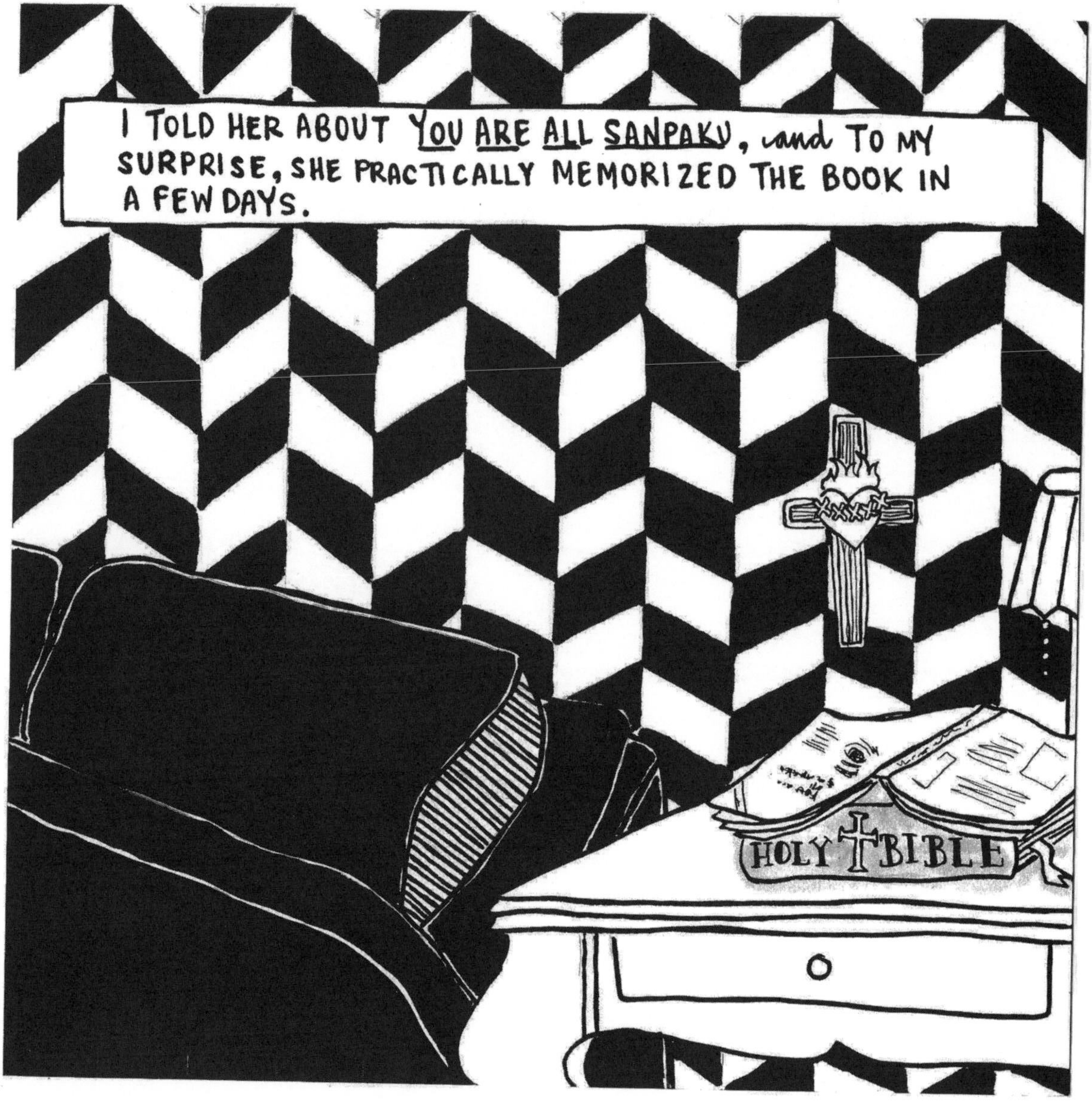
I TOLD HER ABOUT YOU ARE ALL SANPAKU, and TO MY SURPRISE, SHE PRACTICALLY MEMORIZED THE BOOK IN A FEW DAYS.
HOLY BIBLE

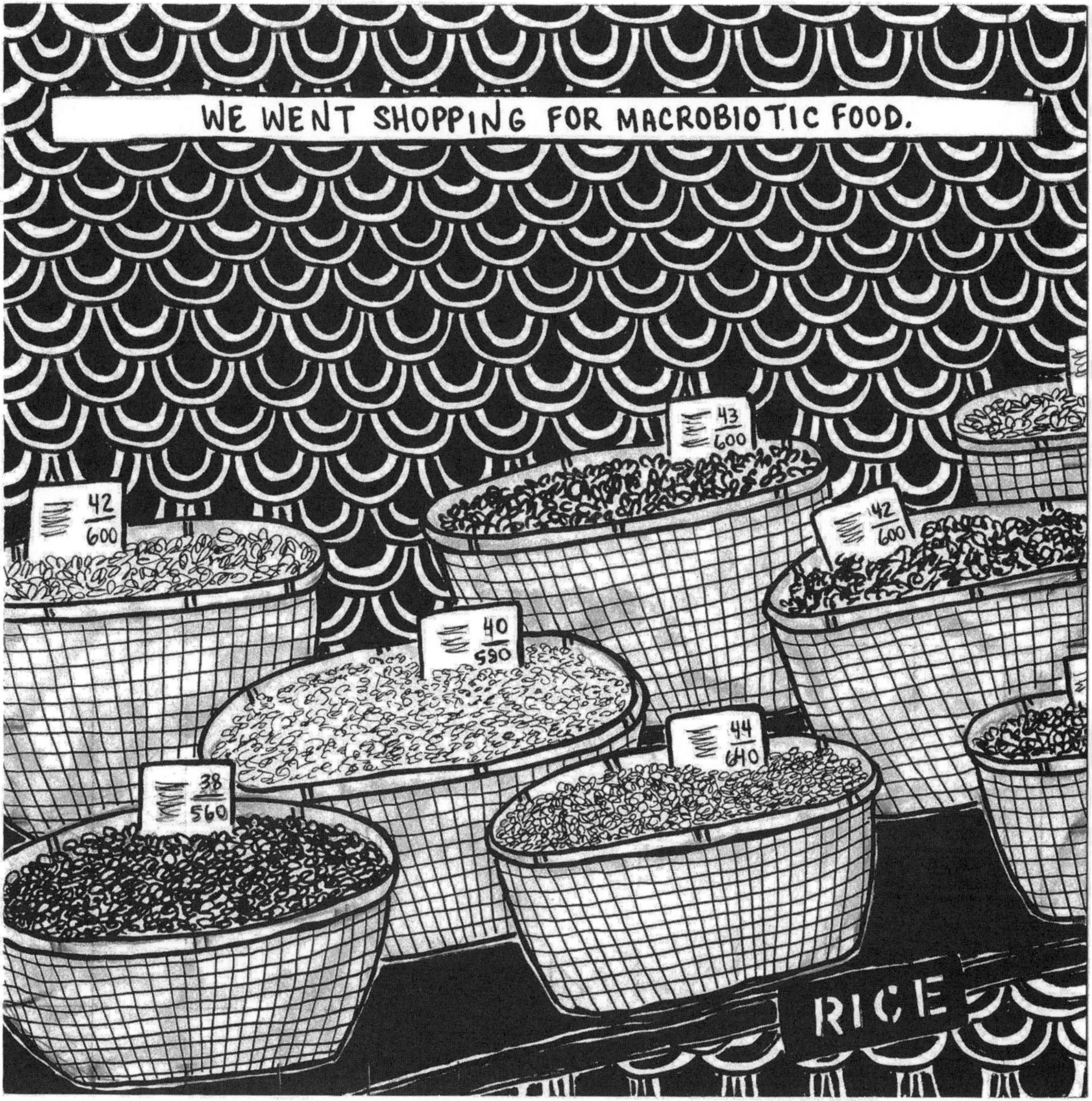
WE WENT SHOPPING FOR MACROBIOTIC FOOD.
43
600
42
600
42
600
40
580
44
640
38
560
RICE

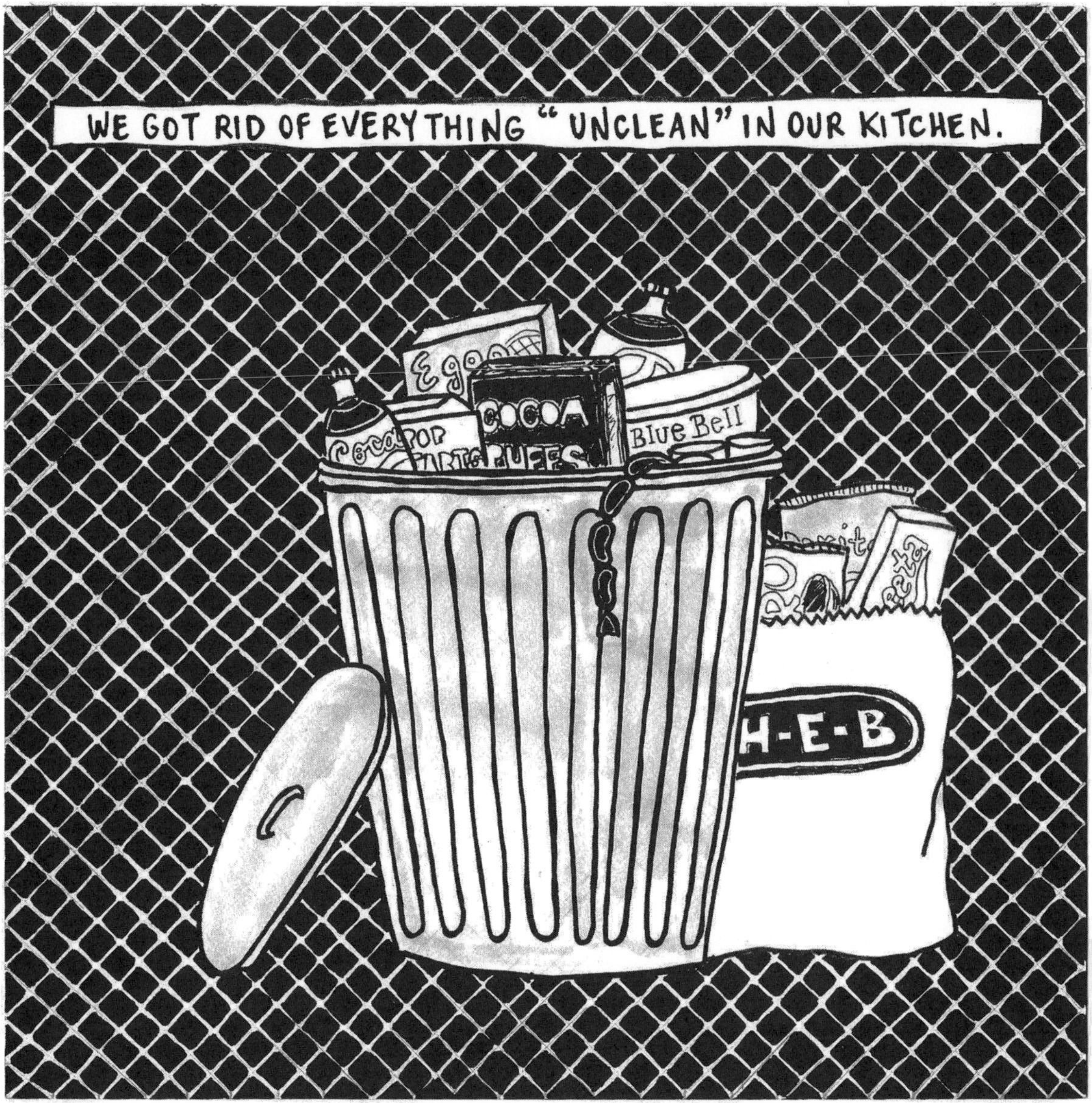
WE GOT RID OF EVERYTHING "UNCLEAN" IN OUR KITCHEN.
COCOA
Blue Bell
H-E-B

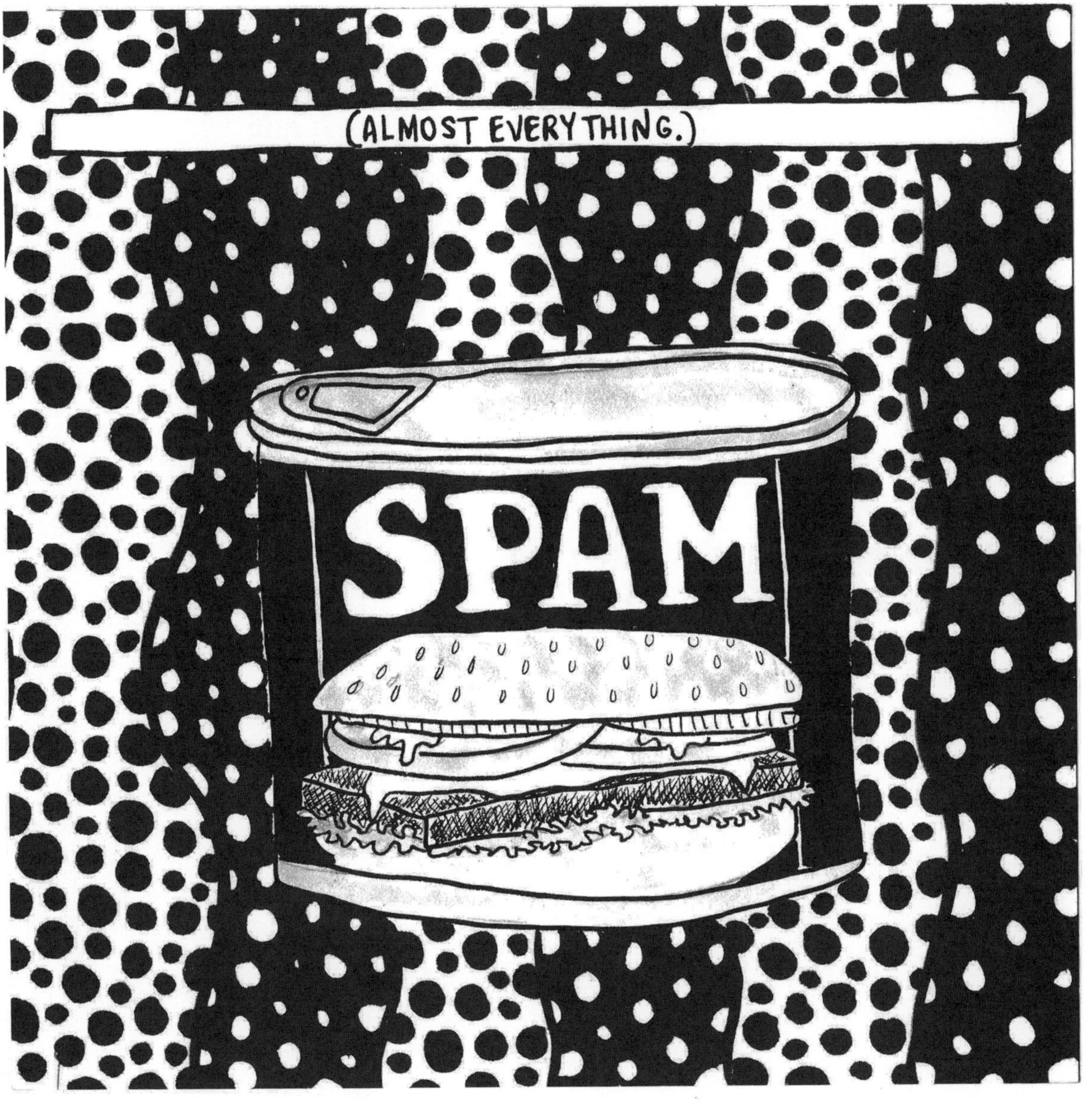
(ALMOST EVERYTHING.)
SPAM

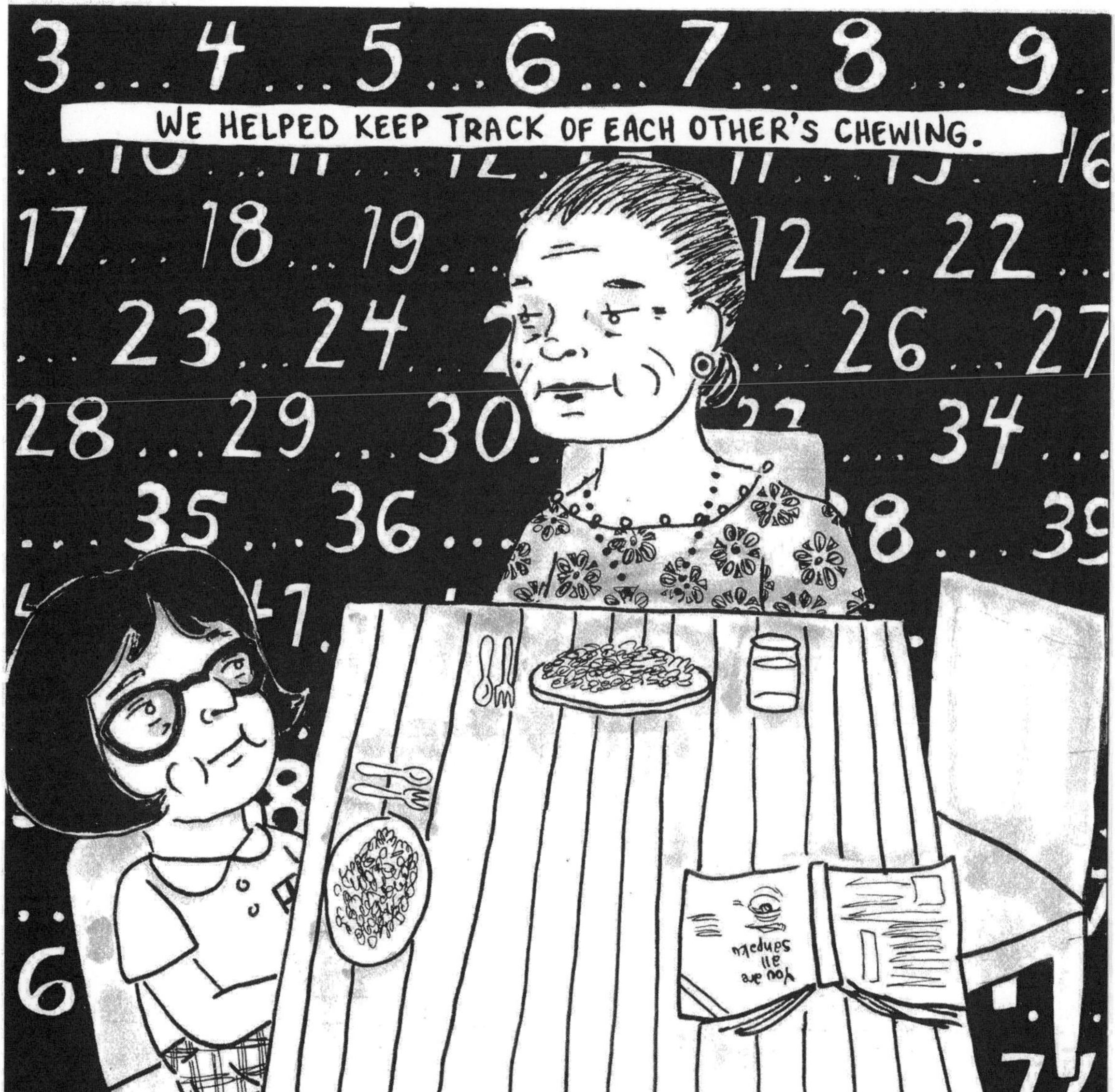
WE HELPED KEEP TRACK OF EACH OTHER'S CHEWING.

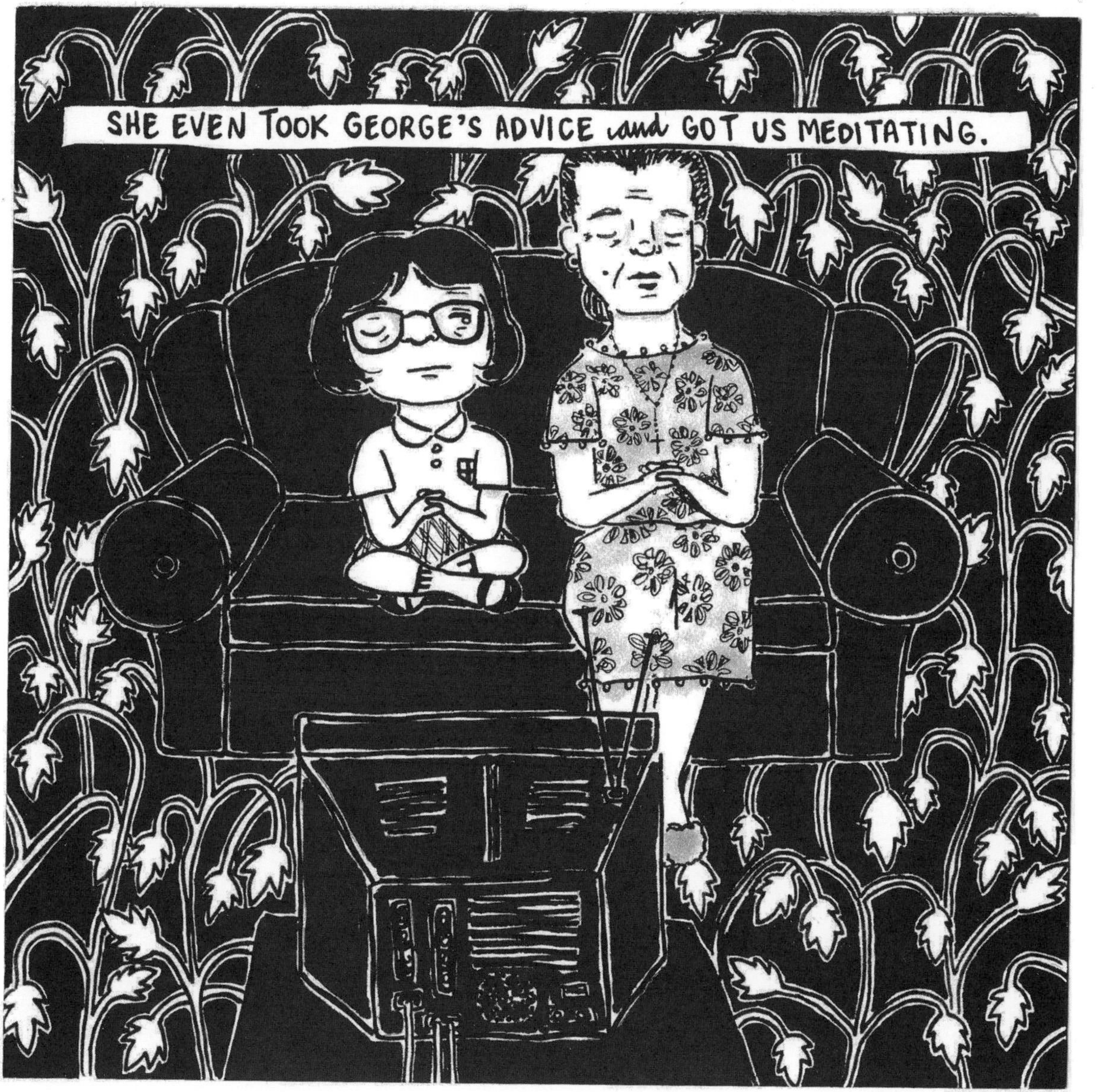
SHE EVEN TOOK GEORGE'S ADVICE and GOT US MEDITATING.

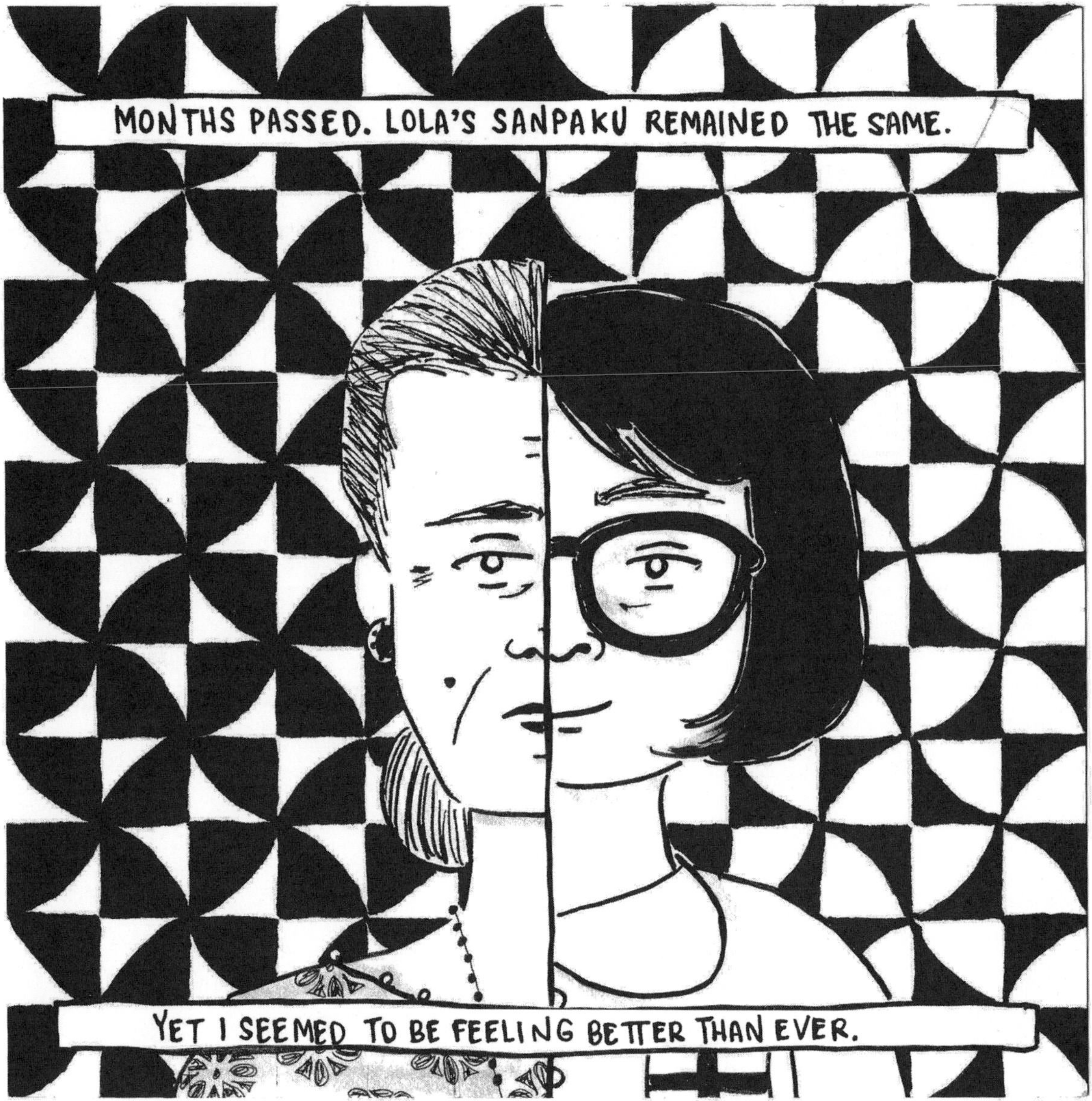
MONTHS PASSED. LOLA'S SANPAKU REMAINED THE SAME.
YET I SEEMED TO BE FEELING BETTER THAN EVER.

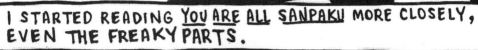

I STARTED READING <u>YOU</u> <u>ARE</u> <u>ALL</u> <u>SANPAKU</u> MORE CLOSELY, EVEN THE FREAKY PARTS.

"A TRULY HEALTHY MAN — LIKE THE ANIMALS — SHOULD NEED NO TOILET PAPER."

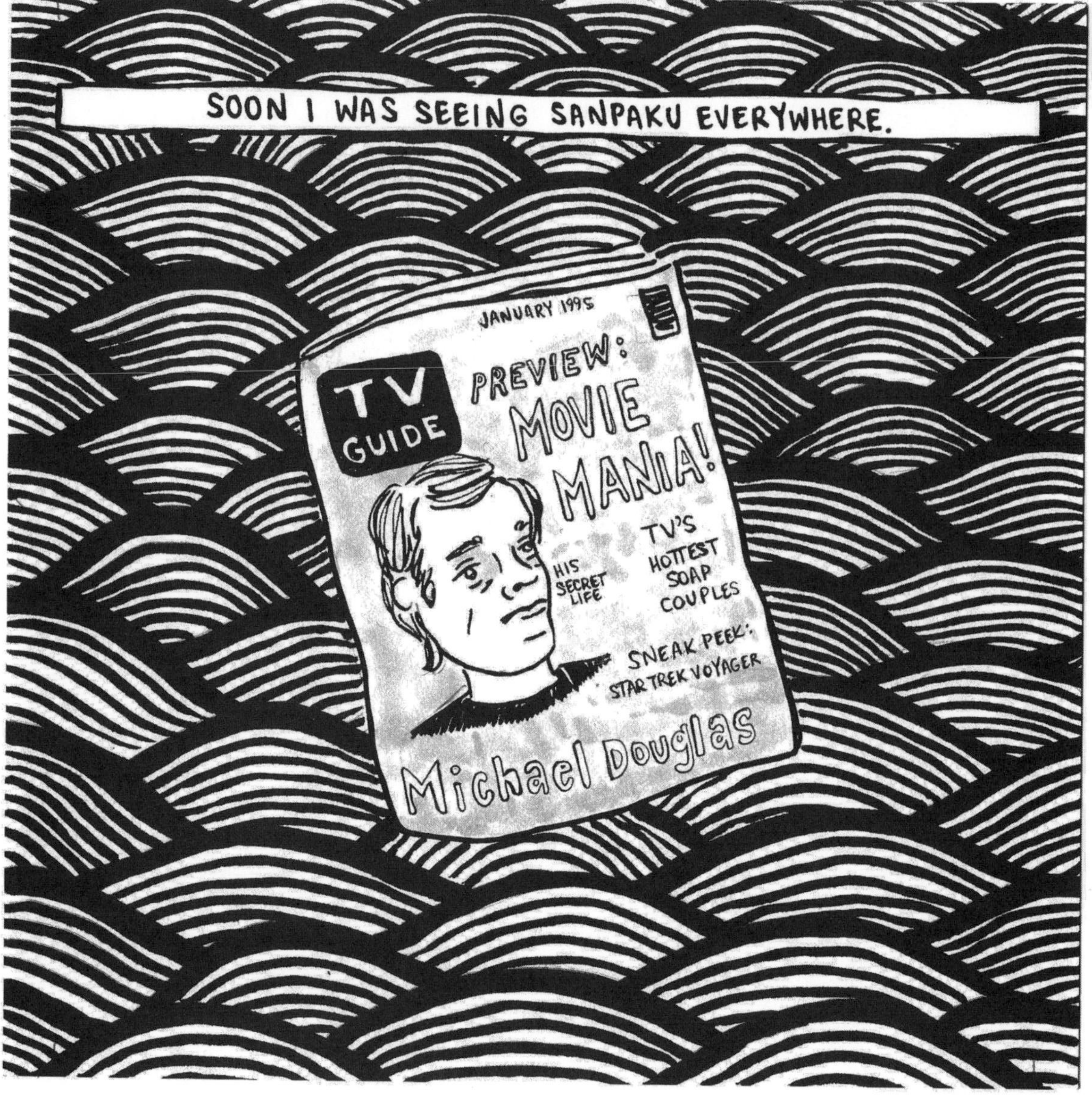
SOON I WAS SEEING SANPAKU EVERYWHERE.
JANUARY 1995
TV GUIDE
PREVIEW:
MOVIE MANIA!
HIS SECRET LIFE
TV'S HOTTEST SOAP COUPLES
SNEAK PEEK: STAR TREK VOYAGER
Michael Douglas

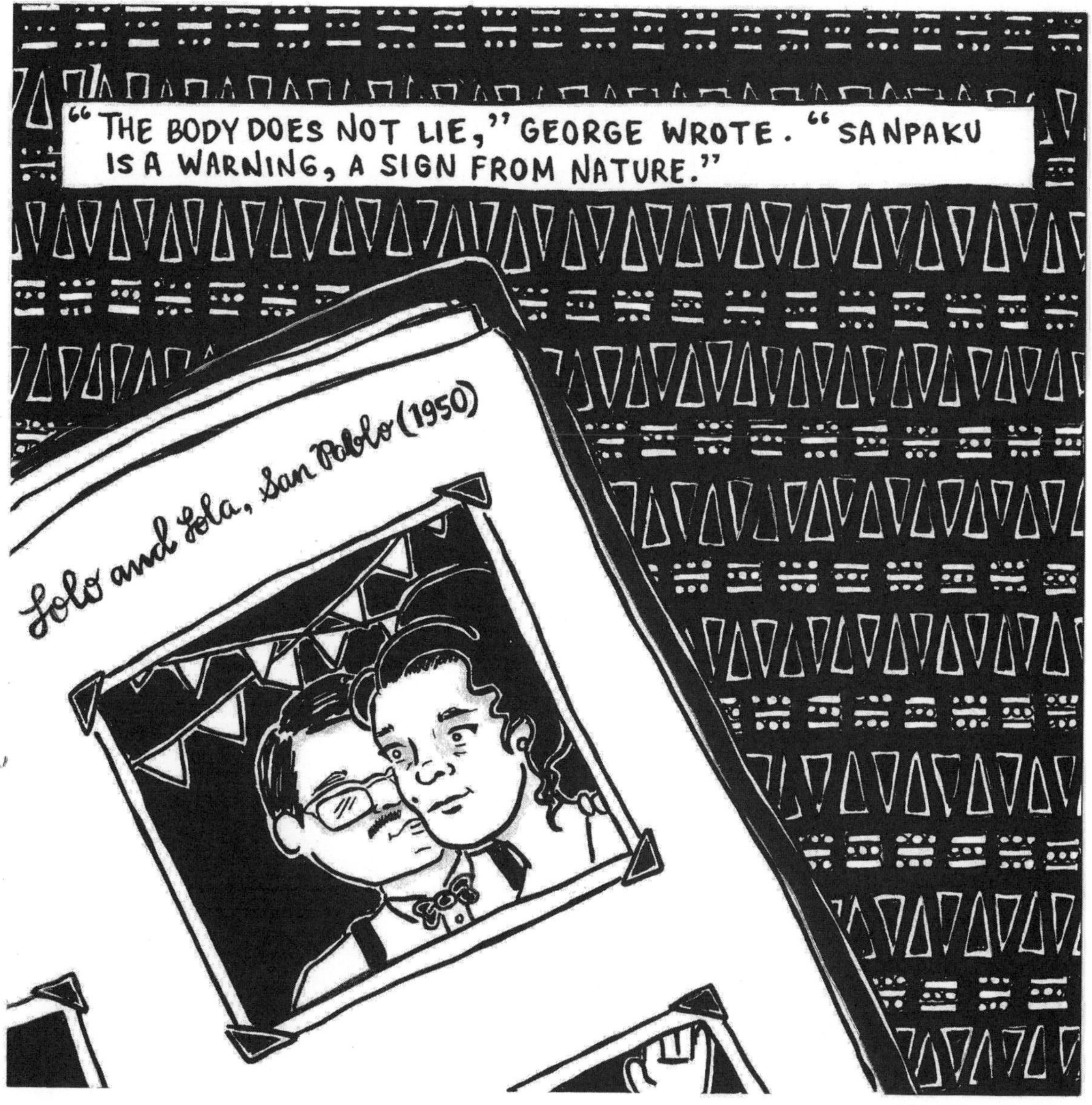
"THE BODY DOES NOT LIE," GEORGE WROTE. "SANPAKU IS A WARNING, A SIGN FROM NATURE."
Lolo and Lola, San Pablo (1950)

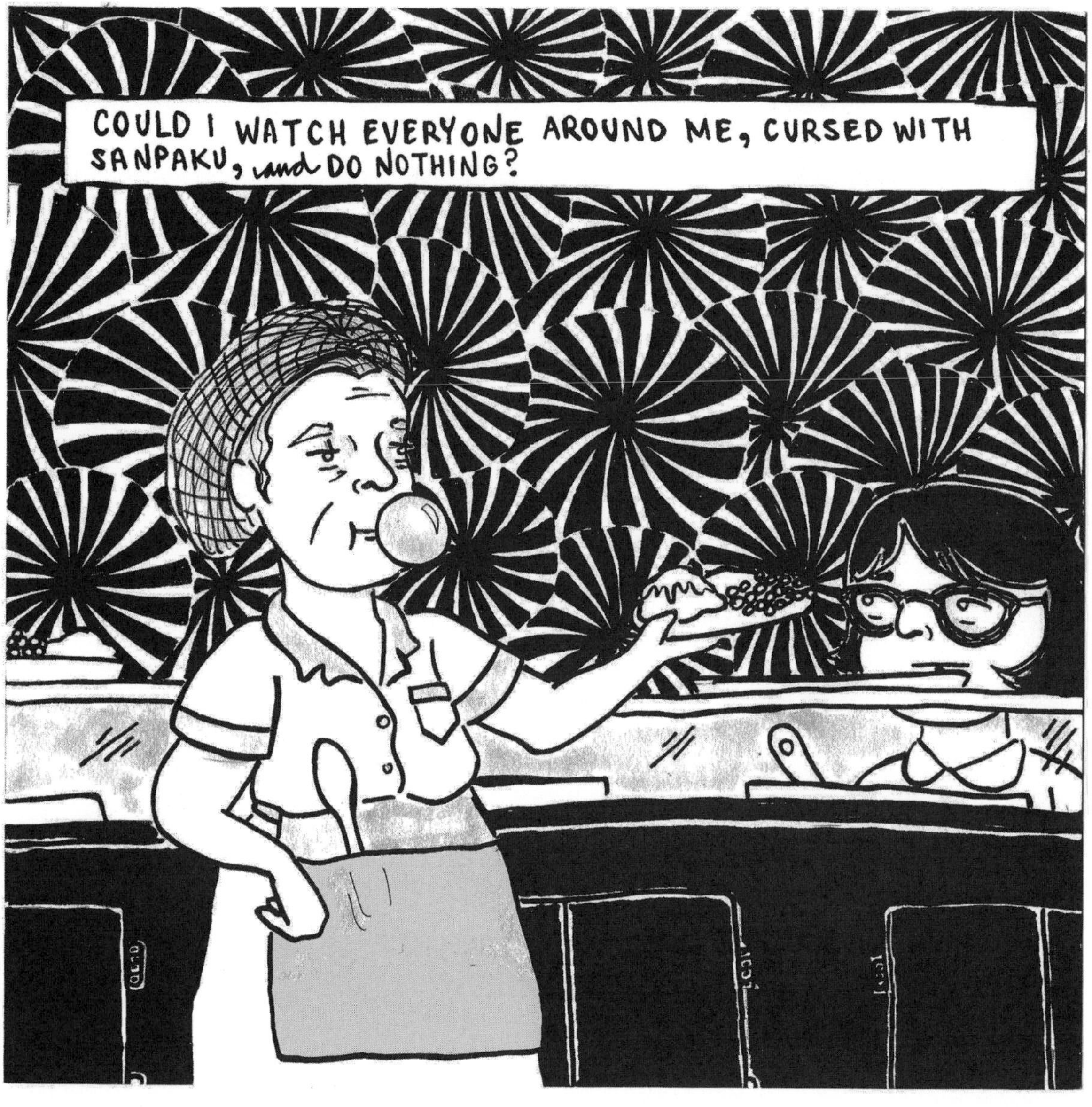
COULD I WATCH EVERYONE AROUND ME, CURSED WITH SANPAKU, and DO NOTHING?

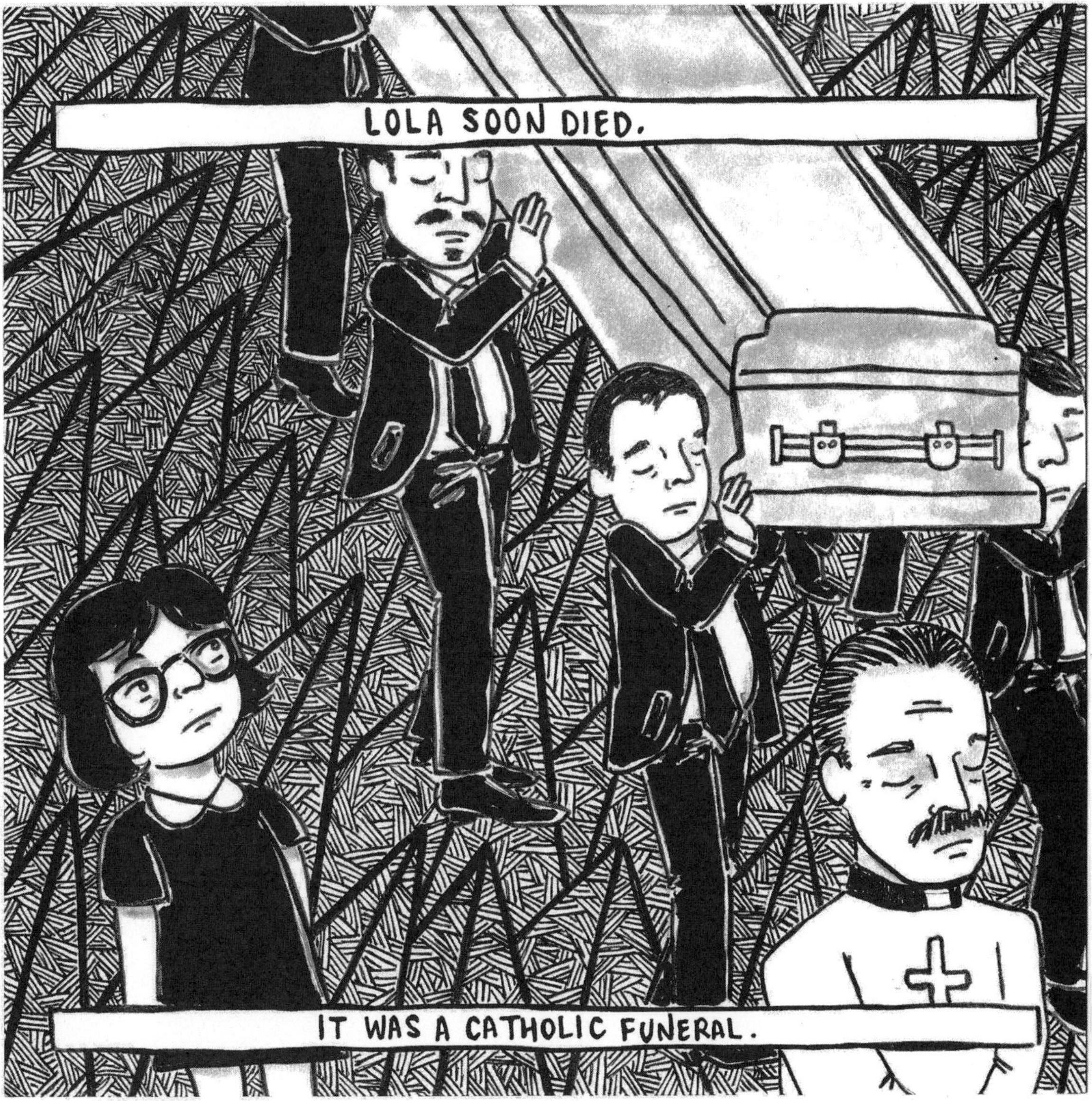
LOLA SOON DIED.
IT WAS A CATHOLIC FUNERAL.

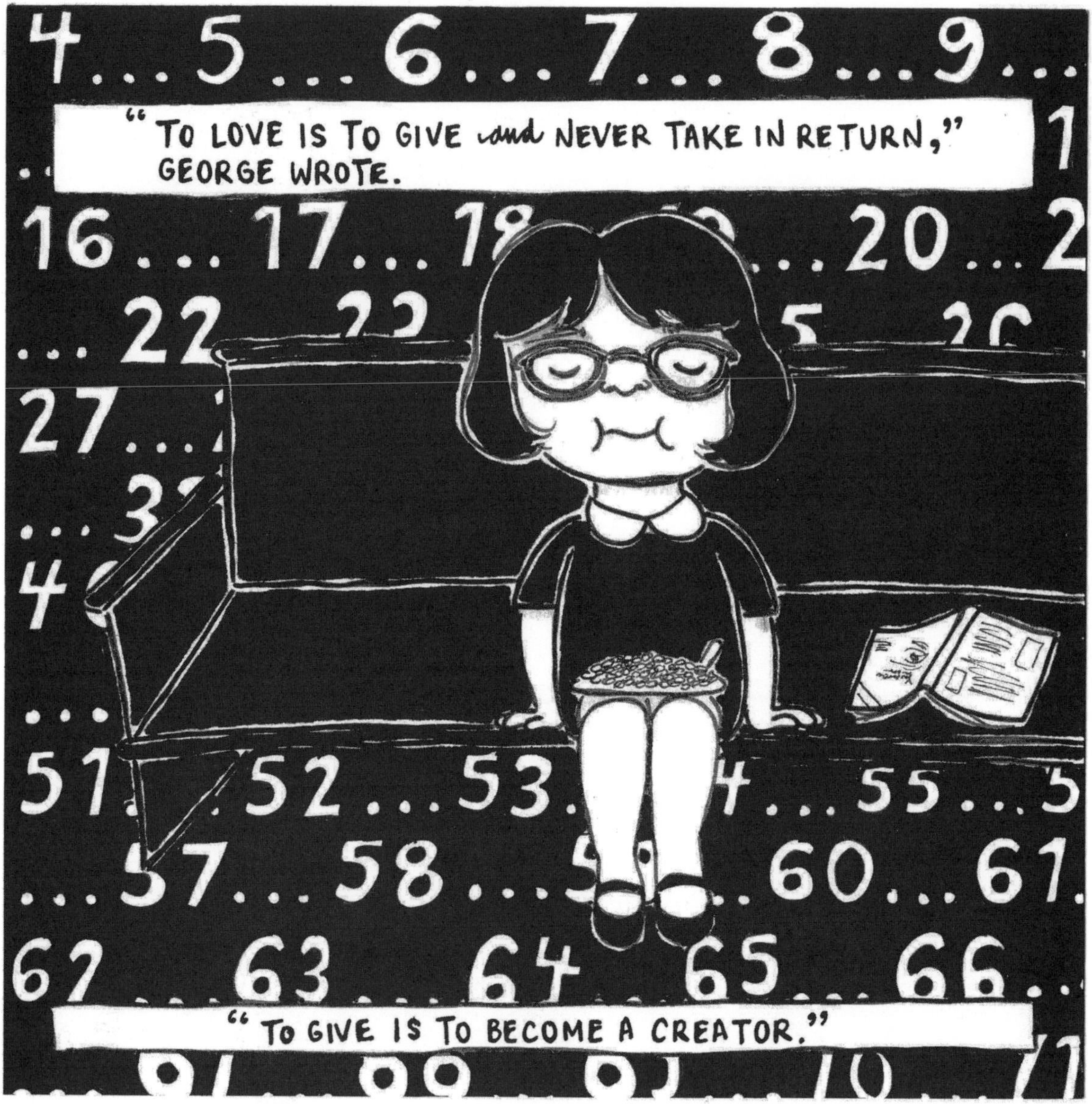
"TO LOVE IS TO GIVE and NEVER TAKE IN RETURN," GEORGE WROTE.
"TO GIVE IS TO BECOME A CREATOR."

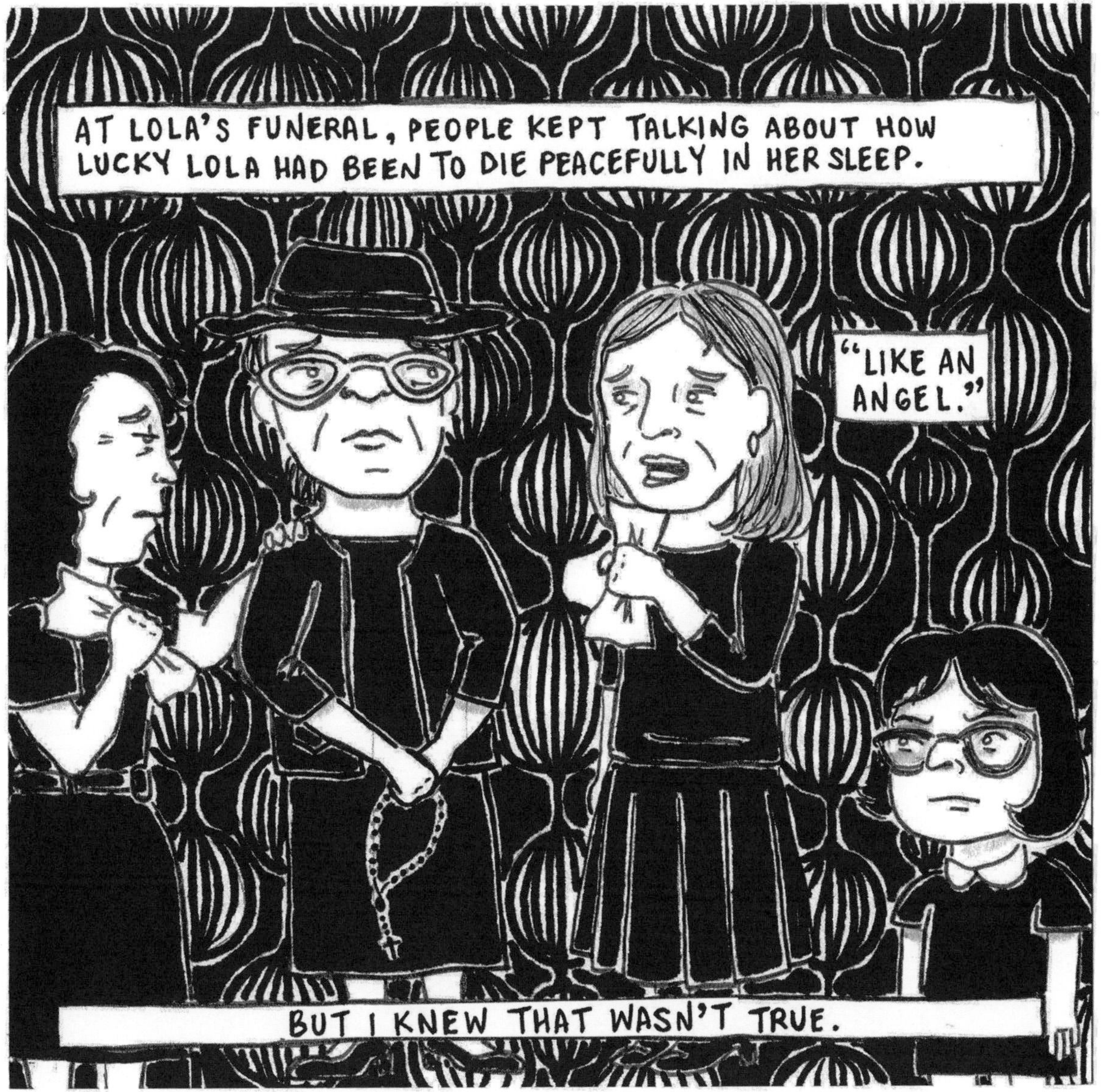
AT LOLA'S FUNERAL, PEOPLE KEPT TALKING ABOUT HOW LUCKY LOLA HAD BEEN TO DIE PEACEFULLY IN HER SLEEP.
"LIKE AN ANGEL."
BUT I KNEW THAT WASN'T TRUE.

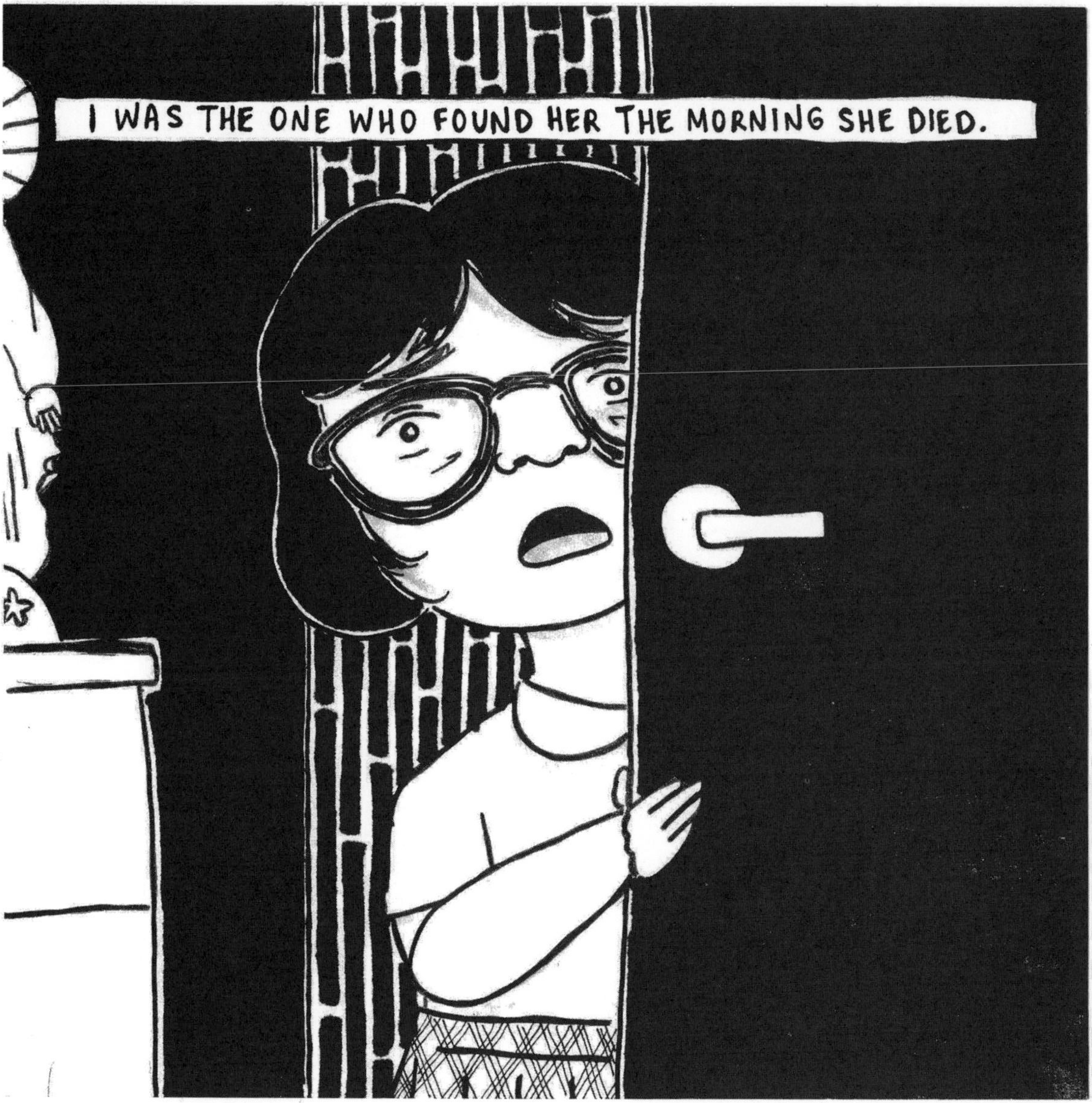
I WAS THE ONE WHO FOUND HER THE MORNING SHE DIED.

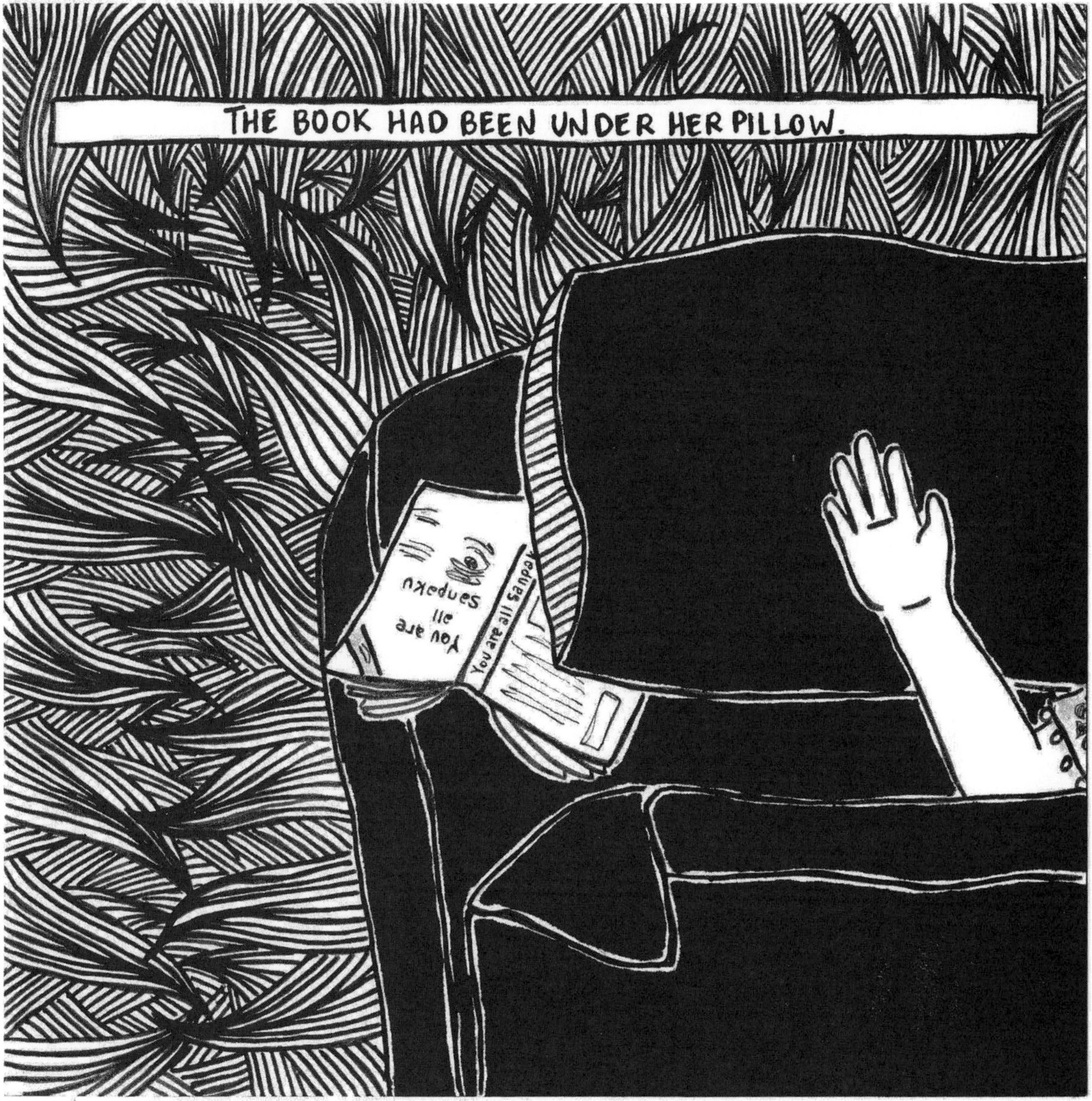
THE BOOK HAD BEEN UNDER HER PILLOW.
You are all sanpaku
You are all Sanpak

SHE HAD BOOKMARKED ONE PAGE.

A Land of Sanpaku

Once we understand this, we have...

...uring our so called incurable ill...

...ure of the simplest m...dy

...turely, because...illn...

...ving graces o...he hu...

...der of the u...se for...

"ILLNESS IS NOT SENT TO US AS A PUNISHMENT, BUT AS A SAVING GRACE. WE HAVE ONLY TO PAY HEED TO OUR BODIES TO KNOW WHAT WE MUST DO."

but it
illness
alarm
as a fir
We hav
Inste
scientif
allopath
delicate t

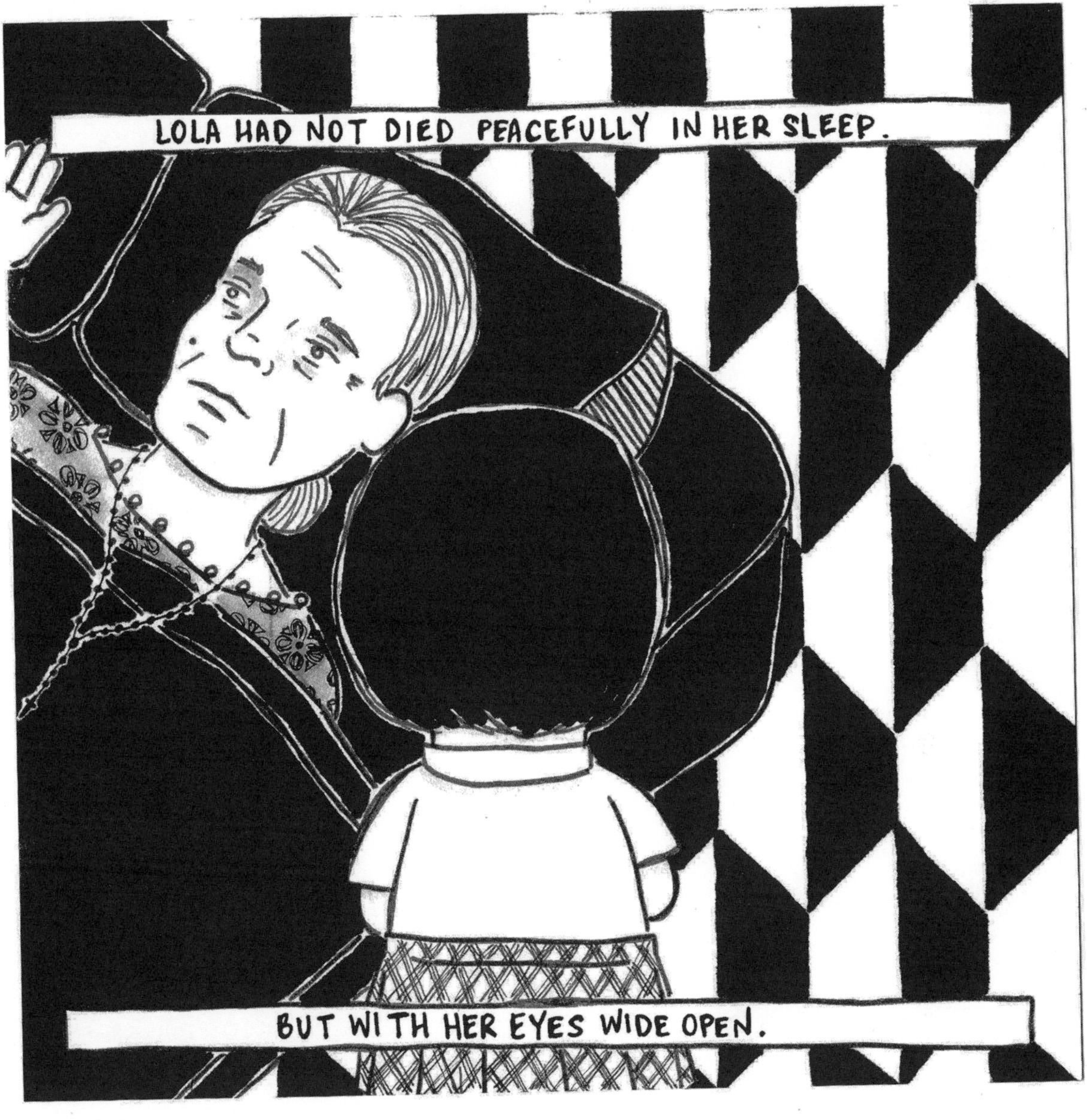
LOLA HAD NOT DIED PEACEFULLY IN HER SLEEP.
BUT WITH HER EYES WIDE OPEN.

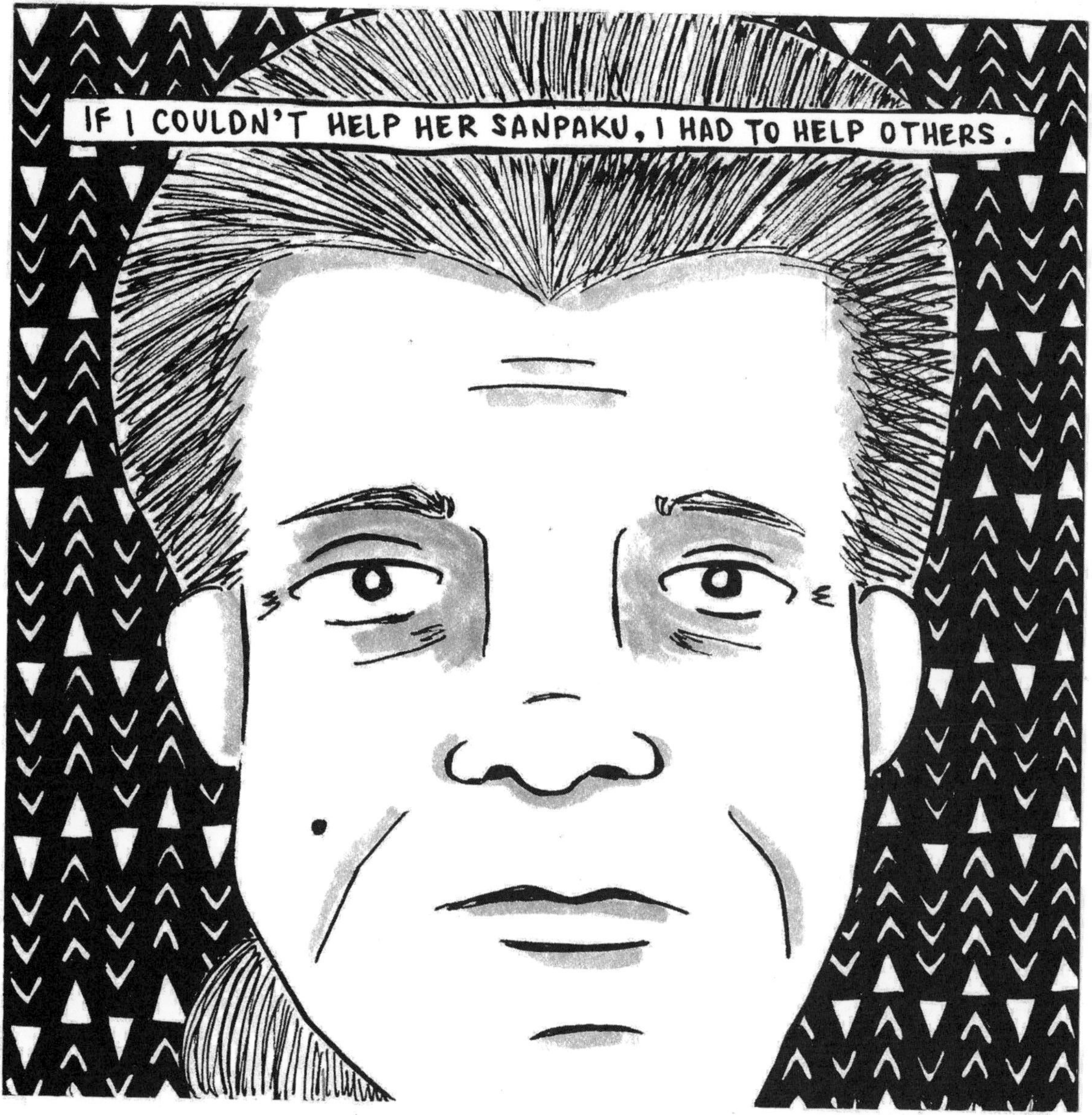
IF I COULDN'T HELP HER SANPAKU, I HAD TO HELP OTHERS.

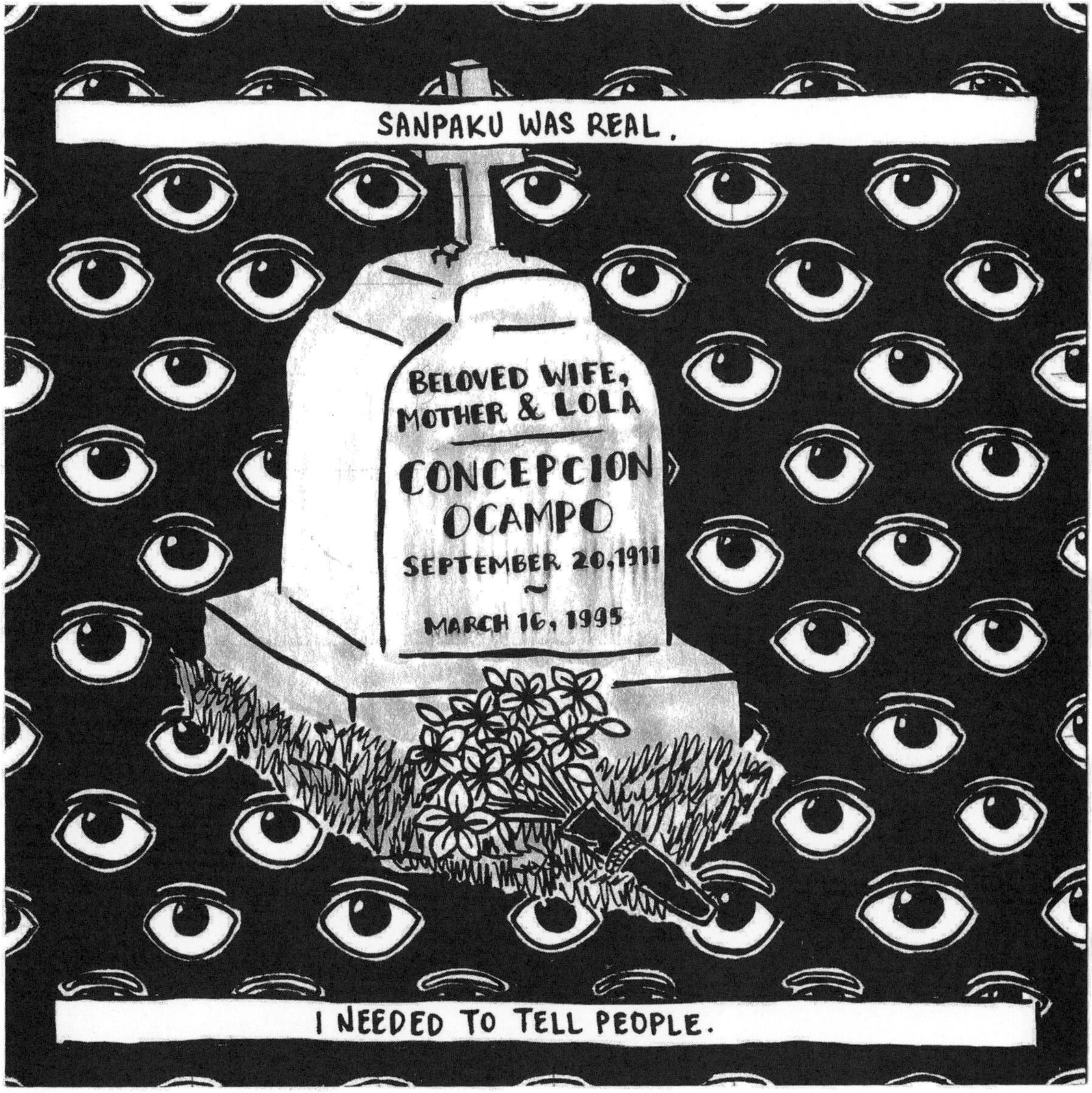
SANPAKU WAS REAL.
BELOVED WIFE, MOTHER & LOLA
CONCEPCION OCAMPO
SEPTEMBER 20, 1911
~
MARCH 16, 1995
I NEEDED TO TELL PEOPLE.

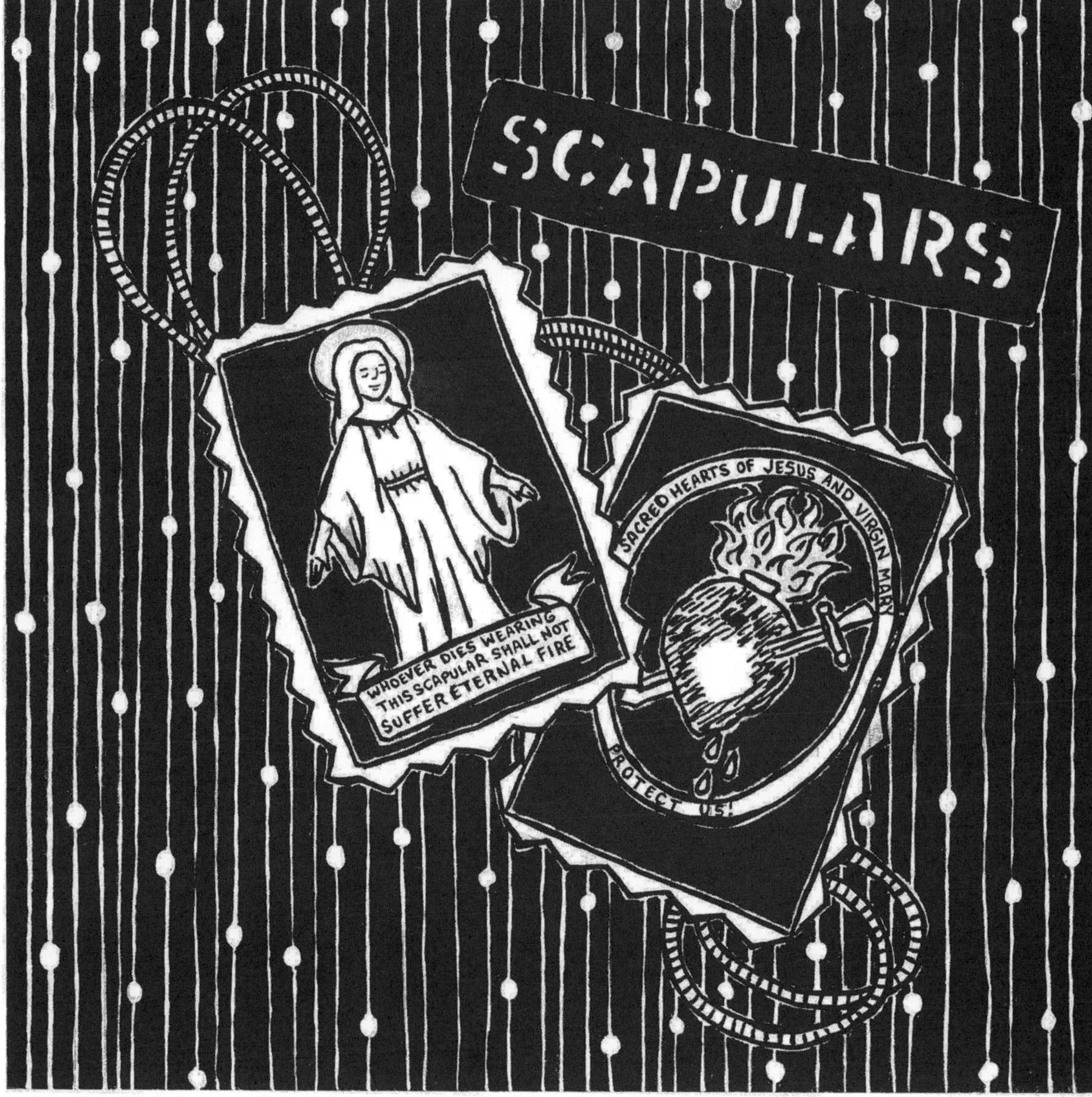
SCAPULARS
WHOEVER DIES WEARING THIS SCAPULAR SHALL NOT SUFFER ETERNAL FIRE
SACRED HEARTS OF JESUS AND VIRGIN MARY
PROTECT US!

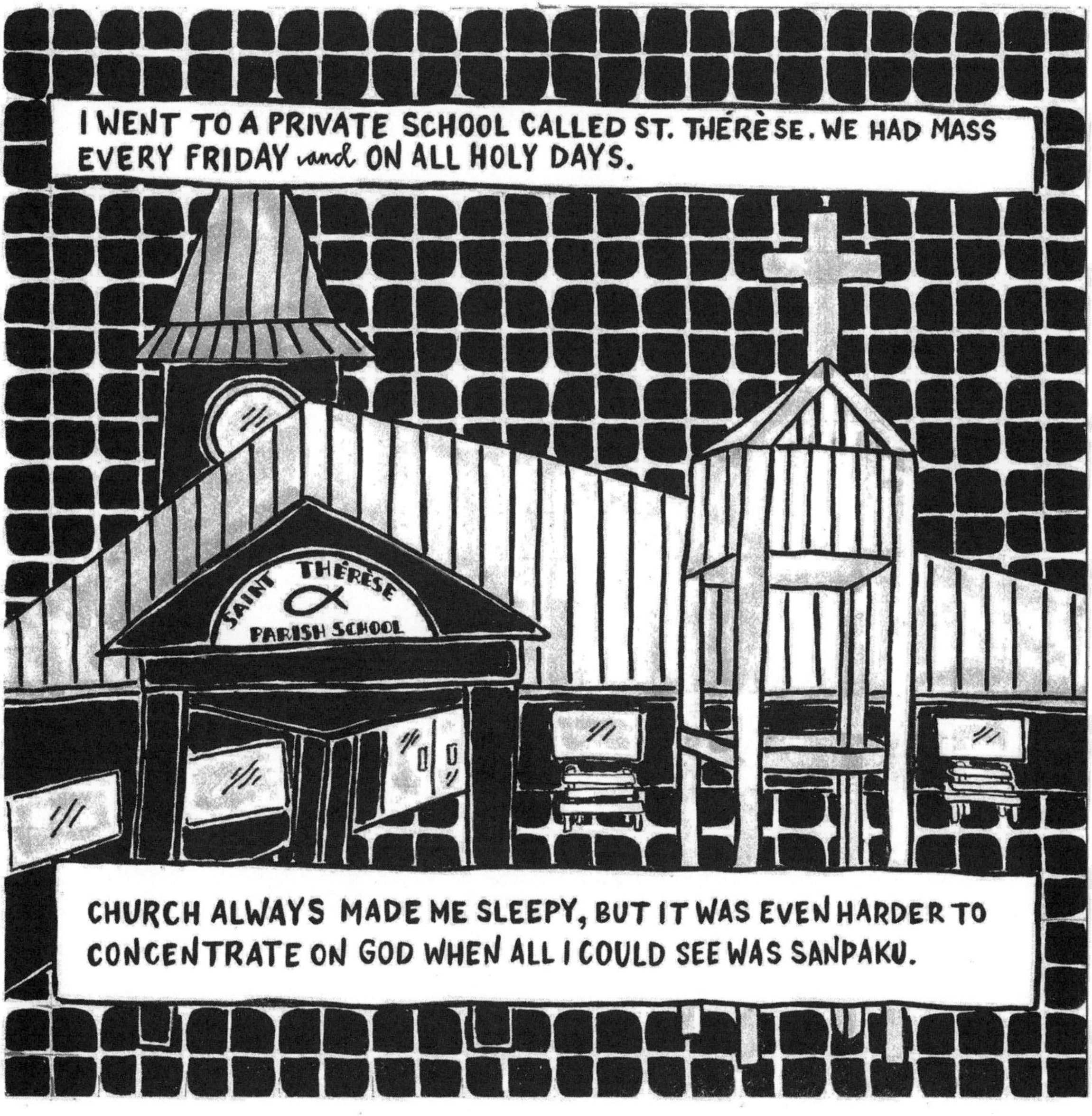
I WENT TO A PRIVATE SCHOOL CALLED ST. THÉRÈSE. WE HAD MASS EVERY FRIDAY and ON ALL HOLY DAYS.
SAINT THÉRÈSE PARISH SCHOOL
CHURCH ALWAYS MADE ME SLEEPY, BUT IT WAS EVEN HARDER TO CONCENTRATE ON GOD WHEN ALL I COULD SEE WAS SANPAKU.

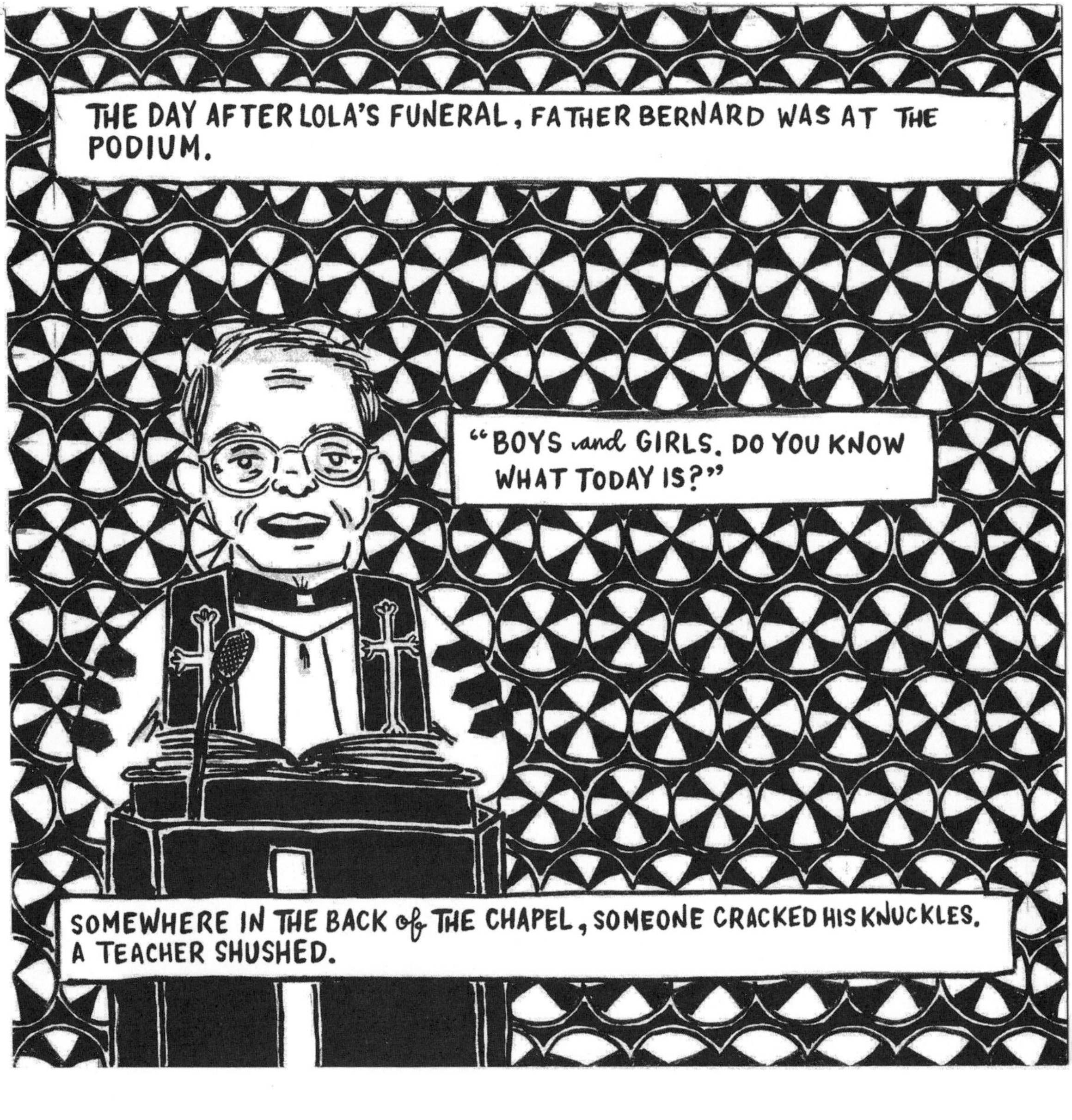
THE DAY AFTER LOLA'S FUNERAL, FATHER BERNARD WAS AT THE PODIUM.
"BOYS and GIRLS. DO YOU KNOW WHAT TODAY IS?"
SOMEWHERE IN THE BACK of THE CHAPEL, SOMEONE CRACKED HIS KNUCKLES. A TEACHER SHUSHED.

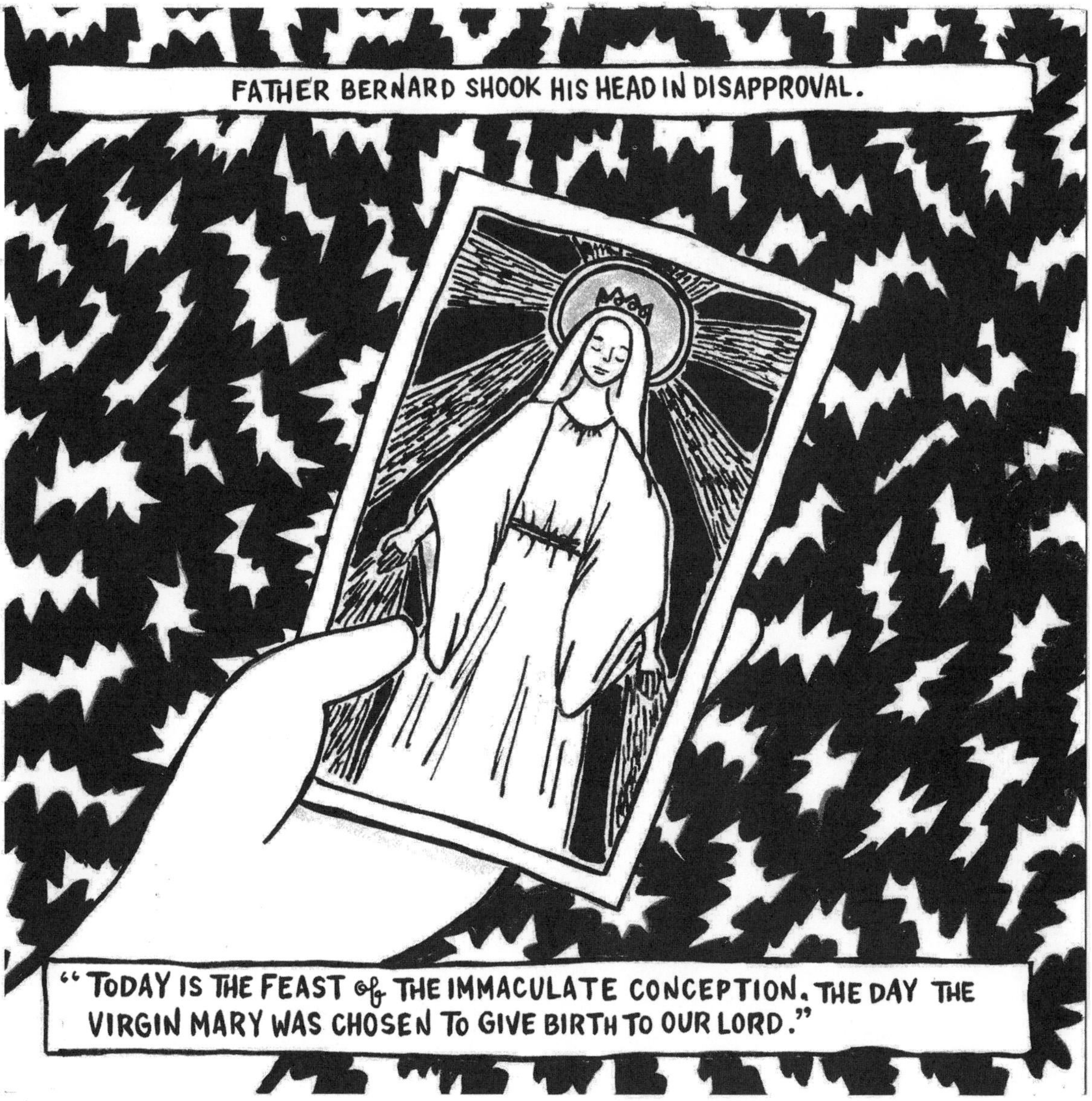
FATHER BERNARD SHOOK HIS HEAD IN DISAPPROVAL.
"TODAY IS THE FEAST of THE IMMACULATE CONCEPTION. THE DAY THE VIRGIN MARY WAS CHOSEN TO GIVE BIRTH TO OUR LORD."

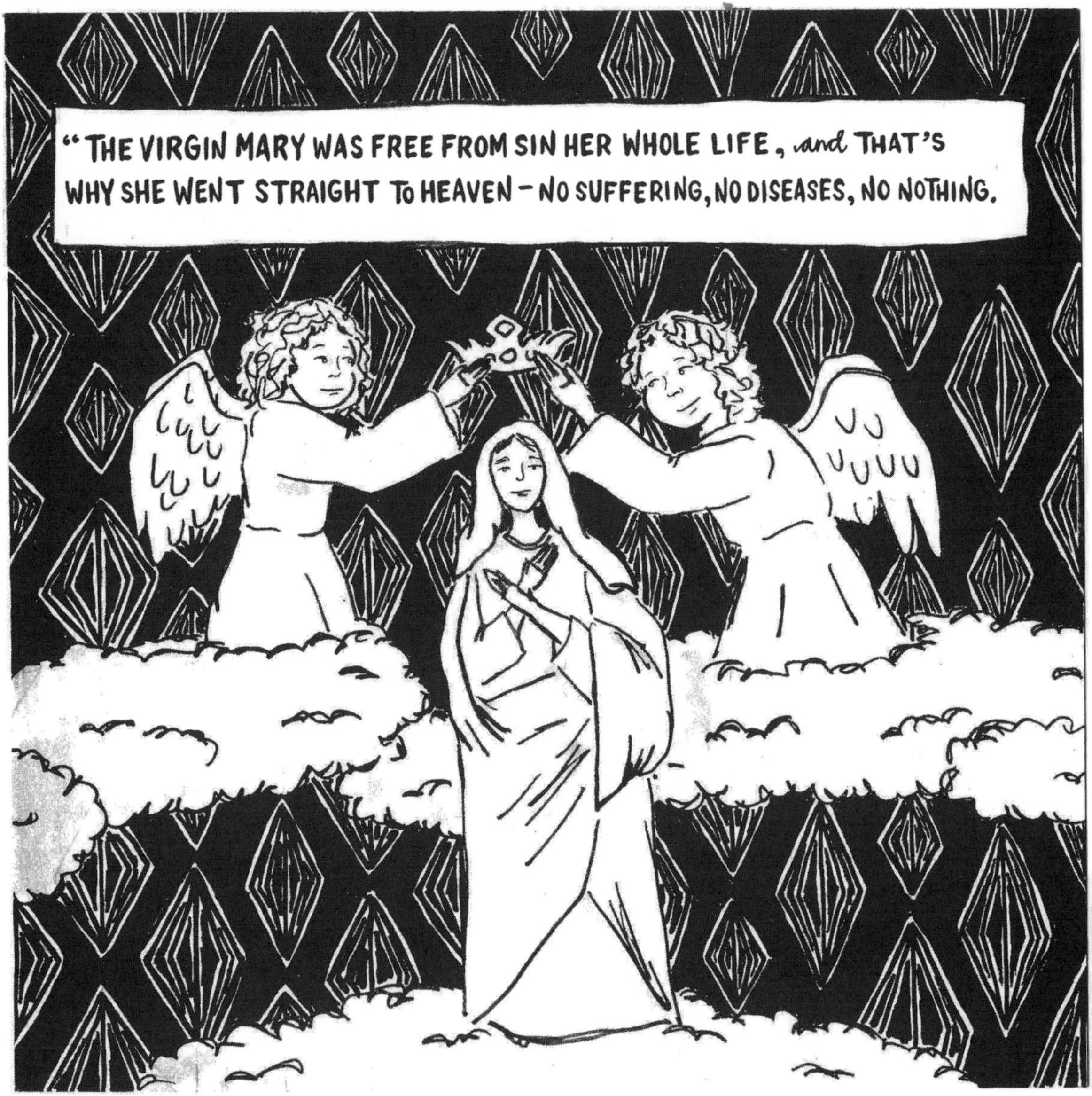
"THE VIRGIN MARY WAS FREE FROM SIN HER WHOLE LIFE, and THAT'S WHY SHE WENT STRAIGHT TO HEAVEN – NO SUFFERING, NO DISEASES, NO NOTHING.

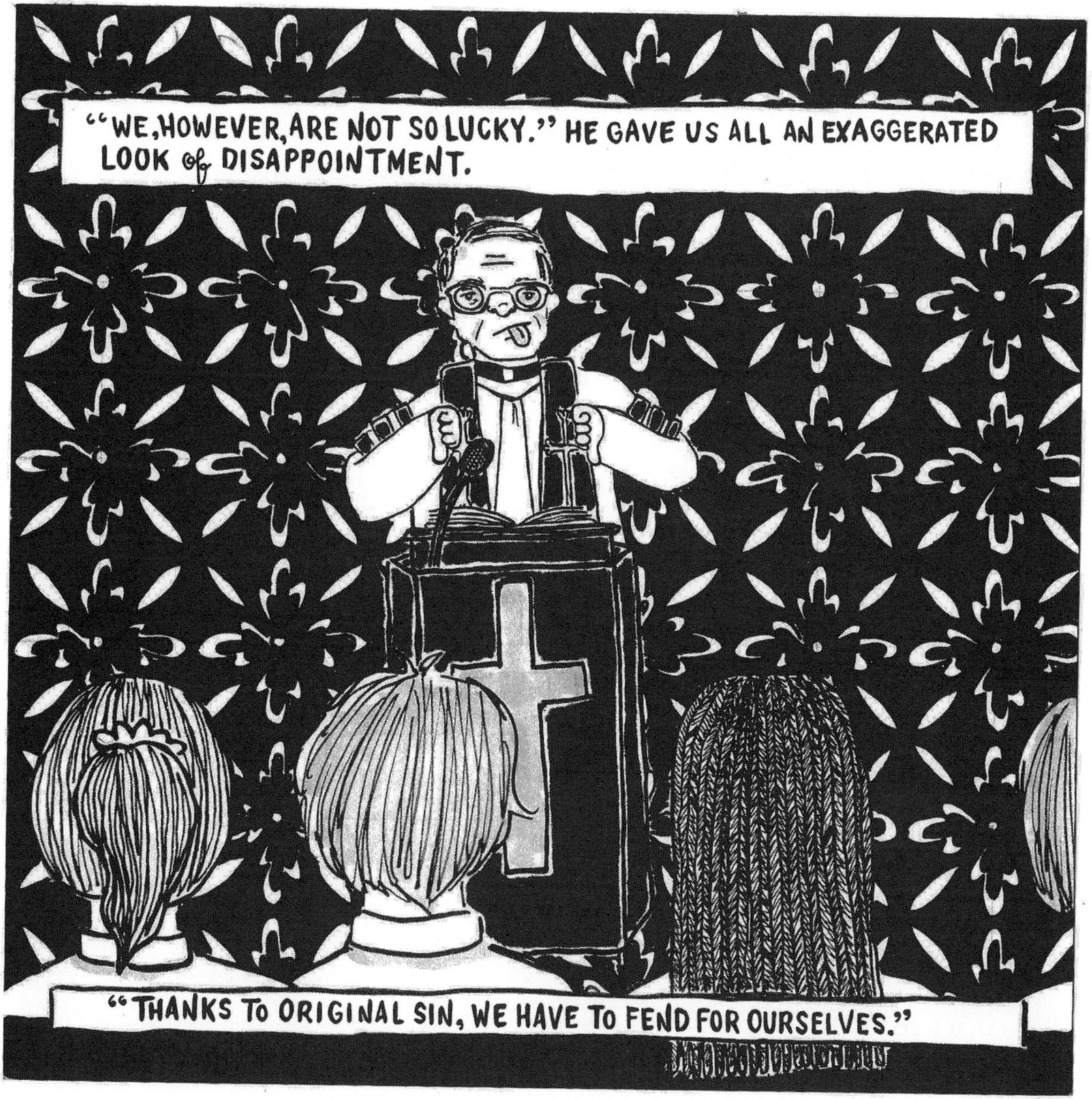
"WE, HOWEVER, ARE NOT SO LUCKY." HE GAVE US ALL AN EXAGGERATED LOOK of DISAPPOINTMENT.
"THANKS TO ORIGINAL SIN, WE HAVE TO FEND FOR OURSELVES."

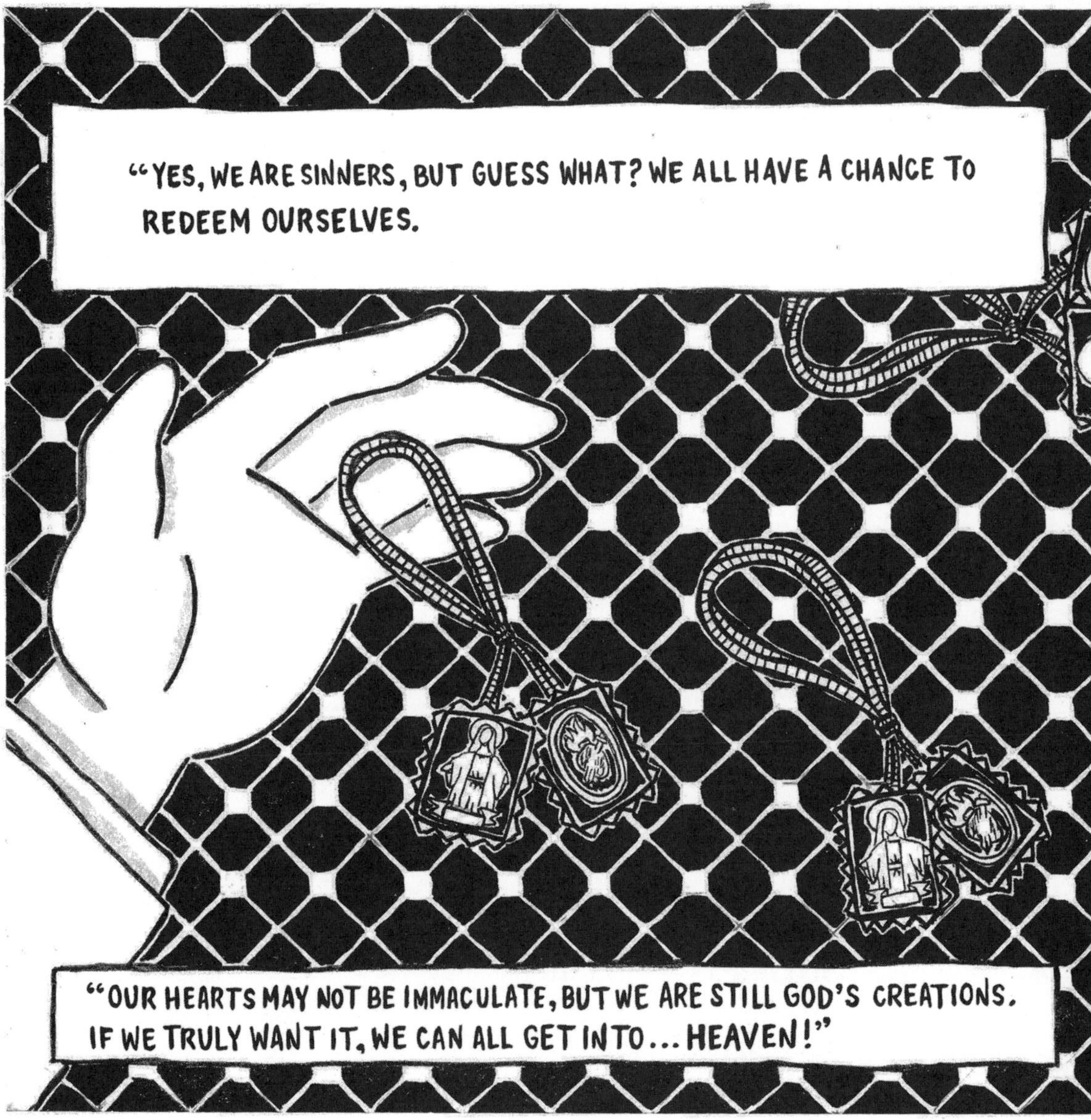
"YES, WE ARE SINNERS, BUT GUESS WHAT? WE ALL HAVE A CHANCE TO REDEEM OURSELVES.
"OUR HEARTS MAY NOT BE IMMACULATE, BUT WE ARE STILL GOD'S CREATIONS. IF WE TRULY WANT IT, WE CAN ALL GET INTO... HEAVEN!"

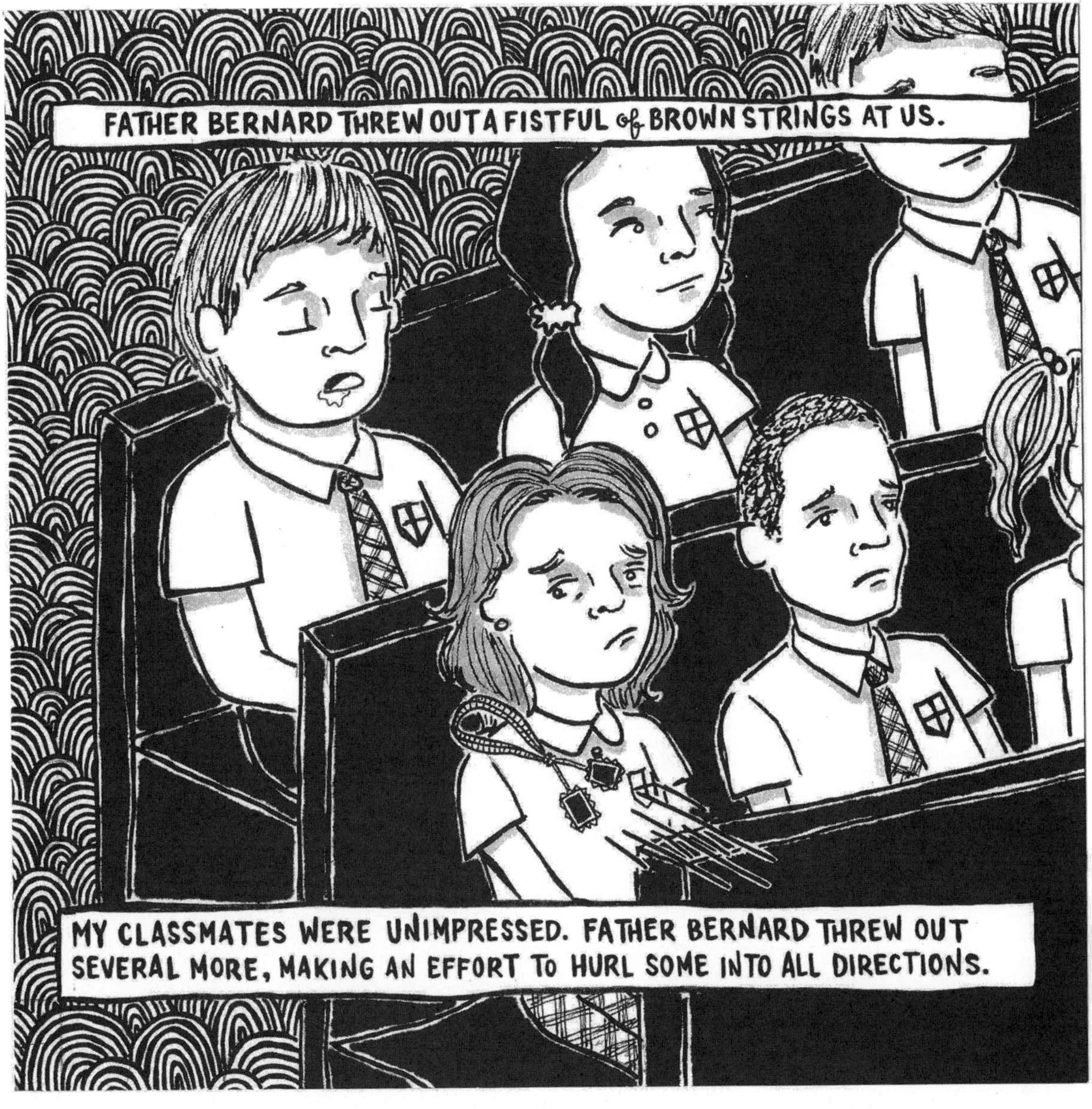
FATHER BERNARD THREW OUT A FISTFUL of BROWN STRINGS AT US.
MY CLASSMATES WERE UNIMPRESSED. FATHER BERNARD THREW OUT SEVERAL MORE, MAKING AN EFFORT TO HURL SOME INTO ALL DIRECTIONS.

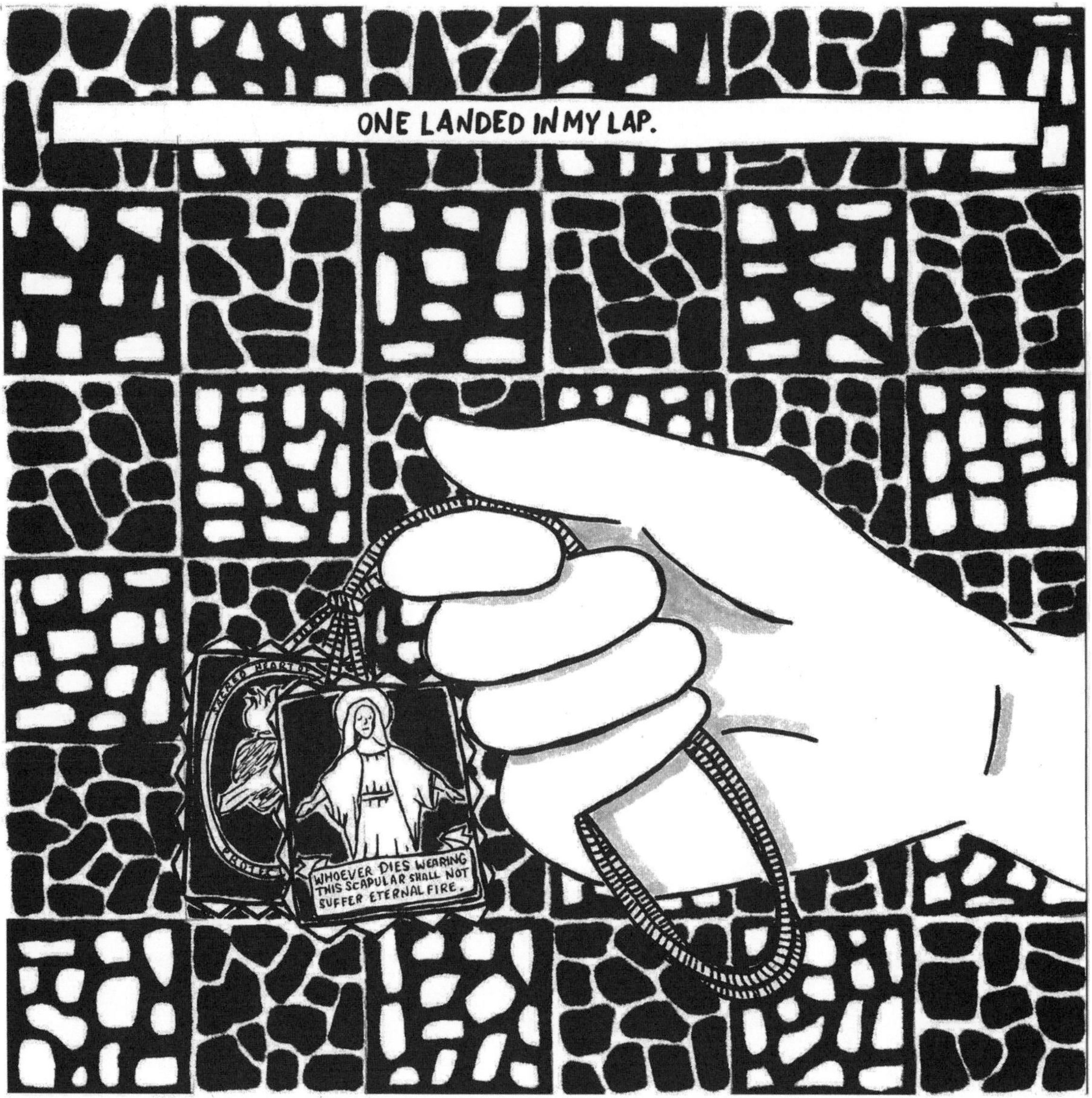
ONE LANDED IN MY LAP.
SACRED HEART OF
WHOEVER DIES WEARING THIS SCAPULAR SHALL NOT SUFFER ETERNAL FIRE.

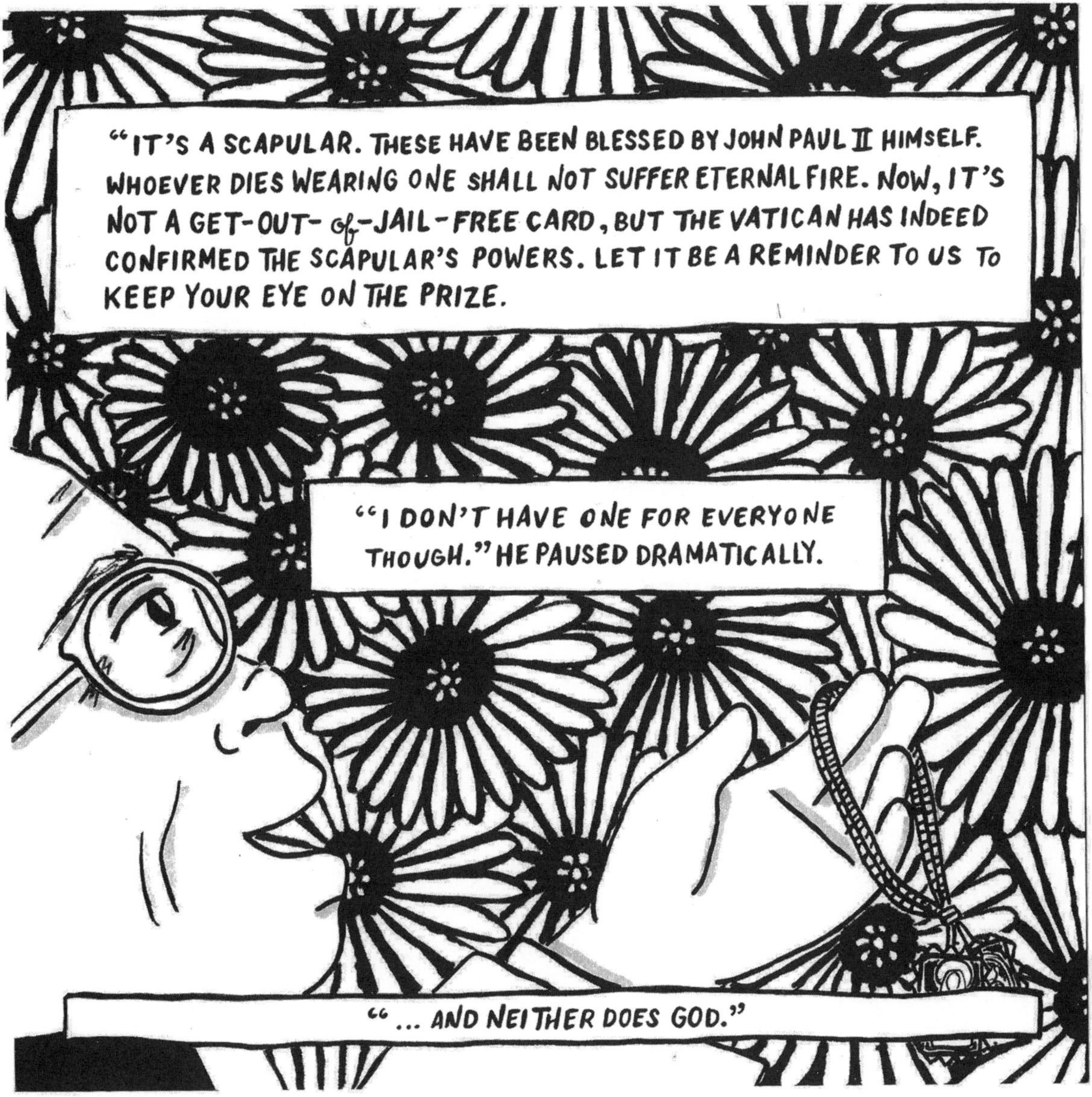
"IT'S A SCAPULAR. THESE HAVE BEEN BLESSED BY JOHN PAUL II HIMSELF. WHOEVER DIES WEARING ONE SHALL NOT SUFFER ETERNAL FIRE. NOW, IT'S NOT A GET-OUT-of-JAIL-FREE CARD, BUT THE VATICAN HAS INDEED CONFIRMED THE SCAPULAR'S POWERS. LET IT BE A REMINDER TO US TO KEEP YOUR EYE ON THE PRIZE.
"I DON'T HAVE ONE FOR EVERYONE THOUGH." HE PAUSED DRAMATICALLY.
"... AND NEITHER DOES GOD."

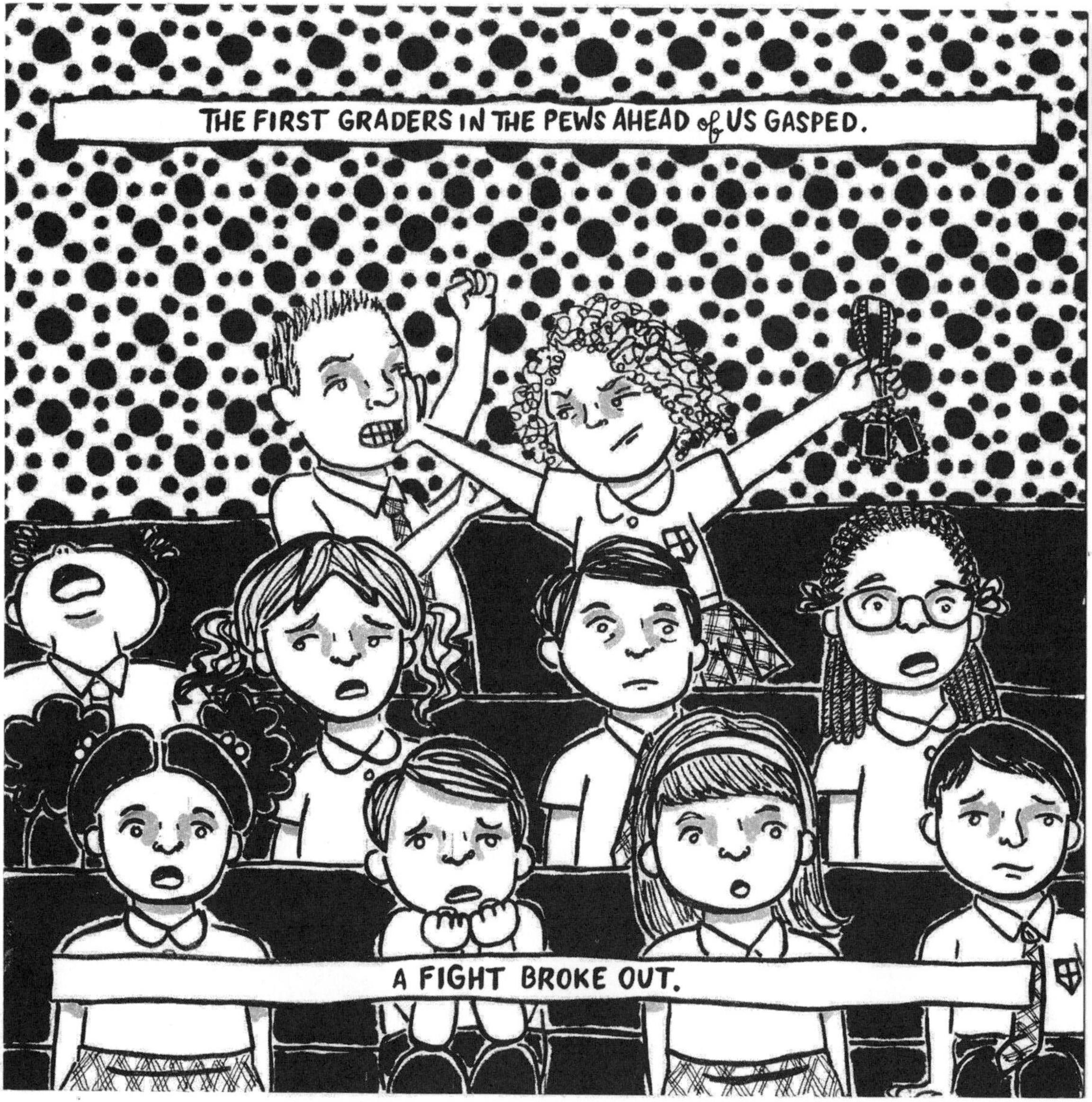
THE FIRST GRADERS IN THE PEWS AHEAD of US GASPED.
A FIGHT BROKE OUT.

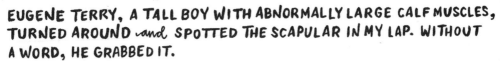

EUGENE TERRY, A TALL BOY WITH ABNORMALLY LARGE CALF MUSCLES, TURNED AROUND *and* SPOTTED THE SCAPULAR IN MY LAP. WITHOUT A WORD, HE GRABBED IT.

HE SNEERED *and* TURNED BACK AROUND.

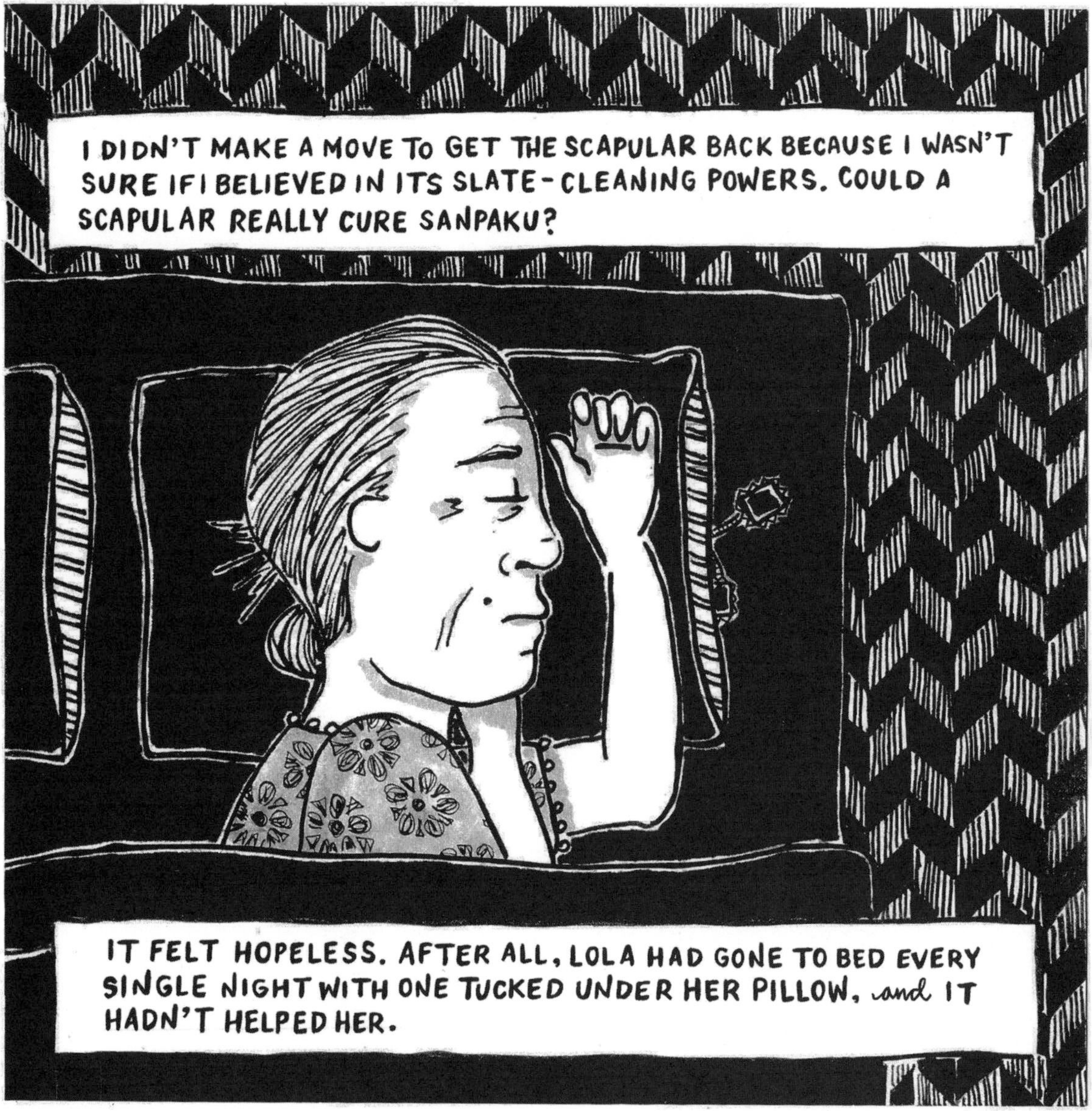
I DIDN'T MAKE A MOVE TO GET THE SCAPULAR BACK BECAUSE I WASN'T SURE IF I BELIEVED IN ITS SLATE-CLEANING POWERS. COULD A SCAPULAR REALLY CURE SANPAKU?
IT FELT HOPELESS. AFTER ALL, LOLA HAD GONE TO BED EVERY SINGLE NIGHT WITH ONE TUCKED UNDER HER PILLOW, and IT HADN'T HELPED HER.

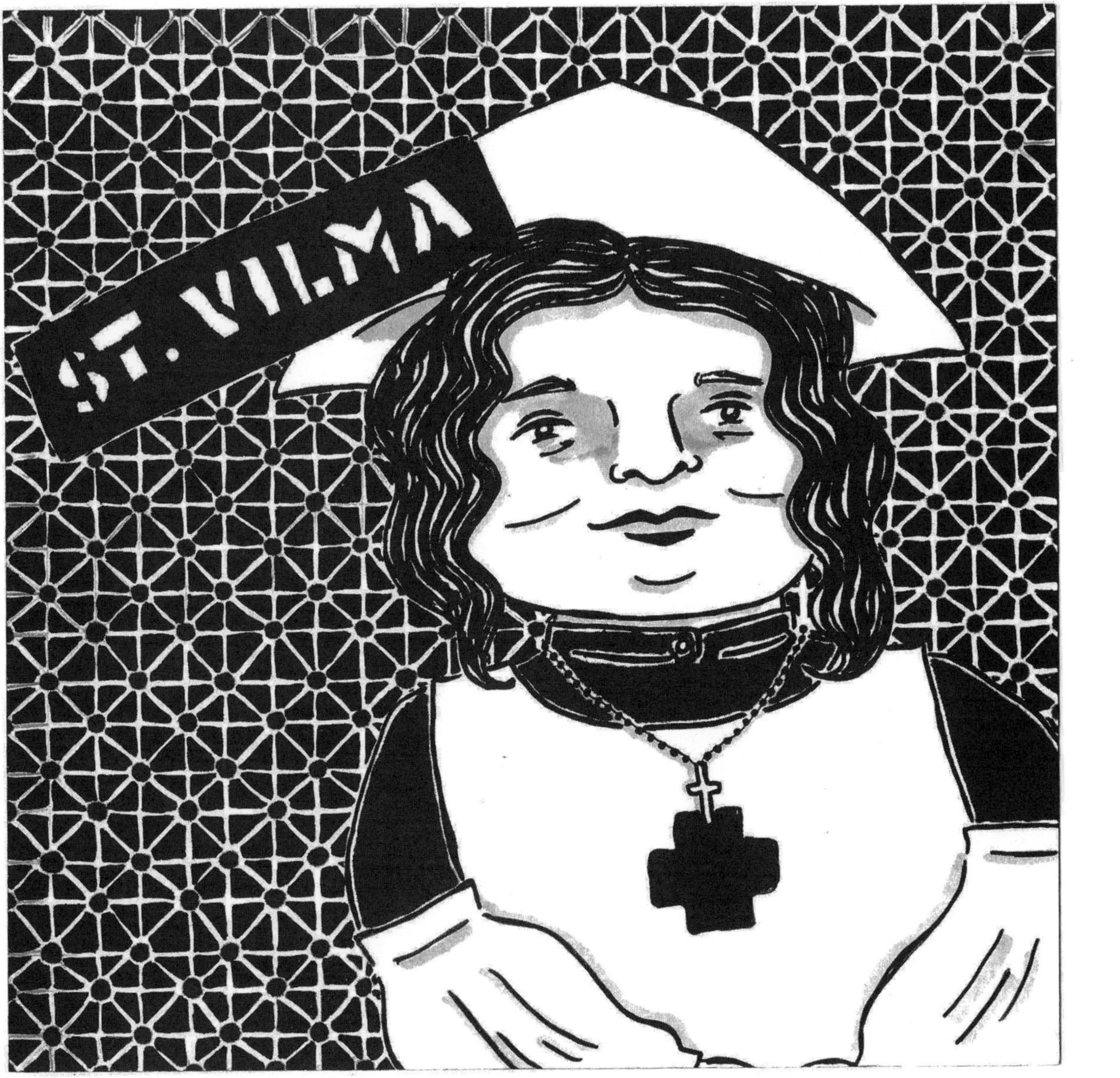
ST. VILMA

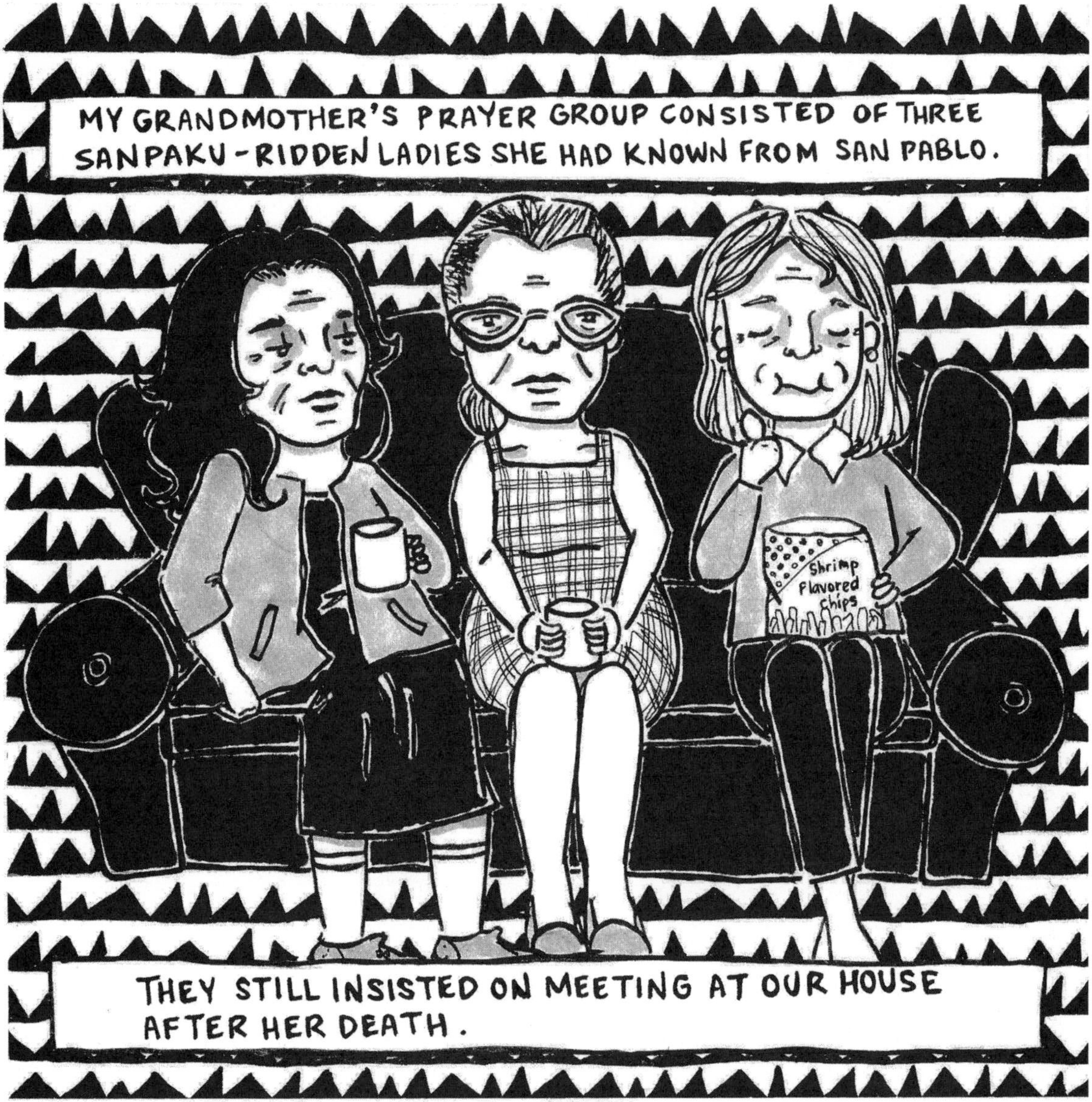
MY GRANDMOTHER'S PRAYER GROUP CONSISTED OF THREE SANPAKU-RIDDEN LADIES SHE HAD KNOWN FROM SAN PABLO.
Shrimp Flavored Chips
THEY STILL INSISTED ON MEETING AT OUR HOUSE AFTER HER DEATH.

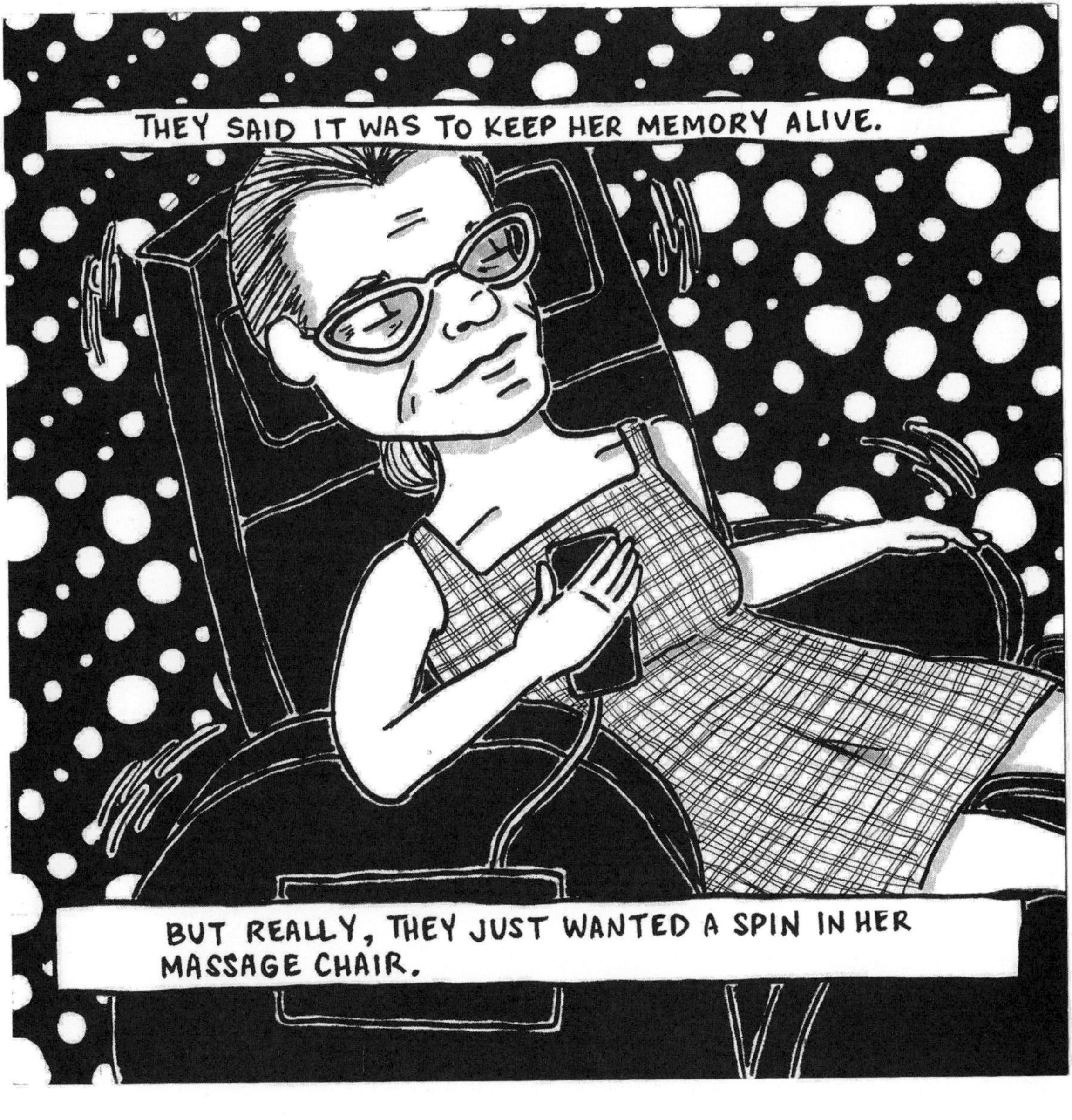
THEY SAID IT WAS TO KEEP HER MEMORY ALIVE.
BUT REALLY, THEY JUST WANTED A SPIN IN HER MASSAGE CHAIR.

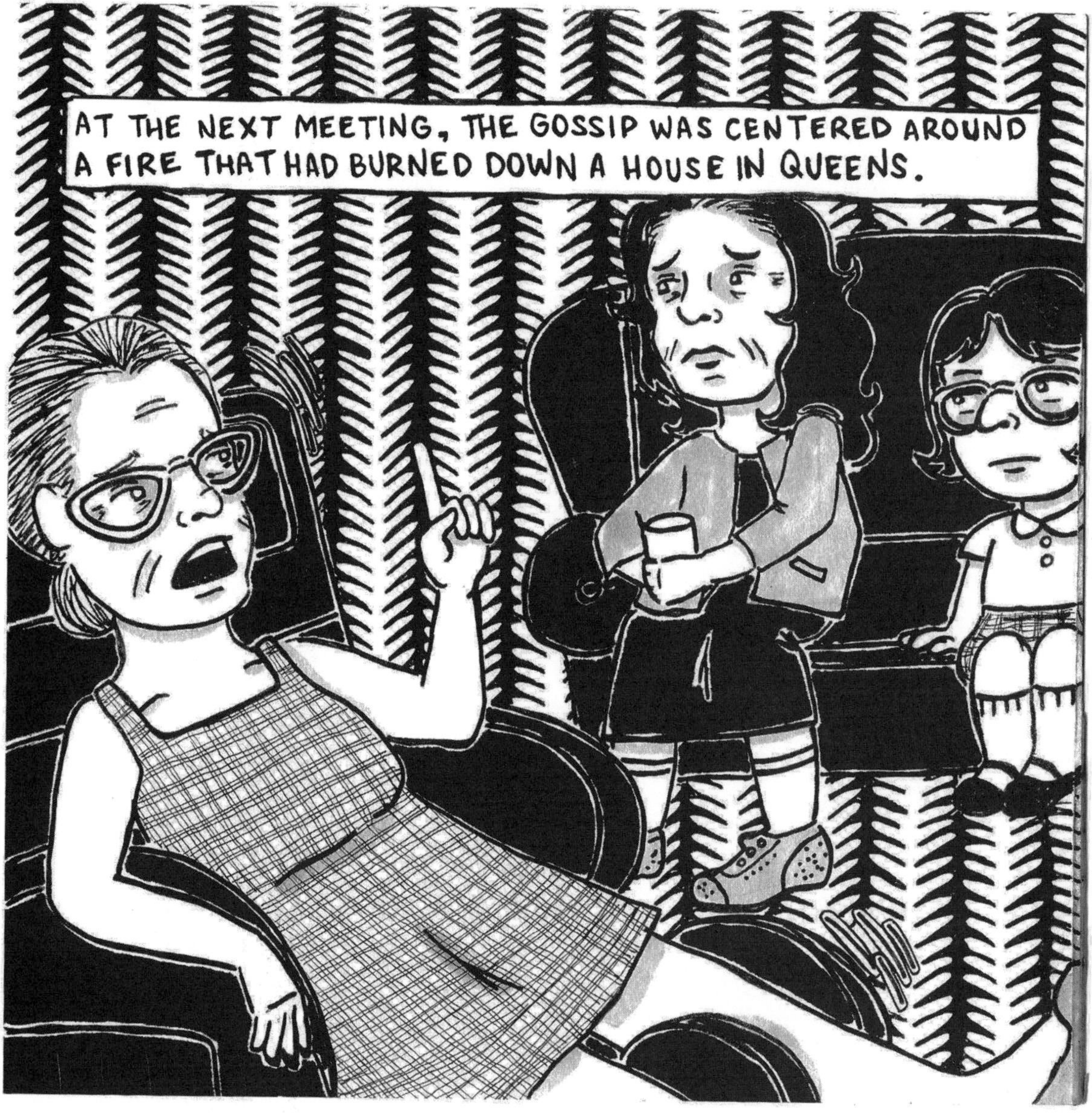
AT THE NEXT MEETING, THE GOSSIP WAS CENTERED AROUND A FIRE THAT HAD BURNED DOWN A HOUSE IN QUEENS.

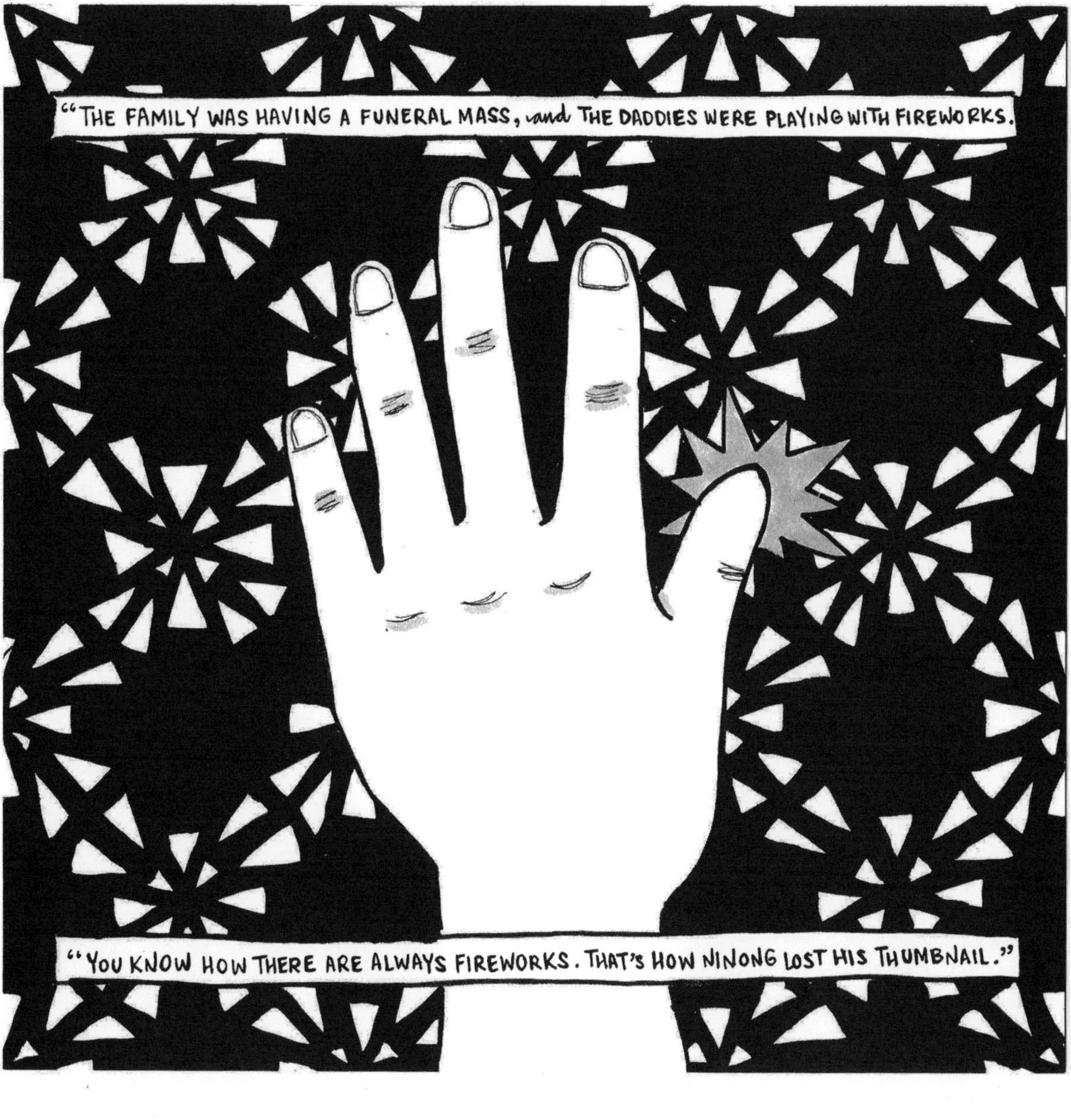
"THE FAMILY WAS HAVING A FUNERAL MASS, and THE DADDIES WERE PLAYING WITH FIREWORKS.
"YOU KNOW HOW THERE ARE ALWAYS FIREWORKS. THAT'S HOW NINONG LOST HIS THUMBNAIL."

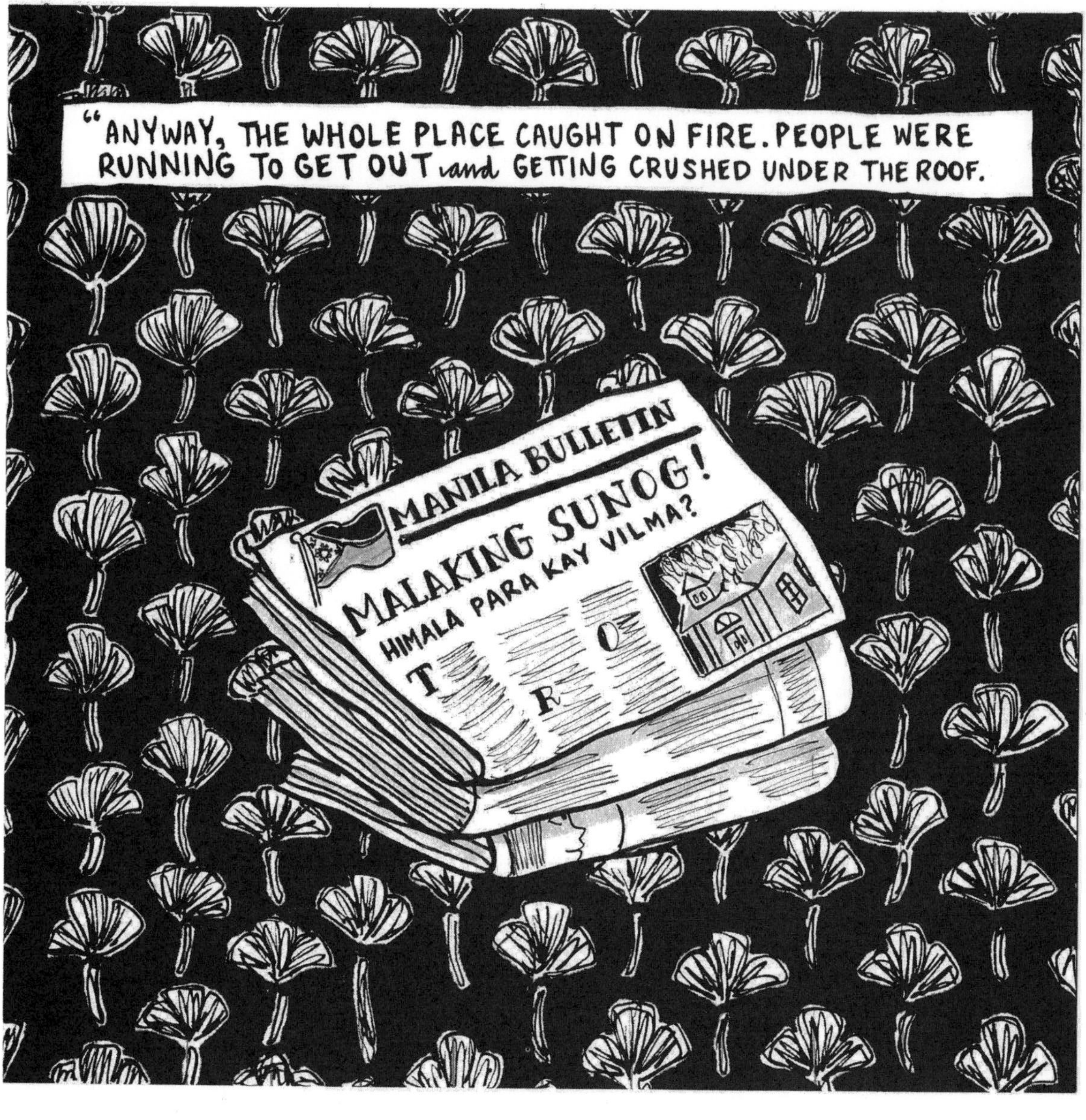
"ANYWAY, THE WHOLE PLACE CAUGHT ON FIRE. PEOPLE WERE RUNNING TO GET OUT and GETTING CRUSHED UNDER THE ROOF.
MANILA BULLETIN
MALAKING SUNOG!
HIMALA PARA KAY VILMA?

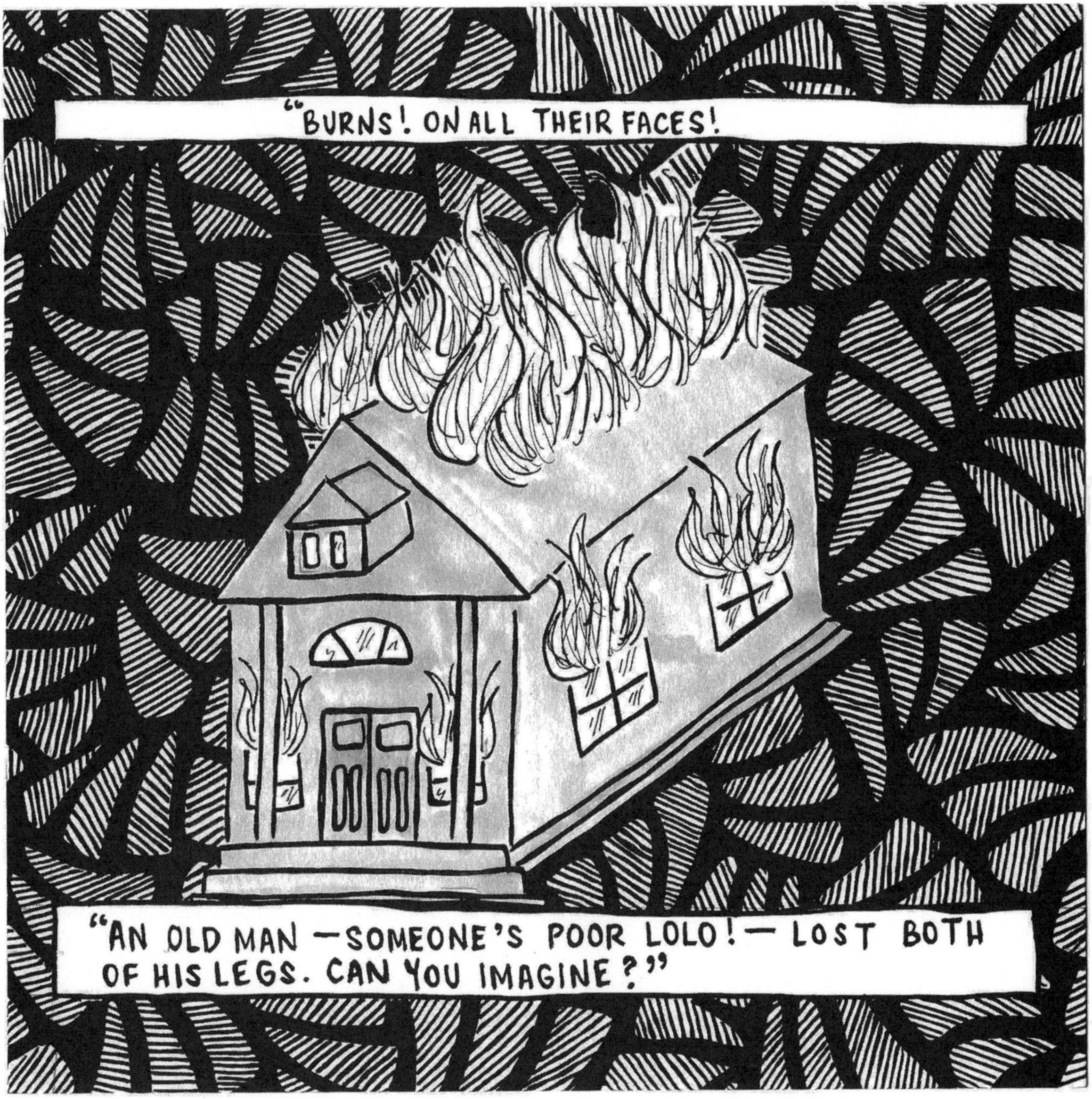
"BURNS! ON ALL THEIR FACES!
"AN OLD MAN —SOMEONE'S POOR LOLO!— LOST BOTH OF HIS LEGS. CAN YOU IMAGINE?"

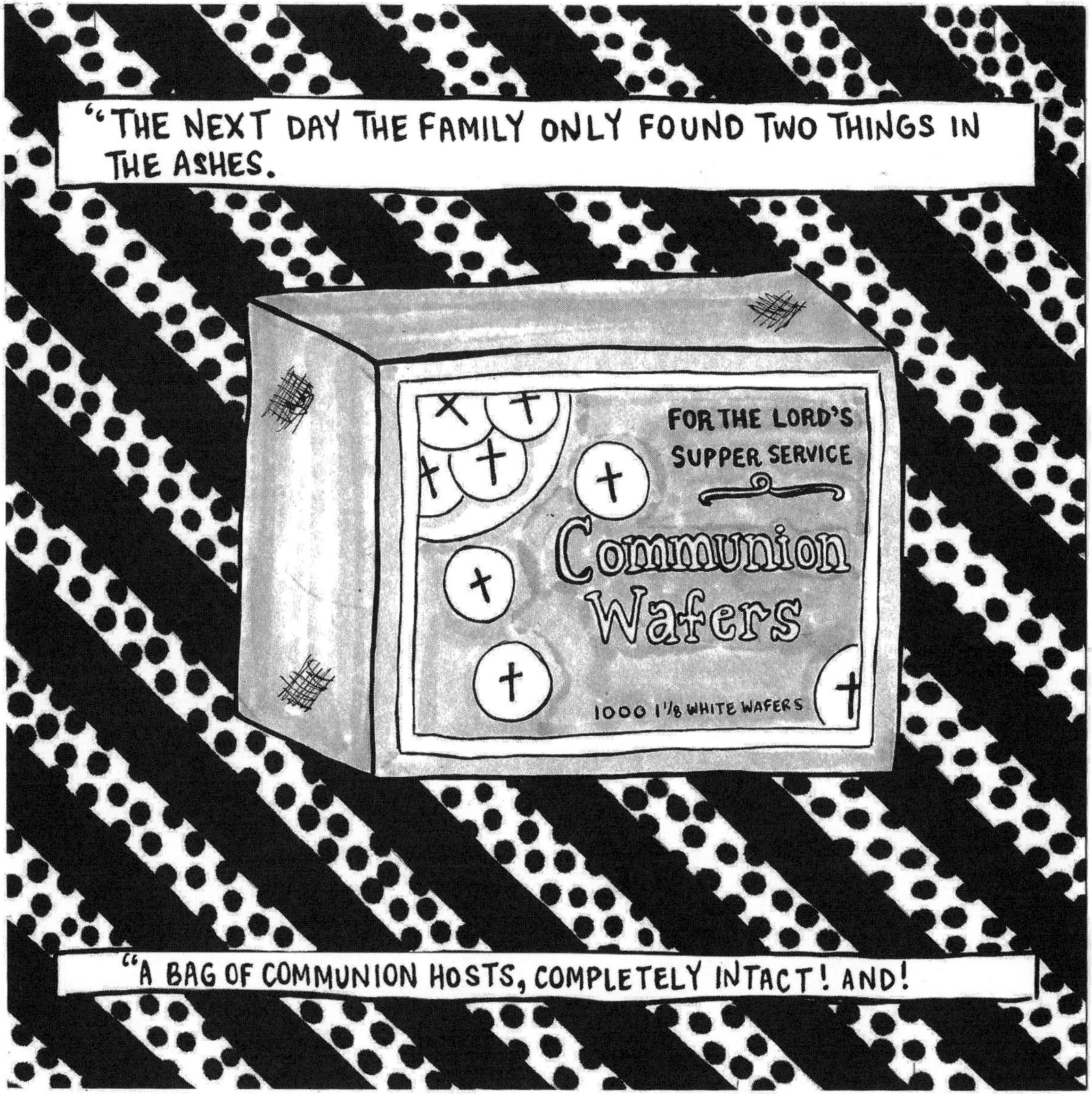
"THE NEXT DAY THE FAMILY ONLY FOUND TWO THINGS IN THE ASHES.
FOR THE LORD'S SUPPER SERVICE
Communion Wafers
1000 1 1/8 WHITE WAFERS
"A BAG OF COMMUNION HOSTS, COMPLETELY INTACT! AND!

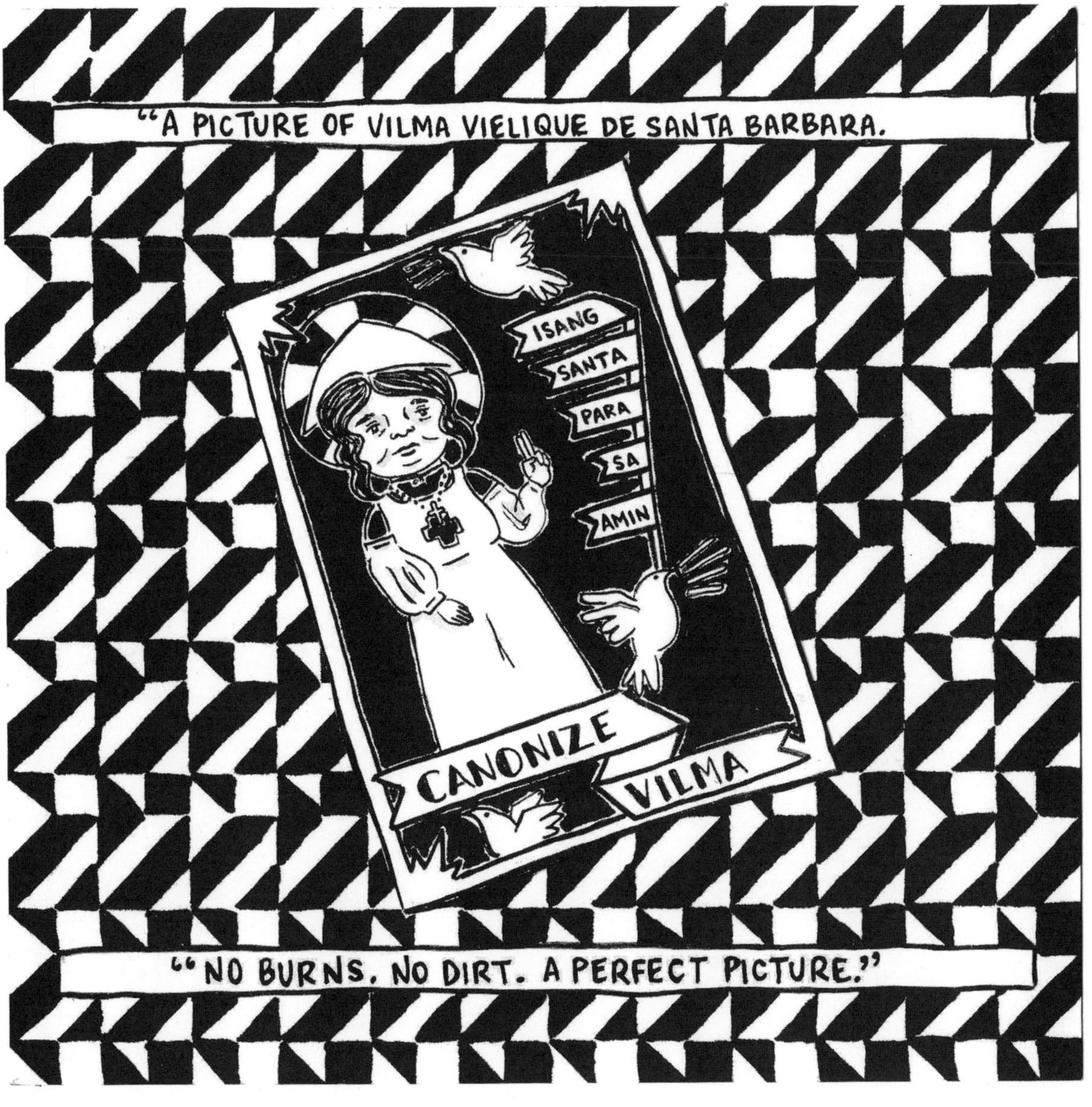
"A PICTURE OF VILMA VIELIQUE DE SANTA BARBARA.
ISANG
SANTA
PARA
SA
AMIN
CANONIZE
VILMA
"NO BURNS. NO DIRT. A PERFECT PICTURE."

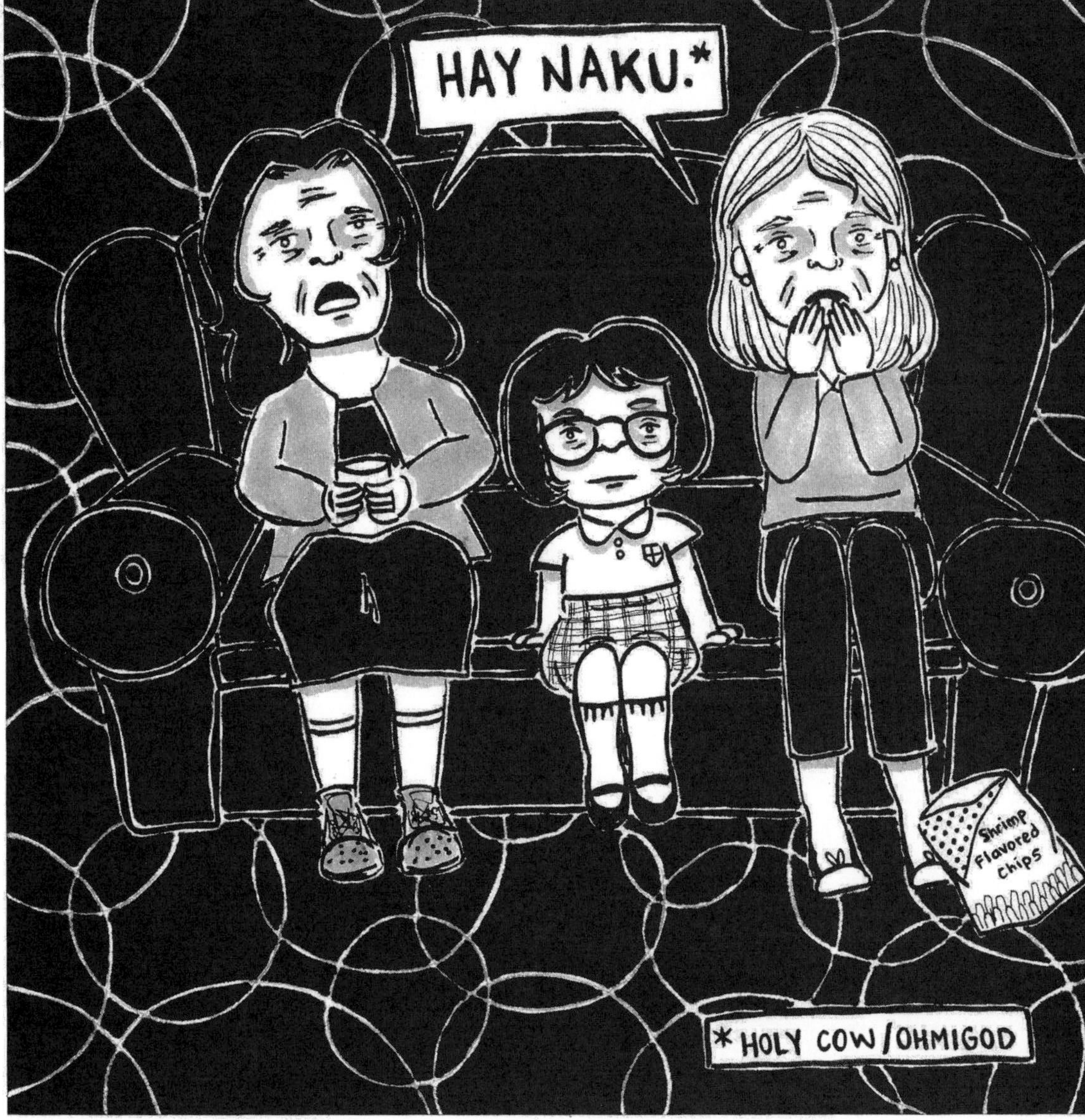
HAY NAKU.*
Shrimp Flavored Chips
* HOLY COW/OHMIGOD

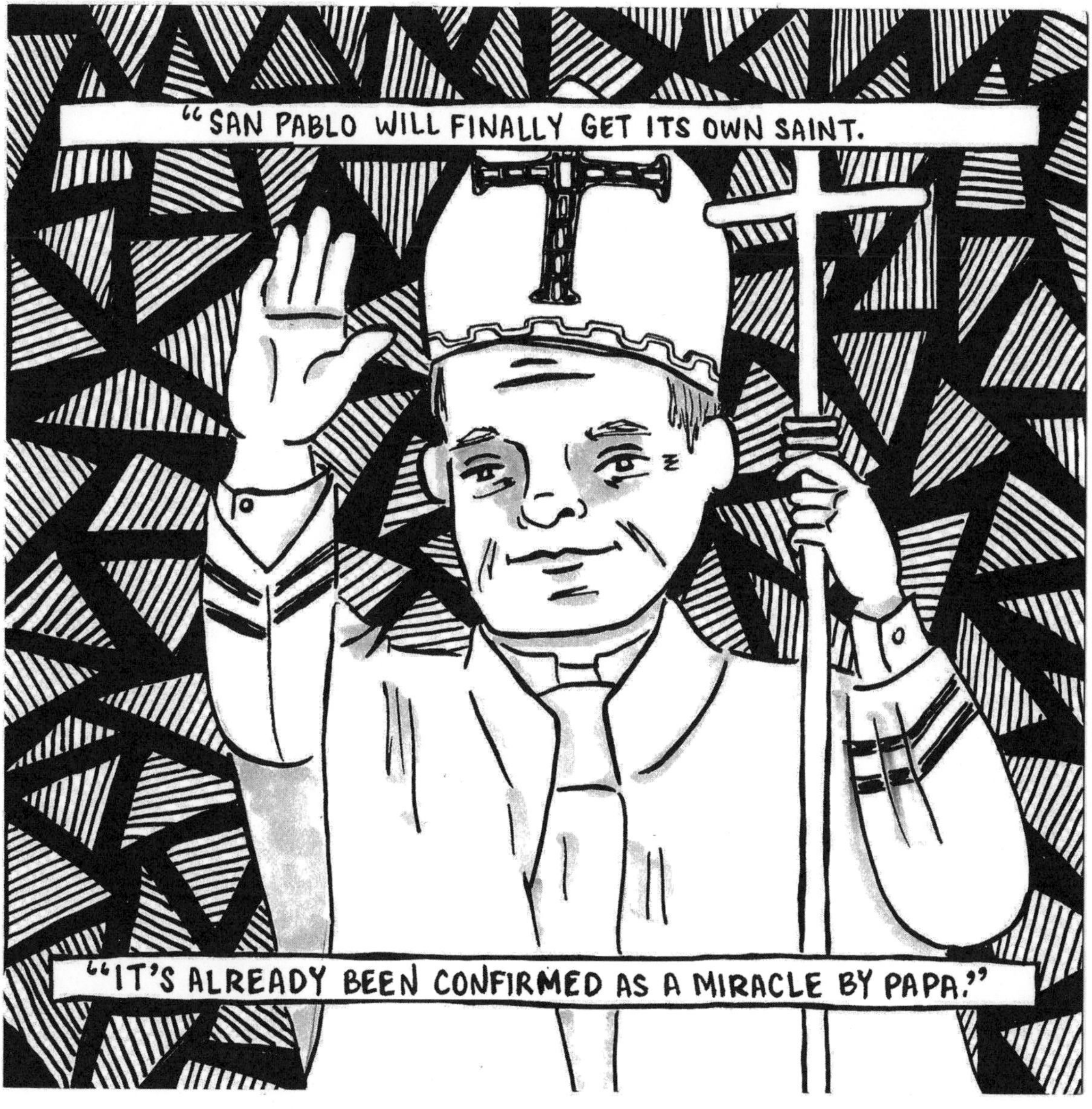
"SAN PABLO WILL FINALLY GET ITS OWN SAINT.
"IT'S ALREADY BEEN CONFIRMED AS A MIRACLE BY PAPA."

I REMEMBERED THAT FOR A TIME, LOLA HAD BEEN VILMA-OBSESSED.
SHE LIT A CANDLE FOR VILMA EVERY SUNDAY.

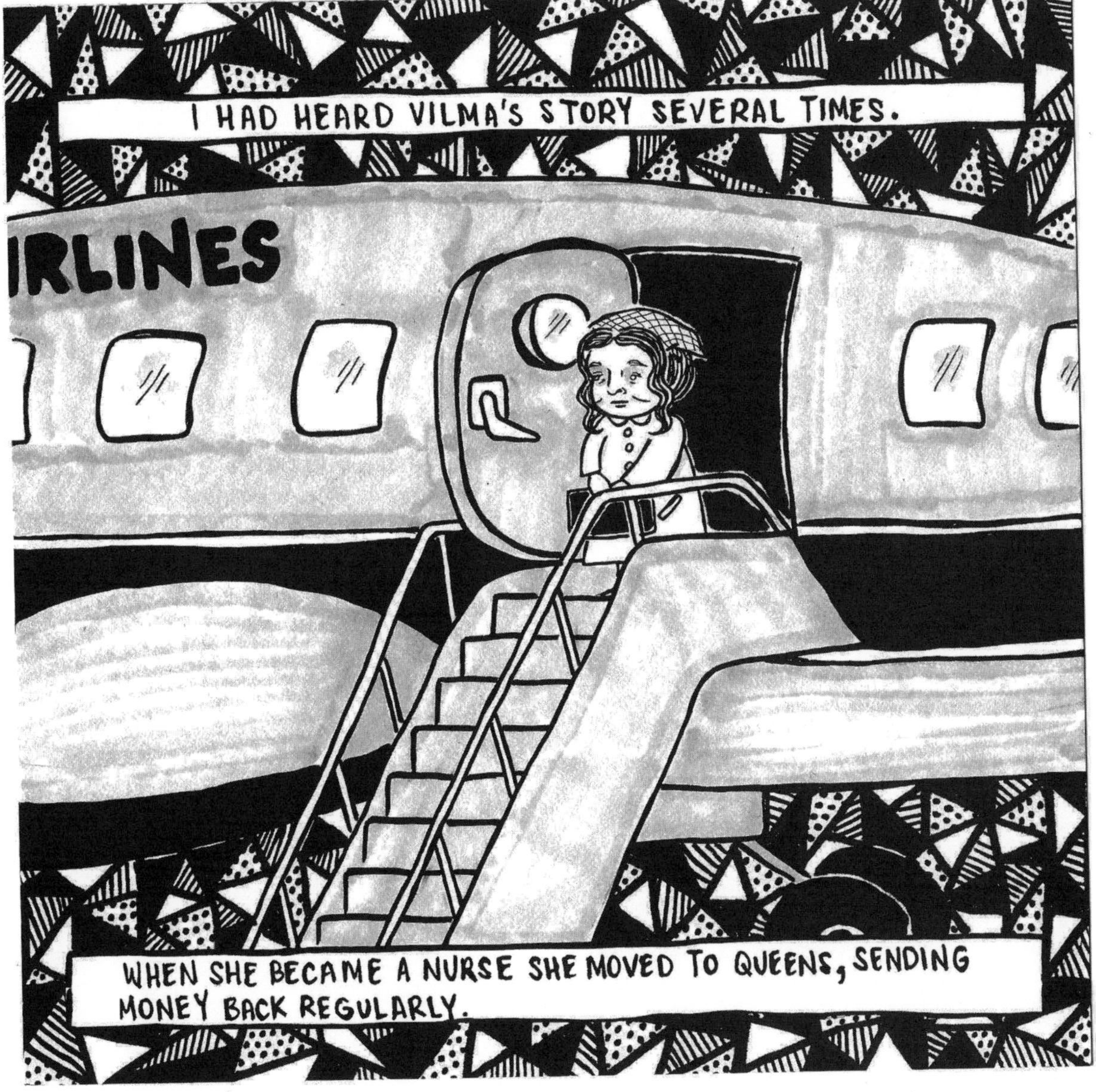
I HAD HEARD VILMA'S STORY SEVERAL TIMES.
IRLINES
WHEN SHE BECAME A NURSE SHE MOVED TO QUEENS, SENDING MONEY BACK REGULARLY.

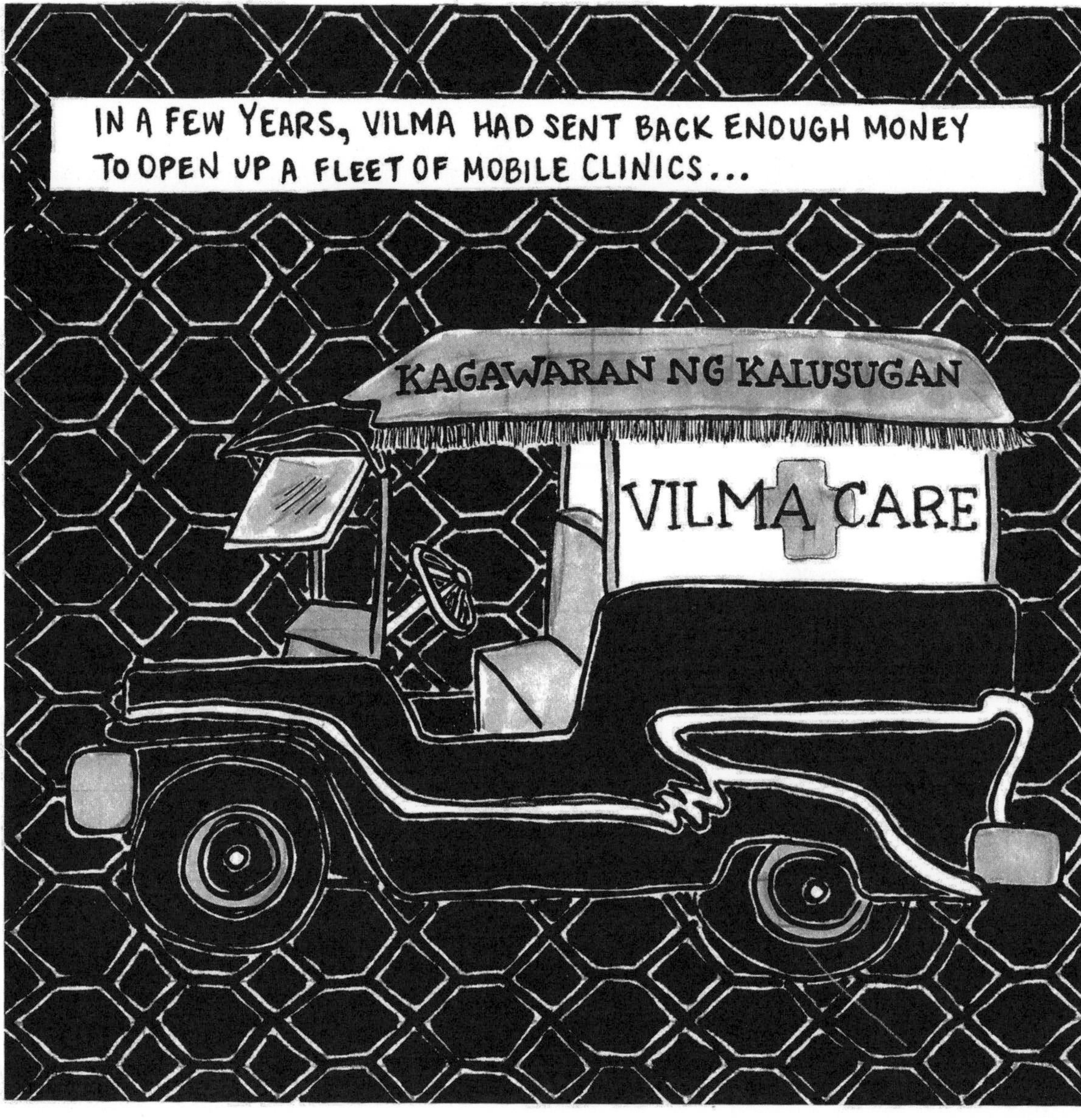
IN A FEW YEARS, VILMA HAD SENT BACK ENOUGH MONEY TO OPEN UP A FLEET OF MOBILE CLINICS...
KAGAWARAN NG KALUSUGAN
VILMA CARE

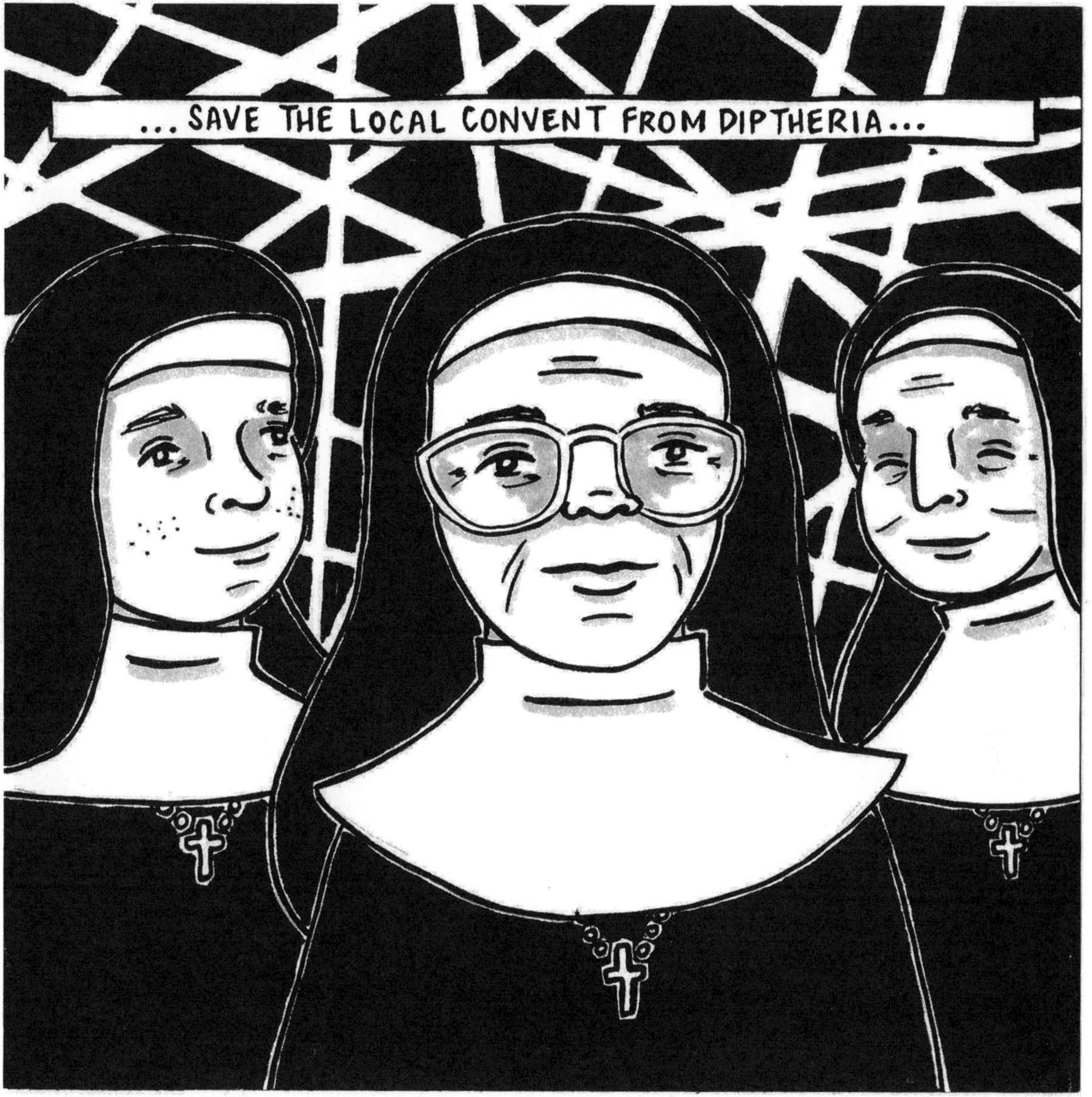
...SAVE THE LOCAL CONVENT FROM DIPTHERIA...

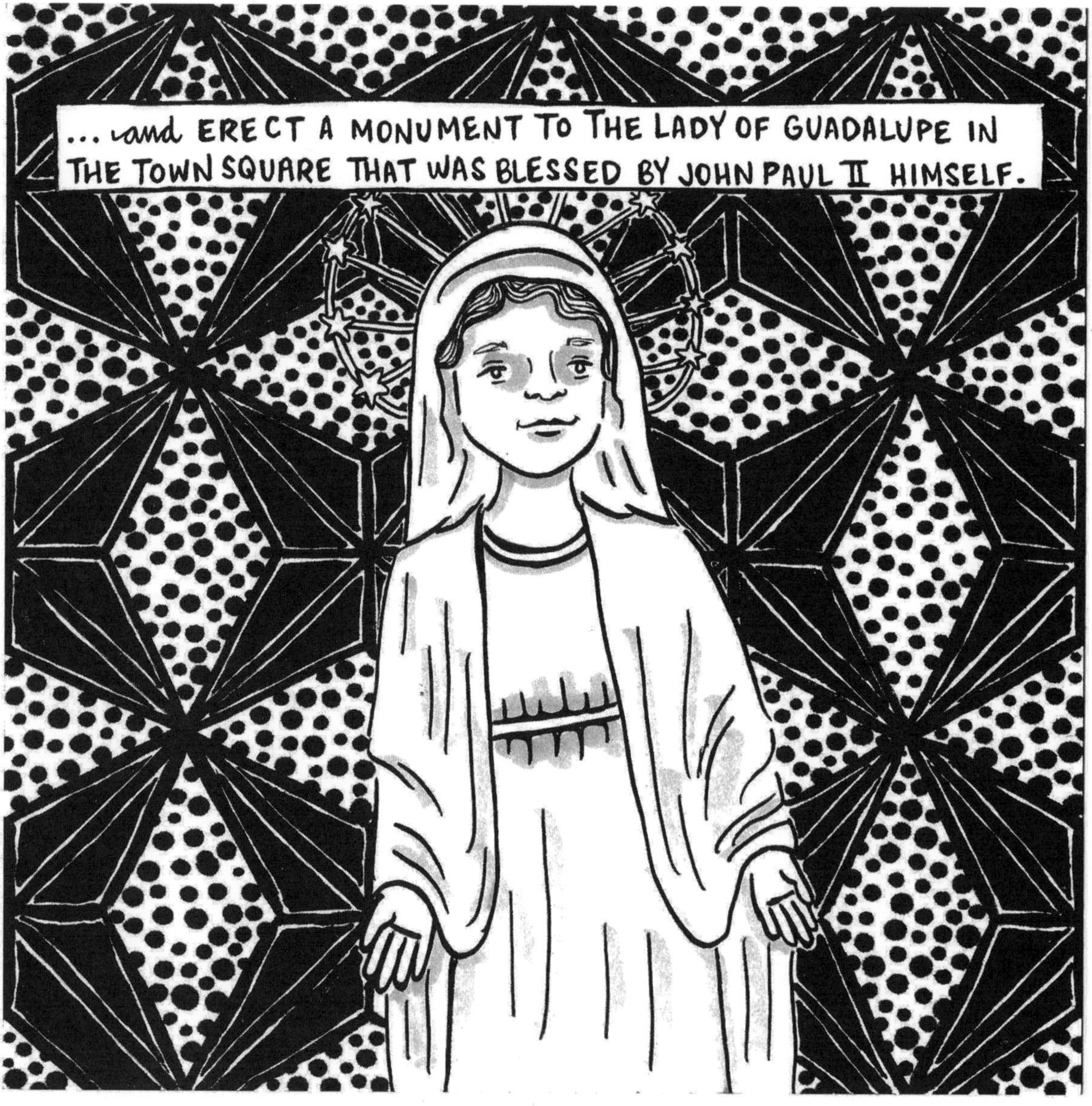
...and ERECT A MONUMENT TO THE LADY OF GUADALUPE IN THE TOWN SQUARE THAT WAS BLESSED BY JOHN PAUL II HIMSELF.

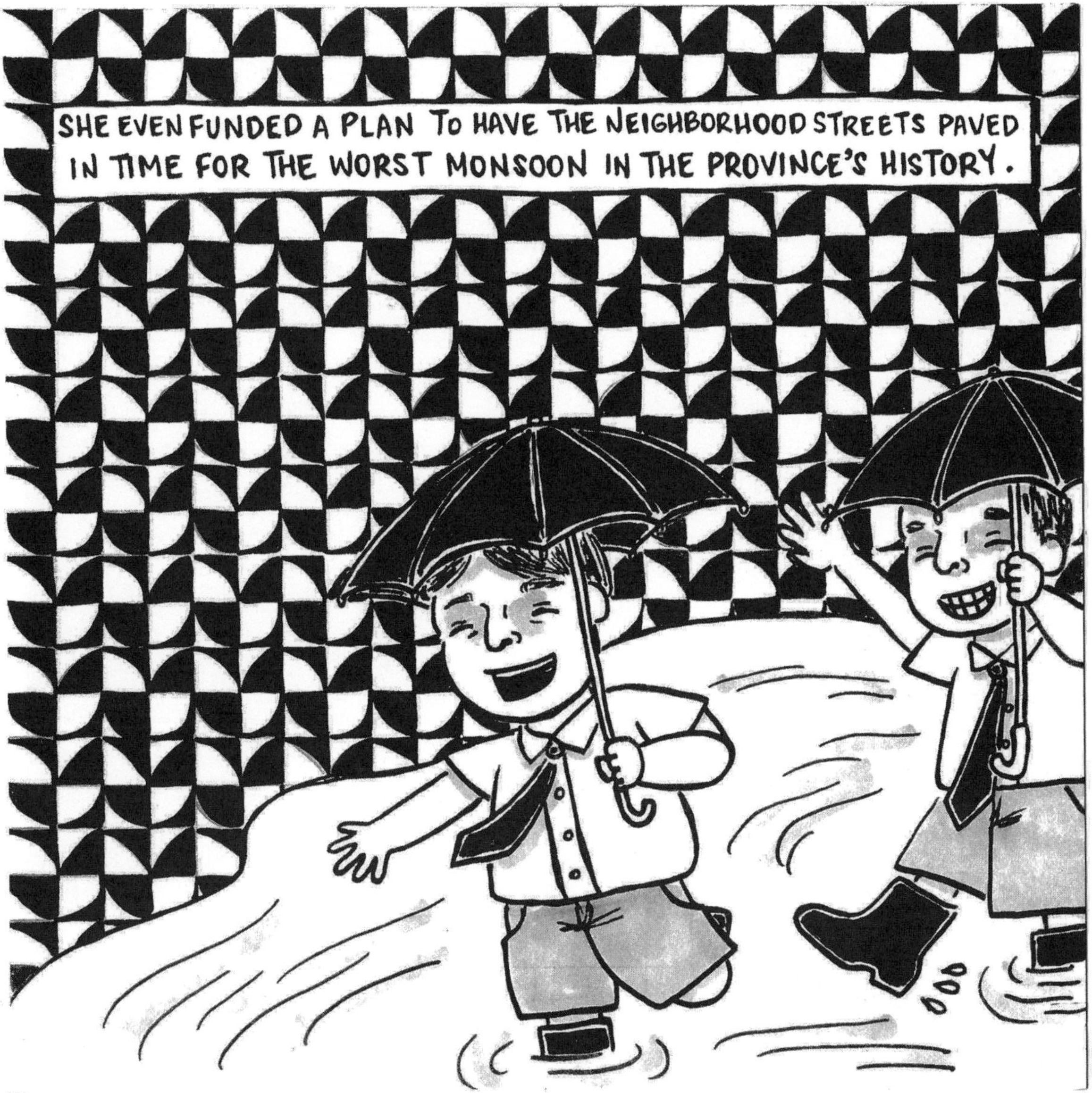
SHE EVEN FUNDED A PLAN TO HAVE THE NEIGHBORHOOD STREETS PAVED IN TIME FOR THE WORST MONSOON IN THE PROVINCE'S HISTORY.

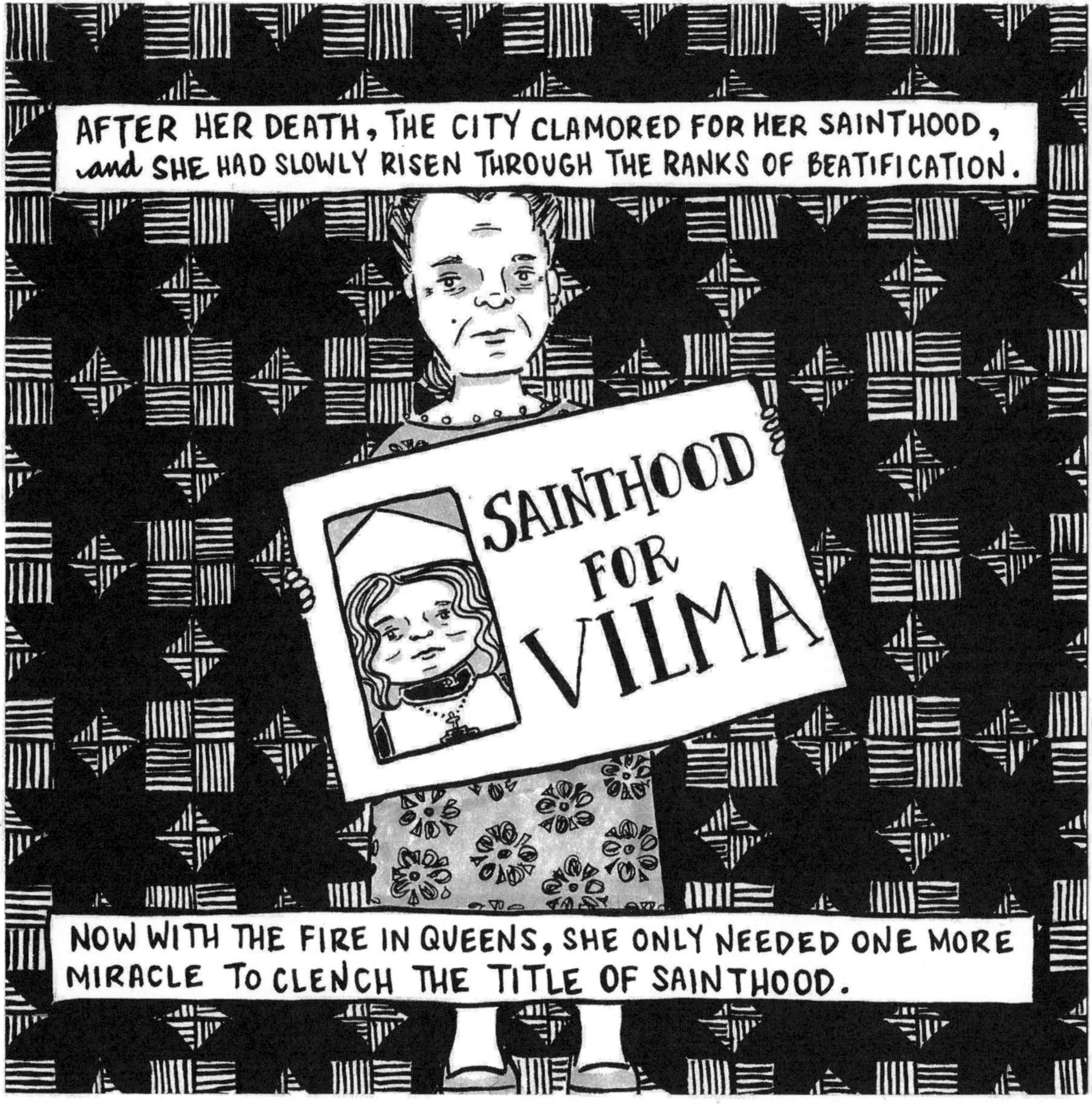
AFTER HER DEATH, THE CITY CLAMORED FOR HER SAINTHOOD, and SHE HAD SLOWLY RISEN THROUGH THE RANKS OF BEATIFICATION.
SAINTHOOD FOR VILMA
NOW WITH THE FIRE IN QUEENS, SHE ONLY NEEDED ONE MORE MIRACLE TO CLENCH THE TITLE OF SAINTHOOD.

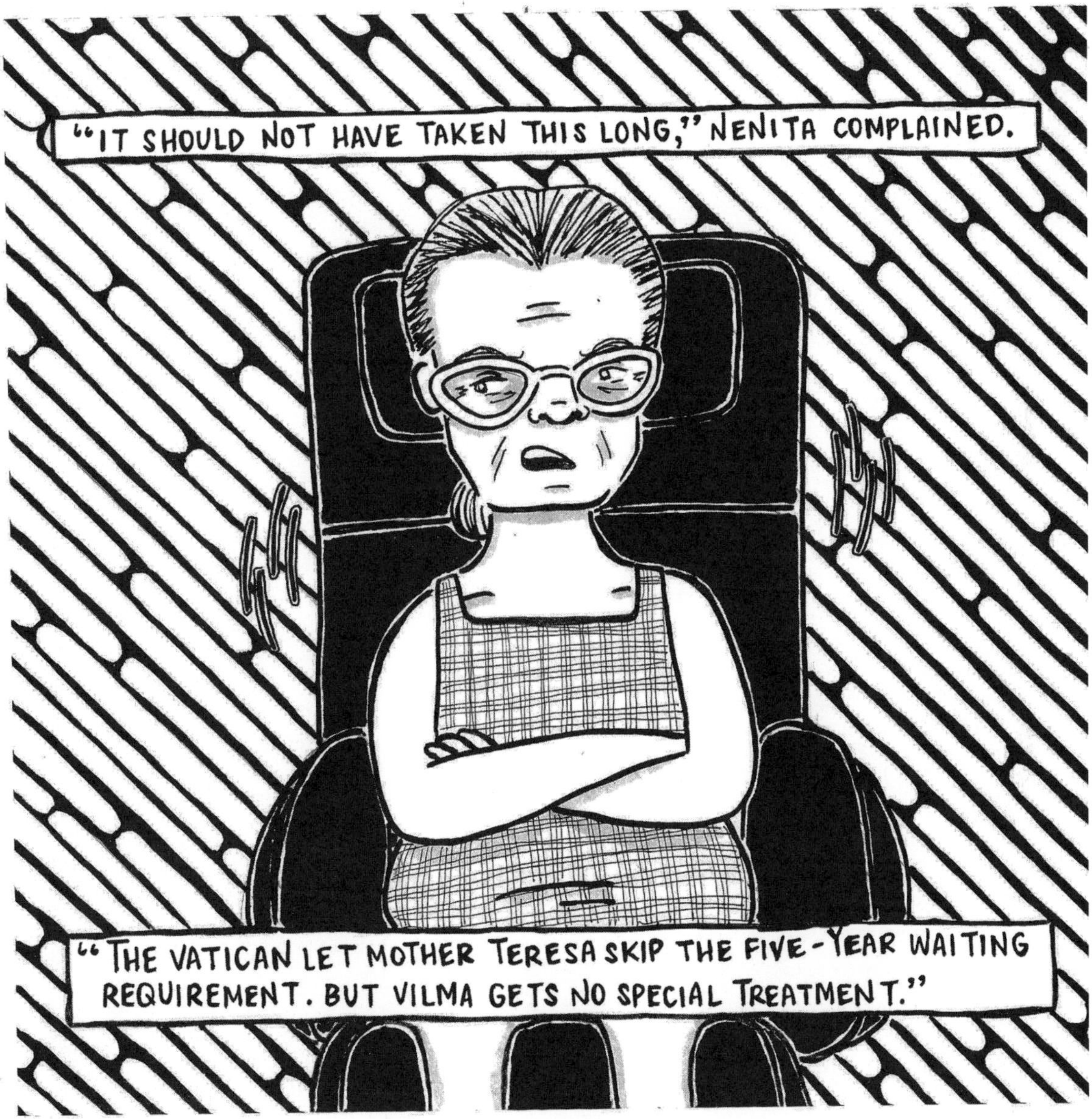
"IT SHOULD NOT HAVE TAKEN THIS LONG," NENITA COMPLAINED.
"THE VATICAN LET MOTHER TERESA SKIP THE FIVE-YEAR WAITING REQUIREMENT. BUT VILMA GETS NO SPECIAL TREATMENT."

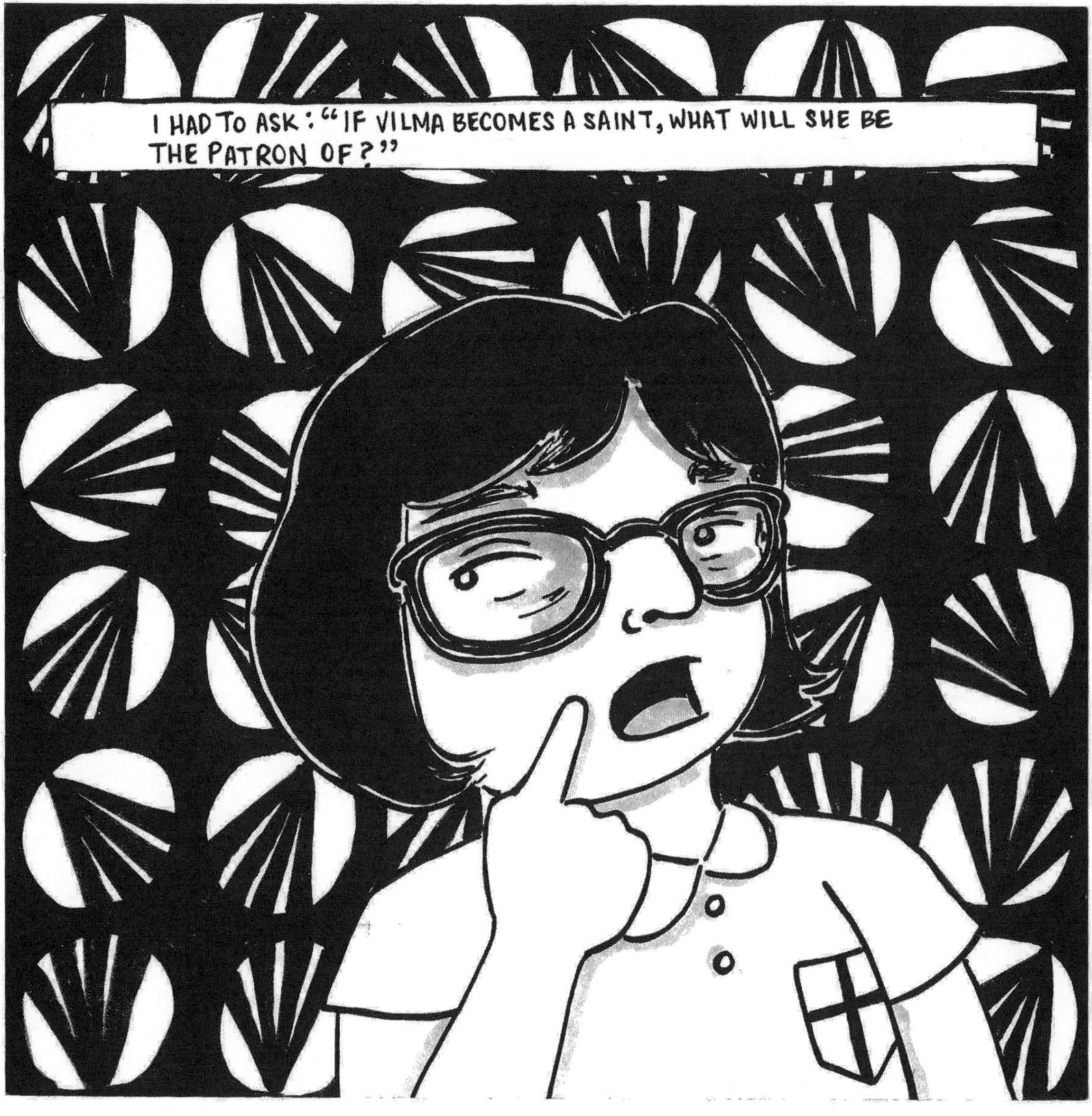
I HAD TO ASK: "IF VILMA BECOMES A SAINT, WHAT WILL SHE BE THE PATRON OF?"

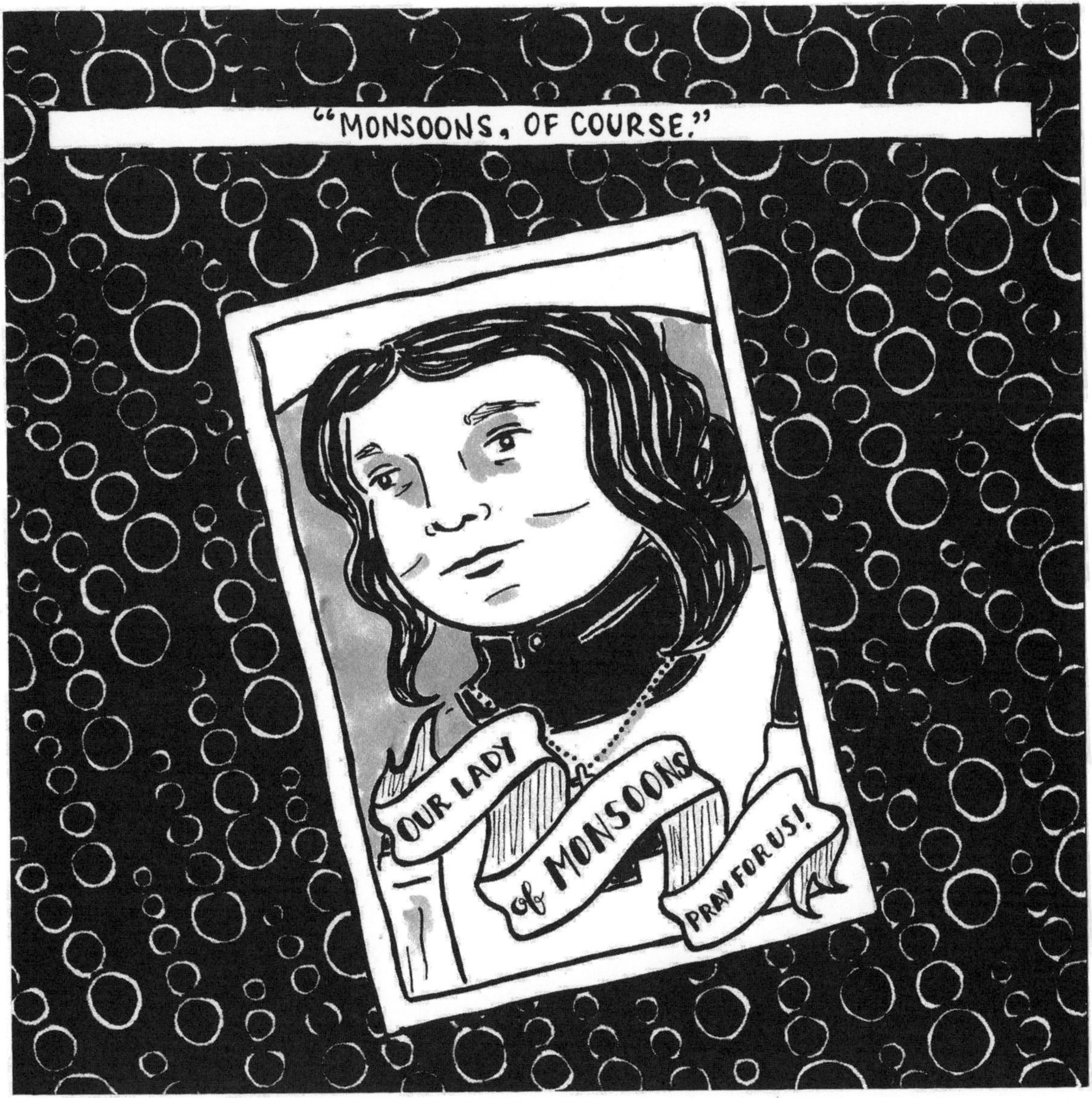
"MONSOONS, OF COURSE."
OUR LADY
of MONSOONS
PRAY FOR US!

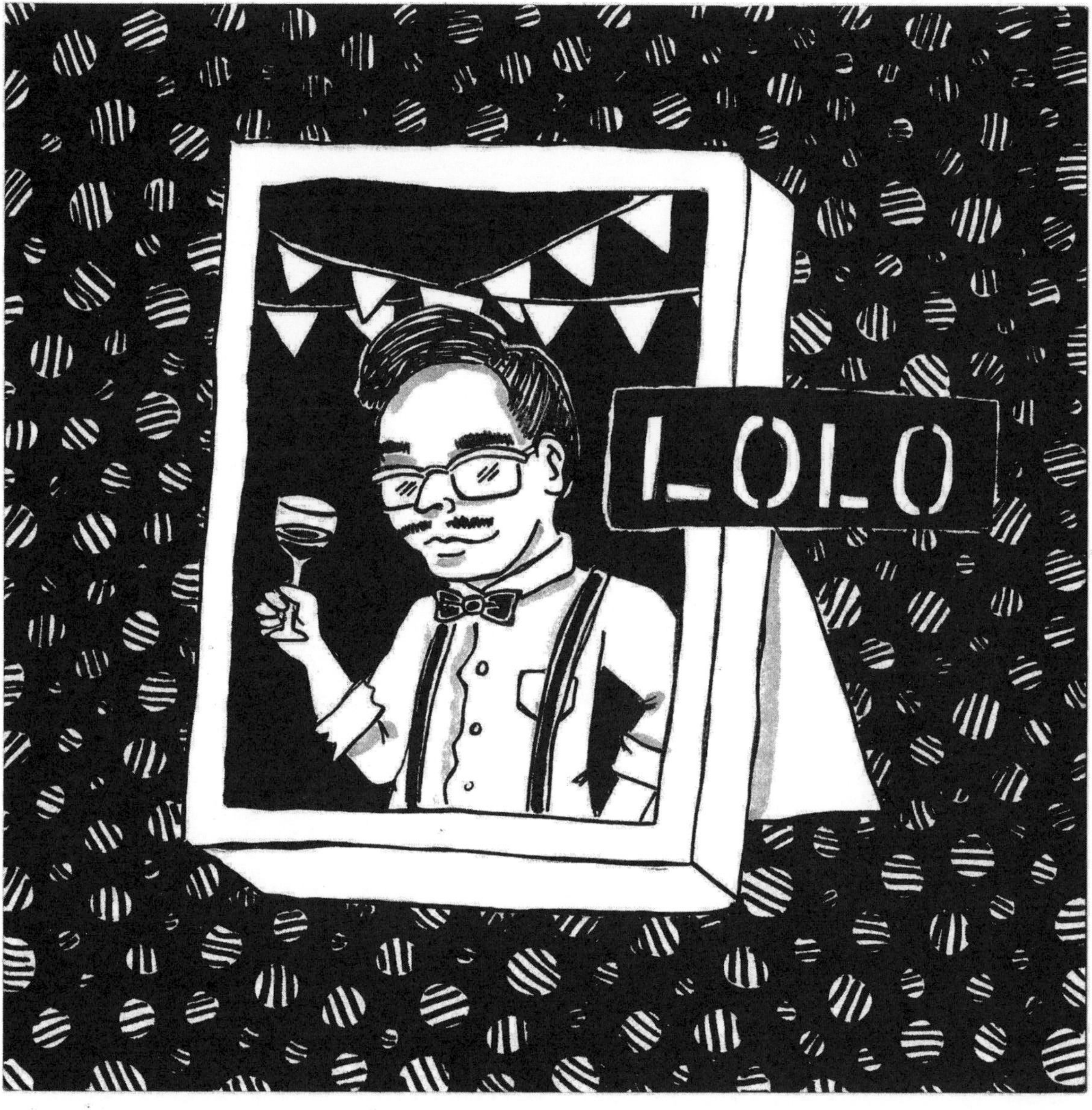
LOLO

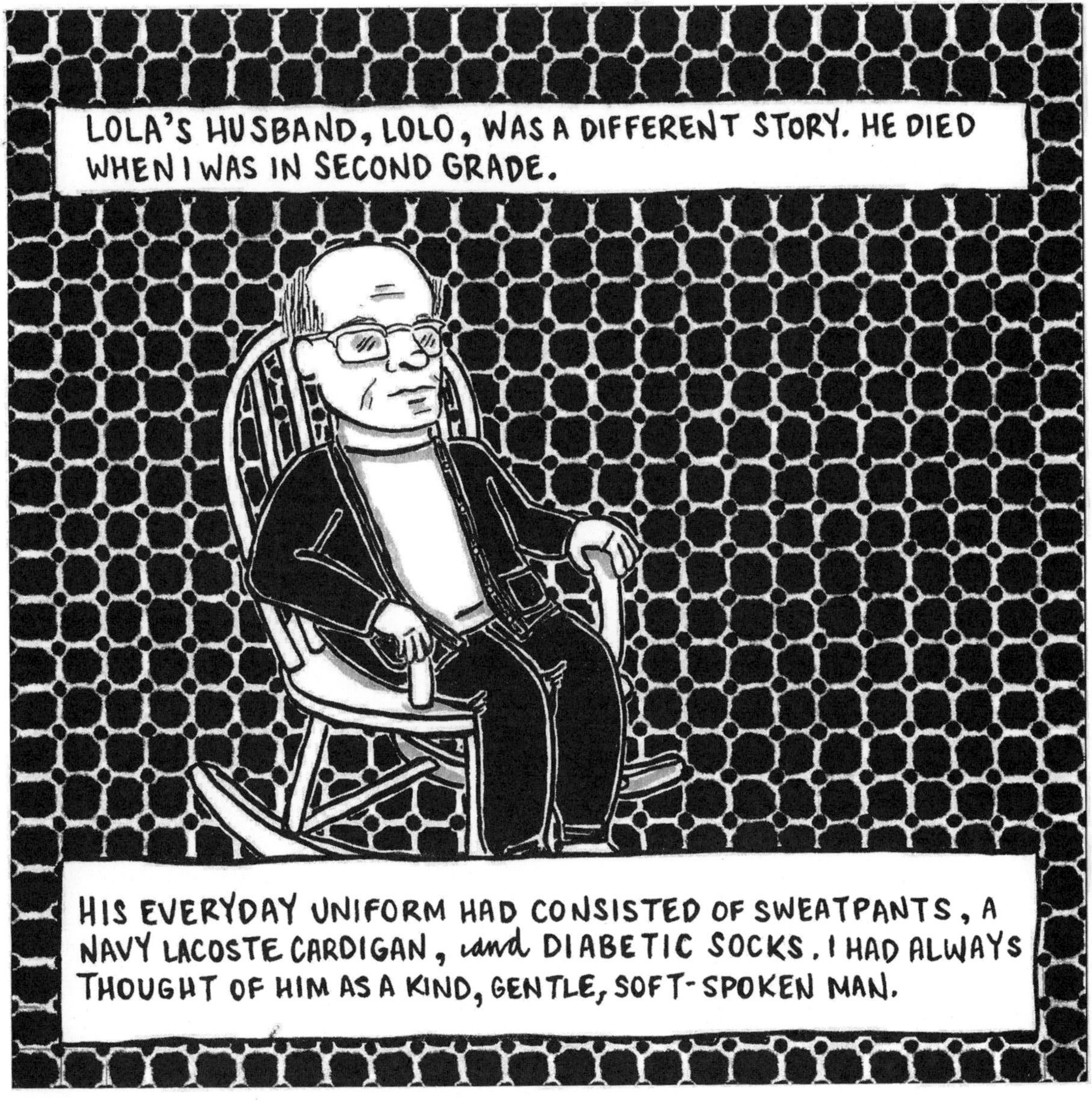
LOLA'S HUSBAND, LOLO, WAS A DIFFERENT STORY. HE DIED WHEN I WAS IN SECOND GRADE.
HIS EVERYDAY UNIFORM HAD CONSISTED OF SWEATPANTS, A NAVY LACOSTE CARDIGAN, and DIABETIC SOCKS. I HAD ALWAYS THOUGHT OF HIM AS A KIND, GENTLE, SOFT-SPOKEN MAN.

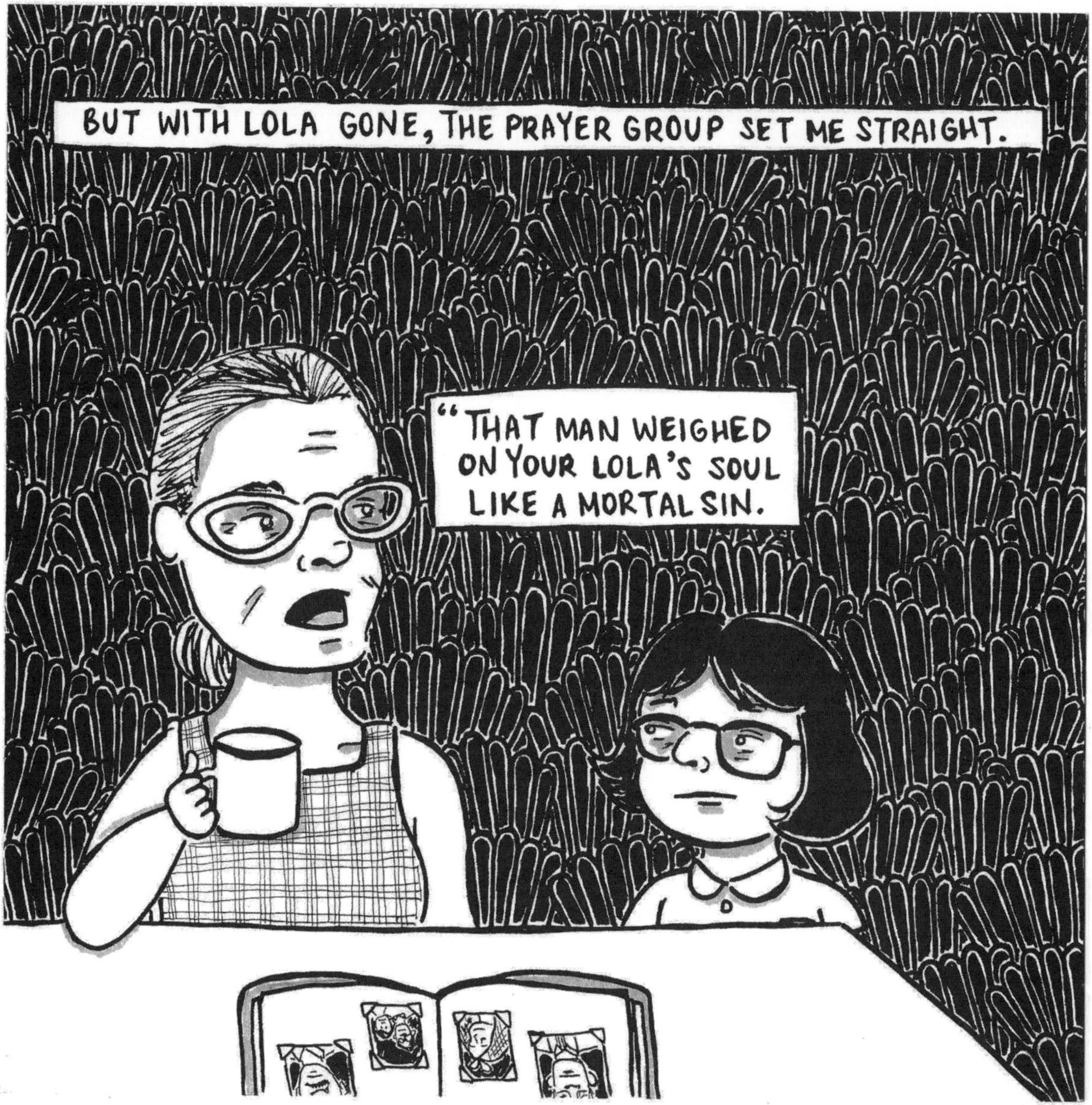
BUT WITH LOLA GONE, THE PRAYER GROUP SET ME STRAIGHT.
"THAT MAN WEIGHED ON YOUR LOLA'S SOUL LIKE A MORTAL SIN.

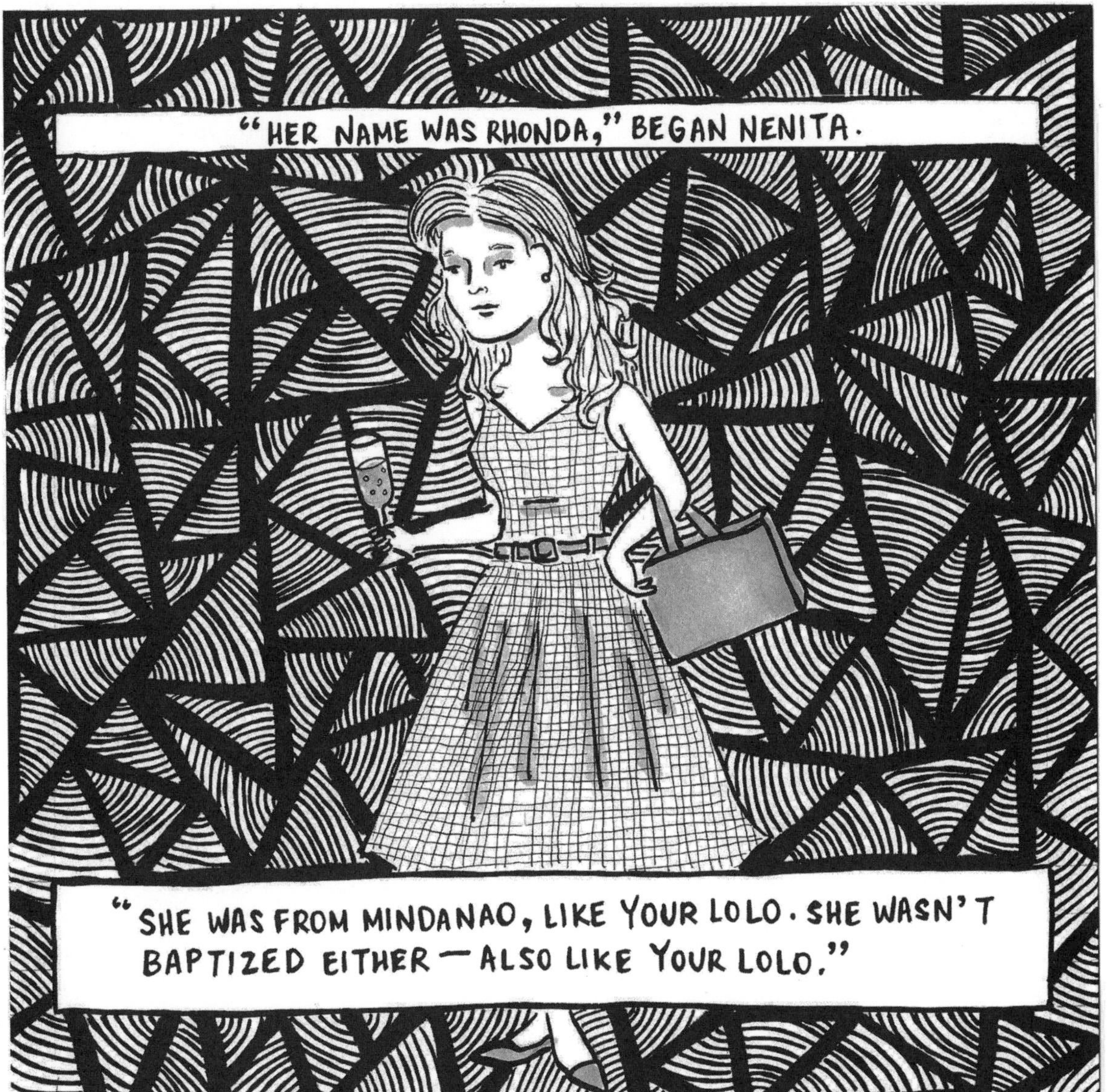
"HER NAME WAS RHONDA," BEGAN NENITA.
"SHE WAS FROM MINDANAO, LIKE YOUR LOLO. SHE WASN'T BAPTIZED EITHER—ALSO LIKE YOUR LOLO."

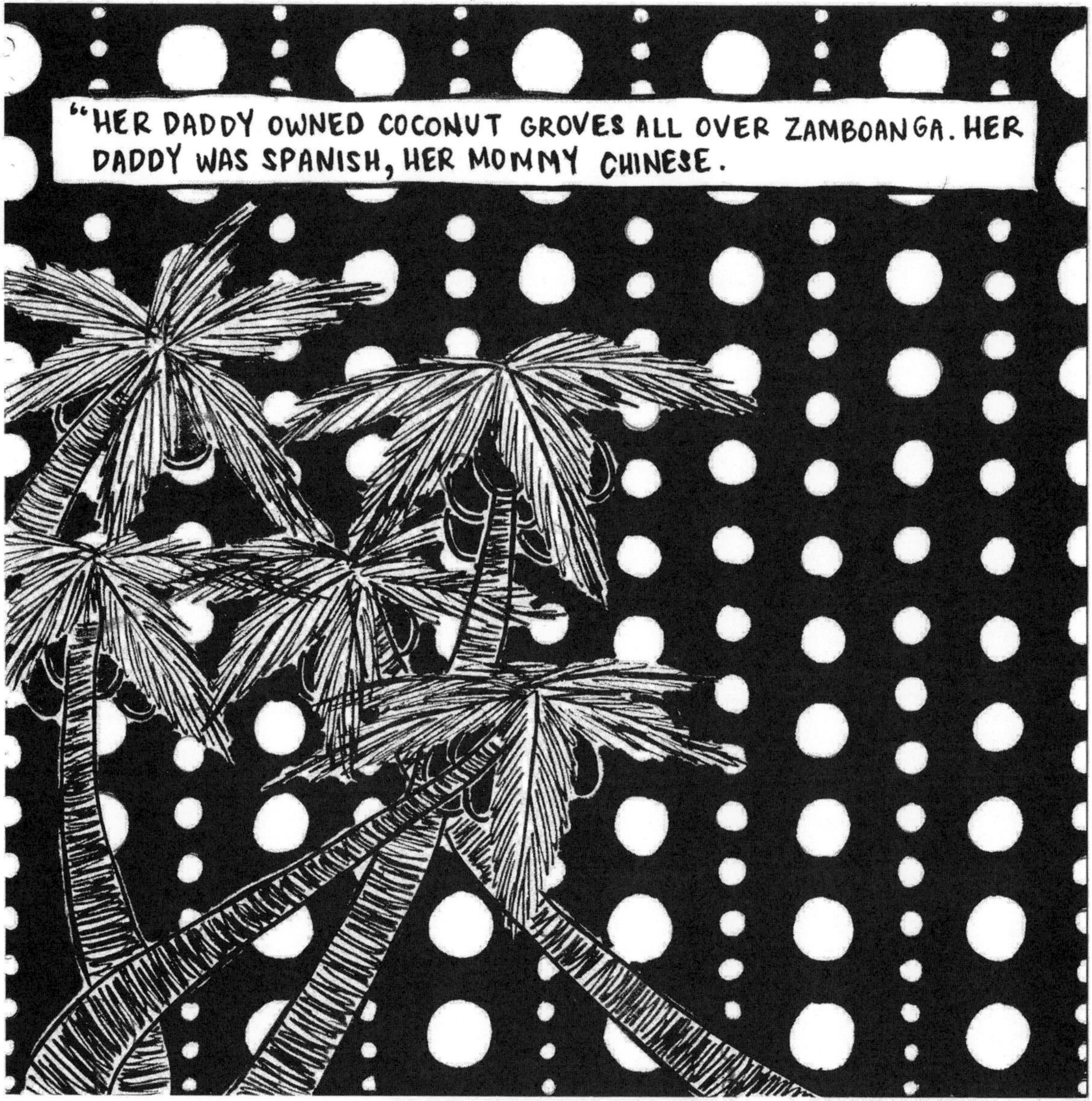
"HER DADDY OWNED COCONUT GROVES ALL OVER ZAMBOANGA. HER DADDY WAS SPANISH, HER MOMMY CHINESE.

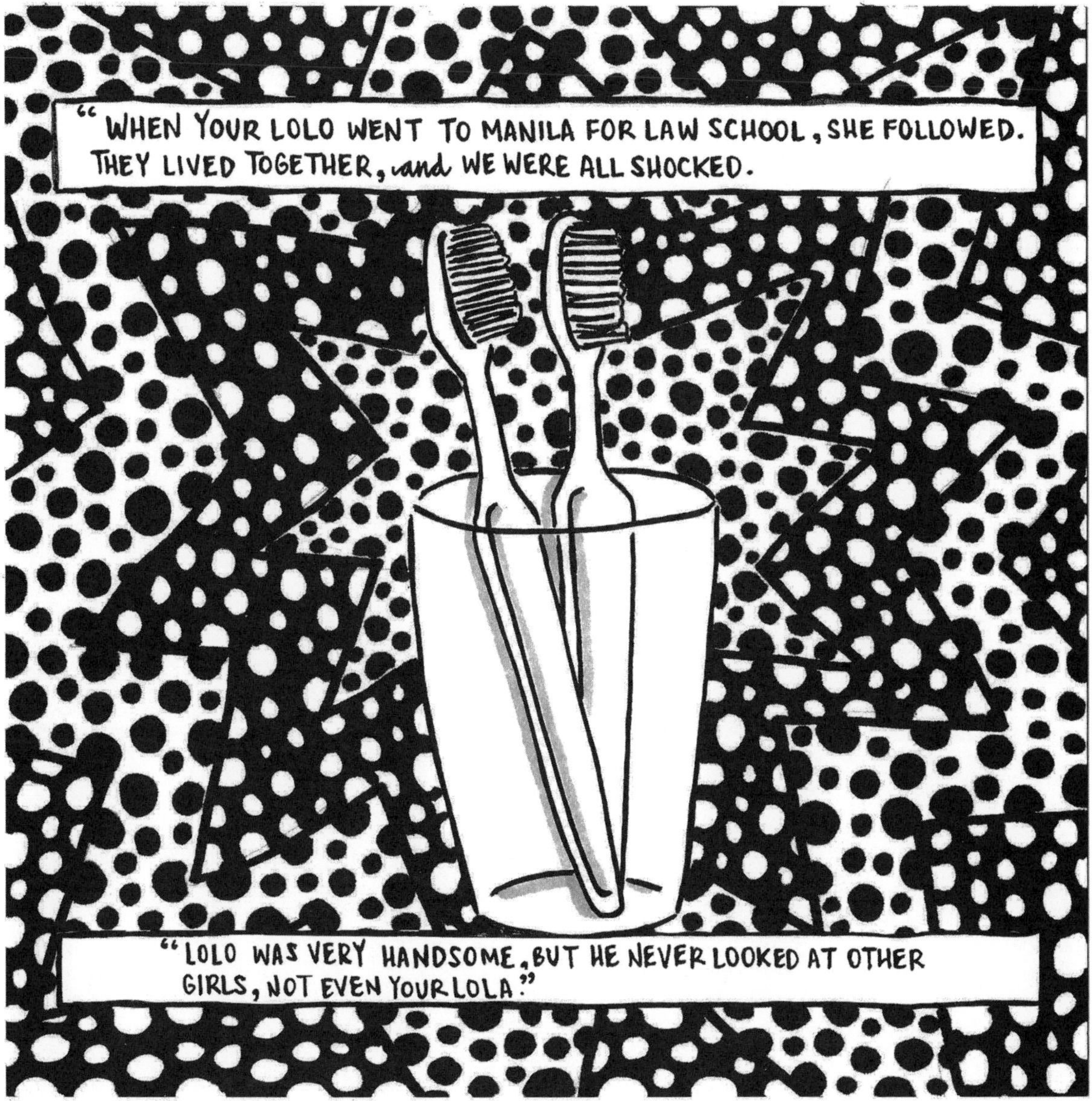
"WHEN YOUR LOLO WENT TO MANILA FOR LAW SCHOOL, SHE FOLLOWED. THEY LIVED TOGETHER, and WE WERE ALL SHOCKED.
"LOLO WAS VERY HANDSOME, BUT HE NEVER LOOKED AT OTHER GIRLS, NOT EVEN YOUR LOLA."

"HE ONLY CARED ABOUT HIS SPANISH-CHINA DOLL. YOU SHOULD'VE SEEN THE WAY THEY DANCED. IT WAS NOT FOR A CHILD'S EYES.

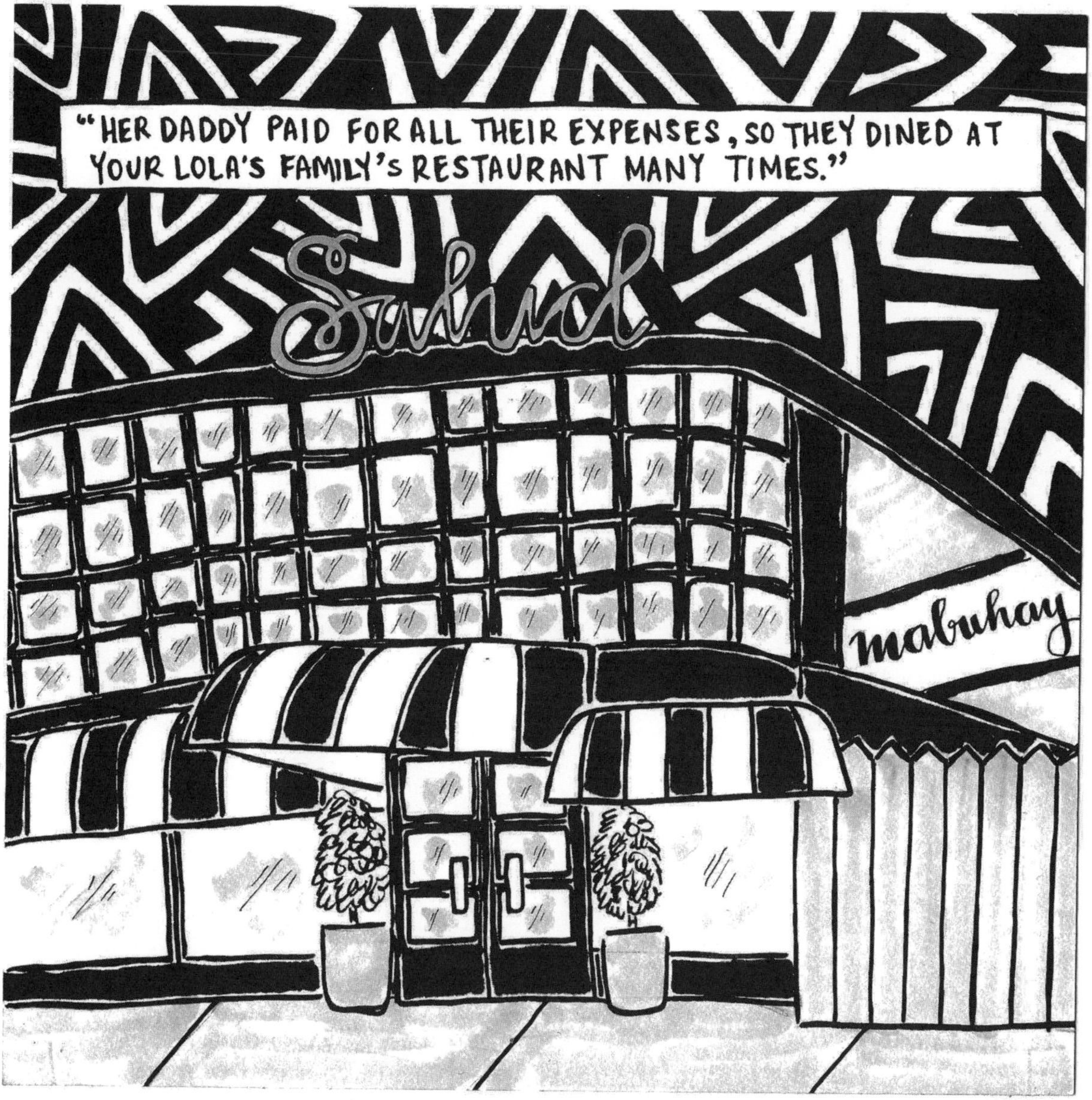
"HER DADDY PAID FOR ALL THEIR EXPENSES, SO THEY DINED AT YOUR LOLA'S FAMILY'S RESTAURANT MANY TIMES."
mabuhay

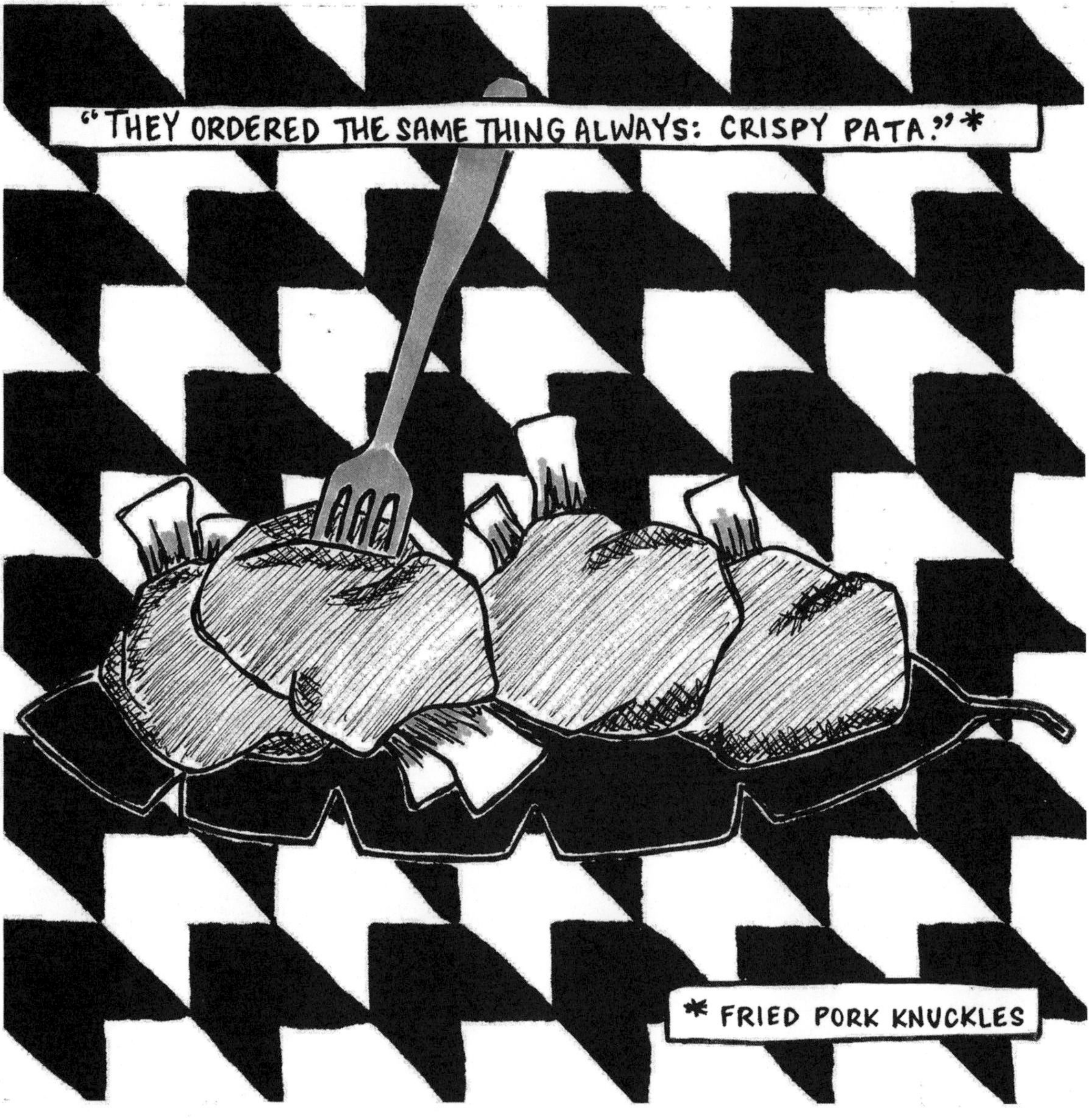
"THEY ORDERED THE SAME THING ALWAYS: CRISPY PATA."*
* FRIED PORK KNUCKLES

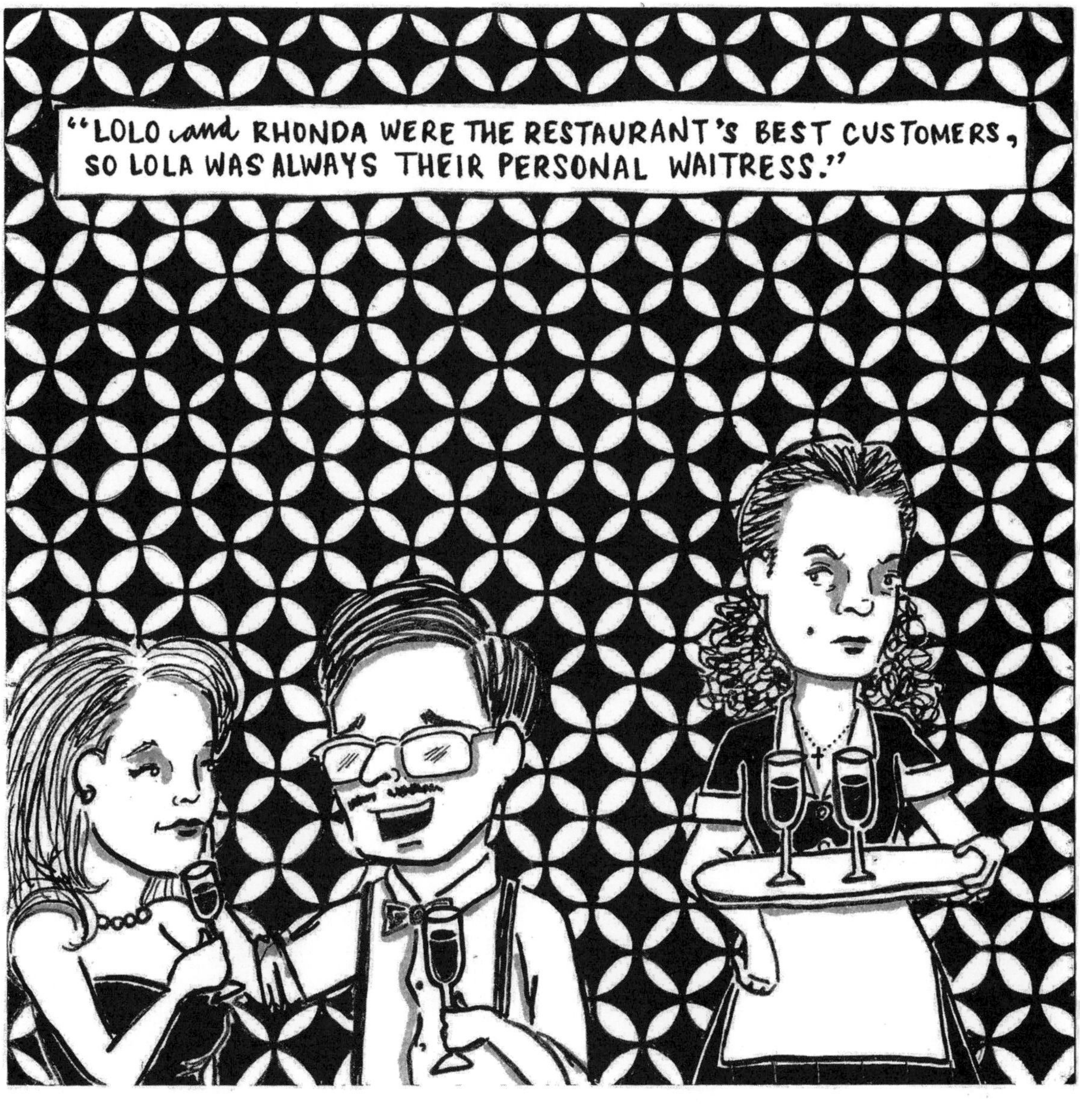
"LOLO and RHONDA WERE THE RESTAURANT'S BEST CUSTOMERS, SO LOLA WAS ALWAYS THEIR PERSONAL WAITRESS."

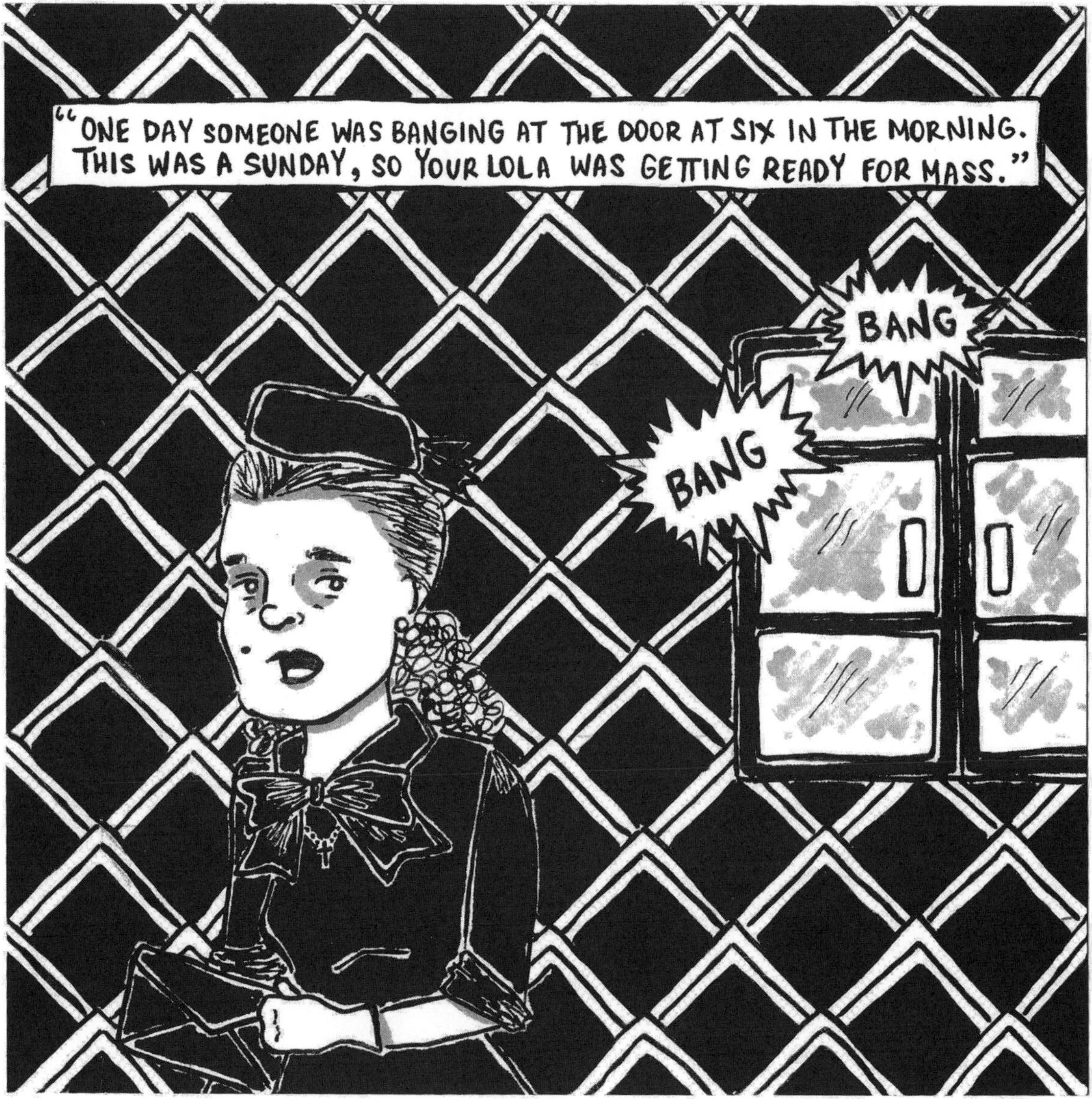
"ONE DAY SOMEONE WAS BANGING AT THE DOOR AT SIX IN THE MORNING. THIS WAS A SUNDAY, SO YOUR LOLA WAS GETTING READY FOR MASS."
BANG
BANG

"IT WAS YOUR LOLO.
"HE WAS ALONE, REEKING OF SAN MIGUEL and CIGARILLOS."

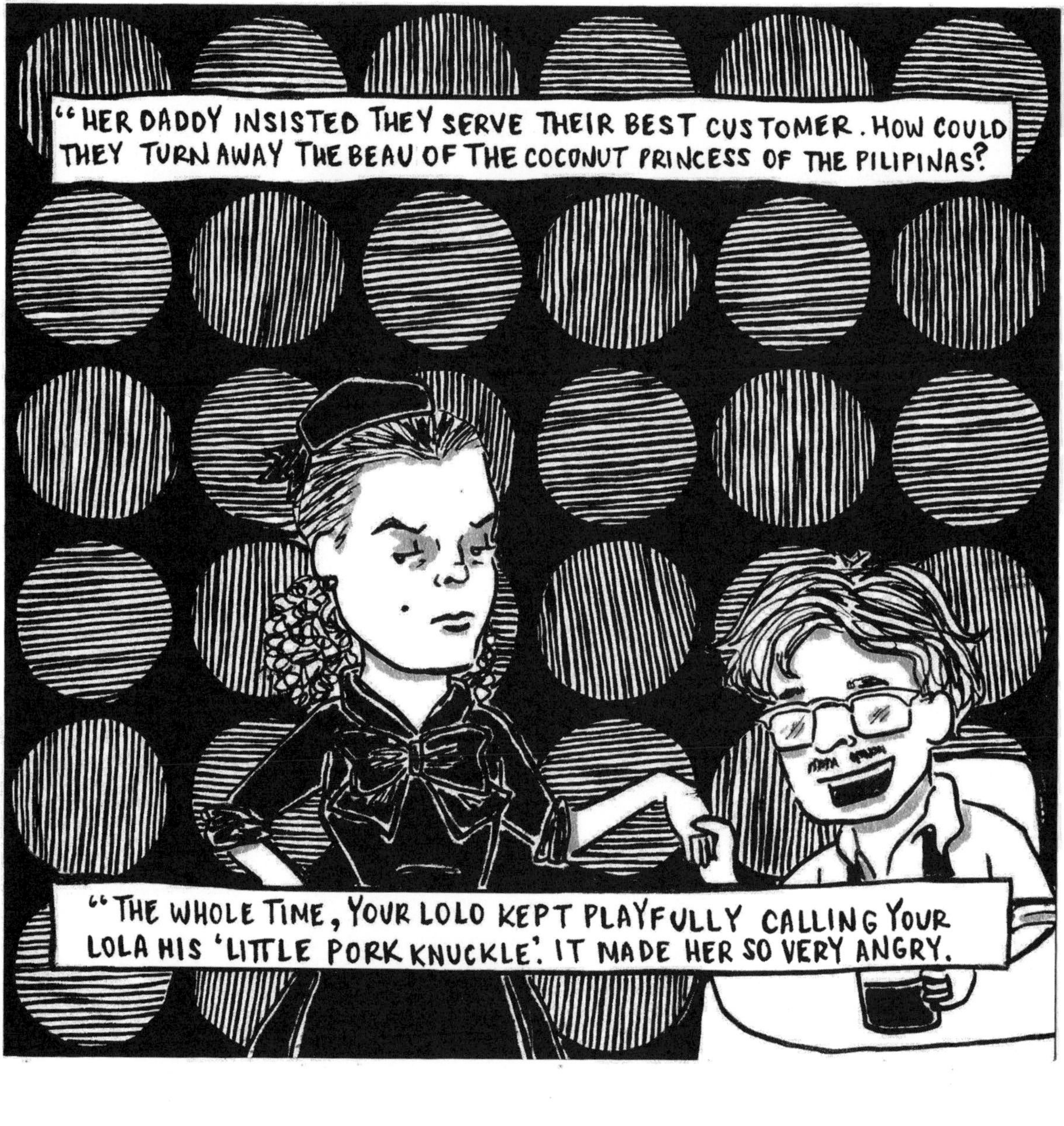
"HER DADDY INSISTED THEY SERVE THEIR BEST CUSTOMER. HOW COULD THEY TURN AWAY THE BEAU OF THE COCONUT PRINCESS OF THE PILIPINAS?
"THE WHOLE TIME, YOUR LOLO KEPT PLAYFULLY CALLING YOUR LOLA HIS 'LITTLE PORK KNUCKLE'. IT MADE HER SO VERY ANGRY.

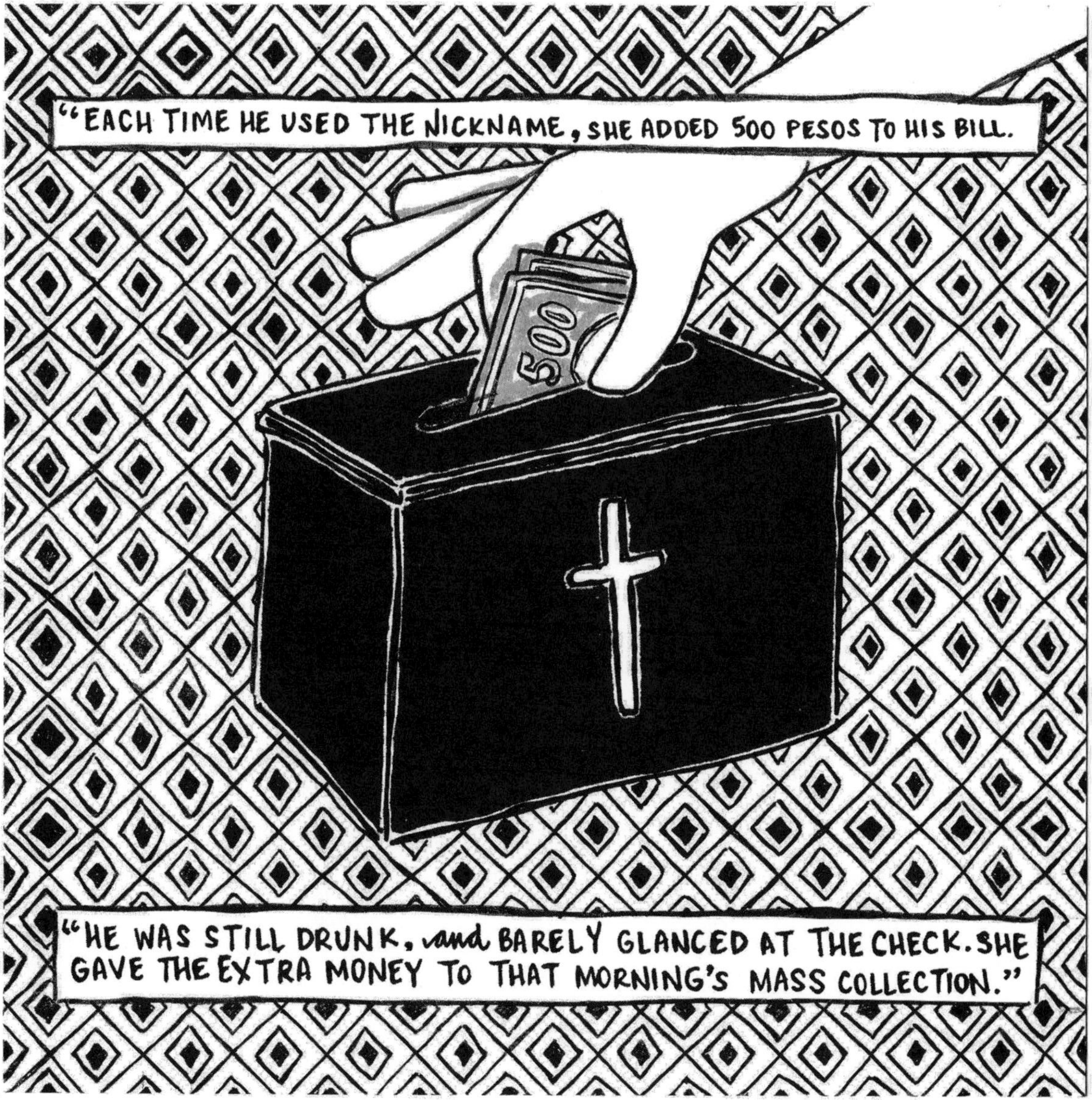
"EACH TIME HE USED THE NICKNAME, SHE ADDED 500 PESOS TO HIS BILL.
500
"HE WAS STILL DRUNK, and BARELY GLANCED AT THE CHECK. SHE GAVE THE EXTRA MONEY TO THAT MORNING'S MASS COLLECTION."

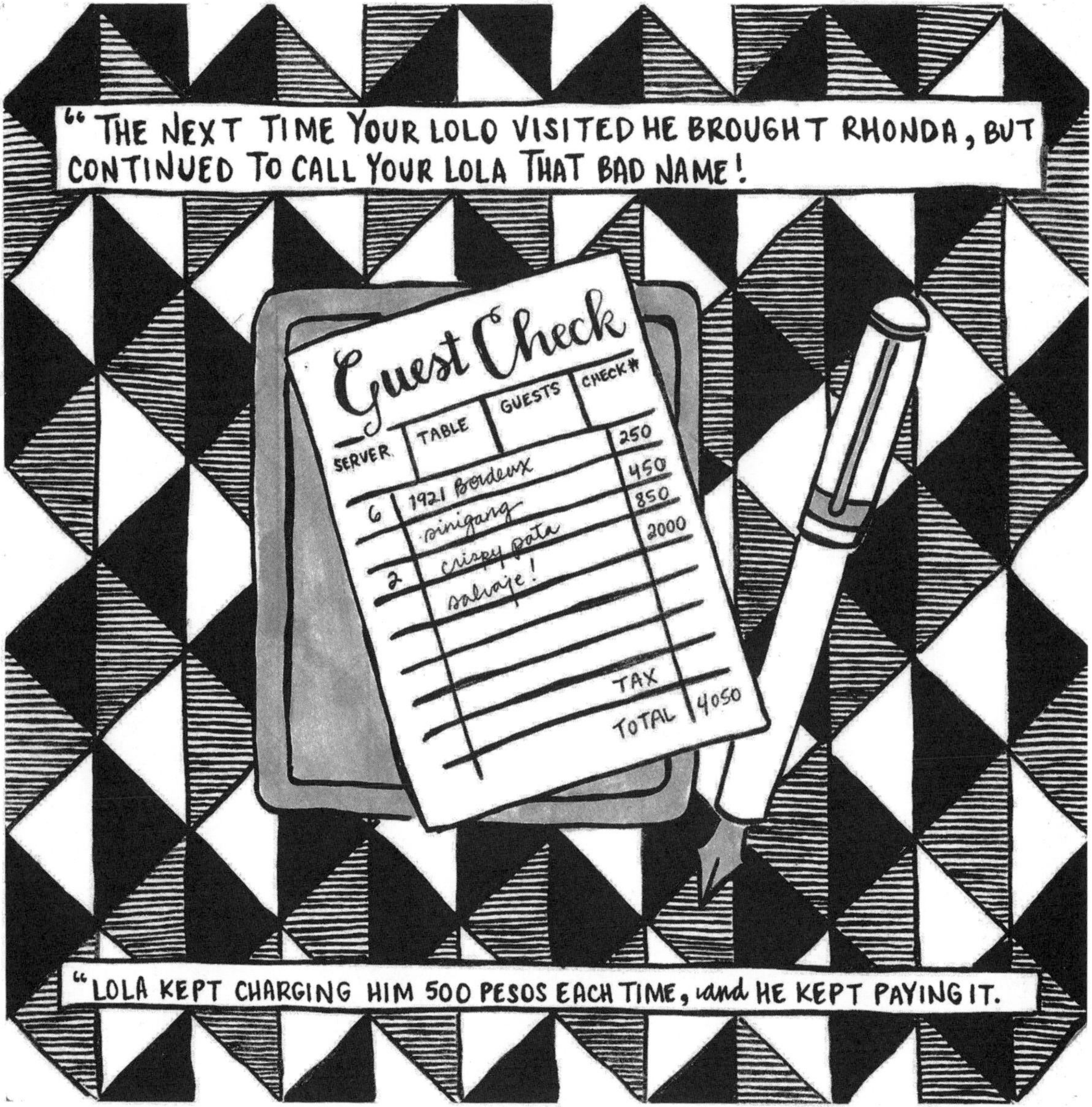
"THE NEXT TIME YOUR LOLO VISITED HE BROUGHT RHONDA, BUT CONTINUED TO CALL YOUR LOLA THAT BAD NAME!
Guest Check
SERVER
TABLE
GUESTS
CHECK #
6
1921 Bordeux
250
sinigang
450
2
crispy pata
850
salvaje!
2000
TAX
TOTAL
4050
"LOLA KEPT CHARGING HIM 500 PESOS EACH TIME, and HE KEPT PAYING IT.

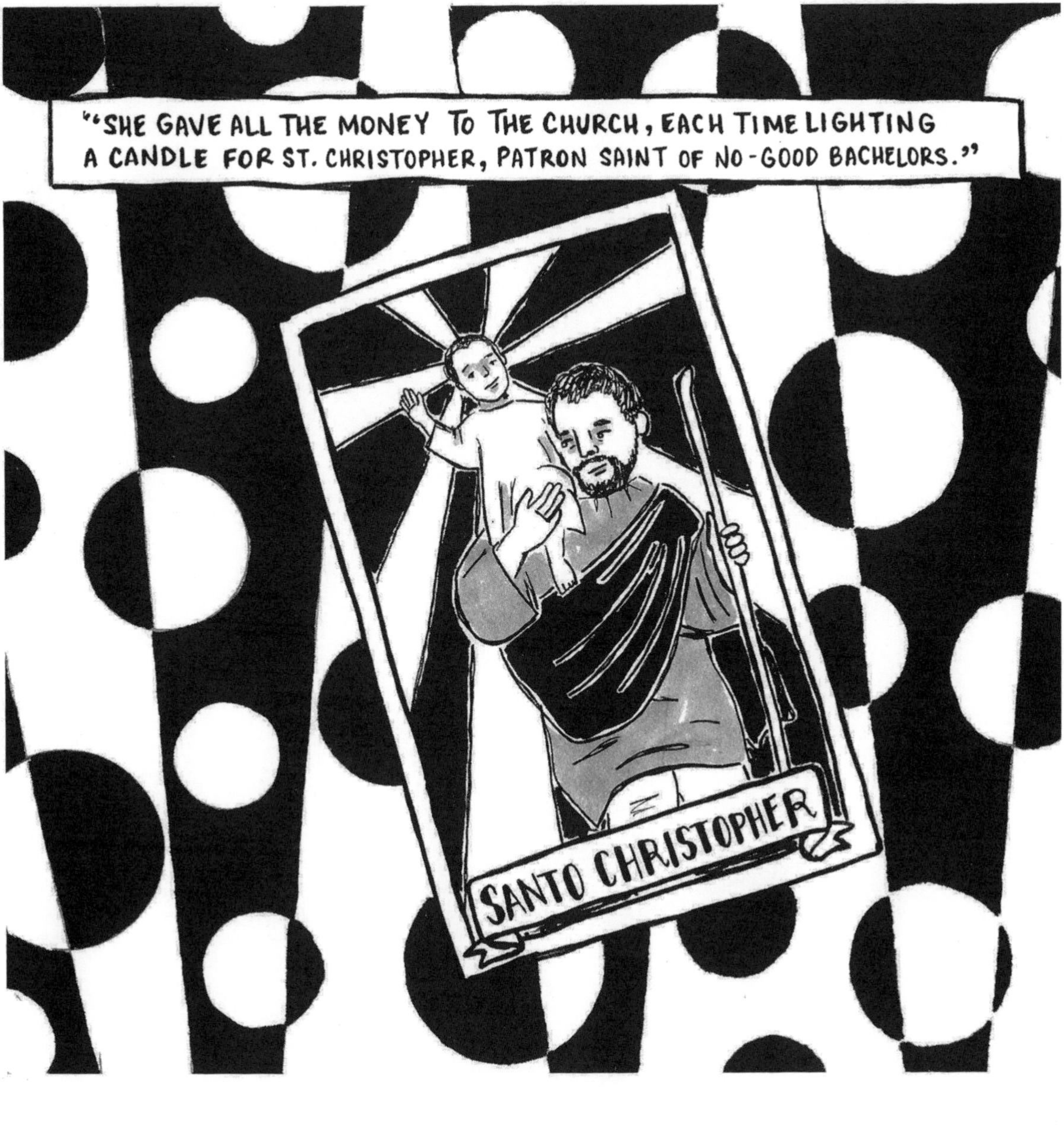
"SHE GAVE ALL THE MONEY TO THE CHURCH, EACH TIME LIGHTING A CANDLE FOR ST. CHRISTOPHER, PATRON SAINT OF NO-GOOD BACHELORS."
SANTO CHRISTOPHER

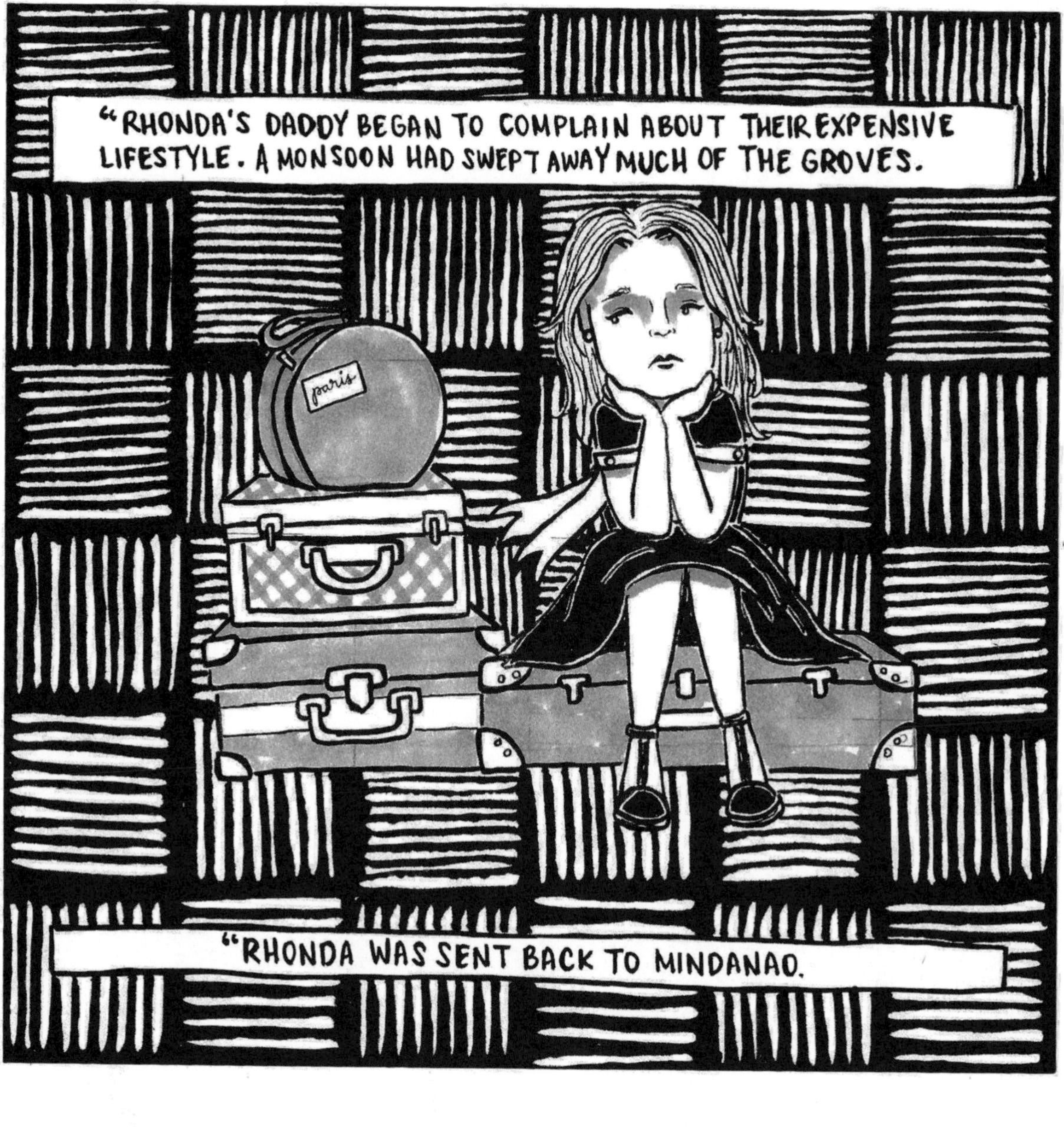
"RHONDA'S DADDY BEGAN TO COMPLAIN ABOUT THEIR EXPENSIVE LIFESTYLE. A MONSOON HAD SWEPT AWAY MUCH OF THE GROVES.
paris
"RHONDA WAS SENT BACK TO MINDANAO.

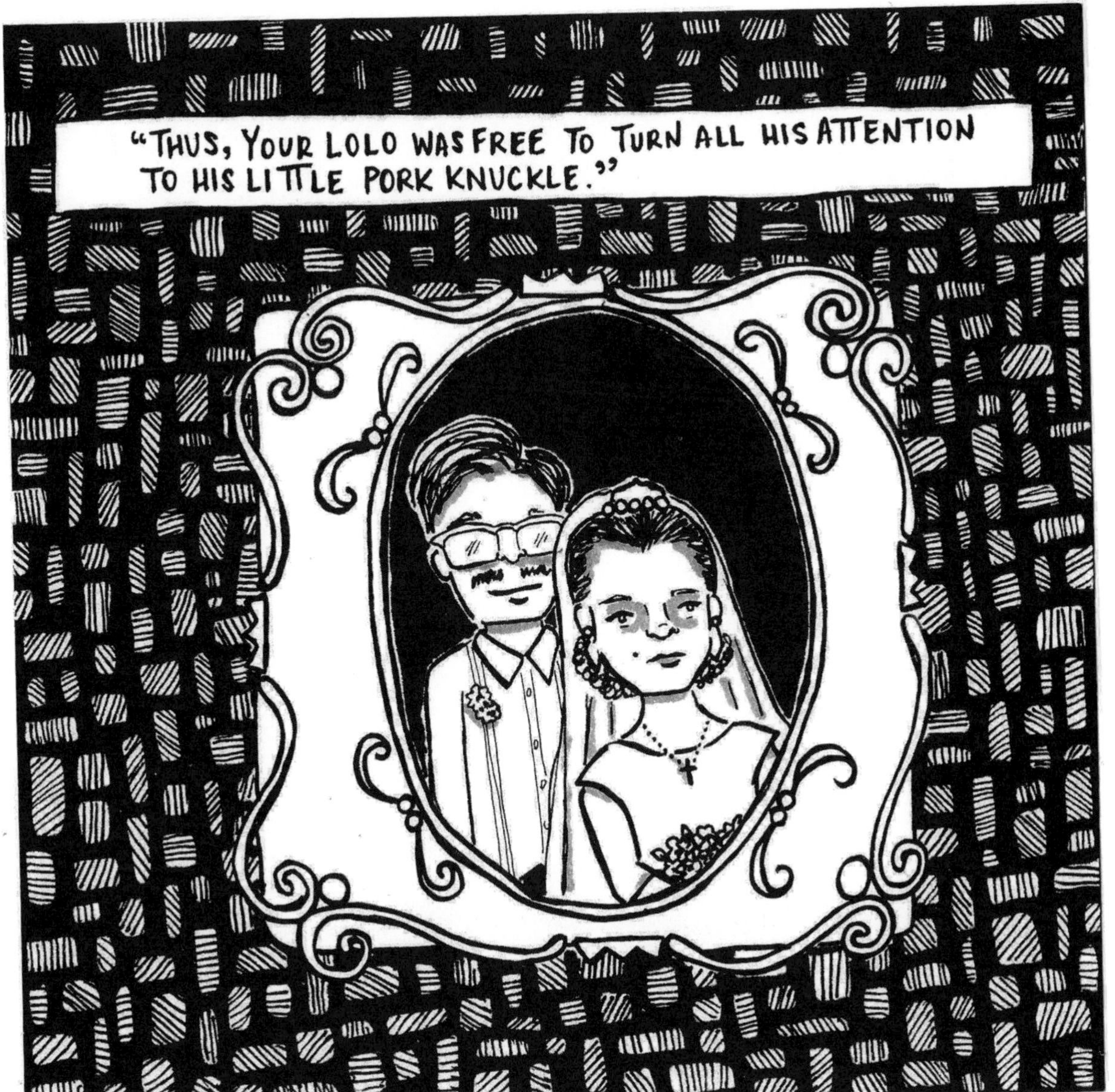
"THUS, YOUR LOLO WAS FREE TO TURN ALL HIS ATTENTION TO HIS LITTLE PORK KNUCKLE."

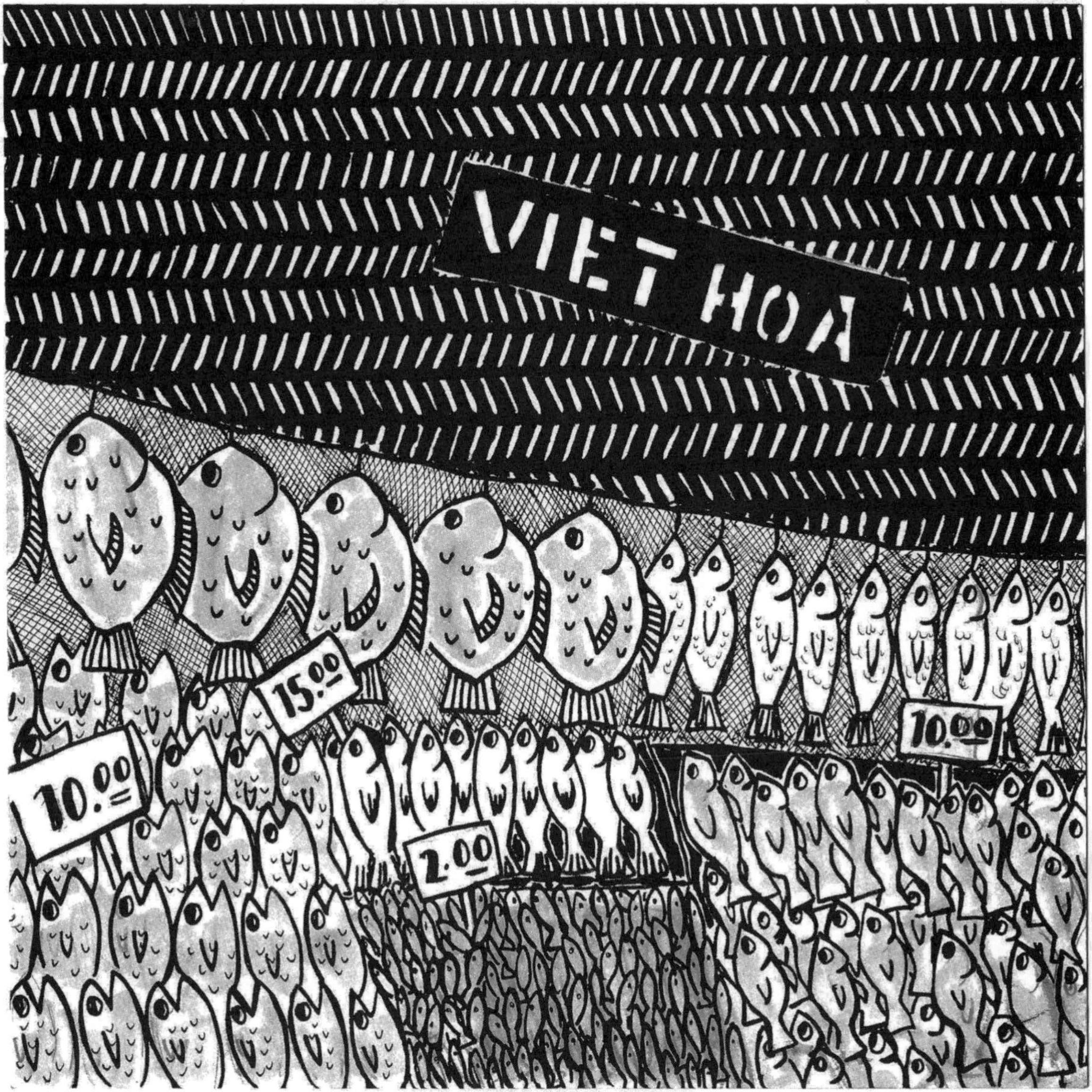
VIET HOA
15.00
10.00
10.00
2.00

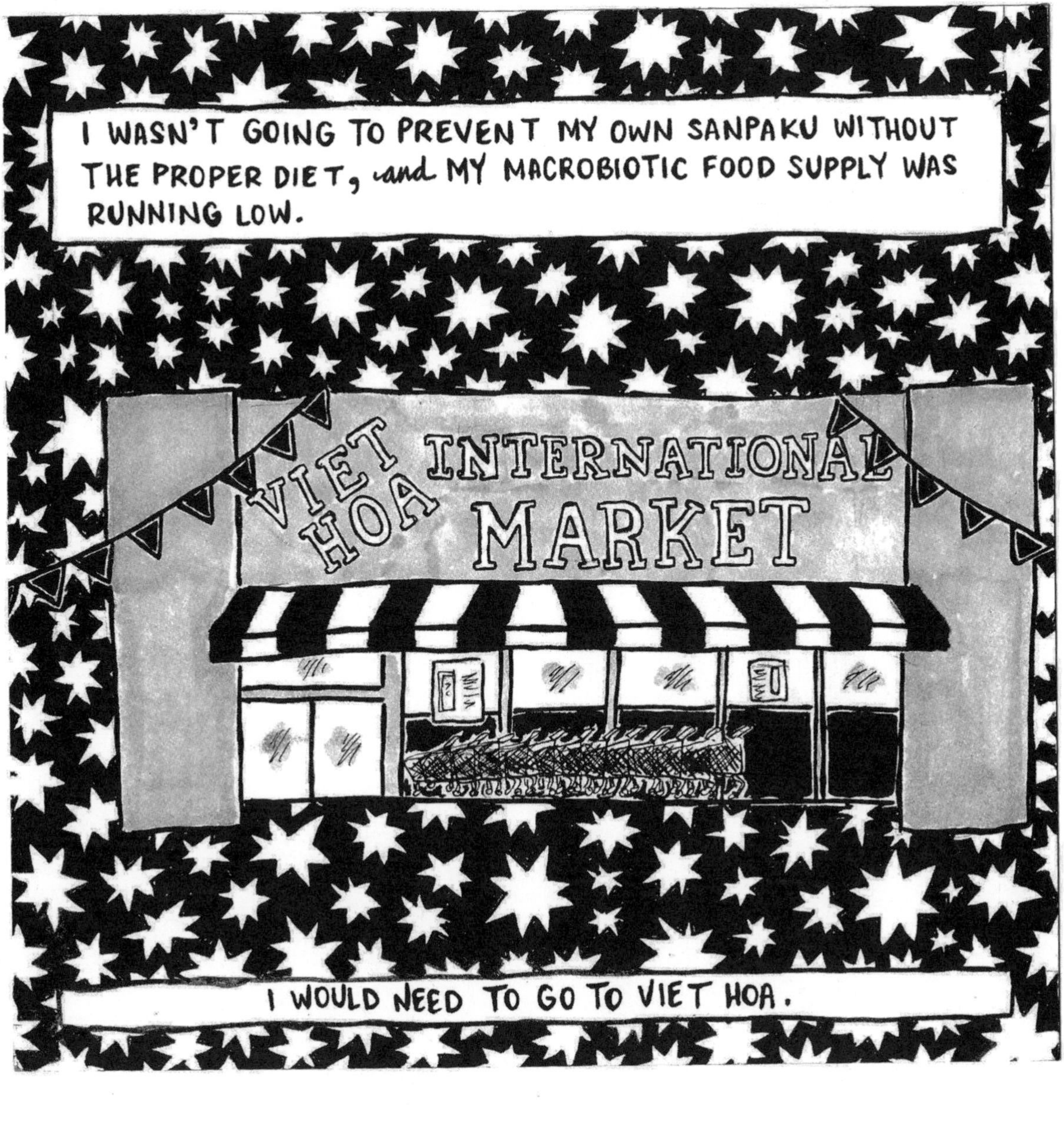
I WASN'T GOING TO PREVENT MY OWN SANPAKU WITHOUT THE PROPER DIET, and MY MACROBIOTIC FOOD SUPPLY WAS RUNNING LOW.
VIET HOA INTERNATIONAL MARKET
I WOULD NEED TO GO TO VIET HOA.

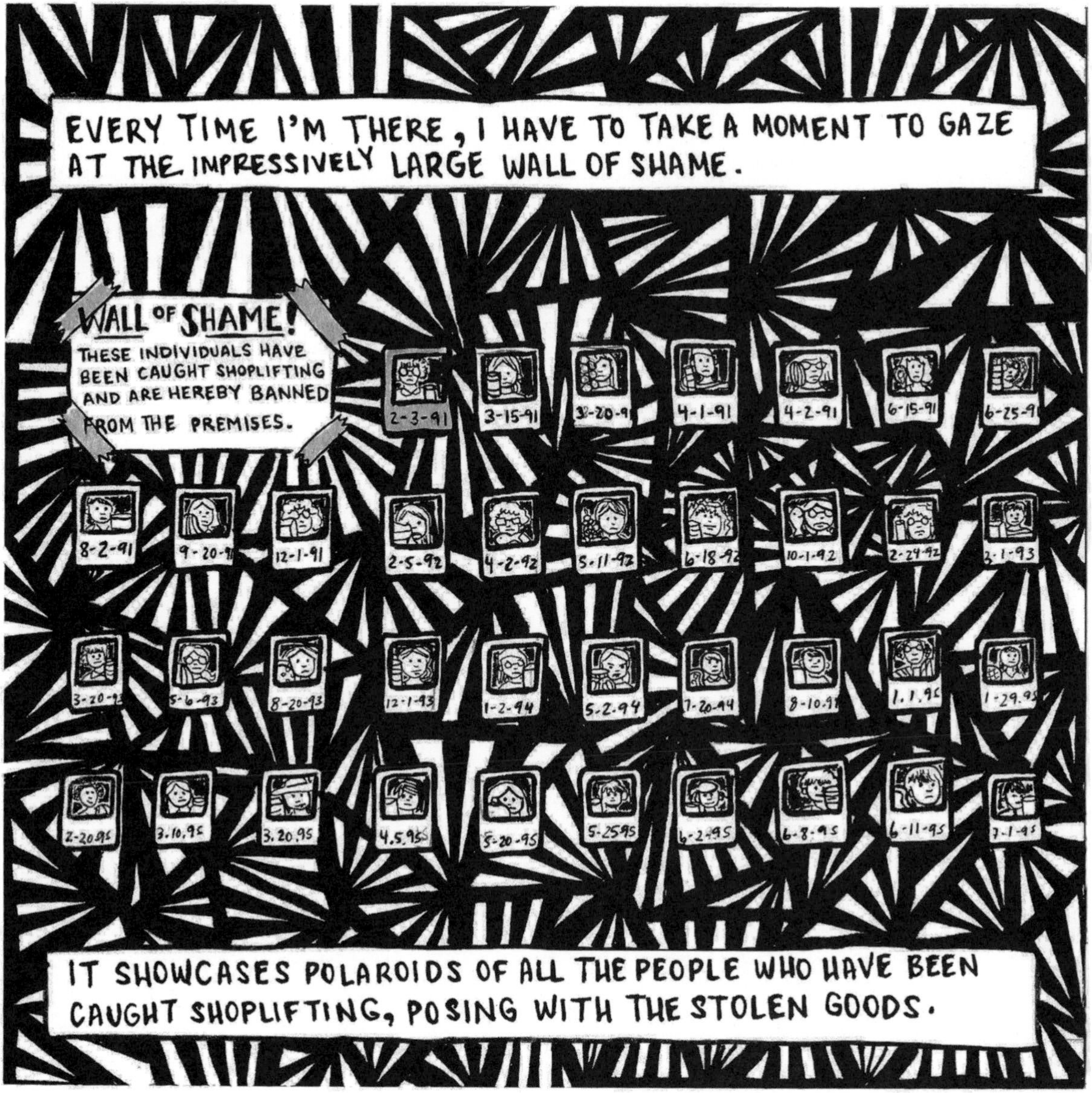
EVERY TIME I'M THERE, I HAVE TO TAKE A MOMENT TO GAZE AT THE IMPRESSIVELY LARGE WALL OF SHAME.
WALL OF SHAME!
THESE INDIVIDUALS HAVE BEEN CAUGHT SHOPLIFTING AND ARE HEREBY BANNED FROM THE PREMISES.
IT SHOWCASES POLAROIDS OF ALL THE PEOPLE WHO HAVE BEEN CAUGHT SHOPLIFTING, POSING WITH THE STOLEN GOODS.

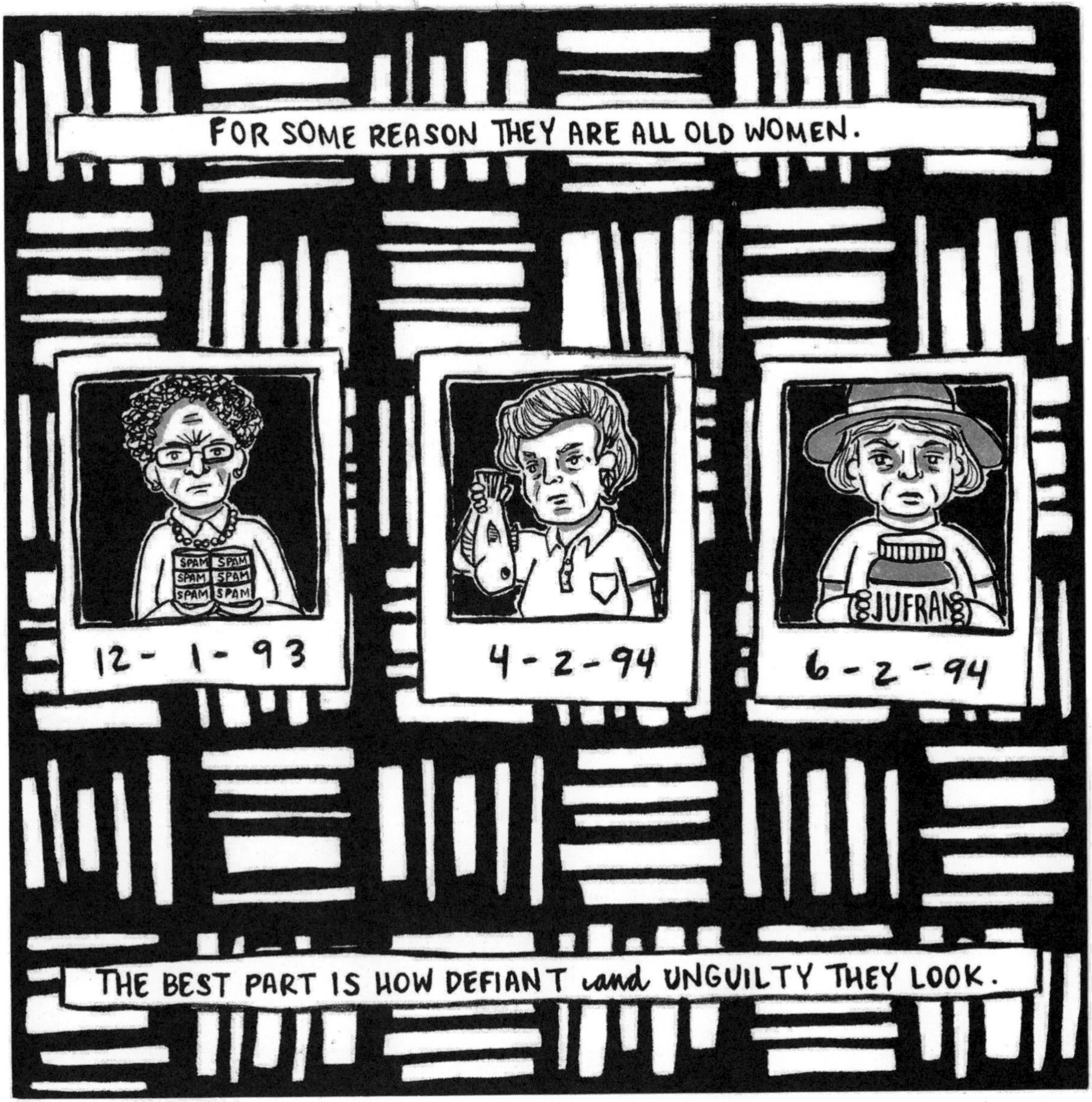
FOR SOME REASON THEY ARE ALL OLD WOMEN.
SPAM SPAM SPAM SPAM SPAM SPAM
12- 1- 93
4-2-94
JUFRAN
6-2-94
THE BEST PART IS HOW DEFIANT and UNGUILTY THEY LOOK.

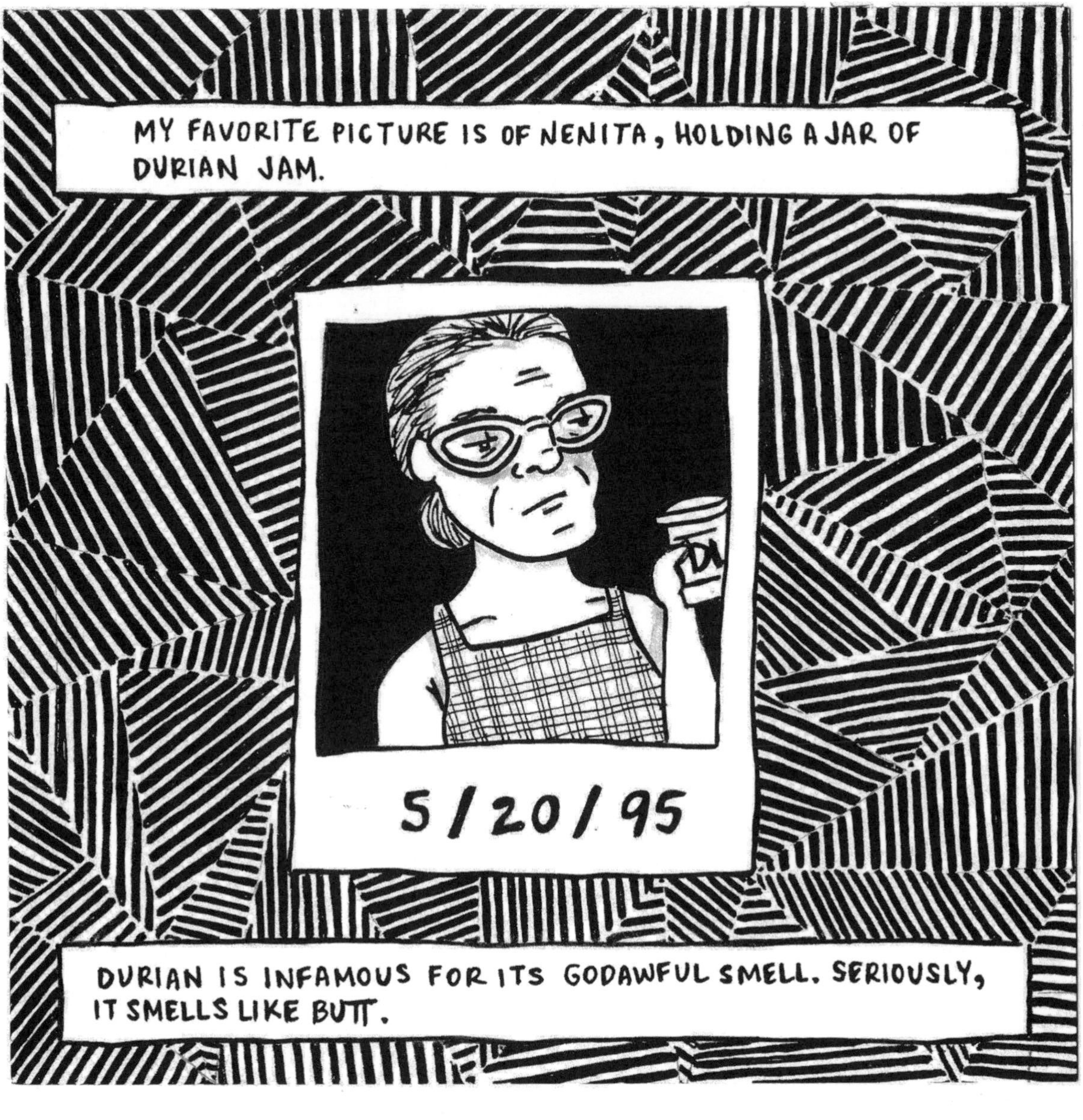
MY FAVORITE PICTURE IS OF NENITA, HOLDING A JAR OF DURIAN JAM.
5/20/95
DURIAN IS INFAMOUS FOR ITS GODAWFUL SMELL. SERIOUSLY, IT SMELLS LIKE BUTT.

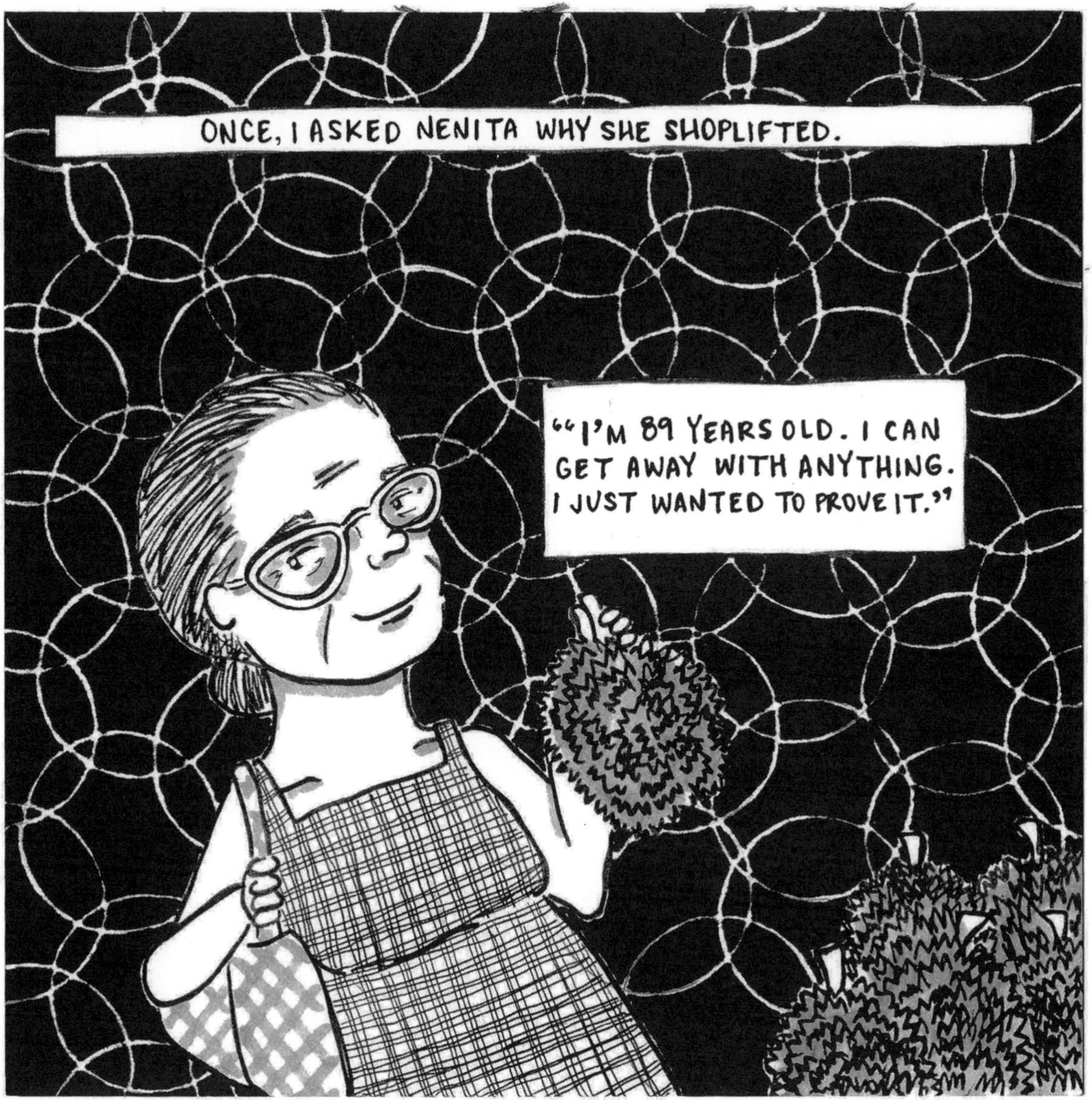
ONCE, I ASKED NENITA WHY SHE SHOPLIFTED.
"I'M 89 YEARS OLD. I CAN GET AWAY WITH ANYTHING. I JUST WANTED TO PROVE IT."

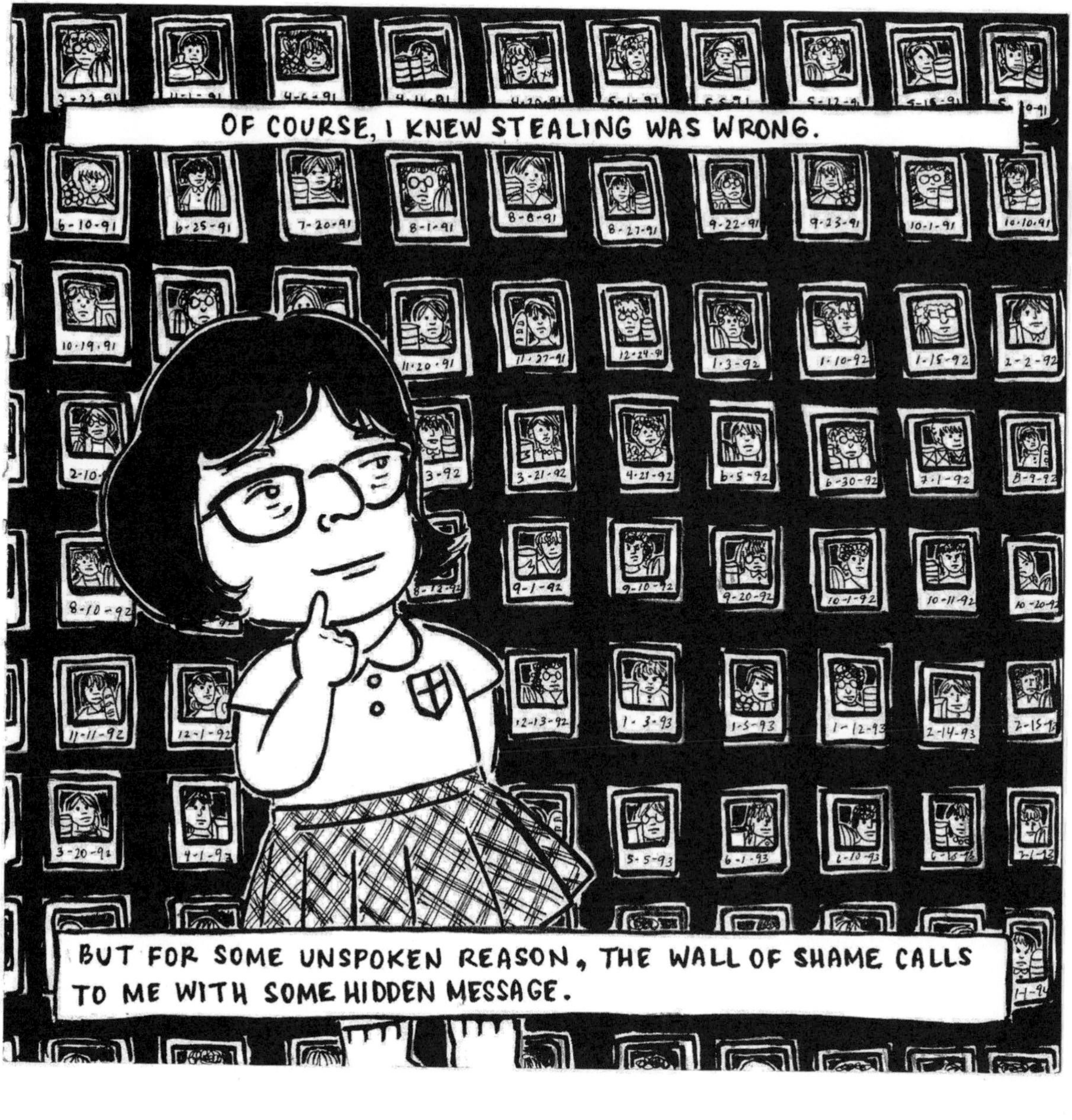
OF COURSE, I KNEW STEALING WAS WRONG.
BUT FOR SOME UNSPOKEN REASON, THE WALL OF SHAME CALLS TO ME WITH SOME HIDDEN MESSAGE.

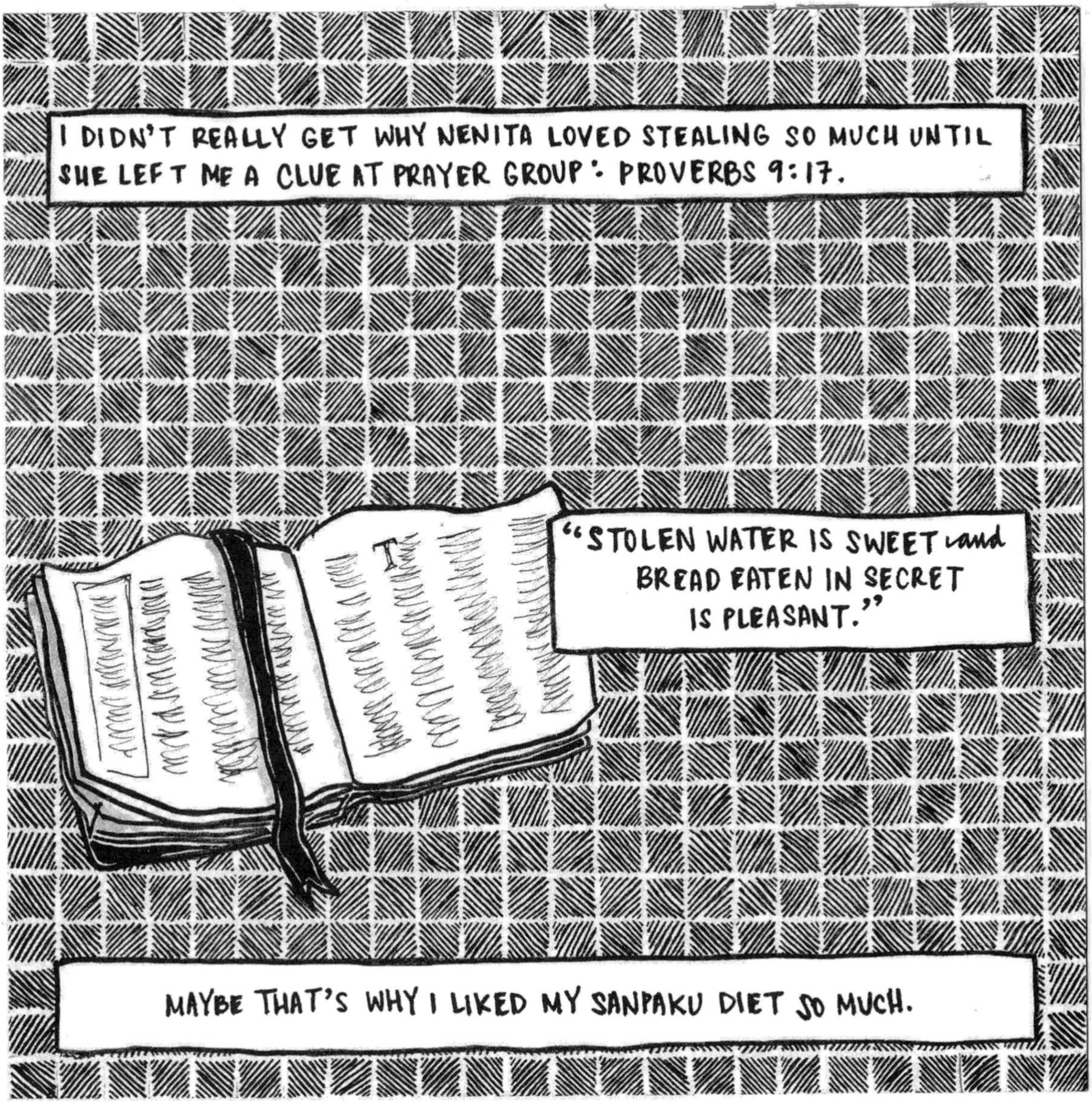
I DIDN'T REALLY GET WHY NENITA LOVED STEALING SO MUCH UNTIL SHE LEFT ME A CLUE AT PRAYER GROUP: PROVERBS 9:17.
"STOLEN WATER IS SWEET and BREAD EATEN IN SECRET IS PLEASANT."
MAYBE THAT'S WHY I LIKED MY SANPAKU DIET SO MUCH.

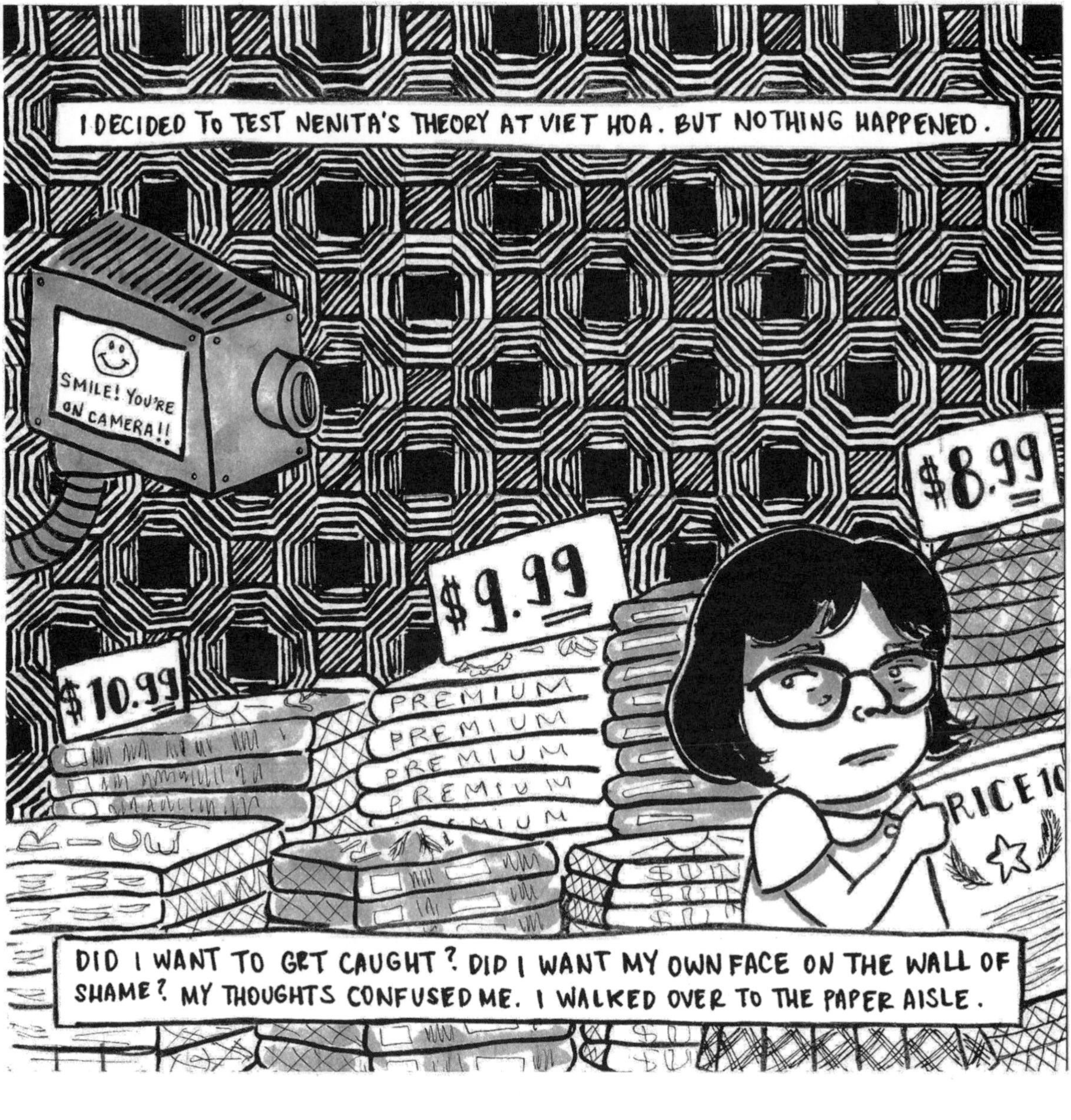
I DECIDED TO TEST NENITA'S THEORY AT VIET HOA. BUT NOTHING HAPPENED.
SMILE! YOU'RE ON CAMERA!!
$8.99
$9.99
$10.99
PREMIUM
PREMIUM
PREMIUM
PREMIUM
RICE10
SUN
DID I WANT TO GET CAUGHT? DID I WANT MY OWN FACE ON THE WALL OF SHAME? MY THOUGHTS CONFUSED ME. I WALKED OVER TO THE PAPER AISLE.

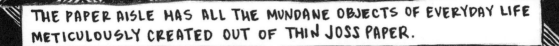

THE PAPER AISLE HAS ALL THE MUNDANE OBJECTS OF EVERYDAY LIFE METICULOUSLY CREATED OUT OF THIN JOSS PAPER.

AT FUNERALS and SPECIAL OCCASIONS, PEOPLE BURN PAPER "GHOST MONEY" and OBJECTS FOR THEIR DEAD LOVED ONES TO HAVE IN THE AFTERLIFE.

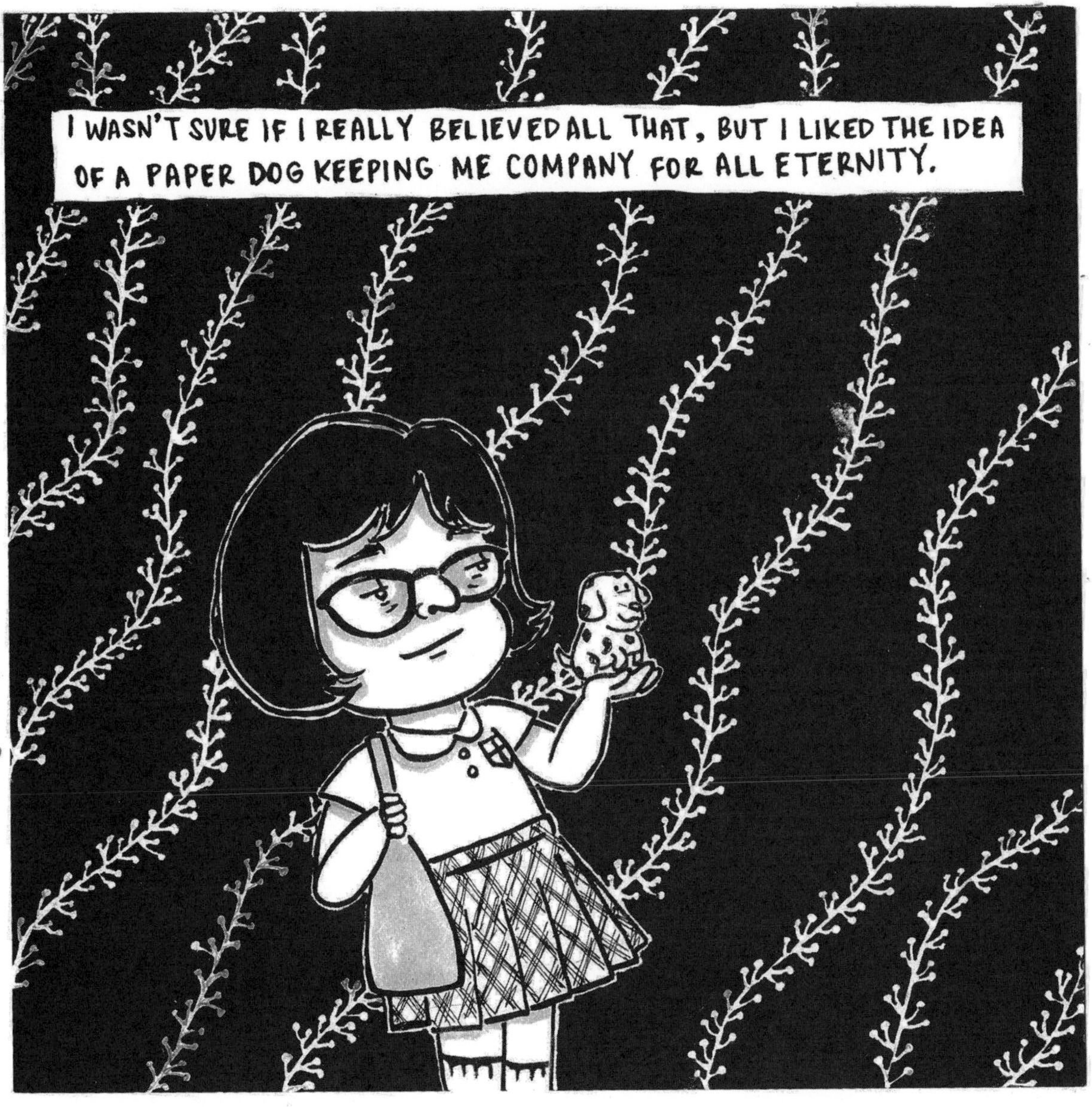
I WASN'T SURE IF I REALLY BELIEVED ALL THAT, BUT I LIKED THE IDEA OF A PAPER DOG KEEPING ME COMPANY FOR ALL ETERNITY.

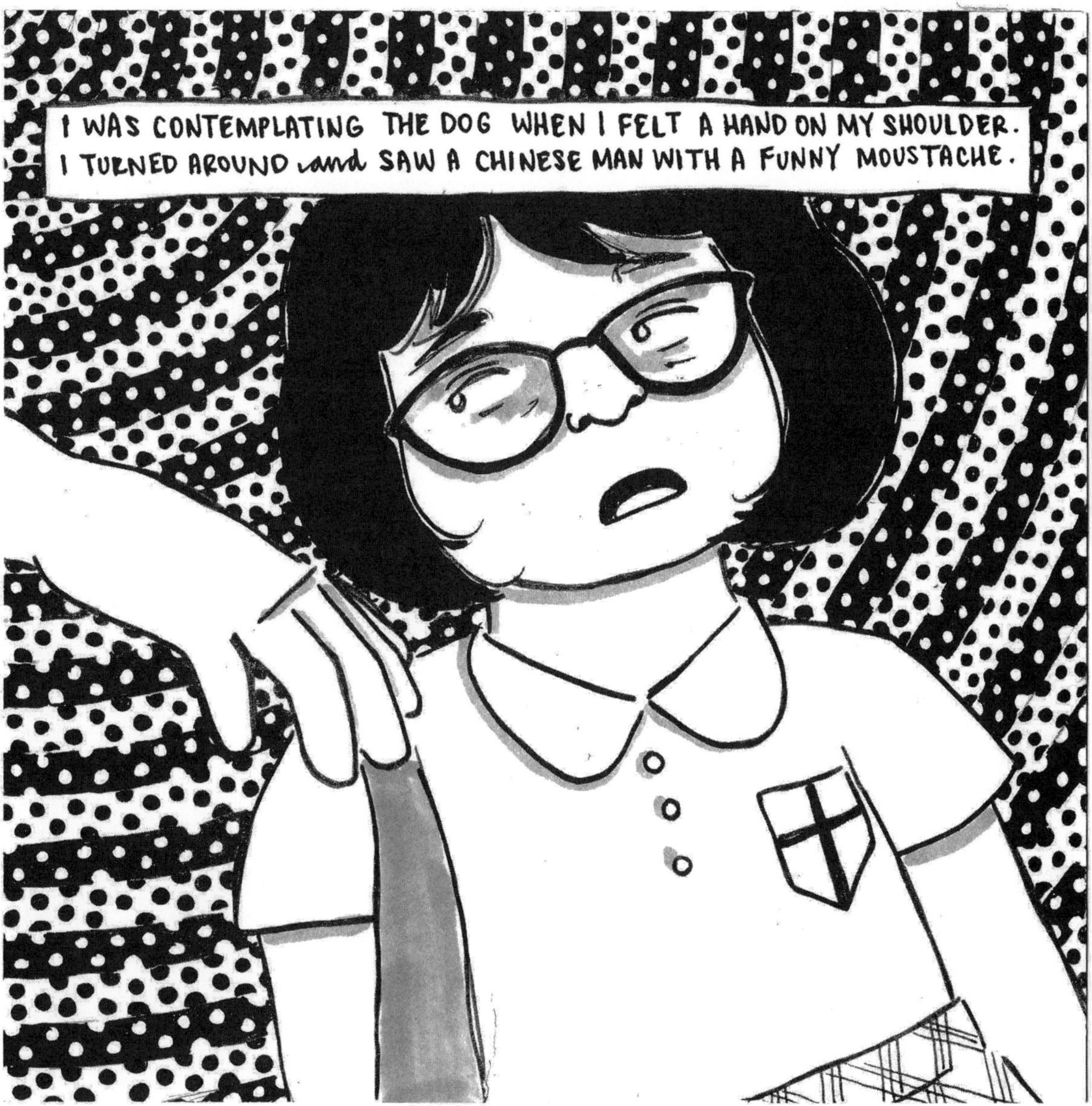
I WAS CONTEMPLATING THE DOG WHEN I FELT A HAND ON MY SHOULDER.
I TURNED AROUND and SAW A CHINESE MAN WITH A FUNNY MOUSTACHE.

HIS NAME TAG READ "HARRY WEI– MANAGER."
"COME WITH ME."
HARRY WEI MANAGER

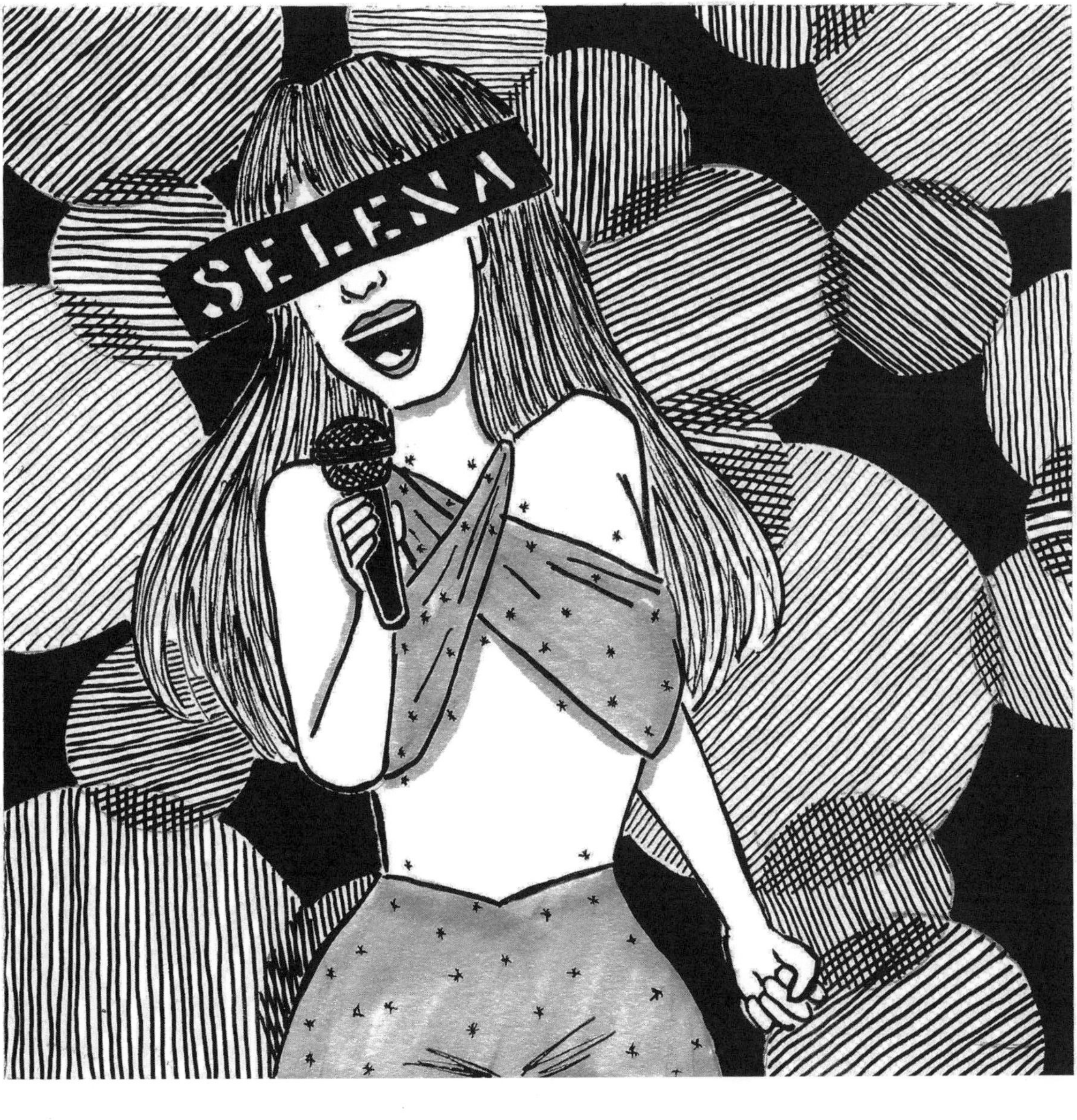
SELENA

HE LED ME TO VIET HOA'S BACKROOM, WHICH I HAD NEVER SEEN.
I WATCHED THE WORKERS UNPACK BOXES and CLEAN VEGETABLES, SINGING ALONG TO THE RADIO, TUNED TO PURO TEJANO 102.9.

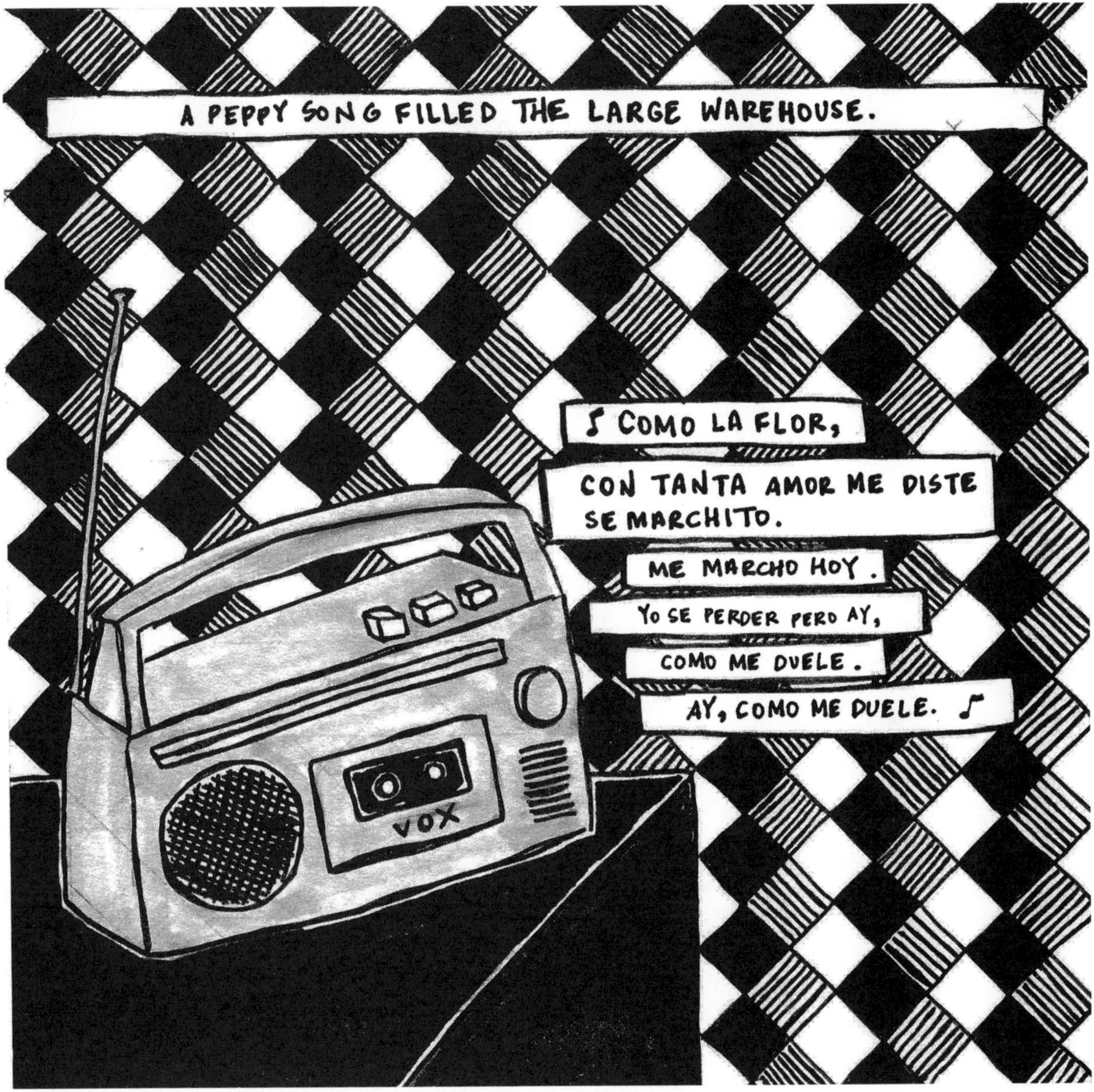
A PEPPY SONG FILLED THE LARGE WAREHOUSE.
♪ COMO LA FLOR,
CON TANTA AMOR ME DISTE SE MARCHITO.
ME MARCHO HOY.
YO SE PERDER PERO AY,
COMO ME DUELE.
AY, COMO ME DUELE. ♪
VOX

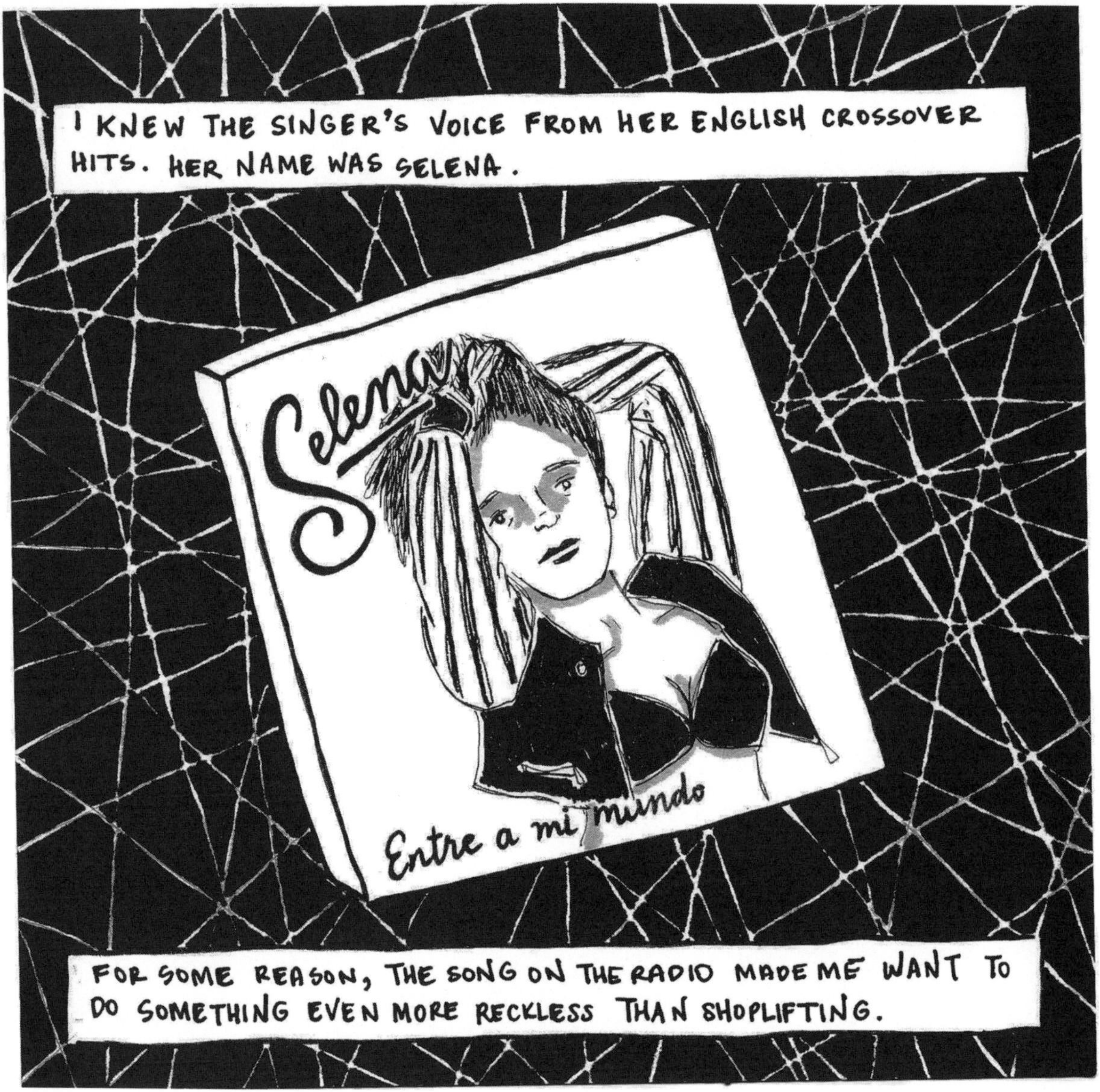
I KNEW THE SINGER'S VOICE FROM HER ENGLISH CROSSOVER HITS. HER NAME WAS SELENA.
Selena
Entre a mi mundo
FOR SOME REASON, THE SONG ON THE RADIO MADE ME WANT TO DO SOMETHING EVEN MORE RECKLESS THAN SHOPLIFTING.

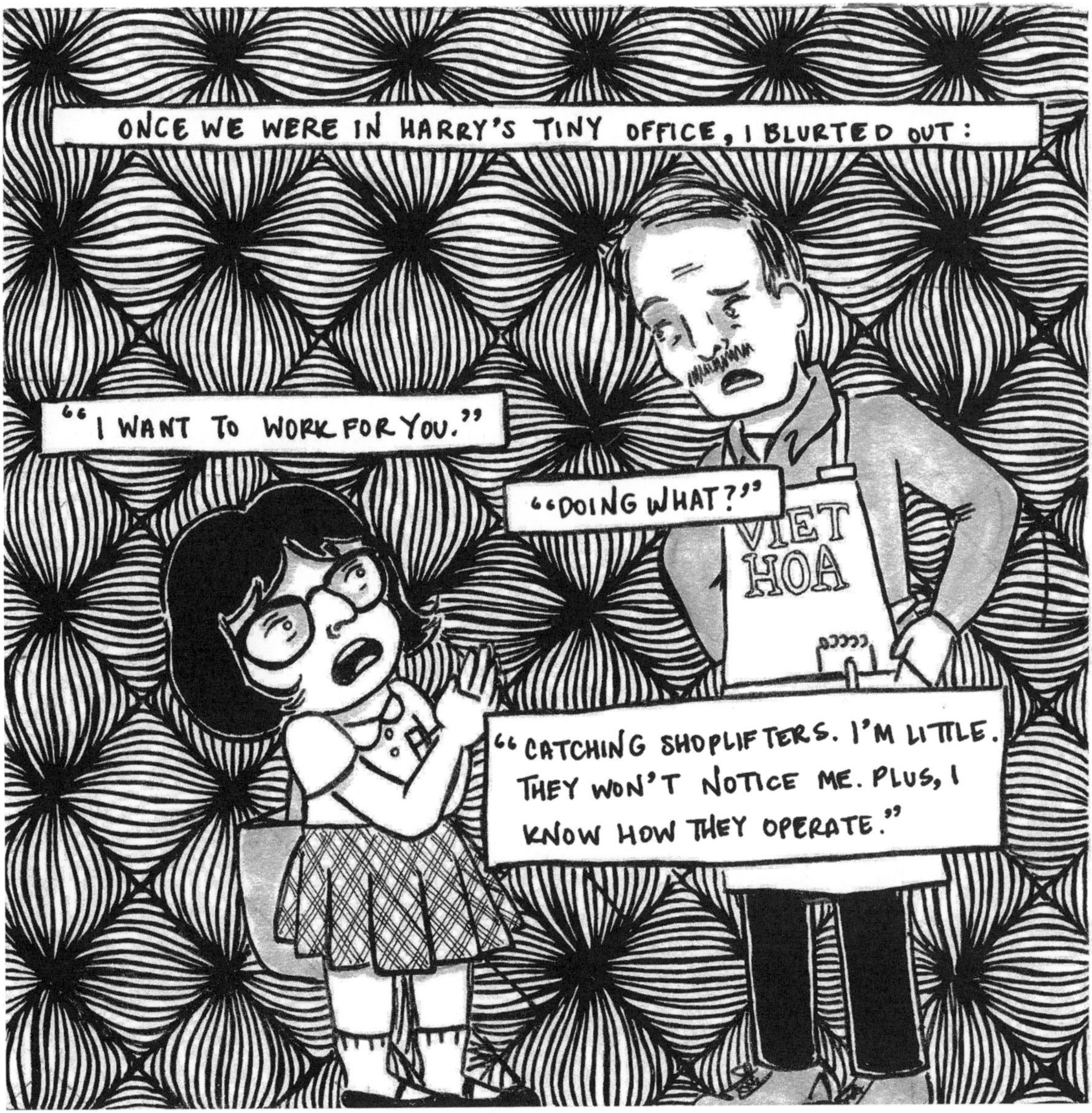
ONCE WE WERE IN HARRY'S TINY OFFICE, I BLURTED OUT:
"I WANT TO WORK FOR YOU."
"DOING WHAT?"
VIET HOA
"CATCHING SHOPLIFTERS. I'M LITTLE. THEY WON'T NOTICE ME. PLUS, I KNOW HOW THEY OPERATE."

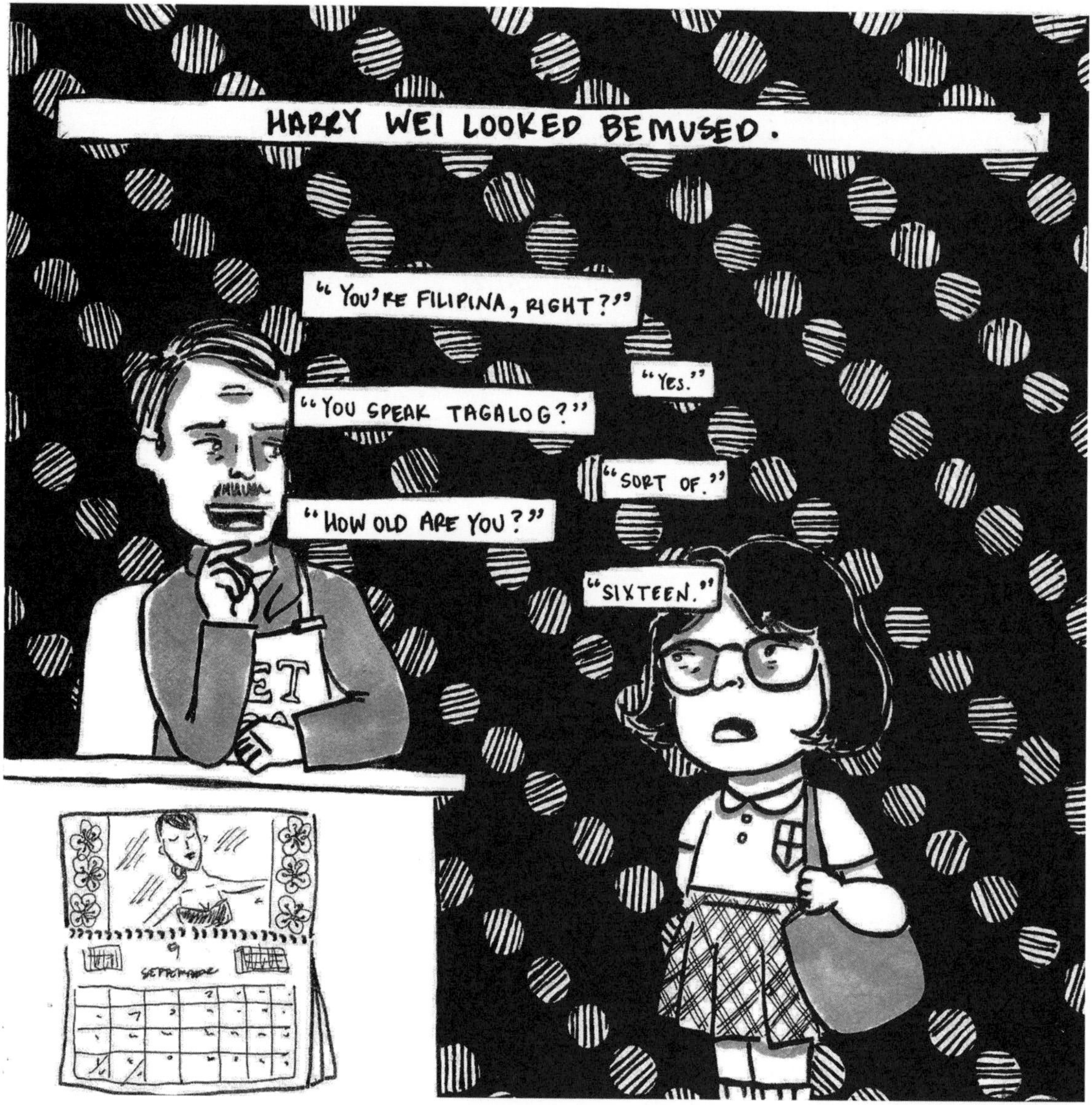
HARRY WEI LOOKED BEMUSED.
"YOU'RE FILIPINA, RIGHT?"
"YES."
"YOU SPEAK TAGALOG?"
"SORT OF."
"HOW OLD ARE YOU?"
"SIXTEEN."

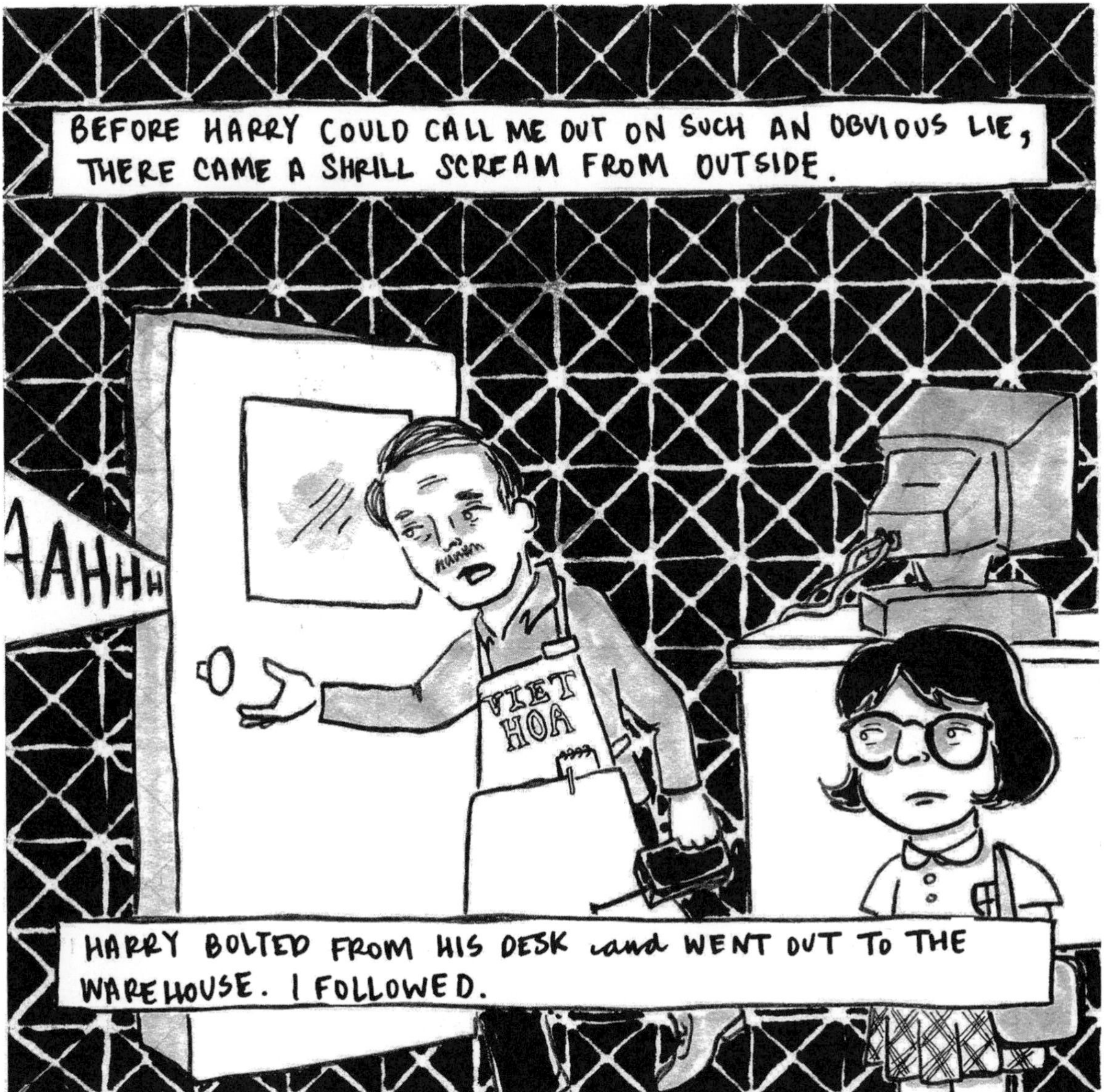
BEFORE HARRY COULD CALL ME OUT ON SUCH AN OBVIOUS LIE, THERE CAME A SHRILL SCREAM FROM OUTSIDE.
AAHHH
VIET HOA
HARRY BOLTED FROM HIS DESK and WENT OUT TO THE WAREHOUSE. I FOLLOWED.

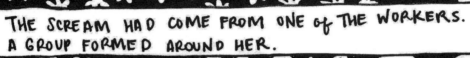

THE SCREAM HAD COME FROM ONE OF THE WORKERS.
A GROUP FORMED AROUND HER.

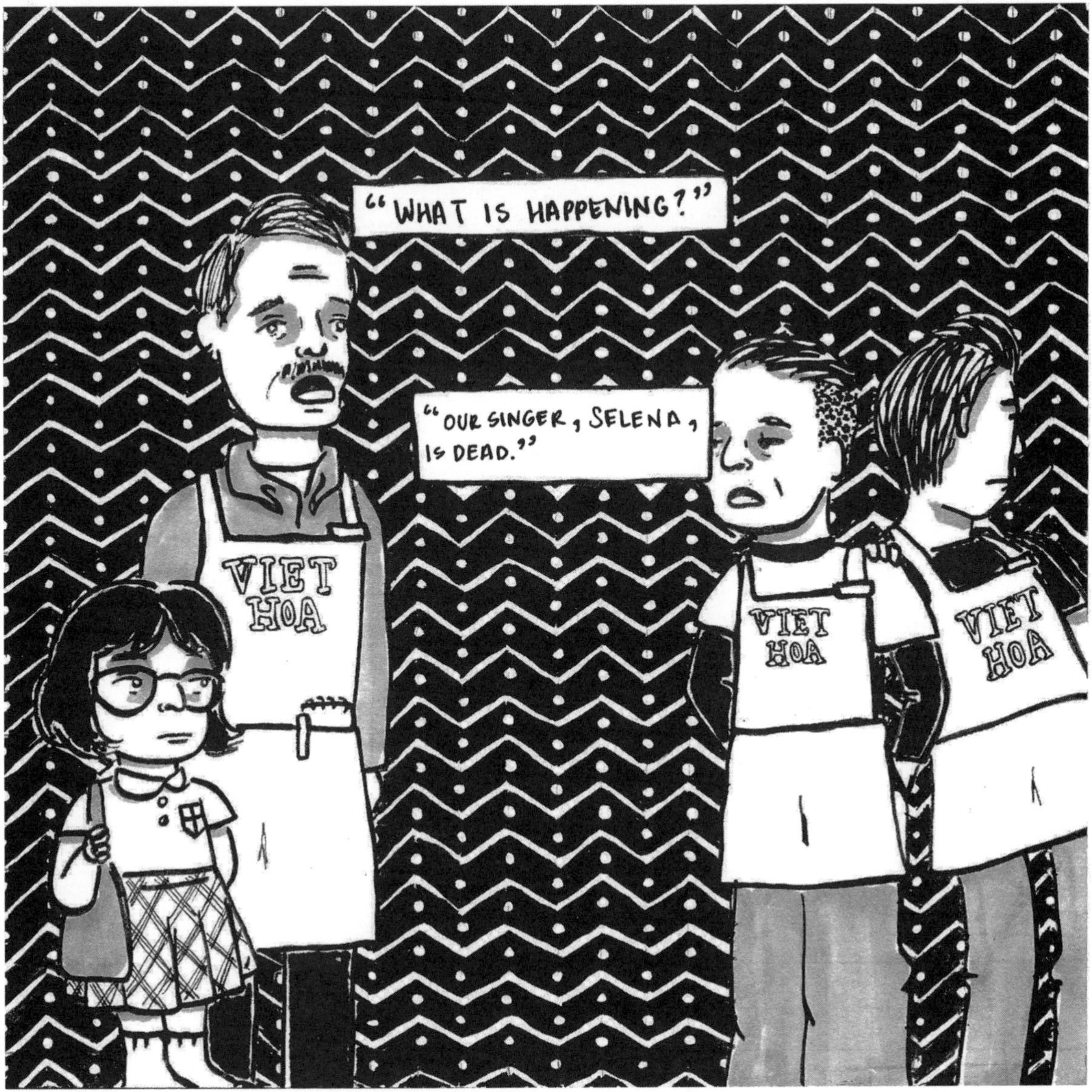
"WHAT IS HAPPENING?"
"OUR SINGER, SELENA, IS DEAD."
VIET HOA
VIET HOA
VIET HOA

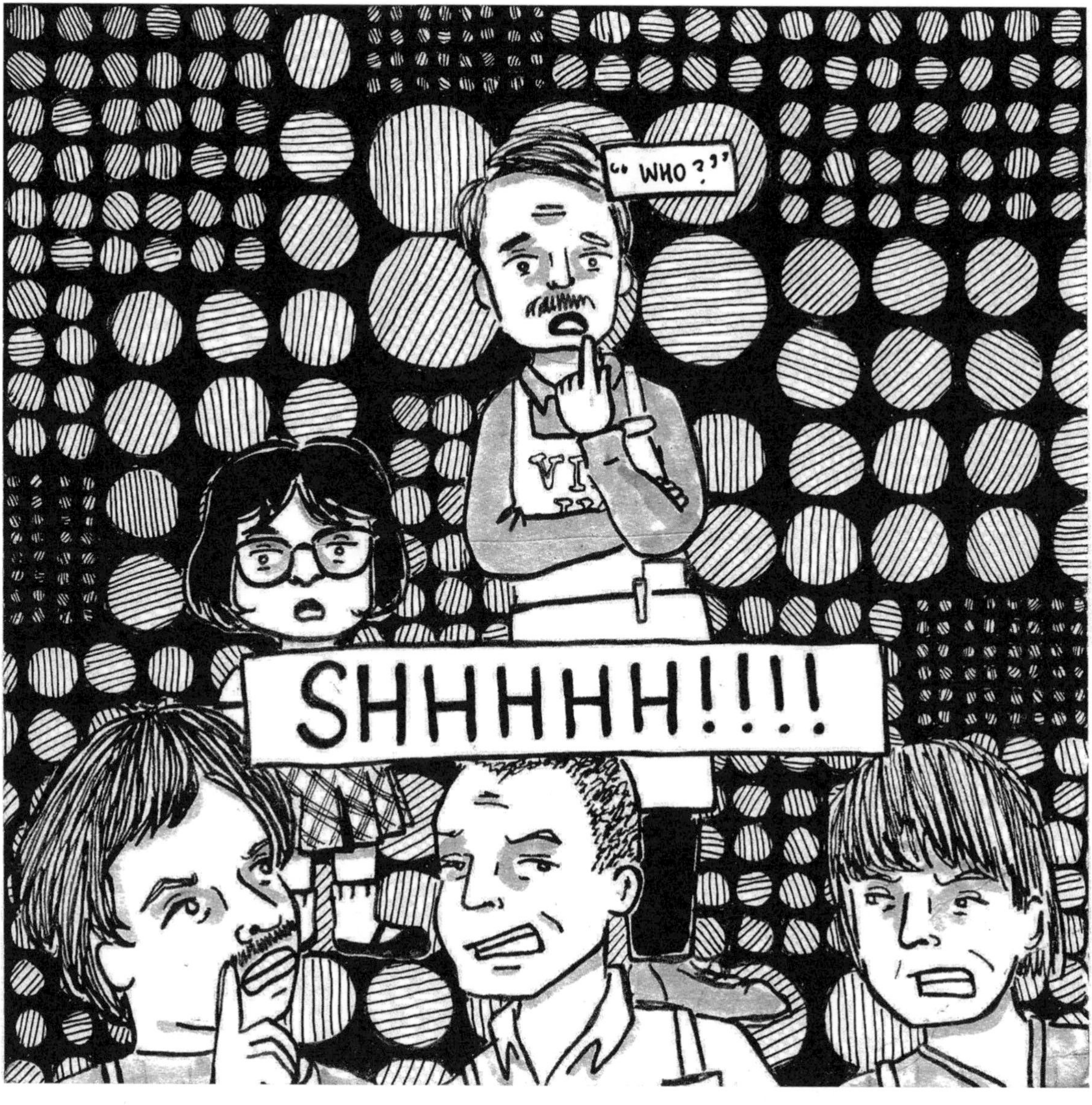
"WHO?"
SHHHHH!!!!

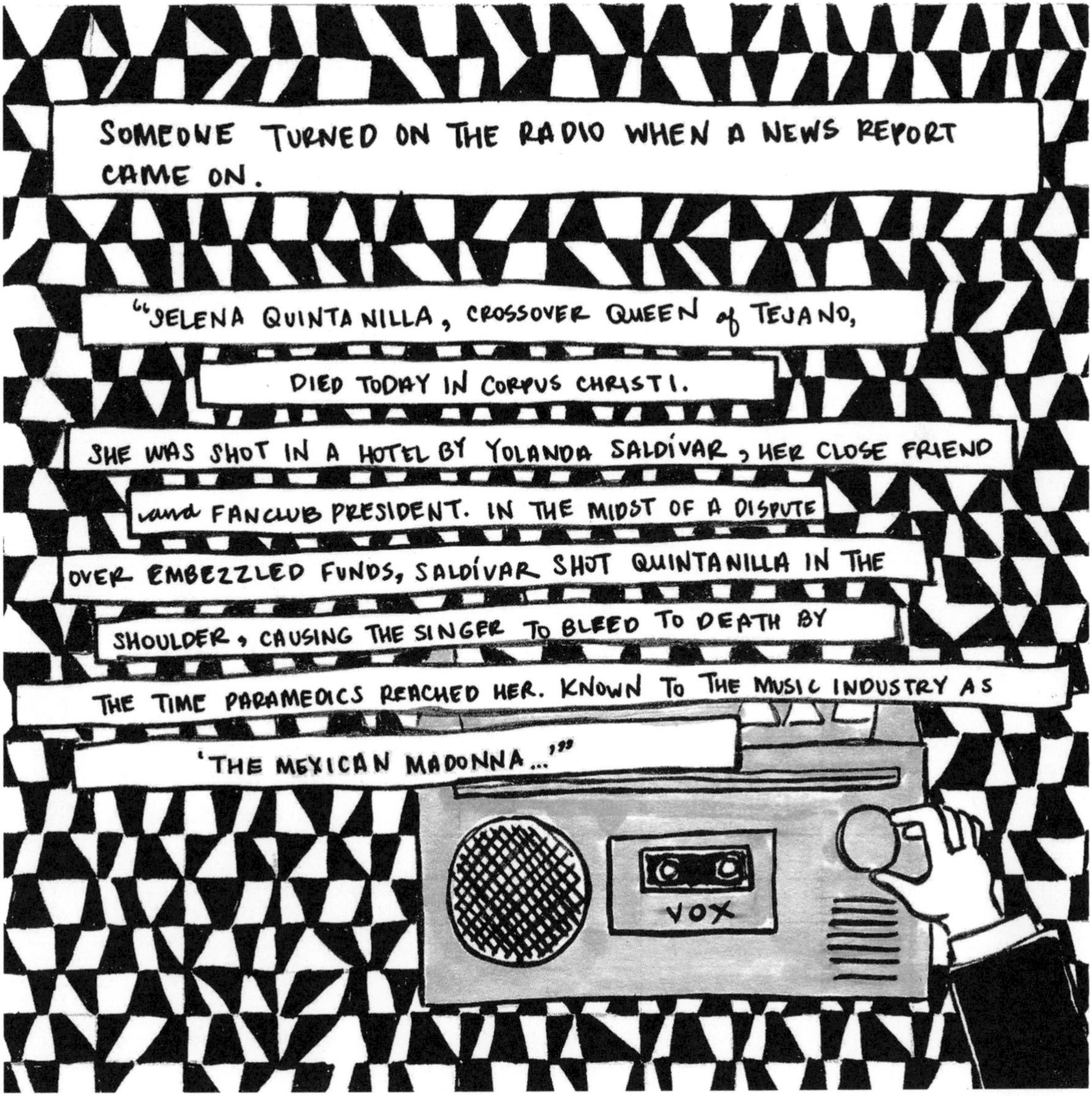
SOMEONE TURNED ON THE RADIO WHEN A NEWS REPORT CAME ON.
"SELENA QUINTANILLA, CROSSOVER QUEEN of TEJANO,
DIED TODAY IN CORPUS CHRISTI.
SHE WAS SHOT IN A HOTEL BY YOLANDA SALDÍVAR, HER CLOSE FRIEND
and FANCLUB PRESIDENT. IN THE MIDST OF A DISPUTE
OVER EMBEZZLED FUNDS, SALDÍVAR SHOT QUINTANILLA IN THE
SHOULDER, CAUSING THE SINGER TO BLEED TO DEATH BY
THE TIME PARAMEDICS REACHED HER. KNOWN TO THE MUSIC INDUSTRY AS
'THE MEXICAN MADONNA...'"
VOX

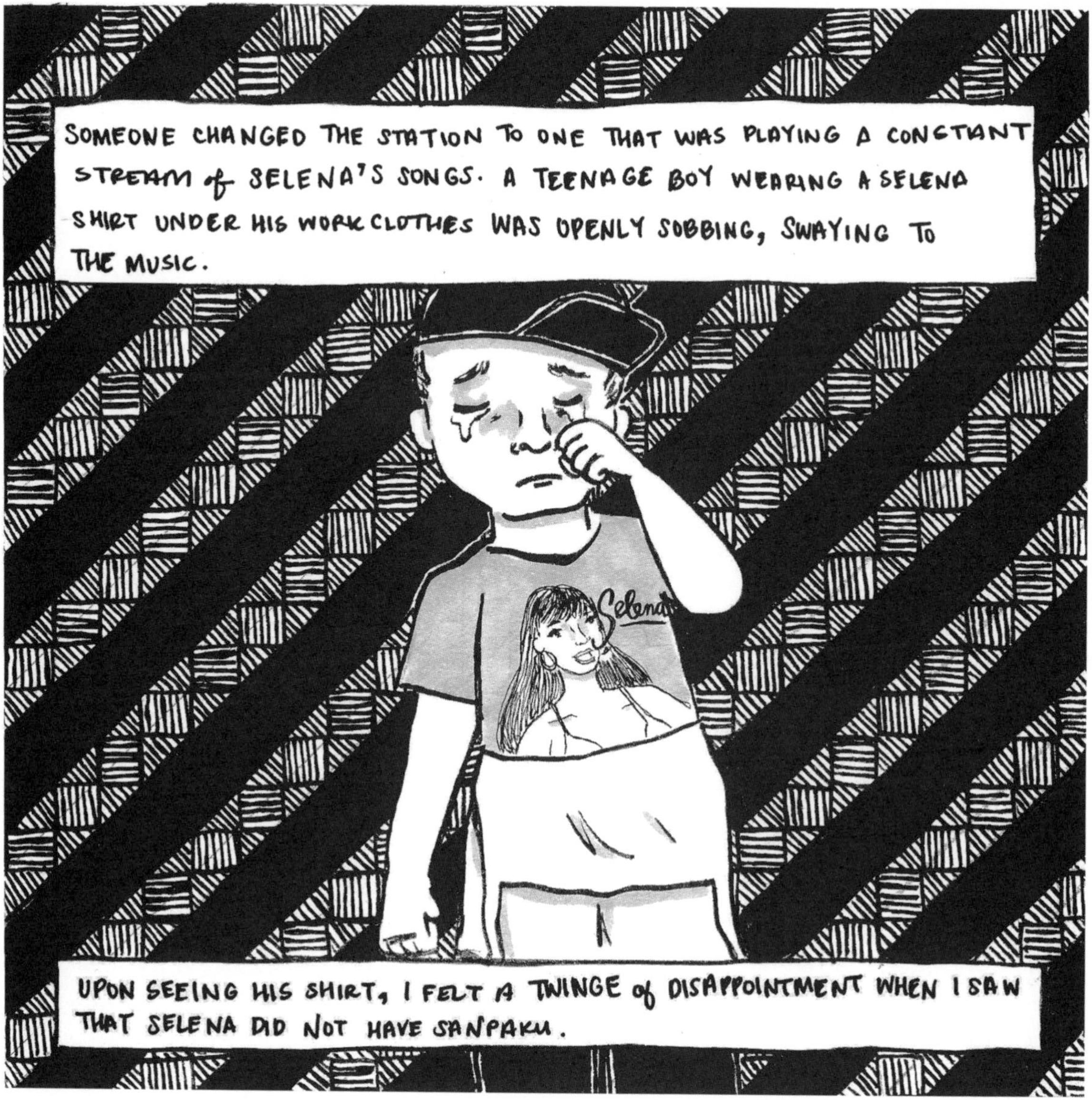
SOMEONE CHANGED THE STATION TO ONE THAT WAS PLAYING A CONSTANT STREAM of SELENA'S SONGS. A TEENAGE BOY WEARING A SELENA SHIRT UNDER HIS WORK CLOTHES WAS OPENLY SOBBING, SWAYING TO THE MUSIC.
Selena
UPON SEEING HIS SHIRT, I FELT A TWINGE of DISAPPOINTMENT WHEN I SAW THAT SELENA DID NOT HAVE SANPAKU.

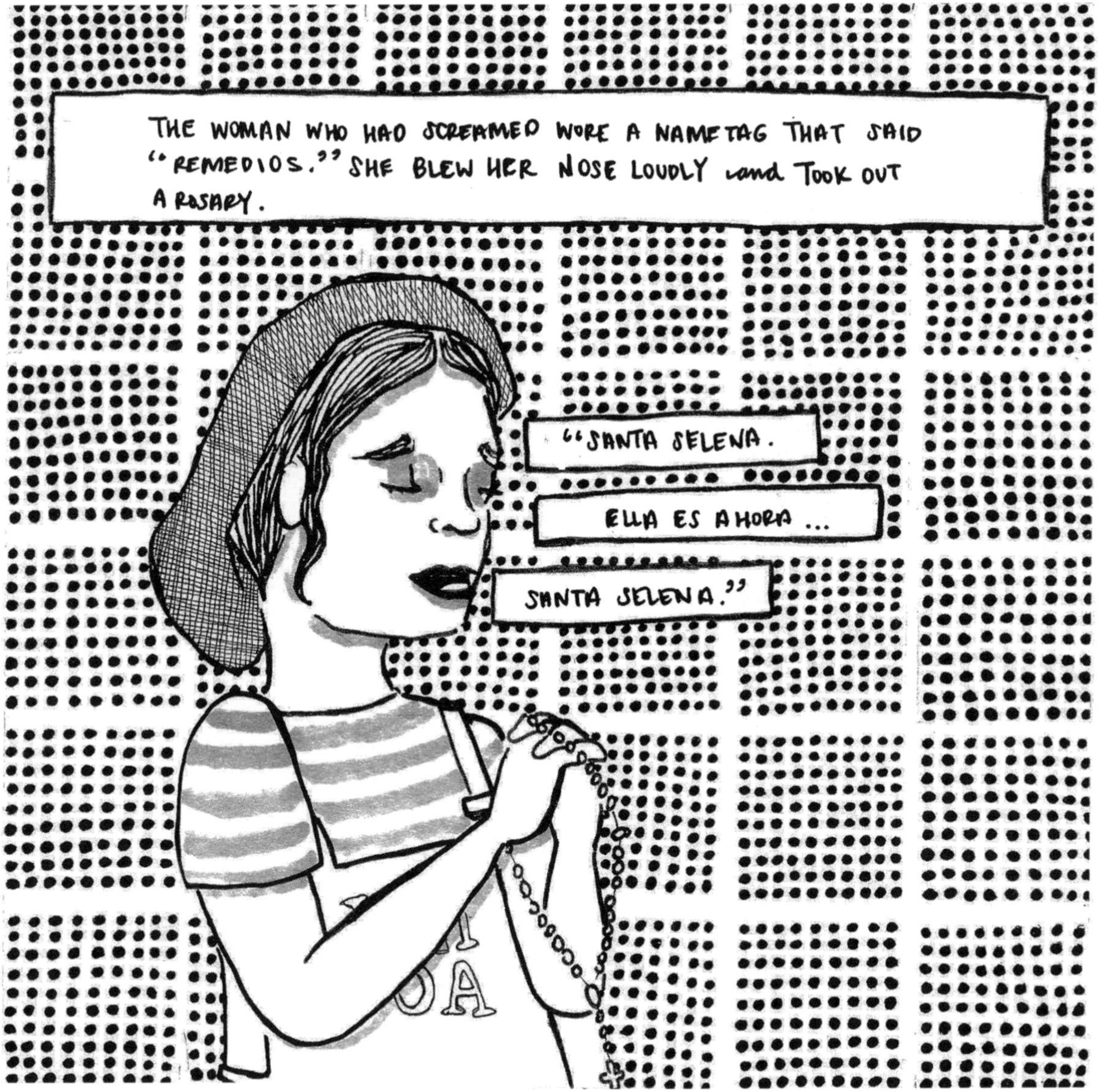
THE WOMAN WHO HAD SCREAMED WORE A NAMETAG THAT SAID "REMEDIOS." SHE BLEW HER NOSE LOUDLY and TOOK OUT A ROSARY.
"SANTA SELENA.
ELLA ES AHORA ...
SANTA SELENA."

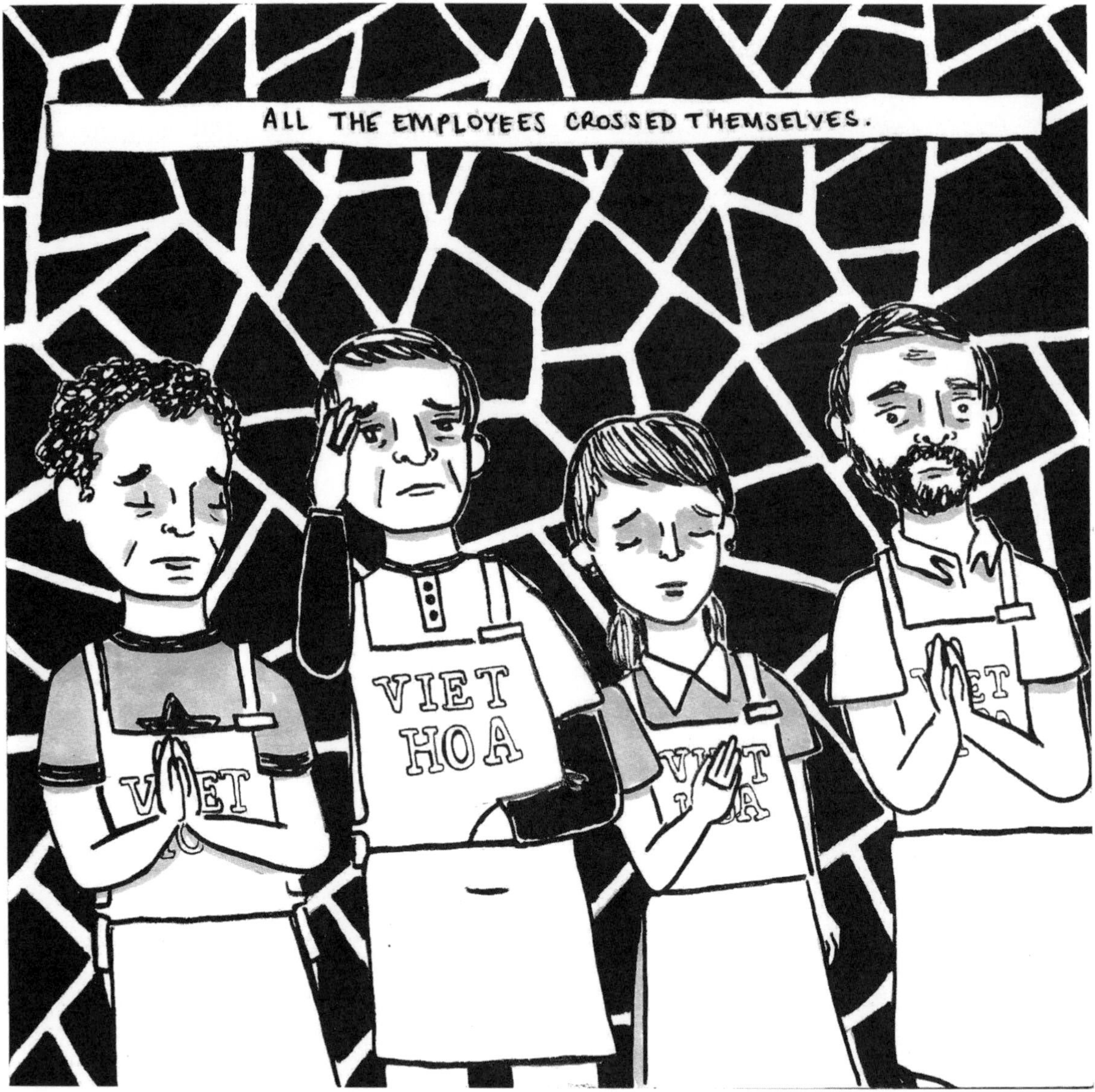
ALL THE EMPLOYEES CROSSED THEMSELVES.
VIET HOA

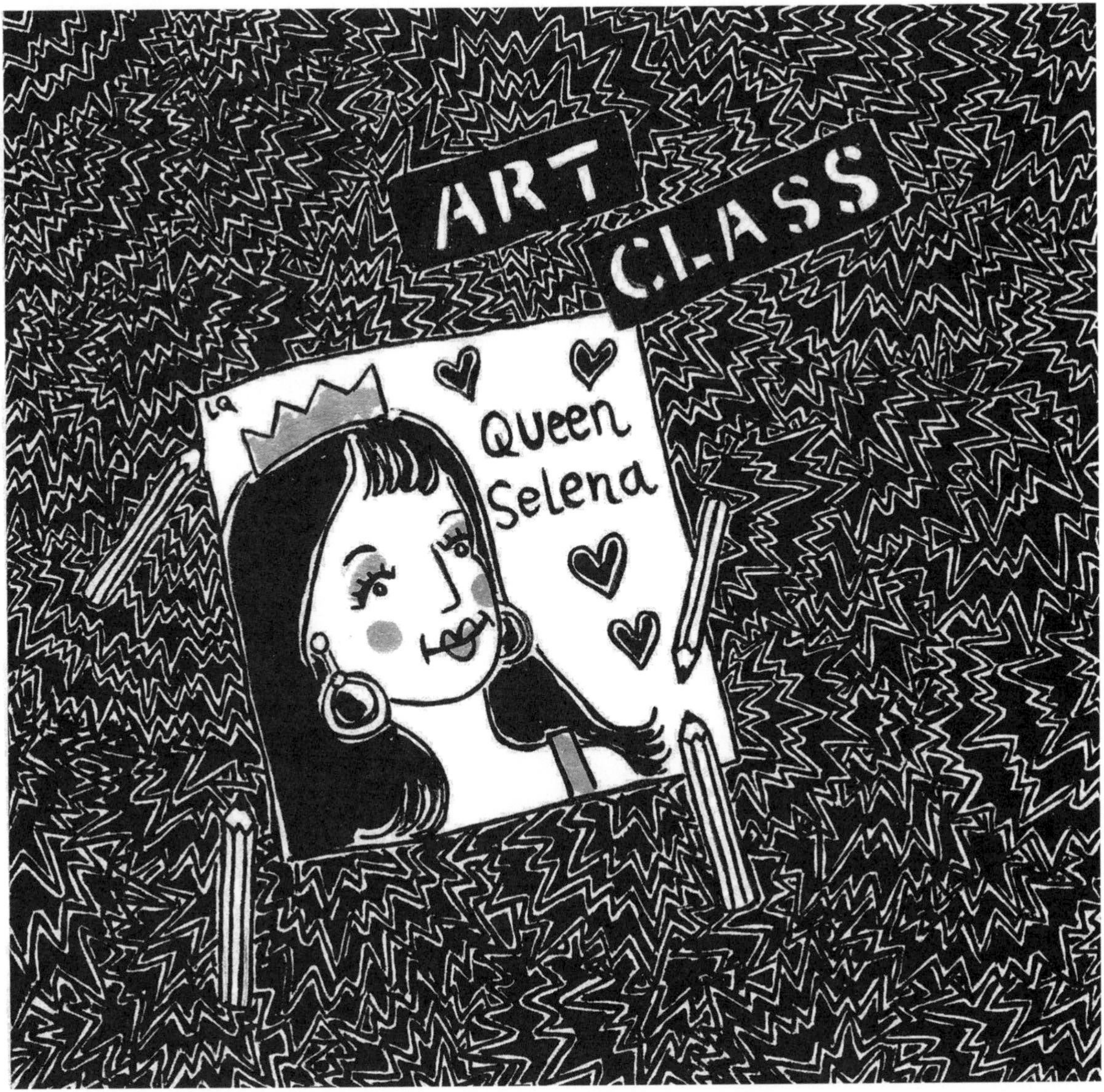
ART CLASS
LQ
Queen Selena

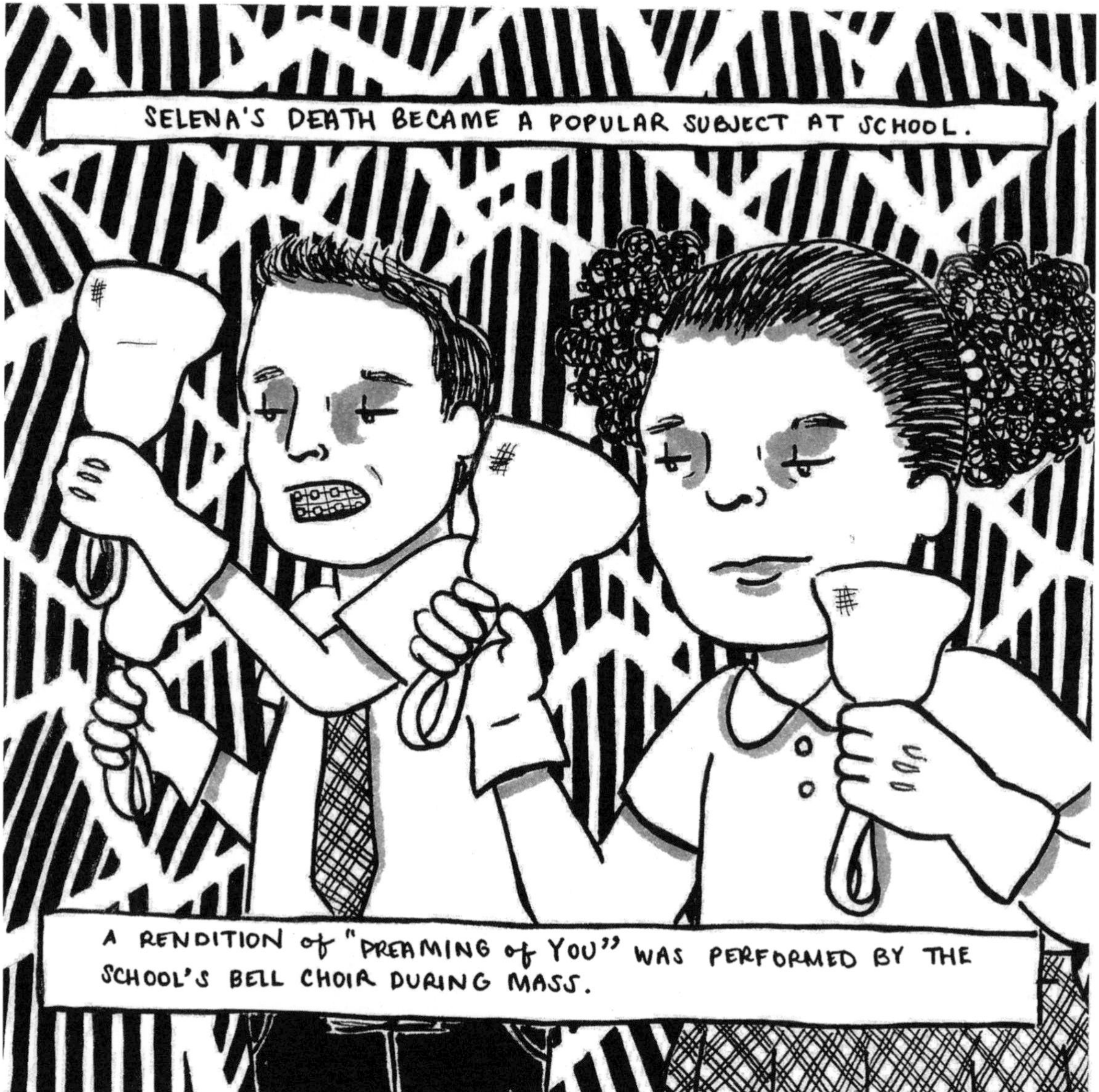
SELENA'S DEATH BECAME A POPULAR SUBJECT AT SCHOOL.
A RENDITION of "DREAMING of YOU" WAS PERFORMED BY THE SCHOOL'S BELL CHOIR DURING MASS.

THE ADVANCED SPANISH CLASSES WROTE POEMS IN MEMORY of SELENA.
Selena
Querida Selena
Como una flor
Eras hermosa
Pero...
Tú moriste
En el invierno
Te extrañamos
Como una flor
Luisa Quiroz

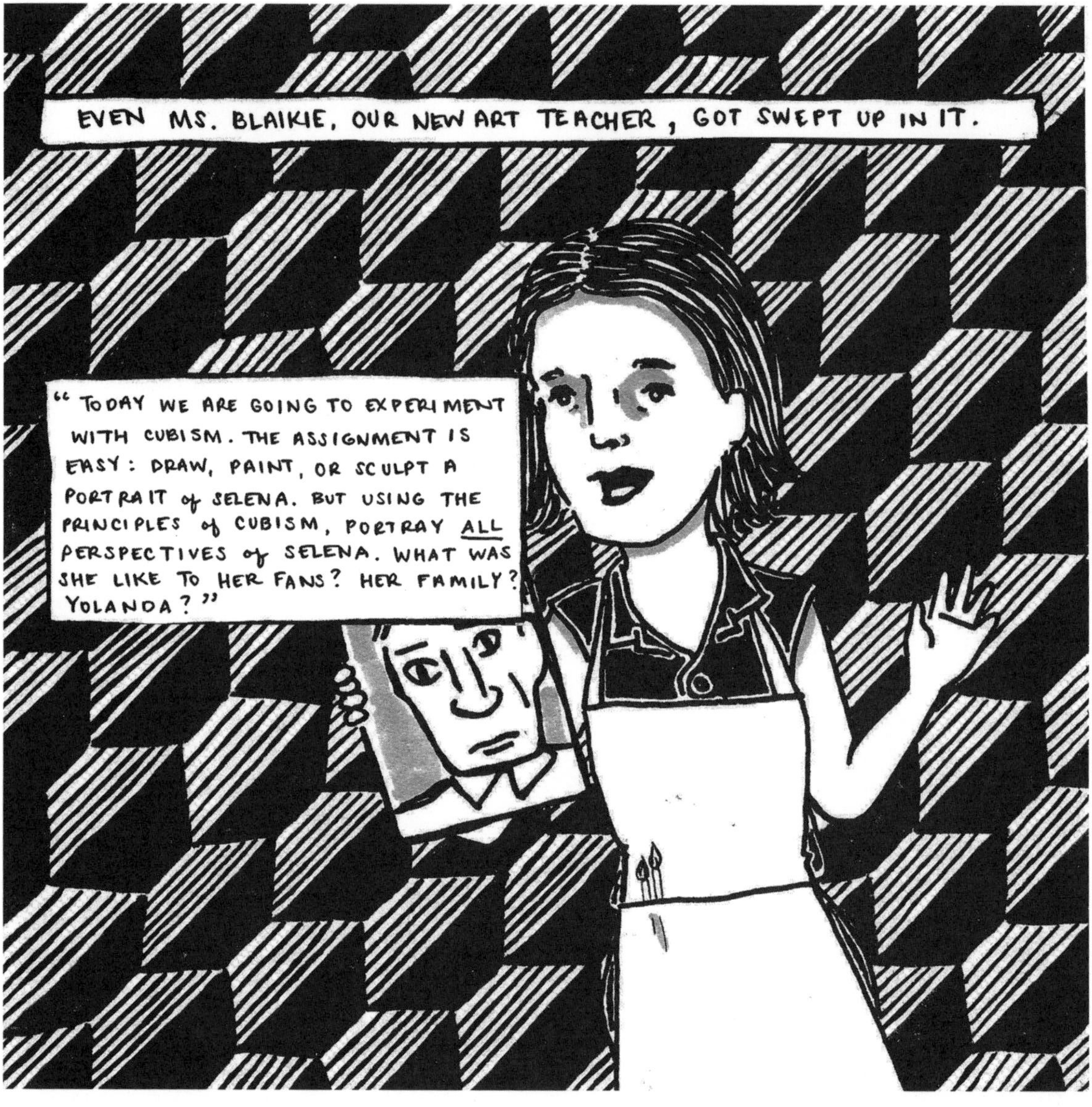
EVEN MS. BLAIKIE, OUR NEW ART TEACHER, GOT SWEPT UP IN IT.
"TODAY WE ARE GOING TO EXPERIMENT WITH CUBISM. THE ASSIGNMENT IS EASY: DRAW, PAINT, OR SCULPT A PORTRAIT of SELENA. BUT USING THE PRINCIPLES of CUBISM, PORTRAY ALL PERSPECTIVES of SELENA. WHAT WAS SHE LIKE TO HER FANS? HER FAMILY? YOLANDA?"

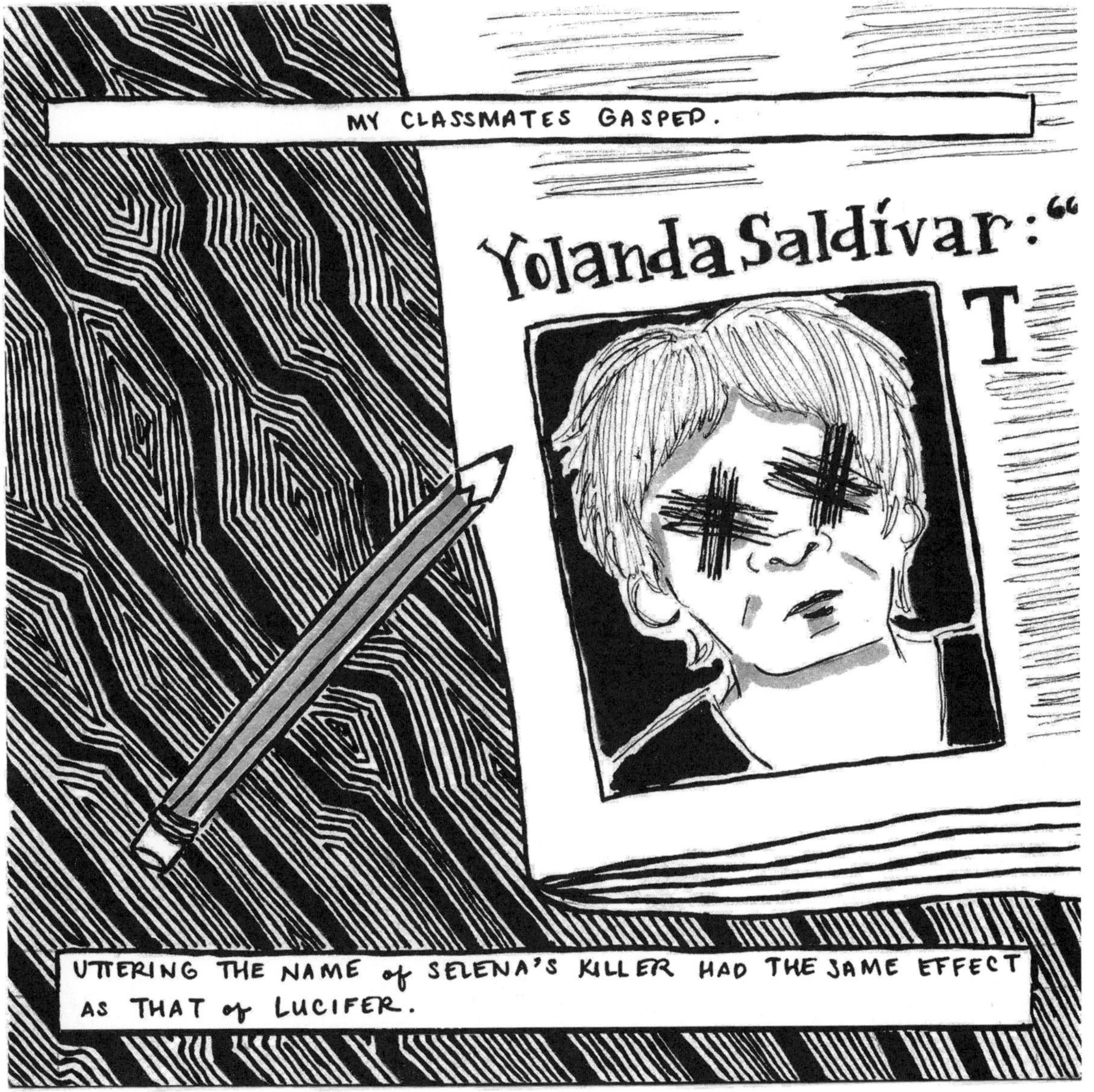
MY CLASSMATES GASPED.
Yolanda Saldívar: "
T
UTTERING THE NAME of SELENA'S KILLER HAD THE SAME EFFECT AS THAT of LUCIFER.

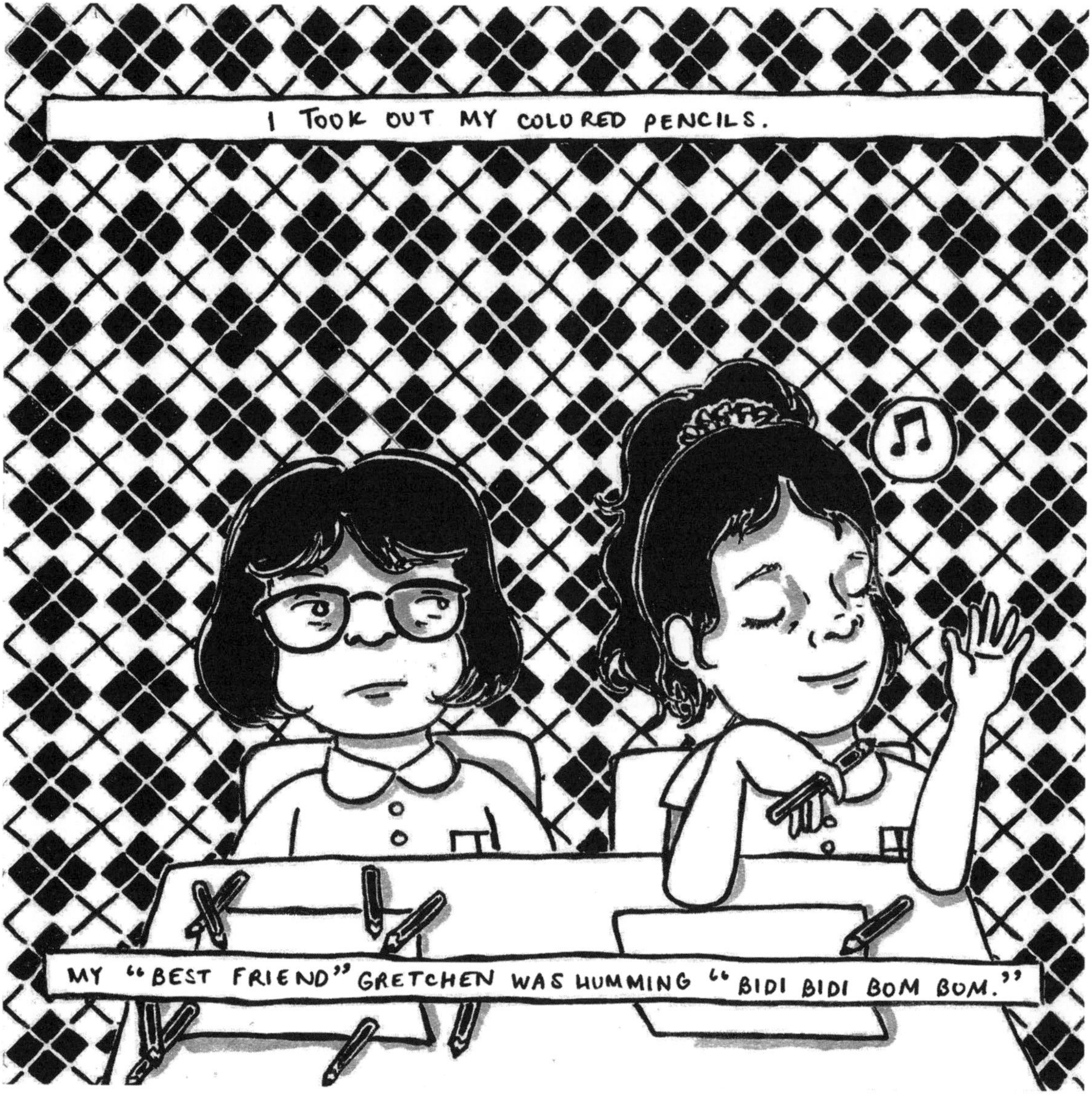
I TOOK OUT MY COLORED PENCILS.
MY "BEST FRIEND" GRETCHEN WAS HUMMING "BIDI BIDI BOM BOM."

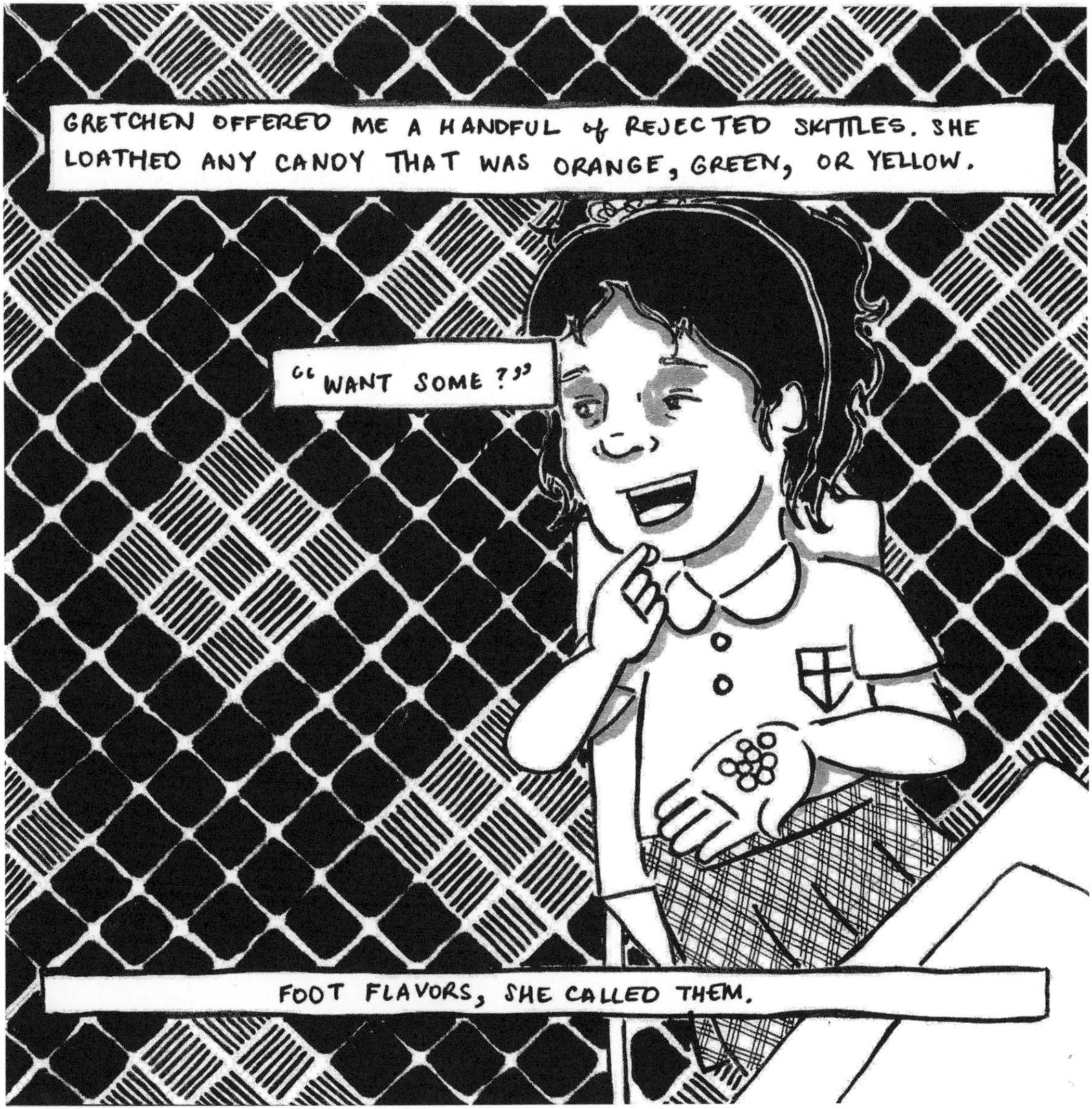
GRETCHEN OFFERED ME A HANDFUL of REJECTED SKITTLES. SHE LOATHED ANY CANDY THAT WAS ORANGE, GREEN, OR YELLOW.
"WANT SOME?"
FOOT FLAVORS, SHE CALLED THEM.

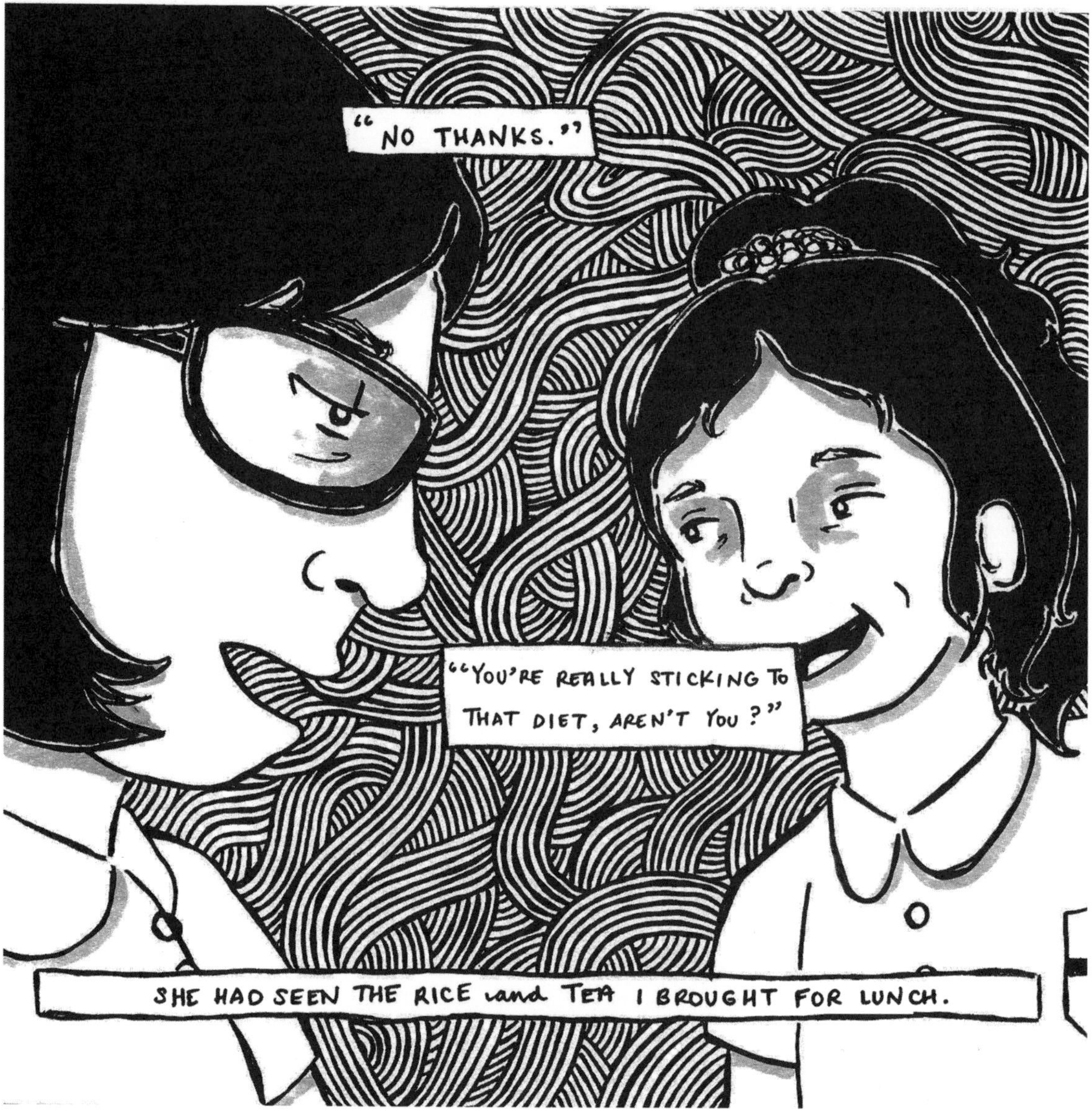
"NO THANKS."
"YOU'RE REALLY STICKING TO THAT DIET, AREN'T YOU?"
SHE HAD SEEN THE RICE and TEA I BROUGHT FOR LUNCH.

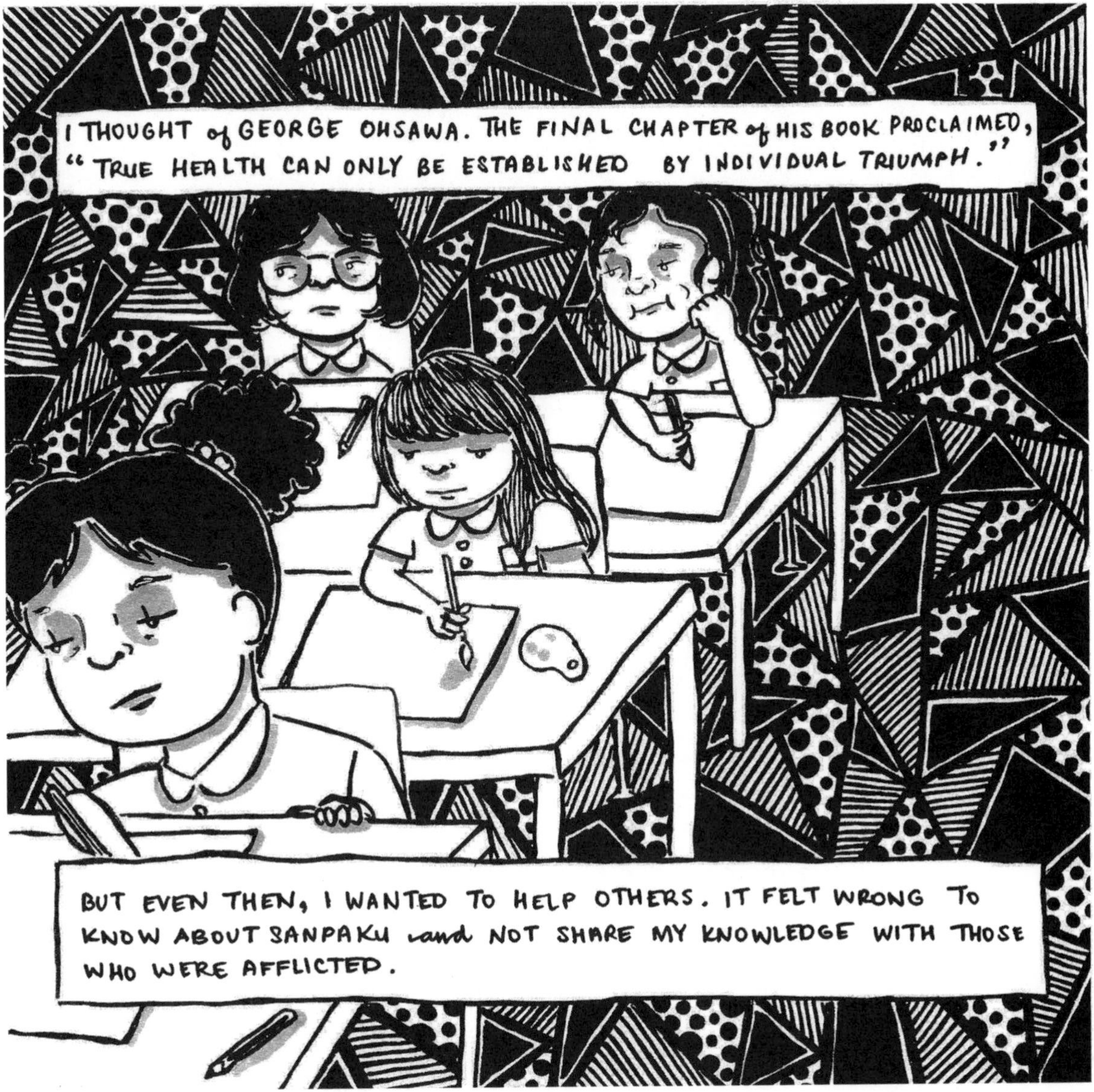
I THOUGHT of GEORGE OHSAWA. THE FINAL CHAPTER of HIS BOOK PROCLAIMED, "TRUE HEALTH CAN ONLY BE ESTABLISHED BY INDIVIDUAL TRIUMPH."
BUT EVEN THEN, I WANTED TO HELP OTHERS. IT FELT WRONG TO KNOW ABOUT SANPAKU and NOT SHARE MY KNOWLEDGE WITH THOSE WHO WERE AFFLICTED.

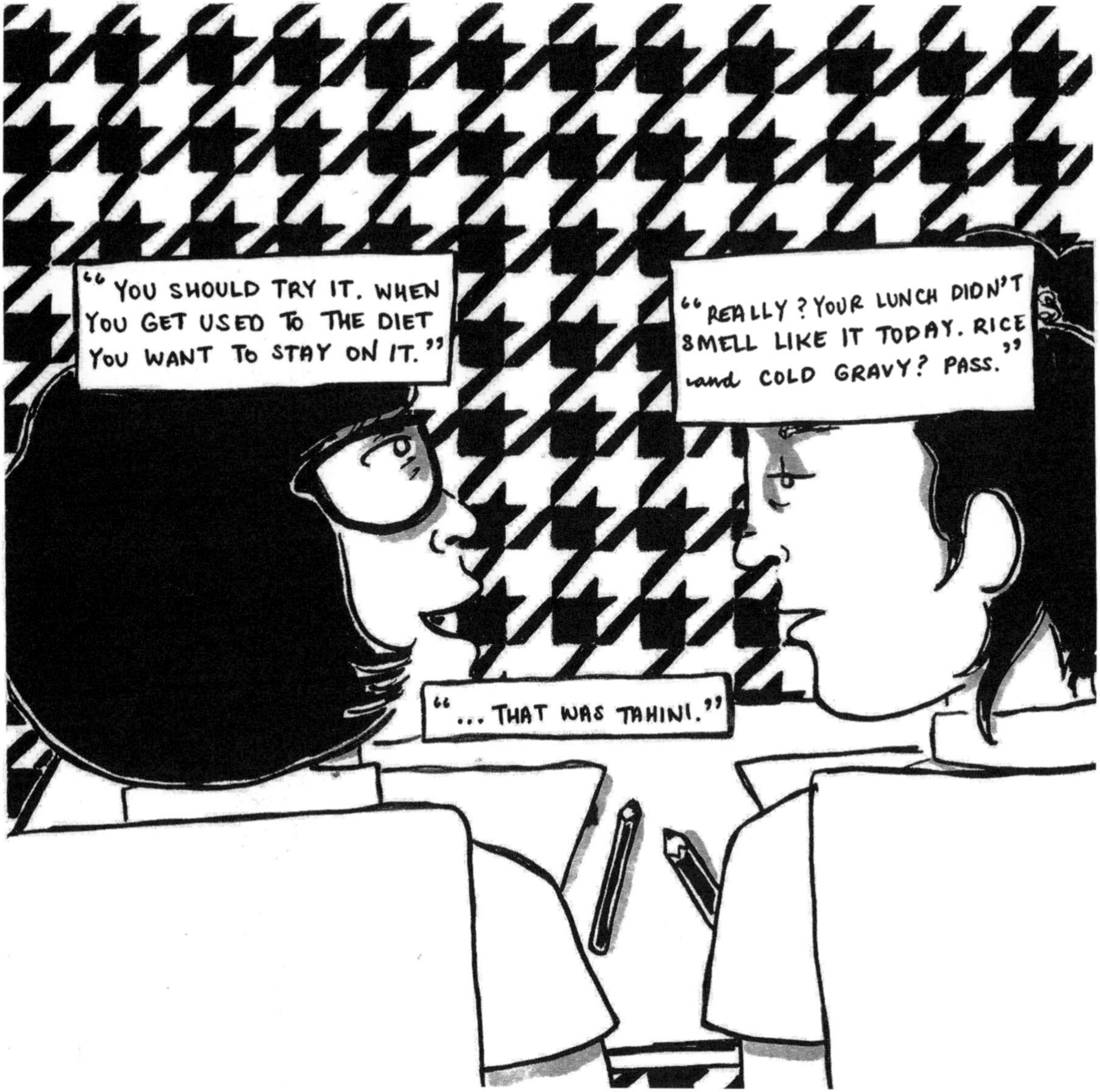
"YOU SHOULD TRY IT. WHEN YOU GET USED TO THE DIET YOU WANT TO STAY ON IT."
"REALLY? YOUR LUNCH DIDN'T SMELL LIKE IT TODAY. RICE and COLD GRAVY? PASS."
"...THAT WAS TAHINI."

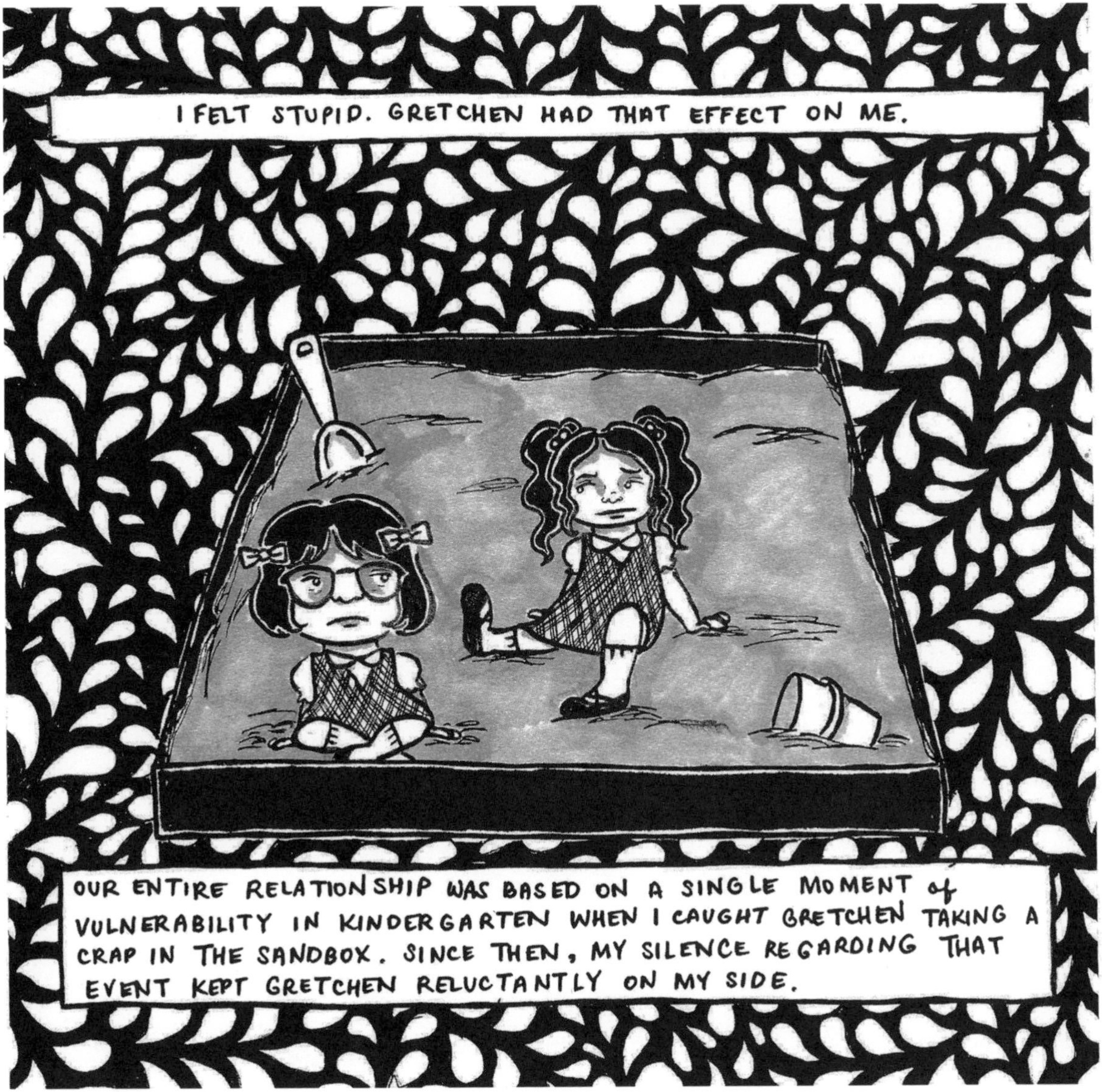
I FELT STUPID. GRETCHEN HAD THAT EFFECT ON ME.
OUR ENTIRE RELATIONSHIP WAS BASED ON A SINGLE MOMENT of VULNERABILITY IN KINDERGARTEN WHEN I CAUGHT GRETCHEN TAKING A CRAP IN THE SANDBOX. SINCE THEN, MY SILENCE REGARDING THAT EVENT KEPT GRETCHEN RELUCTANTLY ON MY SIDE.

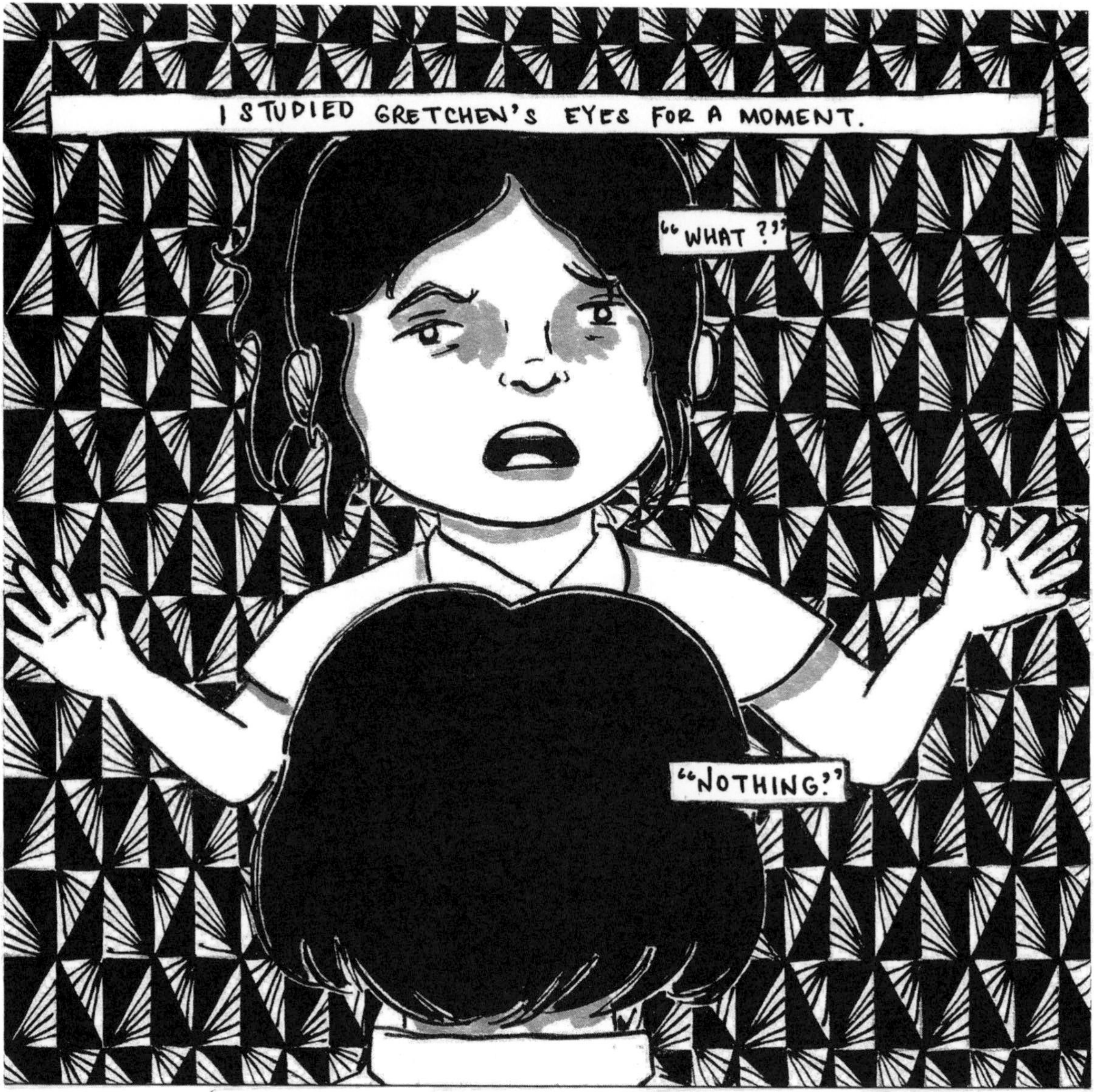
I STUDIED GRETCHEN'S EYES FOR A MOMENT.
"WHAT?"
"NOTHING."

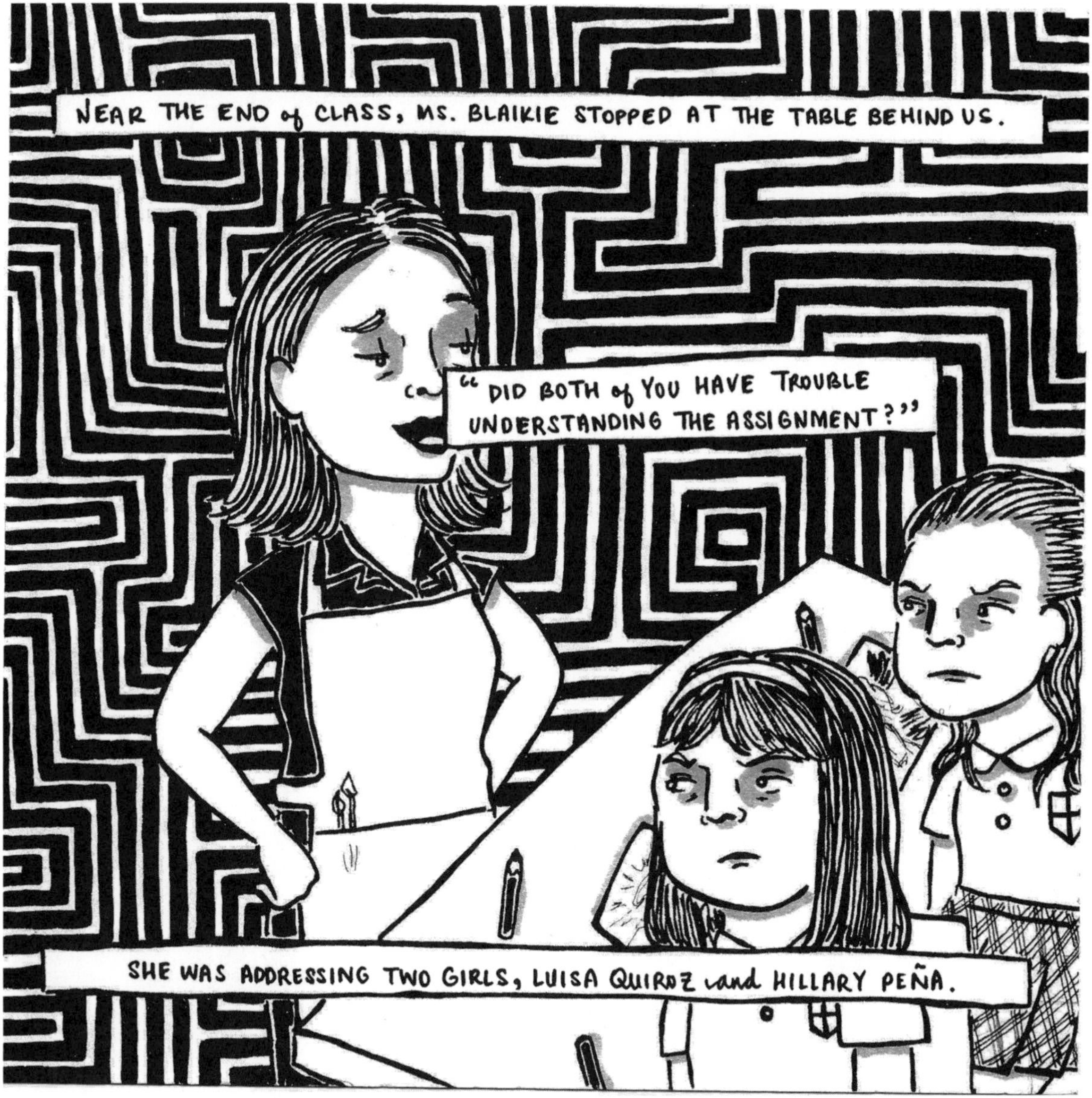
NEAR THE END of CLASS, MS. BLAIKIE STOPPED AT THE TABLE BEHIND US.
"DID BOTH of YOU HAVE TROUBLE UNDERSTANDING THE ASSIGNMENT?"
SHE WAS ADDRESSING TWO GIRLS, LUISA QUIROZ and HILLARY PEÑA.

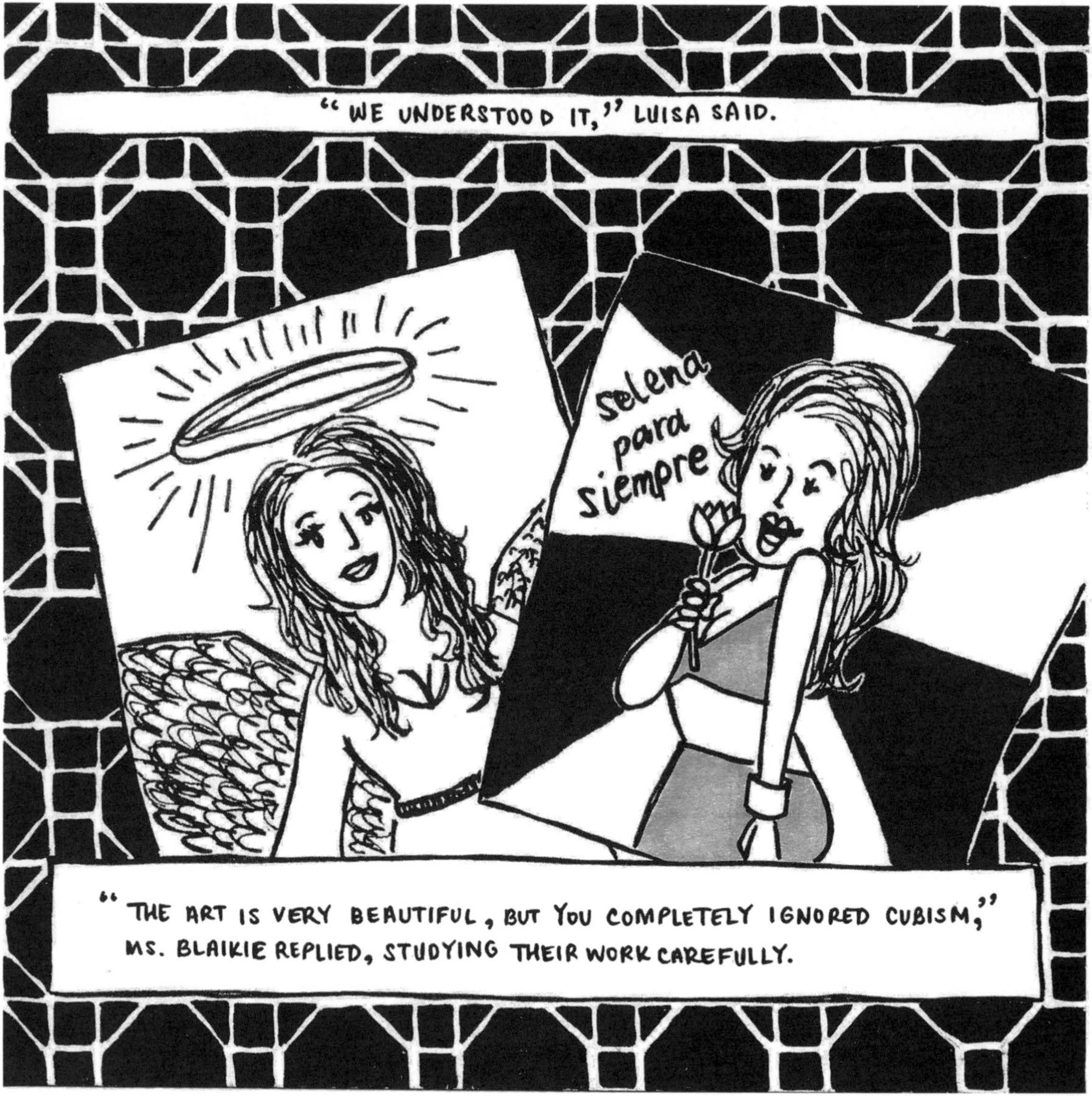
"WE UNDERSTOOD IT," LUISA SAID.
selena para siempre
"THE ART IS VERY BEAUTIFUL, BUT YOU COMPLETELY IGNORED CUBISM," MS. BLAIKIE REPLIED, STUDYING THEIR WORK CAREFULLY.

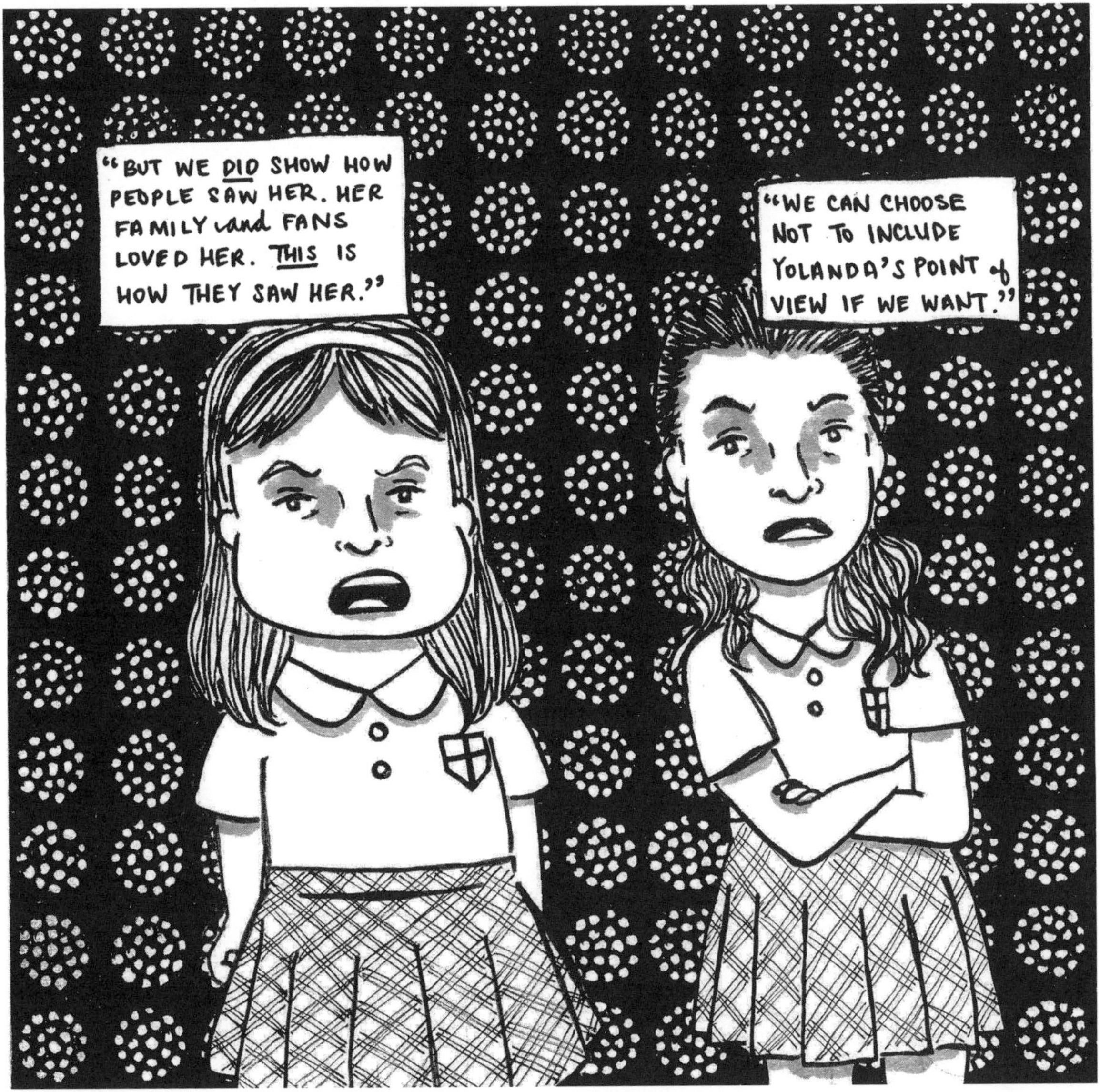
"BUT WE DID SHOW HOW PEOPLE SAW HER. HER FAMILY and FANS LOVED HER. THIS IS HOW THEY SAW HER."
"WE CAN CHOOSE NOT TO INCLUDE YOLANDA'S POINT of VIEW IF WE WANT."

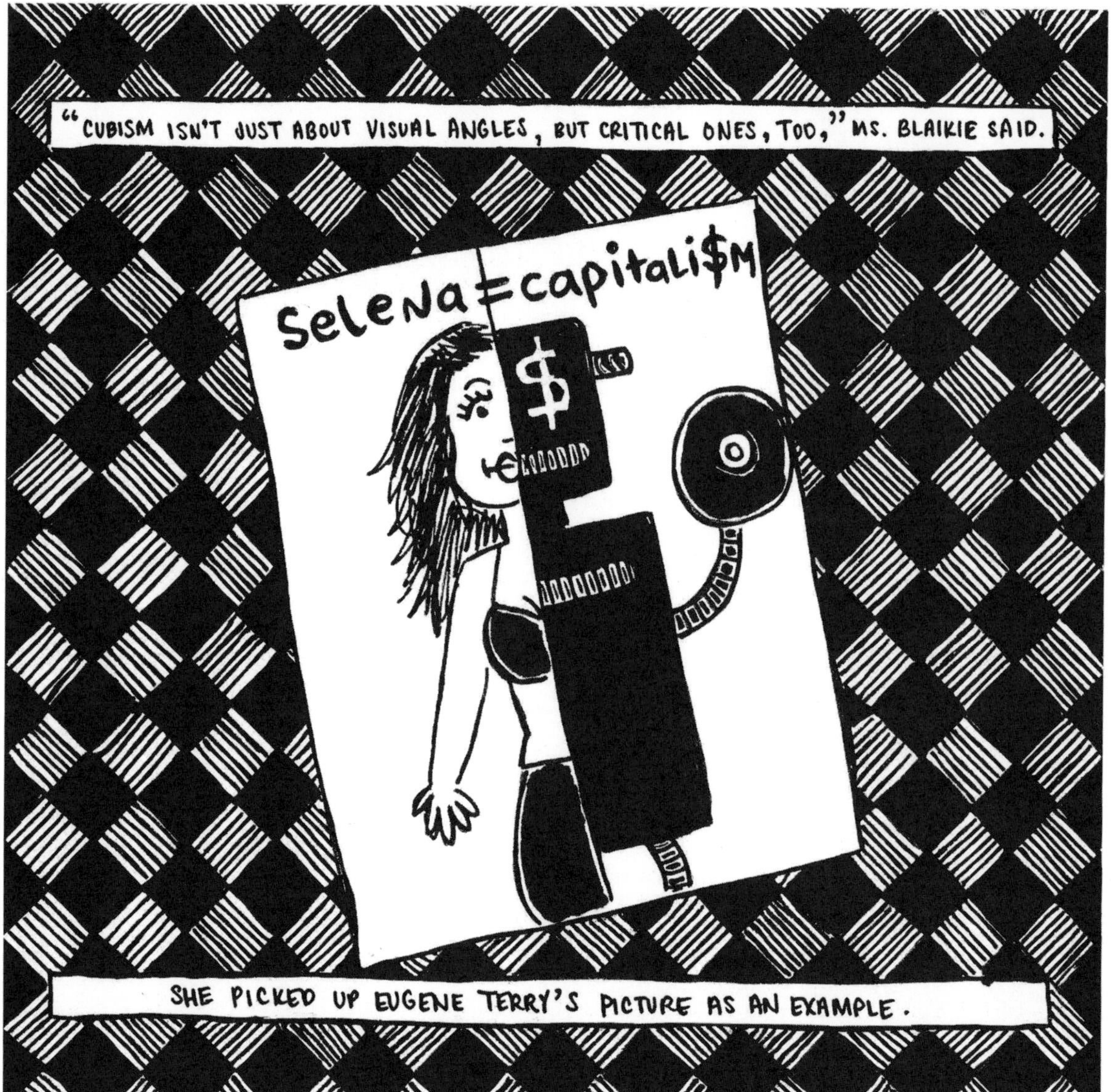
"CUBISM ISN'T JUST ABOUT VISUAL ANGLES, BUT CRITICAL ONES, TOO," MS. BLAIKIE SAID.
Selena=capitali$M
$
SHE PICKED UP EUGENE TERRY'S PICTURE AS AN EXAMPLE.

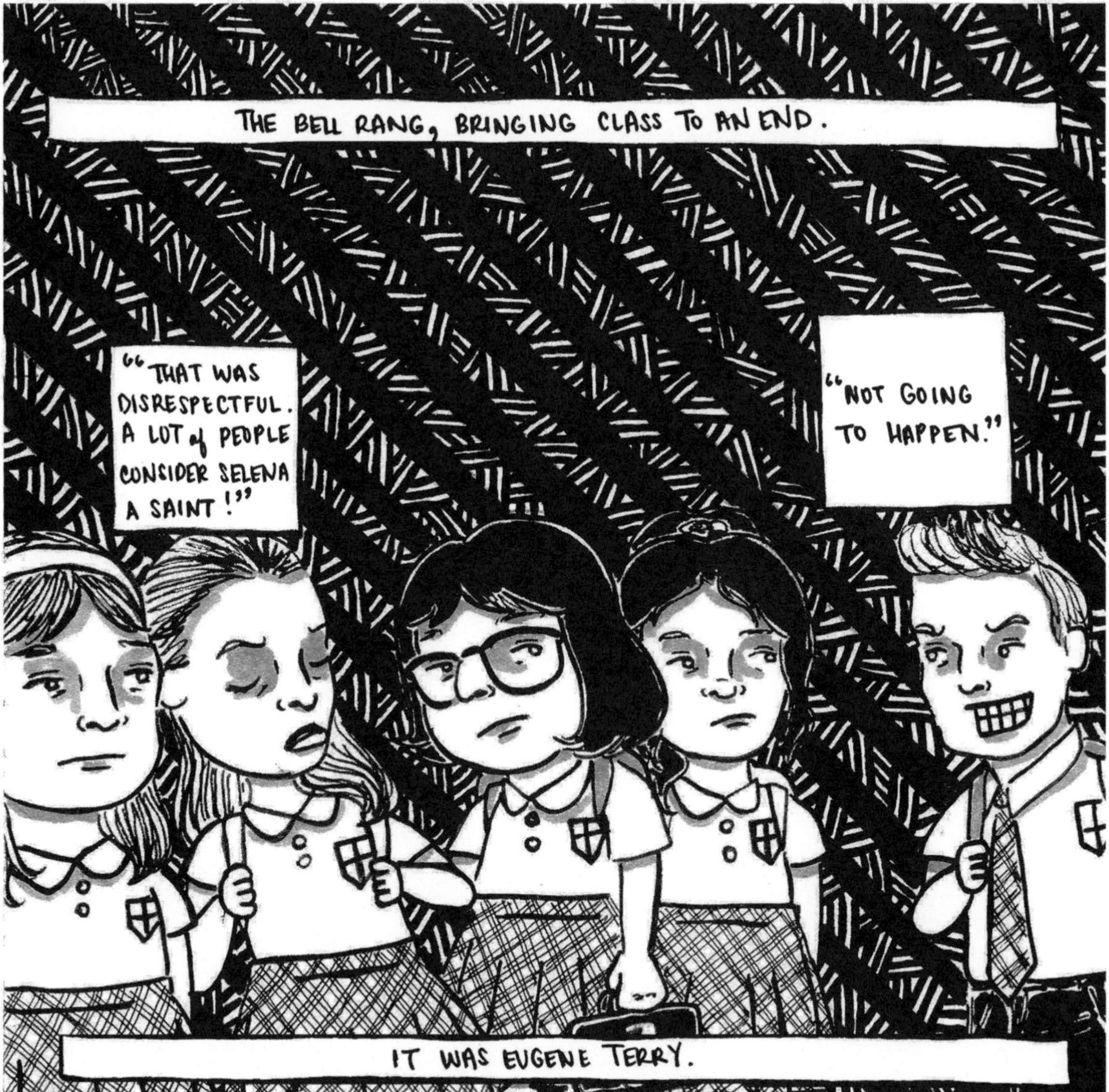
THE BELL RANG, BRINGING CLASS TO AN END.
"THAT WAS DISRESPECTFUL. A LOT of PEOPLE CONSIDER SELENA A SAINT!"
"NOT GOING TO HAPPEN."
IT WAS EUGENE TERRY.

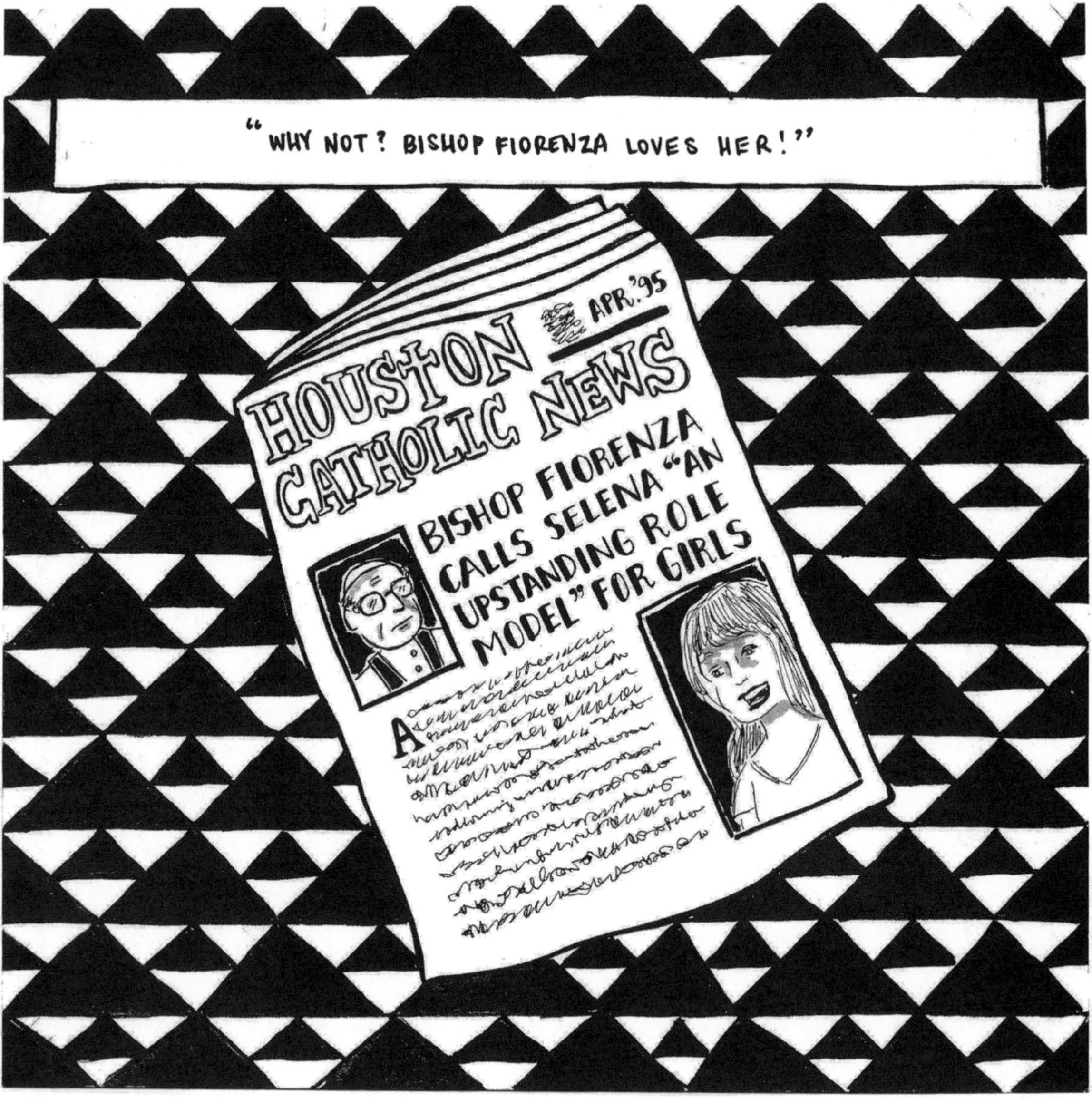
"WHY NOT? BISHOP FIORENZA LOVES HER!"
APR. '95
HOUSTON CATHOLIC NEWS
BISHOP FIORENZA CALLS SELENA "AN UPSTANDING ROLE MODEL" FOR GIRLS

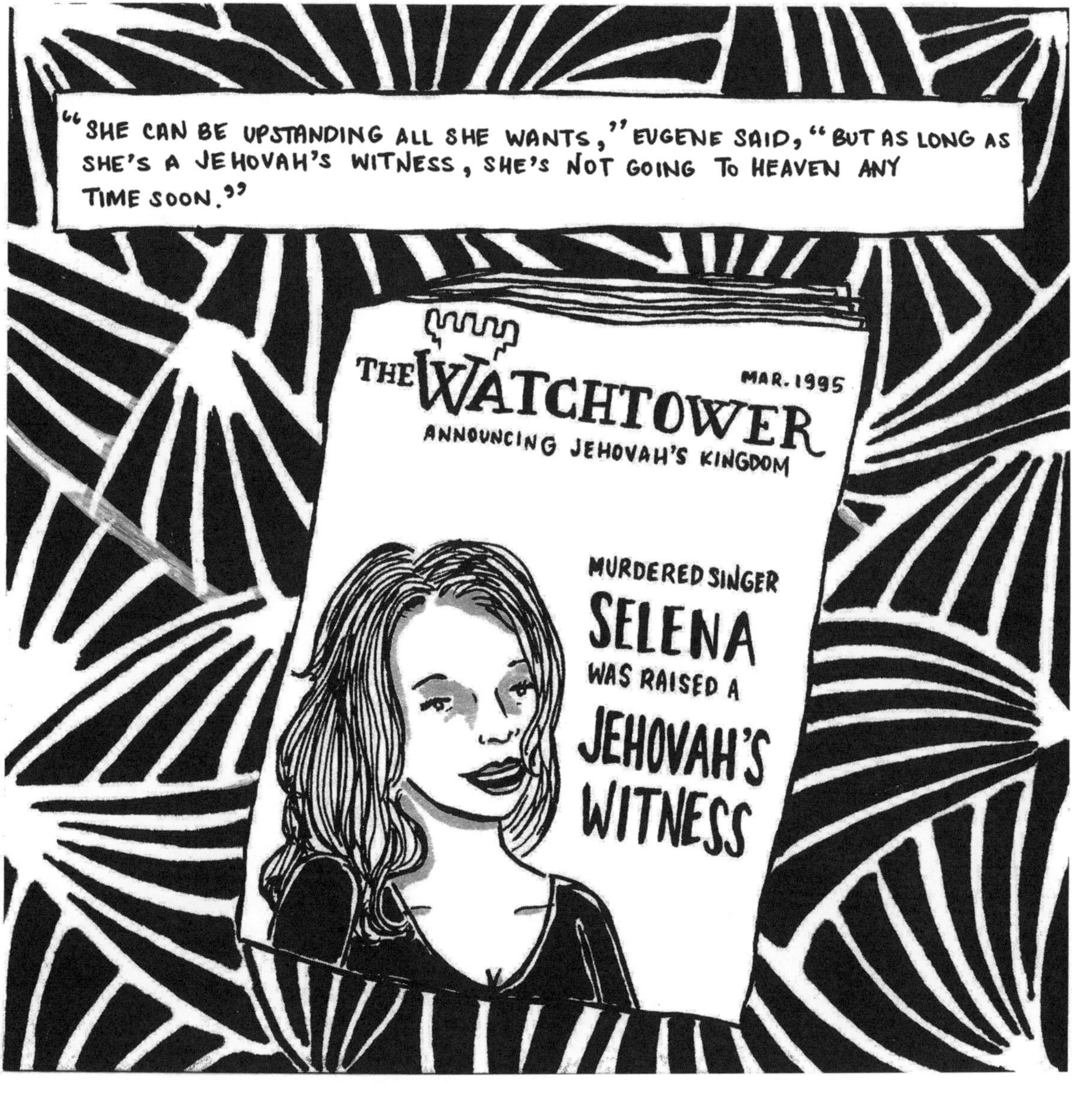
"SHE CAN BE UPSTANDING ALL SHE WANTS," EUGENE SAID, "BUT AS LONG AS SHE'S A JEHOVAH'S WITNESS, SHE'S NOT GOING TO HEAVEN ANY TIME SOON."
THE WATCHTOWER
MAR. 1995
ANNOUNCING JEHOVAH'S KINGDOM
MURDERED SINGER SELENA WAS RAISED A JEHOVAH'S WITNESS

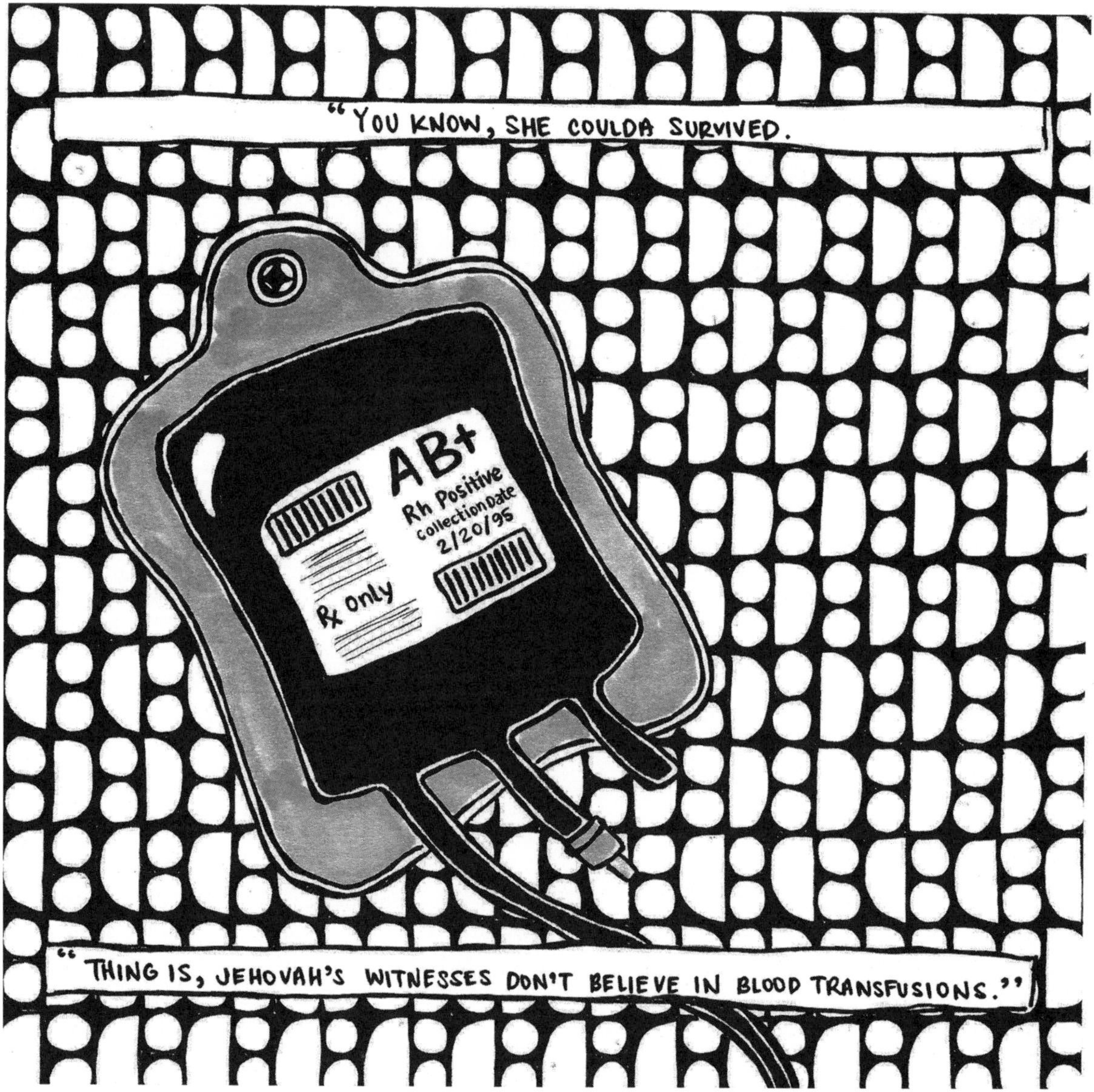
"YOU KNOW, SHE COULDA SURVIVED.
AB+
Rh Positive
Collection Date
2/20/95
℞ only
"THING IS, JEHOVAH'S WITNESSES DON'T BELIEVE IN BLOOD TRANSFUSIONS."

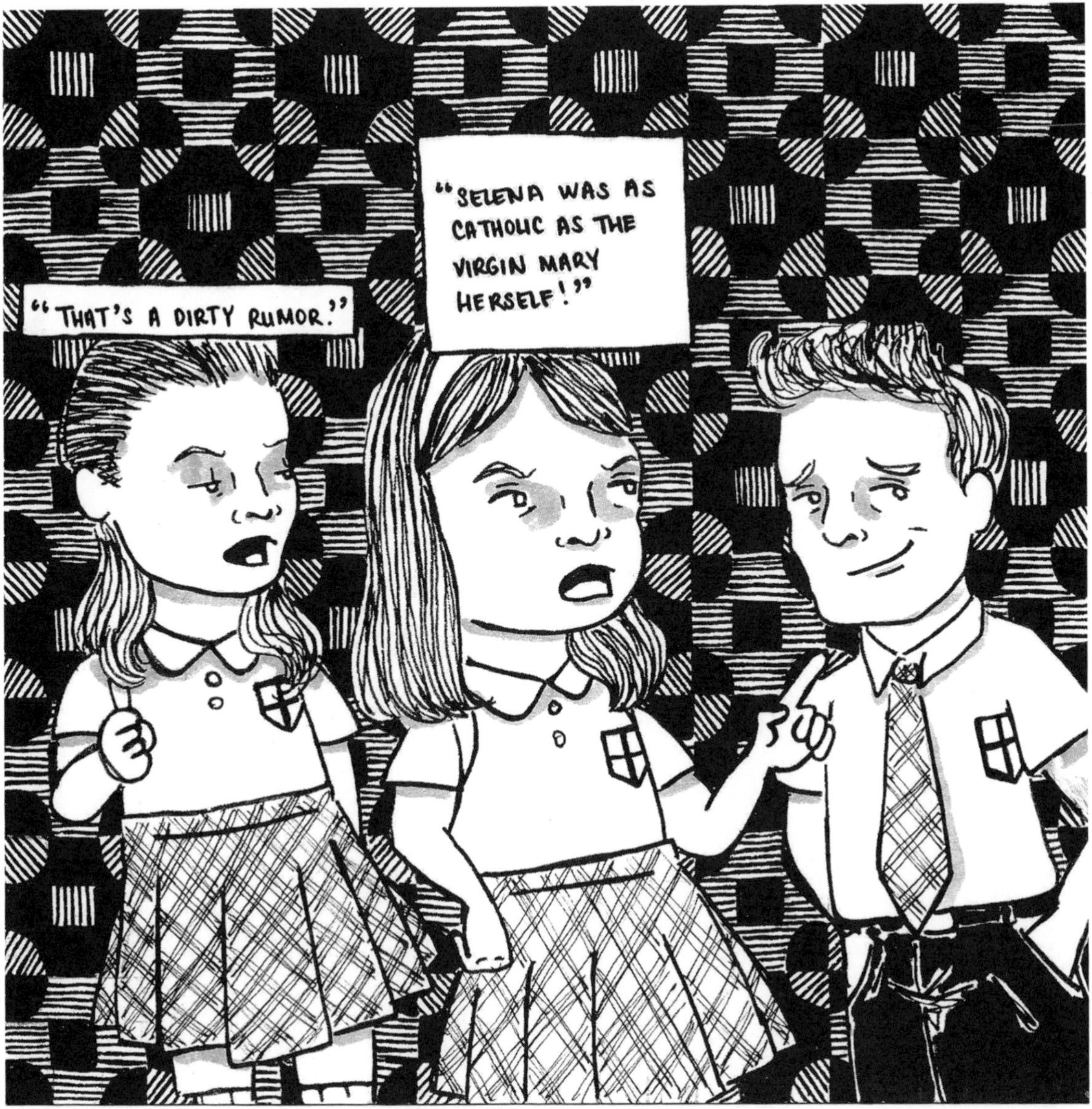
"THAT'S A DIRTY RUMOR."
"SELENA WAS AS CATHOLIC AS THE VIRGIN MARY HERSELF!"

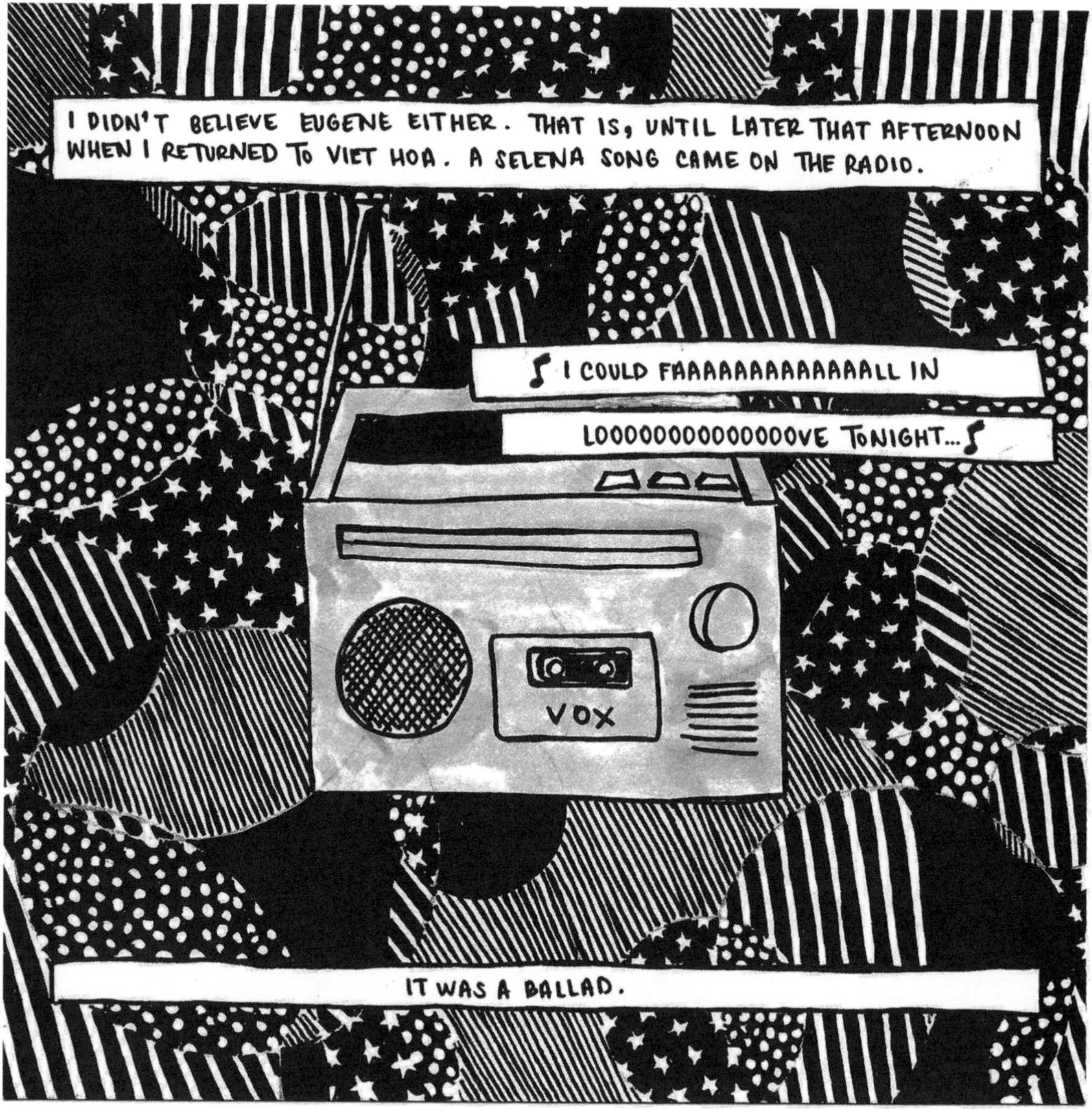
I DIDN'T BELIEVE EUGENE EITHER. THAT IS, UNTIL LATER THAT AFTERNOON WHEN I RETURNED TO VIET HOA. A SELENA SONG CAME ON THE RADIO.
♪ I COULD FAAAAAAAAAAAAALL IN
LOOOOOOOOOOOOOOVE TONIGHT... ♪
VOX
IT WAS A BALLAD.

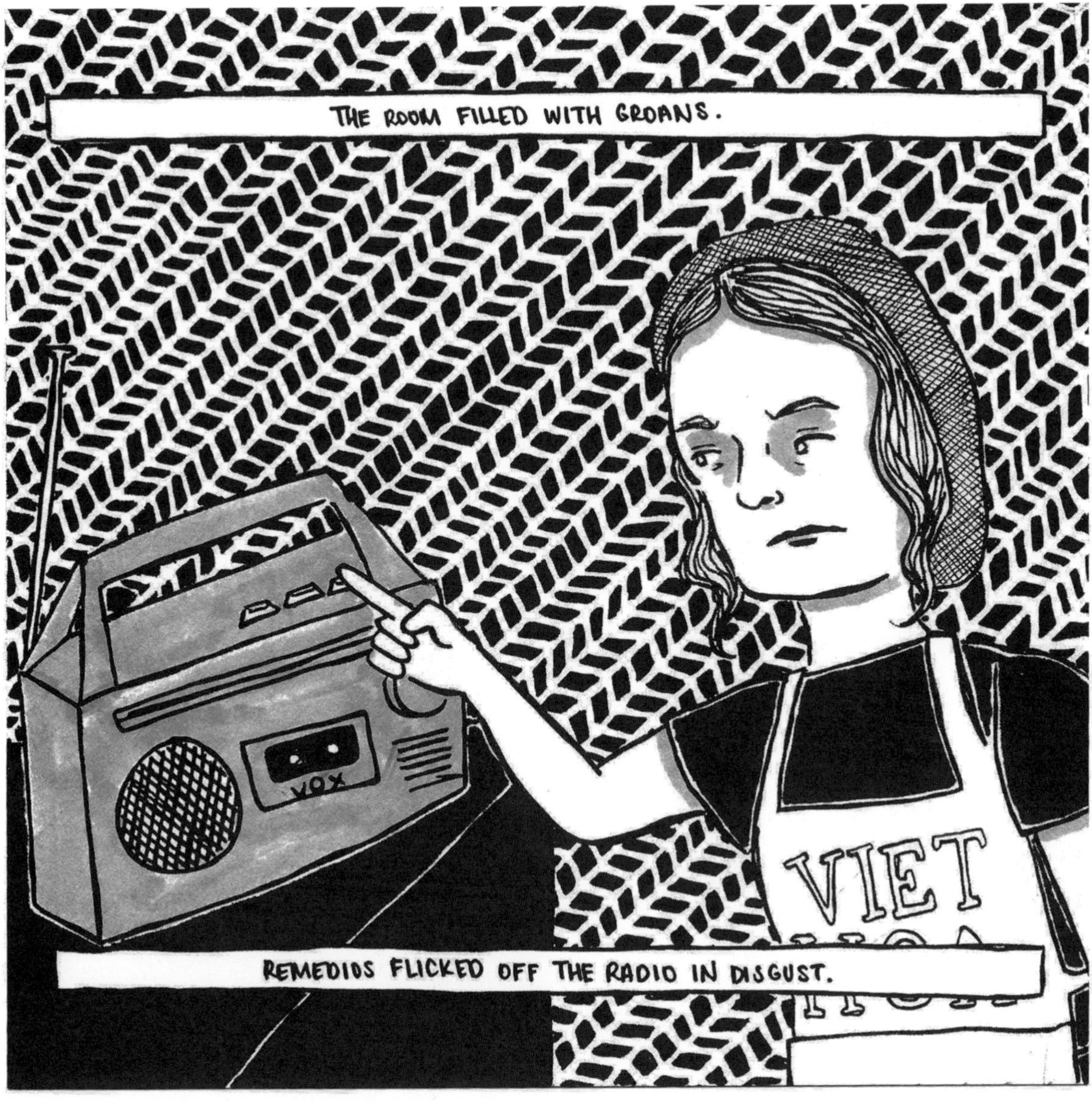
THE ROOM FILLED WITH GROANS.
VOX
VIET
REMEDIOS FLICKED OFF THE RADIO IN DISGUST.

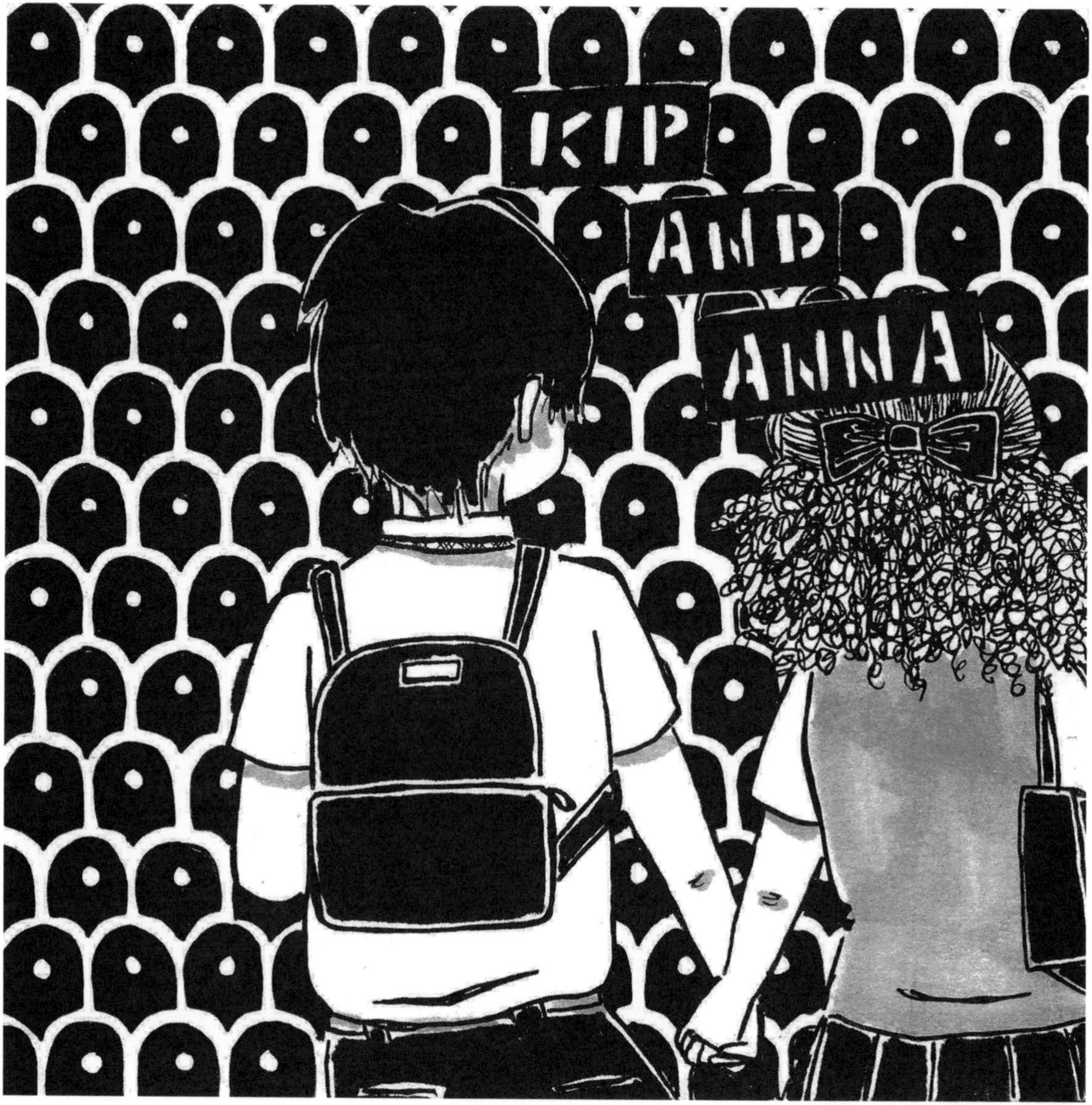
KIP
AND
ANNA

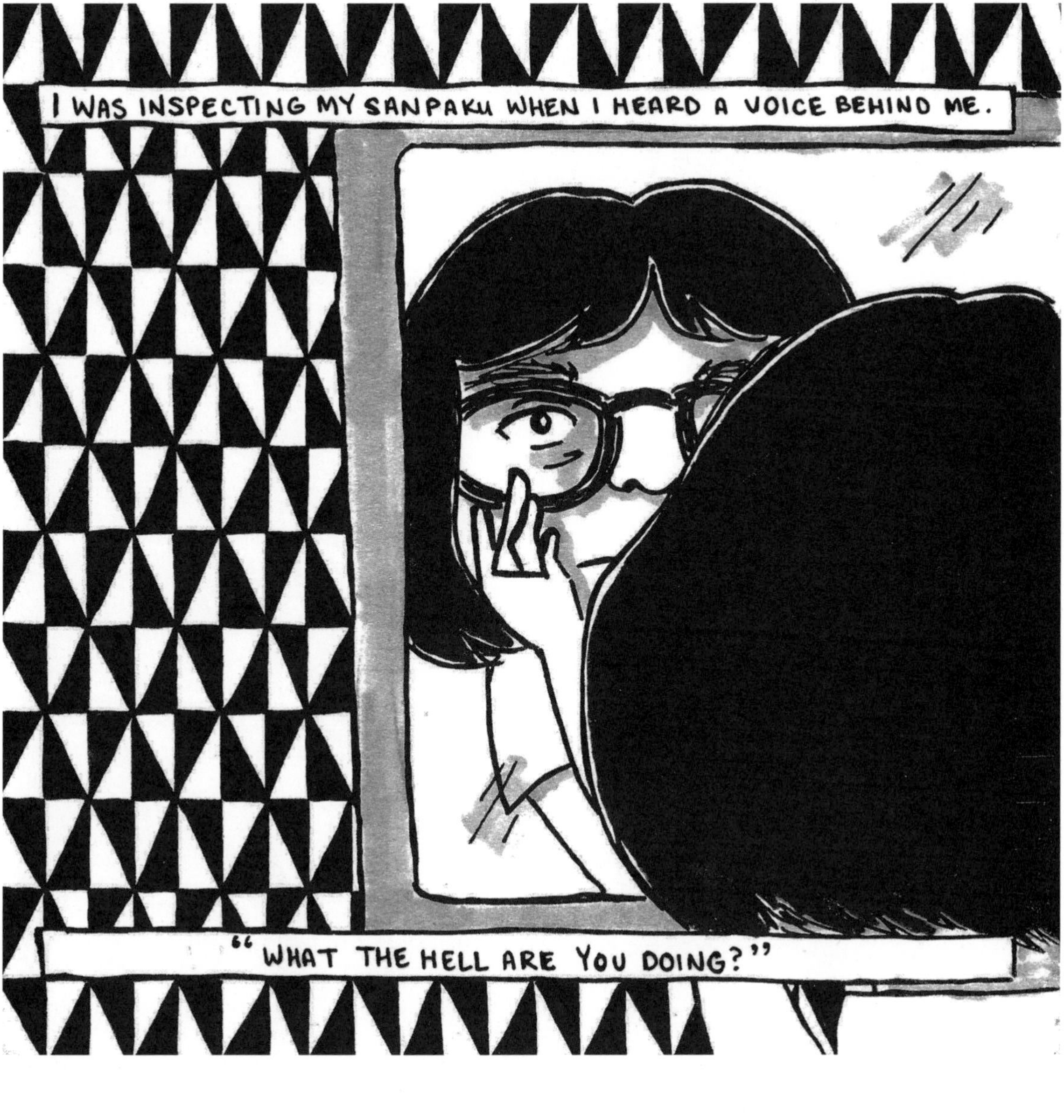
I WAS INSPECTING MY SANPAKU WHEN I HEARD A VOICE BEHIND ME.
"WHAT THE HELL ARE YOU DOING?"

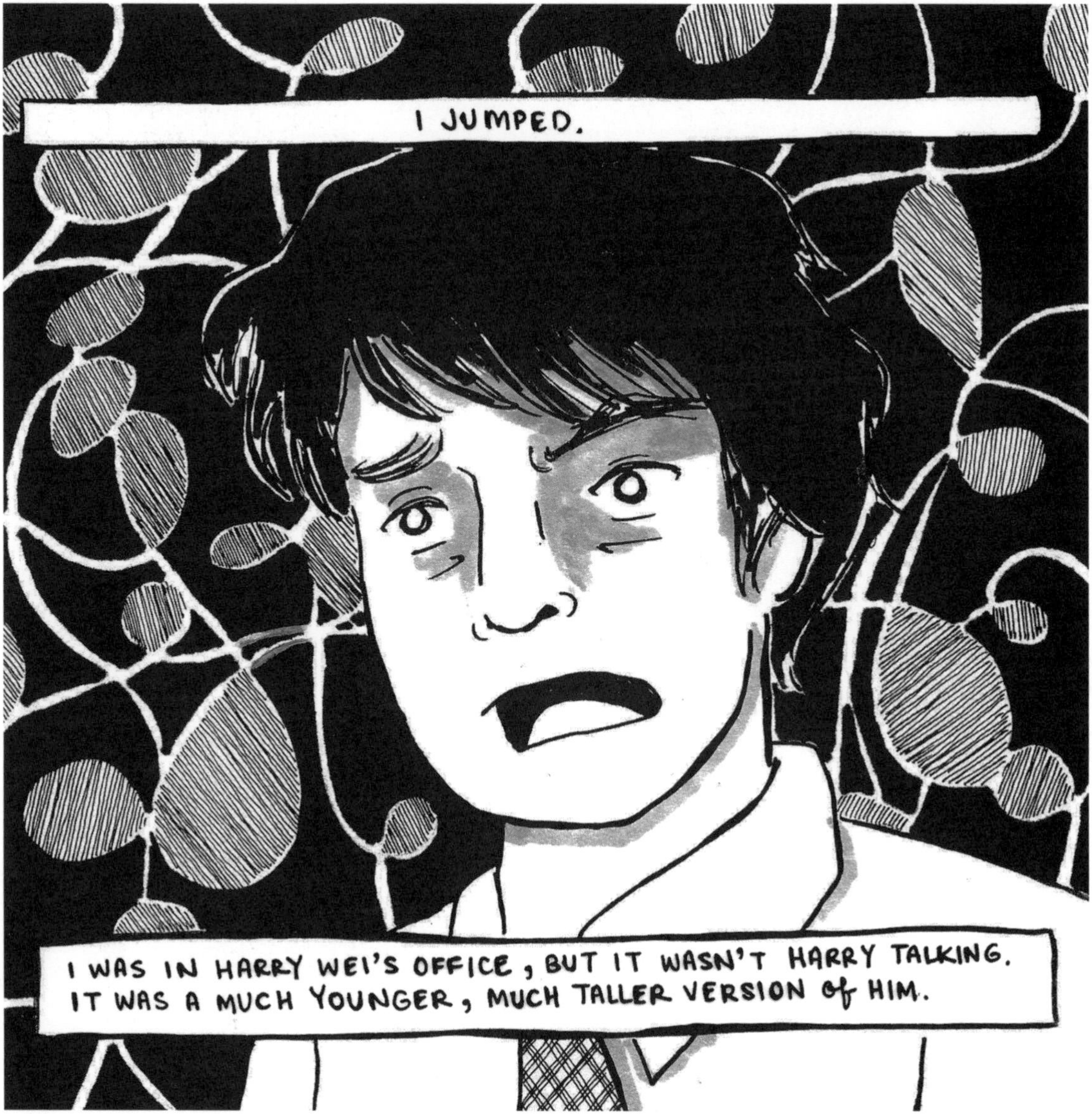
I JUMPED.
I WAS IN HARRY WEI'S OFFICE, BUT IT WASN'T HARRY TALKING. IT WAS A MUCH YOUNGER, MUCH TALLER VERSION OF HIM.

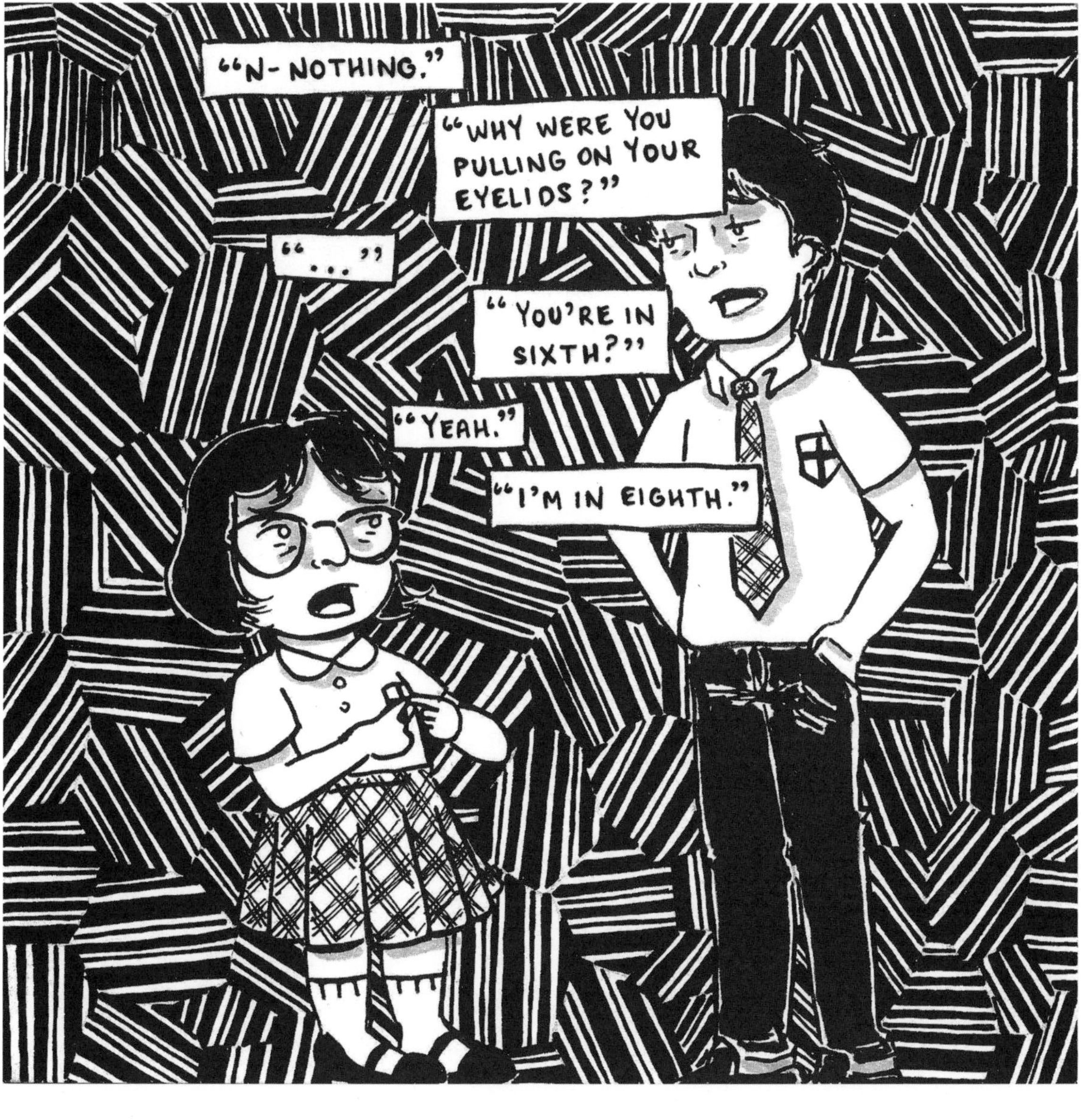
"N-NOTHING."
"WHY WERE YOU PULLING ON YOUR EYELIDS?"
"..."
"YOU'RE IN SIXTH?"
"YEAH."
"I'M IN EIGHTH."

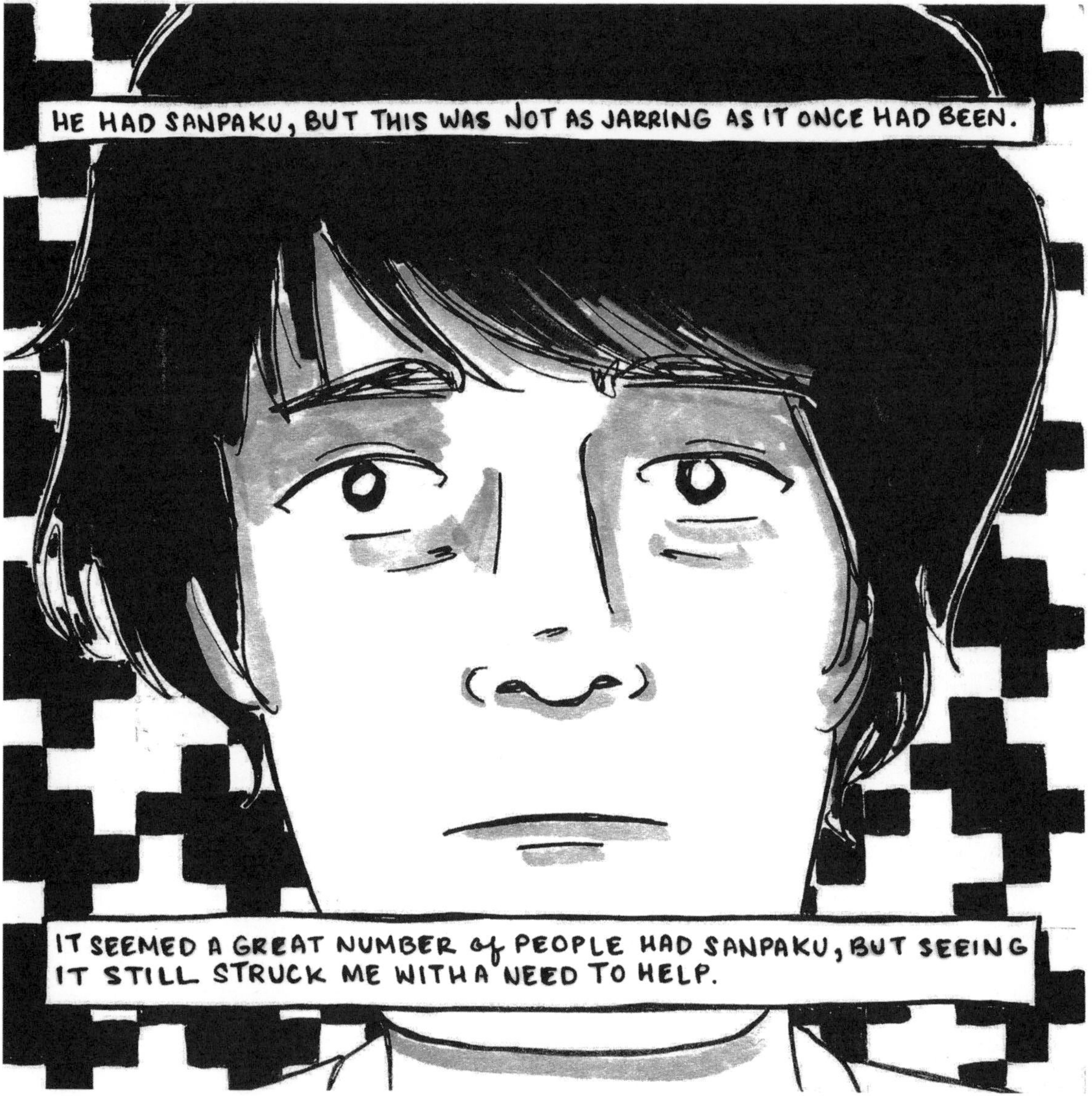
HE HAD SANPAKU, BUT THIS WAS NOT AS JARRING AS IT ONCE HAD BEEN.
IT SEEMED A GREAT NUMBER of PEOPLE HAD SANPAKU, BUT SEEING IT STILL STRUCK ME WITH A NEED TO HELP.

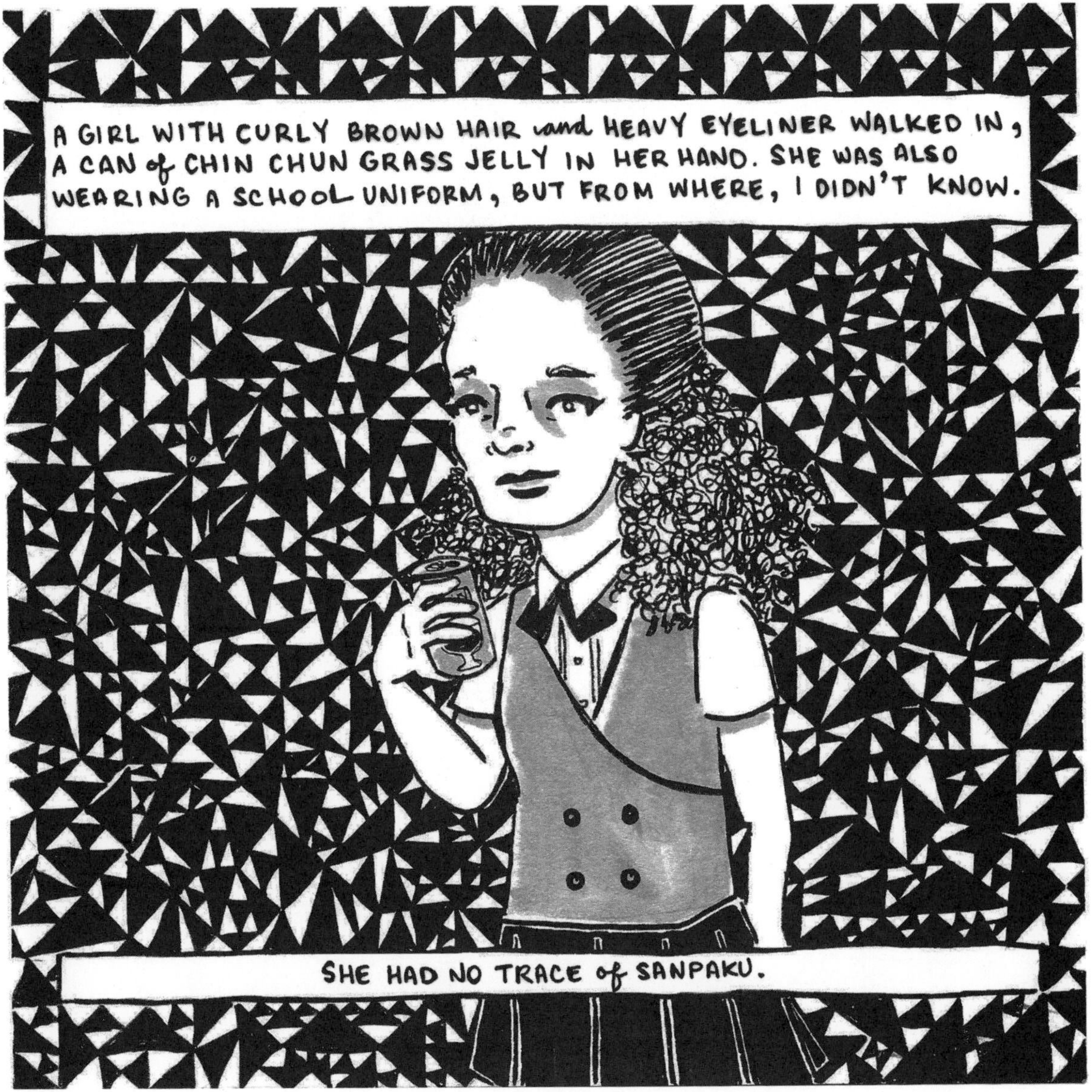
A GIRL WITH CURLY BROWN HAIR and HEAVY EYELINER WALKED IN, A CAN of CHIN CHUN GRASS JELLY IN HER HAND. SHE WAS ALSO WEARING A SCHOOL UNIFORM, BUT FROM WHERE, I DIDN'T KNOW.
SHE HAD NO TRACE of SANPAKU.

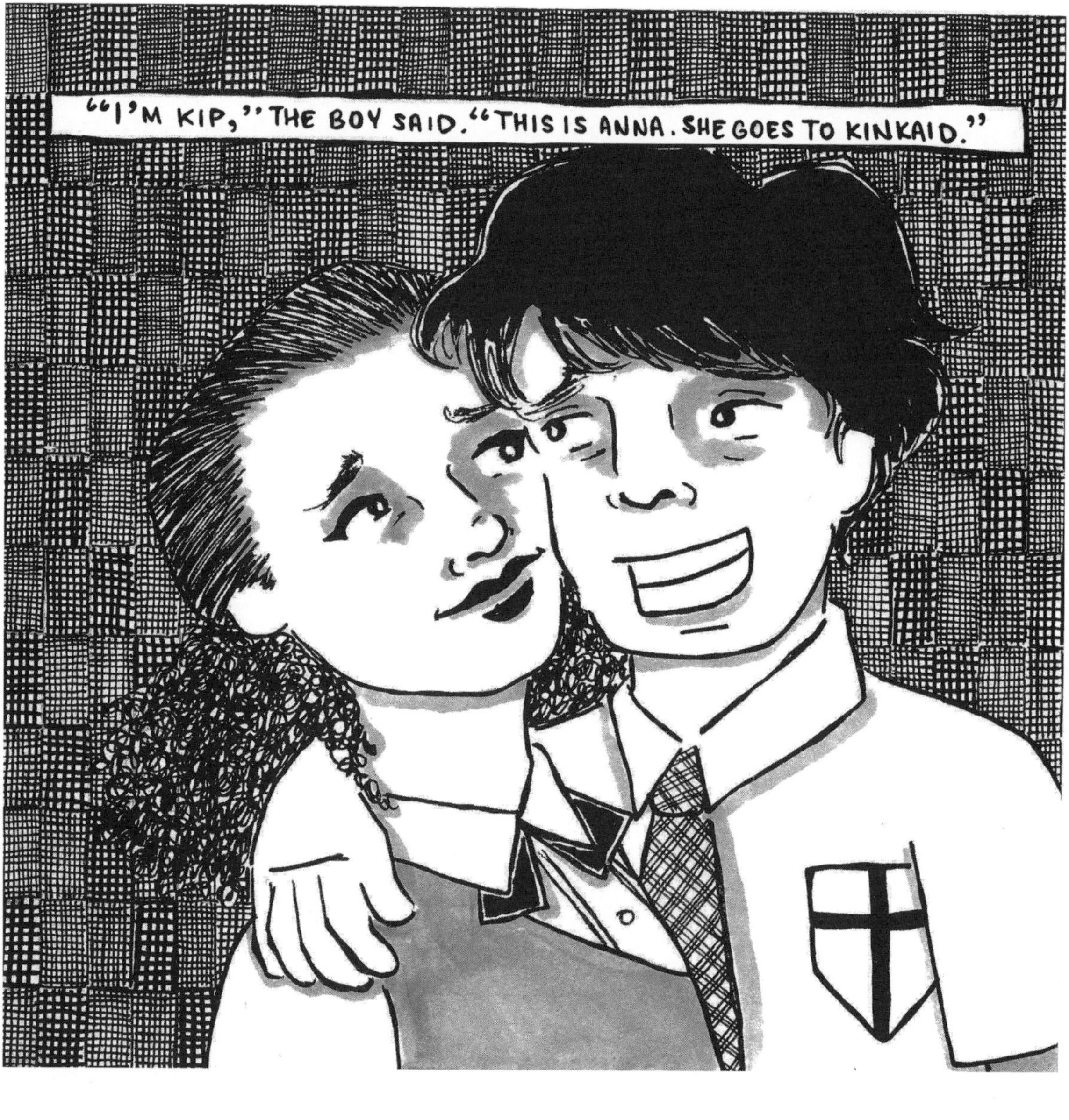
"I'M KIP," THE BOY SAID. "THIS IS ANNA. SHE GOES TO KINKAID."

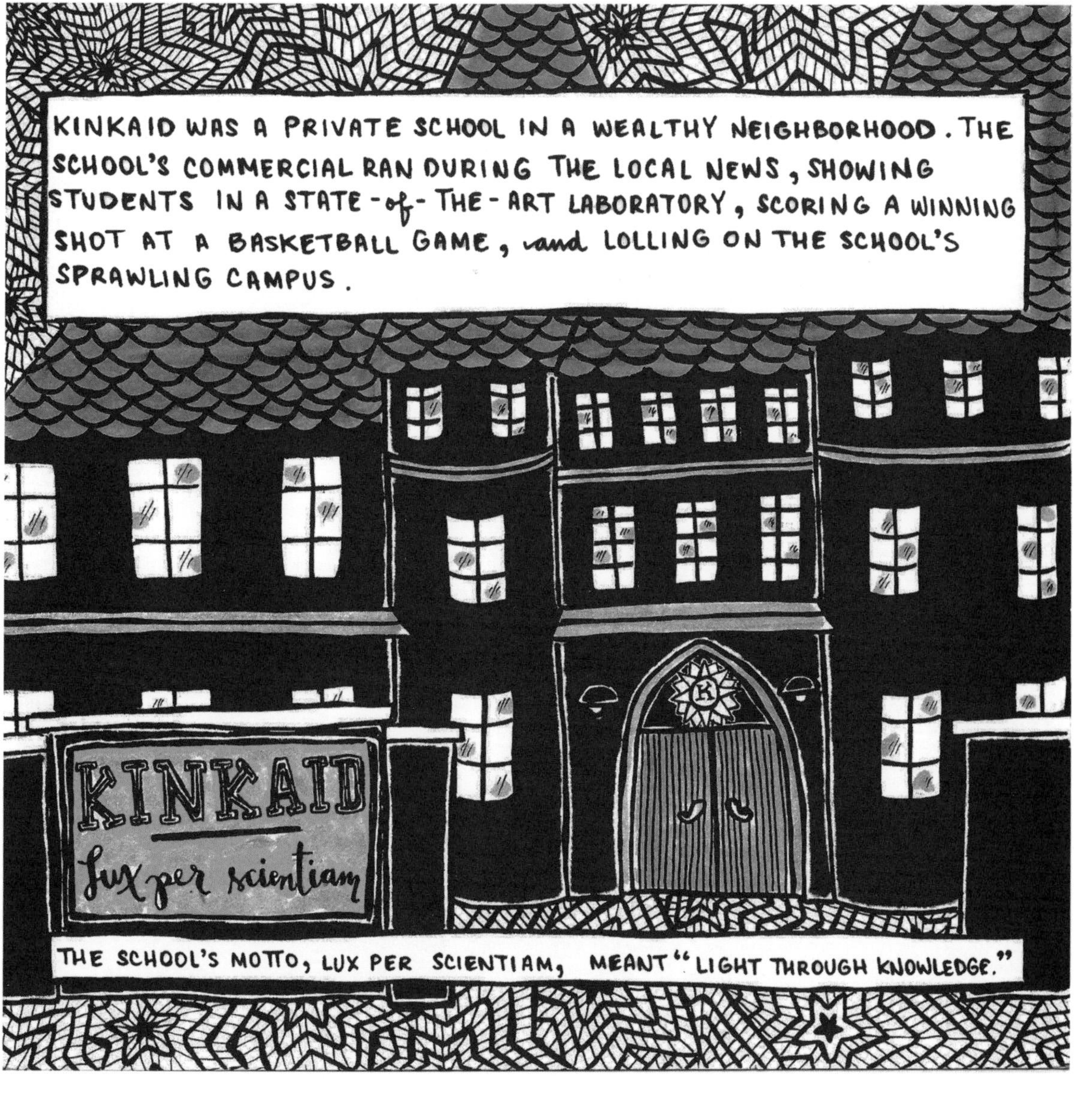
KINKAID WAS A PRIVATE SCHOOL IN A WEALTHY NEIGHBORHOOD. THE SCHOOL'S COMMERCIAL RAN DURING THE LOCAL NEWS, SHOWING STUDENTS IN A STATE-of-THE-ART LABORATORY, SCORING A WINNING SHOT AT A BASKETBALL GAME, and LOLLING ON THE SCHOOL'S SPRAWLING CAMPUS.
KINKAID
Lux per scientiam
THE SCHOOL'S MOTTO, LUX PER SCIENTIAM, MEANT "LIGHT THROUGH KNOWLEDGE."

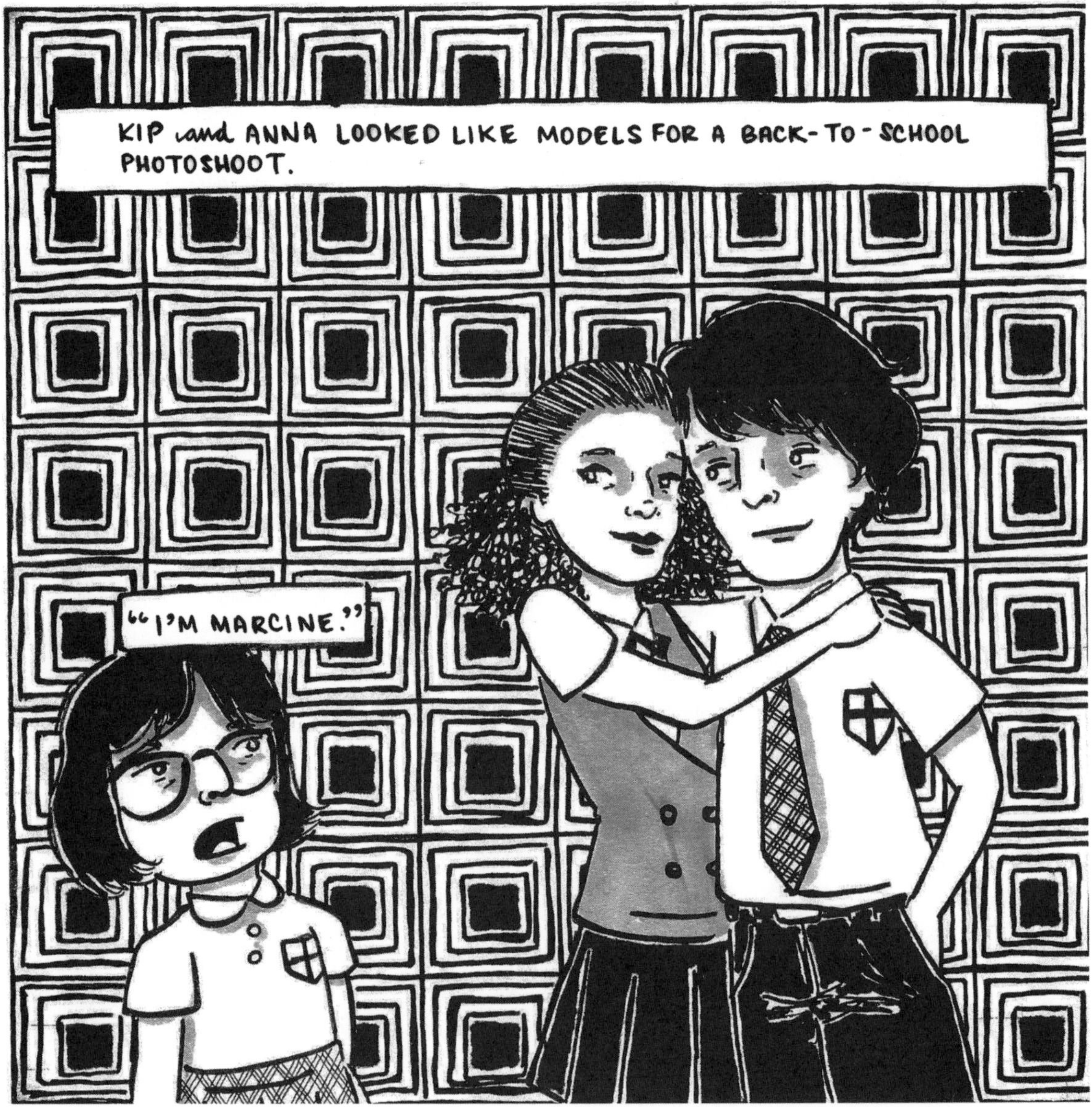
KIP and ANNA LOOKED LIKE MODELS FOR A BACK-TO-SCHOOL PHOTOSHOOT.
"I'M MARCINE."

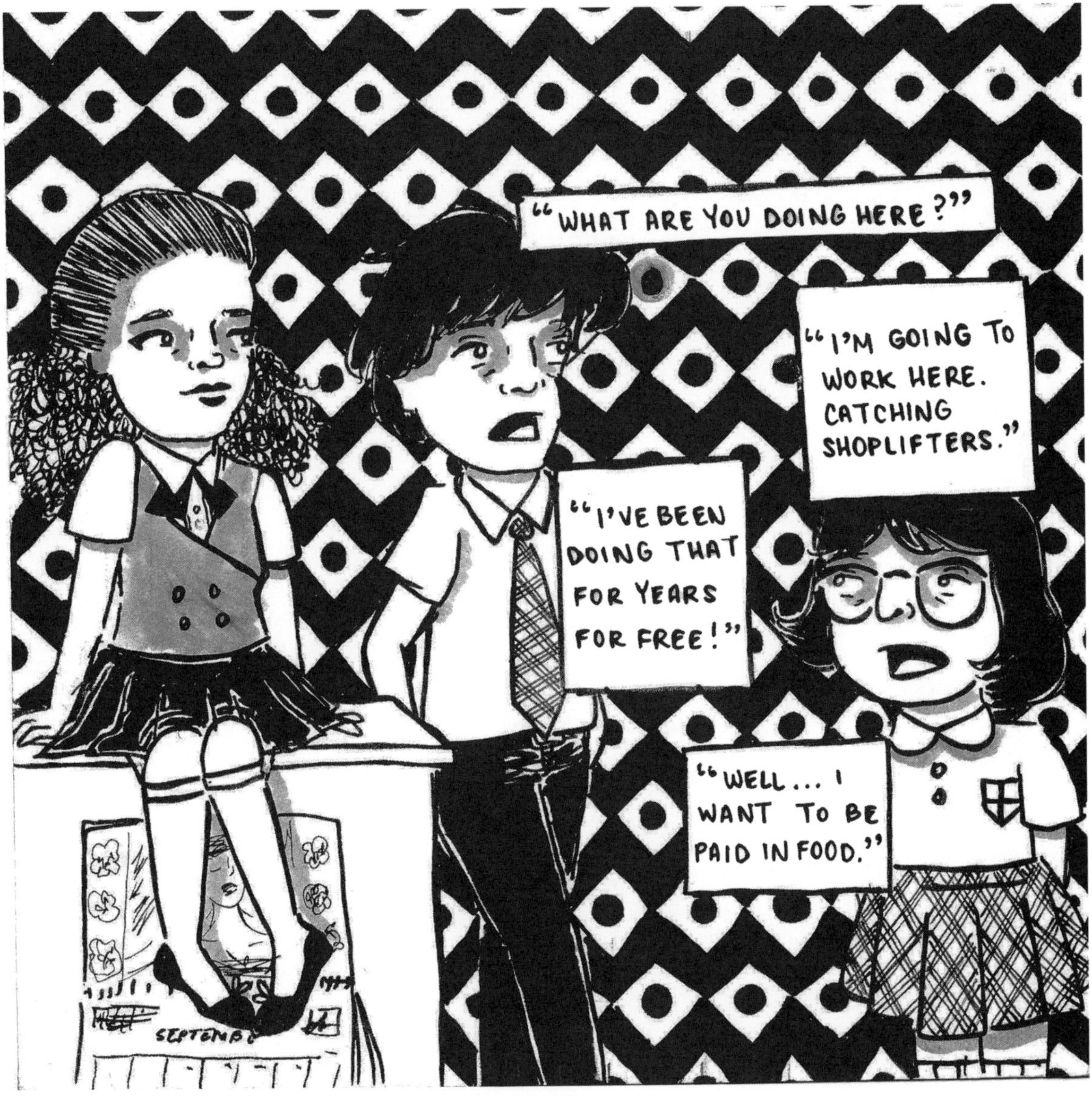
"WHAT ARE YOU DOING HERE?"
"I'M GOING TO WORK HERE. CATCHING SHOPLIFTERS."
"I'VE BEEN DOING THAT FOR YEARS FOR FREE!"
"WELL... I WANT TO BE PAID IN FOOD."

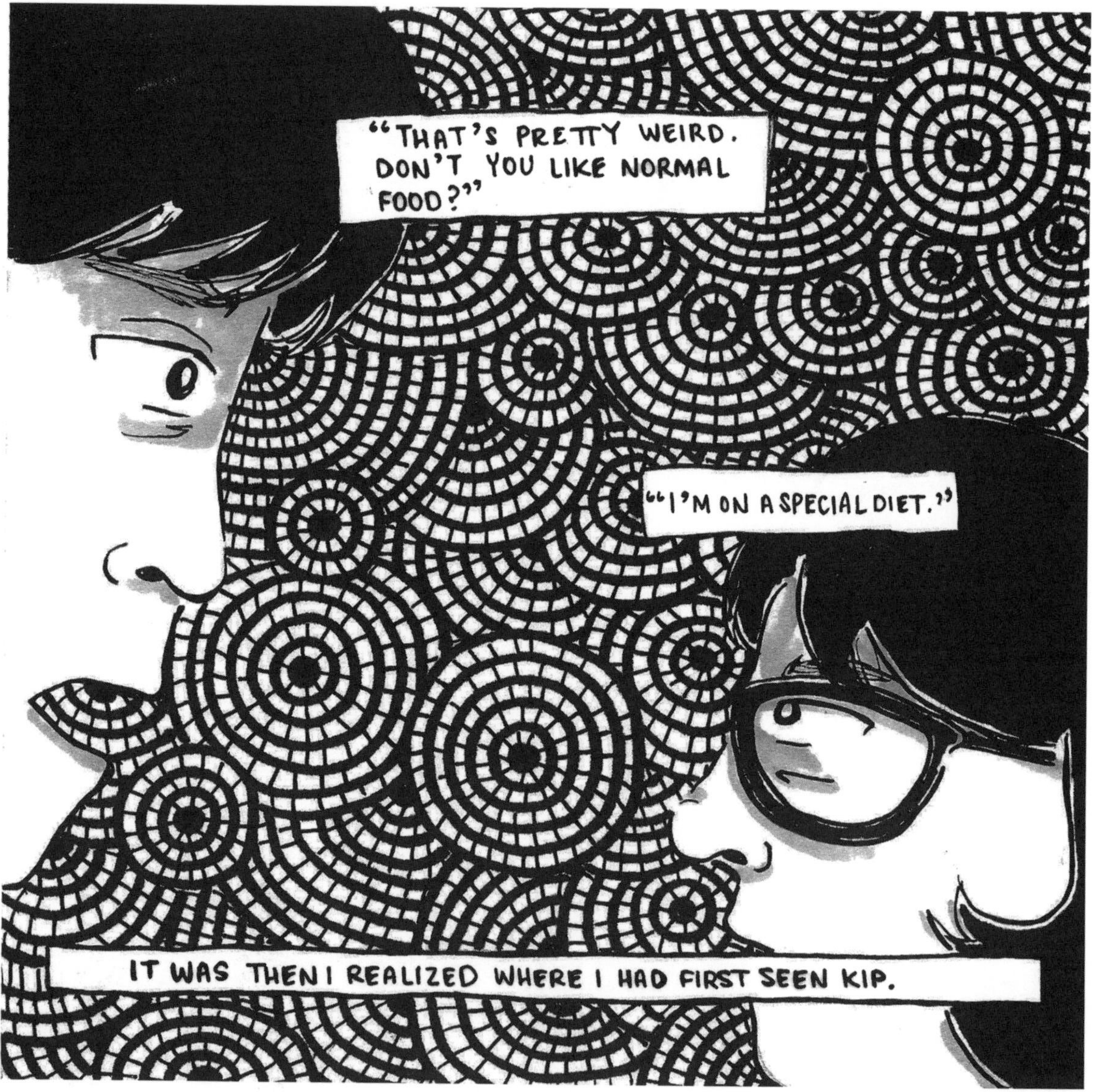
"THAT'S PRETTY WEIRD. DON'T YOU LIKE NORMAL FOOD?"
"I'M ON A SPECIAL DIET."
IT WAS THEN I REALIZED WHERE I HAD FIRST SEEN KIP.

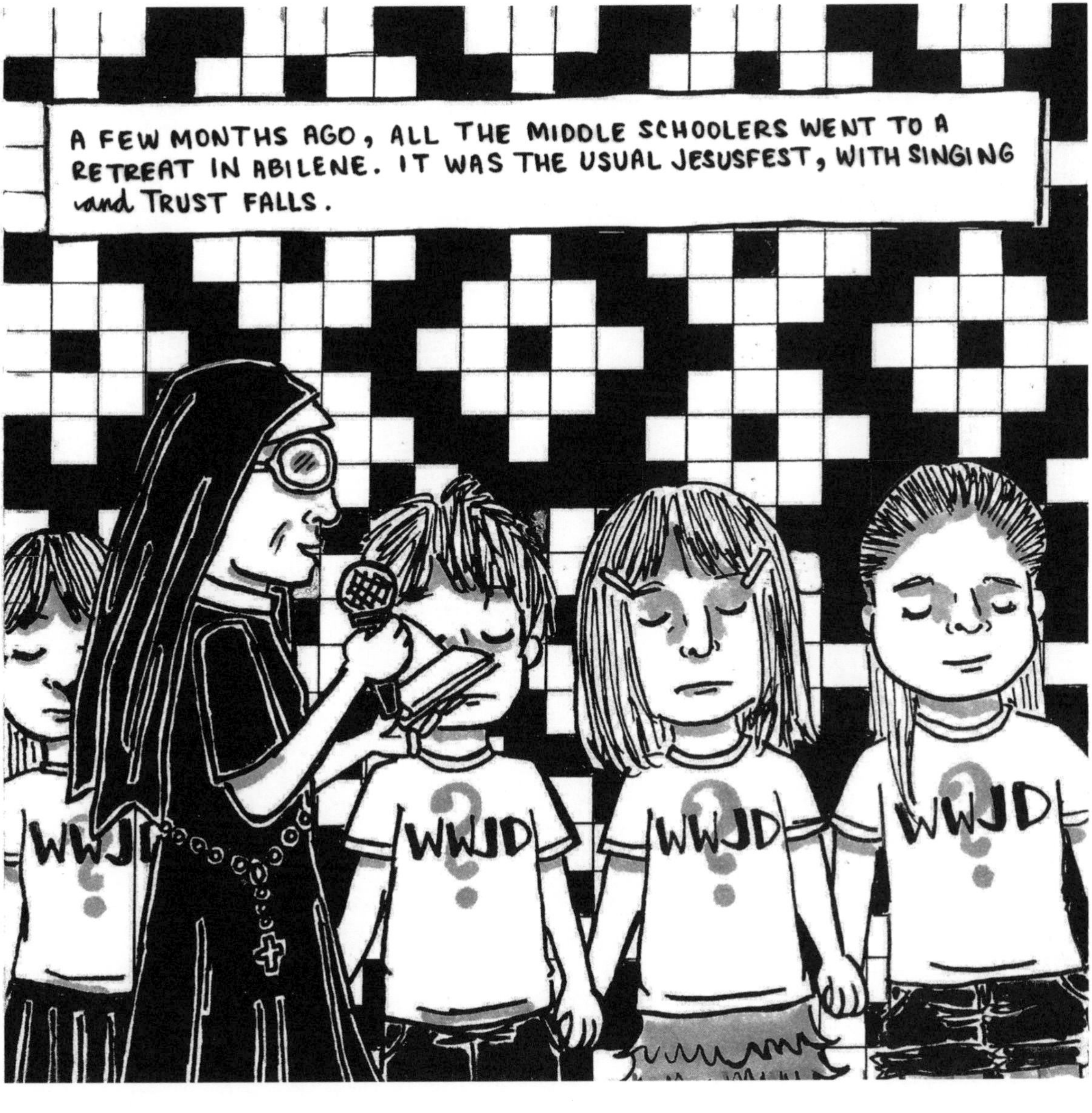
A FEW MONTHS AGO, ALL THE MIDDLE SCHOOLERS WENT TO A RETREAT IN ABILENE. IT WAS THE USUAL JESUSFEST, WITH SINGING and TRUST FALLS.
WWJD
WWJD
WWJD
WWJD

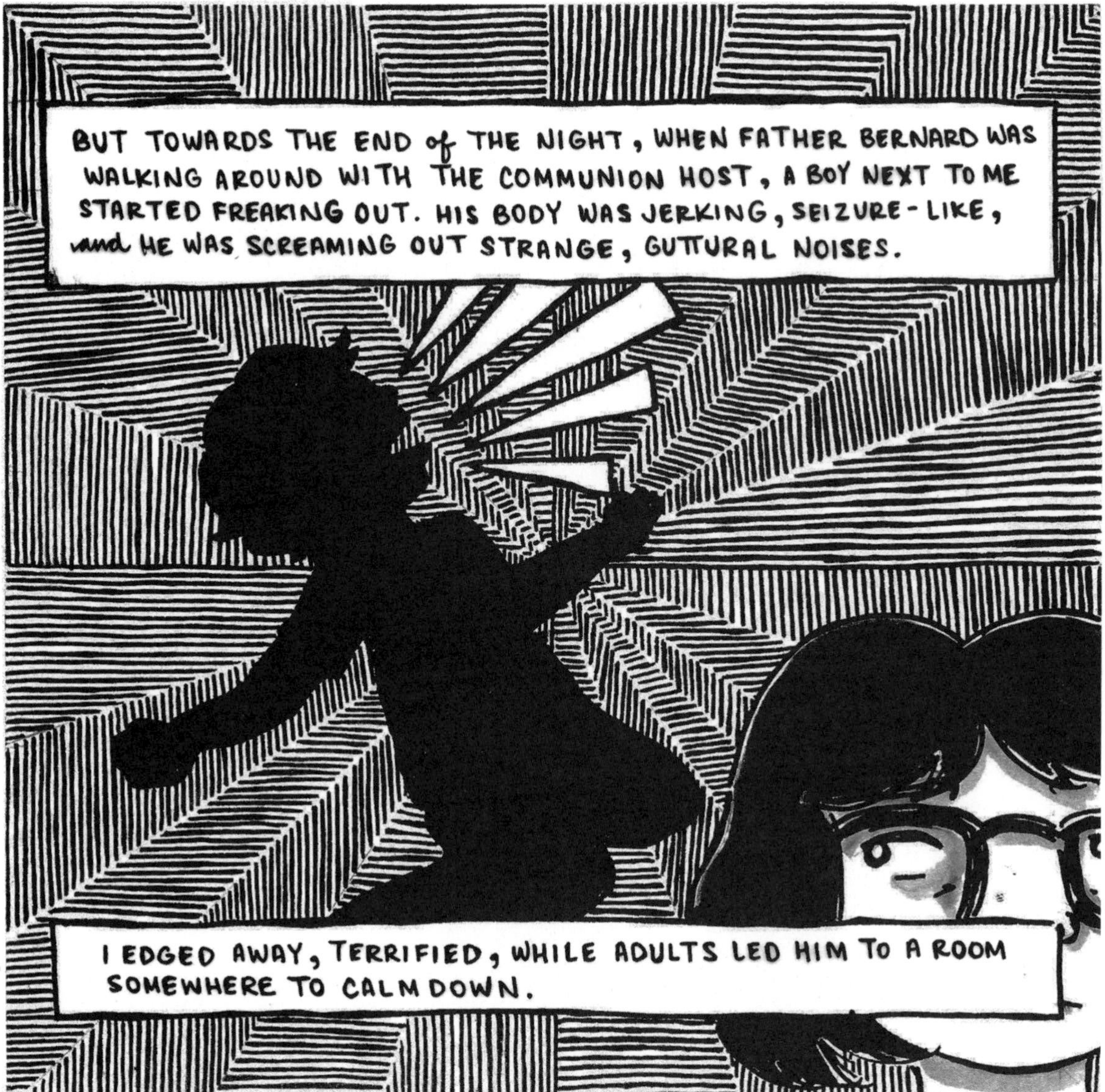
BUT TOWARDS THE END of THE NIGHT, WHEN FATHER BERNARD WAS WALKING AROUND WITH THE COMMUNION HOST, A BOY NEXT TO ME STARTED FREAKING OUT. HIS BODY WAS JERKING, SEIZURE-LIKE, and HE WAS SCREAMING OUT STRANGE, GUTTURAL NOISES.
I EDGED AWAY, TERRIFIED, WHILE ADULTS LED HIM TO A ROOM SOMEWHERE TO CALM DOWN.

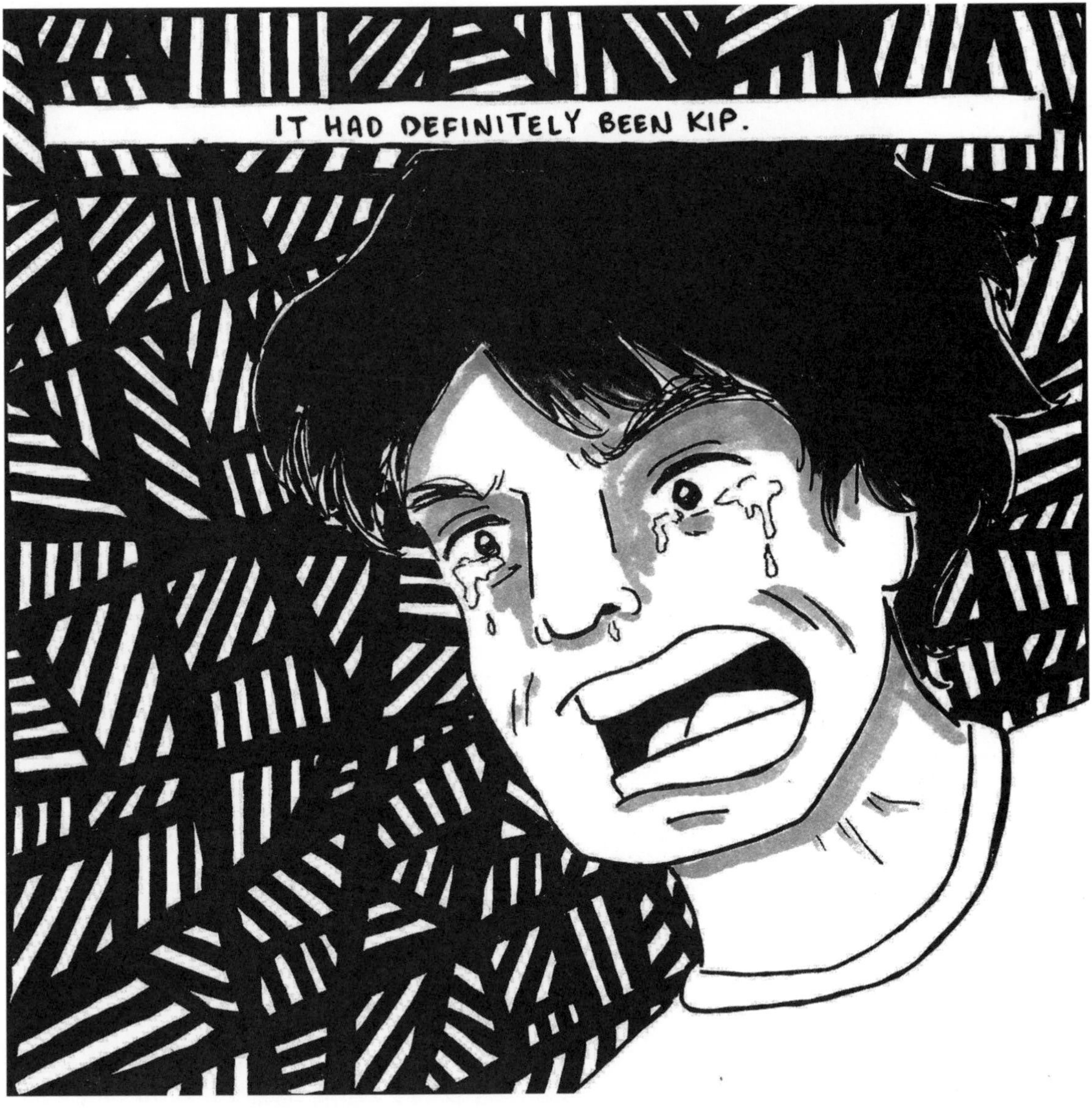
IT HAD DEFINITELY BEEN KIP.

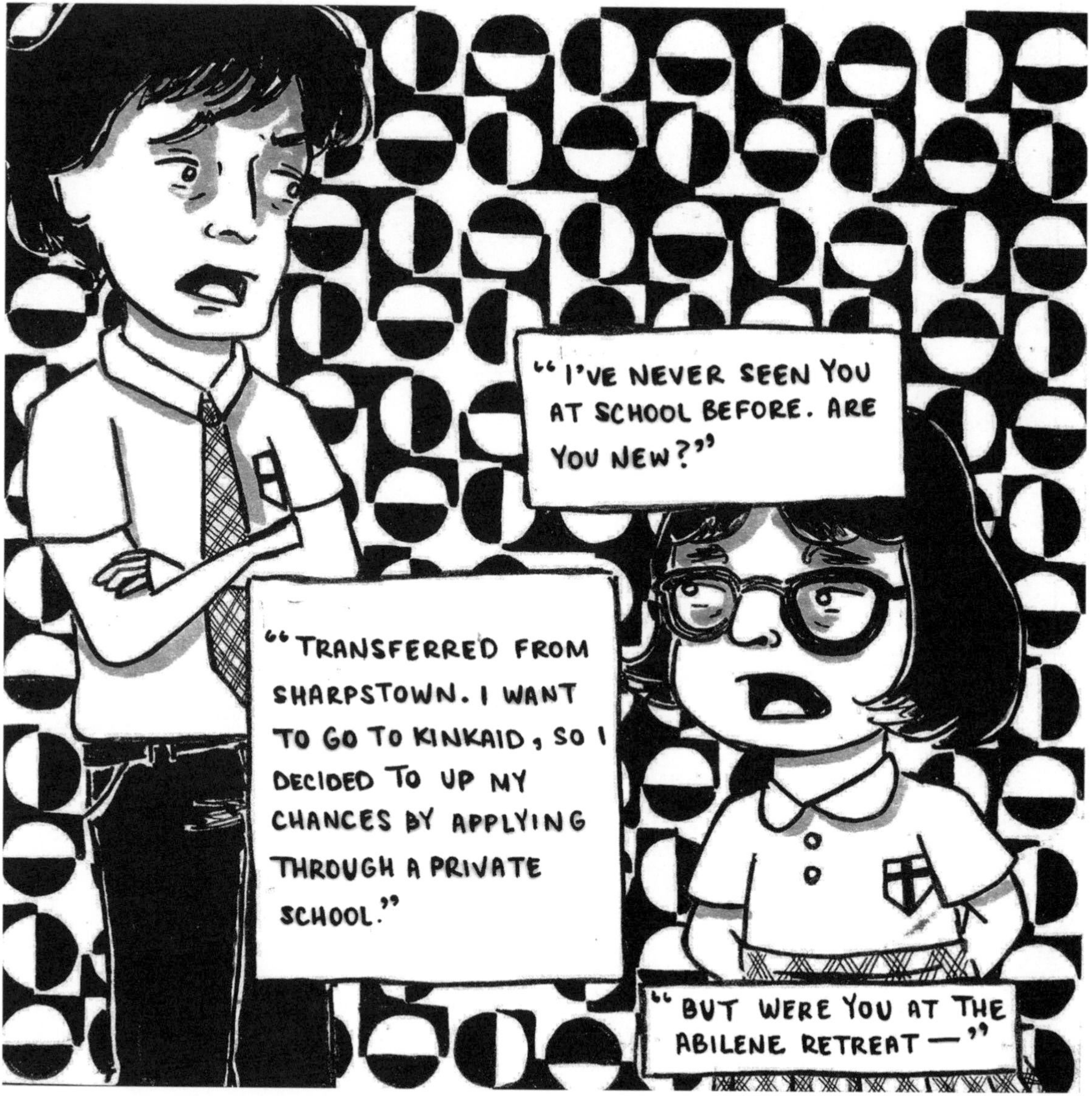
"I'VE NEVER SEEN YOU AT SCHOOL BEFORE. ARE YOU NEW?"
"TRANSFERRED FROM SHARPSTOWN. I WANT TO GO TO KINKAID, SO I DECIDED TO UP MY CHANCES BY APPLYING THROUGH A PRIVATE SCHOOL."
"BUT WERE YOU AT THE ABILENE RETREAT—"

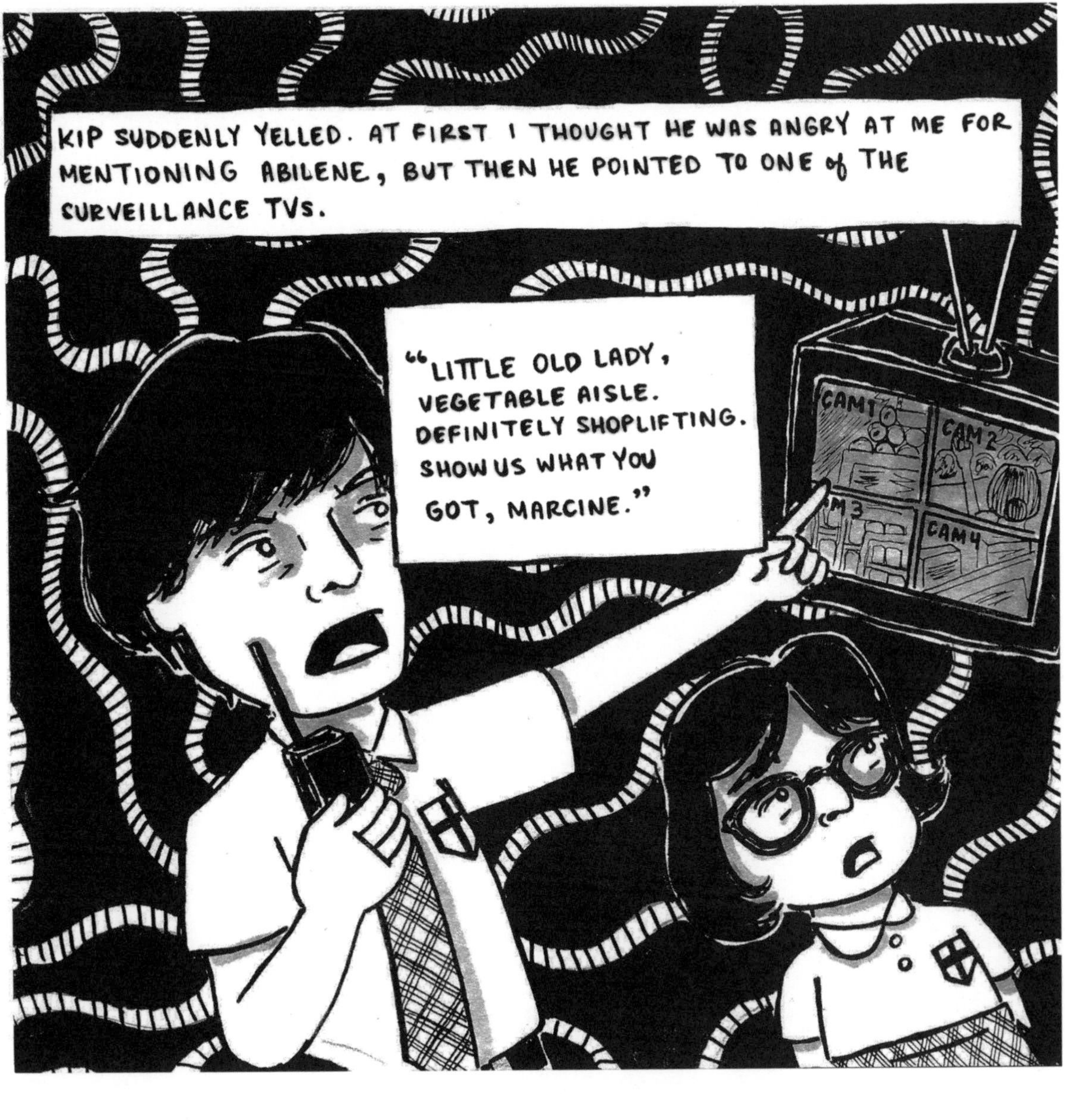
KIP SUDDENLY YELLED. AT FIRST I THOUGHT HE WAS ANGRY AT ME FOR MENTIONING ABILENE, BUT THEN HE POINTED TO ONE of THE SURVEILLANCE TVs.
"LITTLE OLD LADY, VEGETABLE AISLE. DEFINITELY SHOPLIFTING. SHOW US WHAT YOU GOT, MARCINE."
CAM1
CAM2
CAM3
CAM4

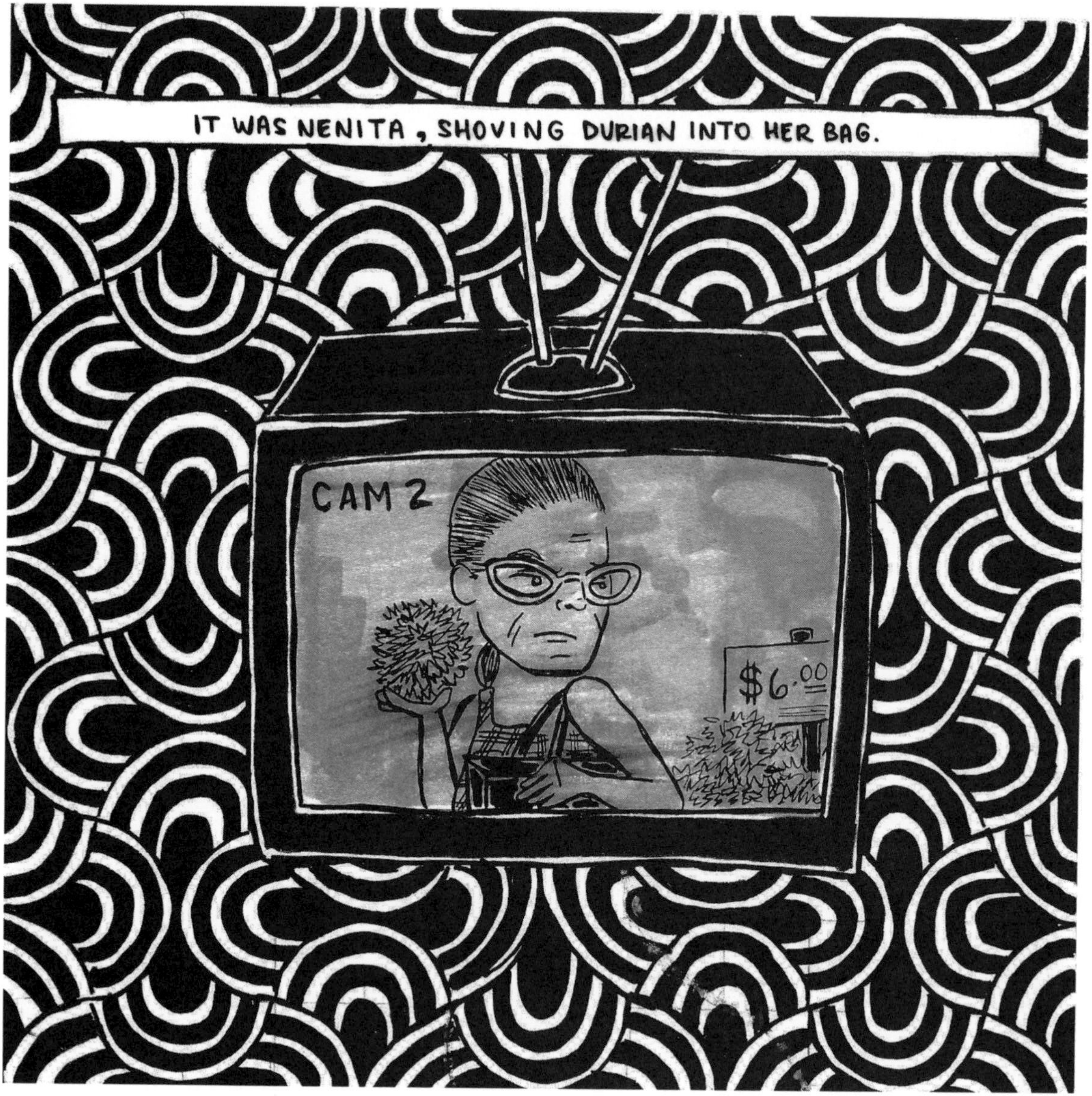
IT WAS NENITA, SHOVING DURIAN INTO HER BAG.
CAM 2
$6.00

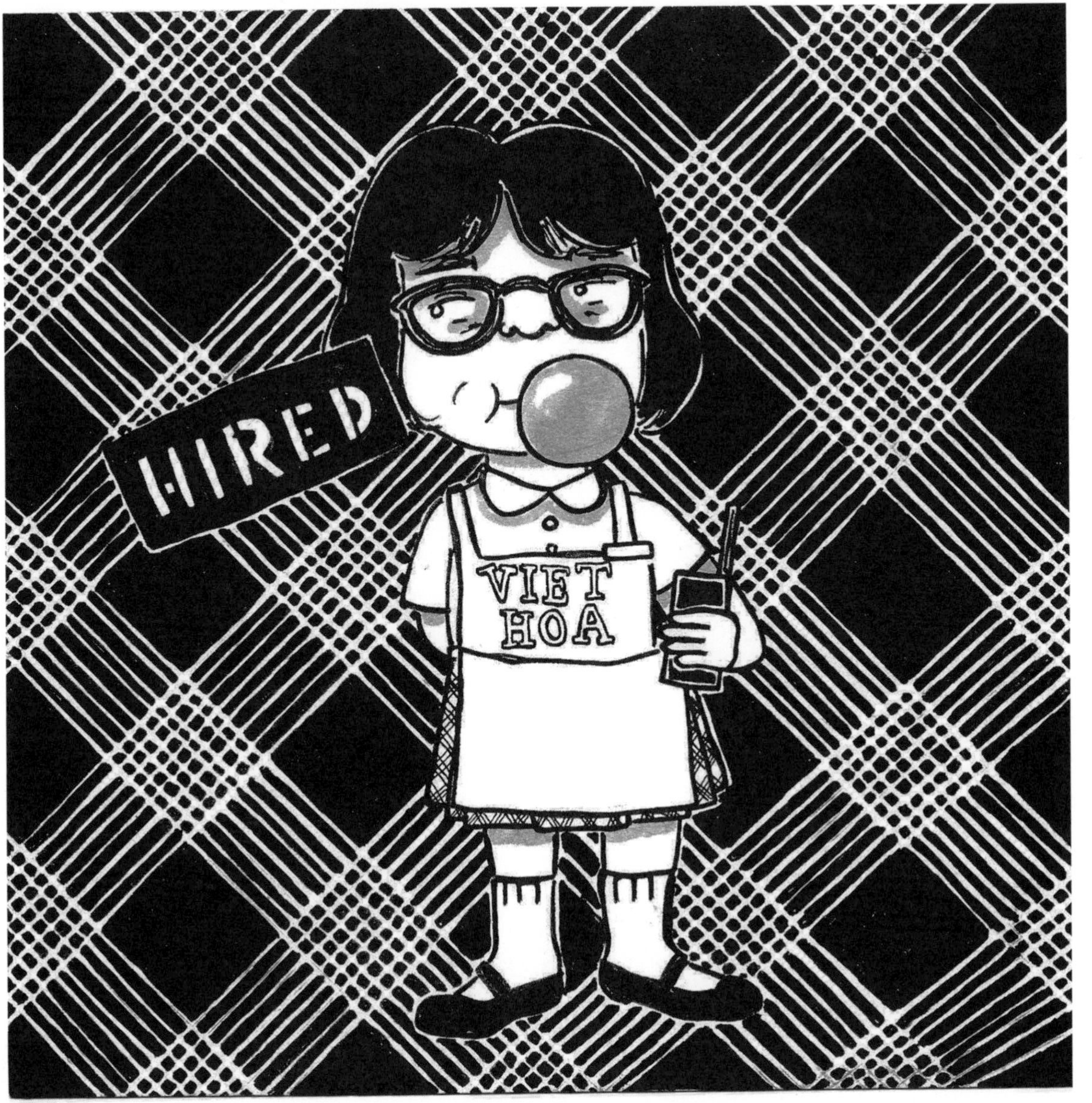
HIRED
VIET
HOA

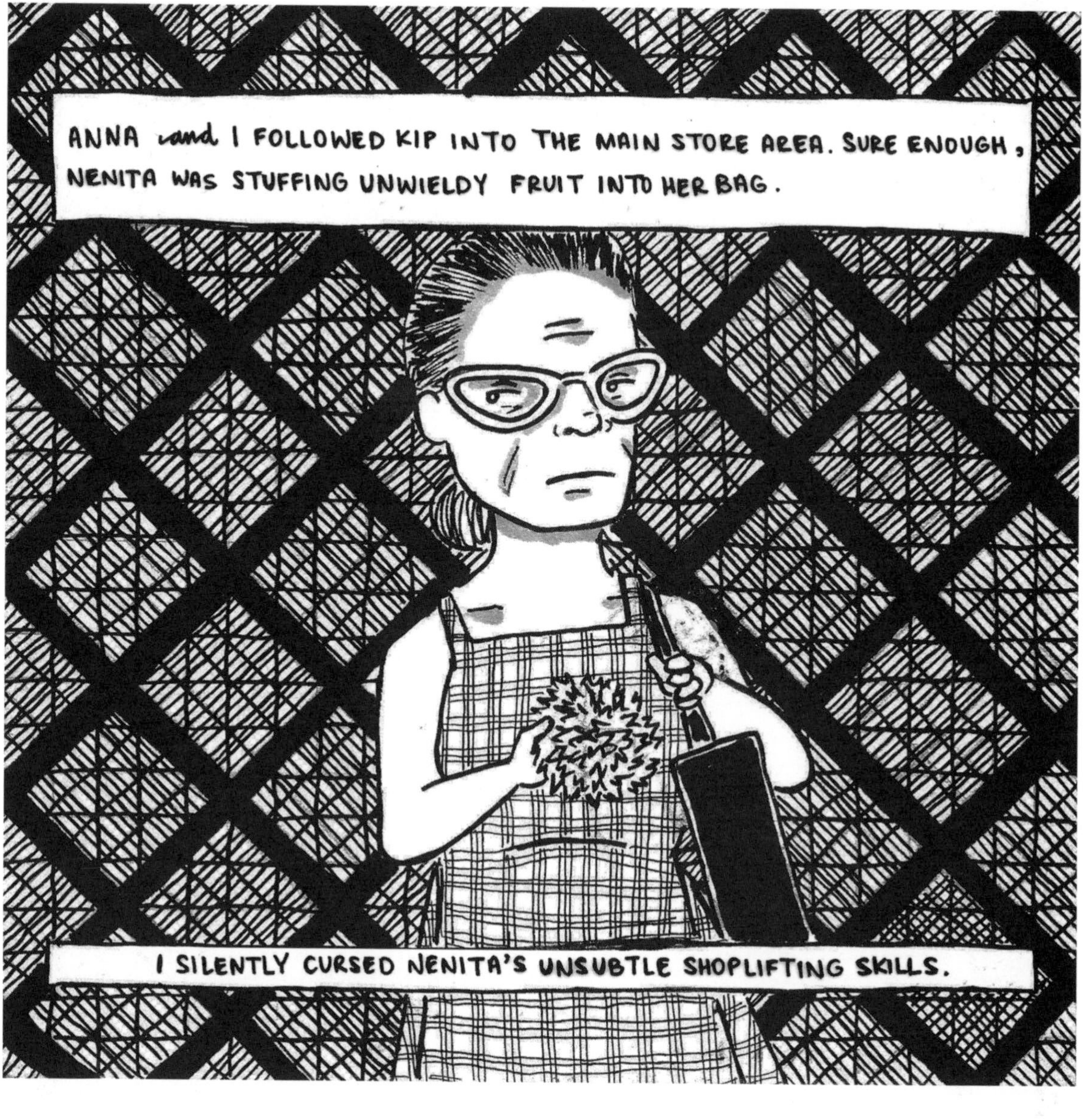
ANNA and I FOLLOWED KIP INTO THE MAIN STORE AREA. SURE ENOUGH, NENITA WAS STUFFING UNWIELDY FRUIT INTO HER BAG.
I SILENTLY CURSED NENITA'S UNSUBTLE SHOPLIFTING SKILLS.

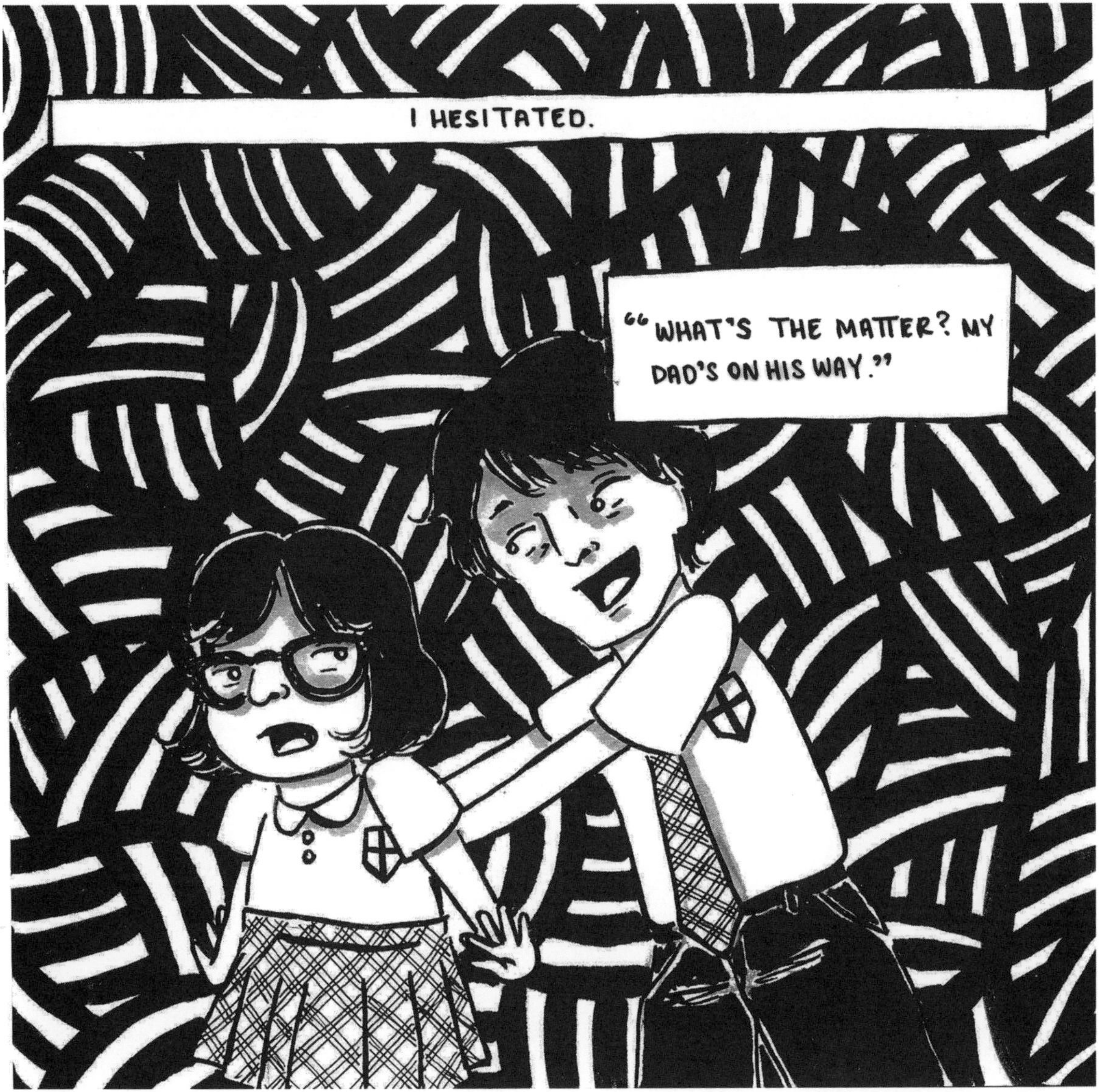
I HESITATED.
"WHAT'S THE MATTER? MY DAD'S ON HIS WAY."

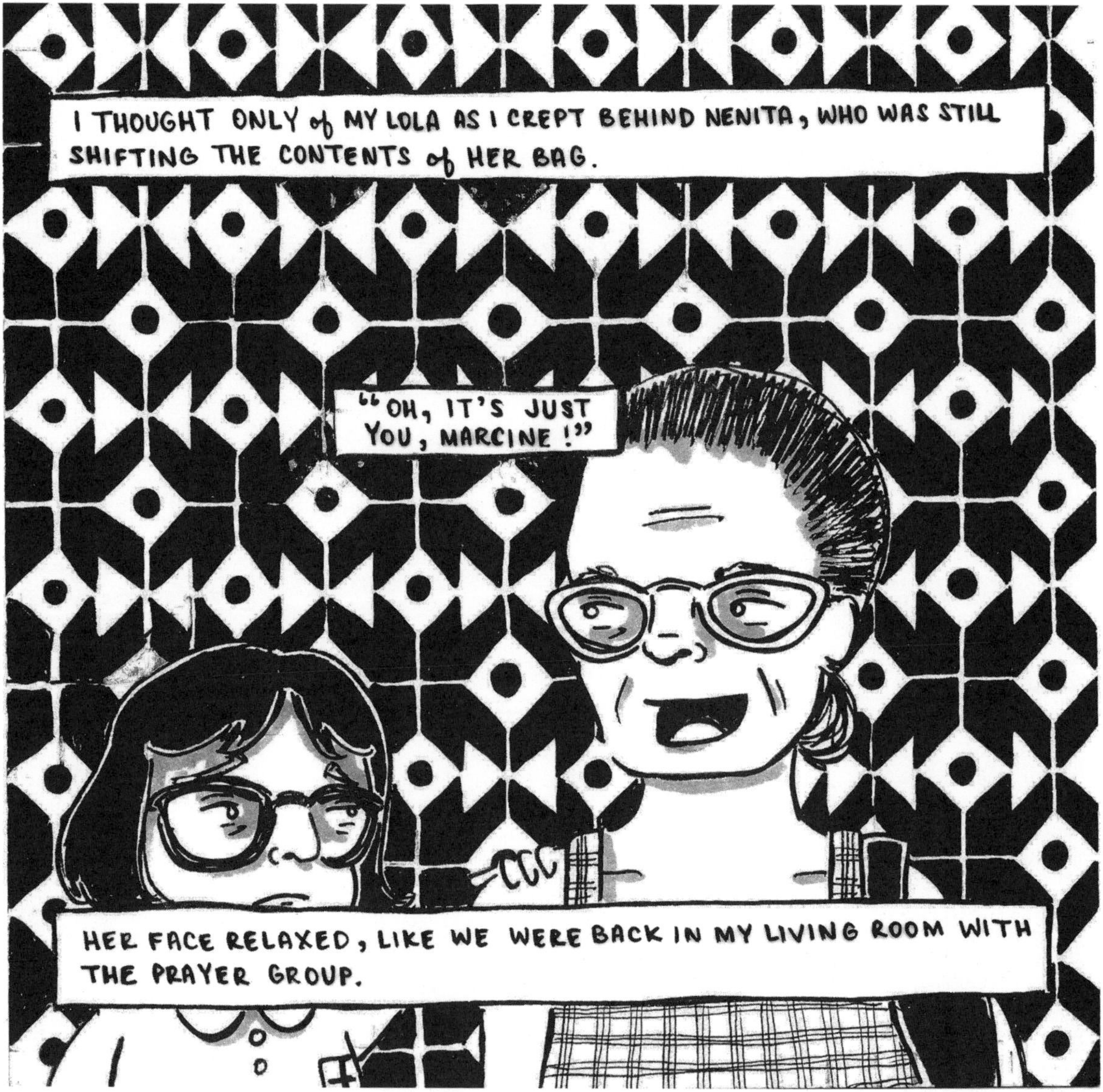
I THOUGHT ONLY of MY LOLA AS I CREPT BEHIND NENITA, WHO WAS STILL SHIFTING THE CONTENTS of HER BAG.
"OH, IT'S JUST YOU, MARCINE!"
HER FACE RELAXED, LIKE WE WERE BACK IN MY LIVING ROOM WITH THE PRAYER GROUP.

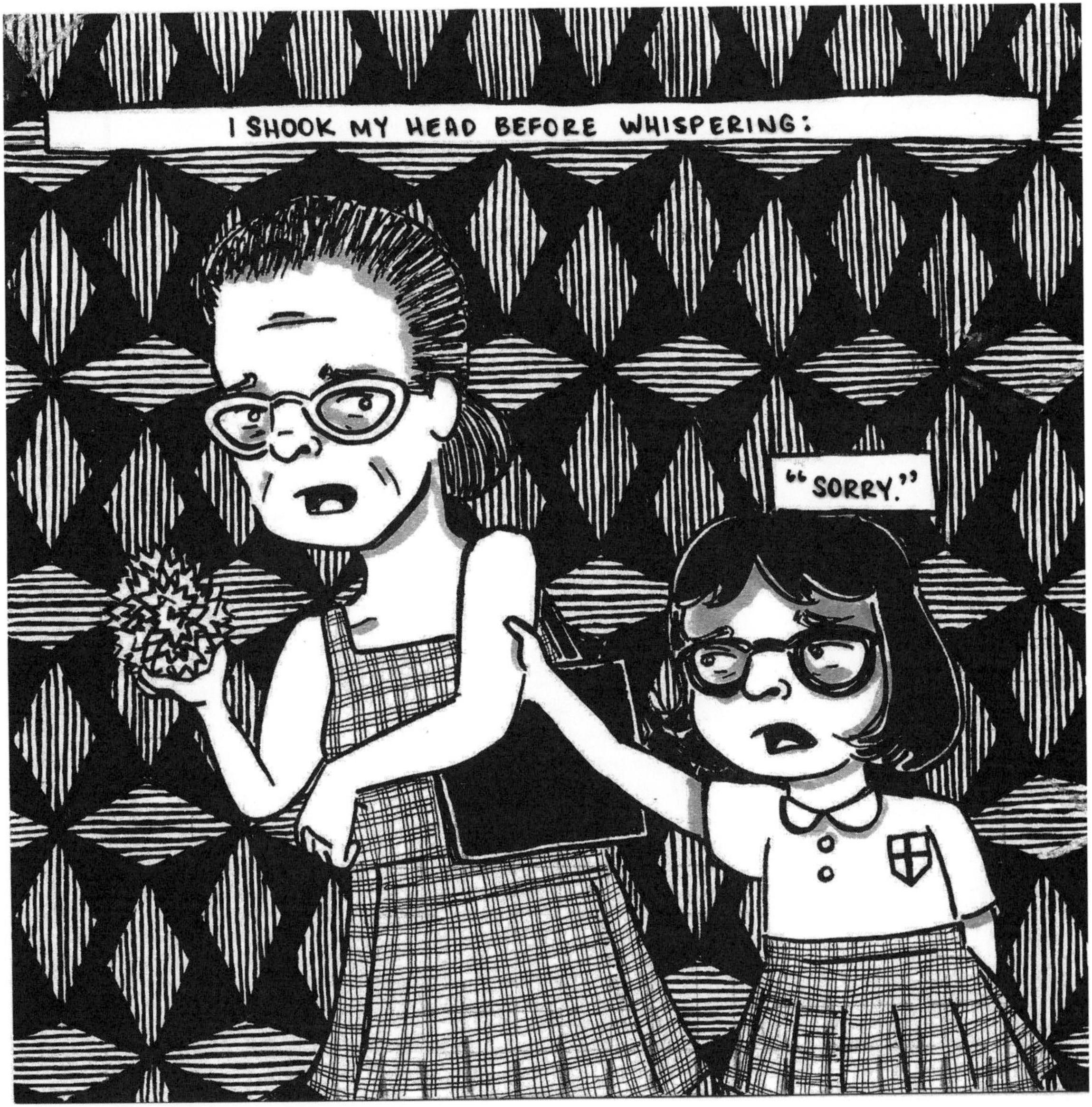
I SHOOK MY HEAD BEFORE WHISPERING:
"SORRY."

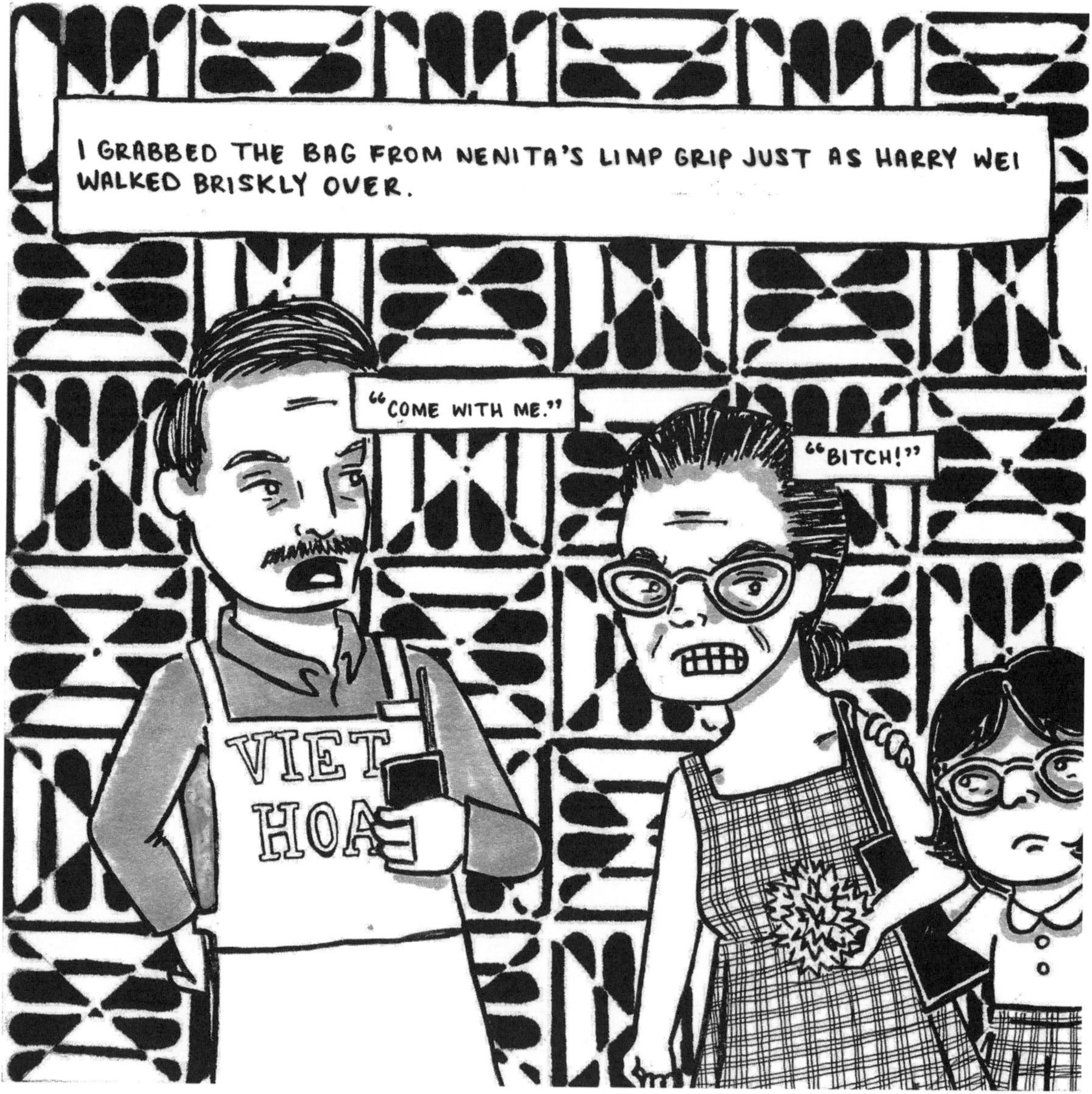
I GRABBED THE BAG FROM NENITA'S LIMP GRIP JUST AS HARRY WEI WALKED BRISKLY OVER.
"COME WITH ME."
"BITCH!"
VIET HOA

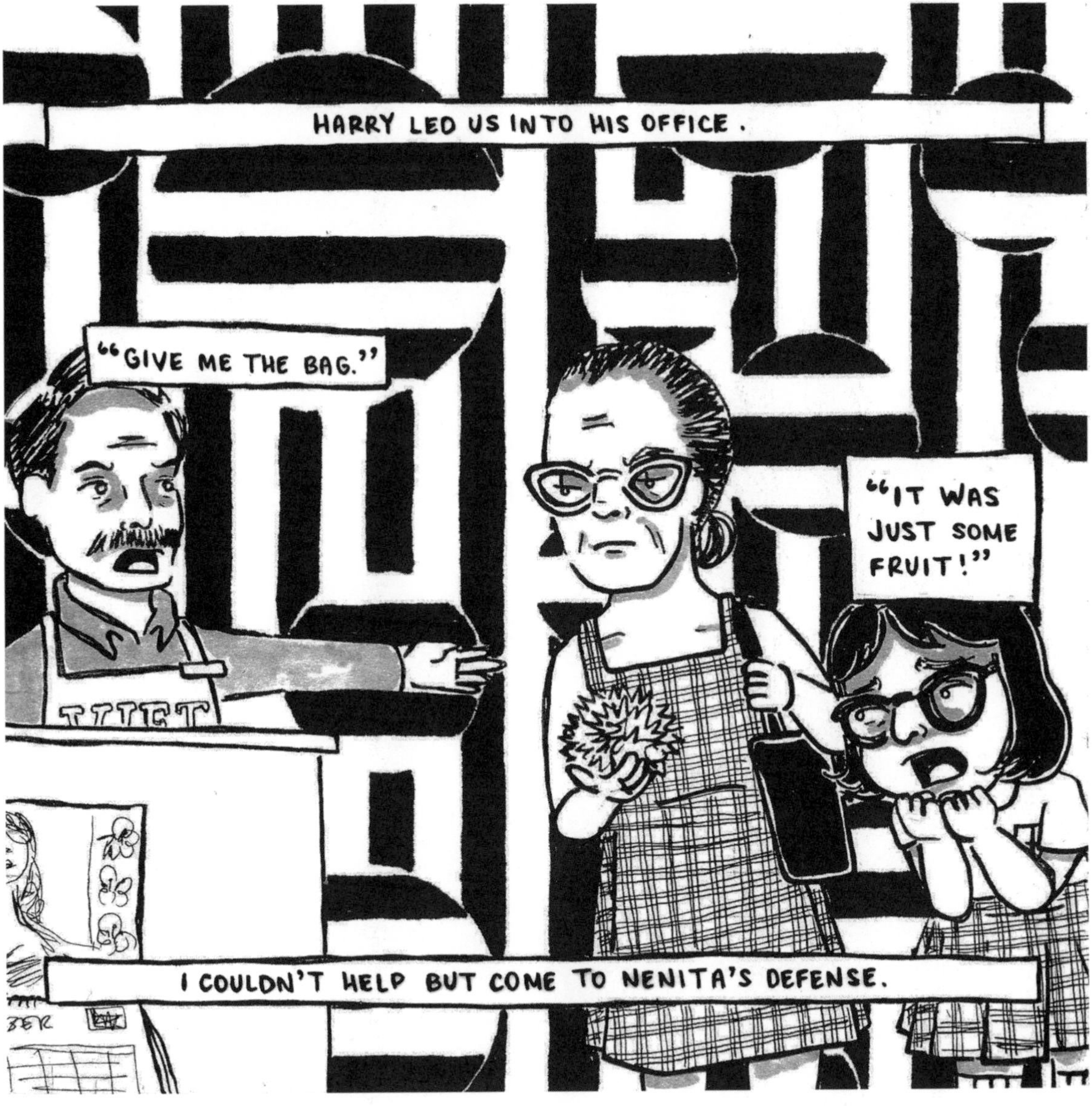
HARRY LED US INTO HIS OFFICE.
"GIVE ME THE BAG."
"IT WAS JUST SOME FRUIT!"
I COULDN'T HELP BUT COME TO NENITA'S DEFENSE.

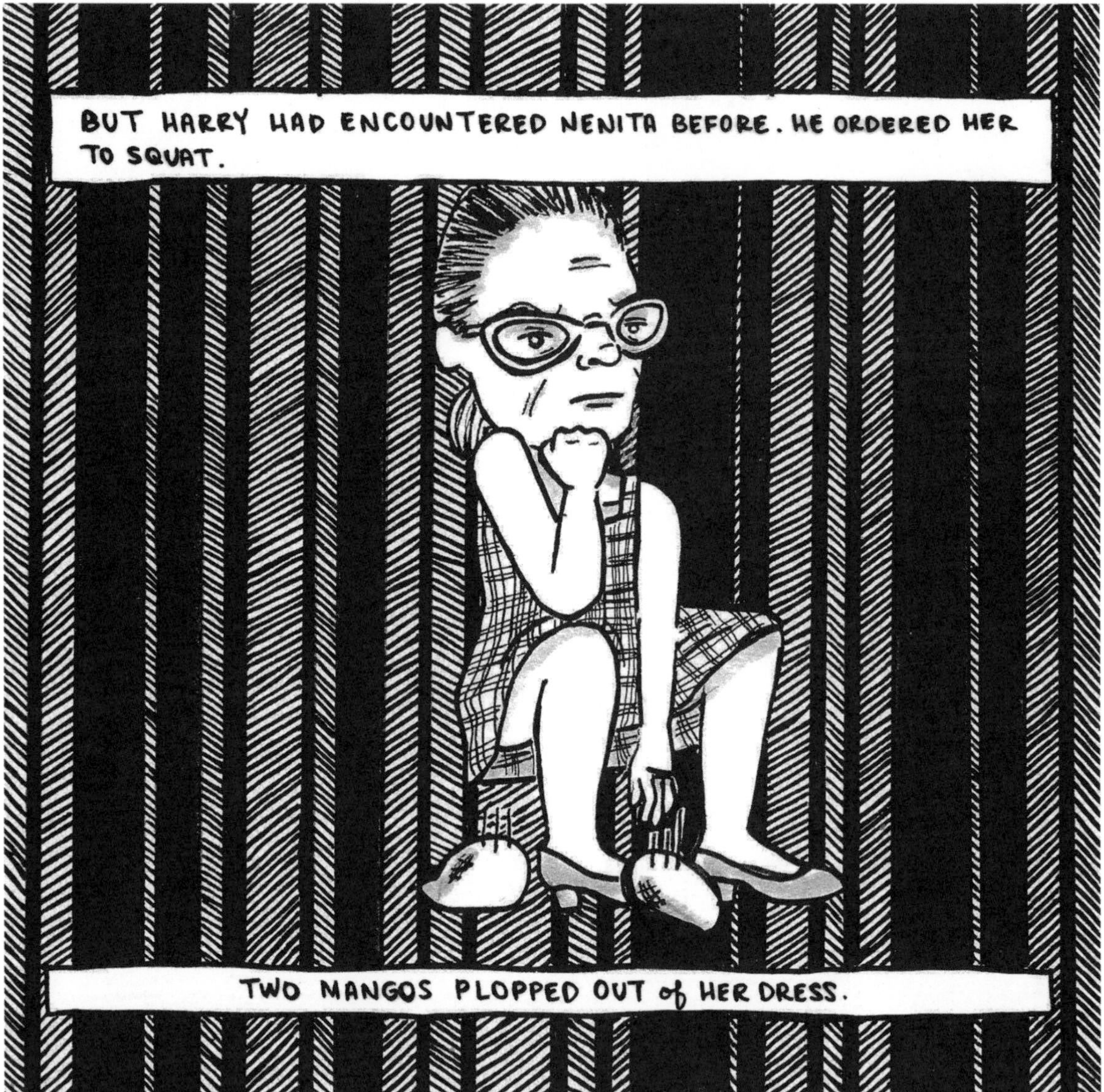
BUT HARRY HAD ENCOUNTERED NENITA BEFORE. HE ORDERED HER TO SQUAT.
TWO MANGOS PLOPPED OUT of HER DRESS.

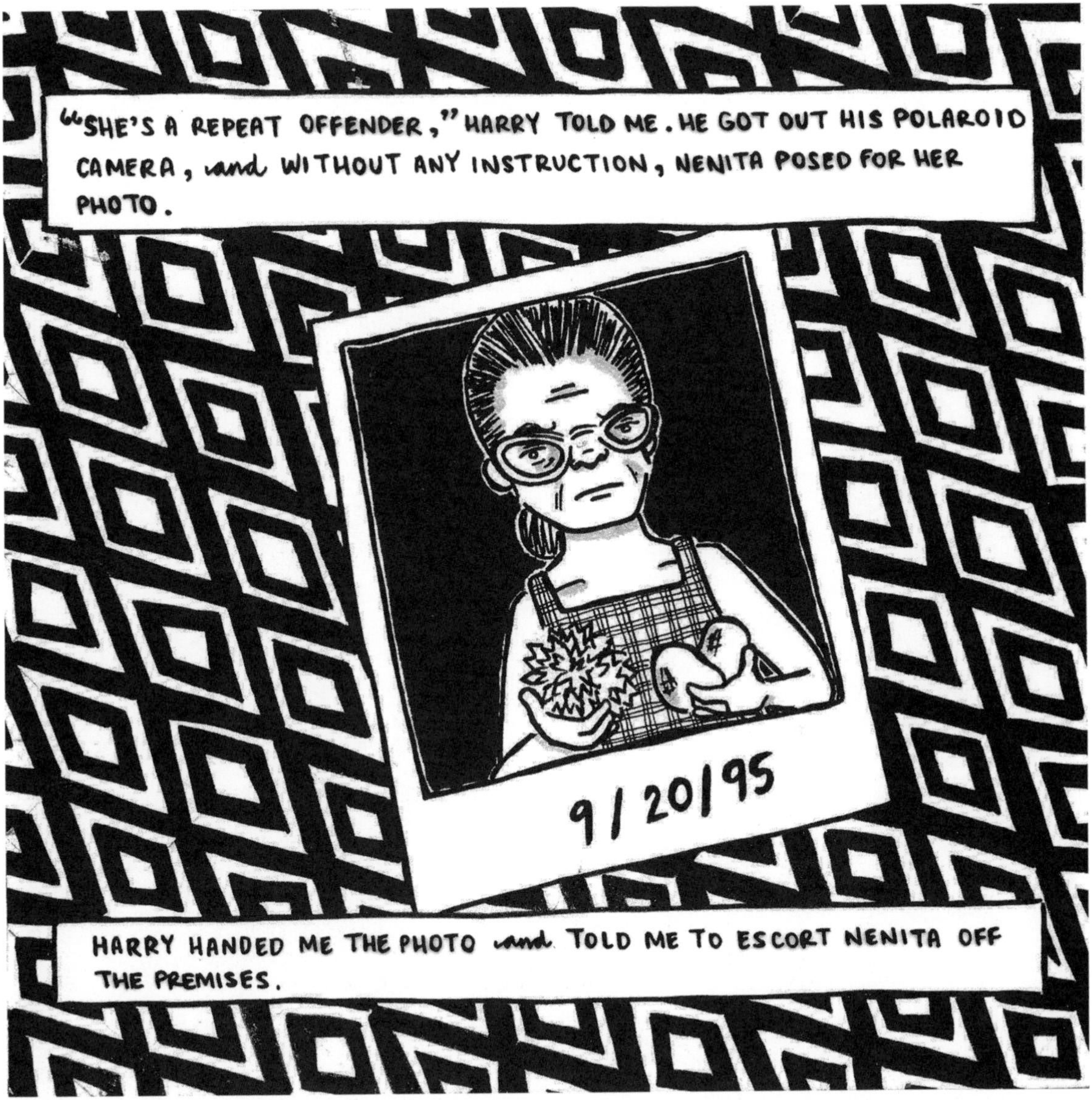
"SHE'S A REPEAT OFFENDER," HARRY TOLD ME. HE GOT OUT HIS POLAROID CAMERA, and WITHOUT ANY INSTRUCTION, NENITA POSED FOR HER PHOTO.
9/20/95
HARRY HANDED ME THE PHOTO and TOLD ME TO ESCORT NENITA OFF THE PREMISES.

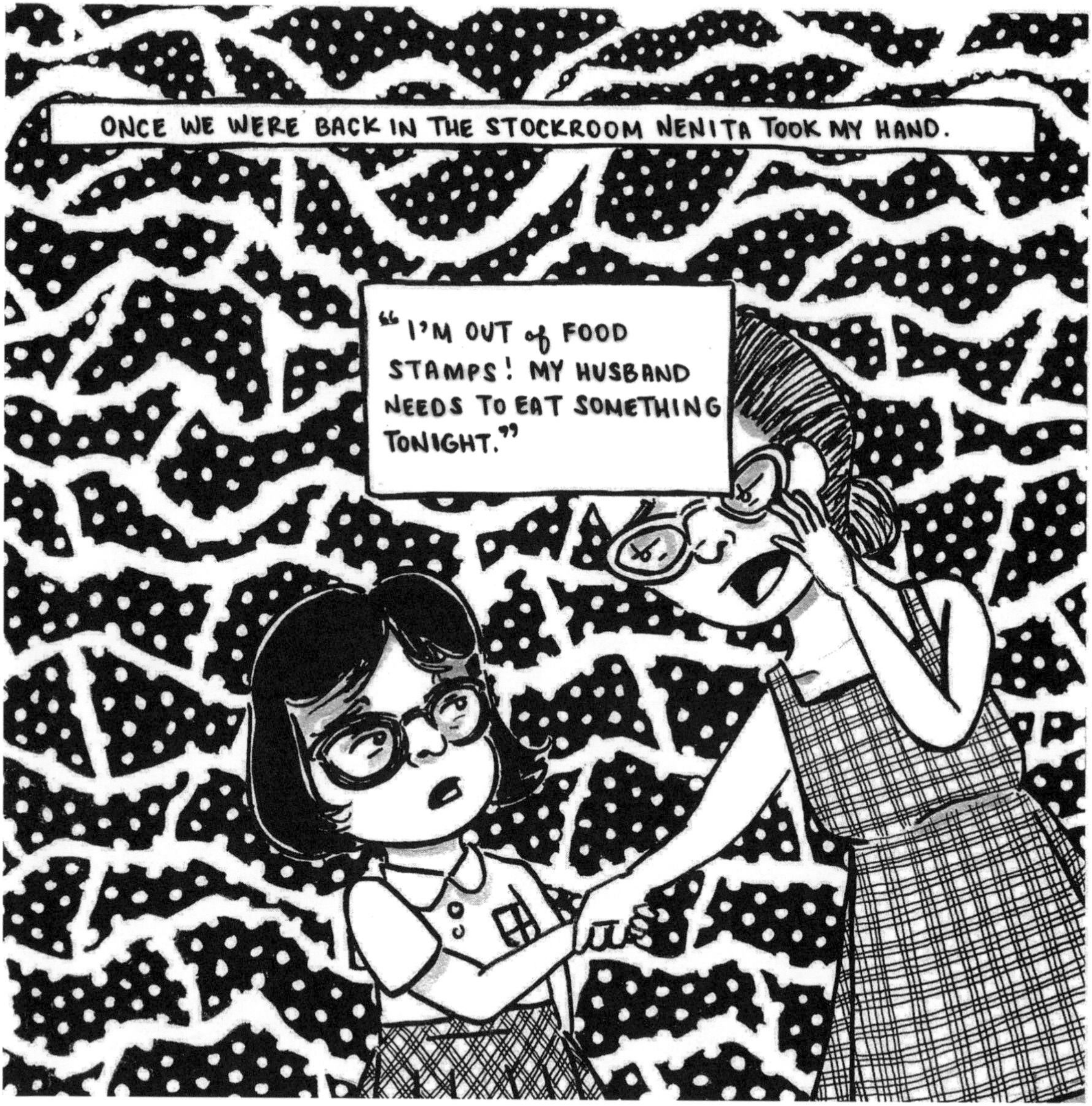
ONCE WE WERE BACK IN THE STOCKROOM NENITA TOOK MY HAND.
"I'M OUT of FOOD STAMPS! MY HUSBAND NEEDS TO EAT SOMETHING TONIGHT."

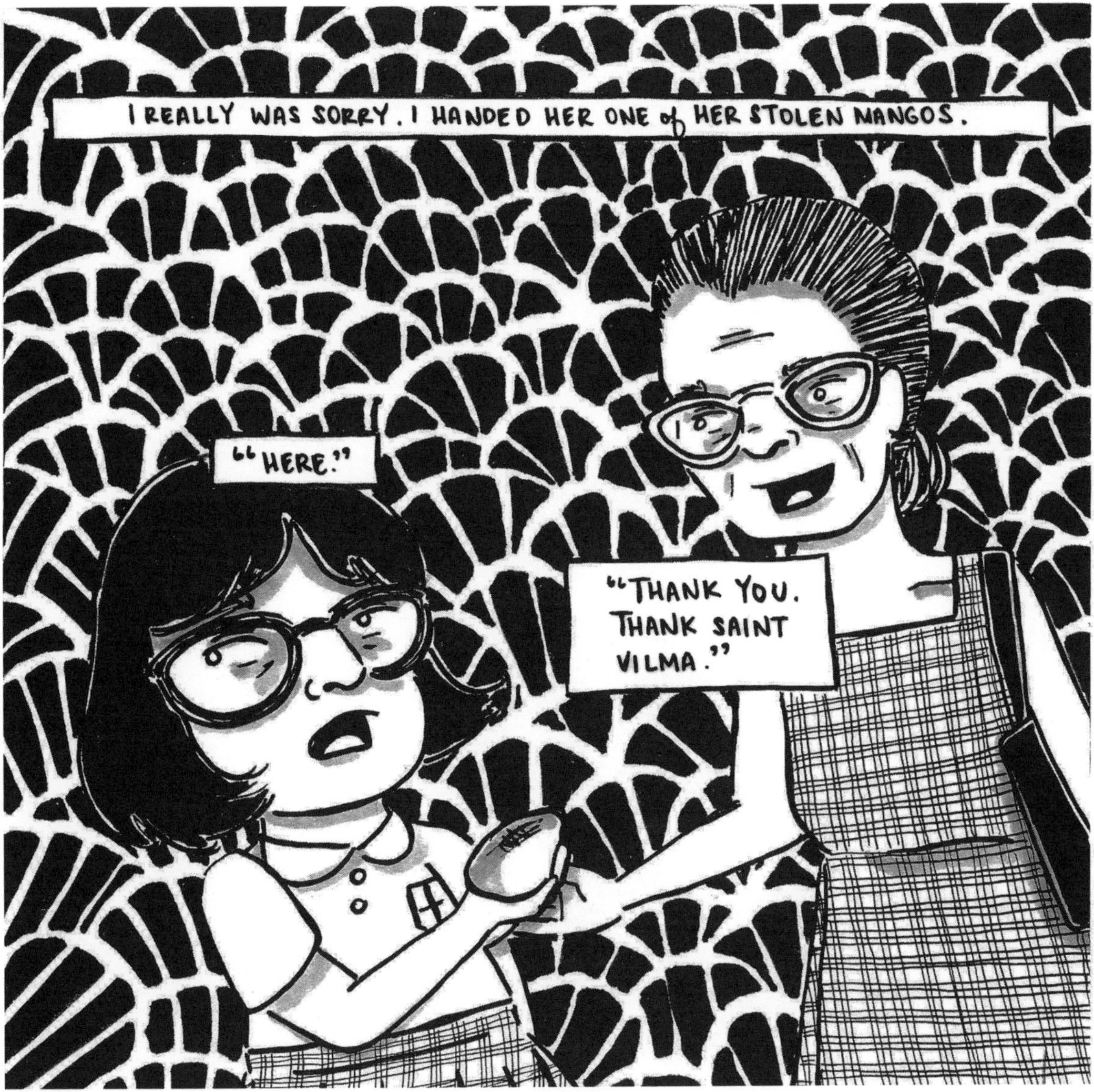
I REALLY WAS SORRY. I HANDED HER ONE of HER STOLEN MANGOS.
"HERE."
"THANK YOU. THANK SAINT VILMA."

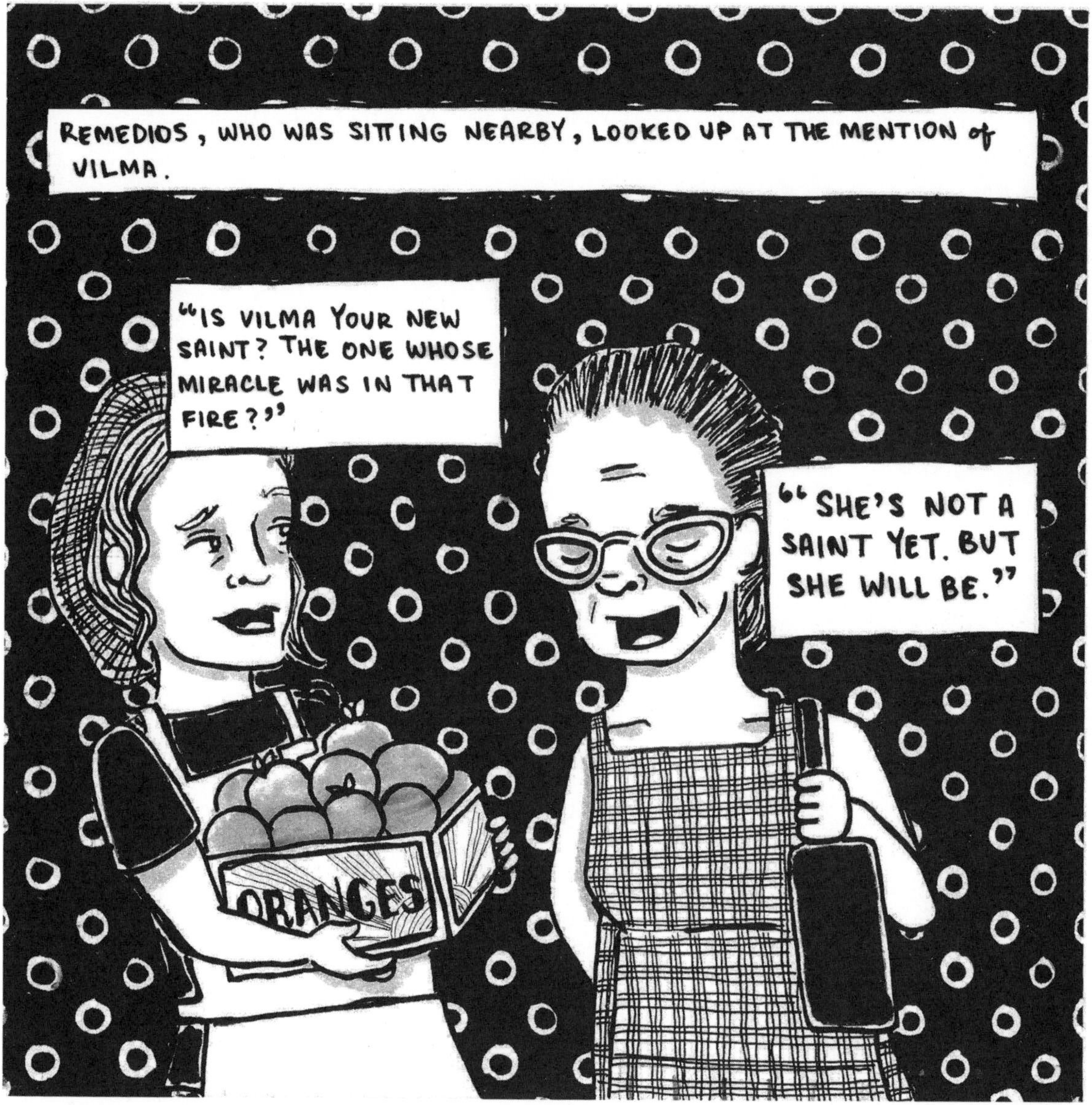
REMEDIOS, WHO WAS SITTING NEARBY, LOOKED UP AT THE MENTION of VILMA.
"IS VILMA YOUR NEW SAINT? THE ONE WHOSE MIRACLE WAS IN THAT FIRE?"
"SHE'S NOT A SAINT YET. BUT SHE WILL BE."
ORANGES

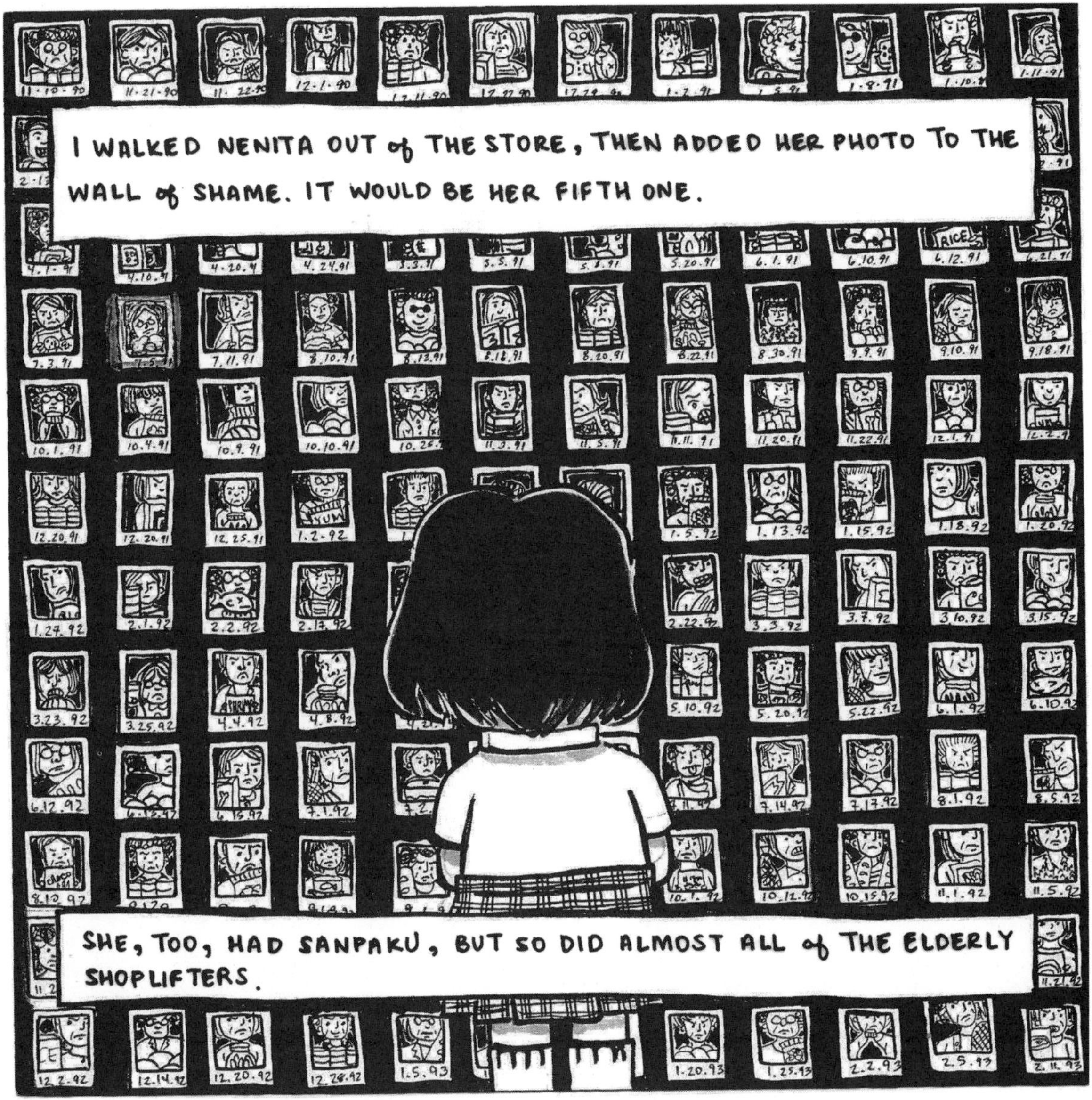
I WALKED NENITA OUT of THE STORE, THEN ADDED HER PHOTO TO THE WALL of SHAME. IT WOULD BE HER FIFTH ONE.
SHE, TOO, HAD SANPAKU, BUT SO DID ALMOST ALL of THE ELDERLY SHOPLIFTERS.

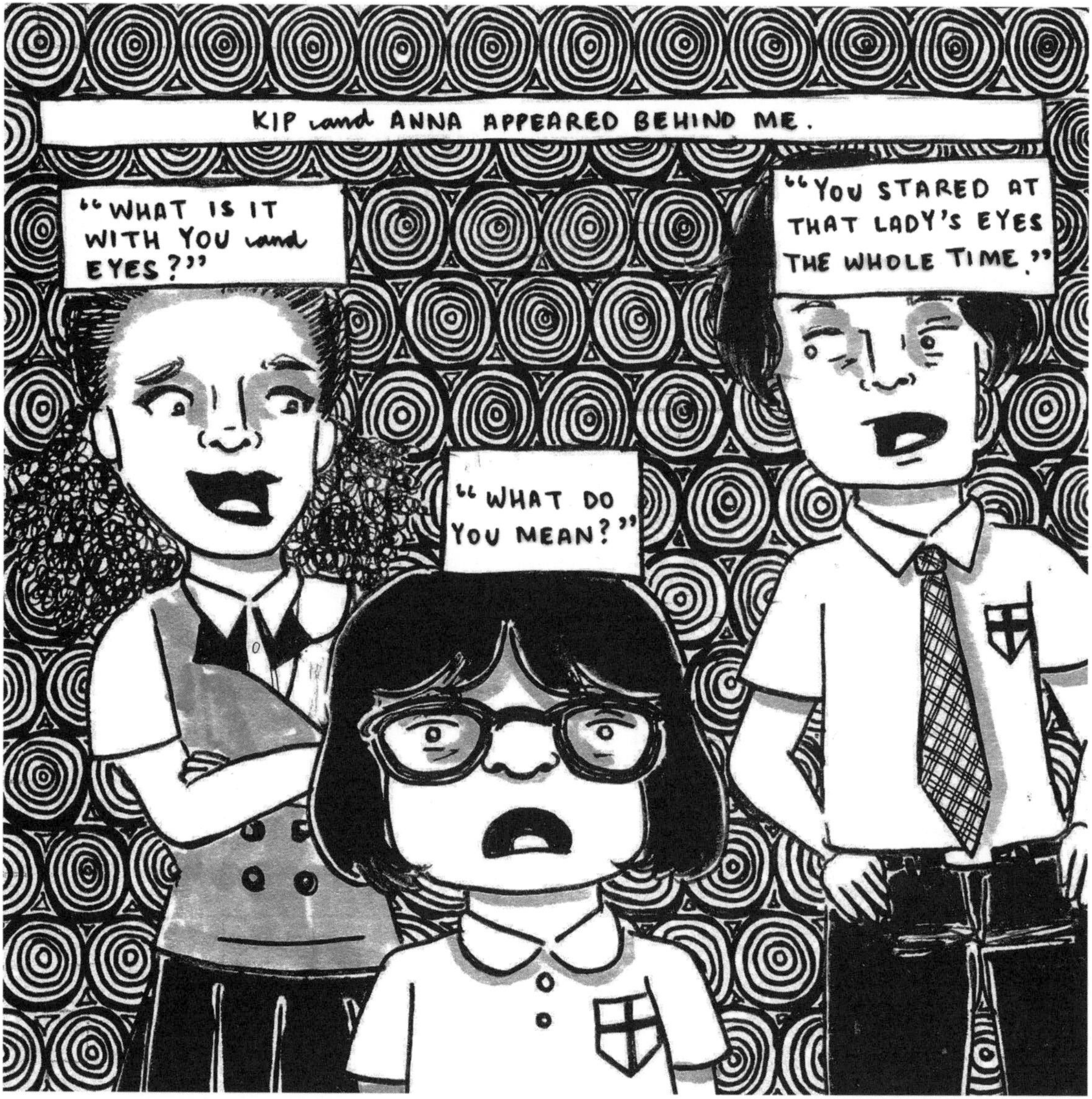
KIP and ANNA APPEARED BEHIND ME.
"WHAT IS IT WITH YOU and EYES?"
"YOU STARED AT THAT LADY'S EYES THE WHOLE TIME."
"WHAT DO YOU MEAN?"

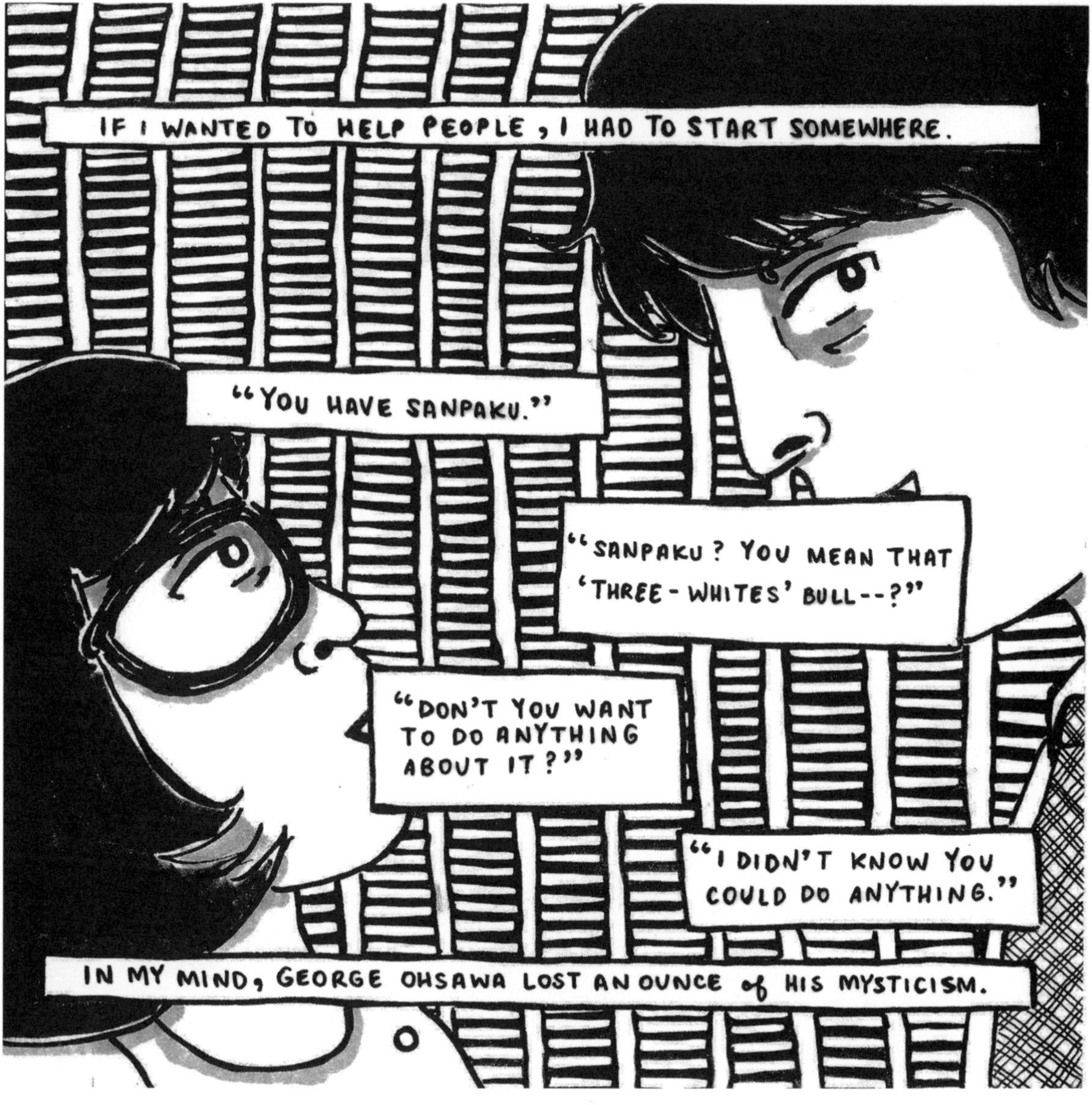
IF I WANTED TO HELP PEOPLE, I HAD TO START SOMEWHERE.
"YOU HAVE SANPAKU."
"SANPAKU? YOU MEAN THAT 'THREE-WHITES' BULL--?"
"DON'T YOU WANT TO DO ANYTHING ABOUT IT?"
"I DIDN'T KNOW YOU COULD DO ANYTHING."
IN MY MIND, GEORGE OHSAWA LOST AN OUNCE of HIS MYSTICISM.

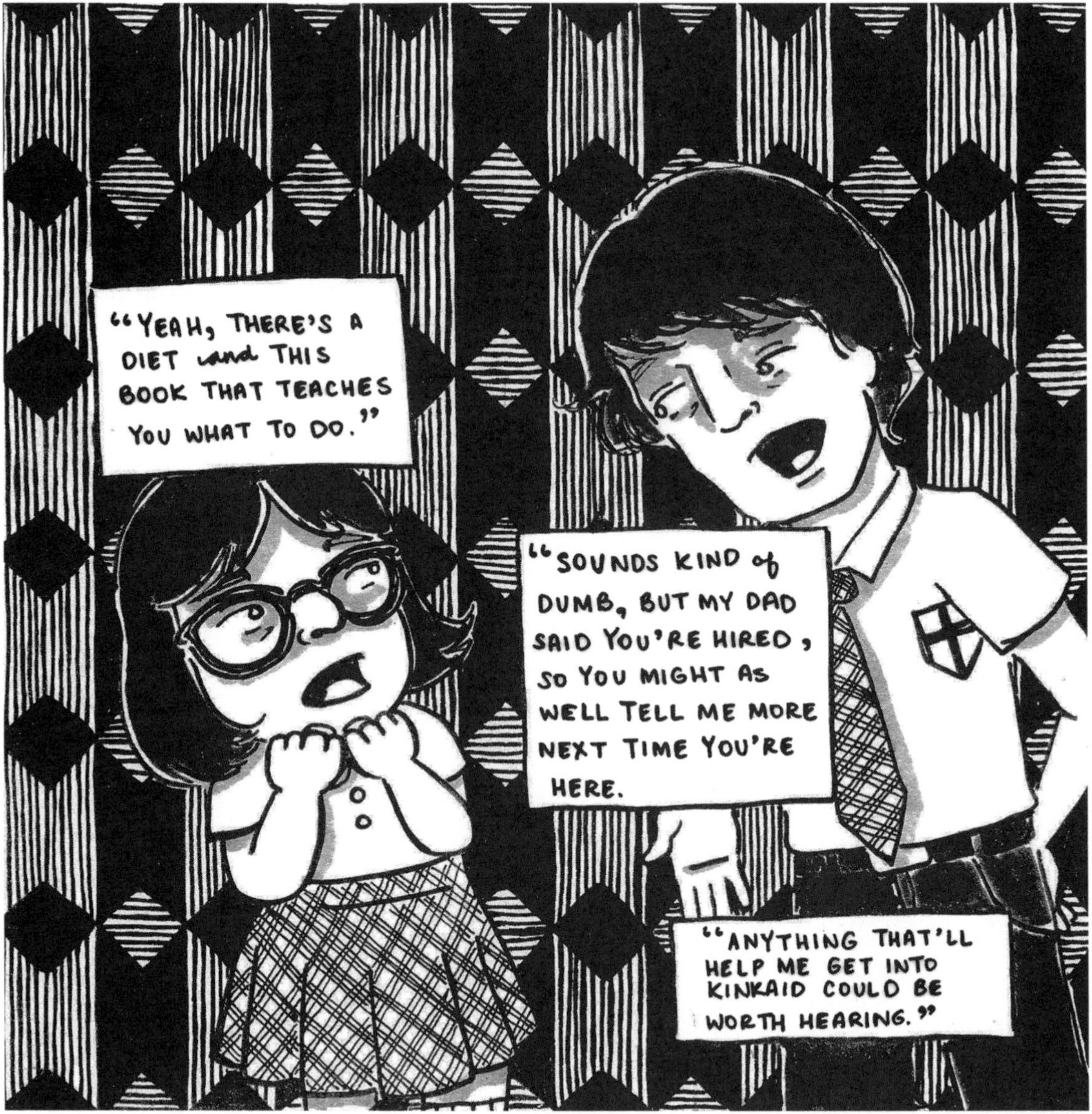
"YEAH, THERE'S A DIET and THIS BOOK THAT TEACHES YOU WHAT TO DO."
"SOUNDS KIND of DUMB, BUT MY DAD SAID YOU'RE HIRED, SO YOU MIGHT AS WELL TELL ME MORE NEXT TIME YOU'RE HERE.
"ANYTHING THAT'LL HELP ME GET INTO KINKAID COULD BE WORTH HEARING."

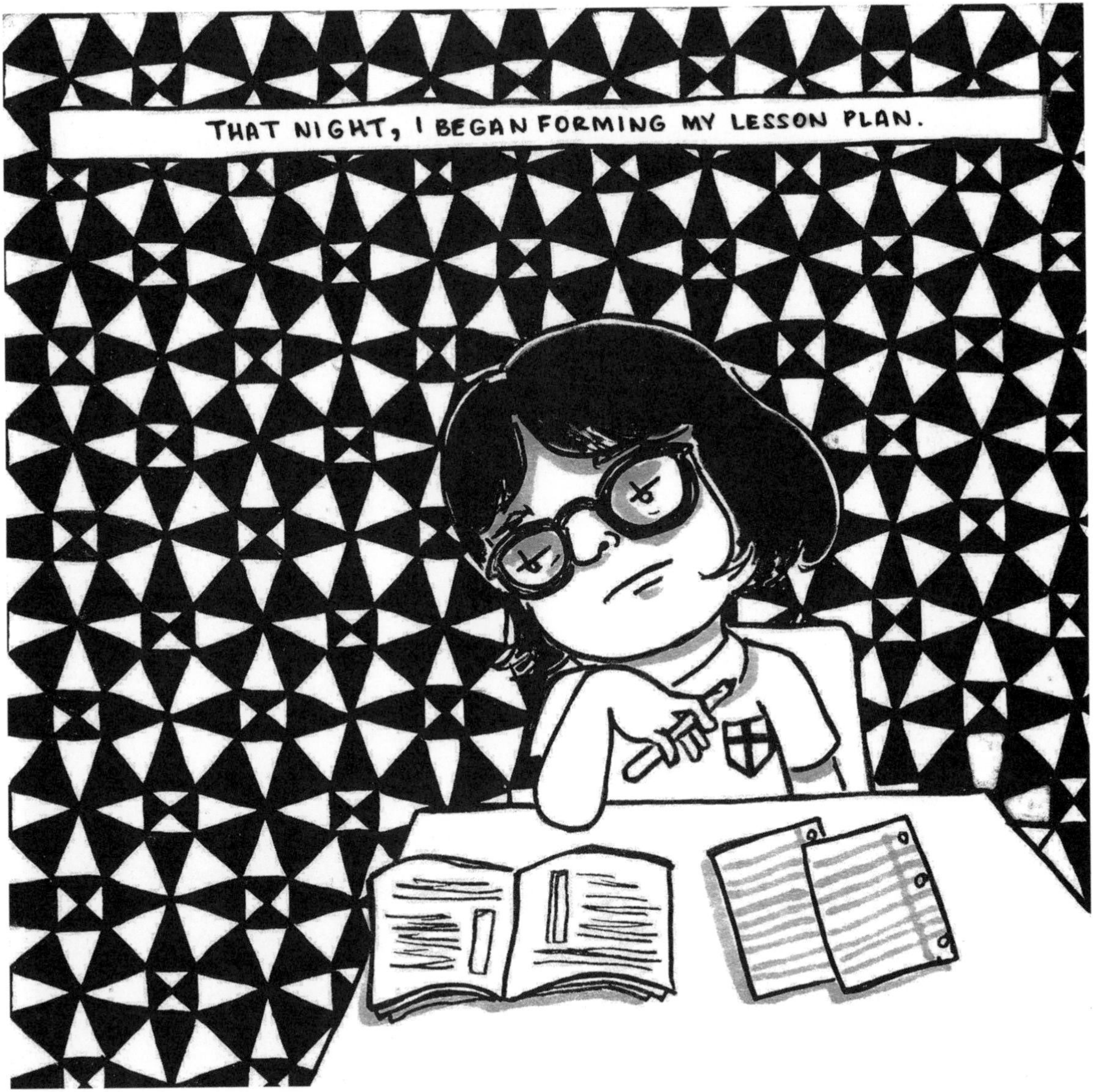
THAT NIGHT, I BEGAN FORMING MY LESSON PLAN.

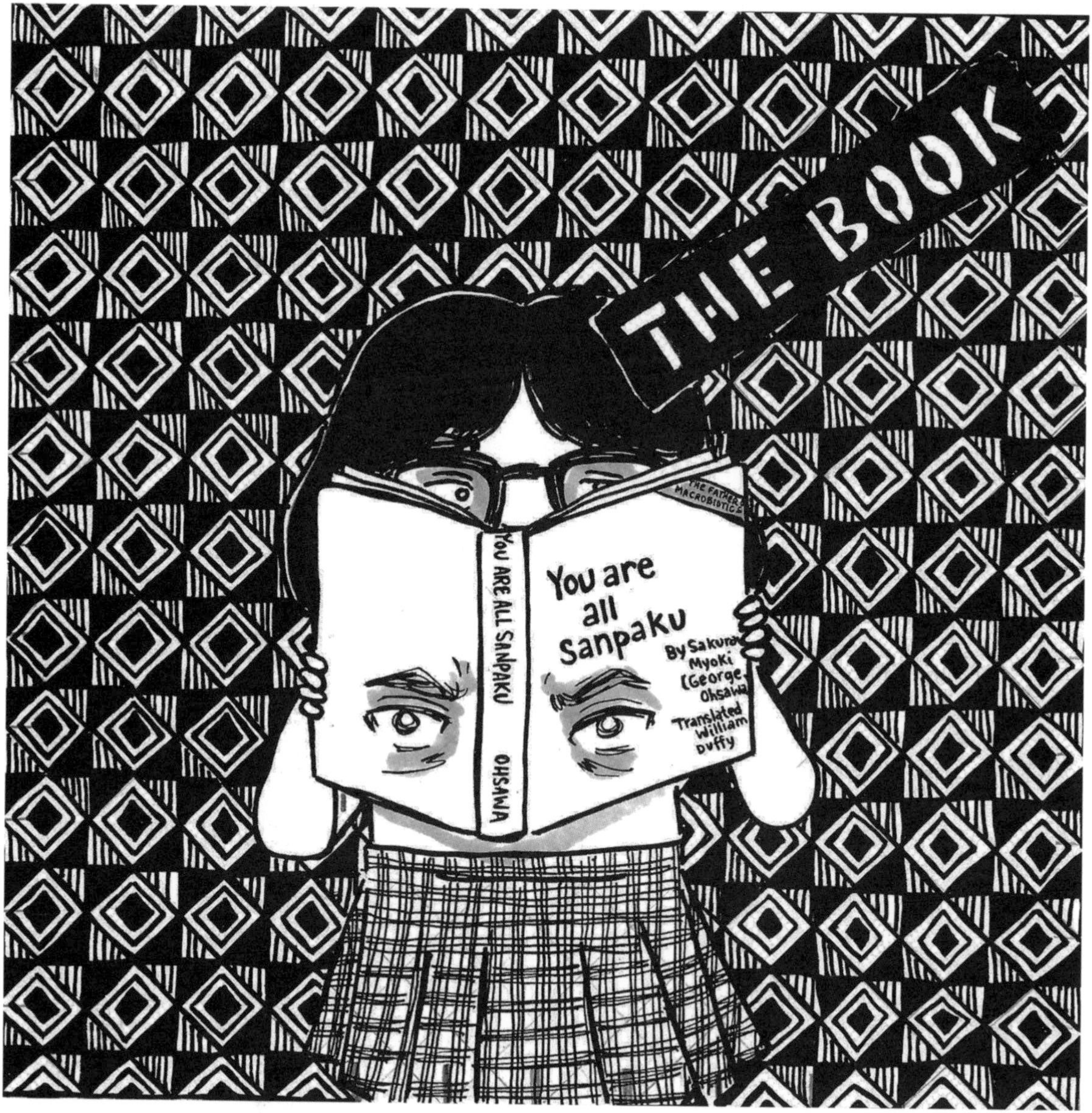
THE BOOK
THE FATHER OF MACROBIOTICS
YOU ARE ALL SANPAKU
OHSAWA
You are all Sanpaku
By Sakurai Myoki (George Ohsawa)
Translated William Duffy

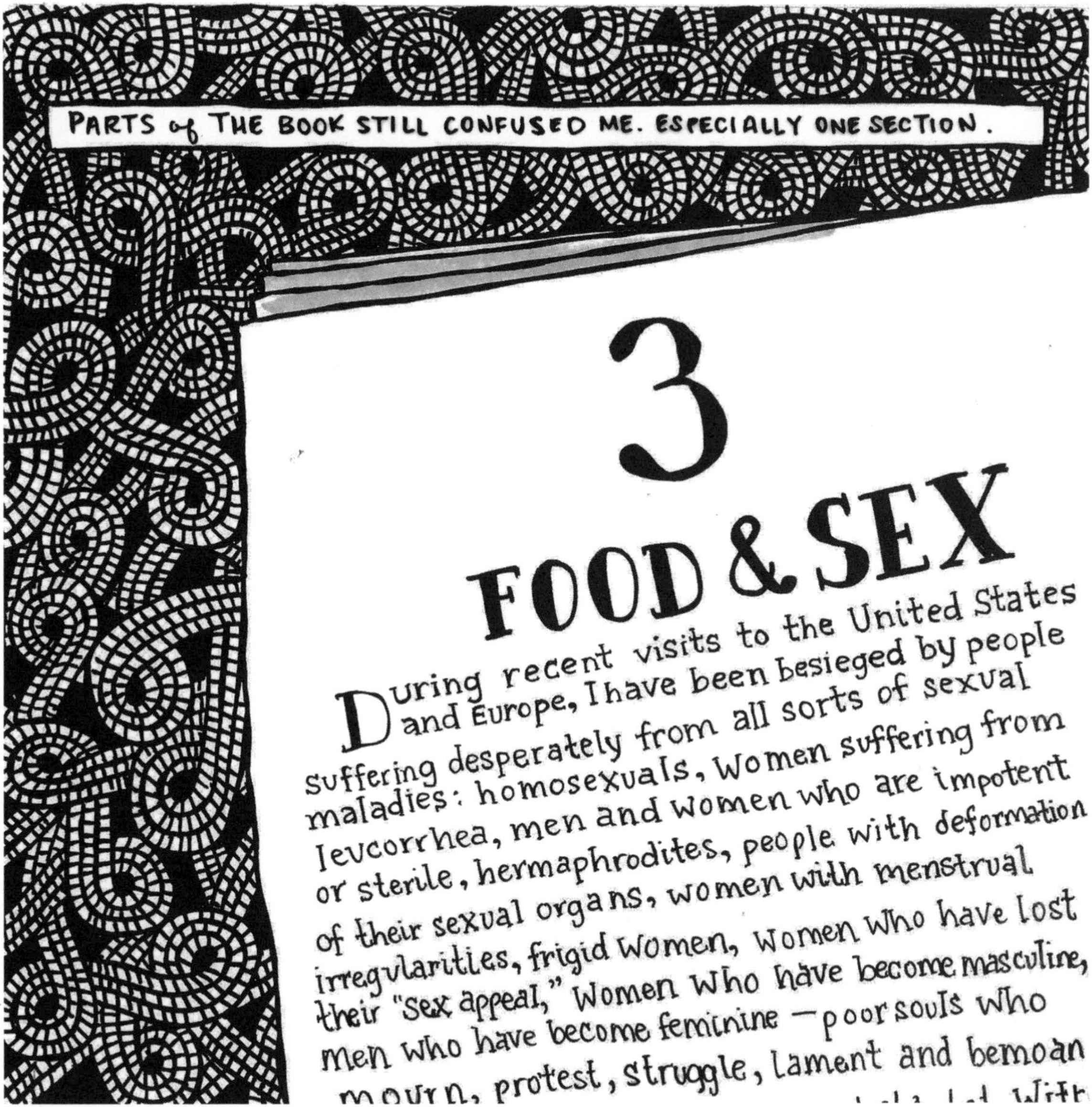
PARTS of THE BOOK STILL CONFUSED ME. ESPECIALLY ONE SECTION.
3
FOOD & SEX
During recent visits to the United States
and Europe, I have been besieged by people
suffering desperately from all sorts of sexual
maladies: homosexuals, women suffering from
leucorrhea, men and women who are impotent
or sterile, hermaphrodites, people with deformation
of their sexual organs, women with menstrual
irregularities, frigid women, women who have lost
their "sex appeal," women who have become masculine,
men who have become feminine — poor souls who
mourn, protest, struggle, lament and bemoan

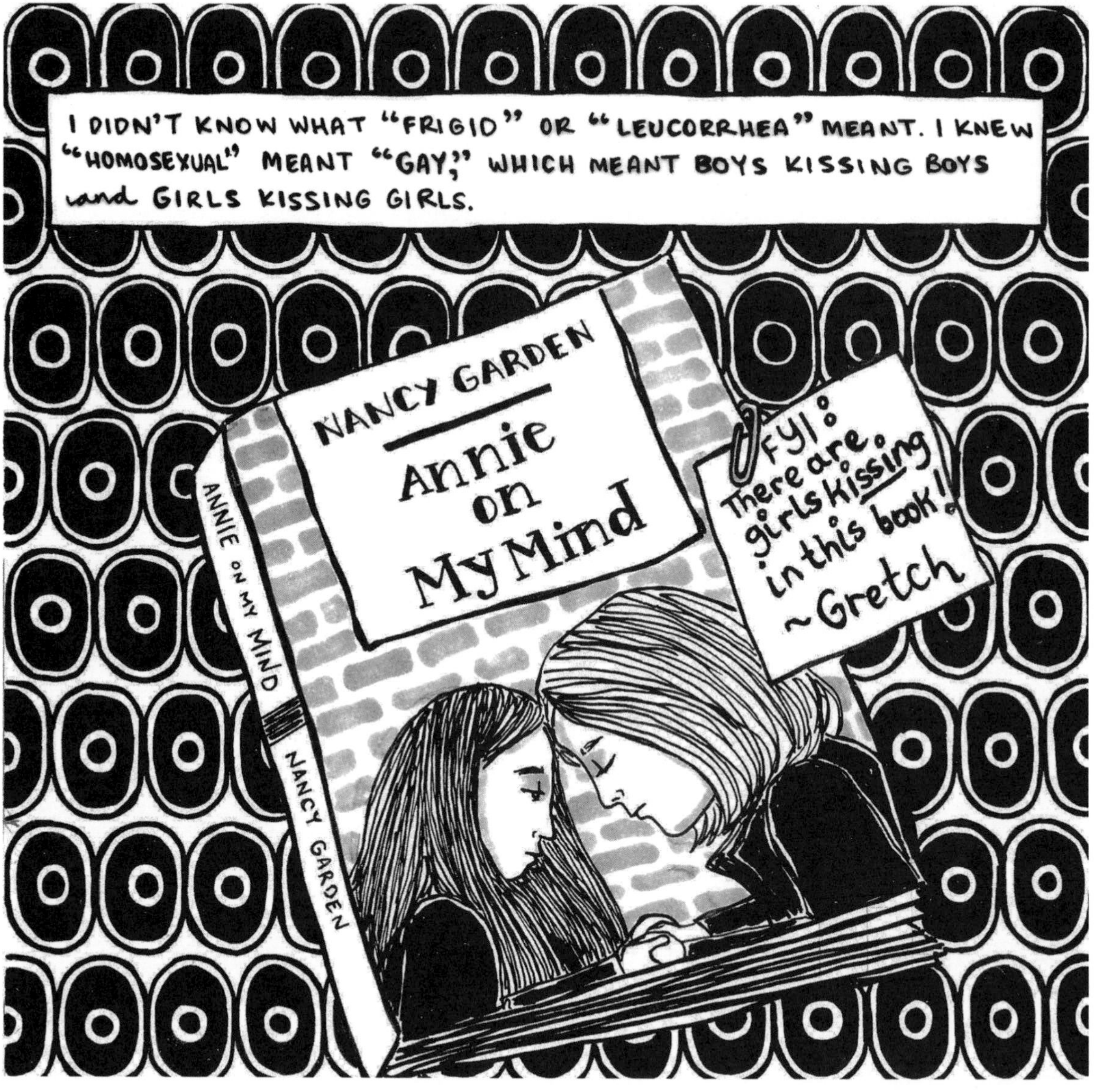
I DIDN'T KNOW WHAT "FRIGID" OR "LEUCORRHEA" MEANT. I KNEW "HOMOSEXUAL" MEANT "GAY," WHICH MEANT BOYS KISSING BOYS and GIRLS KISSING GIRLS.
NANCY GARDEN
Annie on My Mind
ANNIE ON MY MIND
NANCY GARDEN
FYI: There are girls kissing in this book! ~Gretch

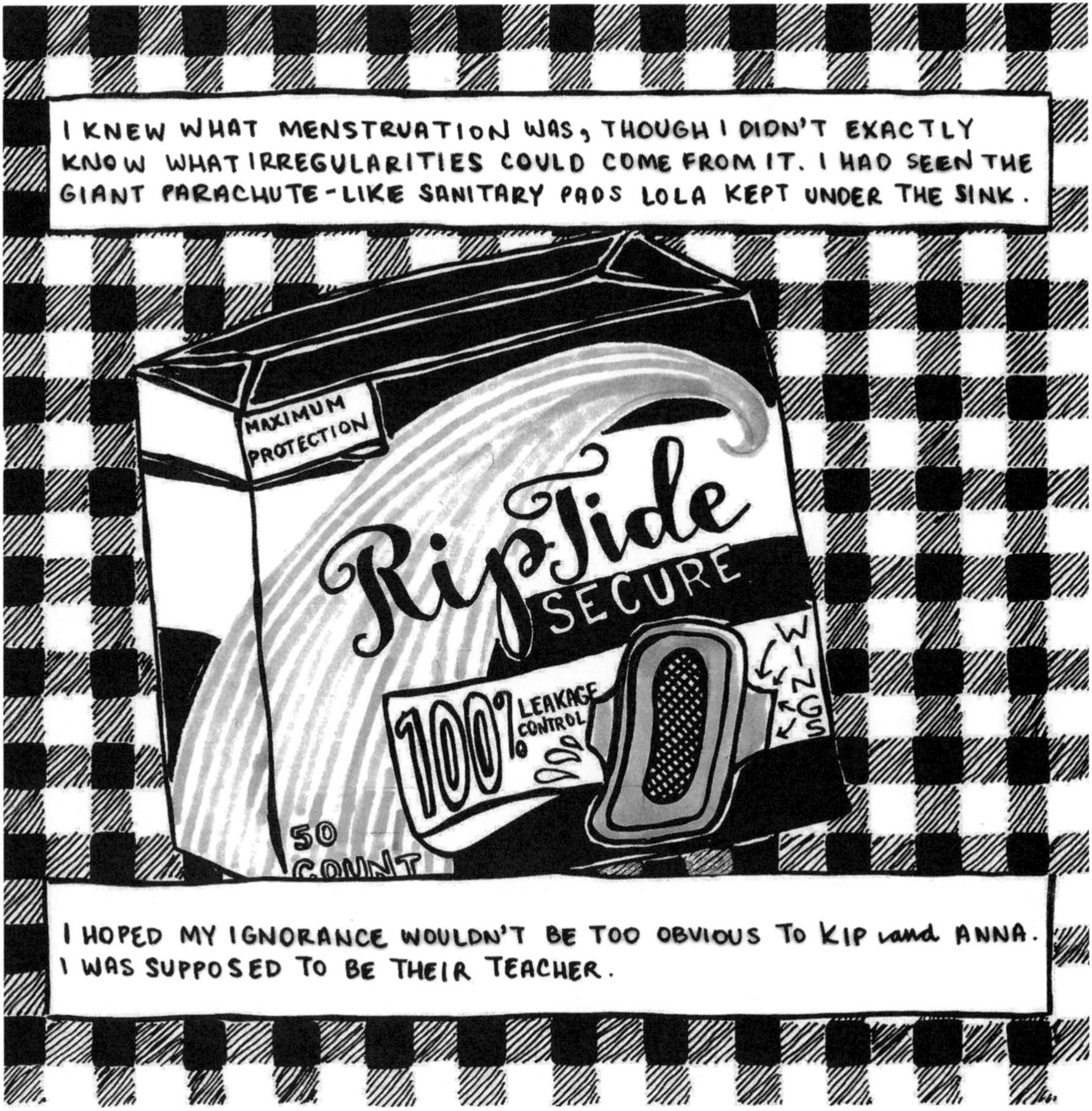
I KNEW WHAT MENSTRUATION WAS, THOUGH I DIDN'T EXACTLY KNOW WHAT IRREGULARITIES COULD COME FROM IT. I HAD SEEN THE GIANT PARACHUTE-LIKE SANITARY PADS LOLA KEPT UNDER THE SINK.
MAXIMUM PROTECTION
RipTide
SECURE
WINGS
100% LEAKAGE CONTROL
50
I HOPED MY IGNORANCE WOULDN'T BE TOO OBVIOUS TO KIP and ANNA. I WAS SUPPOSED TO BE THEIR TEACHER.

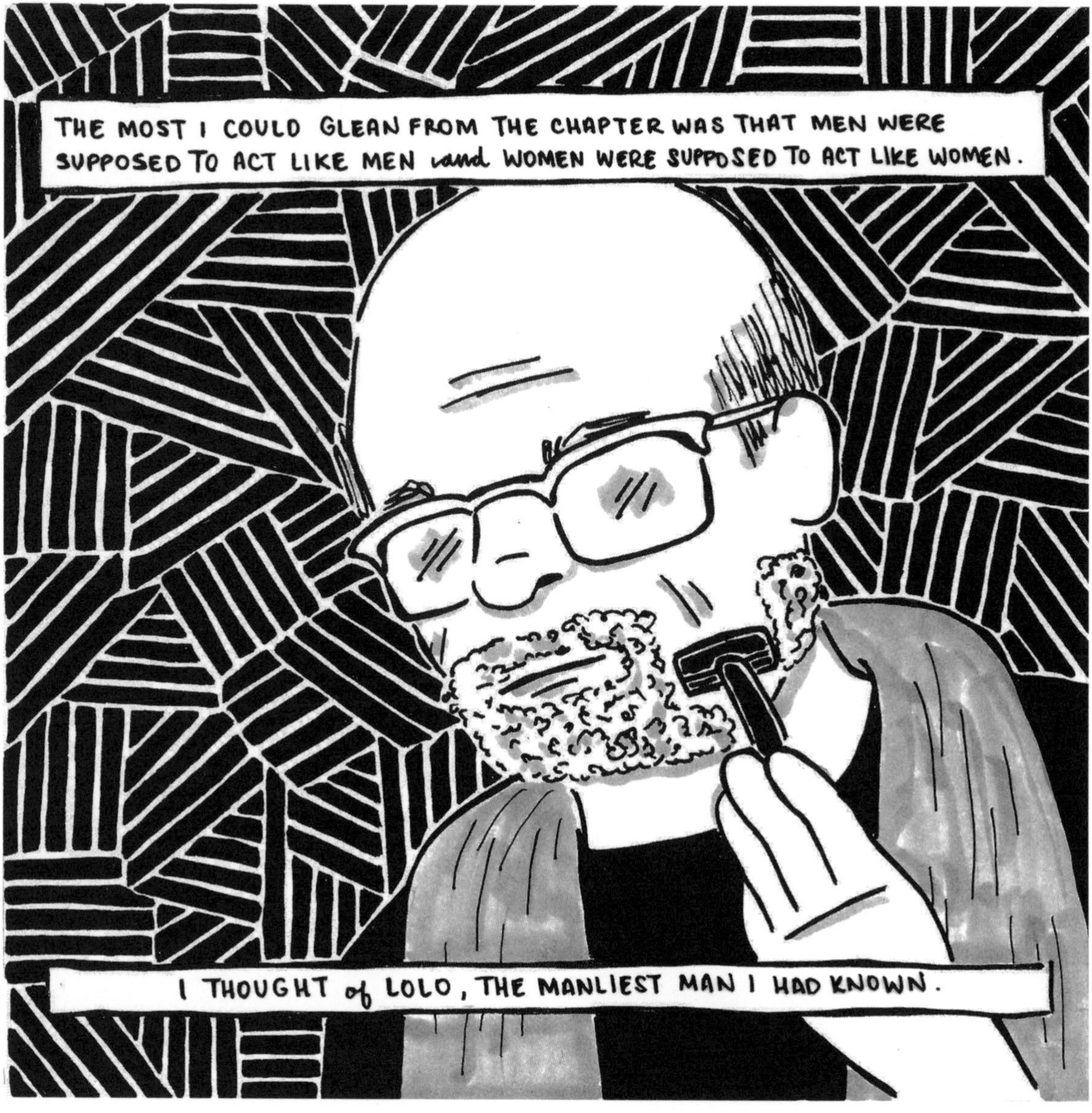
THE MOST I COULD GLEAN FROM THE CHAPTER WAS THAT MEN WERE SUPPOSED TO ACT LIKE MEN and WOMEN WERE SUPPOSED TO ACT LIKE WOMEN.
I THOUGHT of LOLO, THE MANLIEST MAN I HAD KNOWN.

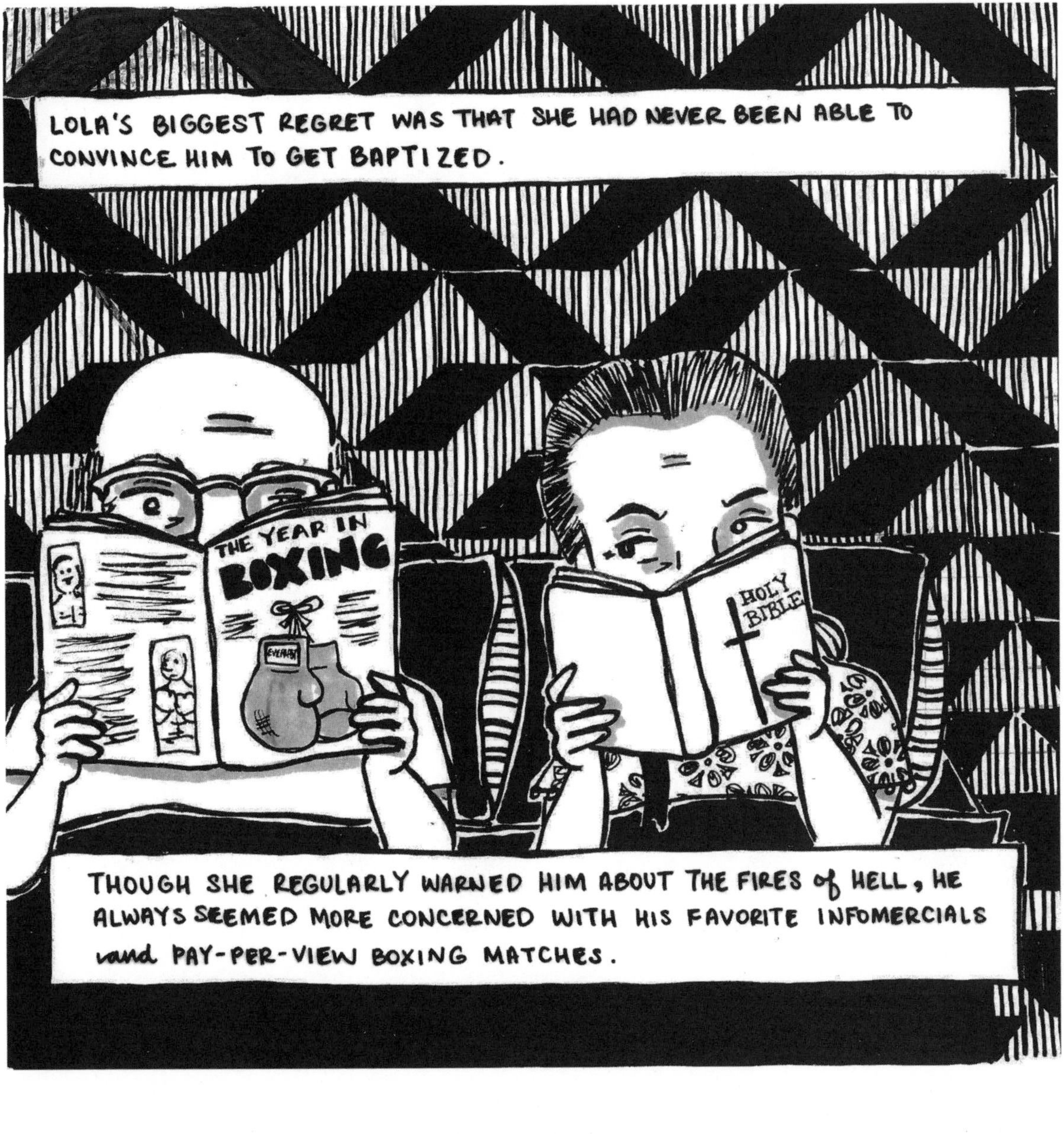
LOLA'S BIGGEST REGRET WAS THAT SHE HAD NEVER BEEN ABLE TO CONVINCE HIM TO GET BAPTIZED.
THE YEAR IN BOXING
EVERLAST
HOLY BIBLE
THOUGH SHE REGULARLY WARNED HIM ABOUT THE FIRES of HELL, HE ALWAYS SEEMED MORE CONCERNED WITH HIS FAVORITE INFOMERCIALS and PAY-PER-VIEW BOXING MATCHES.

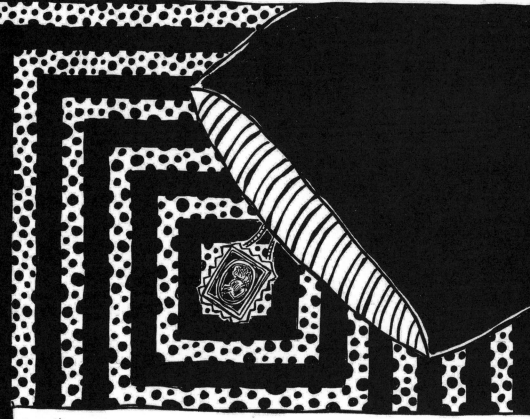

THE NAGGING NEVER SEEMED TO WORK.

AND YET, WHEN WE CLEANED OUT HIS THINGS AFTER HIS DEATH, WE FOUND A SCAPULAR UNDER HIS PILLOW.

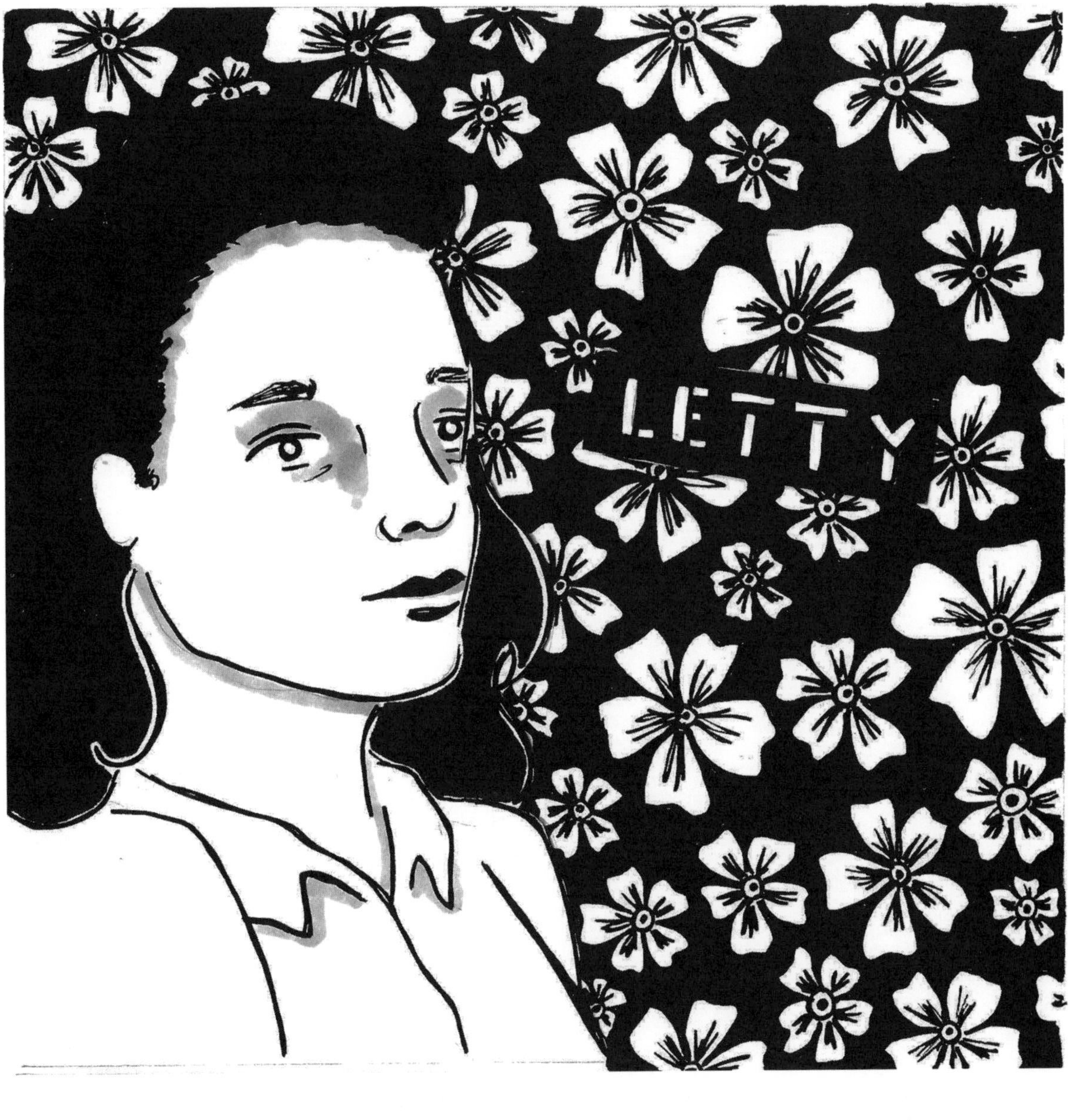
LETTY

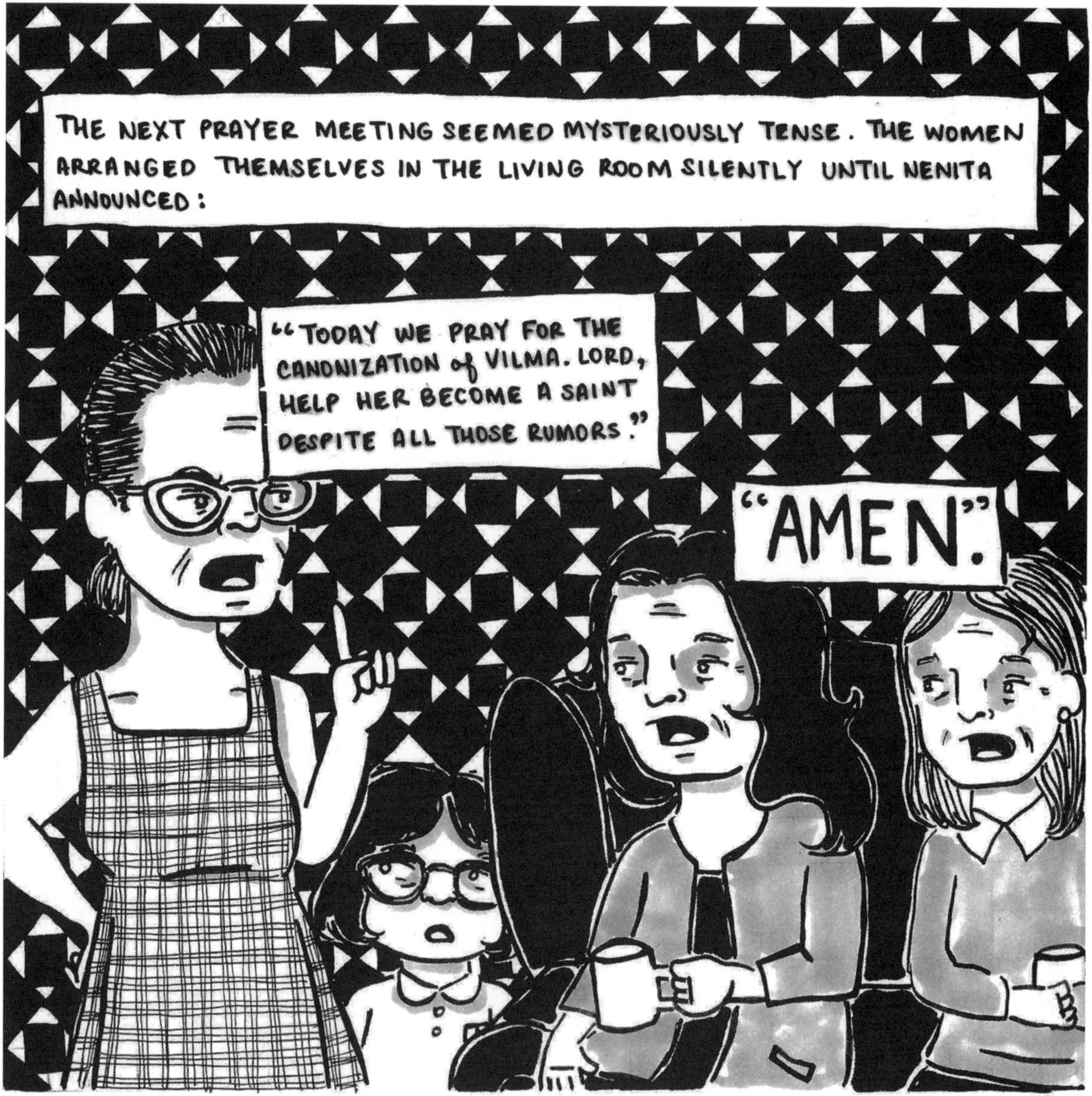
THE NEXT PRAYER MEETING SEEMED MYSTERIOUSLY TENSE. THE WOMEN ARRANGED THEMSELVES IN THE LIVING ROOM SILENTLY UNTIL NENITA ANNOUNCED:
"TODAY WE PRAY FOR THE CANONIZATION of VILMA. LORD, HELP HER BECOME A SAINT DESPITE ALL THOSE RUMORS."
"AMEN."

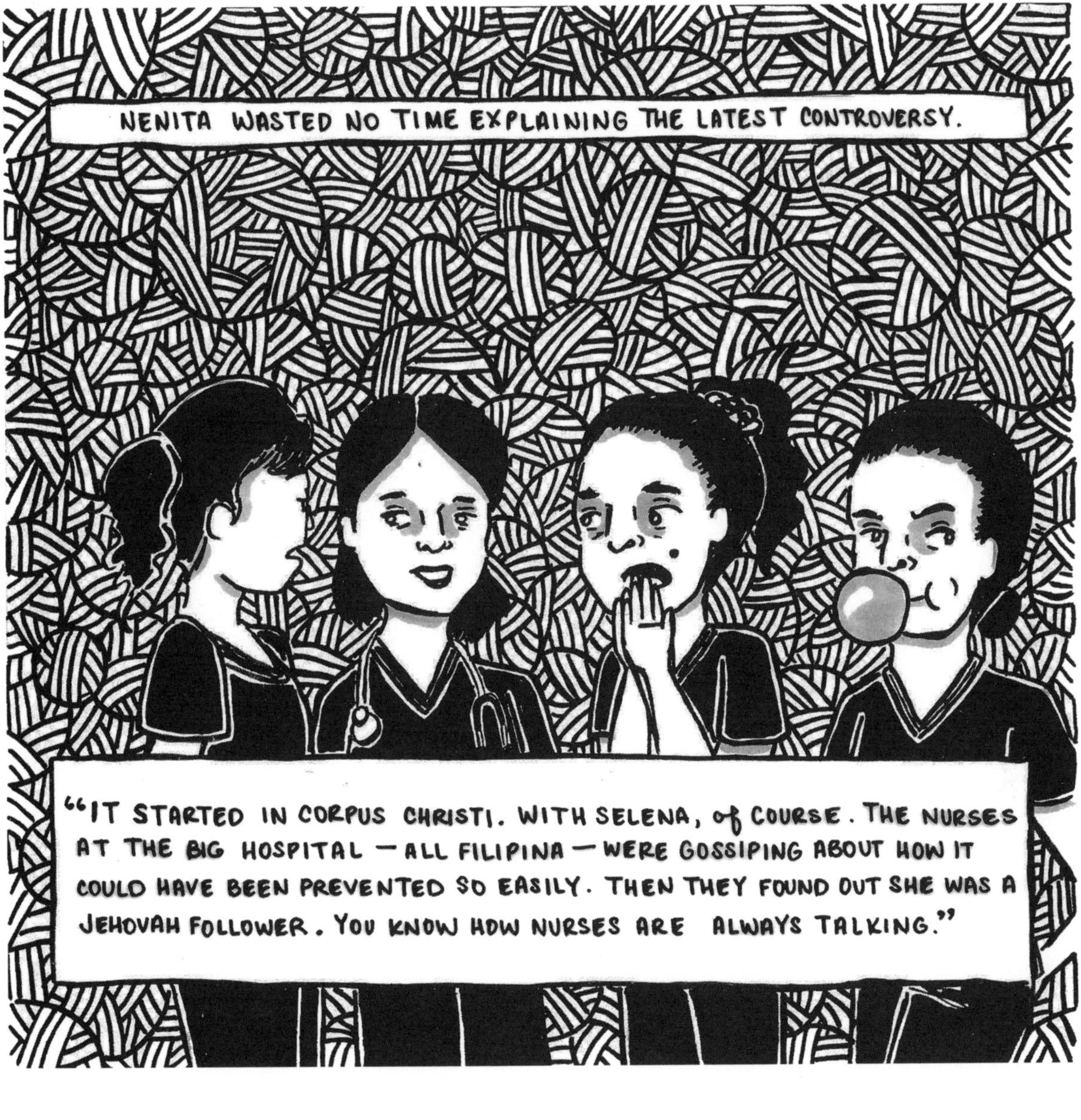
NENITA WASTED NO TIME EXPLAINING THE LATEST CONTROVERSY.
"IT STARTED IN CORPUS CHRISTI. WITH SELENA, of COURSE. THE NURSES AT THE BIG HOSPITAL — ALL FILIPINA — WERE GOSSIPING ABOUT HOW IT COULD HAVE BEEN PREVENTED SO EASILY. THEN THEY FOUND OUT SHE WAS A JEHOVAH FOLLOWER. YOU KNOW HOW NURSES ARE ALWAYS TALKING."

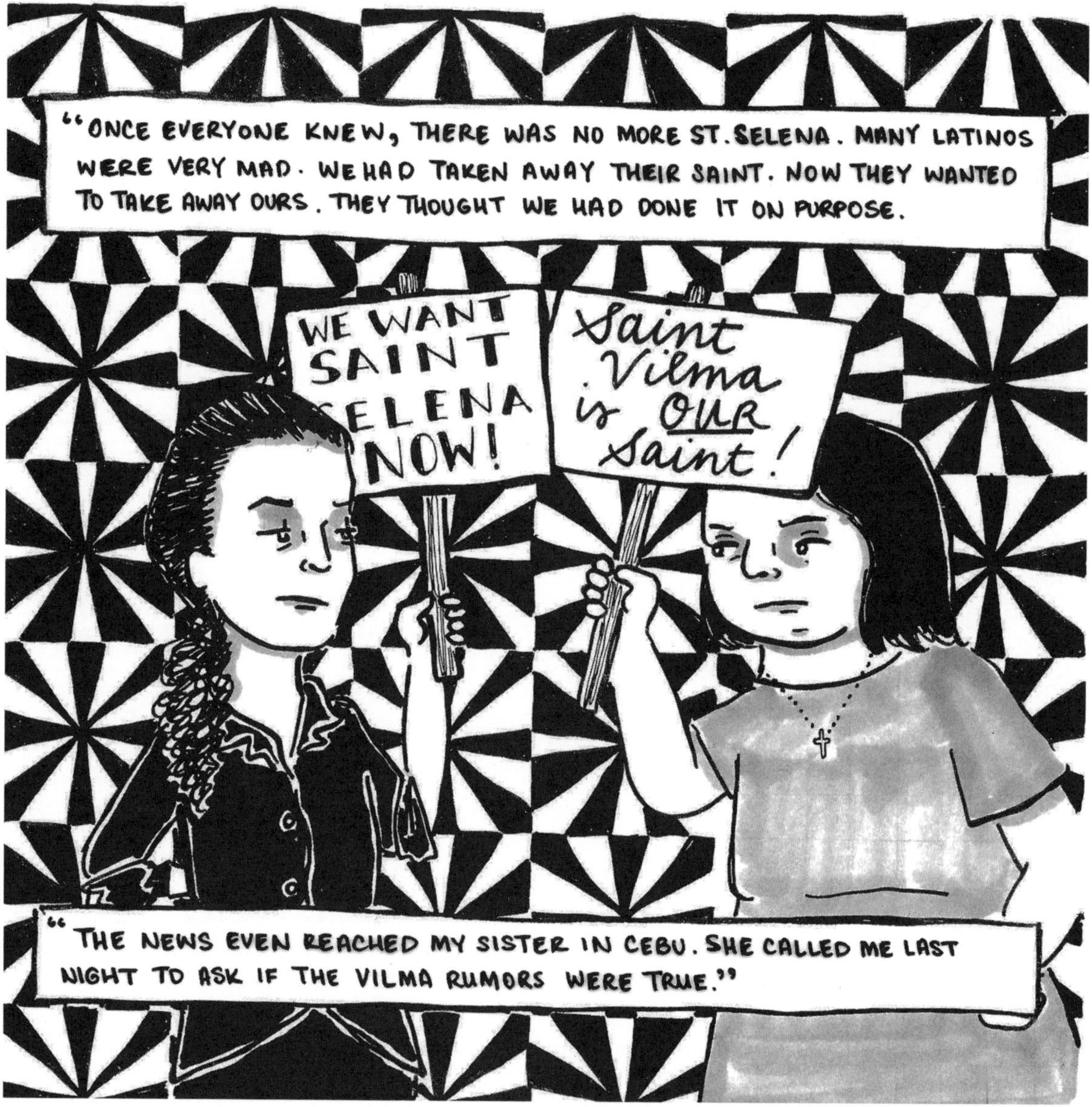
"ONCE EVERYONE KNEW, THERE WAS NO MORE ST. SELENA. MANY LATINOS WERE VERY MAD. WE HAD TAKEN AWAY THEIR SAINT. NOW THEY WANTED TO TAKE AWAY OURS. THEY THOUGHT WE HAD DONE IT ON PURPOSE.
WE WANT SAINT SELENA NOW!
Saint Vilma is OUR Saint!
"THE NEWS EVEN REACHED MY SISTER IN CEBU. SHE CALLED ME LAST NIGHT TO ASK IF THE VILMA RUMORS WERE TRUE."

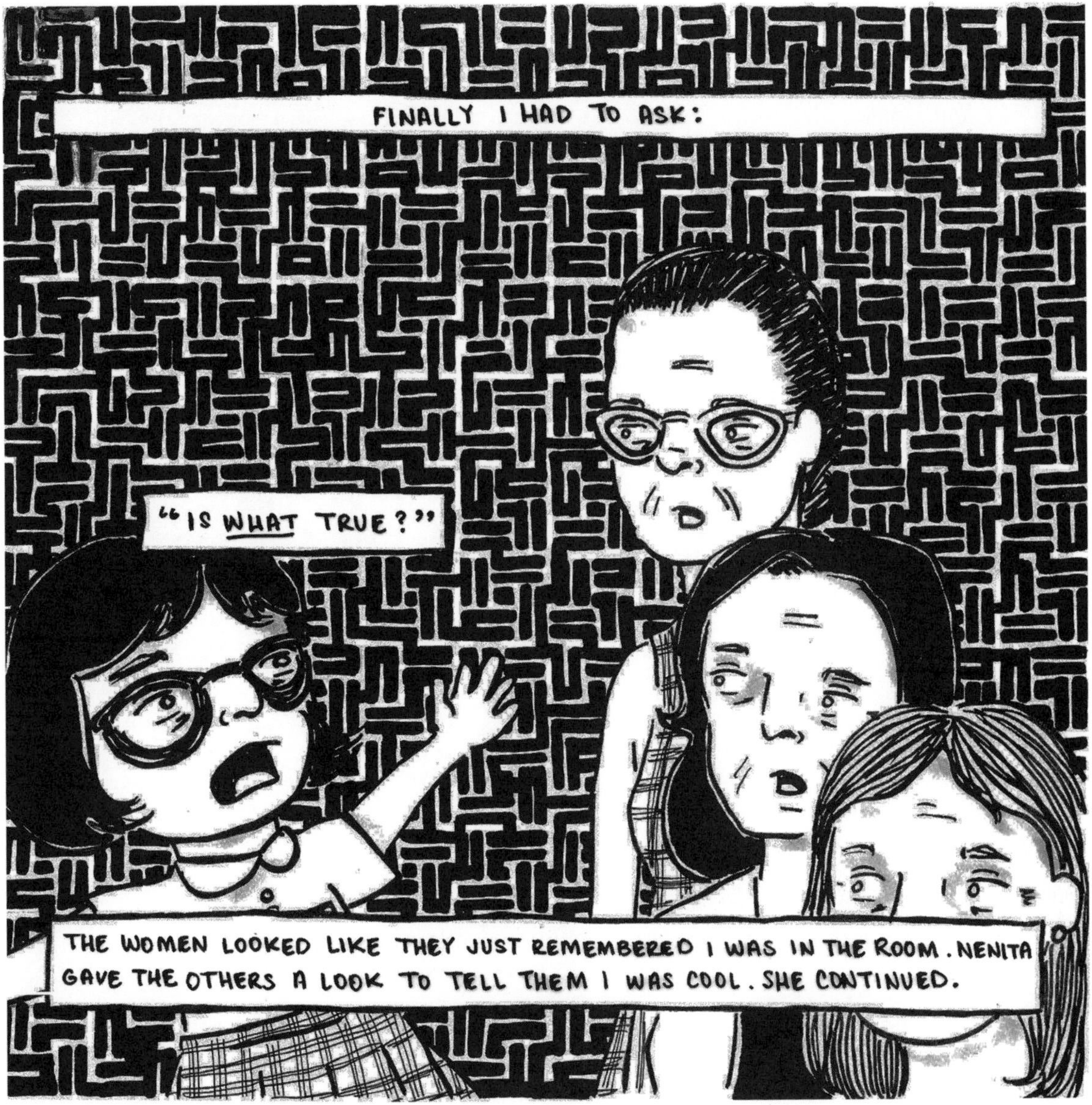
FINALLY I HAD TO ASK:
"IS WHAT TRUE?"
THE WOMEN LOOKED LIKE THEY JUST REMEMBERED I WAS IN THE ROOM. NENITA GAVE THE OTHERS A LOOK TO TELL THEM I WAS COOL. SHE CONTINUED.

"AS YOU KNOW, ST. VILMA HAD A BEAUTIFUL STATUE of THE LADY of GUADALUPE BUILT IN THE MIDDLE of SAN PABLO. IT WAS THE PRIDE of THE TOWN."
MAHAL KA NAMIN, PAPA
"WHEN IT WAS ANNOUNCED JOHN PAUL II WAS VISITING, THE TOWN WAS SO, SO HAPPY. IT WAS LIKE A HOLIDAY!"

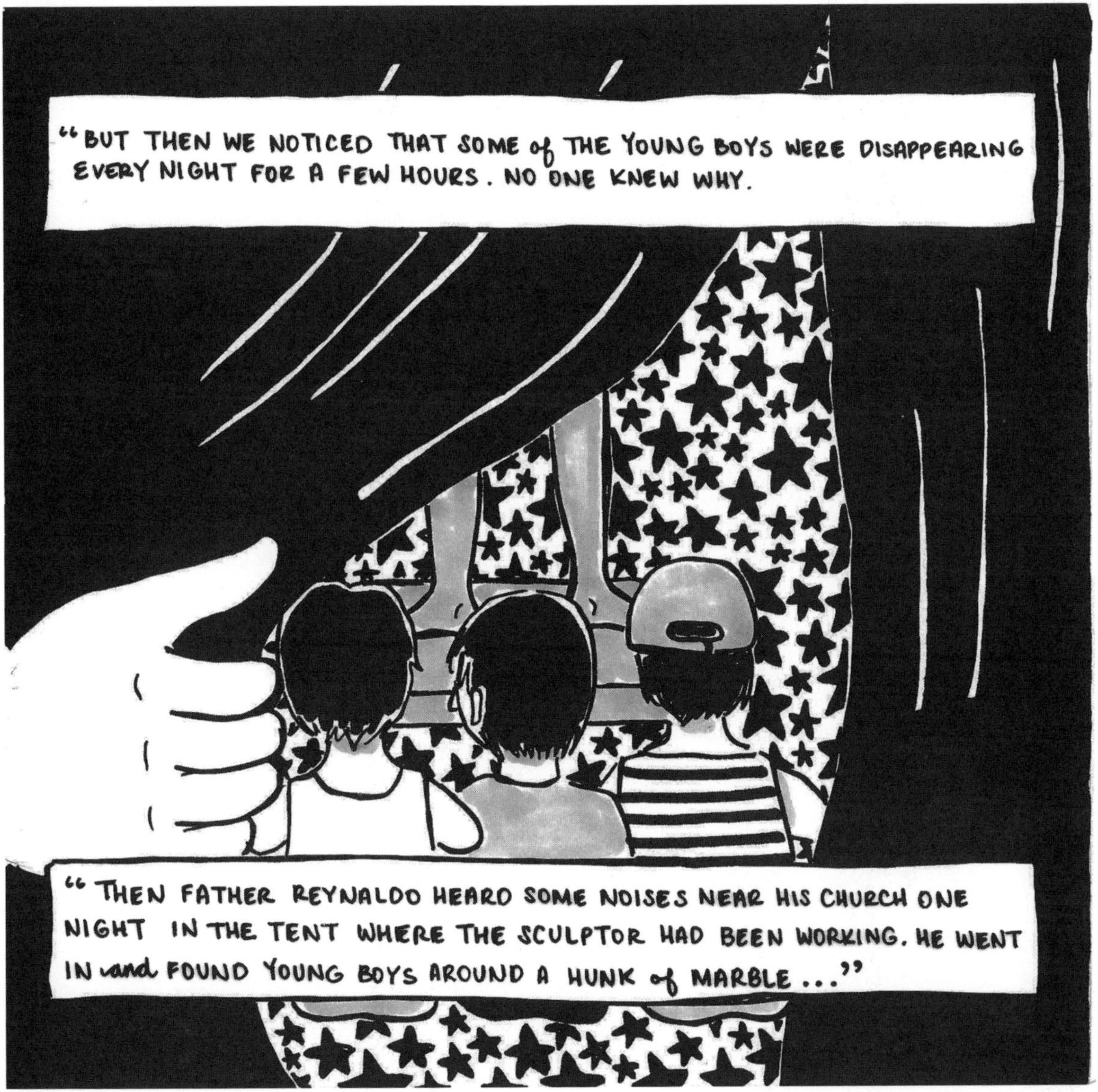
"BUT THEN WE NOTICED THAT SOME of THE YOUNG BOYS WERE DISAPPEARING EVERY NIGHT FOR A FEW HOURS. NO ONE KNEW WHY.
"THEN FATHER REYNALDO HEARD SOME NOISES NEAR HIS CHURCH ONE NIGHT IN THE TENT WHERE THE SCULPTOR HAD BEEN WORKING. HE WENT IN and FOUND YOUNG BOYS AROUND A HUNK of MARBLE..."

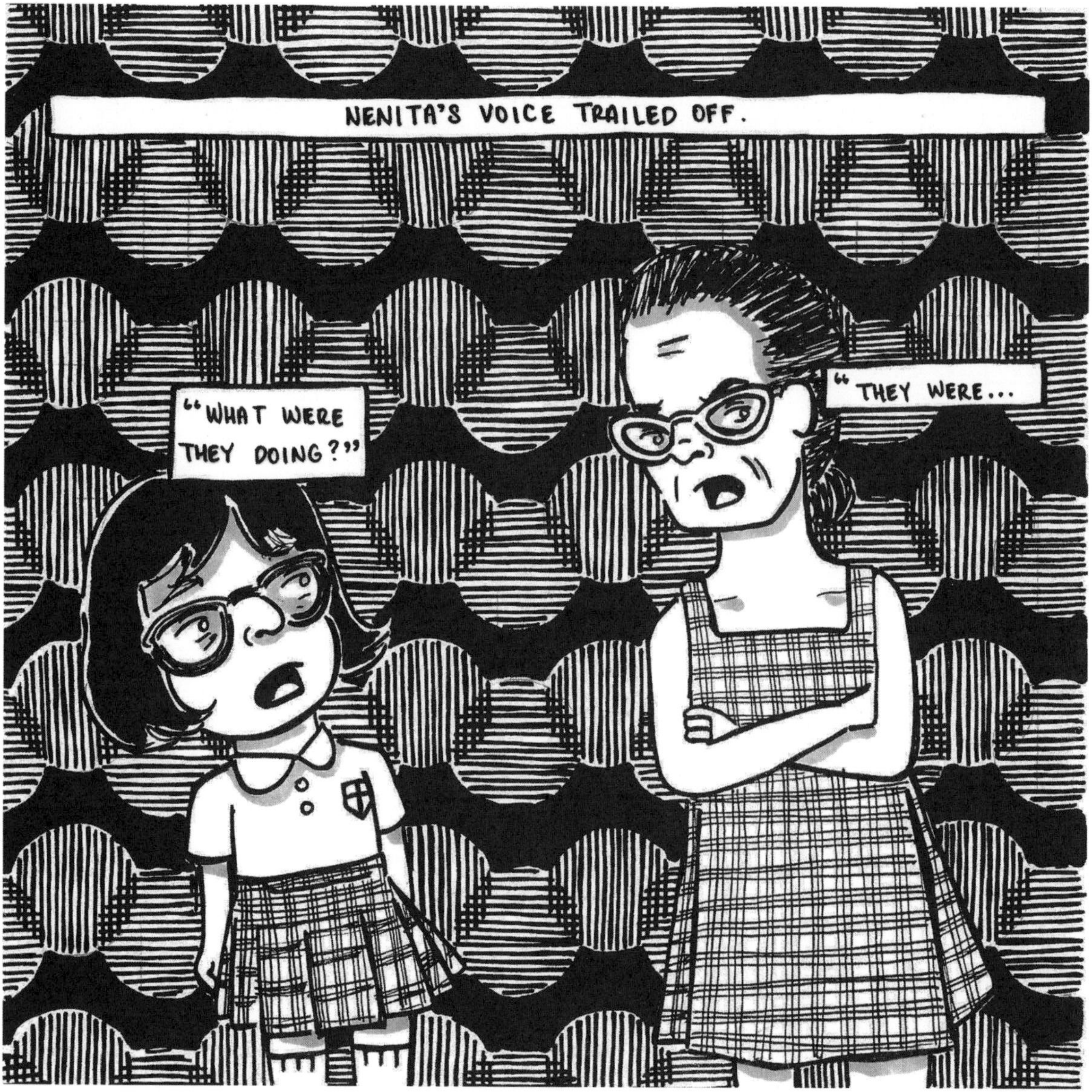
NENITA'S VOICE TRAILED OFF.
"WHAT WERE THEY DOING?"
"THEY WERE...

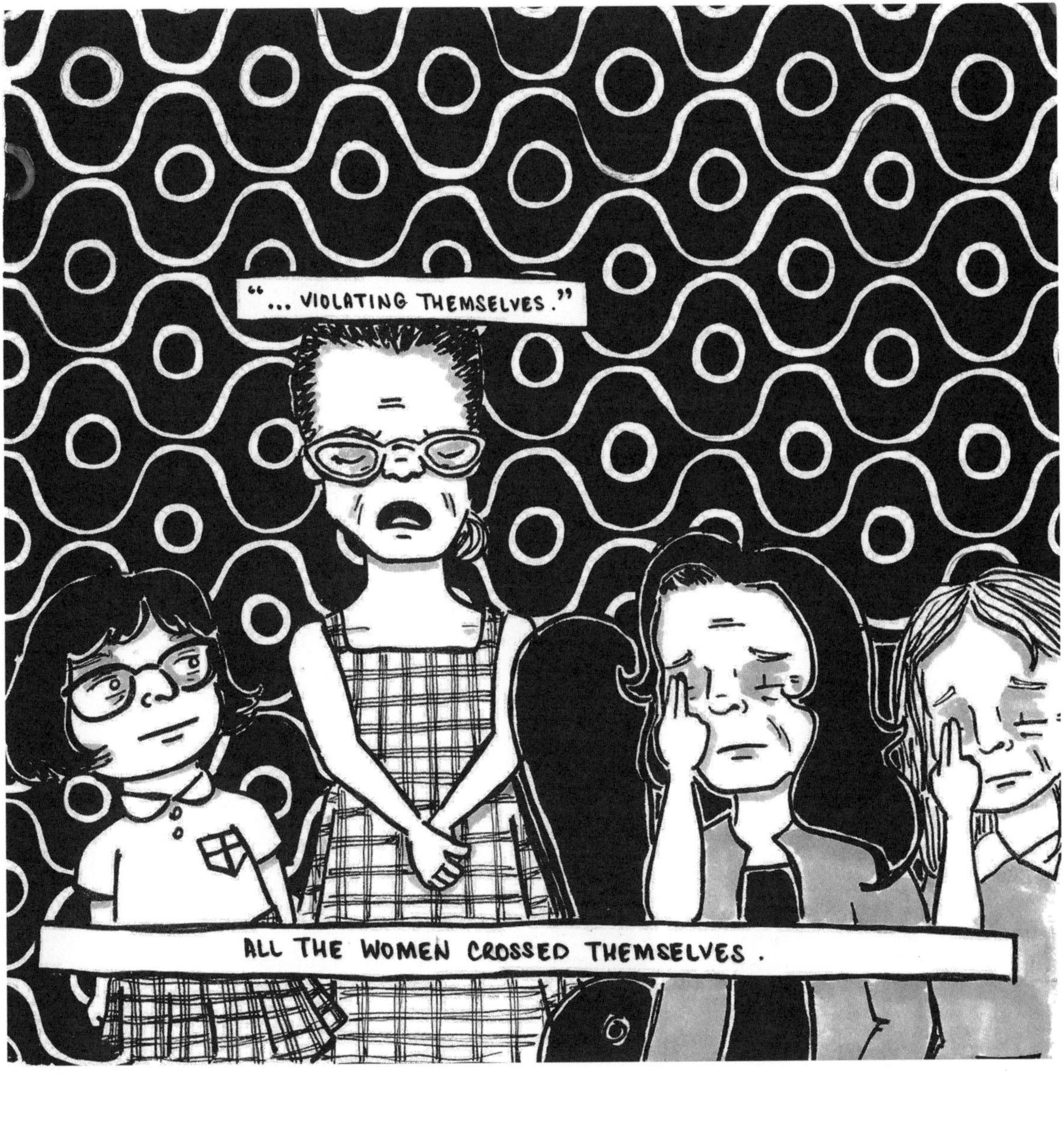
"... VIOLATING THEMSELVES."
ALL THE WOMEN CROSSED THEMSELVES.

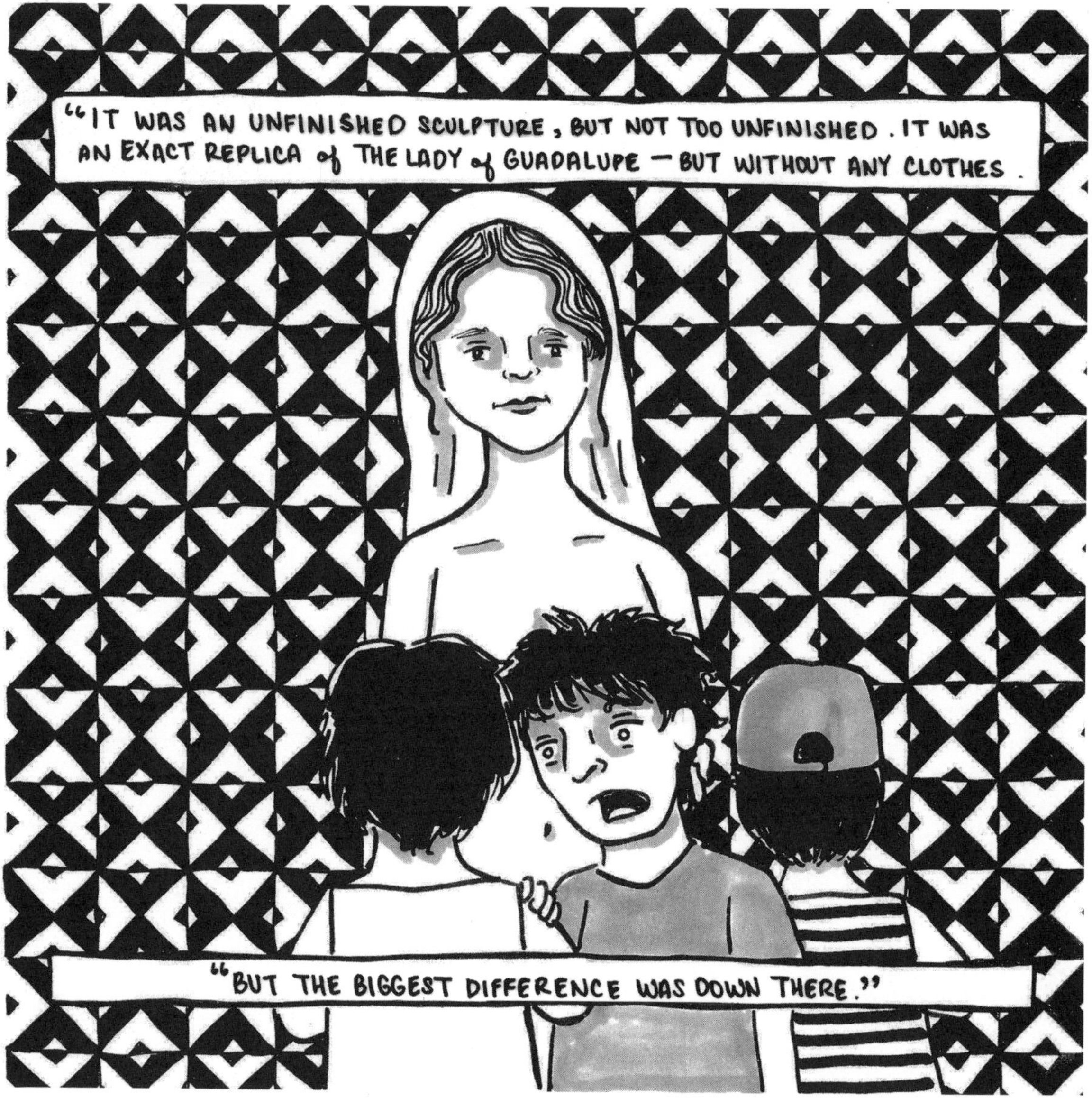
"IT WAS AN UNFINISHED SCULPTURE, BUT NOT TOO UNFINISHED. IT WAS AN EXACT REPLICA of THE LADY of GUADALUPE — BUT WITHOUT ANY CLOTHES.
"BUT THE BIGGEST DIFFERENCE WAS DOWN THERE."

I PROBABLY LOOKED CONFUSED BECAUSE NENITA STAGE-WHISPERED:
"A MARBLE VAGINA!!"

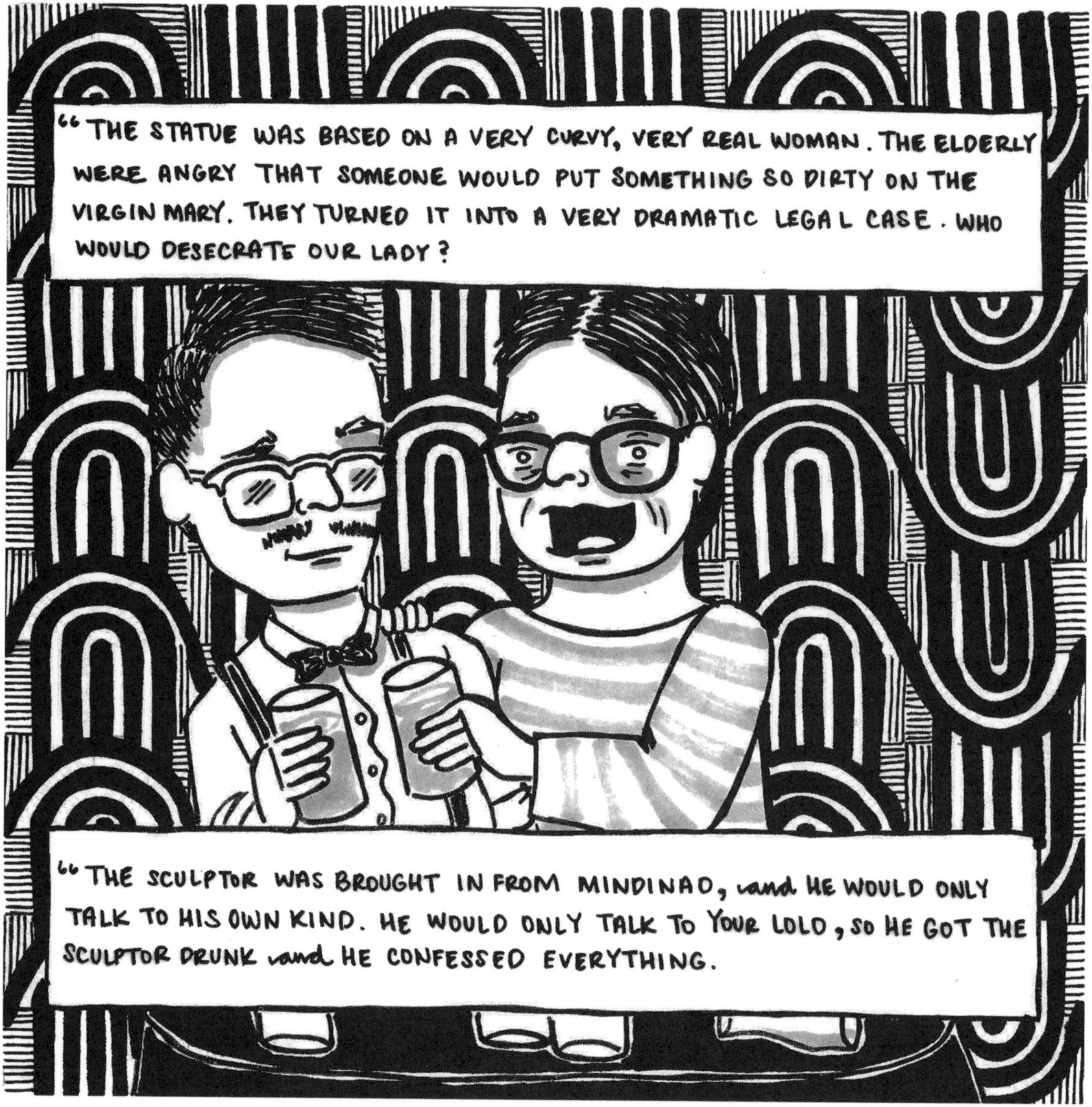
"THE STATUE WAS BASED ON A VERY CURVY, VERY REAL WOMAN. THE ELDERLY WERE ANGRY THAT SOMEONE WOULD PUT SOMETHING SO DIRTY ON THE VIRGIN MARY. THEY TURNED IT INTO A VERY DRAMATIC LEGAL CASE. WHO WOULD DESECRATE OUR LADY?
"THE SCULPTOR WAS BROUGHT IN FROM MINDINAO, and HE WOULD ONLY TALK TO HIS OWN KIND. HE WOULD ONLY TALK TO YOUR LOLO, SO HE GOT THE SCULPTOR DRUNK and HE CONFESSED EVERYTHING.

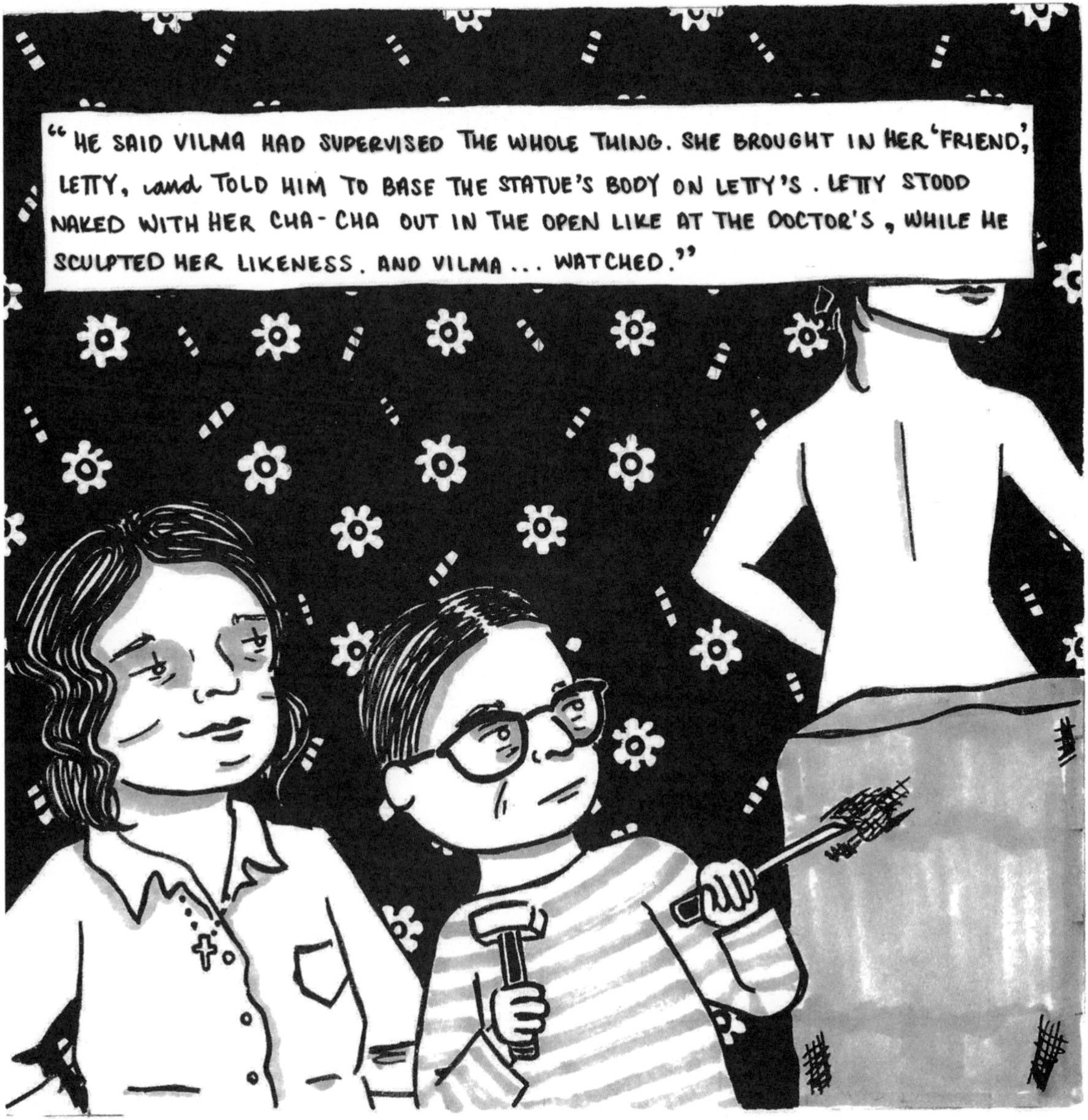
"HE SAID VILMA HAD SUPERVISED THE WHOLE THING. SHE BROUGHT IN HER 'FRIEND', LETTY, and TOLD HIM TO BASE THE STATUE'S BODY ON LETTY'S. LETTY STOOD NAKED WITH HER CHA-CHA OUT IN THE OPEN LIKE AT THE DOCTOR'S, WHILE HE SCULPTED HER LIKENESS. AND VILMA... WATCHED."

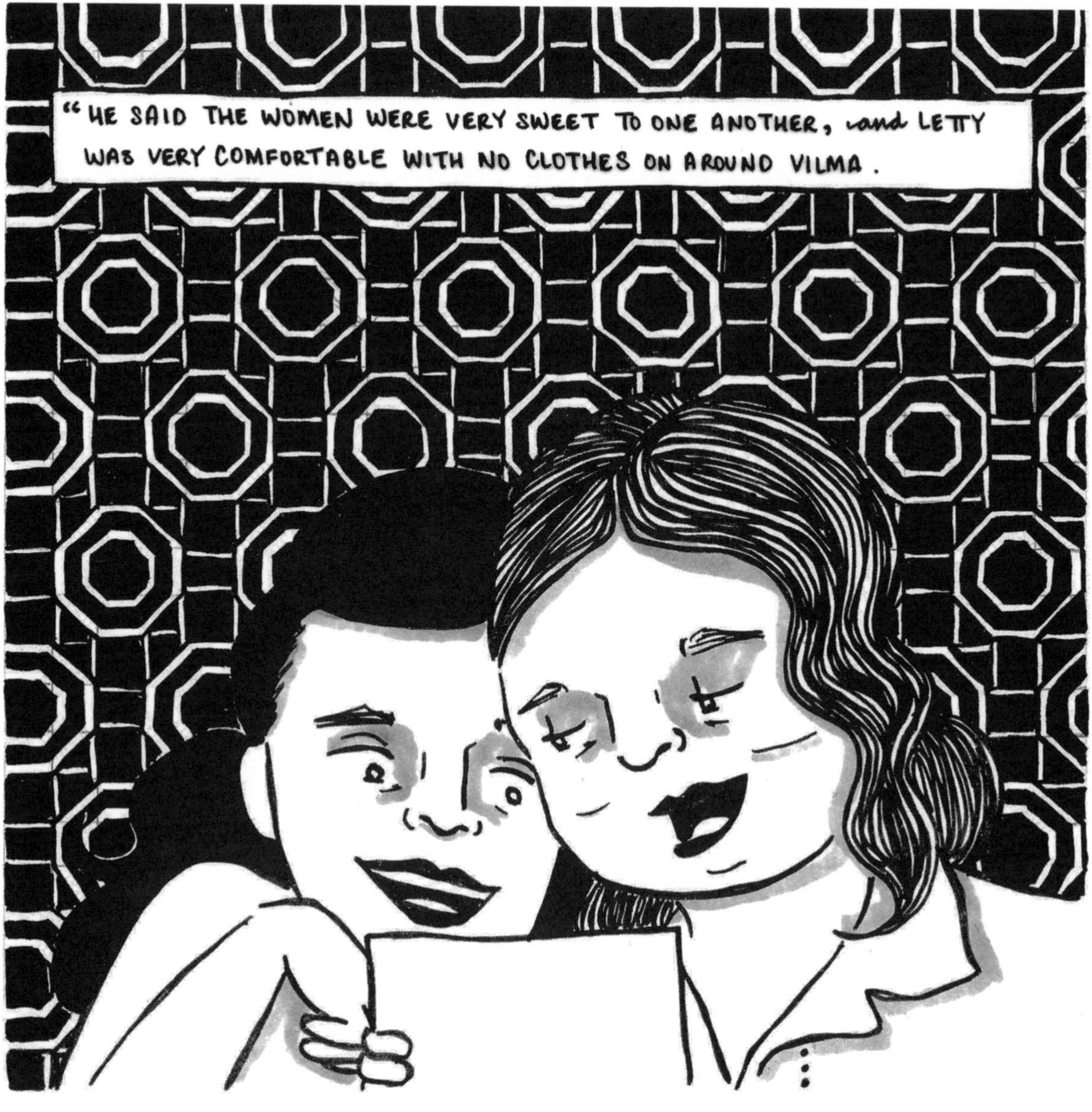
"HE SAID THE WOMEN WERE VERY SWEET TO ONE ANOTHER, and LETTY WAS VERY COMFORTABLE WITH NO CLOTHES ON AROUND VILMA.

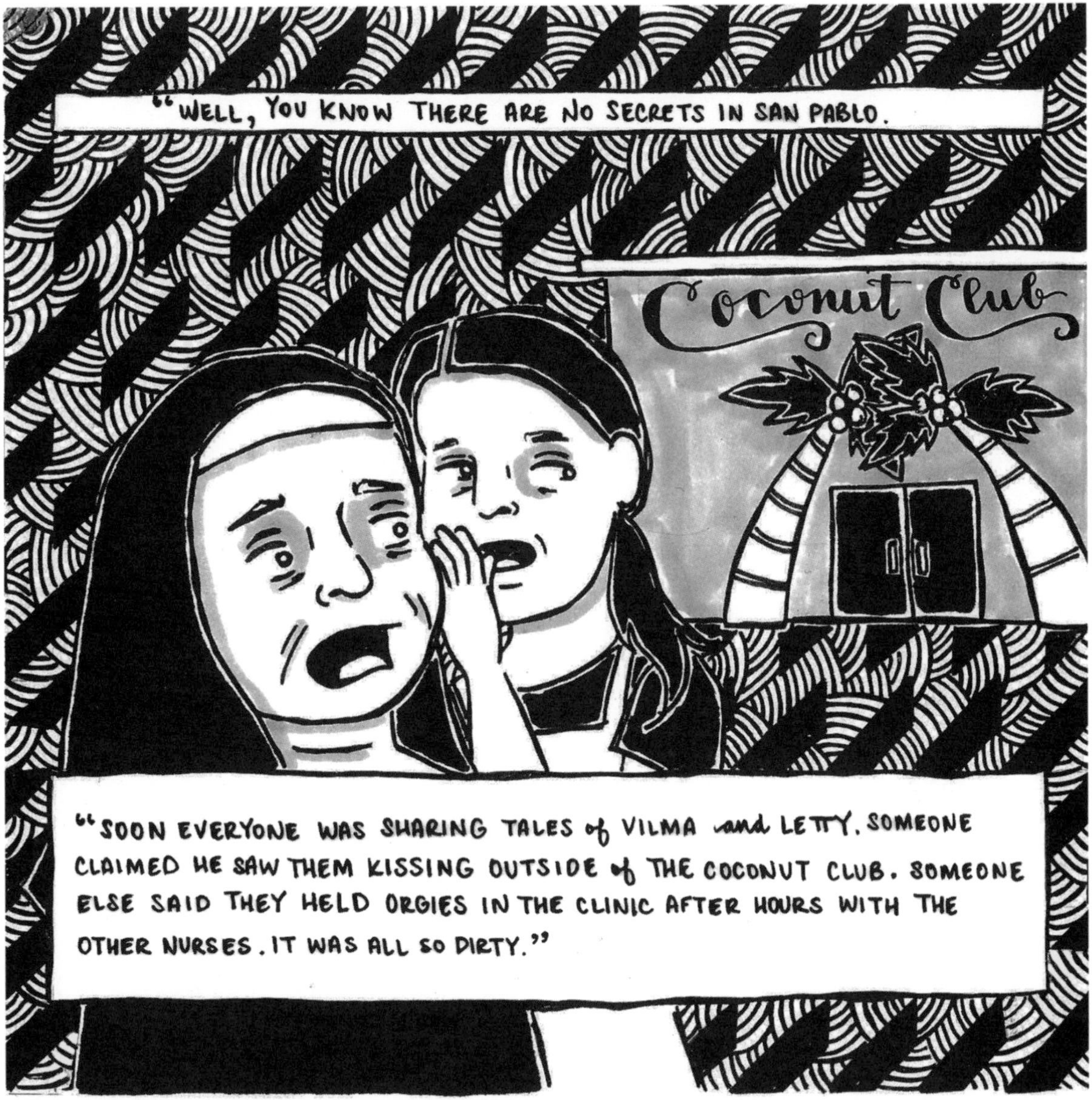
"WELL, YOU KNOW THERE ARE NO SECRETS IN SAN PABLO.
Coconut Club
"SOON EVERYONE WAS SHARING TALES of VILMA and LETTY. SOMEONE CLAIMED HE SAW THEM KISSING OUTSIDE of THE COCONUT CLUB. SOMEONE ELSE SAID THEY HELD ORGIES IN THE CLINIC AFTER HOURS WITH THE OTHER NURSES. IT WAS ALL SO DIRTY."

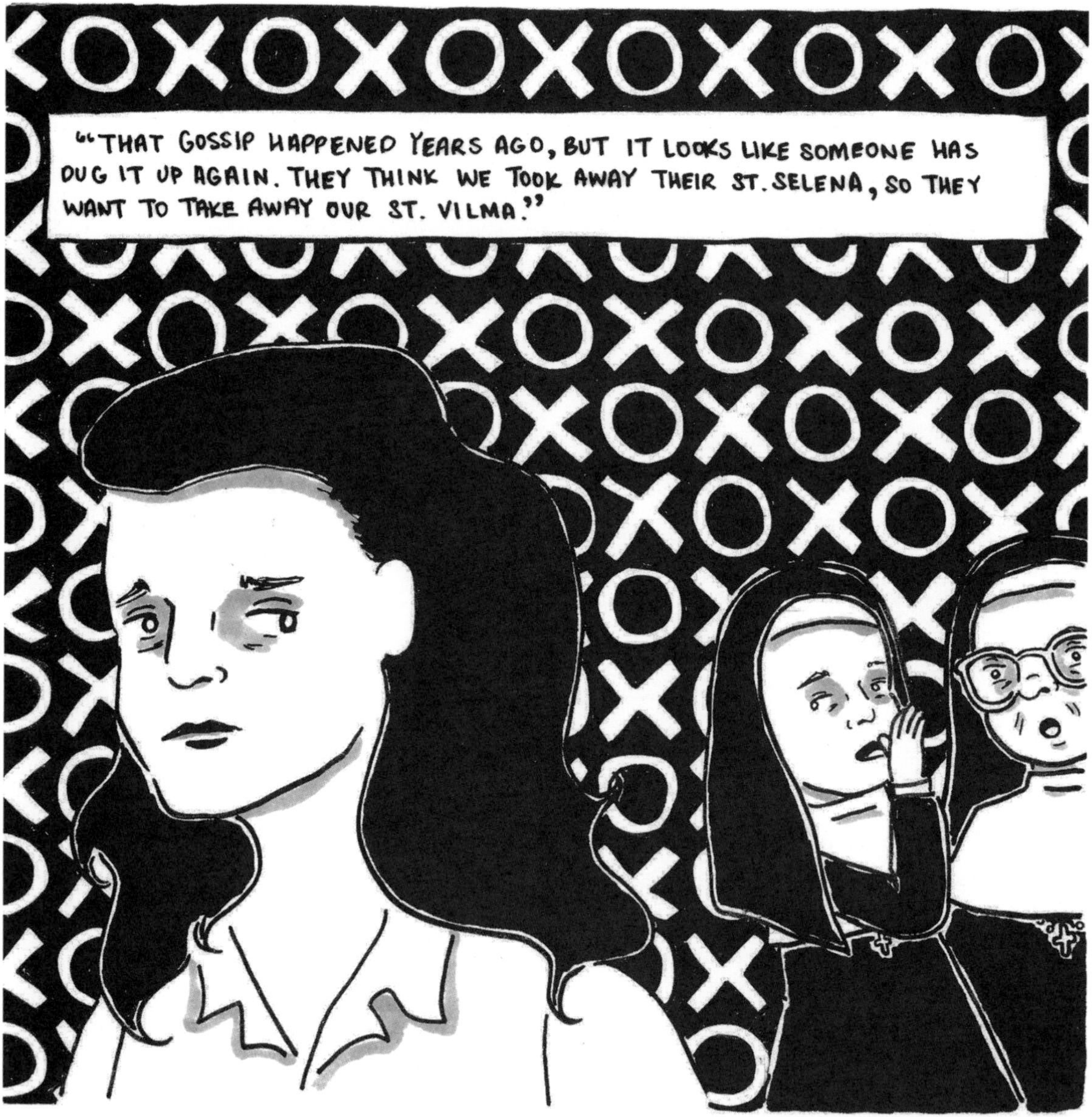
"THAT GOSSIP HAPPENED YEARS AGO, BUT IT LOOKS LIKE SOMEONE HAS DUG IT UP AGAIN. THEY THINK WE TOOK AWAY THEIR ST. SELENA, SO THEY WANT TO TAKE AWAY OUR ST. VILMA."

NENITA SHOOK HER HEAD IN DISGUST.
"SINFUL. SO SINFUL."
SHE PULLED A DURIAN OUT of HER BAG.

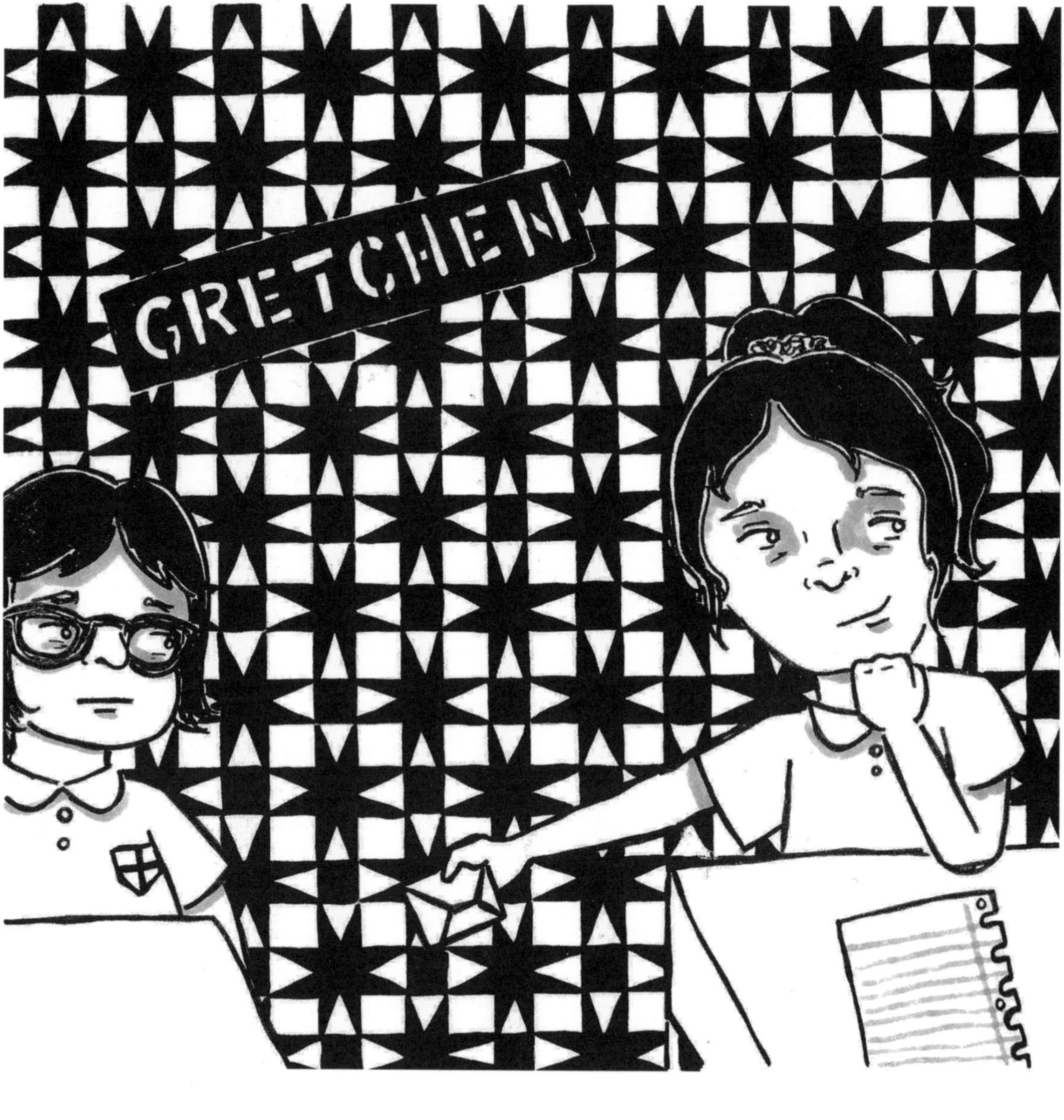
GRETCHEN

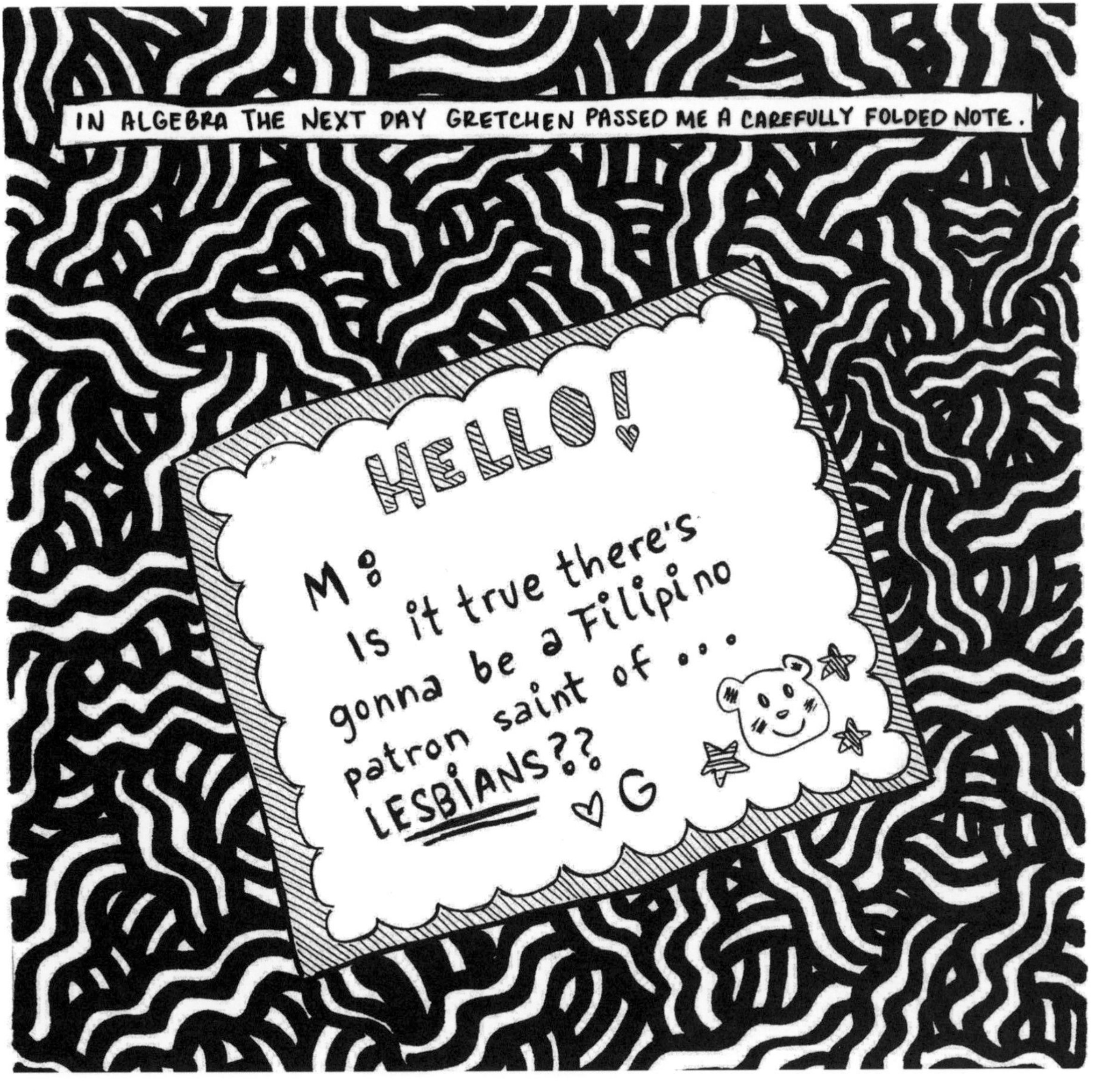
IN ALGEBRA THE NEXT DAY GRETCHEN PASSED ME A CAREFULLY FOLDED NOTE.
HELLO!
M:
Is it true there's gonna be a Filipino patron saint of ... LESBIANS??
♡ G

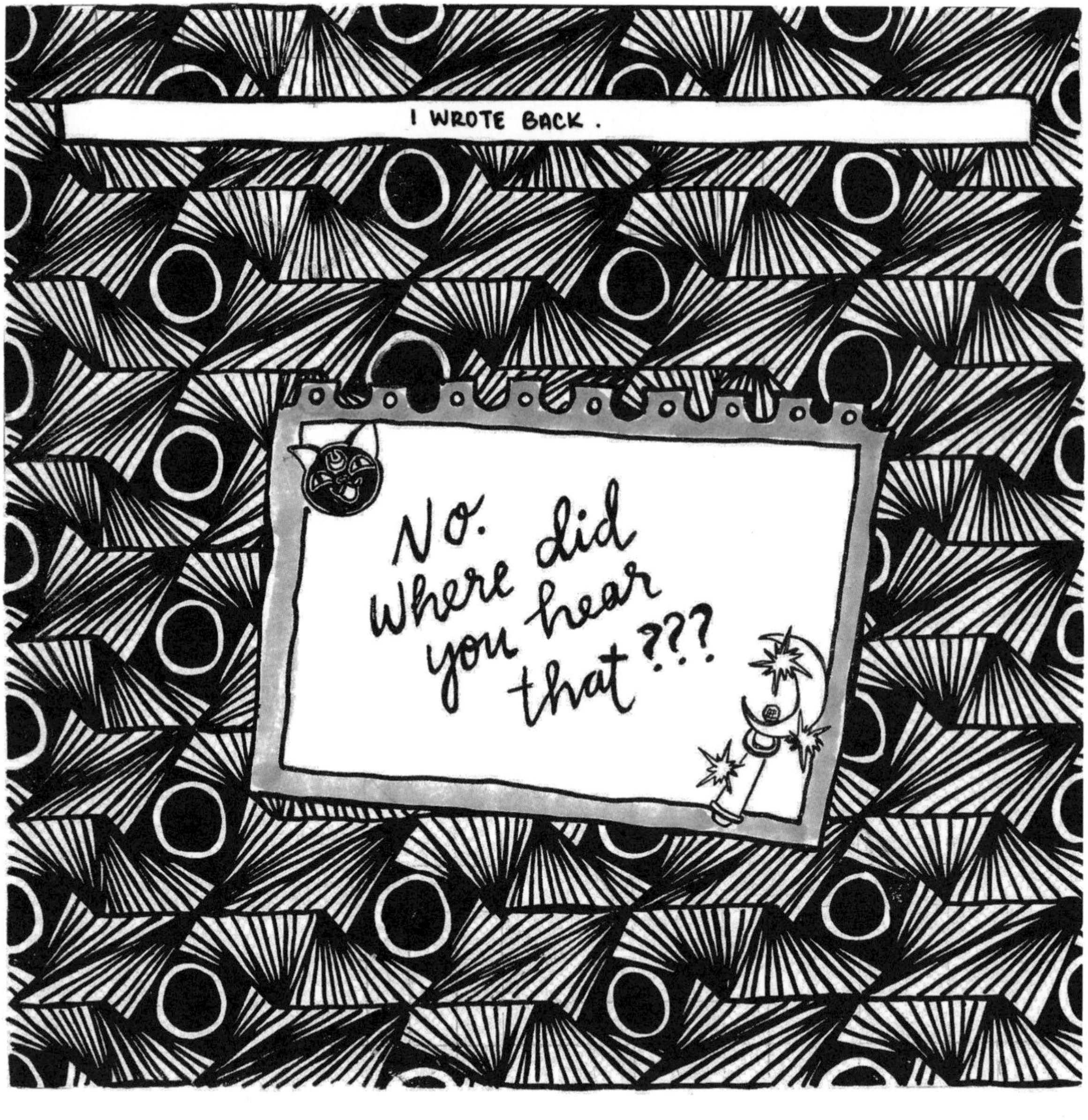
I WROTE BACK.
No. where did you hear that???

I PEERED BACK INTO MY TEXTBOOK, WHICH WAS PROPPED UP ON MY LAP, HIDING MY COPY of YOU ARE ALL SANPAKU. I WAS BRUSHING UP ON THE DIET CHAPTER IN PREPARATION FOR MY LESSON WITH KIP AFTER SCHOOL.

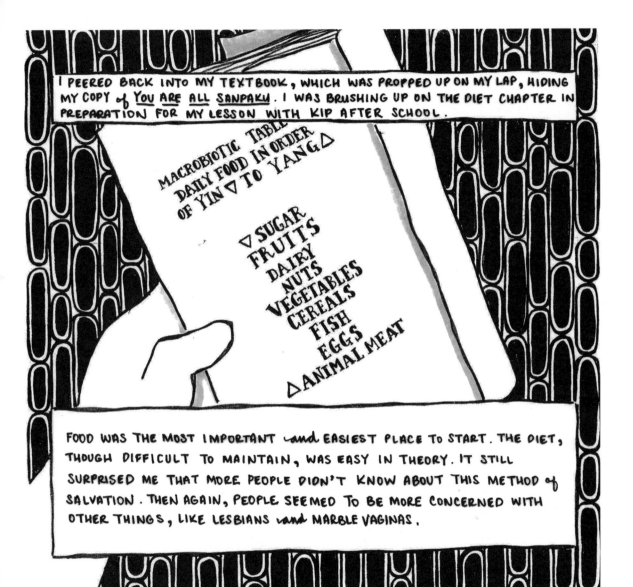

MACROBIOTIC TABLE
DAILY FOOD IN ORDER
OF YIN ▽ TO YANG △

▽ SUGAR
FRUITS
DAIRY
NUTS
VEGETABLES
CEREALS
FISH
EGGS
△ ANIMAL MEAT

FOOD WAS THE MOST IMPORTANT and EASIEST PLACE TO START. THE DIET, THOUGH DIFFICULT TO MAINTAIN, WAS EASY IN THEORY. IT STILL SURPRISED ME THAT MORE PEOPLE DIDN'T KNOW ABOUT THIS METHOD of SALVATION. THEN AGAIN, PEOPLE SEEMED TO BE MORE CONCERNED WITH OTHER THINGS, LIKE LESBIANS and MARBLE VAGINAS.

GRETCHEN'S REPLY SLID UNDER MY ELBOW.
HELLO!
Bishop Fiorenza came to our house last night for dinner. He said she even had a LOVER!!!
HELLO!
Didn't your grandma pray to her or something? That's gross!!!

It's just a rumor spread by the people who were mad about Selena being a Jehovah's Witness!
HELLO!
Selena being a JW turned out to be totally true tho! I've seen photos of this Velma lady too...
HELLO!
She was DEF a lesbian. They all dress like boys and they're always staring at girls.
HELLO!
Remember Lydia from 2nd grade? TOTAL LESBO, She tried to hold my hand during square dancing ALL THE TIME!!

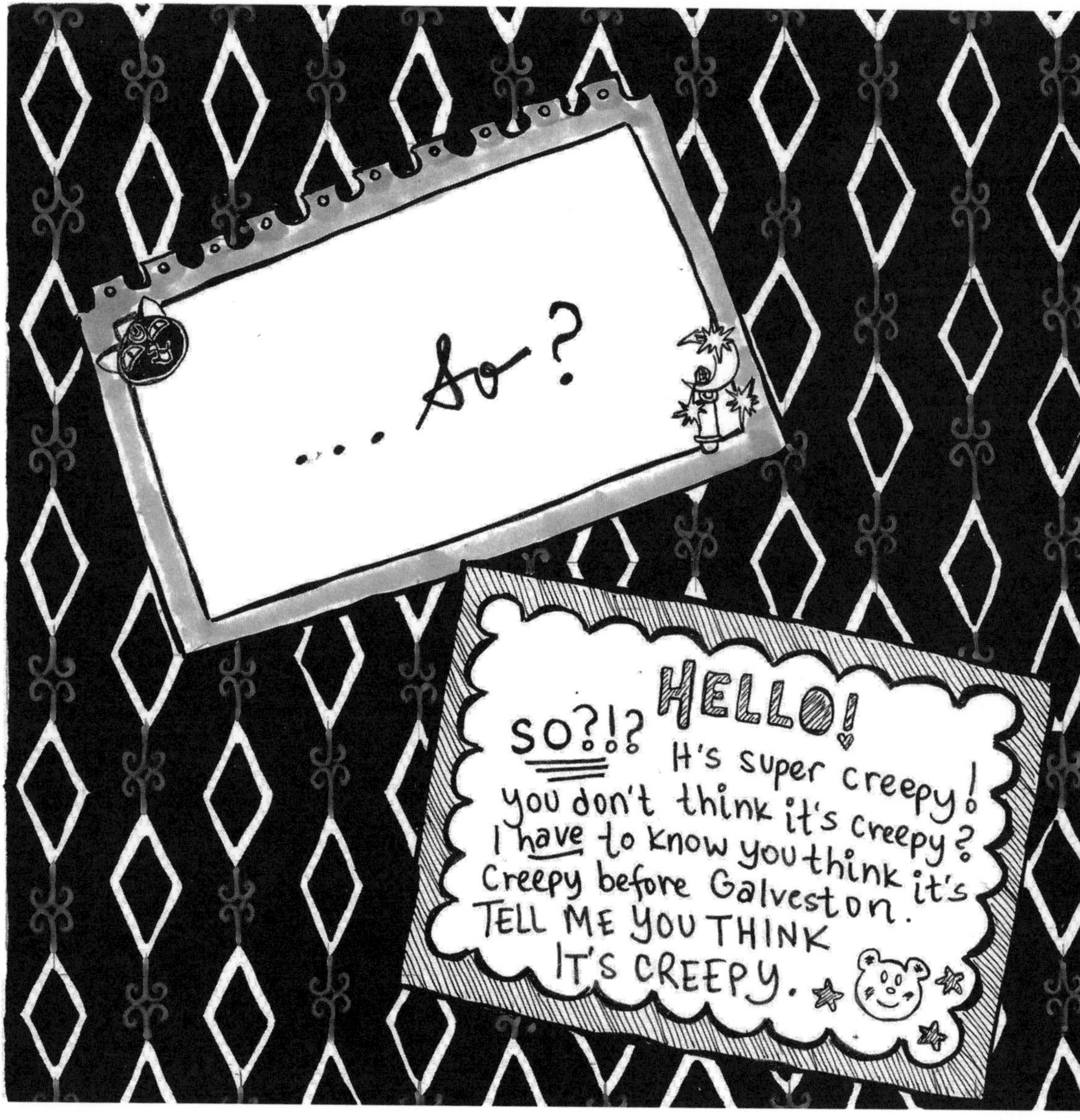
. . . So?
HELLO!
SO?!? It's super creepy!
you don't think it's creepy?
I have to know you think it's
creepy before Galveston.
TELL ME YOU THINK
IT'S CREEPY.

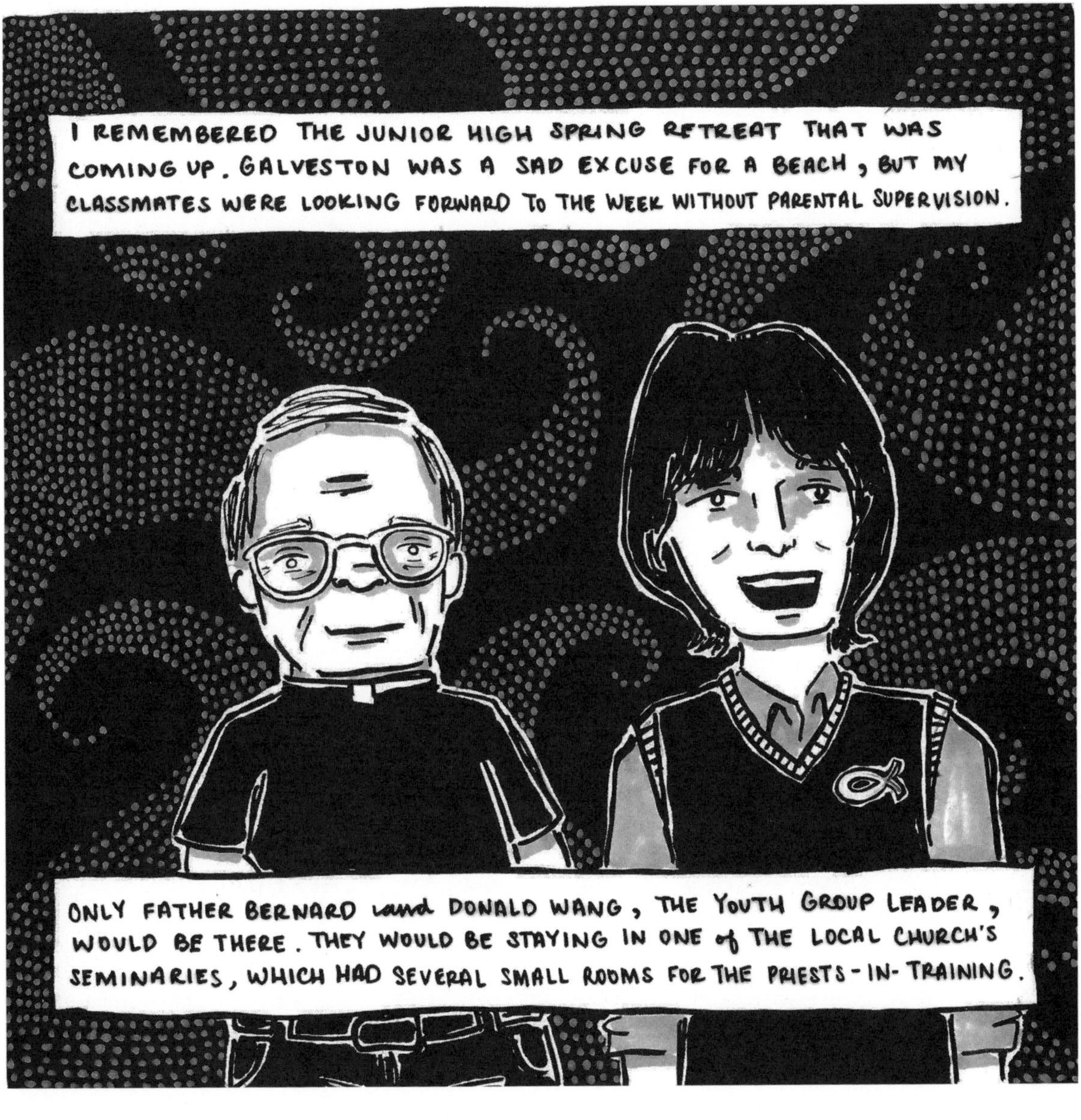
I REMEMBERED THE JUNIOR HIGH SPRING RETREAT THAT WAS COMING UP. GALVESTON WAS A SAD EXCUSE FOR A BEACH, BUT MY CLASSMATES WERE LOOKING FORWARD TO THE WEEK WITHOUT PARENTAL SUPERVISION.
ONLY FATHER BERNARD and DONALD WANG, THE YOUTH GROUP LEADER, WOULD BE THERE. THEY WOULD BE STAYING IN ONE of THE LOCAL CHURCH'S SEMINARIES, WHICH HAD SEVERAL SMALL ROOMS FOR THE PRIESTS-IN-TRAINING.

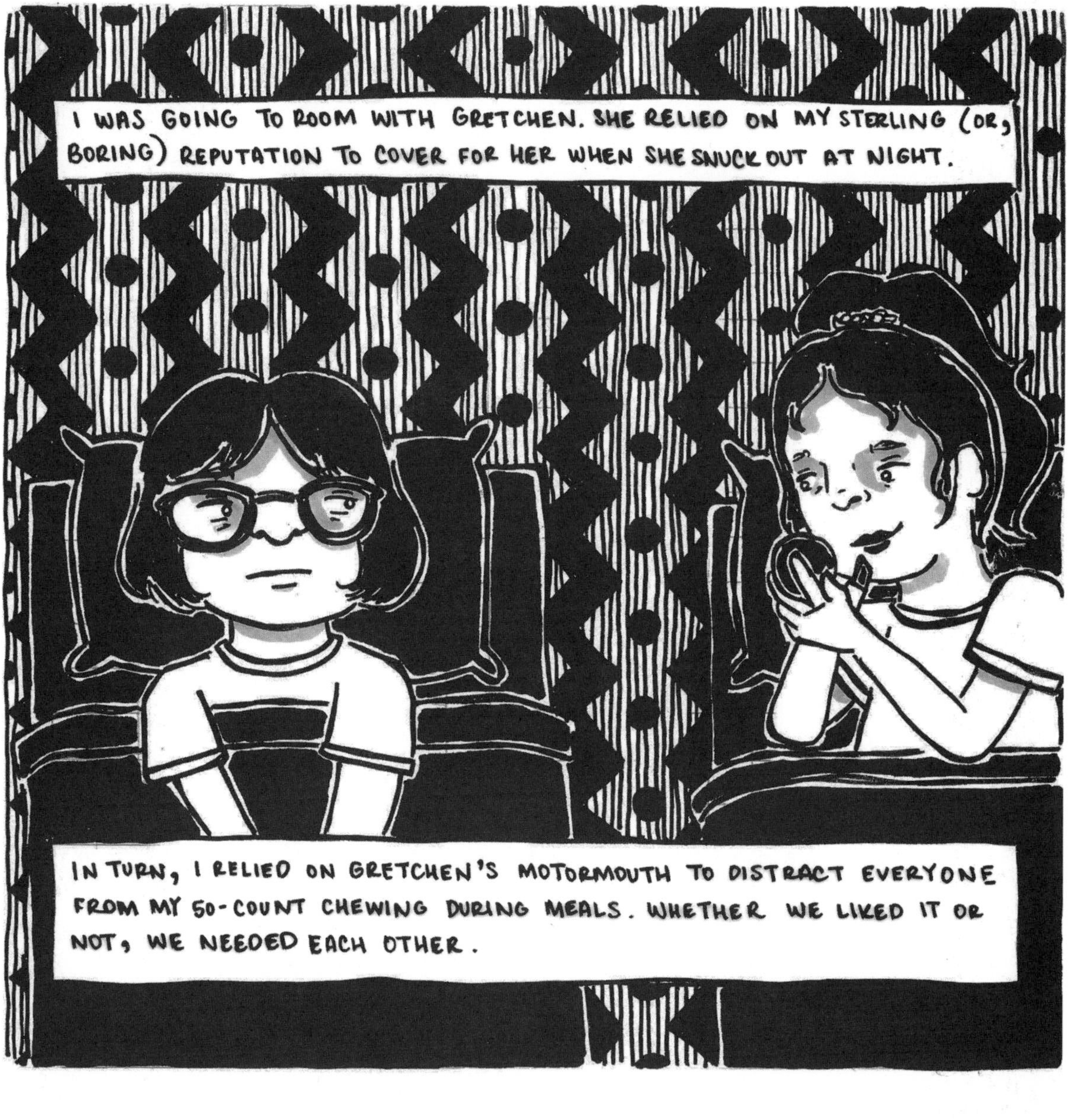
I WAS GOING TO ROOM WITH GRETCHEN. SHE RELIED ON MY STERLING (OR, BORING) REPUTATION TO COVER FOR HER WHEN SHE SNUCK OUT AT NIGHT.
IN TURN, I RELIED ON GRETCHEN'S MOTORMOUTH TO DISTRACT EVERYONE FROM MY 50-COUNT CHEWING DURING MEALS. WHETHER WE LIKED IT OR NOT, WE NEEDED EACH OTHER.

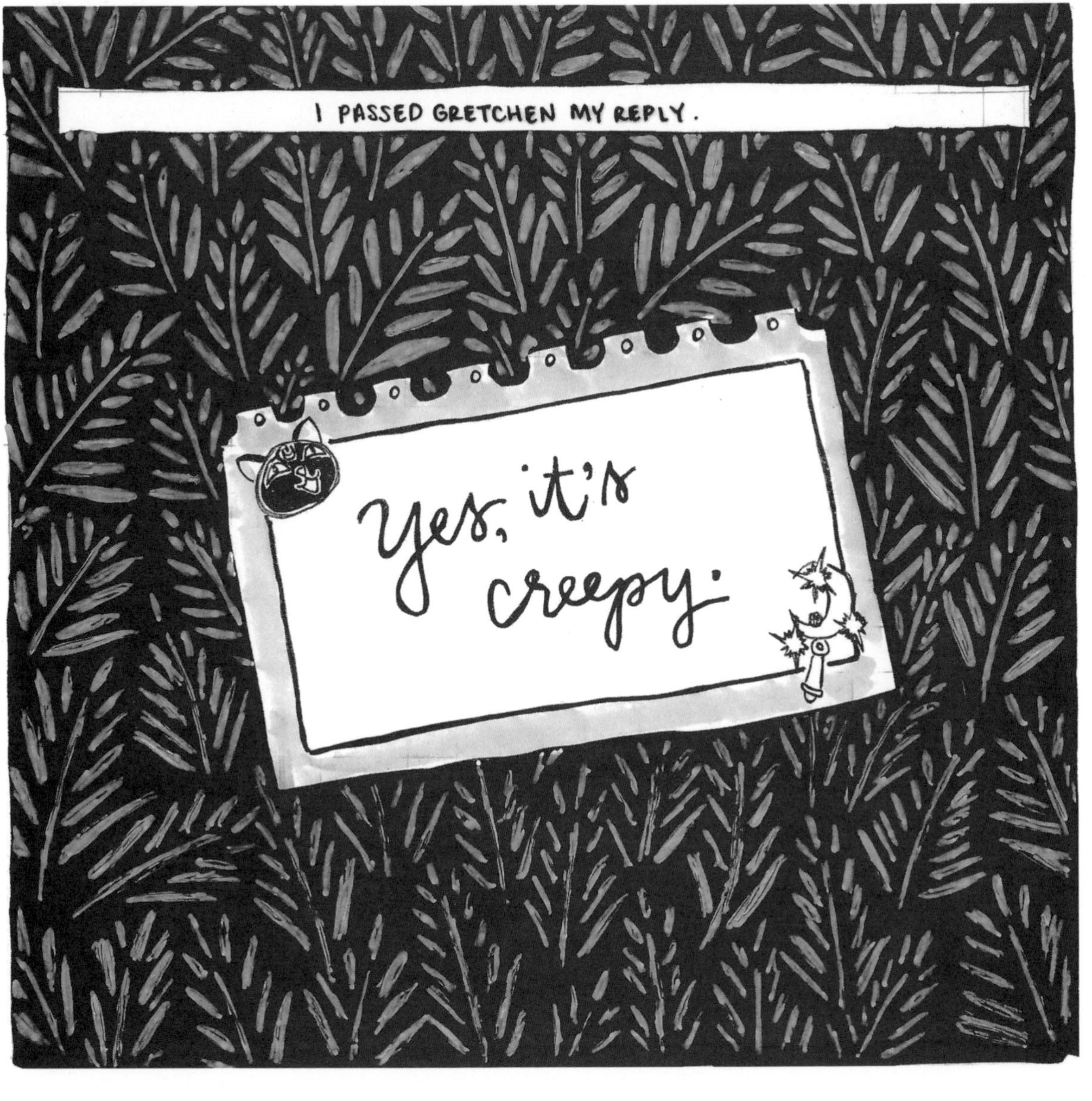
I PASSED GRETCHEN MY REPLY.
Yes, it's creepy.

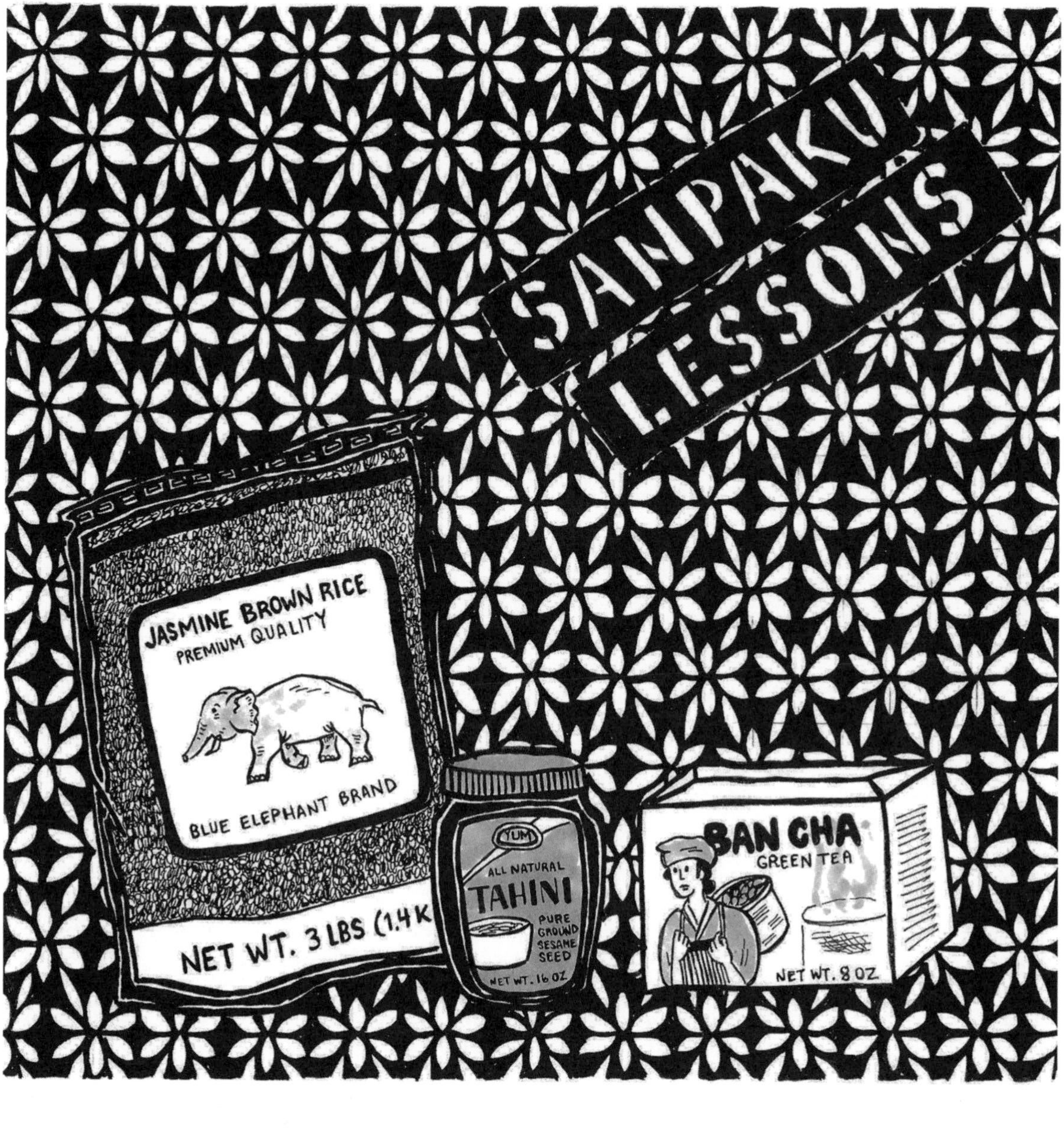
SANPAKU
LESSONS
JASMINE BROWN RICE
PREMIUM QUALITY
BLUE ELEPHANT BRAND
NET WT. 3 LBS (1.4 K
YUM
ALL NATURAL
TAHINI
PURE GROUND SESAME SEED
NET WT. 16 OZ
BAN CHA
GREEN TEA
NET WT. 8 OZ

THE NEXT DAY I RETURNED TO VIET HOA FOR KIP'S FIRST LESSON.
"OKAY, GET RID of MY SANPAKU."
I GAVE KIP A LIBRARY COPY of YOU ARE ALL SANPAKU.

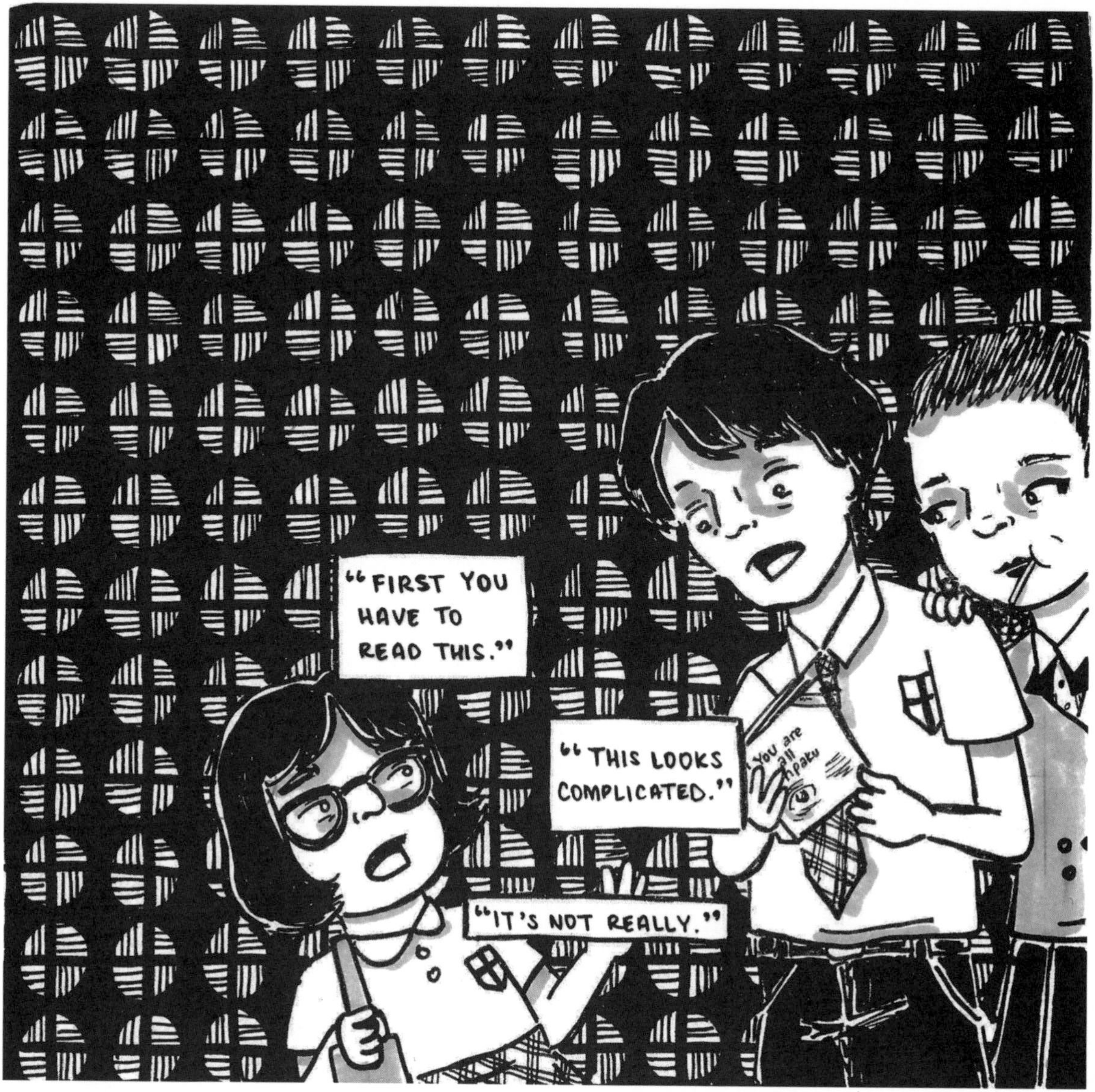
"FIRST YOU HAVE TO READ THIS."
"THIS LOOKS COMPLICATED."
"IT'S NOT REALLY."
You are all

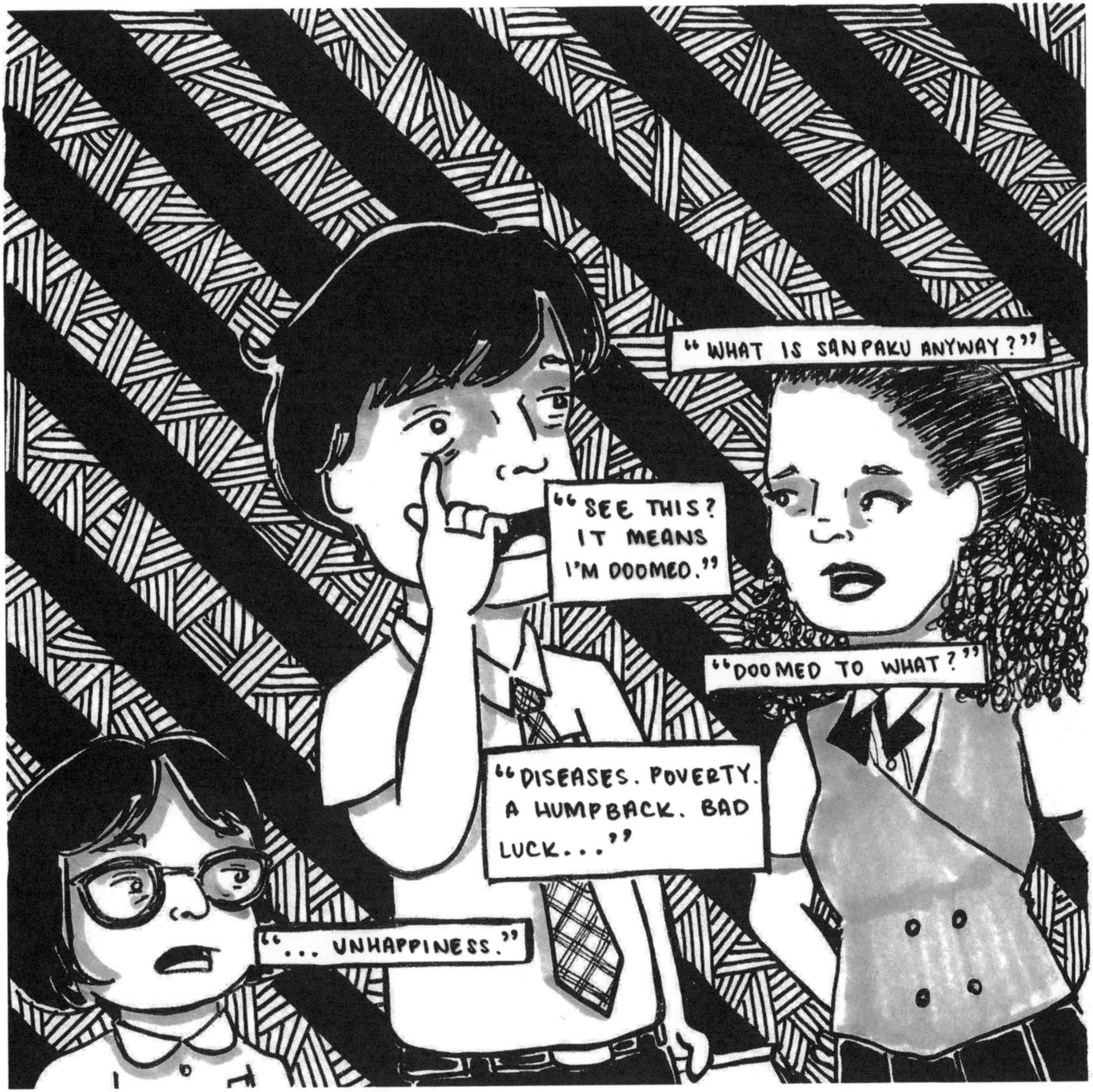
"WHAT IS SANPAKU ANYWAY?"
"SEE THIS? IT MEANS I'M DOOMED."
"DOOMED TO WHAT?"
"DISEASES. POVERTY. A HUMPBACK. BAD LUCK..."
"... UNHAPPINESS."

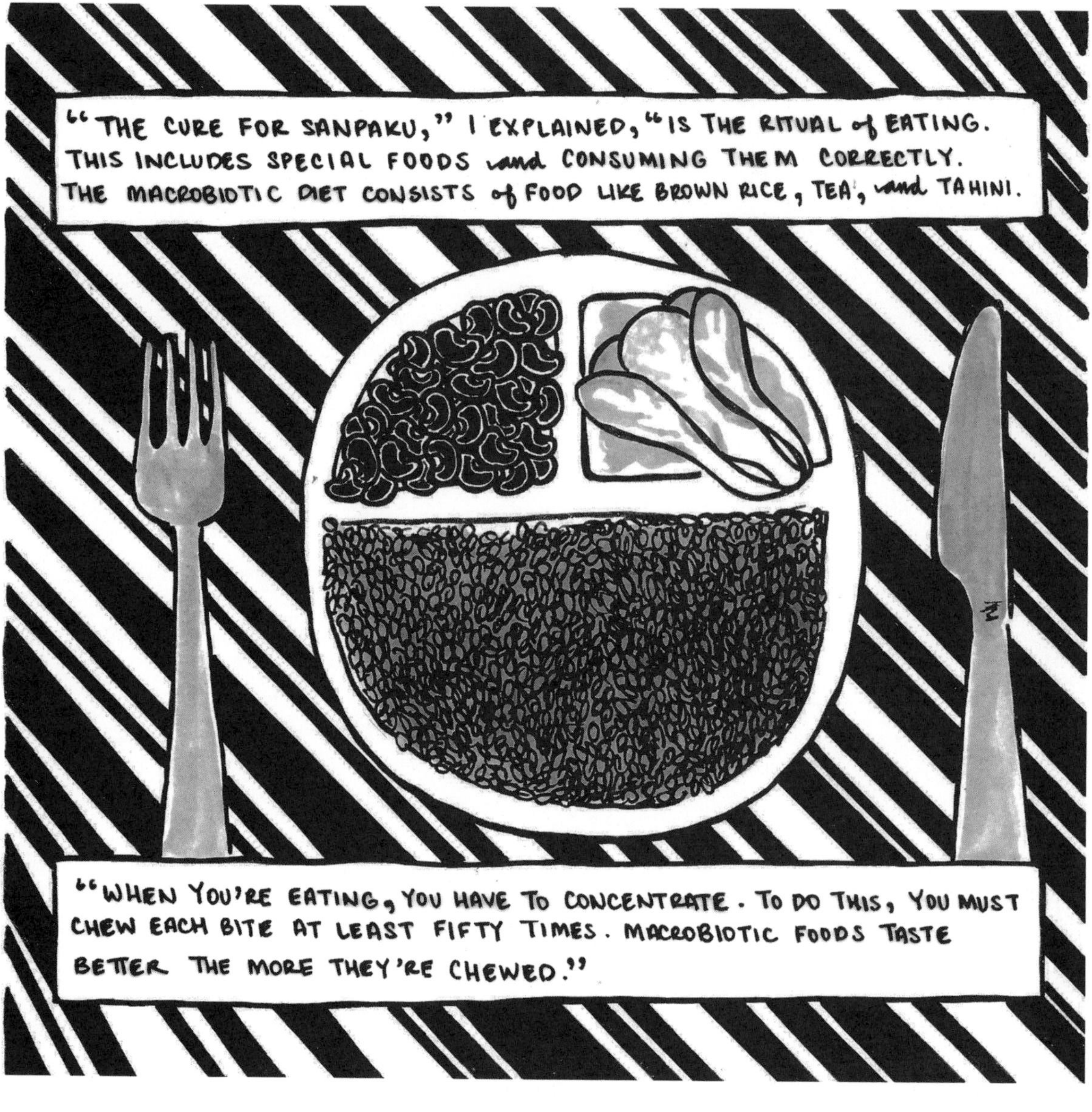
"THE CURE FOR SANPAKU," I EXPLAINED, "IS THE RITUAL of EATING. THIS INCLUDES SPECIAL FOODS and CONSUMING THEM CORRECTLY. THE MACROBIOTIC DIET CONSISTS of FOOD LIKE BROWN RICE, TEA, and TAHINI.
"WHEN YOU'RE EATING, YOU HAVE TO CONCENTRATE. TO DO THIS, YOU MUST CHEW EACH BITE AT LEAST FIFTY TIMES. MACROBIOTIC FOODS TASTE BETTER THE MORE THEY'RE CHEWED."

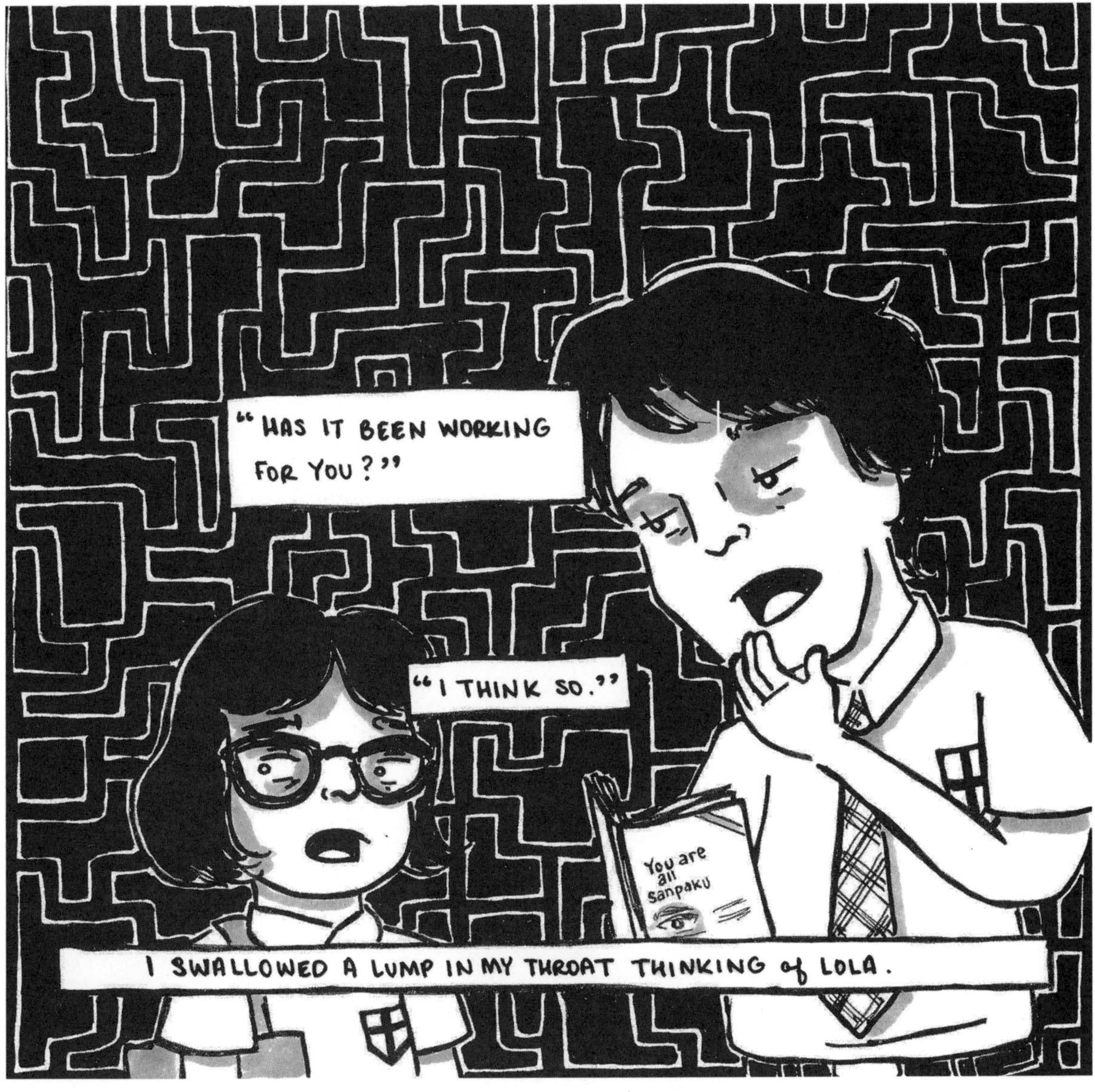
"HAS IT BEEN WORKING FOR YOU?"
"I THINK SO."
You are all Sanpaku
I SWALLOWED A LUMP IN MY THROAT THINKING of LOLA.

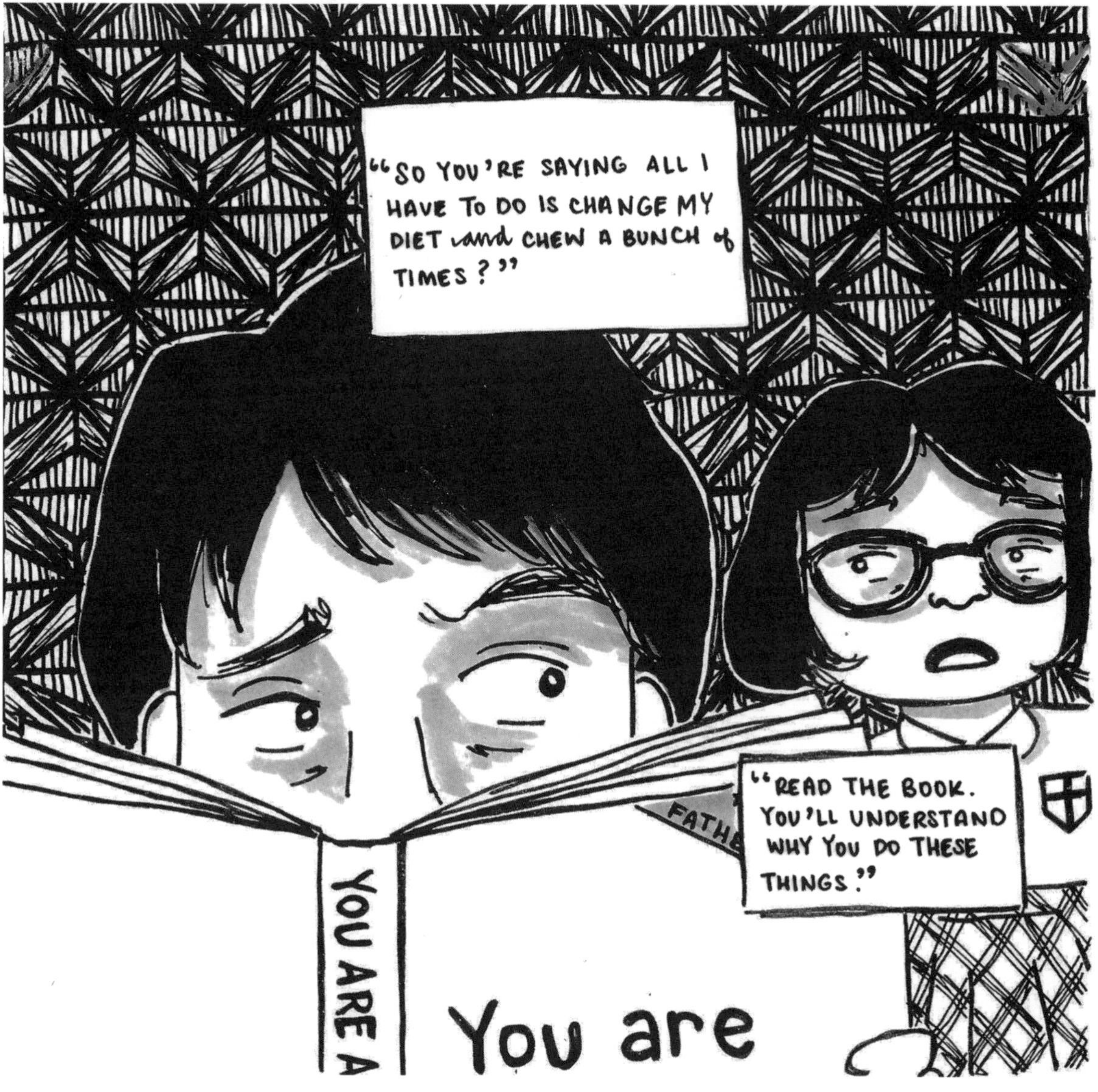
"SO YOU'RE SAYING ALL I HAVE TO DO IS CHANGE MY DIET and CHEW A BUNCH of TIMES?"
"READ THE BOOK. YOU'LL UNDERSTAND WHY YOU DO THESE THINGS."
FATHE
YOU ARE A
You are

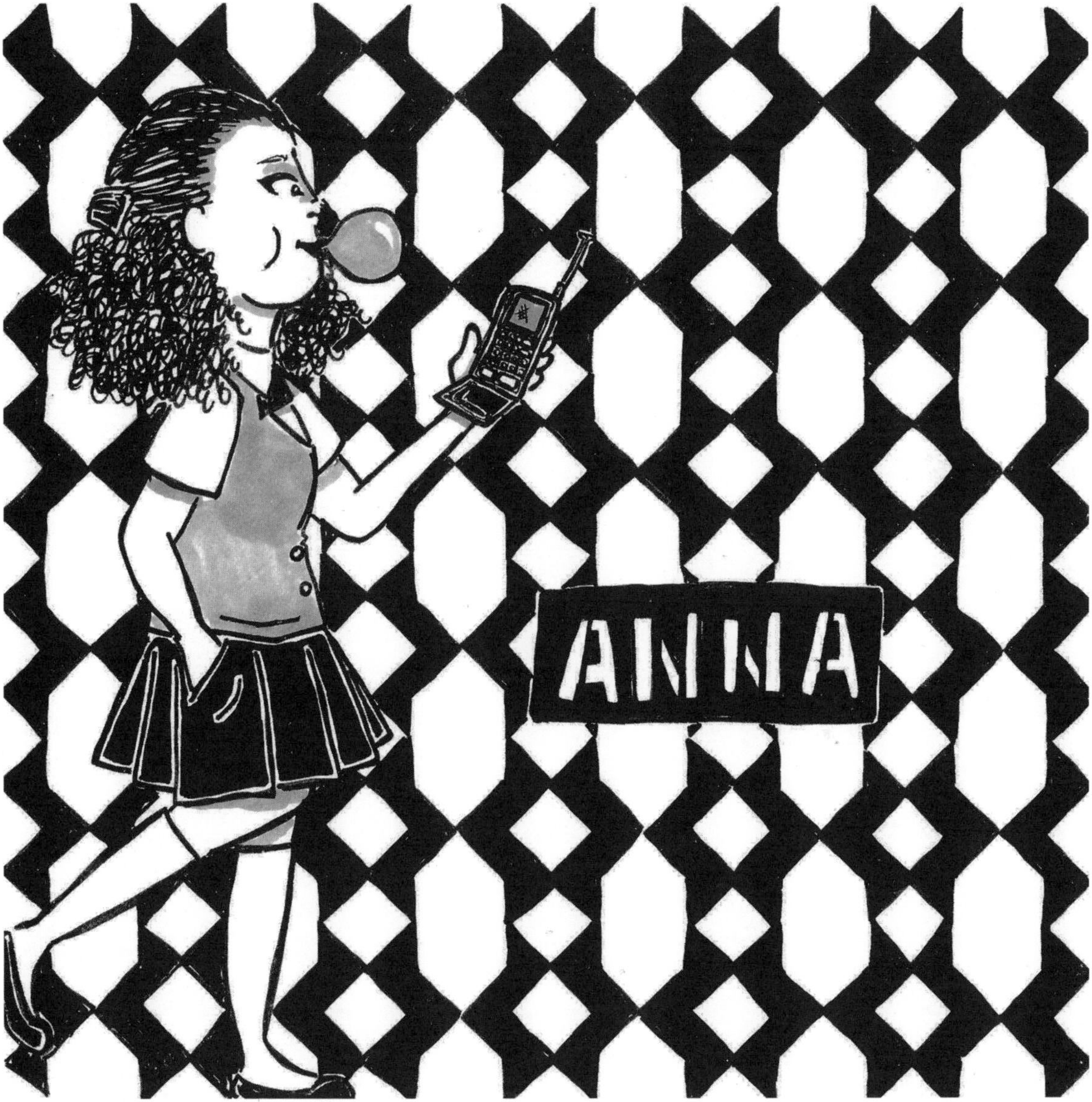
ANNA

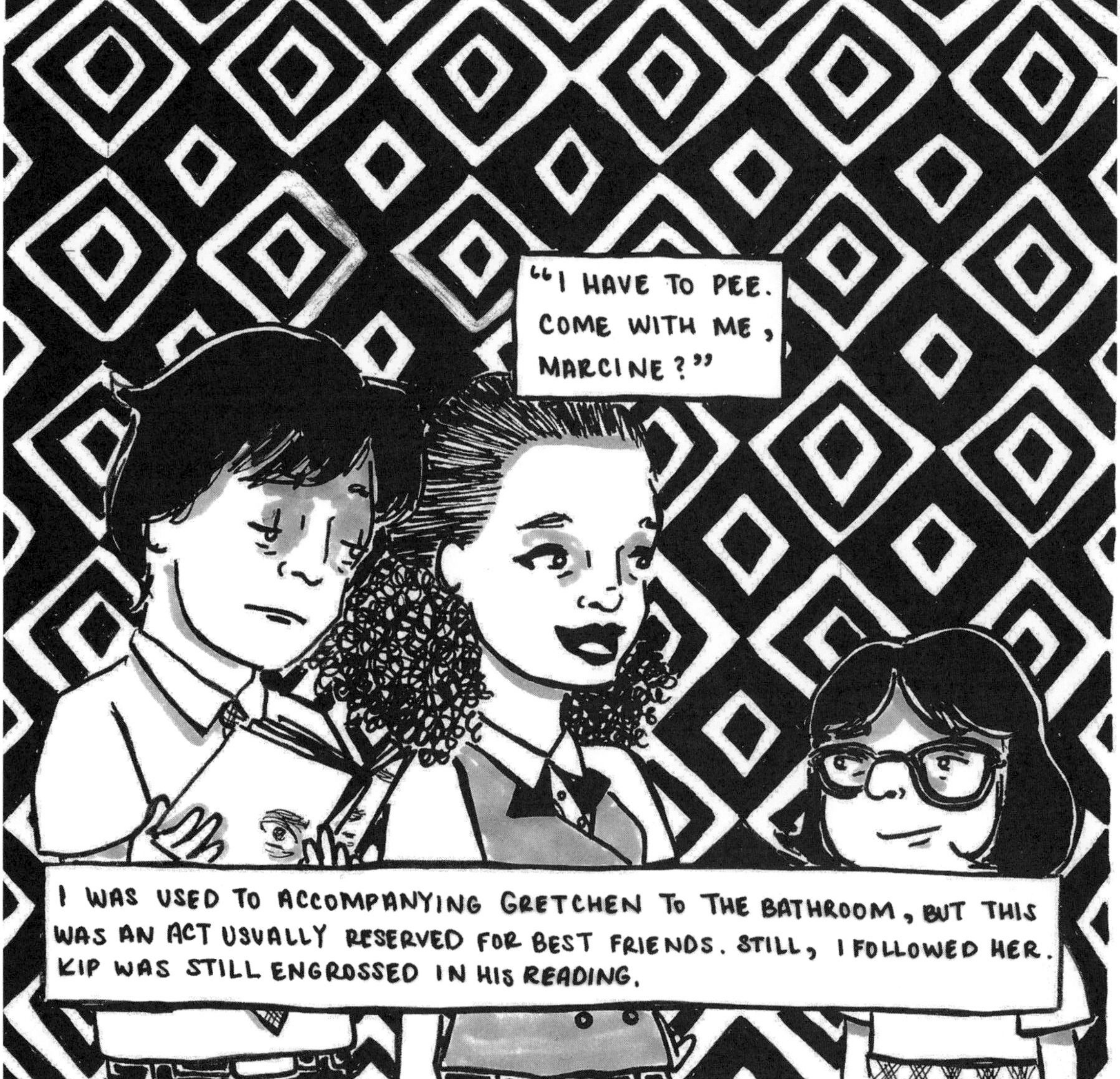
"I HAVE TO PEE. COME WITH ME, MARCINE?"
I WAS USED TO ACCOMPANYING GRETCHEN TO THE BATHROOM, BUT THIS WAS AN ACT USUALLY RESERVED FOR BEST FRIENDS. STILL, I FOLLOWED HER. KIP WAS STILL ENGROSSED IN HIS READING.

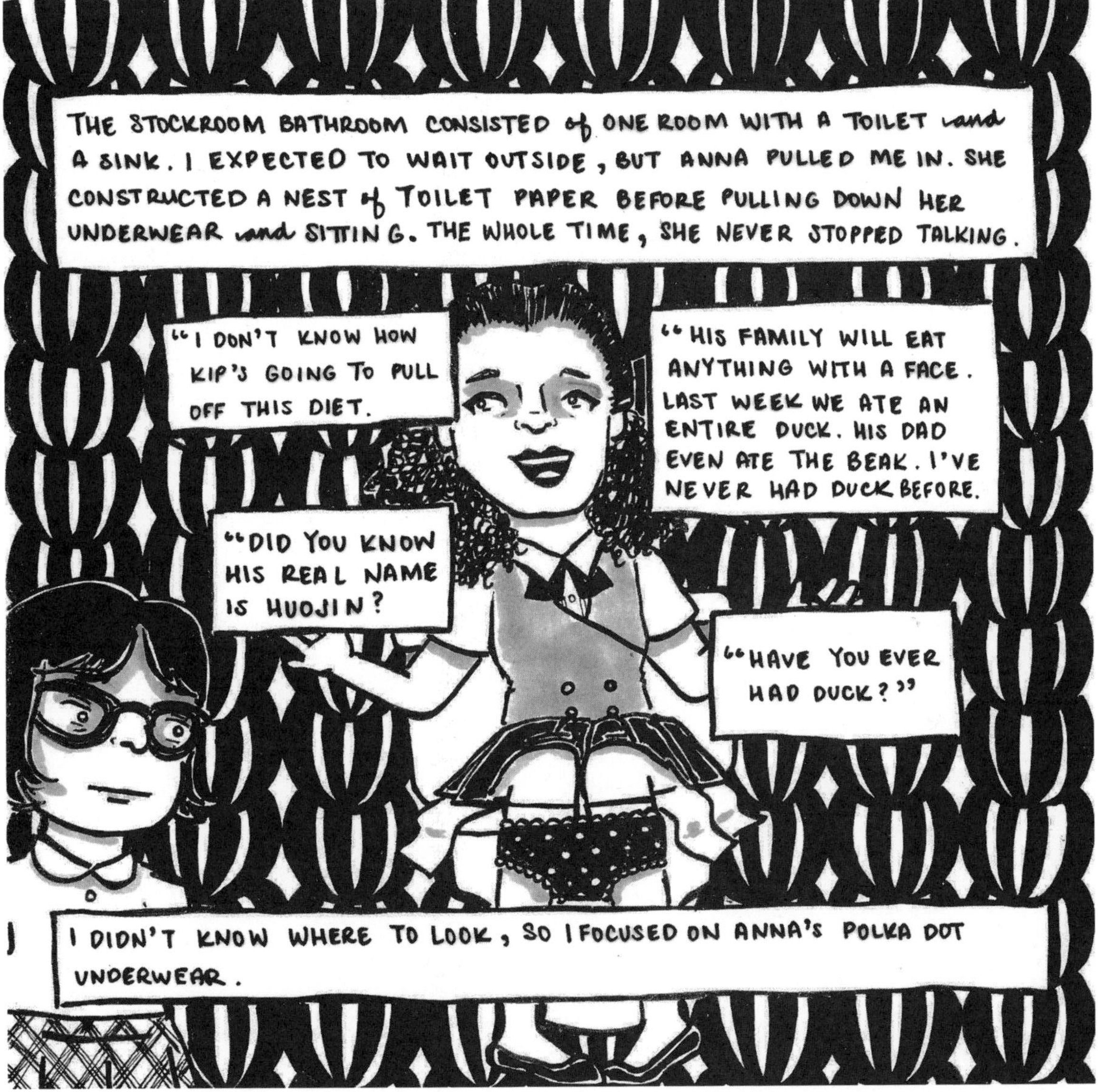
THE STOCKROOM BATHROOM CONSISTED of ONE ROOM WITH A TOILET and A SINK. I EXPECTED TO WAIT OUTSIDE, BUT ANNA PULLED ME IN. SHE CONSTRUCTED A NEST of TOILET PAPER BEFORE PULLING DOWN HER UNDERWEAR and SITTING. THE WHOLE TIME, SHE NEVER STOPPED TALKING.
"I DON'T KNOW HOW KIP'S GOING TO PULL OFF THIS DIET.
"HIS FAMILY WILL EAT ANYTHING WITH A FACE. LAST WEEK WE ATE AN ENTIRE DUCK. HIS DAD EVEN ATE THE BEAK. I'VE NEVER HAD DUCK BEFORE.
"DID YOU KNOW HIS REAL NAME IS HUOJIN?
"HAVE YOU EVER HAD DUCK?"
I DIDN'T KNOW WHERE TO LOOK, SO I FOCUSED ON ANNA'S POLKA DOT UNDERWEAR.

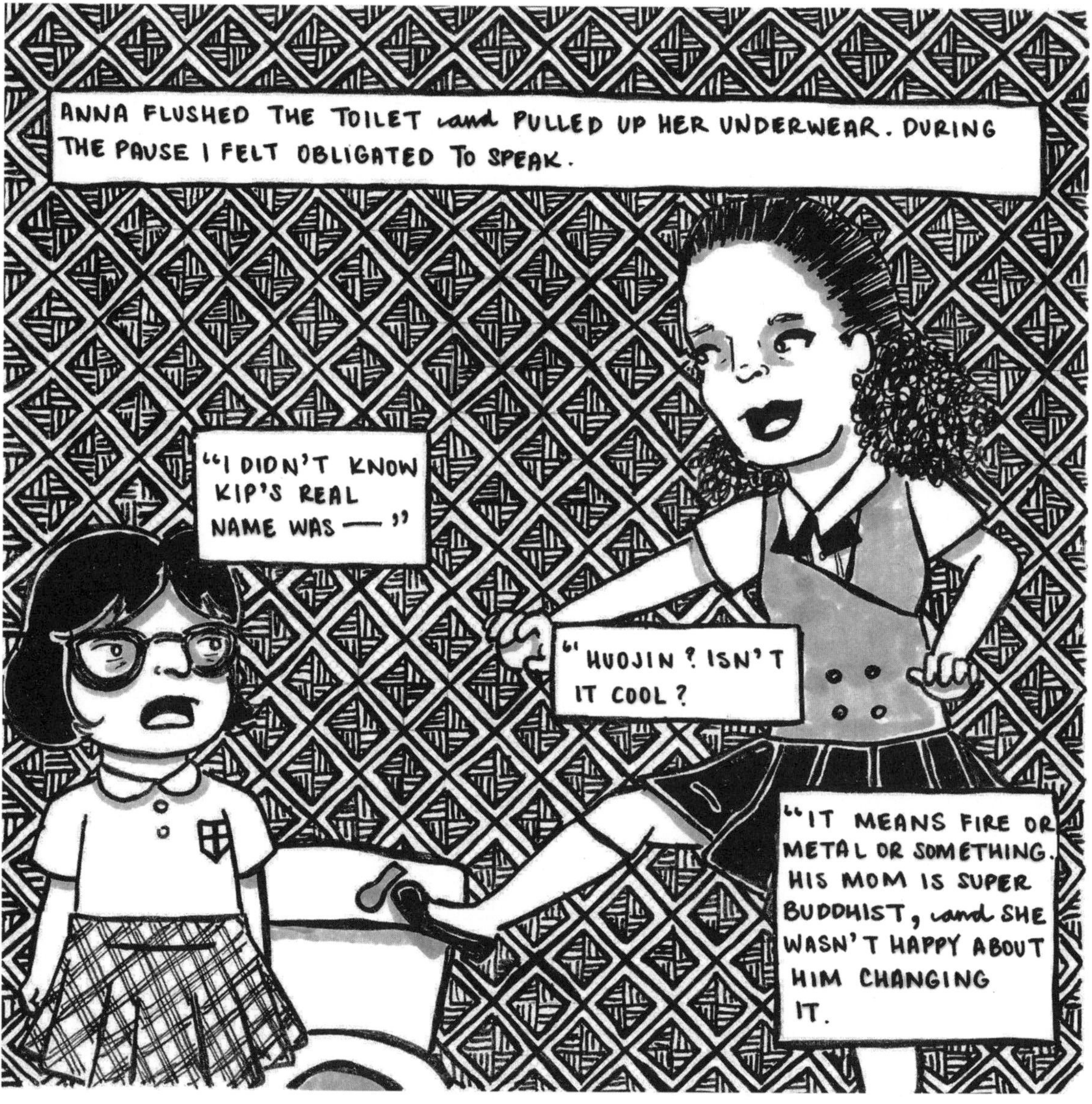
ANNA FLUSHED THE TOILET and PULLED UP HER UNDERWEAR. DURING THE PAUSE I FELT OBLIGATED TO SPEAK.
"I DIDN'T KNOW KIP'S REAL NAME WAS—"
"HUOJIN? ISN'T IT COOL?
"IT MEANS FIRE OR METAL OR SOMETHING. HIS MOM IS SUPER BUDDHIST, and SHE WASN'T HAPPY ABOUT HIM CHANGING IT.

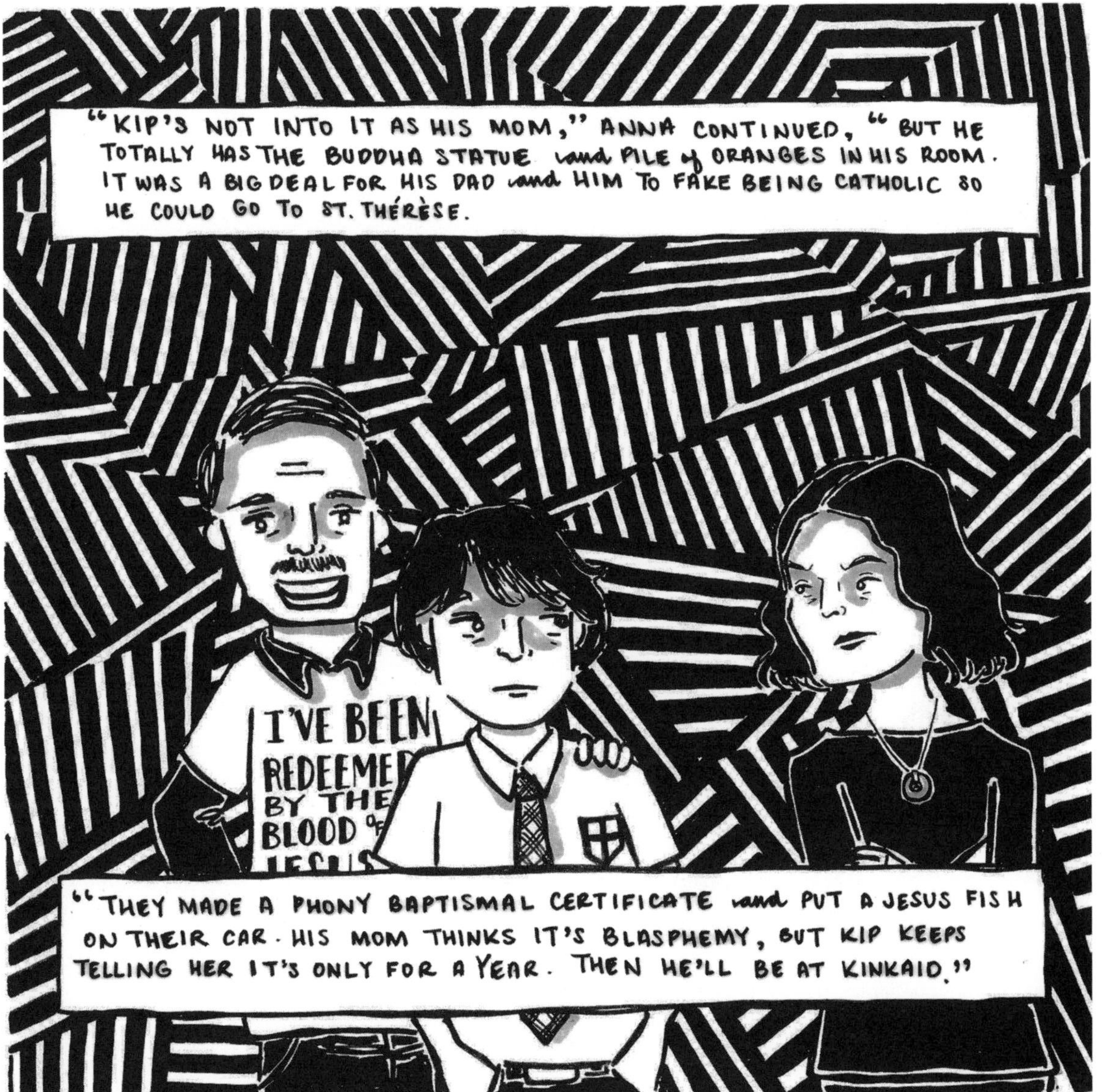
"KIP'S NOT INTO IT AS HIS MOM," ANNA CONTINUED, "BUT HE TOTALLY HAS THE BUDDHA STATUE and PILE of ORANGES IN HIS ROOM. IT WAS A BIG DEAL FOR HIS DAD and HIM TO FAKE BEING CATHOLIC SO HE COULD GO TO ST. THÉRÈSE.
I'VE BEEN REDEEMED BY THE BLOOD of JESUS
"THEY MADE A PHONY BAPTISMAL CERTIFICATE and PUT A JESUS FISH ON THEIR CAR. HIS MOM THINKS IT'S BLASPHEMY, BUT KIP KEEPS TELLING HER IT'S ONLY FOR A YEAR. THEN HE'LL BE AT KINKAID."

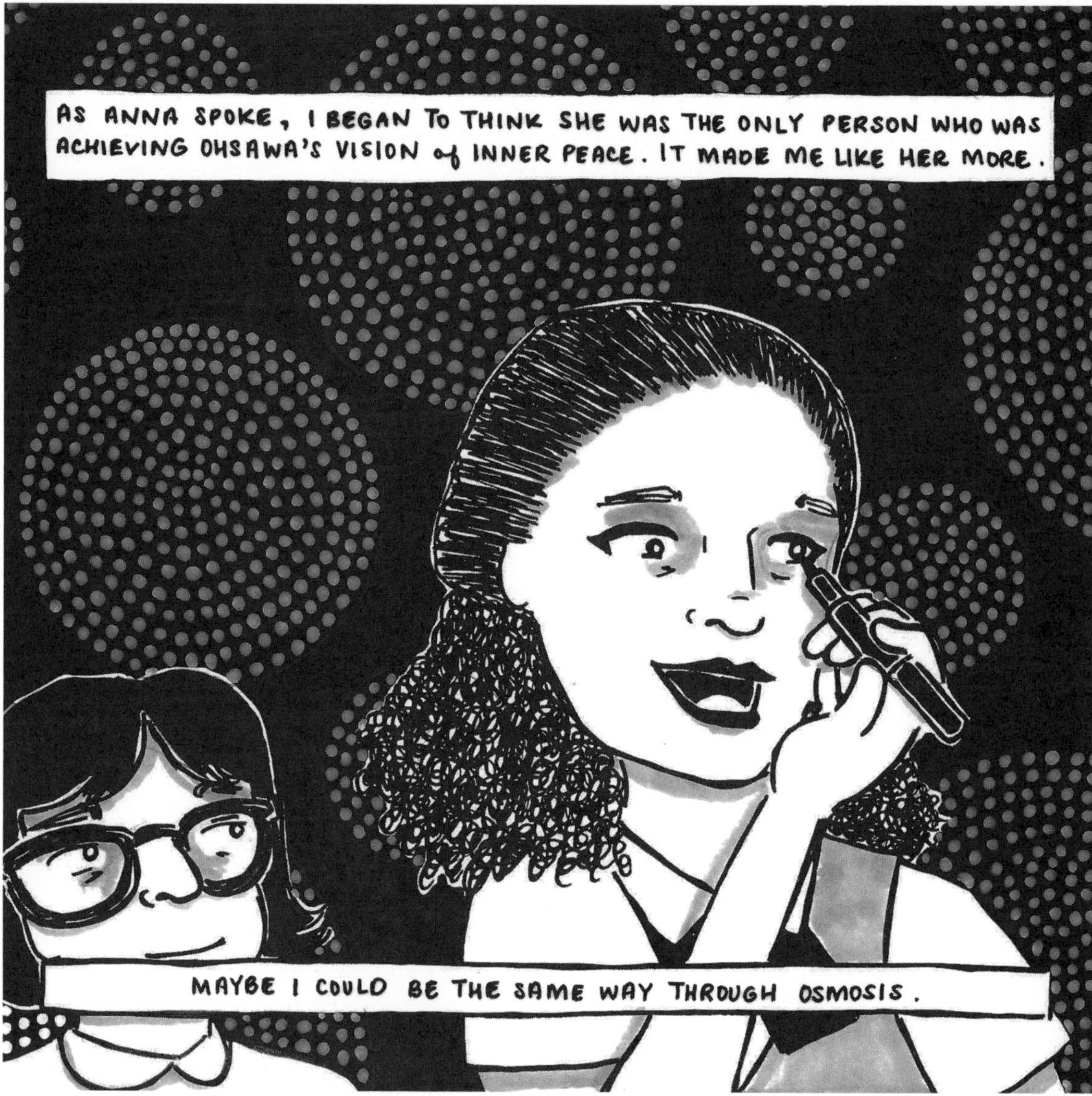
AS ANNA SPOKE, I BEGAN TO THINK SHE WAS THE ONLY PERSON WHO WAS ACHIEVING OHSAWA'S VISION of INNER PEACE. IT MADE ME LIKE HER MORE.
MAYBE I COULD BE THE SAME WAY THROUGH OSMOSIS.

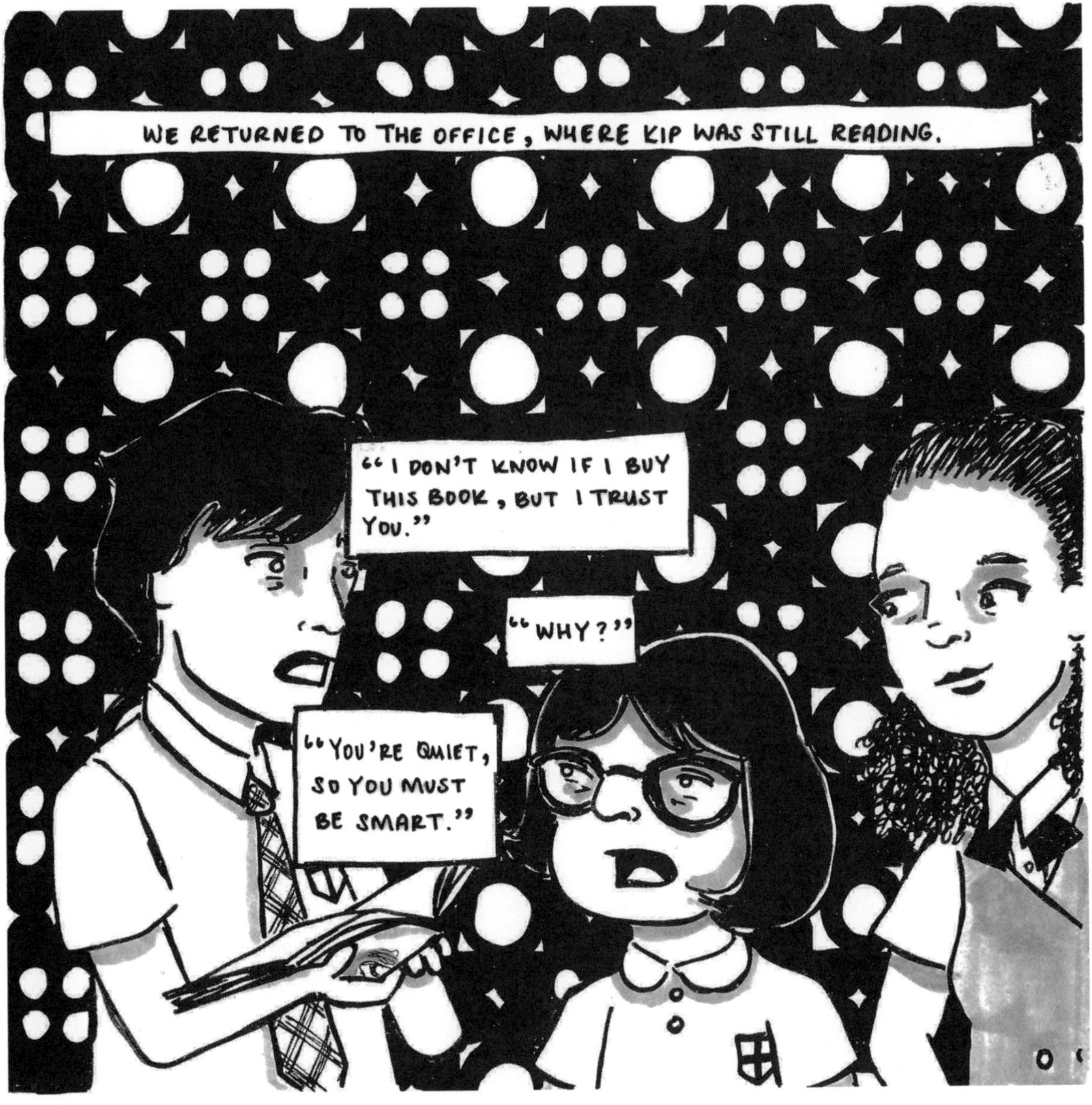
WE RETURNED TO THE OFFICE, WHERE KIP WAS STILL READING.
"I DON'T KNOW IF I BUY THIS BOOK, BUT I TRUST YOU."
"WHY?"
"YOU'RE QUIET, SO YOU MUST BE SMART."

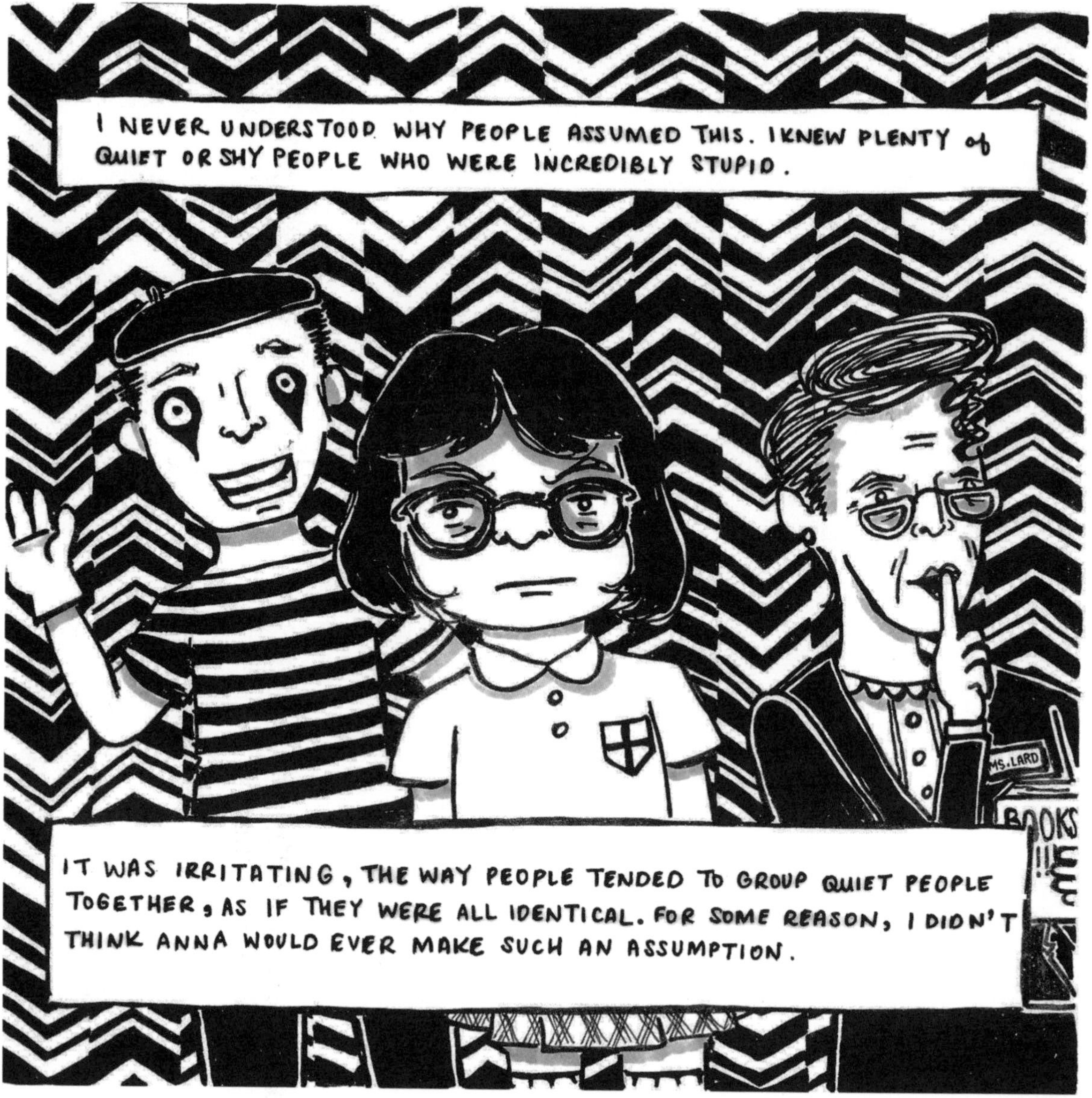
I NEVER UNDERSTOOD WHY PEOPLE ASSUMED THIS. I KNEW PLENTY of QUIET OR SHY PEOPLE WHO WERE INCREDIBLY STUPID.
MS. LARD
BOOKS
IT WAS IRRITATING, THE WAY PEOPLE TENDED TO GROUP QUIET PEOPLE TOGETHER, AS IF THEY WERE ALL IDENTICAL. FOR SOME REASON, I DIDN'T THINK ANNA WOULD EVER MAKE SUCH AN ASSUMPTION.

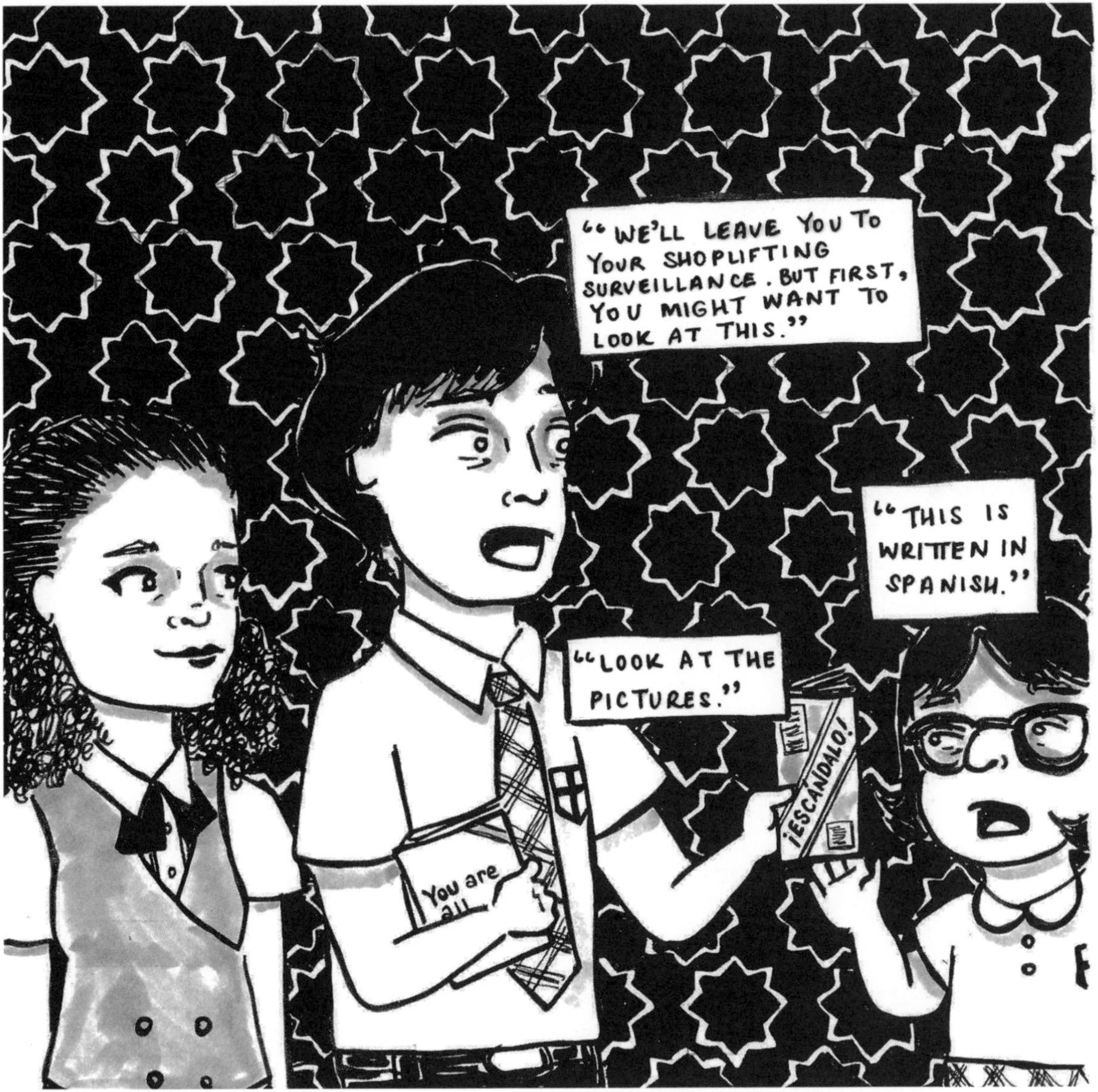
"WE'LL LEAVE YOU TO YOUR SHOPLIFTING SURVEILLANCE. BUT FIRST, YOU MIGHT WANT TO LOOK AT THIS."
"THIS IS WRITTEN IN SPANISH."
"LOOK AT THE PICTURES."
¡ESCÁNDALO!
You are all

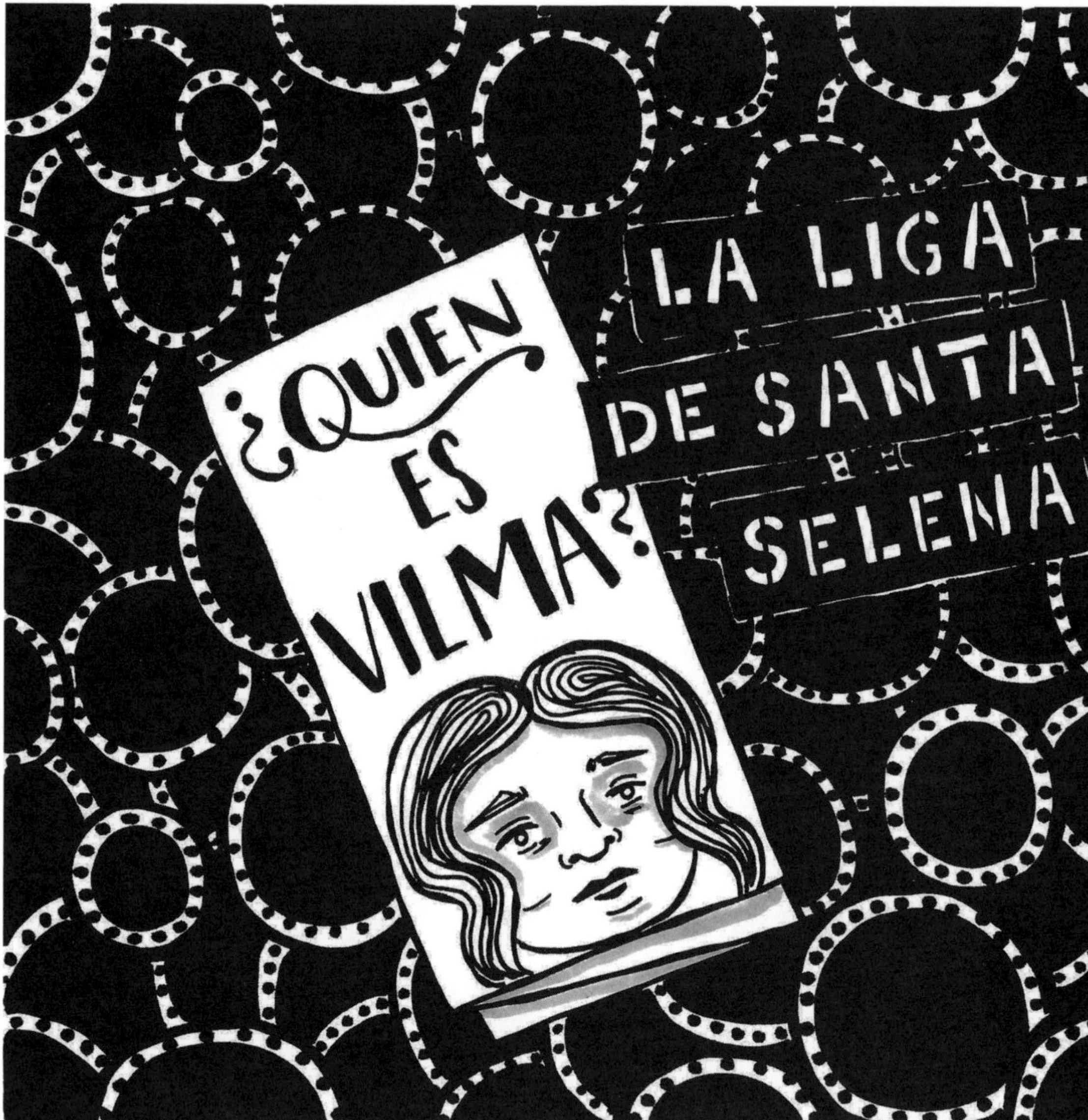
¿QUIEN ES VILMA?
LA LIGA DE SANTA SELENA

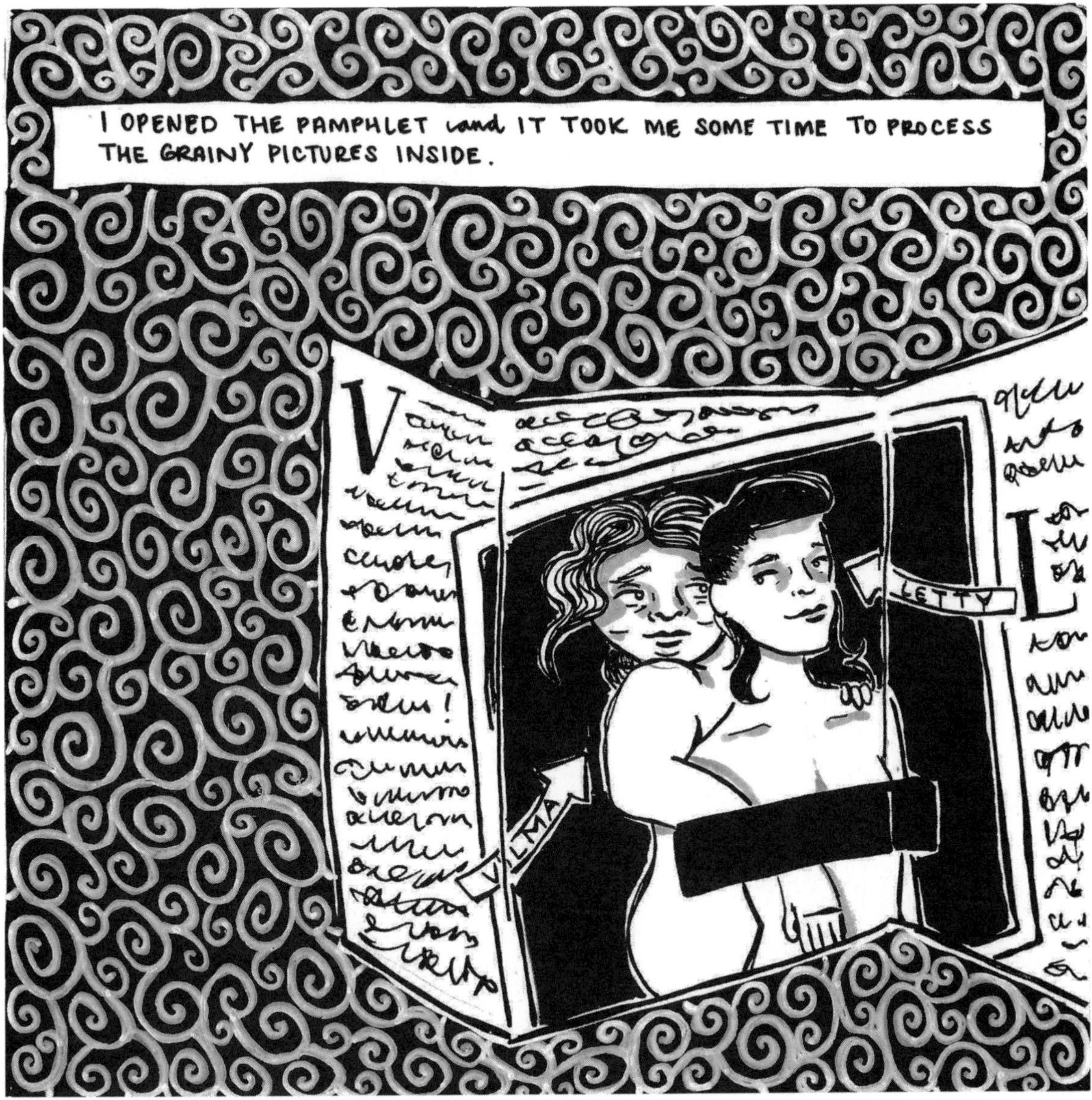
I OPENED THE PAMPHLET and IT TOOK ME SOME TIME TO PROCESS THE GRAINY PICTURES INSIDE.
LETTY
VILMA

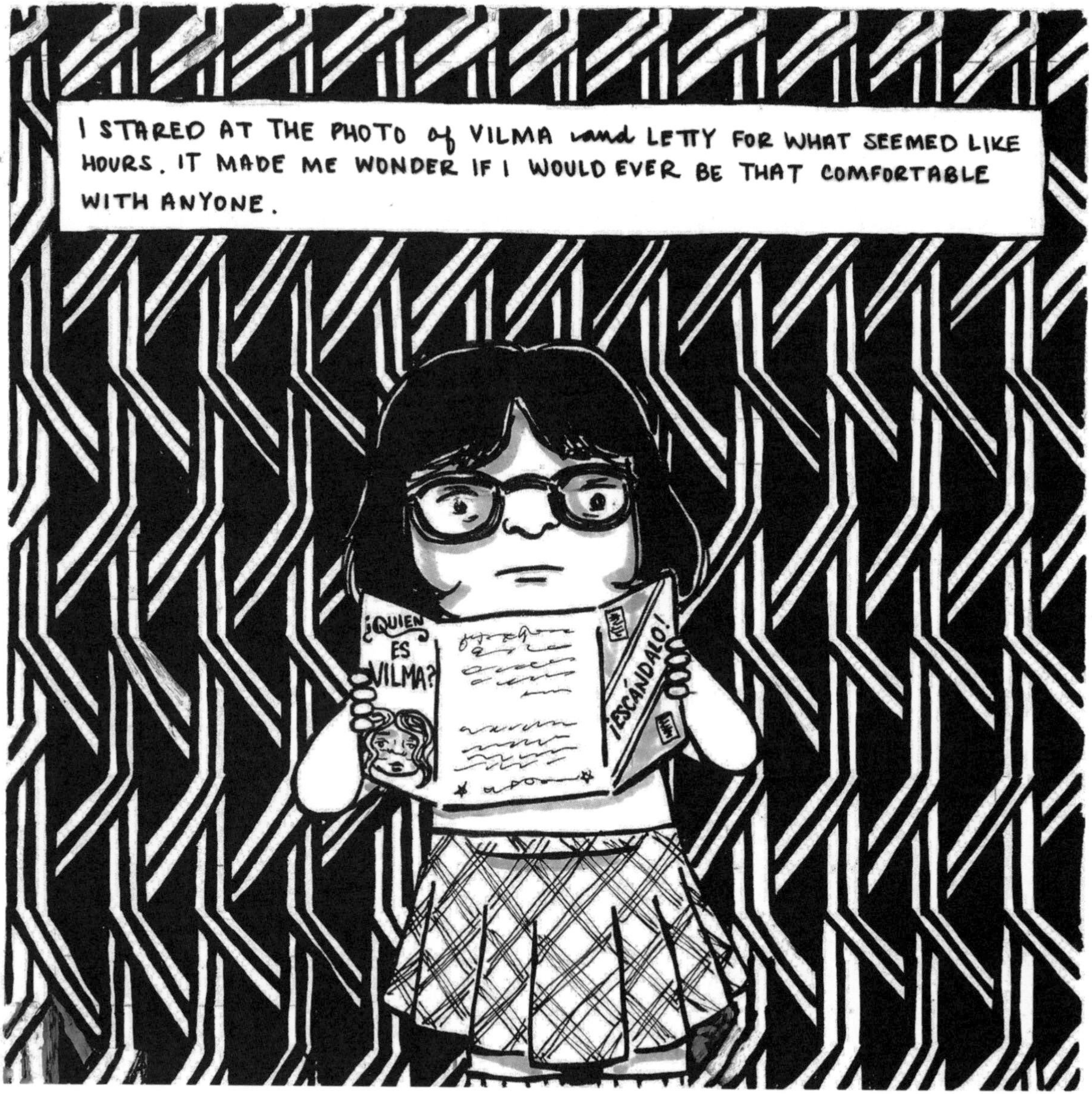
I STARED AT THE PHOTO of VILMA and LETTY FOR WHAT SEEMED LIKE HOURS. IT MADE ME WONDER IF I WOULD EVER BE THAT COMFORTABLE WITH ANYONE.
¿QUIEN ES VILMA?
¡ESCÁNDALO!

I TURNED IT OVER and WAS MET WITH WORDS IN ENGLISH.
¿QUIEN ES VILMA?
LEE AHORA
¡ESCÁNDALO!
"If there is a man who lies with a man as those who lie with a woman, both of them have committed a detestable act; they shall surely be put to death. Their bloodguiltiness is upon them."
–Leviticus 20:13
ATTENTION: There is currently someone about to be canonized who is a proven homosexual. To stop this shame from happening, write to Bishop Fiorenza NOW to stop Vilma Vielique de Santa Barbara from dirtying the realm of canonized saints.
★DISTRIBUIDO POR LA LIGA DE SANTA SELENA★

I LOOKED BACK AT THE PHOTO of LETTY and VILMA, UNABLE TO RELATE THE WORDS "DETESTABLE" and "BLOODGUILTNESS" TO THEIR CALM FACES.
las dos mujeres trabajar
la gente los veía todos
es la
de la
OF COURSE, THEY BOTH HAD SANPAKU.

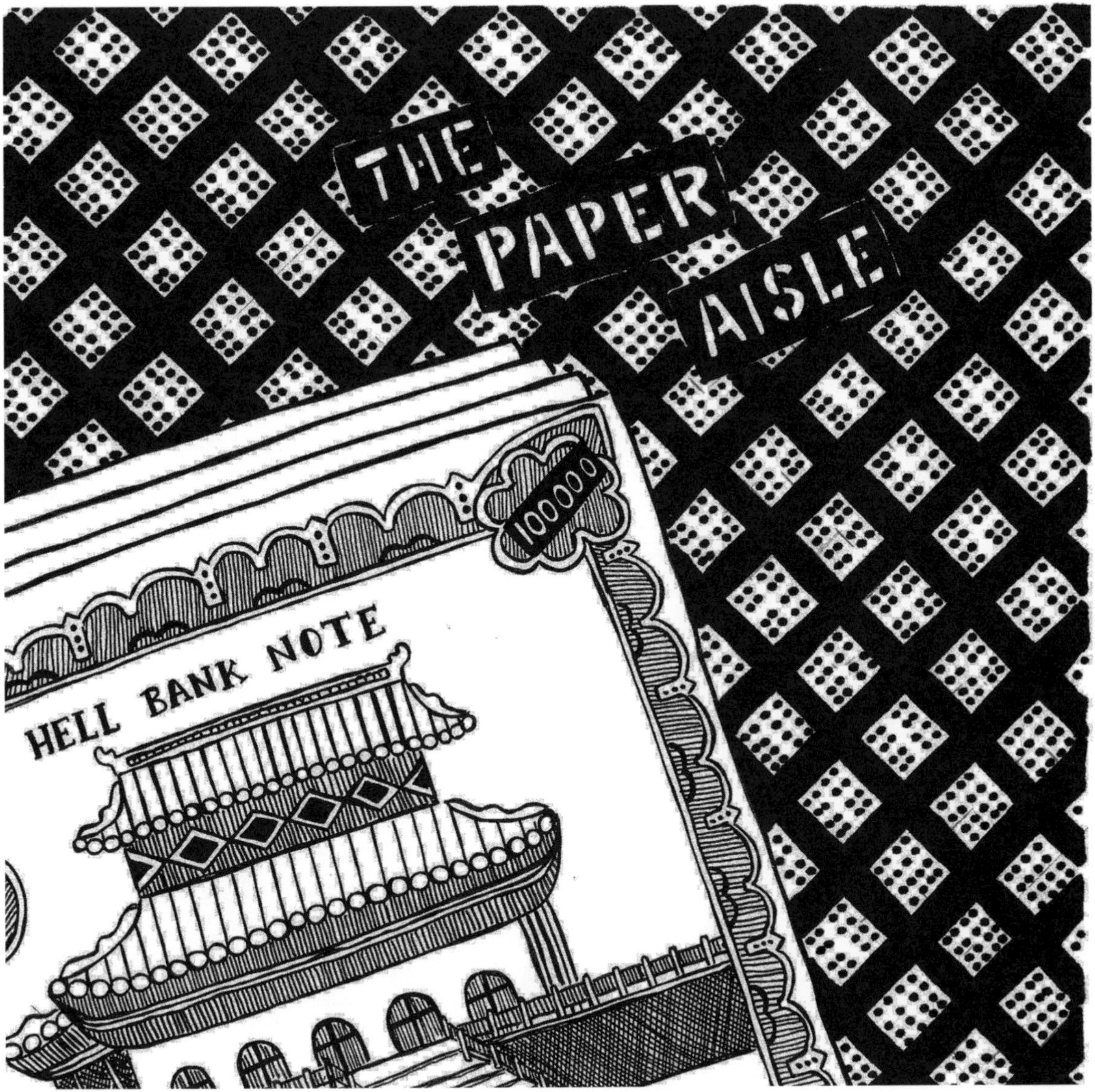
THE
PAPER
AISLE
100000
HELL BANK NOTE

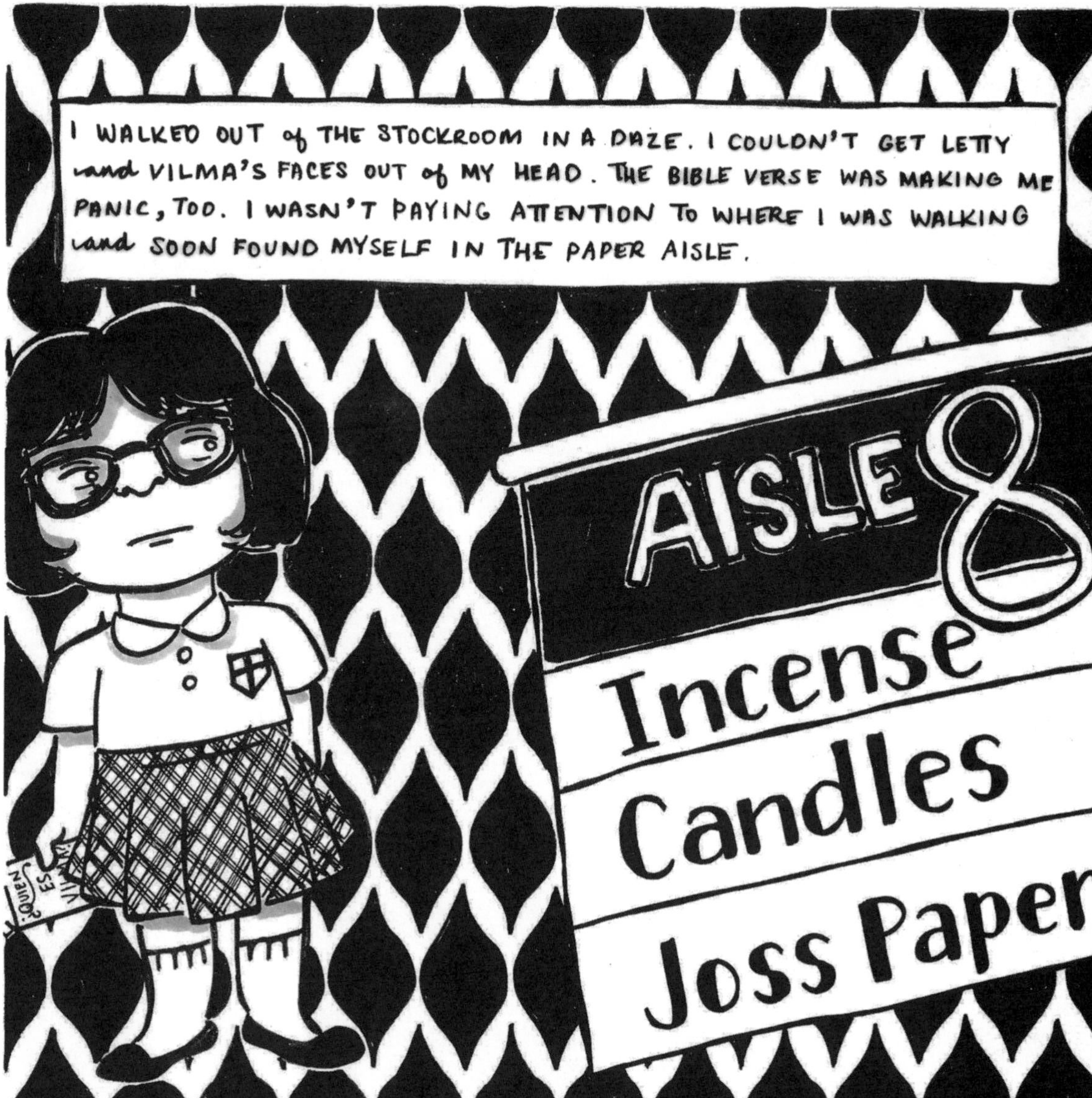
I WALKED OUT of THE STOCKROOM IN A DAZE. I COULDN'T GET LETTY and VILMA'S FACES OUT of MY HEAD. THE BIBLE VERSE WAS MAKING ME PANIC, TOO. I WASN'T PAYING ATTENTION TO WHERE I WAS WALKING and SOON FOUND MYSELF IN THE PAPER AISLE.
¿QUIEN ES
AISLE 8
Incense
Candles
Joss Paper

I PICKED UP THE SMALL PAPER DOG I HAD STUDIED THE FIRST TIME HARRY WEI CAUGHT ME SHOPLIFTING.
I PUT IT IN MY POCKET.

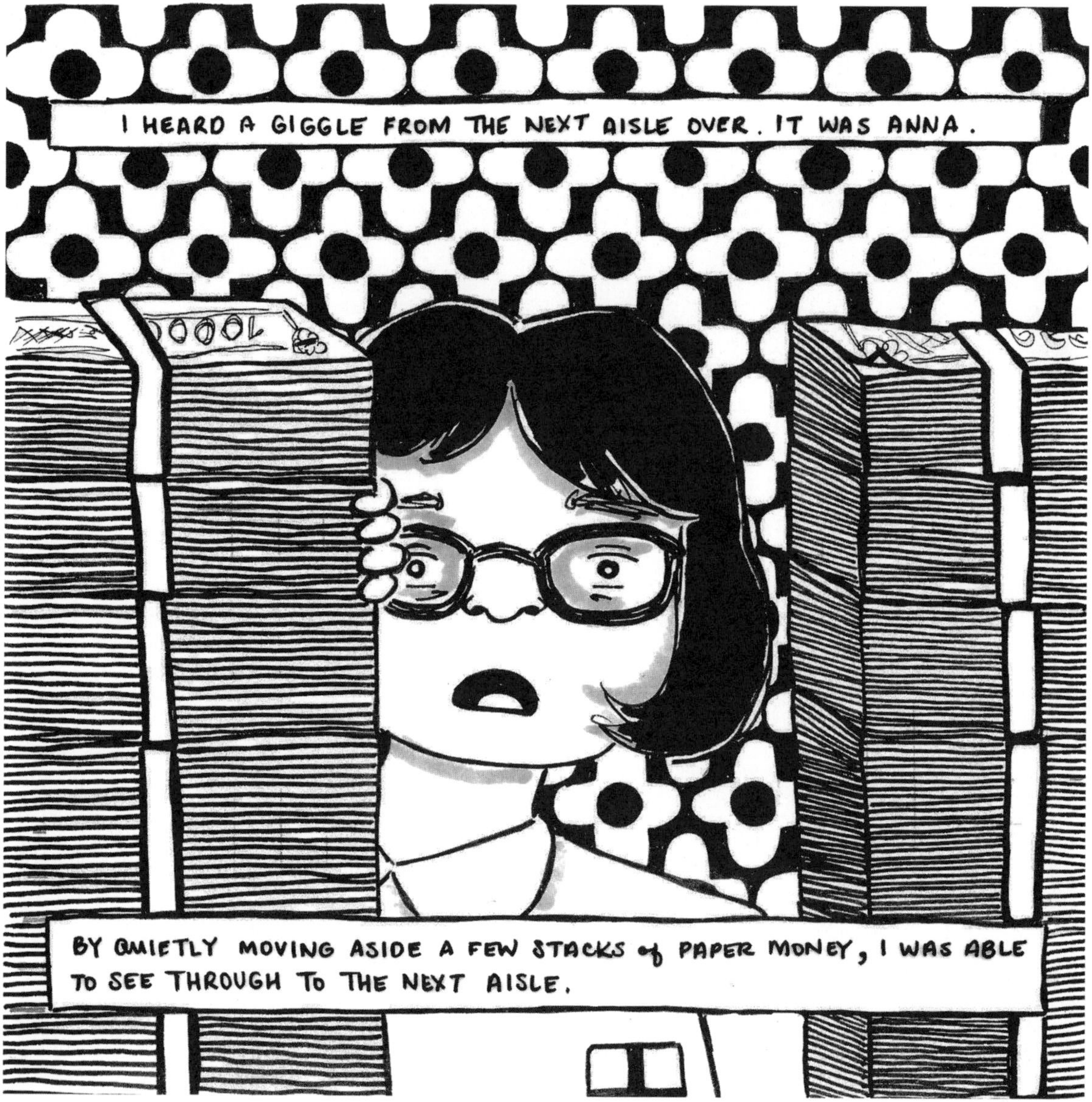
I HEARD A GIGGLE FROM THE NEXT AISLE OVER. IT WAS ANNA.
BY QUIETLY MOVING ASIDE A FEW STACKS of PAPER MONEY, I WAS ABLE TO SEE THROUGH TO THE NEXT AISLE.

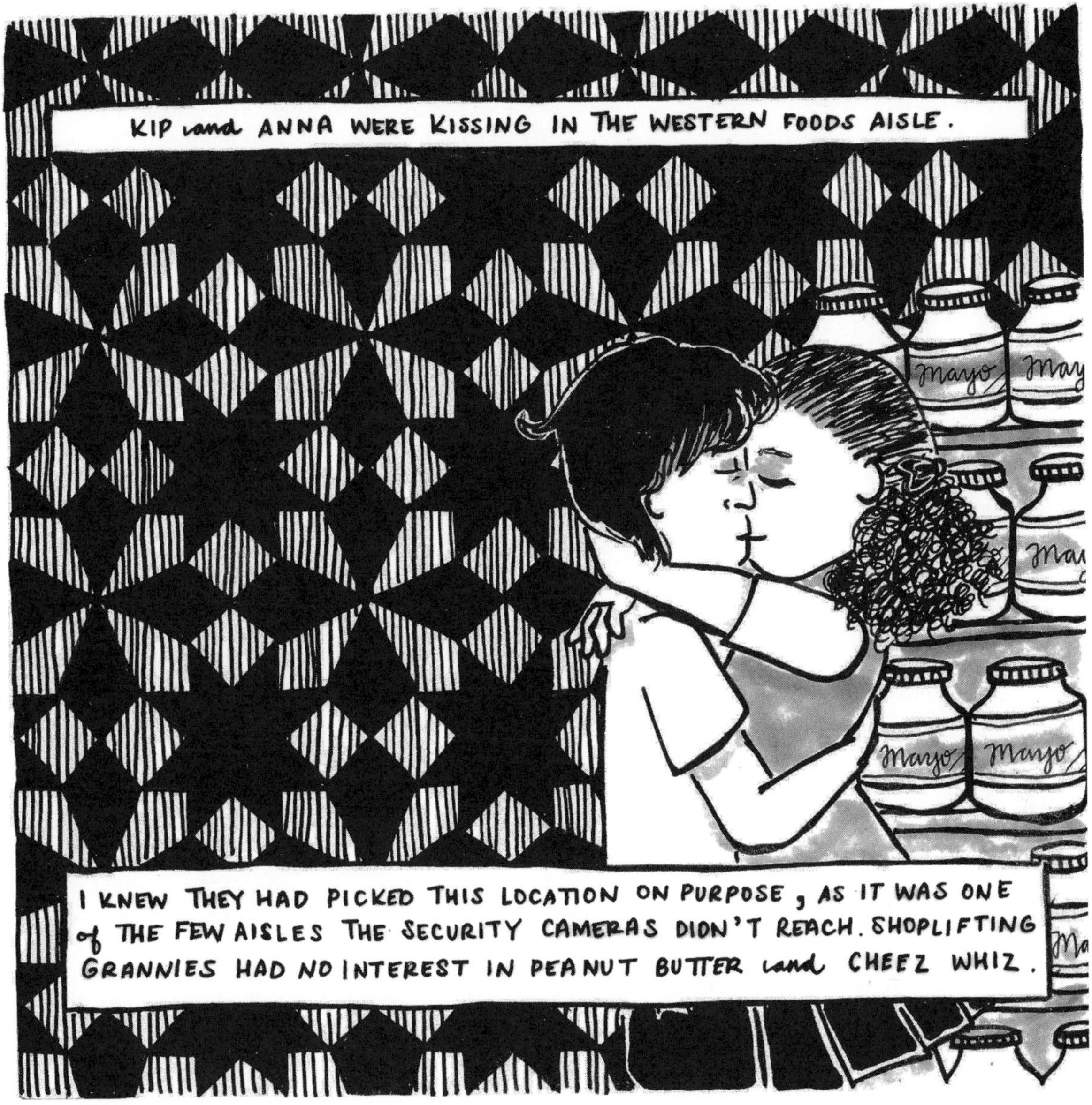
KIP and ANNA WERE KISSING IN THE WESTERN FOODS AISLE.
Mayo
Mayo
Mayo
Mayo
Mayo
I KNEW THEY HAD PICKED THIS LOCATION ON PURPOSE, AS IT WAS ONE of THE FEW AISLES THE SECURITY CAMERAS DIDN'T REACH. SHOPLIFTING GRANNIES HAD NO INTEREST IN PEANUT BUTTER and CHEEZ WHIZ.

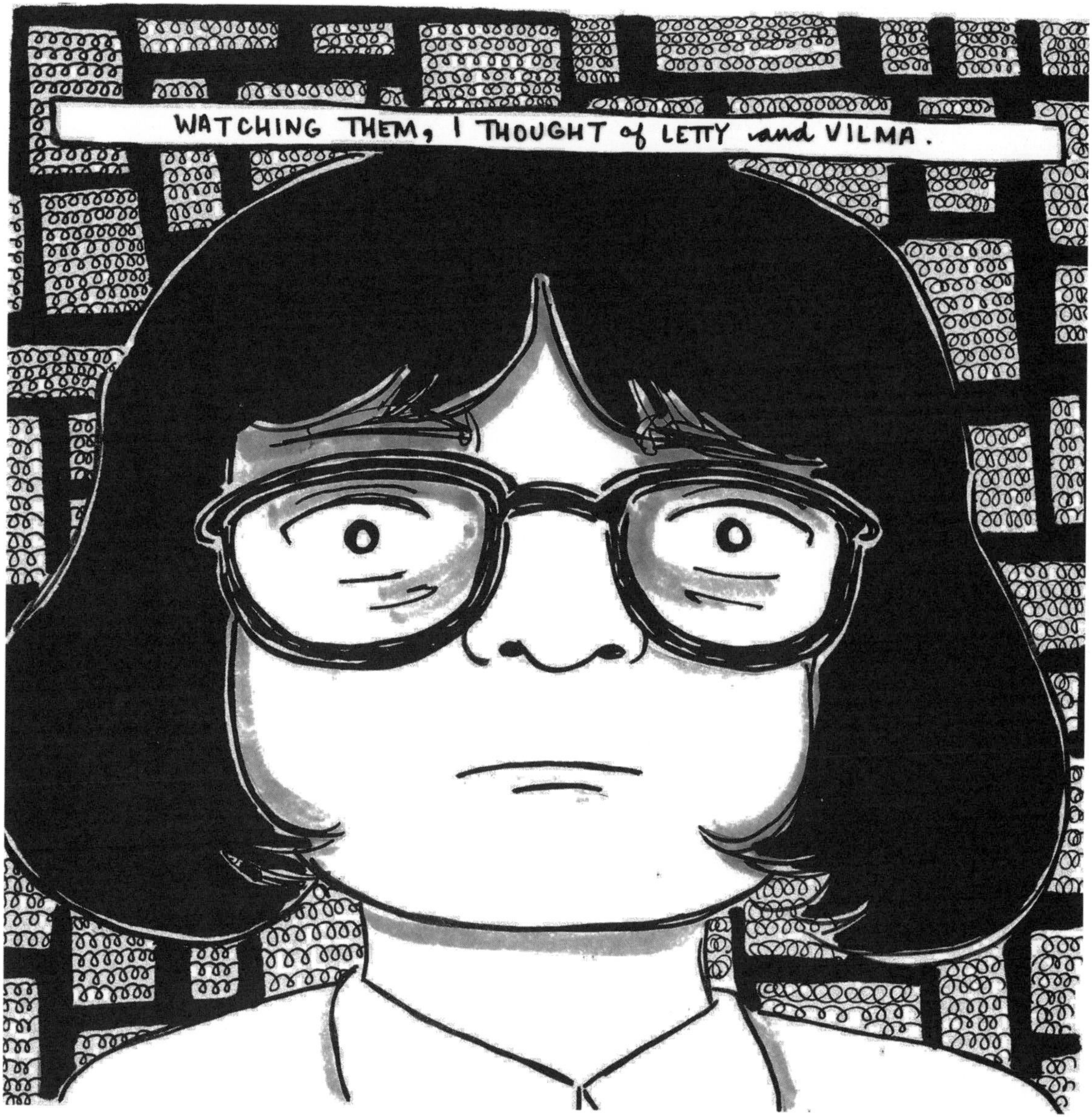
WATCHING THEM, I THOUGHT of LETTY and VILMA.

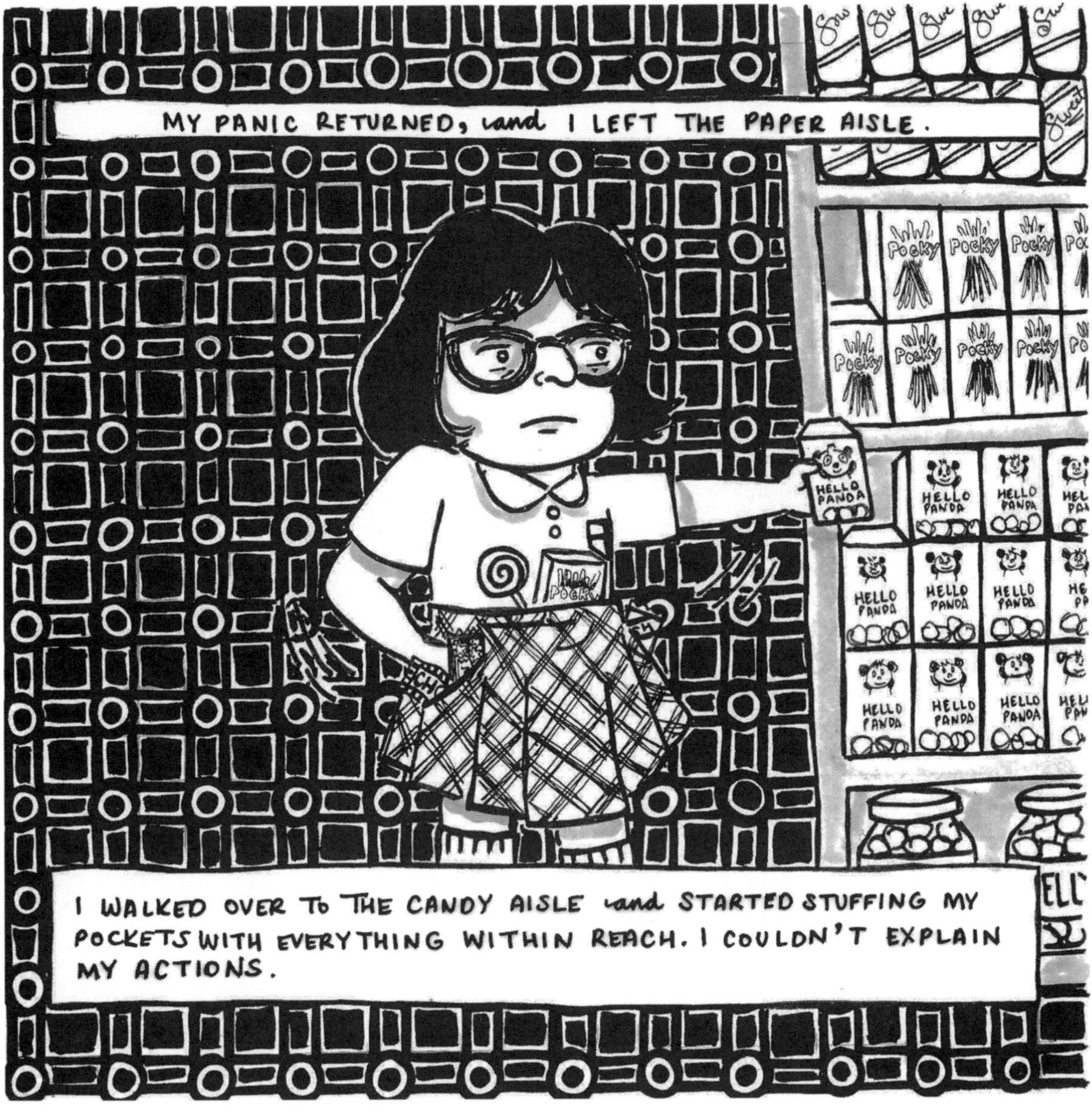
MY PANIC RETURNED, and I LEFT THE PAPER AISLE.
I WALKED OVER TO THE CANDY AISLE and STARTED STUFFING MY POCKETS WITH EVERYTHING WITHIN REACH. I COULDN'T EXPLAIN MY ACTIONS.
Pocky
HELLO PANDA

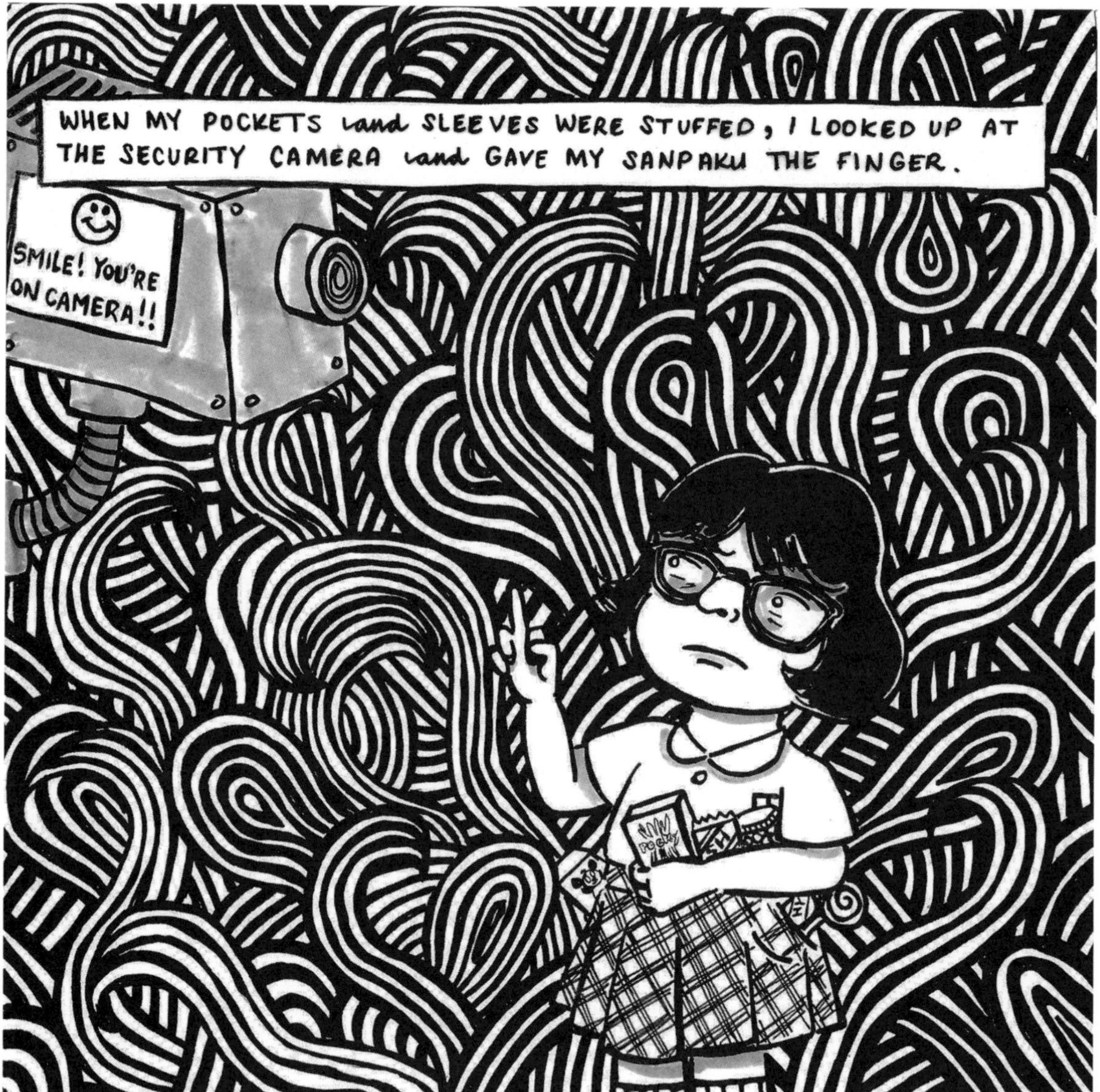
WHEN MY POCKETS and SLEEVES WERE STUFFED, I LOOKED UP AT THE SECURITY CAMERA and GAVE MY SANPAKU THE FINGER.
SMILE! YOU'RE ON CAMERA!!
POCKY

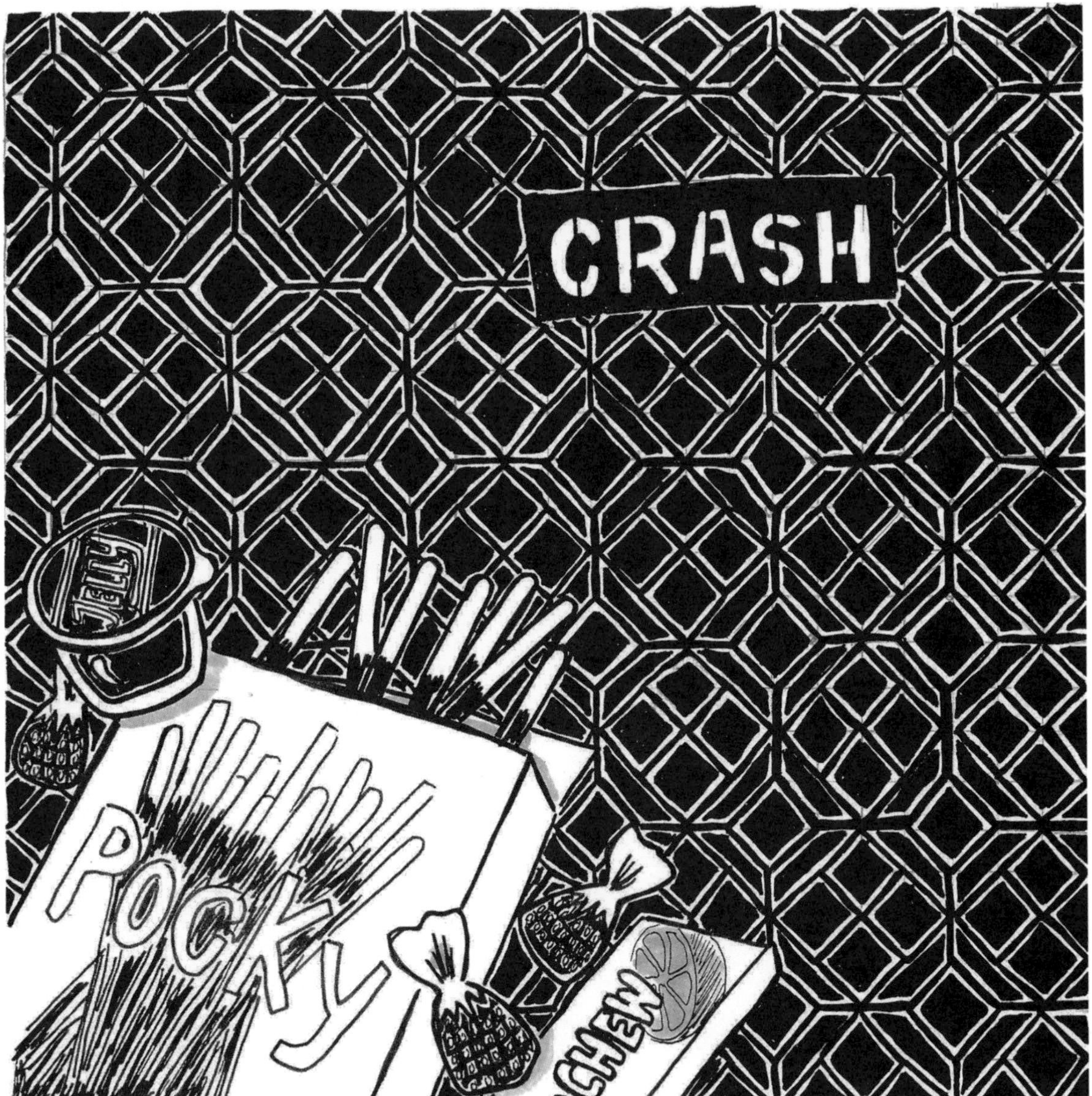
CRASH
POCKY
CHEW

I WAS HALFWAY OUT THE DOOR WHEN I HEARD A VOICE BEHIND ME.
"SHOPLIFTER!"
VIET HOA
I BEGAN RUNNING DOWN THE MOSTLY VACANT PARKING LOT. I TURNED AROUND TO SEE HARRY CHASING ME.

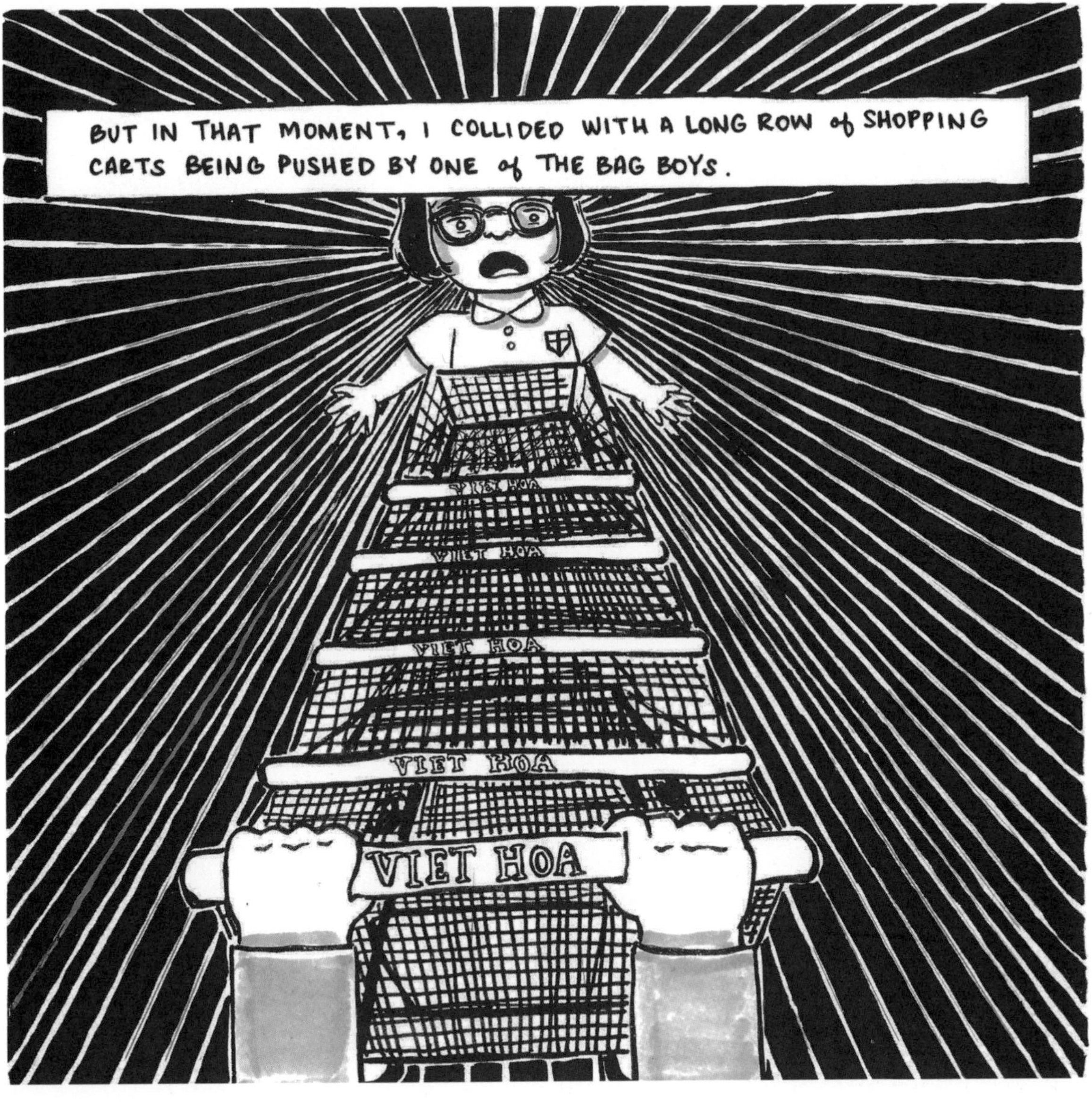
BUT IN THAT MOMENT, I COLLIDED WITH A LONG ROW of SHOPPING CARTS BEING PUSHED BY ONE of THE BAG BOYS.
VIET HOA
VIET HOA
VIET HOA
VIET HOA
VIET HOA

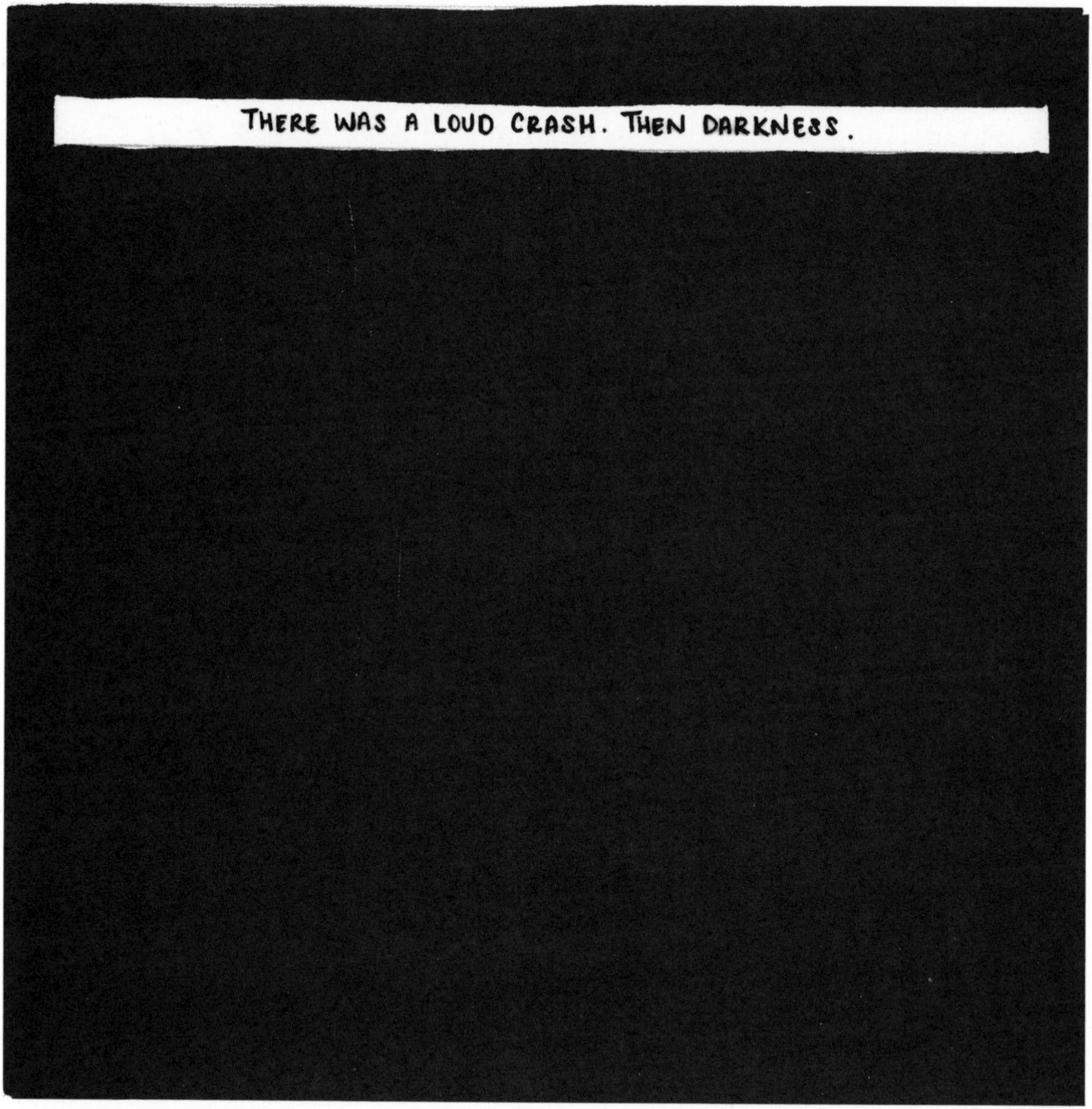
THERE WAS A LOUD CRASH. THEN DARKNESS.

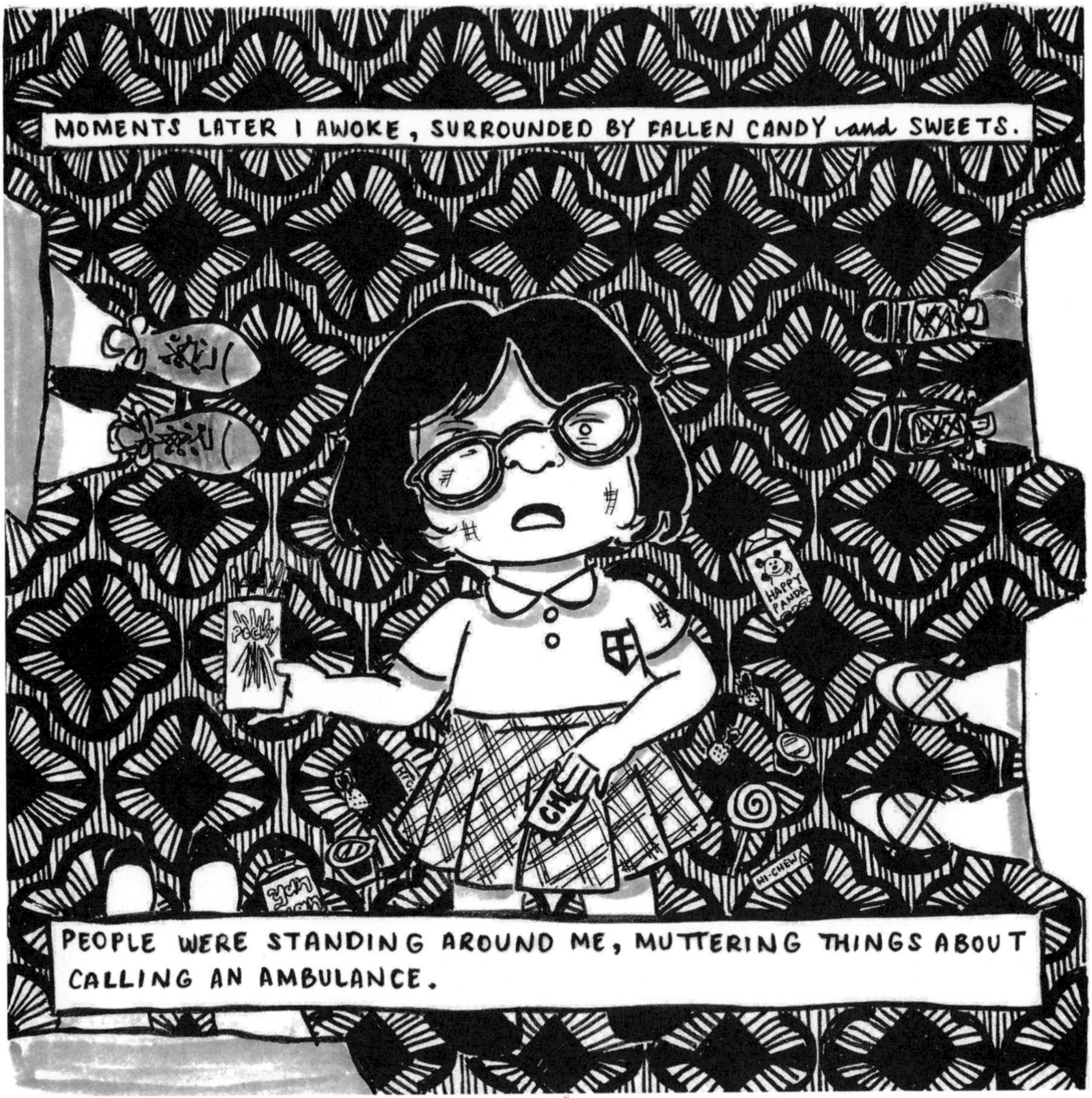
MOMENTS LATER I AWOKE, SURROUNDED BY FALLEN CANDY and SWEETS.
Pocky
HAPPY PANDA
HI-CHEW
PEOPLE WERE STANDING AROUND ME, MUTTERING THINGS ABOUT CALLING AN AMBULANCE.

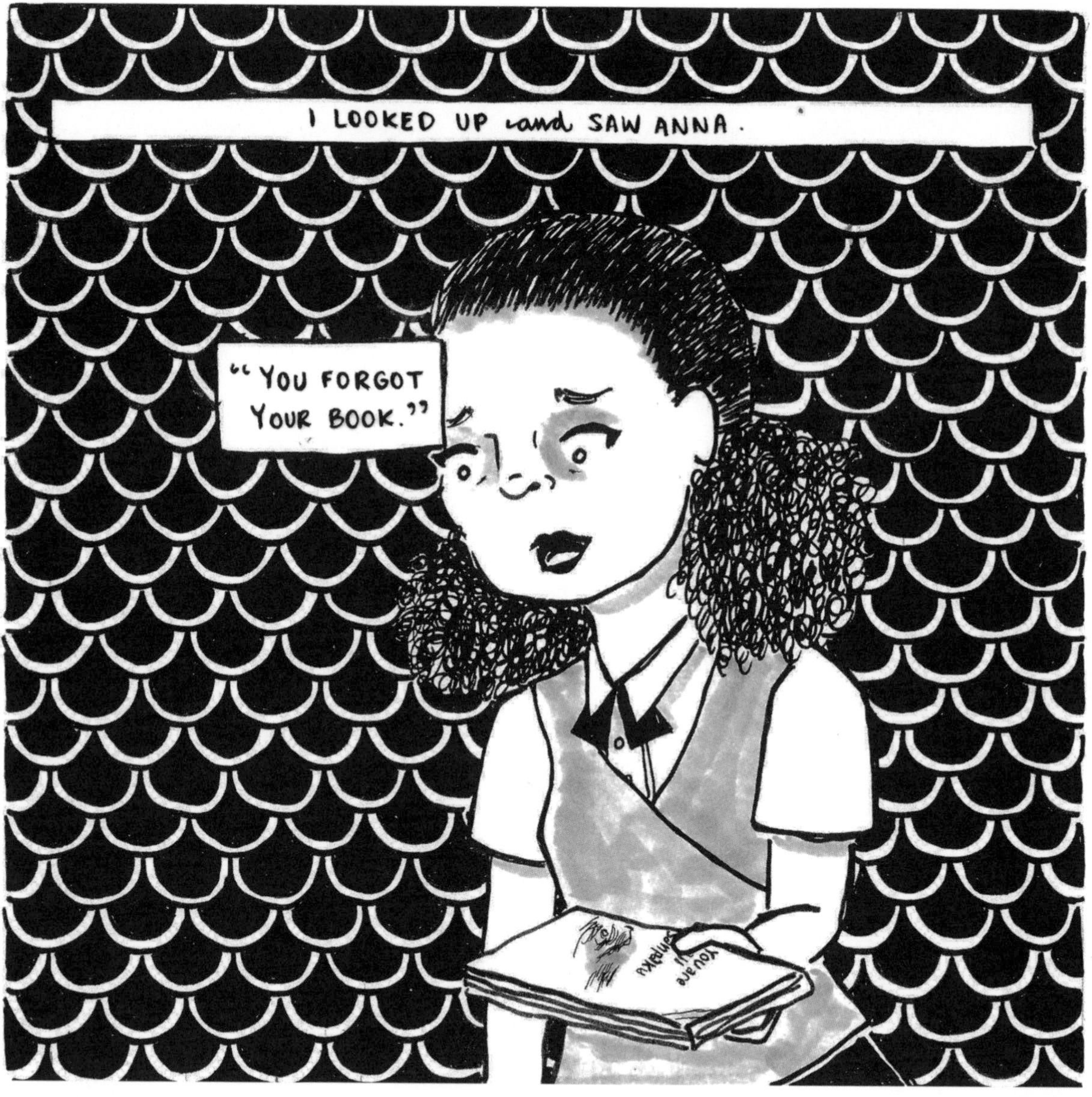
I LOOKED UP and SAW ANNA.
"YOU FORGOT YOUR BOOK."

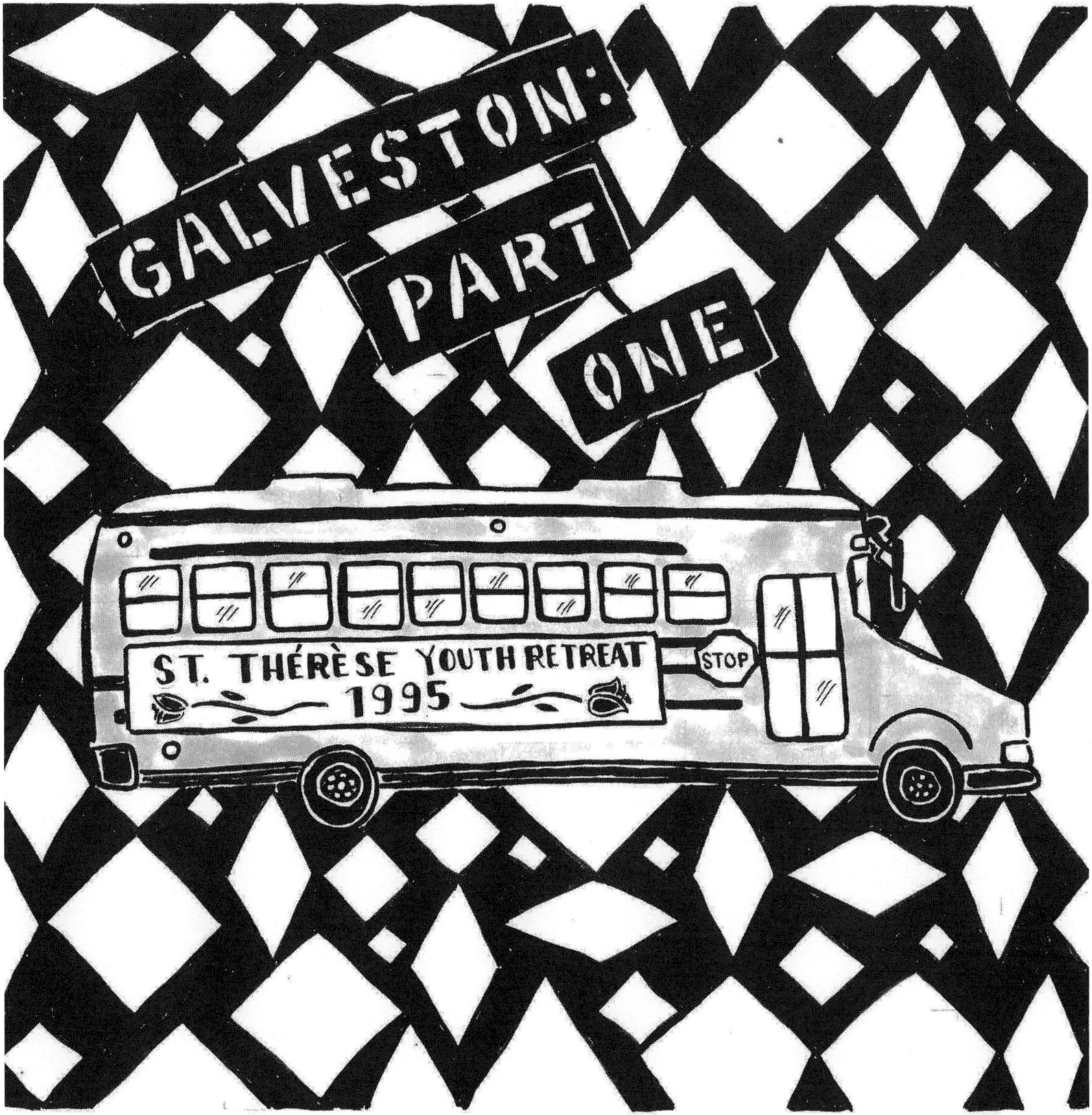
GALVESTON:
PART
ONE
ST. THÉRÈSE YOUTH RETREAT
1995
STOP

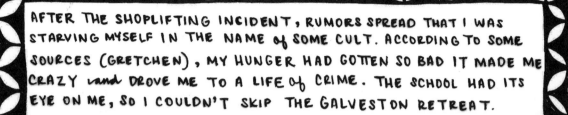

AFTER THE SHOPLIFTING INCIDENT, RUMORS SPREAD THAT I WAS STARVING MYSELF IN THE NAME of SOME CULT. ACCORDING TO SOME SOURCES (GRETCHEN), MY HUNGER HAD GOTTEN SO BAD IT MADE ME CRAZY and DROVE ME TO A LIFE of CRIME. THE SCHOOL HAD ITS EYE ON ME, SO I COULDN'T SKIP THE GALVESTON RETREAT.

BUT I WAS DREADING IT A LITTLE LESS NOW THAT I'VE GIVEN UP ON THE SANPAKU DIET.

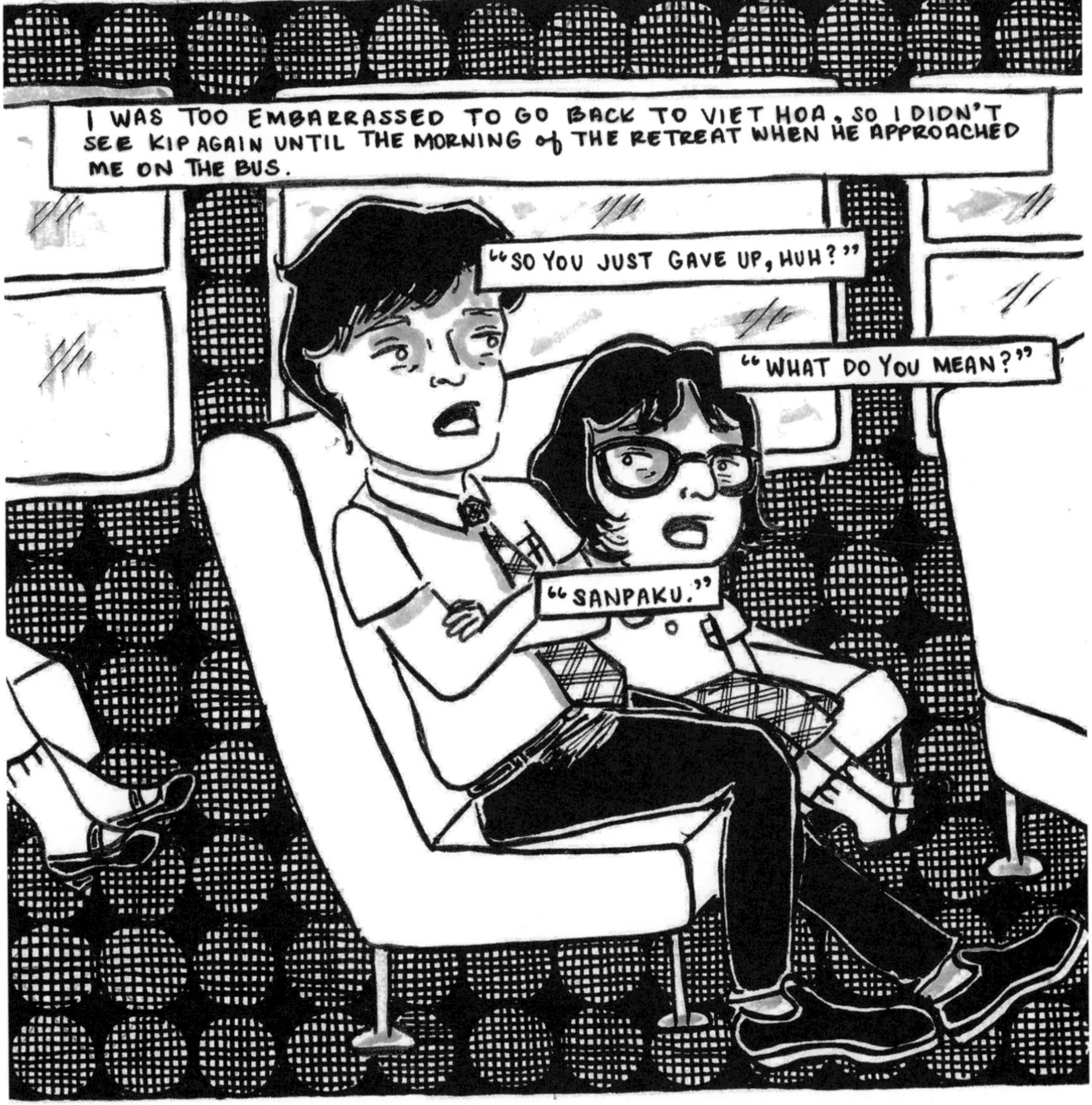
I WAS TOO EMBARRASSED TO GO BACK TO VIET HOA, SO I DIDN'T SEE KIP AGAIN UNTIL THE MORNING of THE RETREAT WHEN HE APPROACHED ME ON THE BUS.
"SO YOU JUST GAVE UP, HUH?"
"WHAT DO YOU MEAN?"
"SANPAKU."

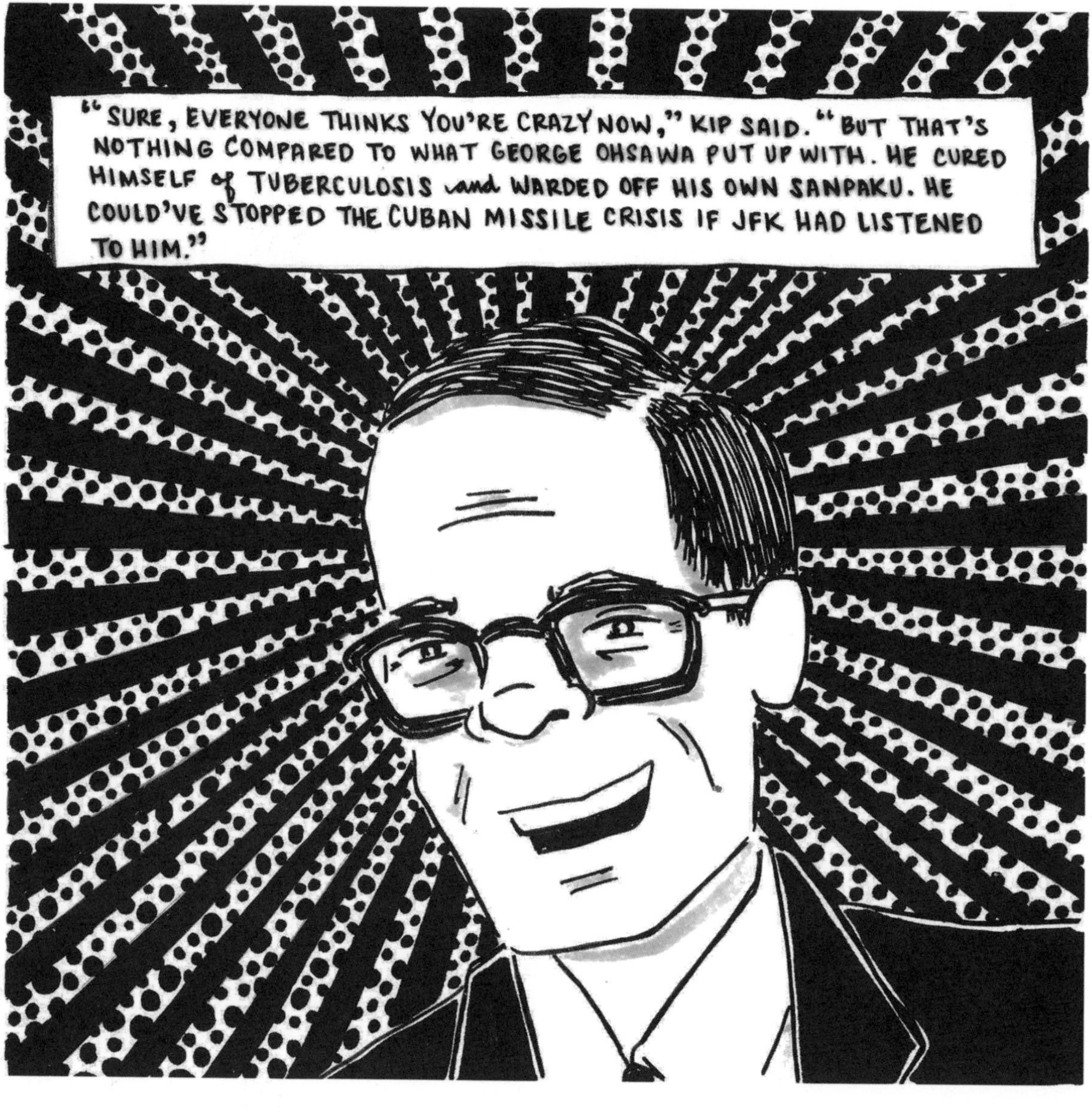
"SURE, EVERYONE THINKS YOU'RE CRAZY NOW," KIP SAID. "BUT THAT'S NOTHING COMPARED TO WHAT GEORGE OHSAWA PUT UP WITH. HE CURED HIMSELF of TUBERCULOSIS and WARDED OFF HIS OWN SANPAKU. HE COULD'VE STOPPED THE CUBAN MISSILE CRISIS IF JFK HAD LISTENED TO HIM."

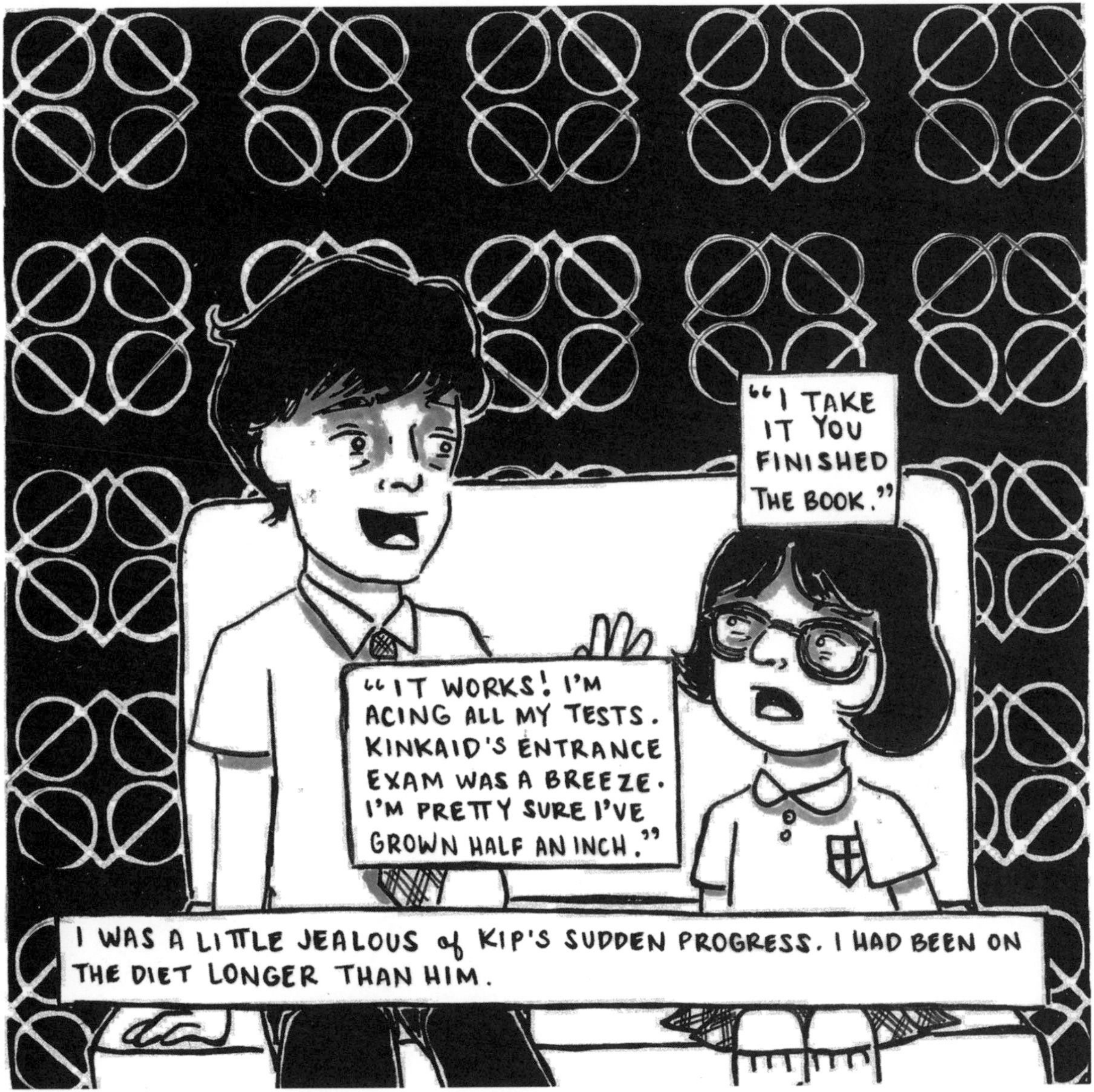
"IT WORKS! I'M ACING ALL MY TESTS. KINKAID'S ENTRANCE EXAM WAS A BREEZE. I'M PRETTY SURE I'VE GROWN HALF AN INCH."
"I TAKE IT YOU FINISHED THE BOOK."
I WAS A LITTLE JEALOUS of KIP'S SUDDEN PROGRESS. I HAD BEEN ON THE DIET LONGER THAN HIM.

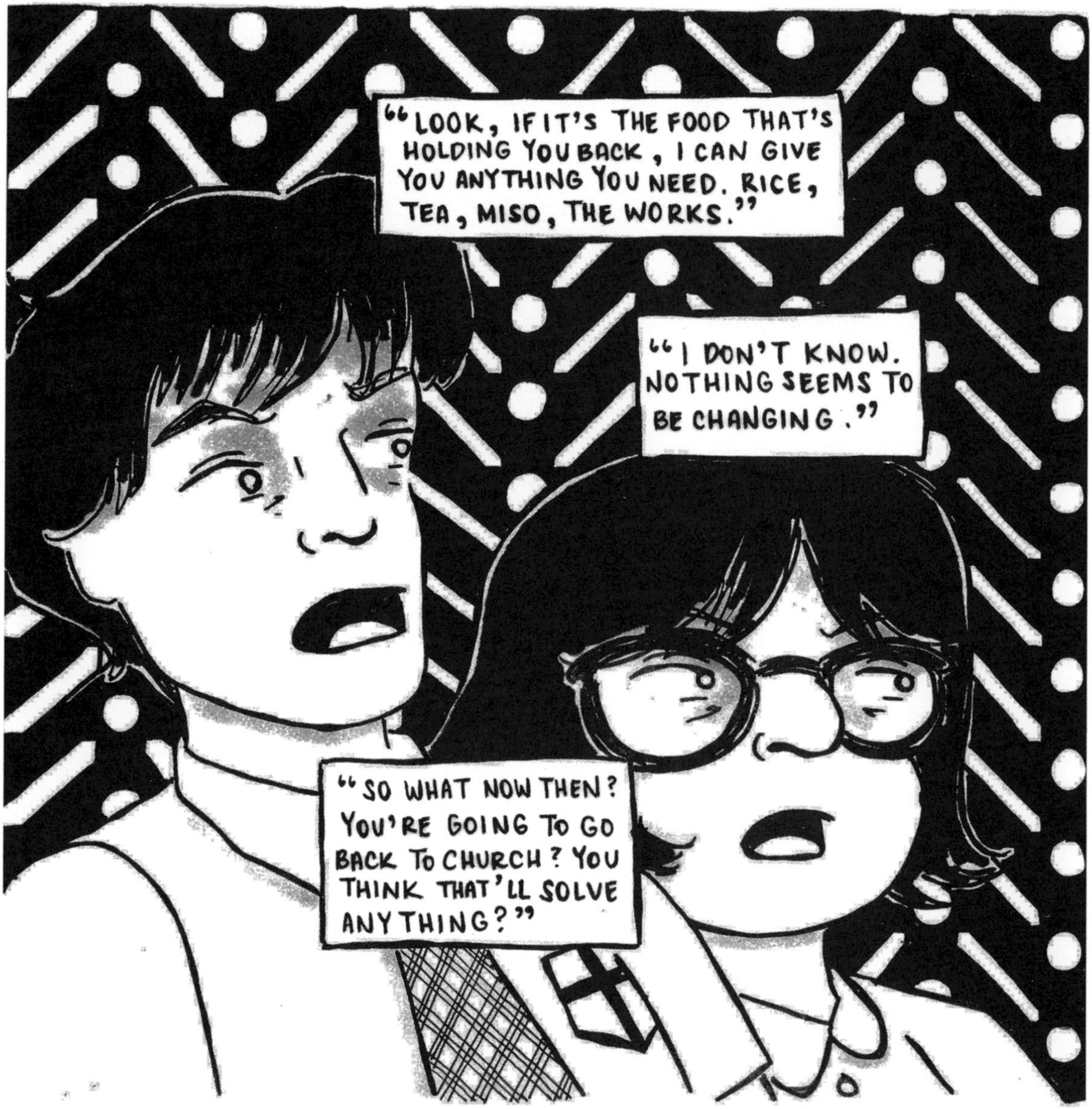
"LOOK, IF IT'S THE FOOD THAT'S HOLDING YOU BACK, I CAN GIVE YOU ANYTHING YOU NEED. RICE, TEA, MISO, THE WORKS."
"I DON'T KNOW. NOTHING SEEMS TO BE CHANGING."
"SO WHAT NOW THEN? YOU'RE GOING TO GO BACK TO CHURCH? YOU THINK THAT'LL SOLVE ANYTHING?"

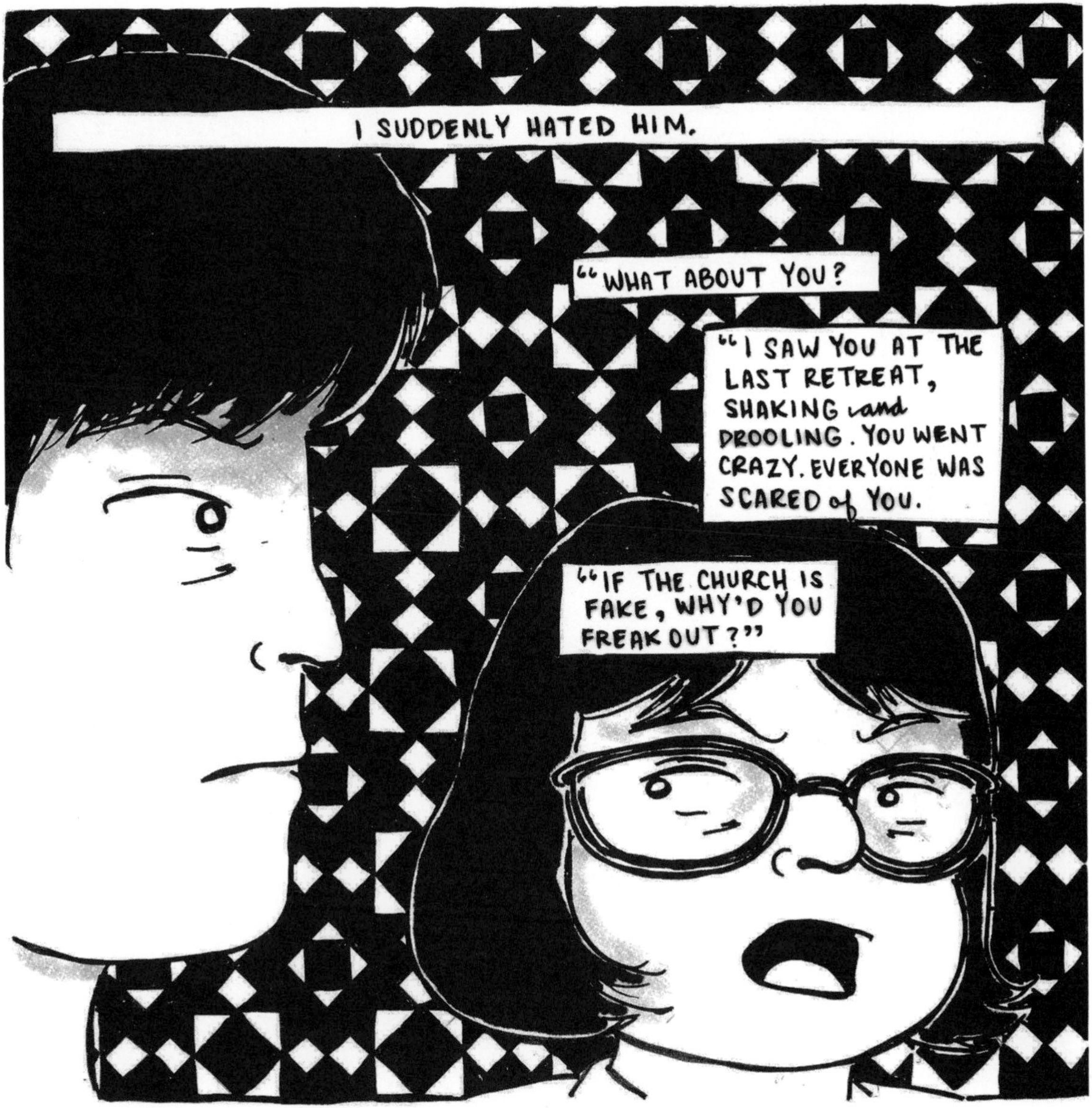
I SUDDENLY HATED HIM.
"WHAT ABOUT YOU?
"I SAW YOU AT THE LAST RETREAT, SHAKING and DROOLING. YOU WENT CRAZY. EVERYONE WAS SCARED of YOU.
"IF THE CHURCH IS FAKE, WHY'D YOU FREAK OUT?"

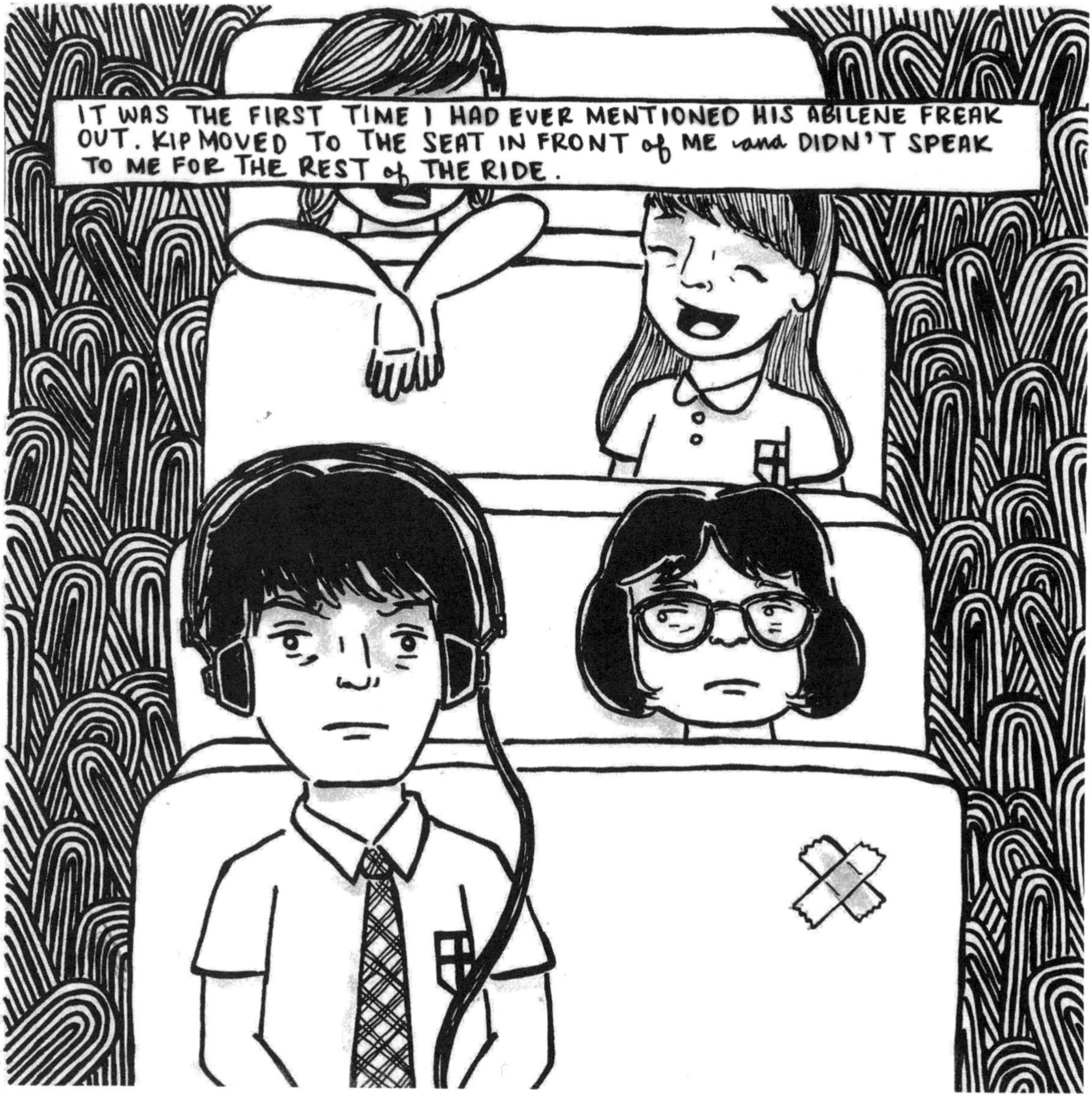
IT WAS THE FIRST TIME I HAD EVER MENTIONED HIS ABILENE FREAK OUT. KIP MOVED TO THE SEAT IN FRONT of ME and DIDN'T SPEAK TO ME FOR THE REST of THE RIDE.

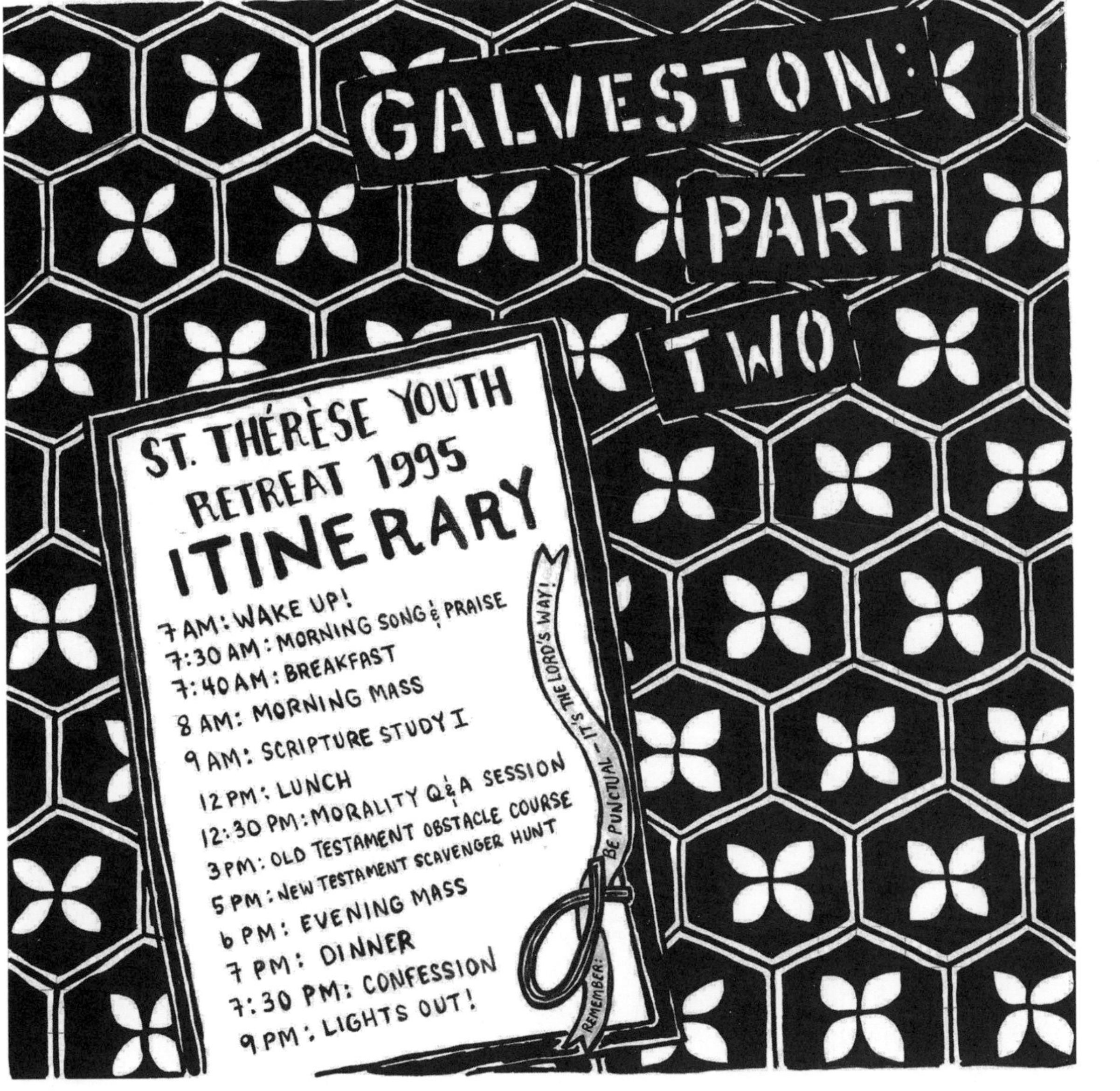
GALVESTON:
PART
TWO
ST. THÉRÈSE YOUTH
RETREAT 1995
ITINERARY
7 AM: WAKE UP!
7:30 AM: MORNING SONG & PRAISE
7:40 AM: BREAKFAST
8 AM: MORNING MASS
9 AM: SCRIPTURE STUDY I
12 PM: LUNCH
12:30 PM: MORALITY Q&A SESSION
3 PM: OLD TESTAMENT OBSTACLE COURSE
5 PM: NEW TESTAMENT SCAVENGER HUNT
6 PM: EVENING MASS
7 PM: DINNER
7:30 PM: CONFESSION
9 PM: LIGHTS OUT!
REMEMBER: BE PUNCTUAL — IT'S THE LORD'S WAY!

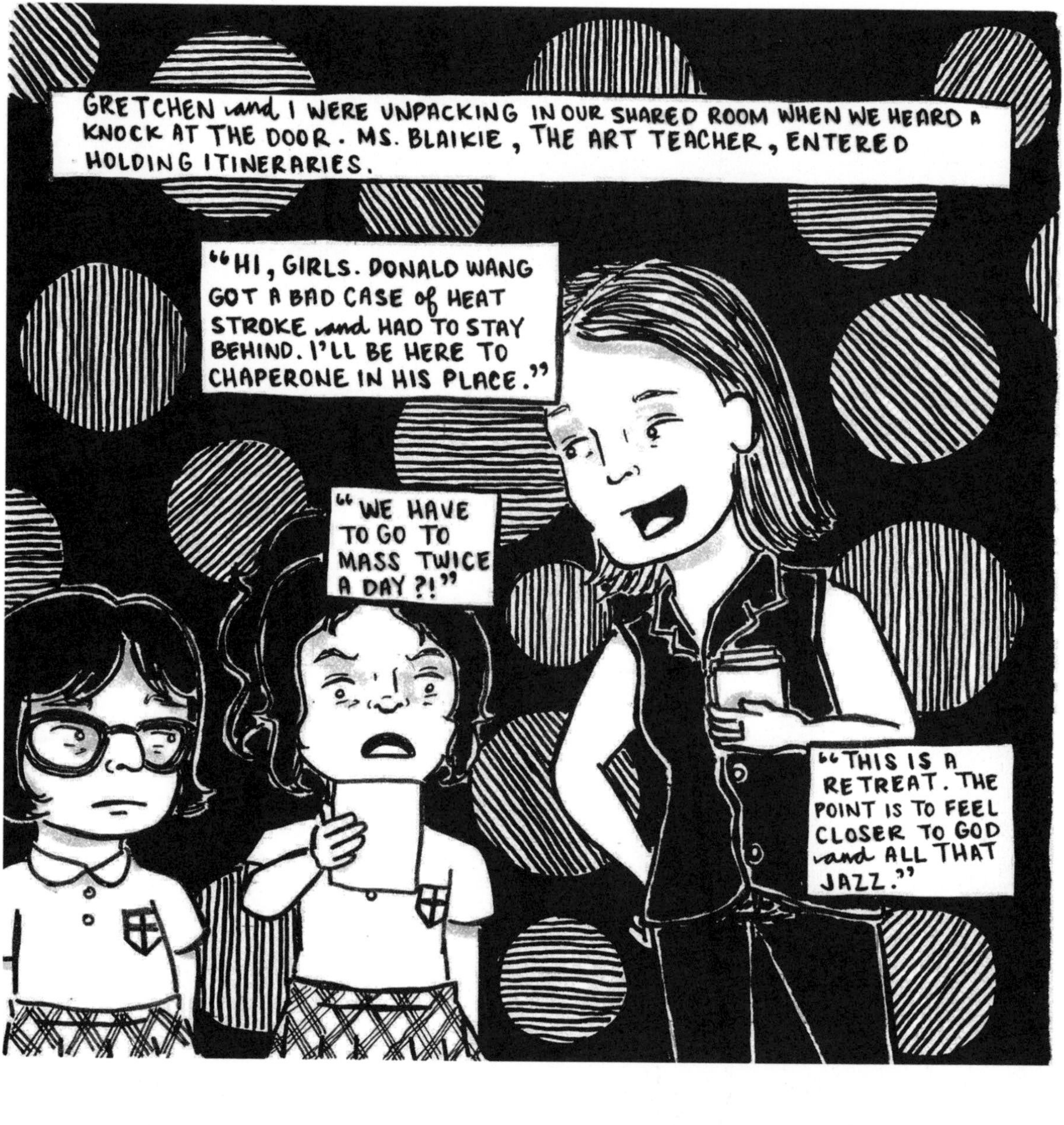
GRETCHEN and I WERE UNPACKING IN OUR SHARED ROOM WHEN WE HEARD A KNOCK AT THE DOOR. MS. BLAIKIE, THE ART TEACHER, ENTERED HOLDING ITINERARIES.
"HI, GIRLS. DONALD WANG GOT A BAD CASE of HEAT STROKE and HAD TO STAY BEHIND. I'LL BE HERE TO CHAPERONE IN HIS PLACE."
"WE HAVE TO GO TO MASS TWICE A DAY?!"
"THIS IS A RETREAT. THE POINT IS TO FEEL CLOSER TO GOD and ALL THAT JAZZ."

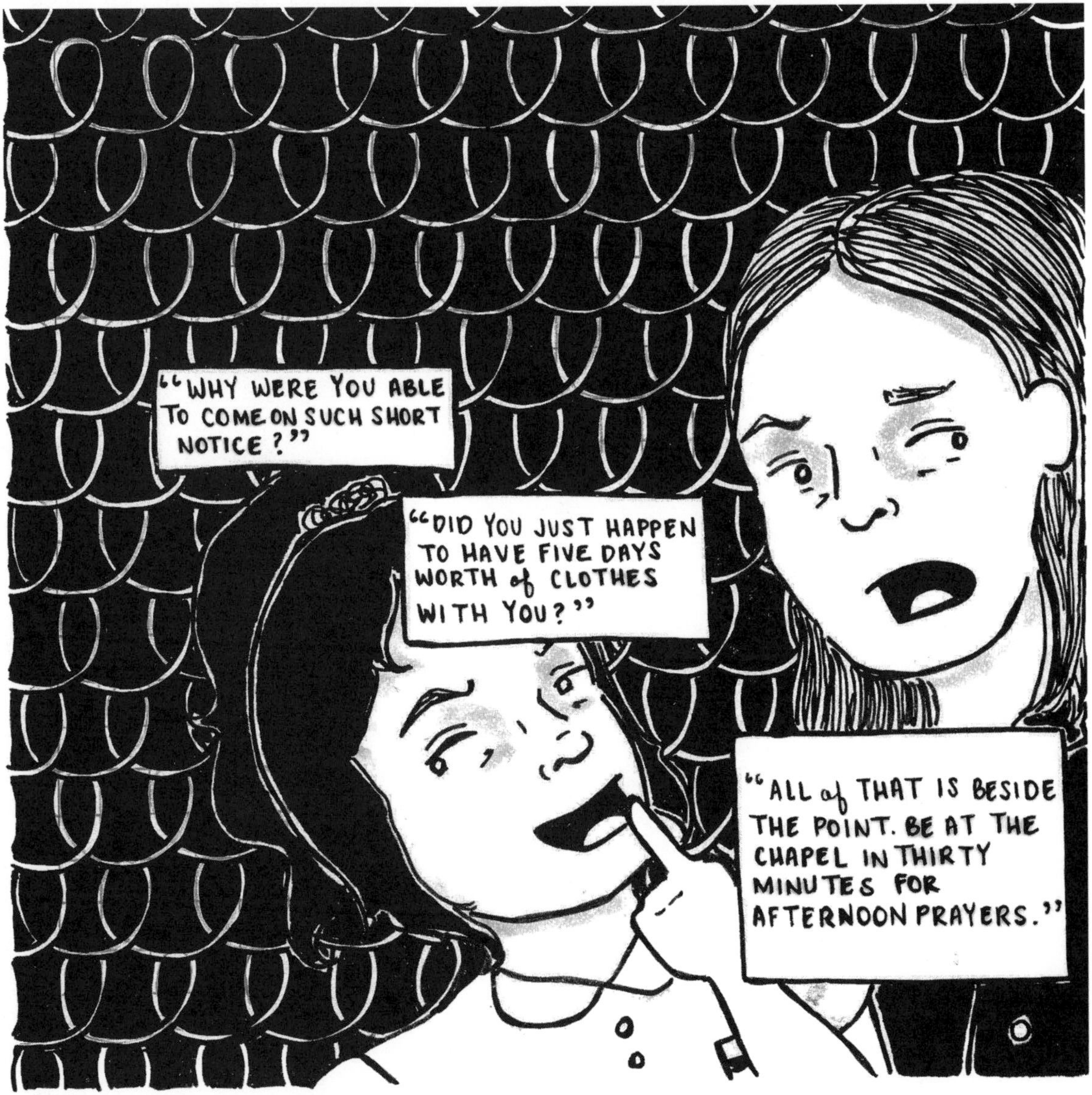
"WHY WERE YOU ABLE TO COME ON SUCH SHORT NOTICE?"
"DID YOU JUST HAPPEN TO HAVE FIVE DAYS WORTH of CLOTHES WITH YOU?"
"ALL of THAT IS BESIDE THE POINT. BE AT THE CHAPEL IN THIRTY MINUTES FOR AFTERNOON PRAYERS."

MS. BLAIKIE PROMPTLY SHUT THE DOOR and LEFT.
"I KNEW IT!"
"WHAT?"
"SHE LIVES IN HER CAR!

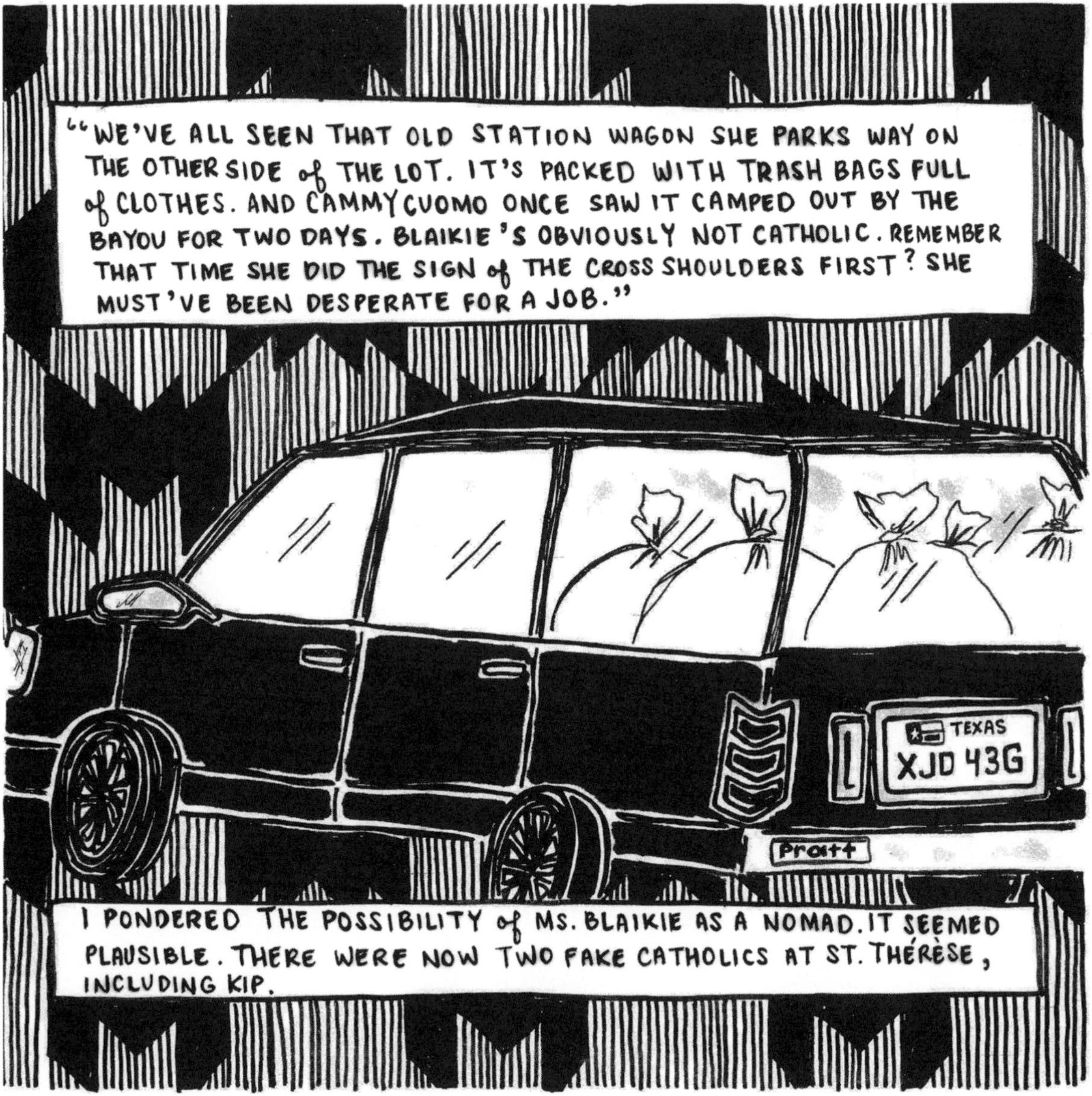
"WE'VE ALL SEEN THAT OLD STATION WAGON SHE PARKS WAY ON THE OTHER SIDE of THE LOT. IT'S PACKED WITH TRASH BAGS FULL of CLOTHES. AND CAMMY CUOMO ONCE SAW IT CAMPED OUT BY THE BAYOU FOR TWO DAYS. BLAIKIE'S OBVIOUSLY NOT CATHOLIC. REMEMBER THAT TIME SHE DID THE SIGN of THE CROSS SHOULDERS FIRST? SHE MUST'VE BEEN DESPERATE FOR A JOB."
TEXAS
XJD 43G
Pratt
I PONDERED THE POSSIBILITY of MS. BLAIKIE AS A NOMAD. IT SEEMED PLAUSIBLE. THERE WERE NOW TWO FAKE CATHOLICS AT ST. THÉRÈSE, INCLUDING KIP.

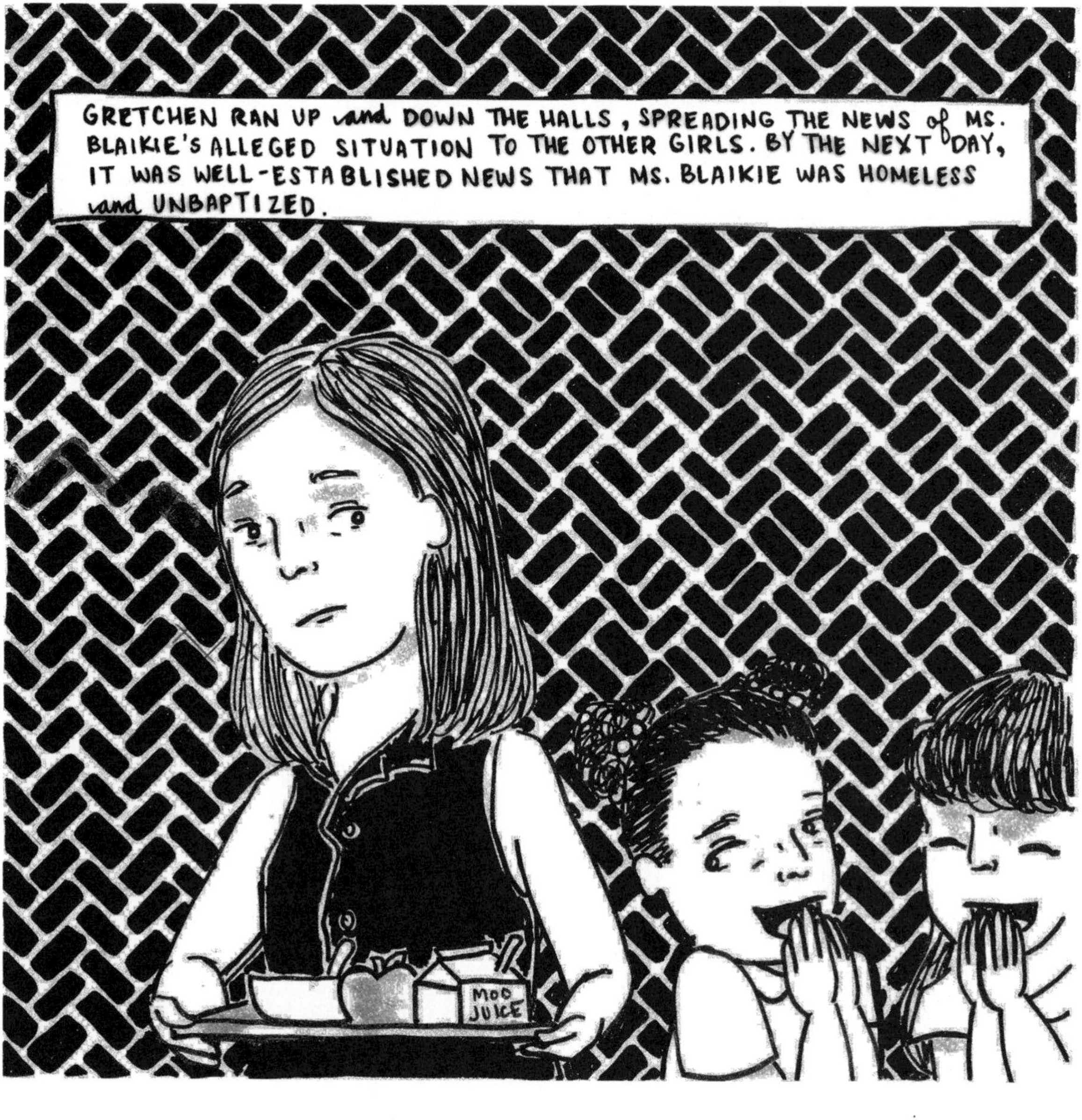
GRETCHEN RAN UP and DOWN THE HALLS, SPREADING THE NEWS of MS. BLAIKIE'S ALLEGED SITUATION TO THE OTHER GIRLS. BY THE NEXT DAY, IT WAS WELL-ESTABLISHED NEWS THAT MS. BLAIKIE WAS HOMELESS and UNBAPTIZED.
MOO JUICE

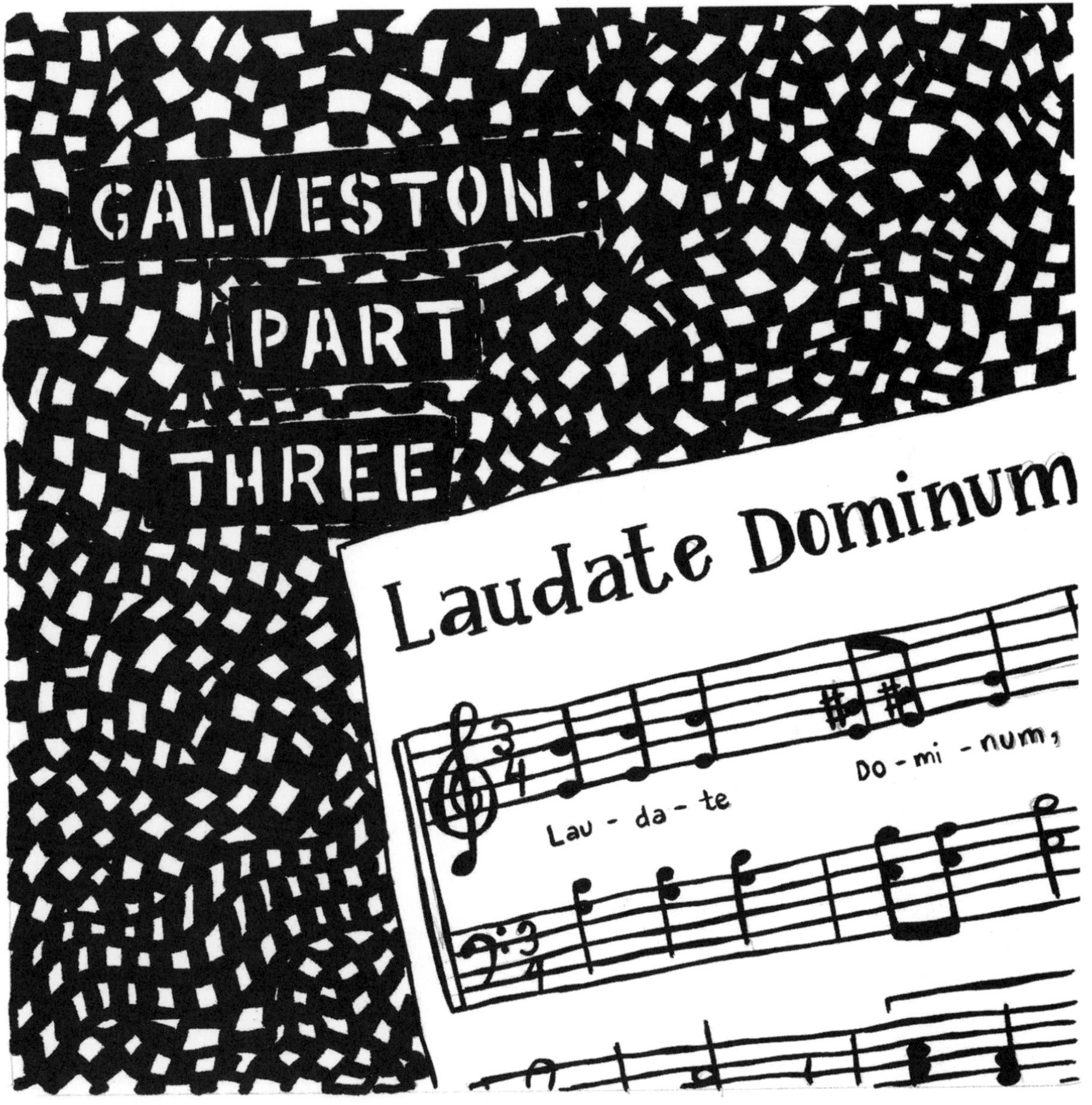
GALVESTON:
PART
THREE
Laudate Dominum
Lau - da - te
Do - mi - num,

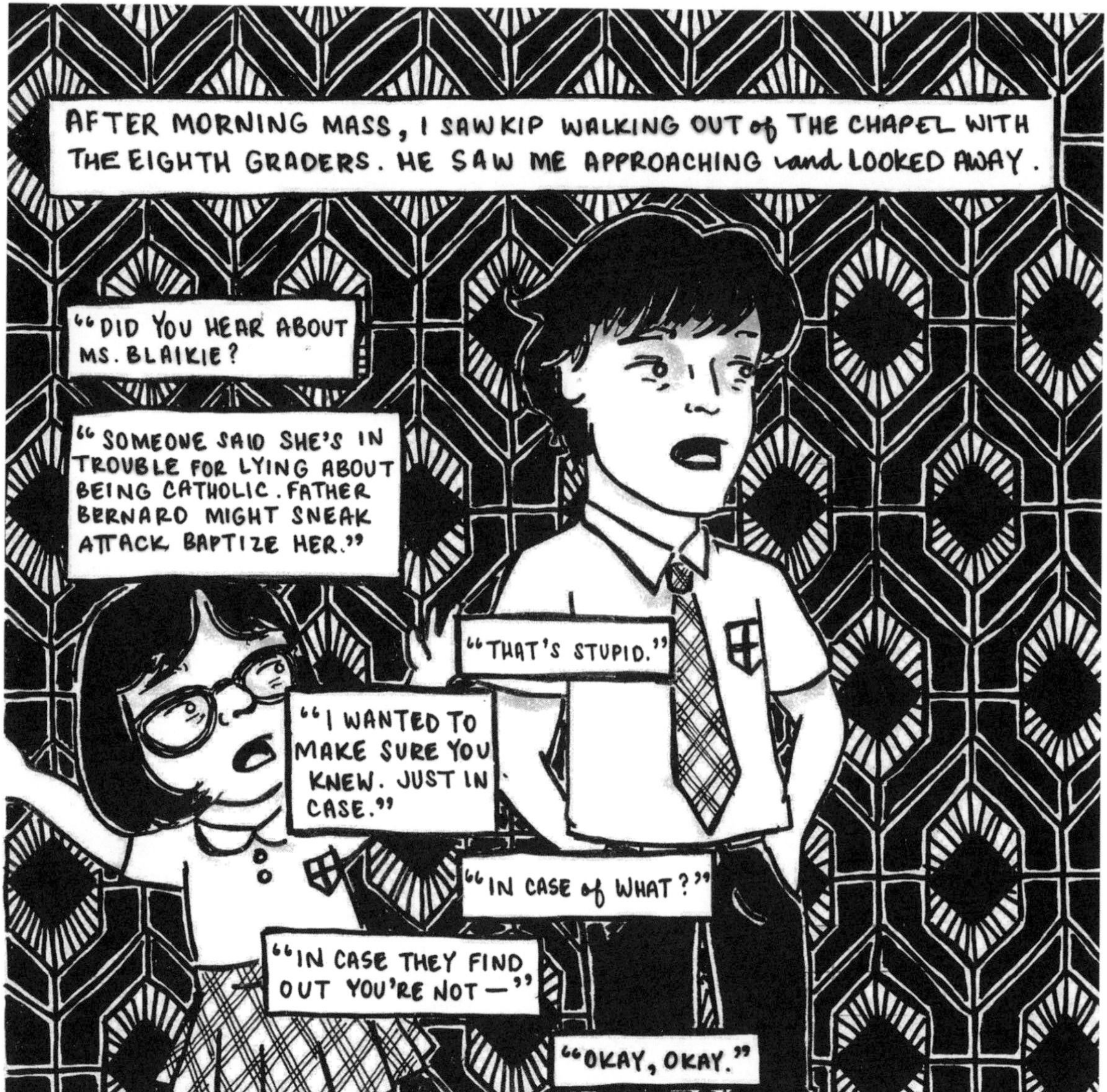
AFTER MORNING MASS, I SAW KIP WALKING OUT of THE CHAPEL WITH THE EIGHTH GRADERS. HE SAW ME APPROACHING and LOOKED AWAY.
"DID YOU HEAR ABOUT MS. BLAIKIE?
"SOMEONE SAID SHE'S IN TROUBLE FOR LYING ABOUT BEING CATHOLIC. FATHER BERNARD MIGHT SNEAK ATTACK BAPTIZE HER."
"THAT'S STUPID."
"I WANTED TO MAKE SURE YOU KNEW. JUST IN CASE."
"IN CASE of WHAT?"
"IN CASE THEY FIND OUT YOU'RE NOT—"
"OKAY, OKAY."

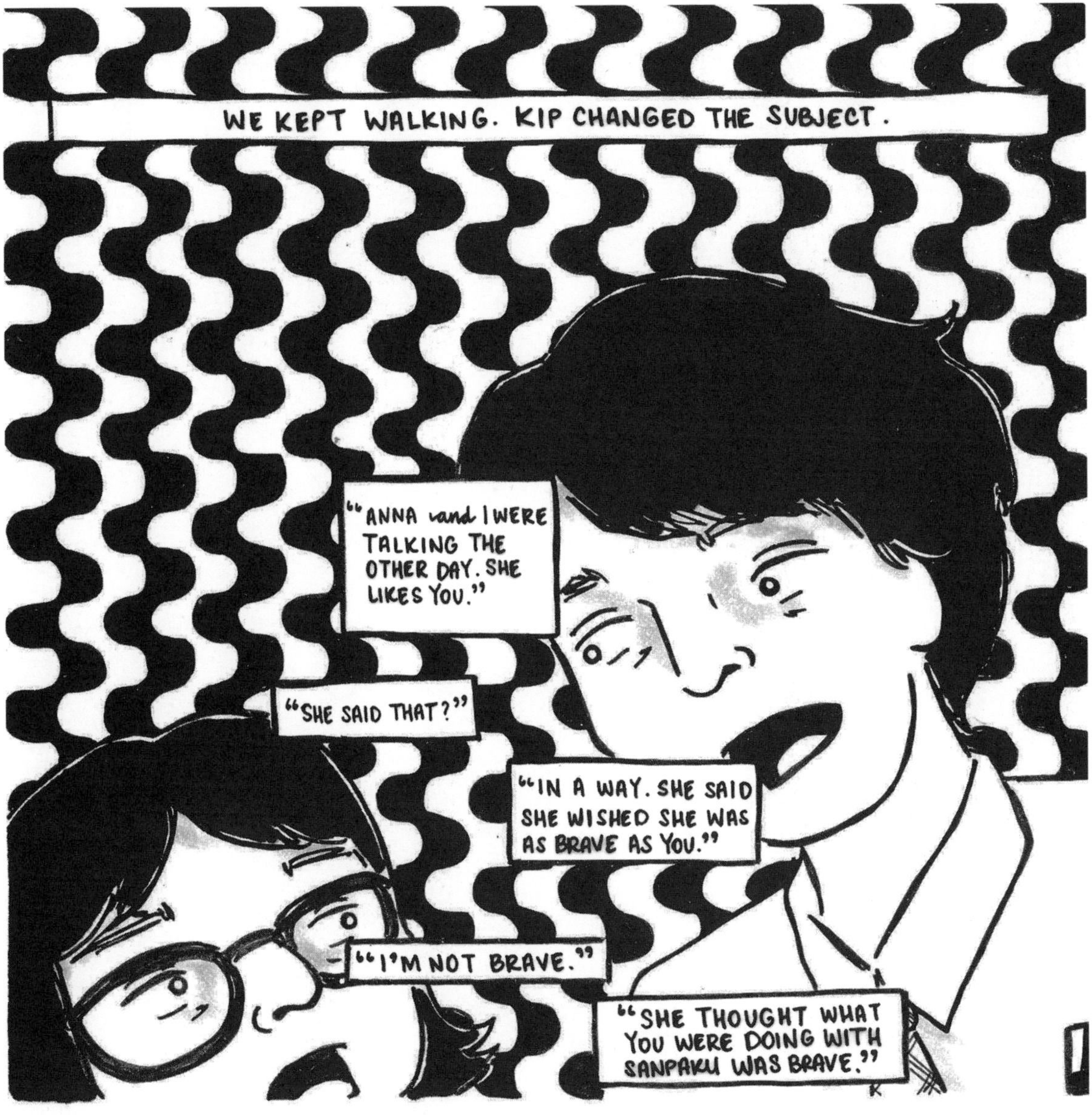
WE KEPT WALKING. KIP CHANGED THE SUBJECT.
"ANNA and I WERE TALKING THE OTHER DAY. SHE LIKES YOU."
"SHE SAID THAT?"
"IN A WAY. SHE SAID SHE WISHED SHE WAS AS BRAVE AS YOU."
"I'M NOT BRAVE."
"SHE THOUGHT WHAT YOU WERE DOING WITH SANPAKU WAS BRAVE."

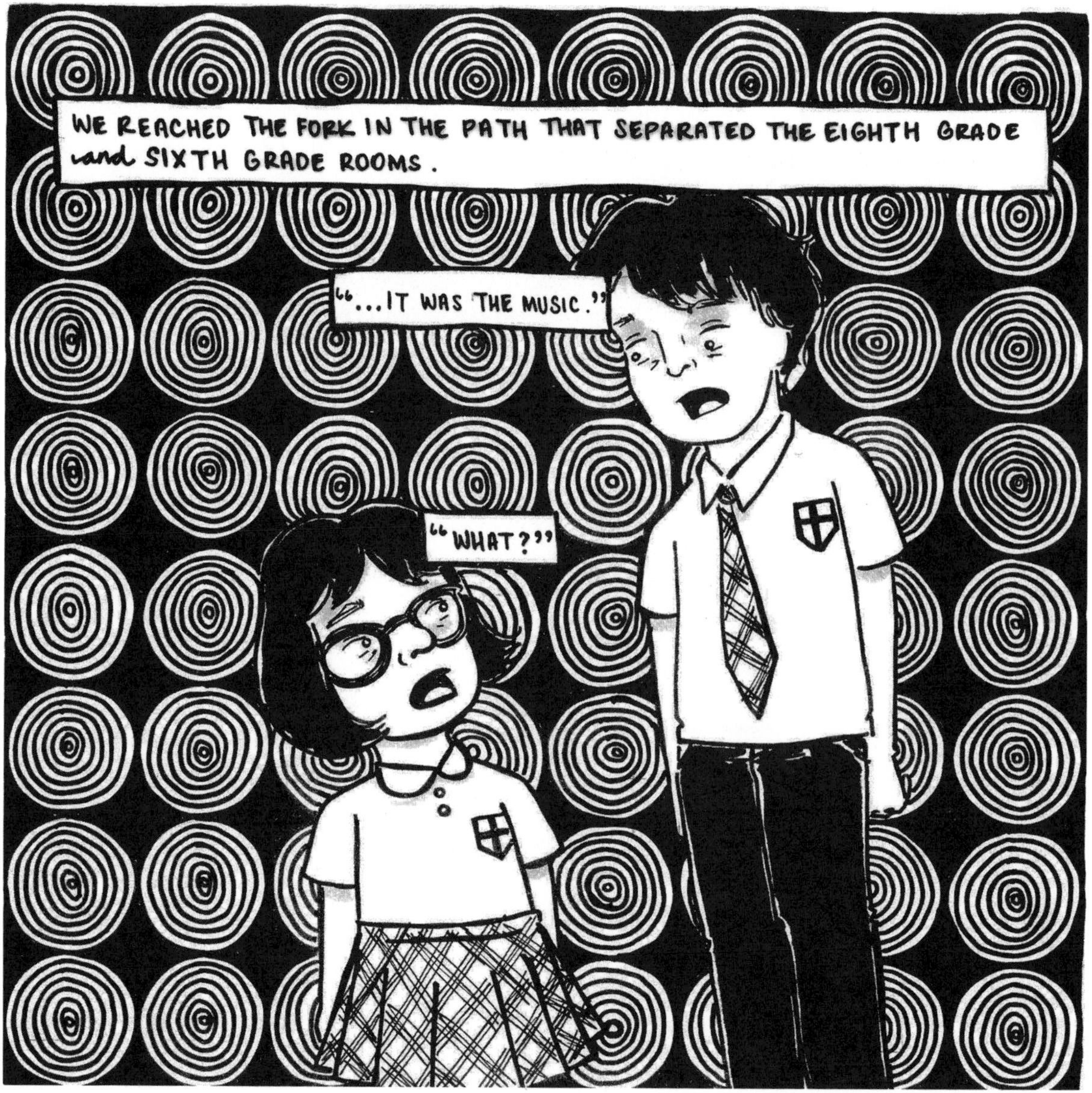
WE REACHED THE FORK IN THE PATH THAT SEPARATED THE EIGHTH GRADE and SIXTH GRADE ROOMS.
"...IT WAS THE MUSIC."
"WHAT?"

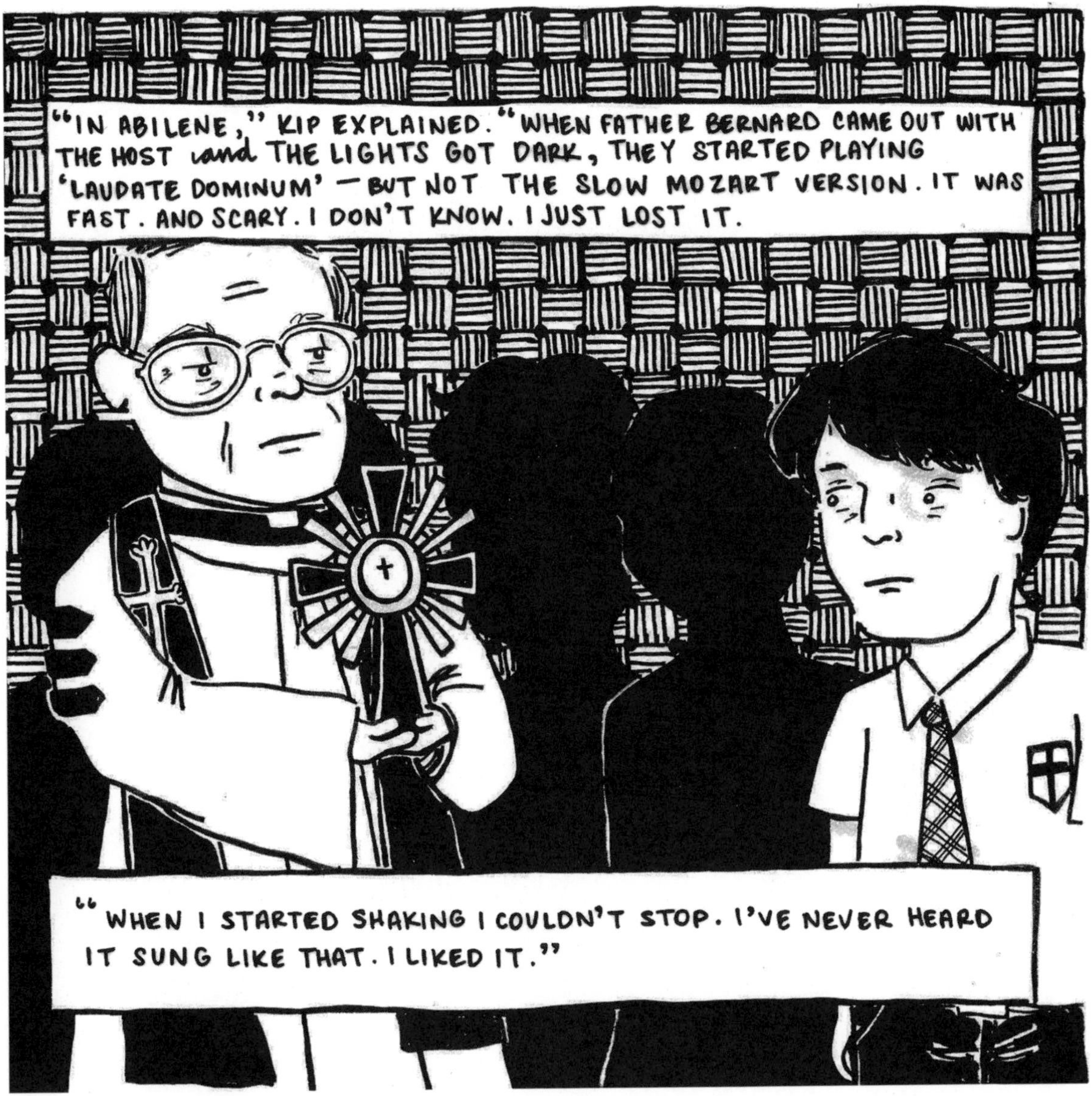
"IN ABILENE," KIP EXPLAINED. "WHEN FATHER BERNARD CAME OUT WITH THE HOST and THE LIGHTS GOT DARK, THEY STARTED PLAYING 'LAUDATE DOMINUM' — BUT NOT THE SLOW MOZART VERSION. IT WAS FAST. AND SCARY. I DON'T KNOW. I JUST LOST IT.
"WHEN I STARTED SHAKING I COULDN'T STOP. I'VE NEVER HEARD IT SUNG LIKE THAT. I LIKED IT."

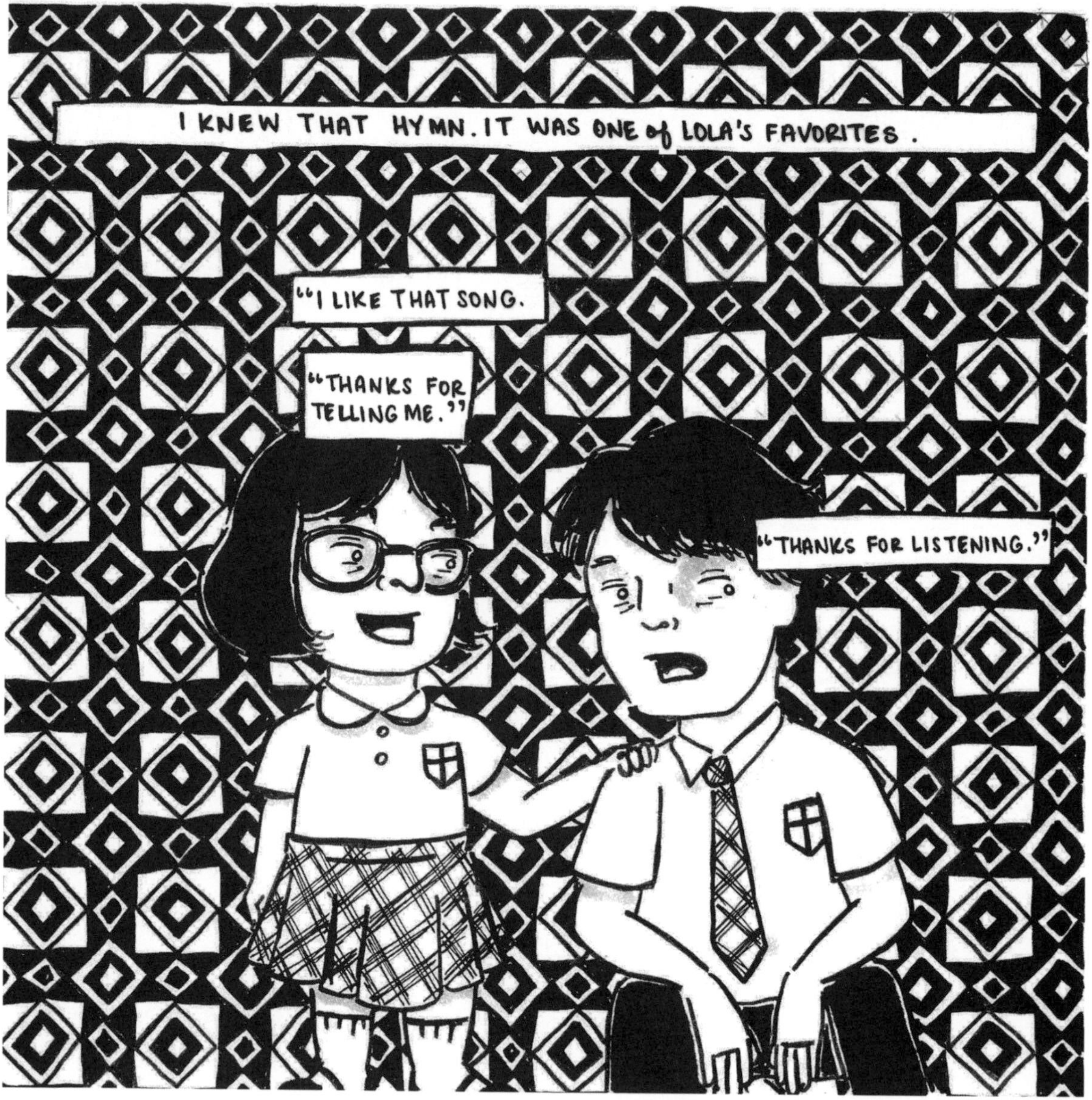
I KNEW THAT HYMN. IT WAS ONE of LOLA'S FAVORITES.
"I LIKE THAT SONG.
"THANKS FOR TELLING ME."
"THANKS FOR LISTENING."

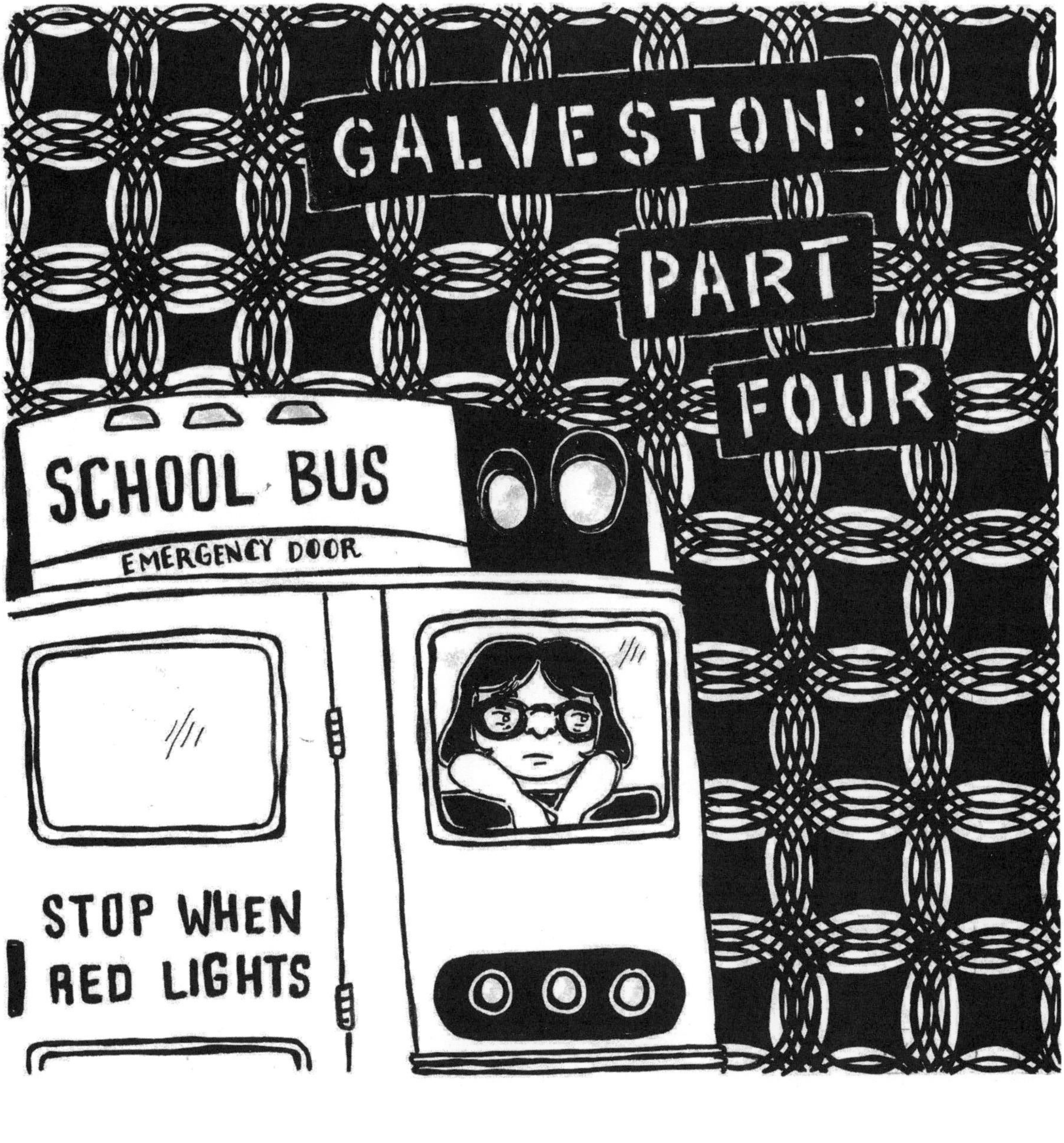
GALVESTON:
PART
FOUR
SCHOOL BUS
EMERGENCY DOOR
STOP WHEN
RED LIGHTS

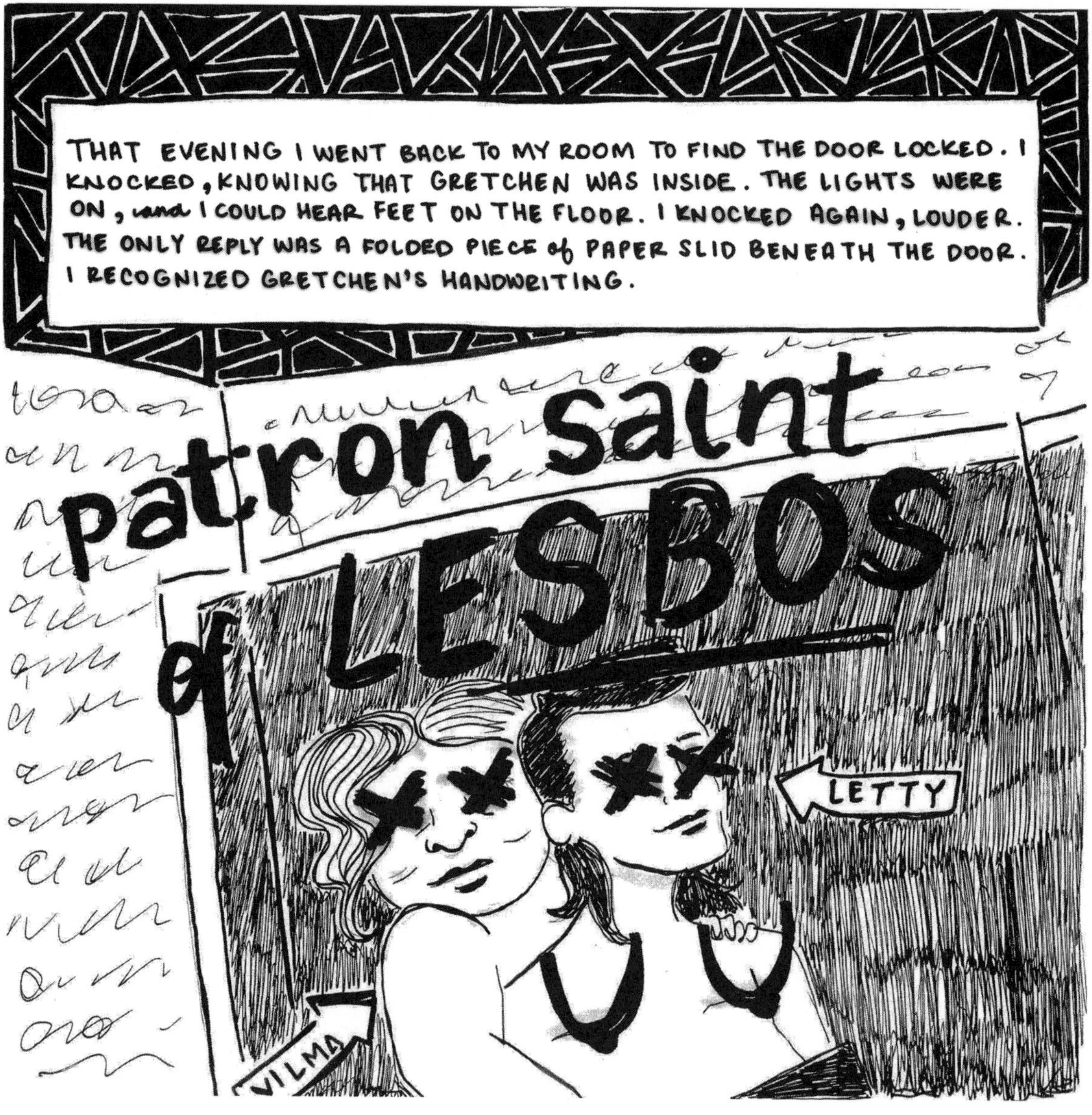
THAT EVENING I WENT BACK TO MY ROOM TO FIND THE DOOR LOCKED. I KNOCKED, KNOWING THAT GRETCHEN WAS INSIDE. THE LIGHTS WERE ON, and I COULD HEAR FEET ON THE FLOOR. I KNOCKED AGAIN, LOUDER. THE ONLY REPLY WAS A FOLDED PIECE of PAPER SLID BENEATH THE DOOR. I RECOGNIZED GRETCHEN'S HANDWRITING.
patron saint of LESBOS
LETTY
VILMA

I HEARD AN ERUPTION of GIGGLES FROM INSIDE THE ROOM.
"IS SHE STILL OUT THERE?"
ROOM 16
"YEAH, SHE'S PROBABLY STILL STARING AT IT."
"SHE PROBABLY LIKES IT!"

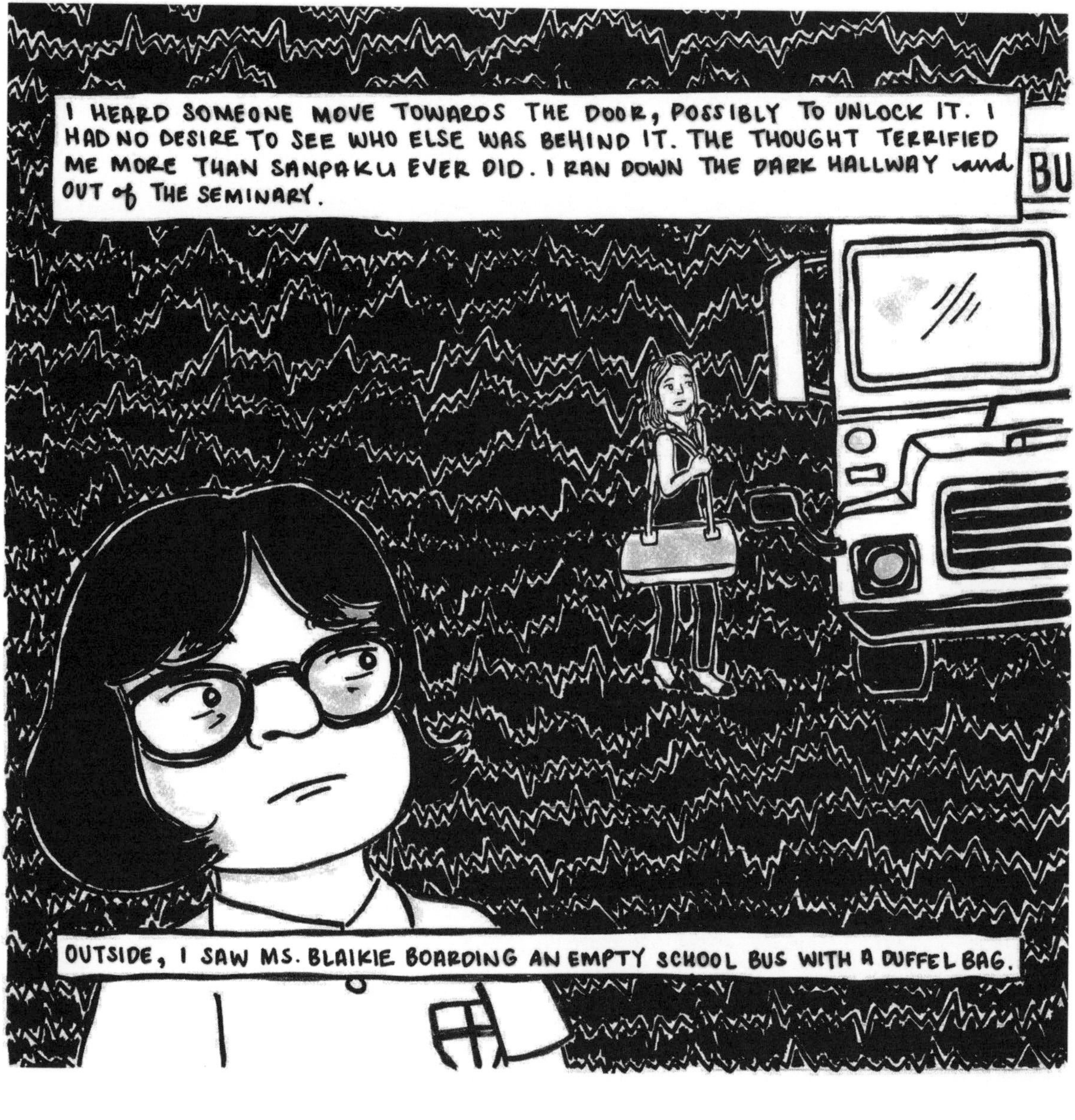
I HEARD SOMEONE MOVE TOWARDS THE DOOR, POSSIBLY TO UNLOCK IT. I HAD NO DESIRE TO SEE WHO ELSE WAS BEHIND IT. THE THOUGHT TERRIFIED ME MORE THAN SANPAKU EVER DID. I RAN DOWN THE DARK HALLWAY and OUT of THE SEMINARY.
OUTSIDE, I SAW MS. BLAIKIE BOARDING AN EMPTY SCHOOL BUS WITH A DUFFEL BAG.

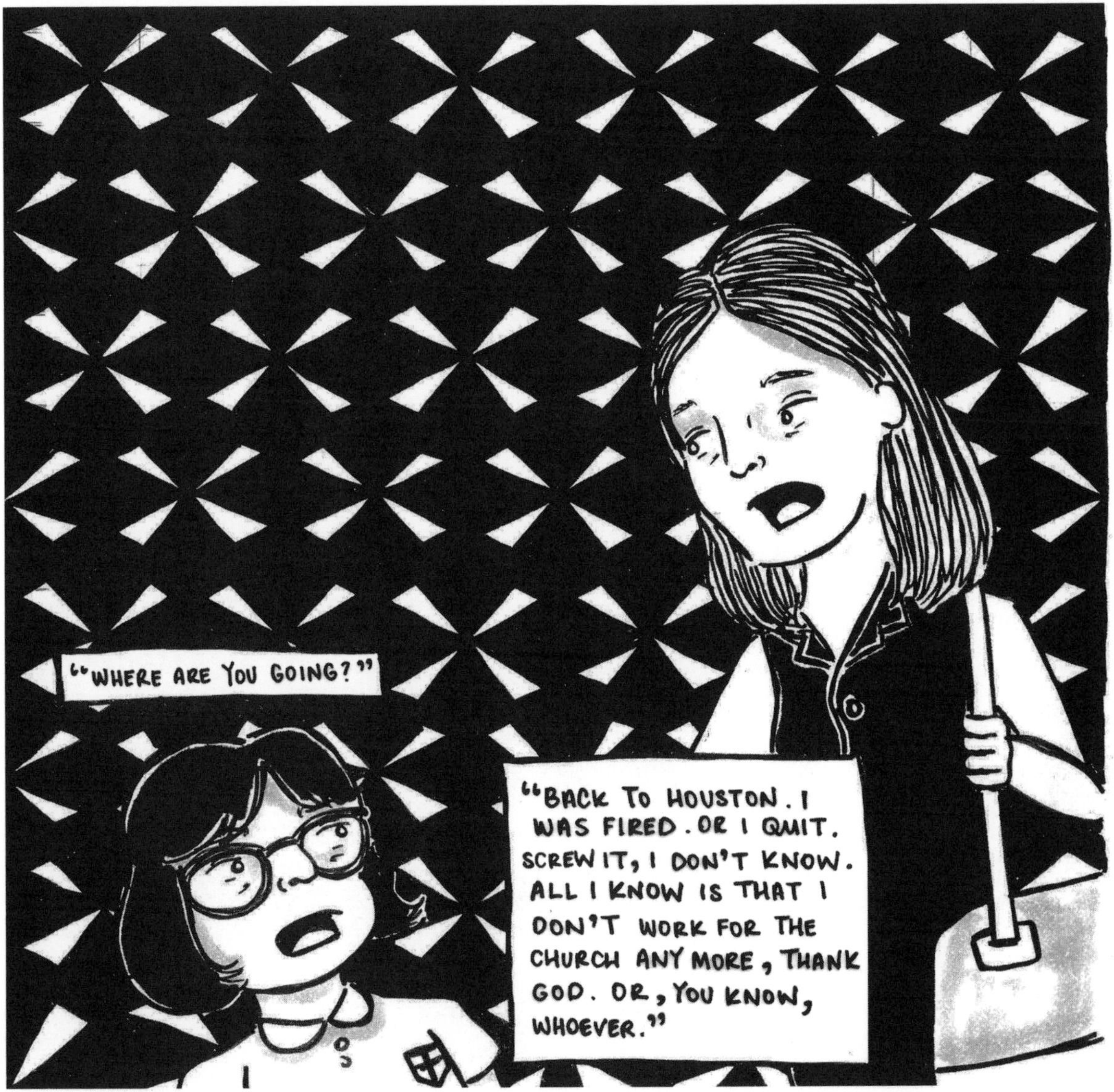
"WHERE ARE YOU GOING?"
"BACK TO HOUSTON. I WAS FIRED. OR I QUIT. SCREW IT, I DON'T KNOW. ALL I KNOW IS THAT I DON'T WORK FOR THE CHURCH ANY MORE, THANK GOD. OR, YOU KNOW, WHOEVER."

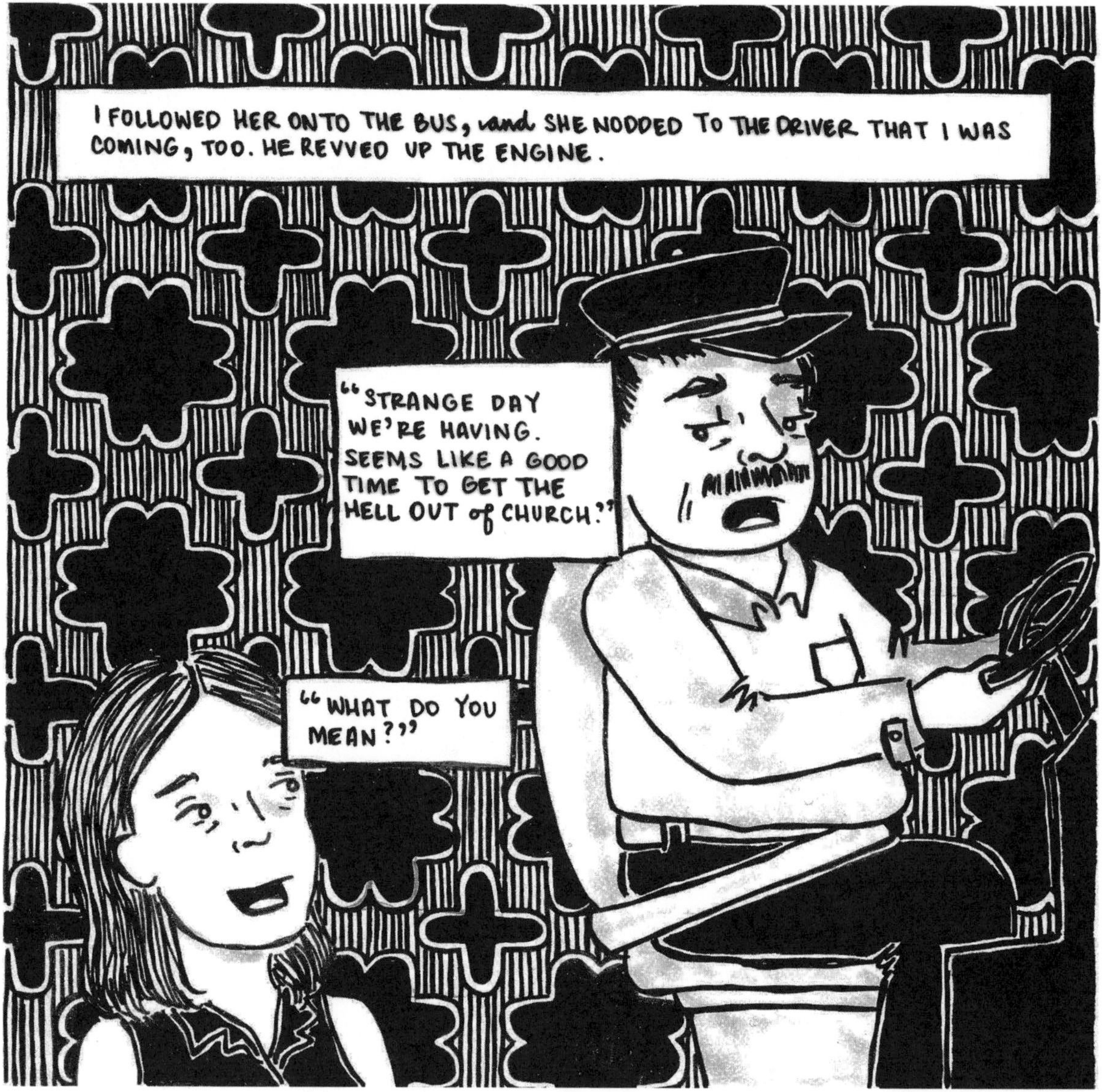
I FOLLOWED HER ONTO THE BUS, and SHE NODDED TO THE DRIVER THAT I WAS COMING, TOO. HE REVVED UP THE ENGINE.
"STRANGE DAY WE'RE HAVING. SEEMS LIKE A GOOD TIME TO GET THE HELL OUT of CHURCH."
"WHAT DO YOU MEAN?"

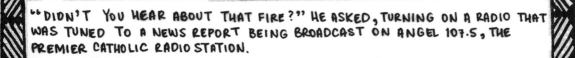

"DIDN'T YOU HEAR ABOUT THAT FIRE?" HE ASKED, TURNING ON A RADIO THAT WAS TUNED TO A NEWS REPORT BEING BROADCAST ON ANGEL 107.5, THE PREMIER CATHOLIC RADIO STATION.
1 2 3 4 5 6
AM/FM
Panasonic
BUS AUDIO
AUX
TUNE
SEEK
107.5
"YOU KNOW, THE ONE IN QUEENS A FEW MONTHS AGO THAT WAS SUPPOSED TO HAVE BEEN A MIRACLE FOR THAT SAINT-IN-THE-MAKING? IT WAS STAGED. THE WHOLE THING WAS PLANNED BY A BUNCH of LOONIES WHO WANTED TO SPEED UP CANONIZATION."

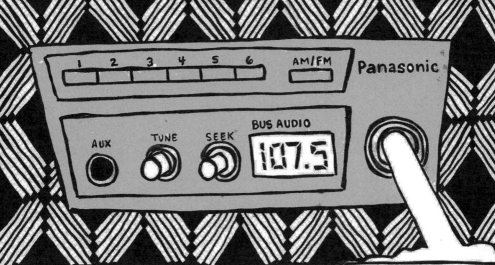

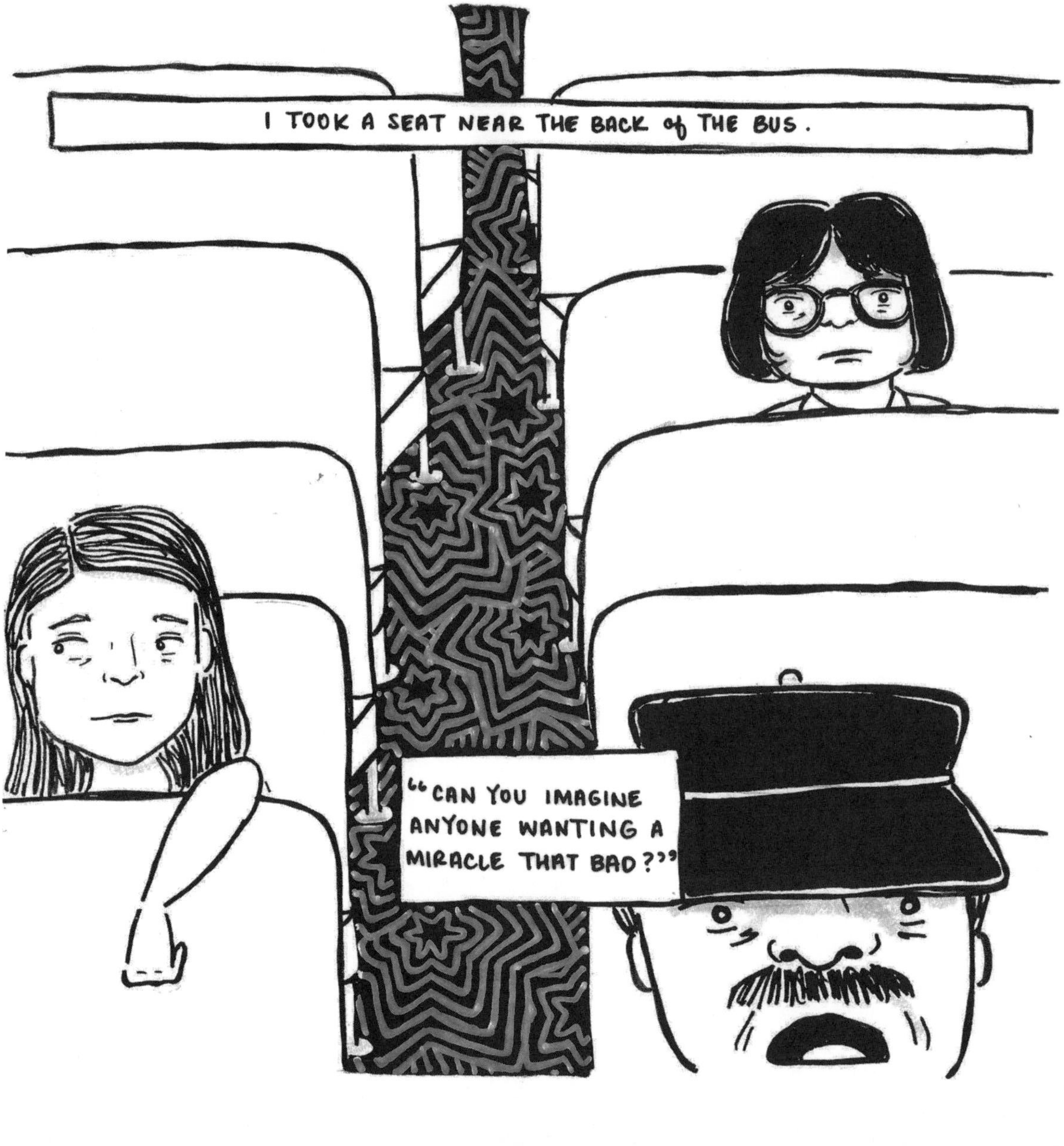
I TOOK A SEAT NEAR THE BACK of THE BUS.
"CAN YOU IMAGINE ANYONE WANTING A MIRACLE THAT BAD?"

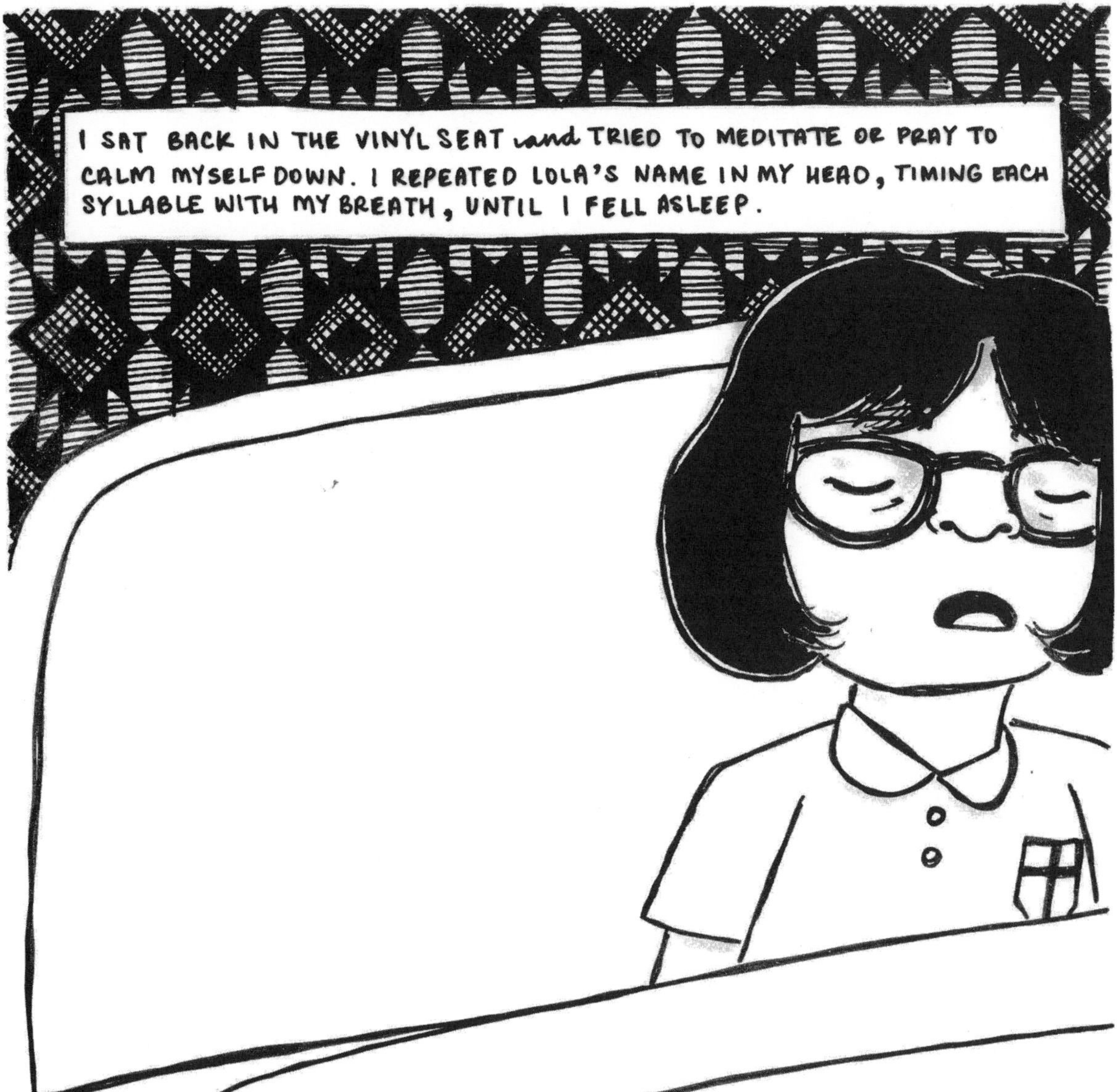
I SAT BACK IN THE VINYL SEAT and TRIED TO MEDITATE OR PRAY TO CALM MYSELF DOWN. I REPEATED LOLA'S NAME IN MY HEAD, TIMING EACH SYLLABLE WITH MY BREATH, UNTIL I FELL ASLEEP.

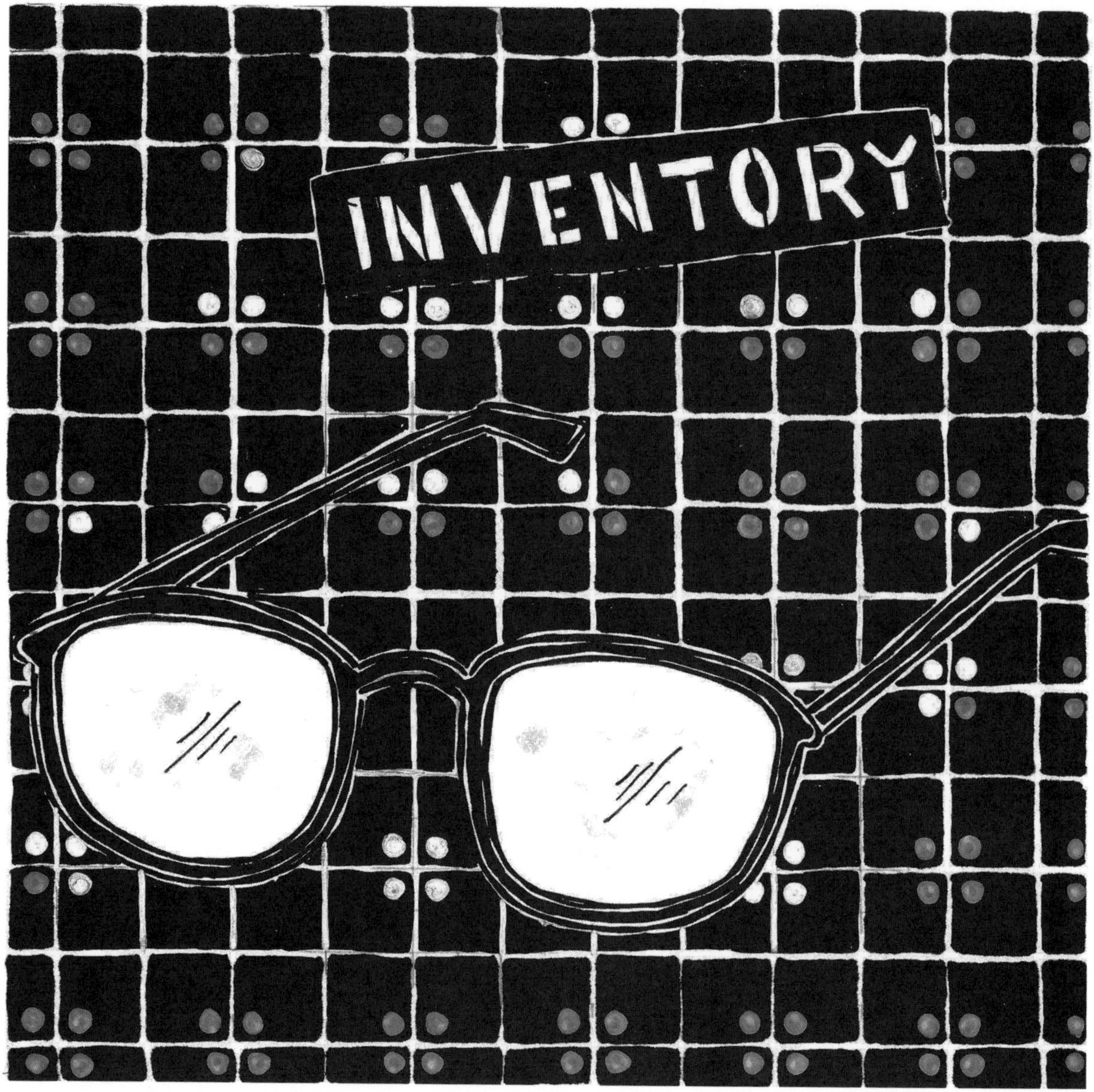
INVENTORY

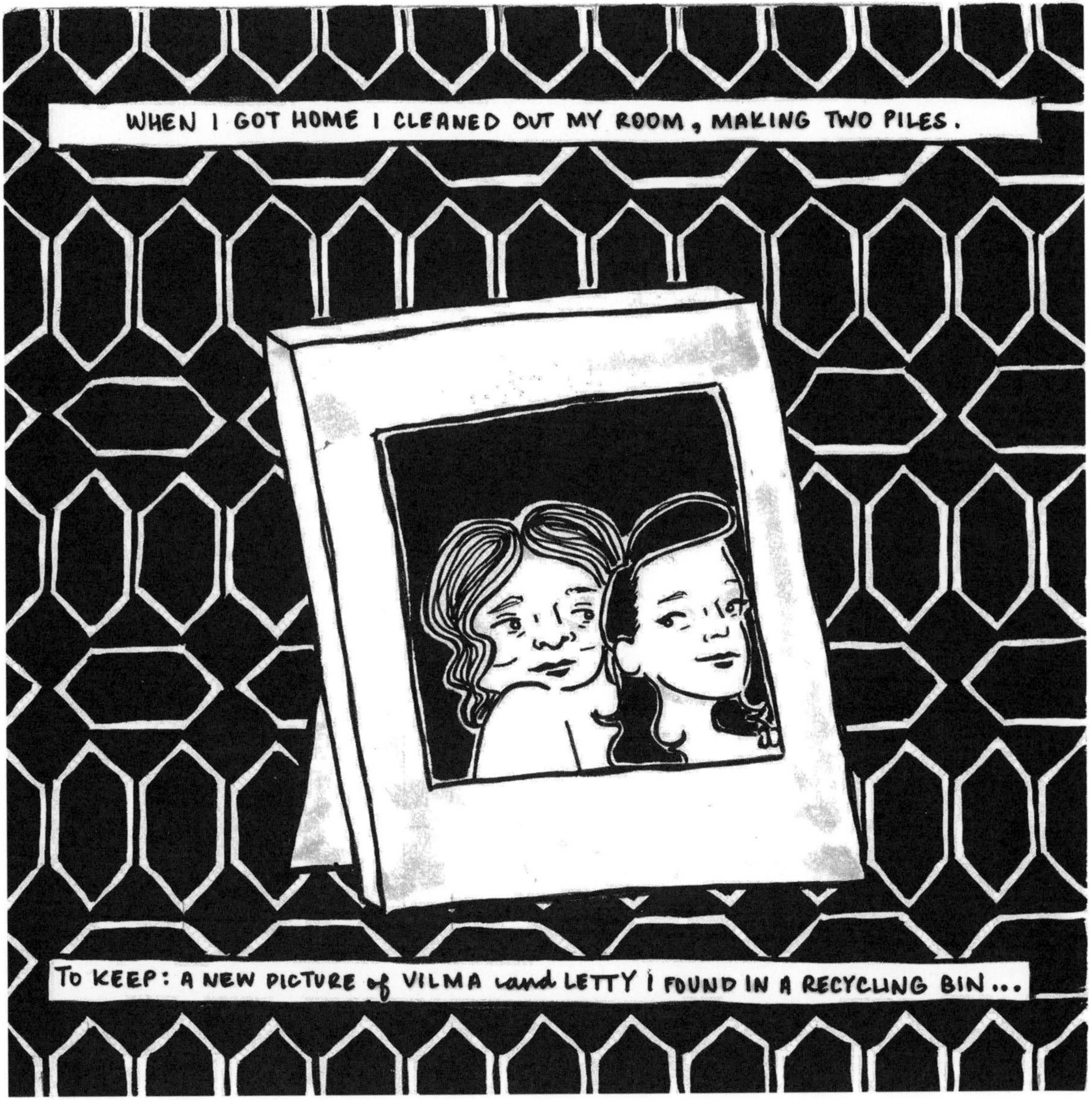
WHEN I GOT HOME I CLEANED OUT MY ROOM, MAKING TWO PILES.
TO KEEP: A NEW PICTURE of VILMA and LETTY I FOUND IN A RECYCLING BIN...

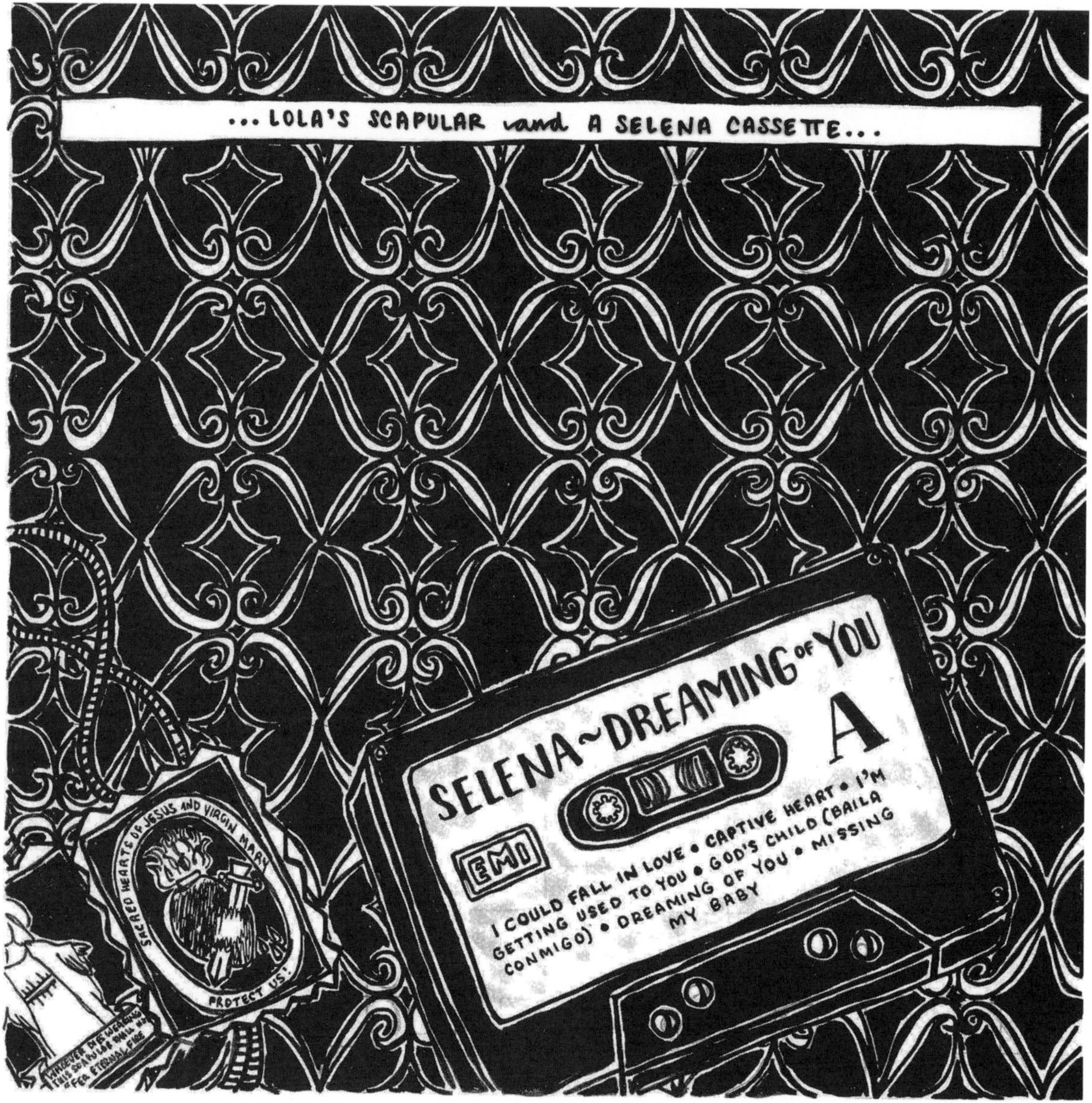
...LOLA'S SCAPULAR and A SELENA CASSETTE...
SACRED HEARTS OF JESUS AND VIRGIN MARY
PROTECT US!
WHOEVER DIES WEARING
THIS SCAPULAR SHALL
ETERNAL FIRE
SELENA ~ DREAMING OF YOU
A
EMI
I COULD FALL IN LOVE • CAPTIVE HEART • I'M GETTING USED TO YOU • GOD'S CHILD (BAILA CONMIGO) • DREAMING OF YOU • MISSING MY BABY

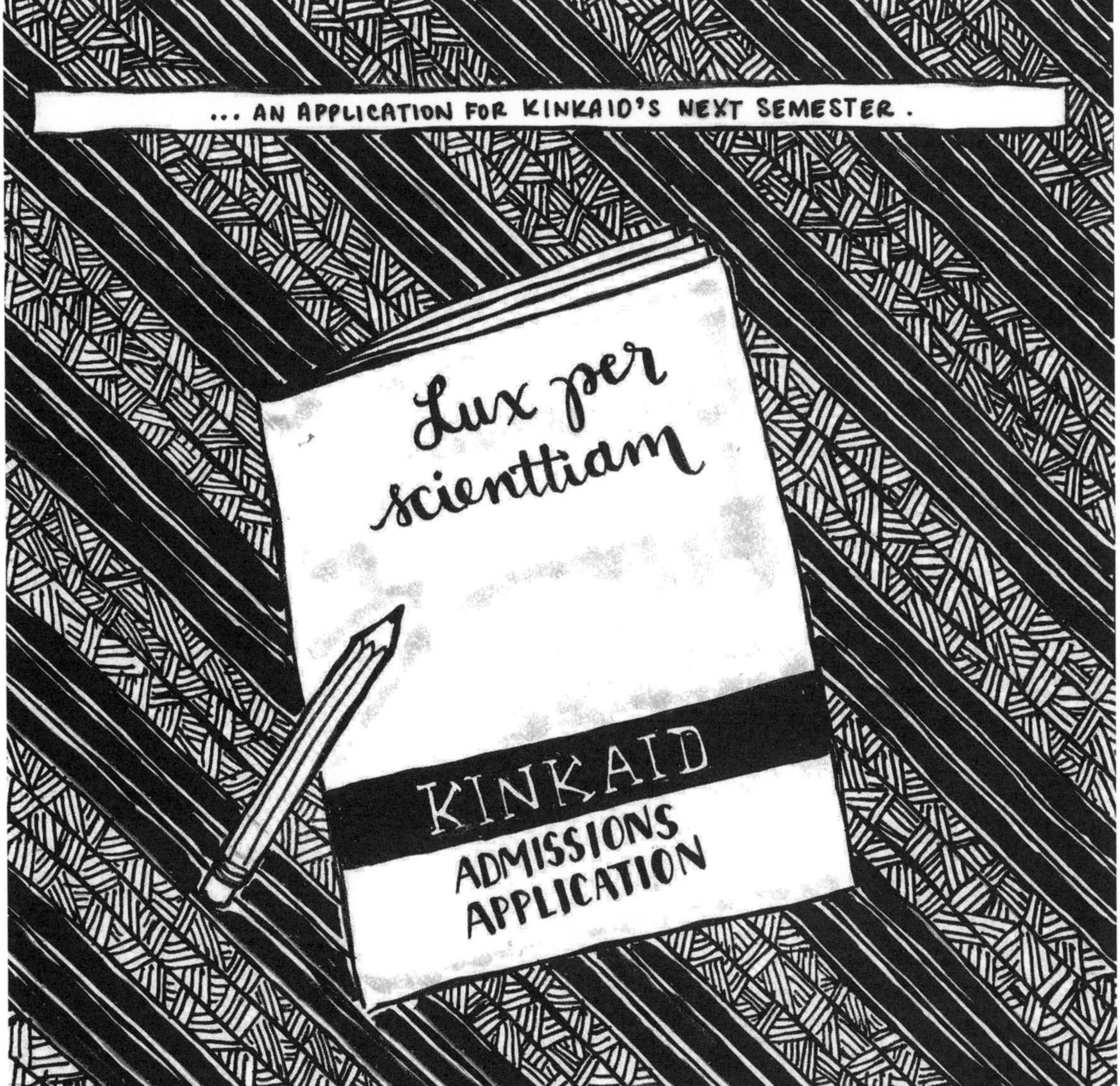
... AN APPLICATION FOR KINKAID'S NEXT SEMESTER.
Lux per scienttiam
KINKAID
ADMISSIONS APPLICATION

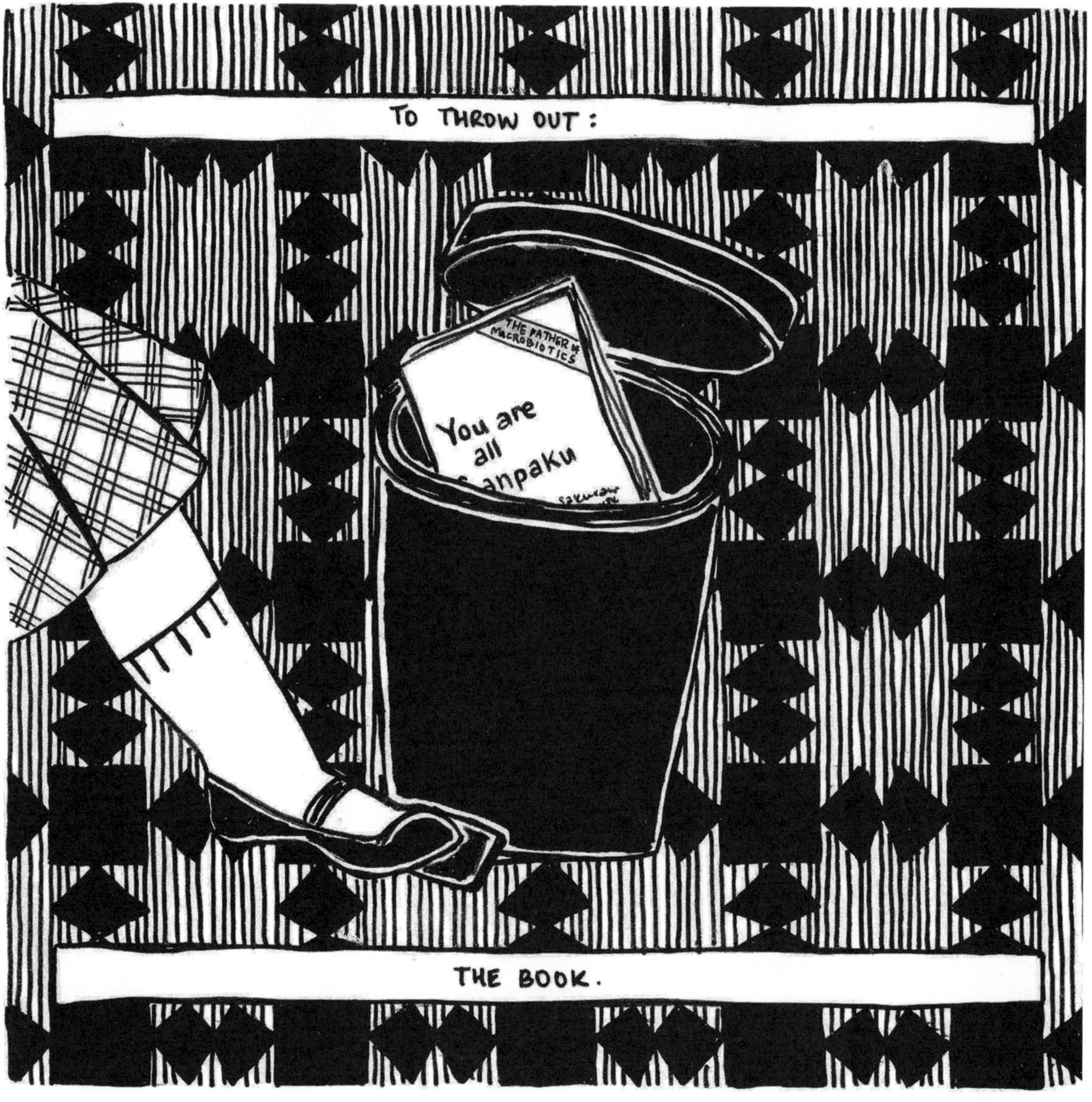
TO THROW OUT:
THE FATHER OF MACROBIOTICS
You are all
THE BOOK.

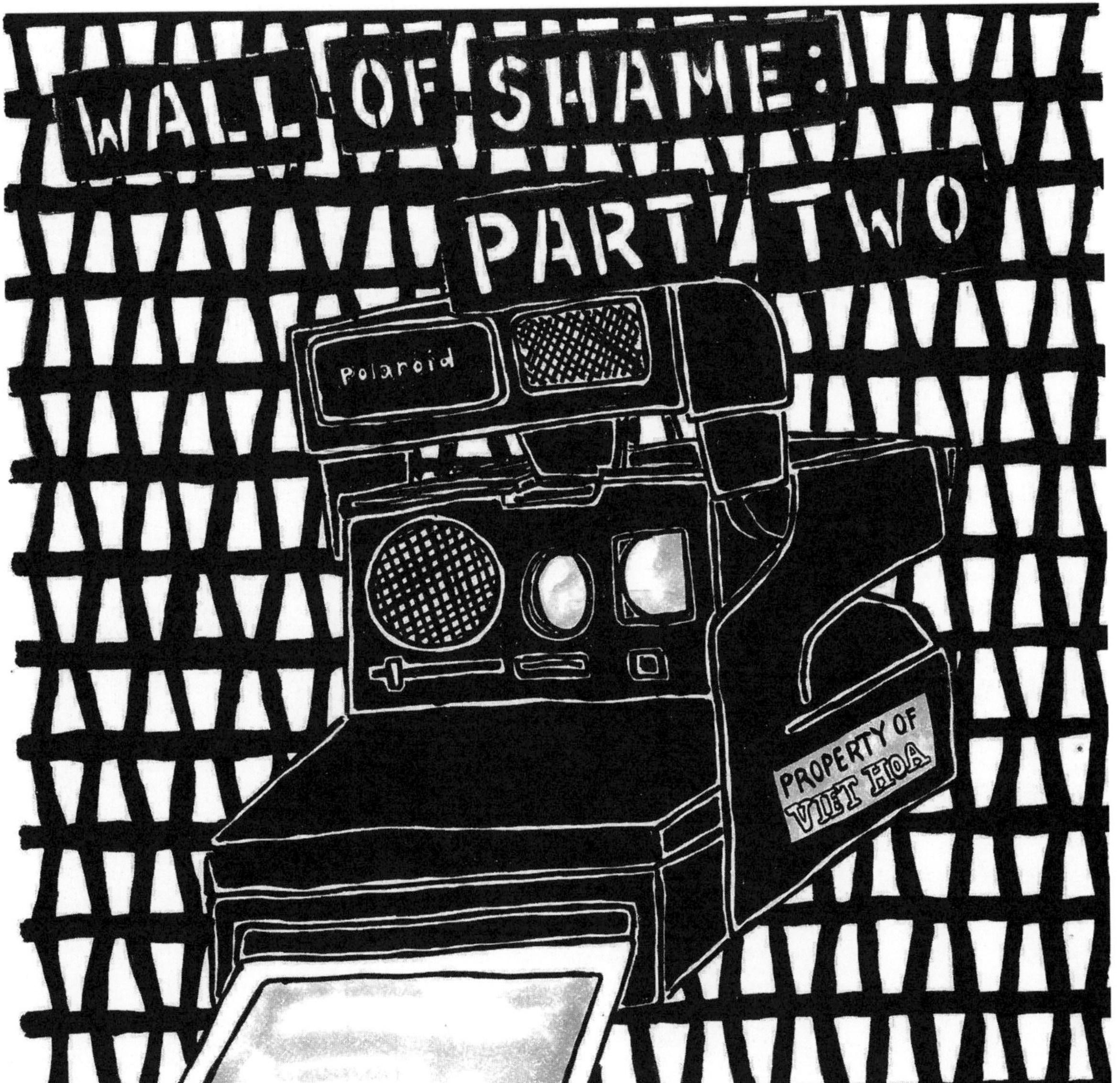
WALL OF SHAME:
PART TWO
Polaroid
PROPERTY OF
VIET HOA

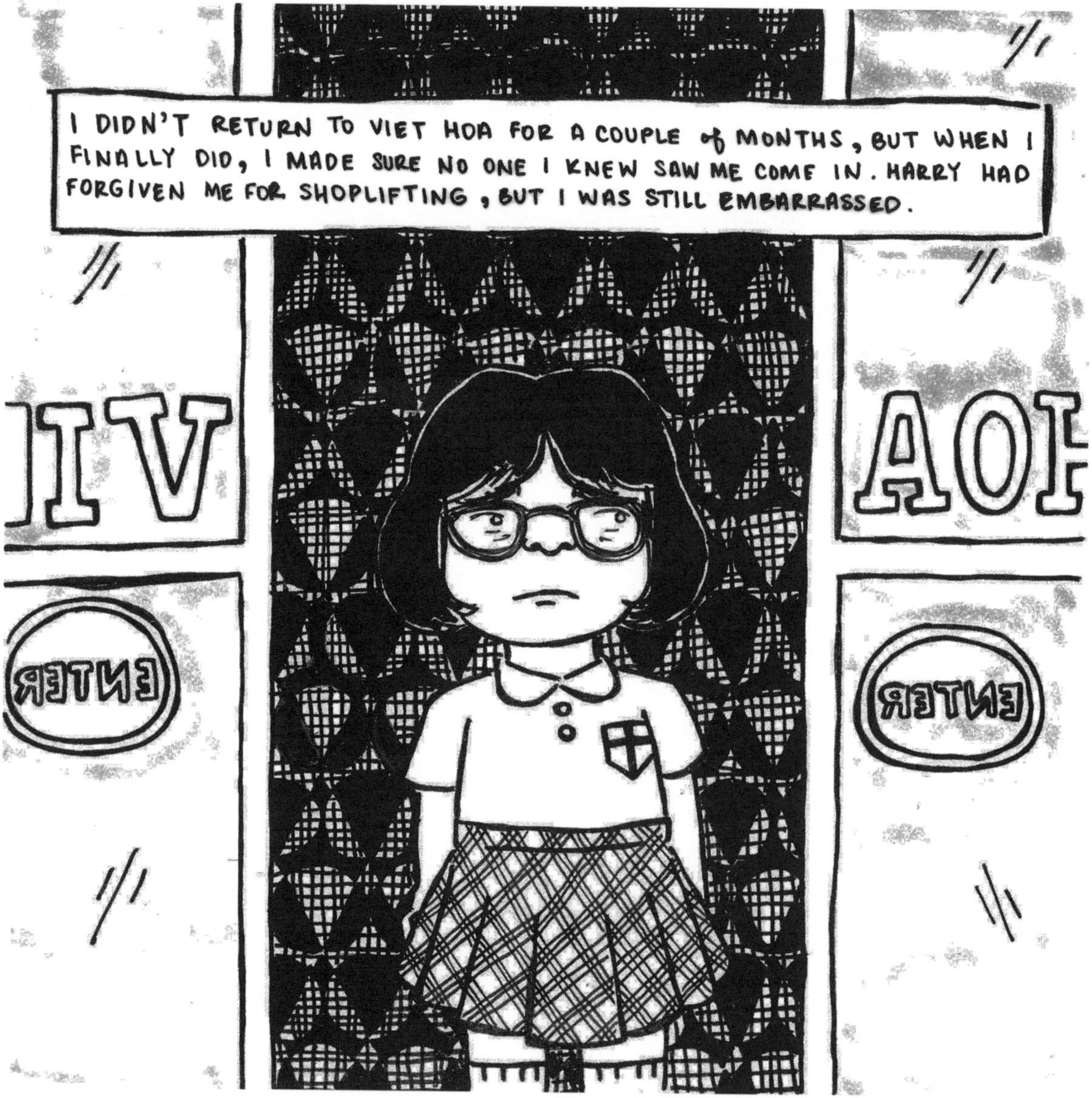
I DIDN'T RETURN TO VIET HOA FOR A COUPLE of MONTHS, BUT WHEN I FINALLY DID, I MADE SURE NO ONE I KNEW SAW ME COME IN. HARRY HAD FORGIVEN ME FOR SHOPLIFTING, BUT I WAS STILL EMBARRASSED.
ENTER
ENTER

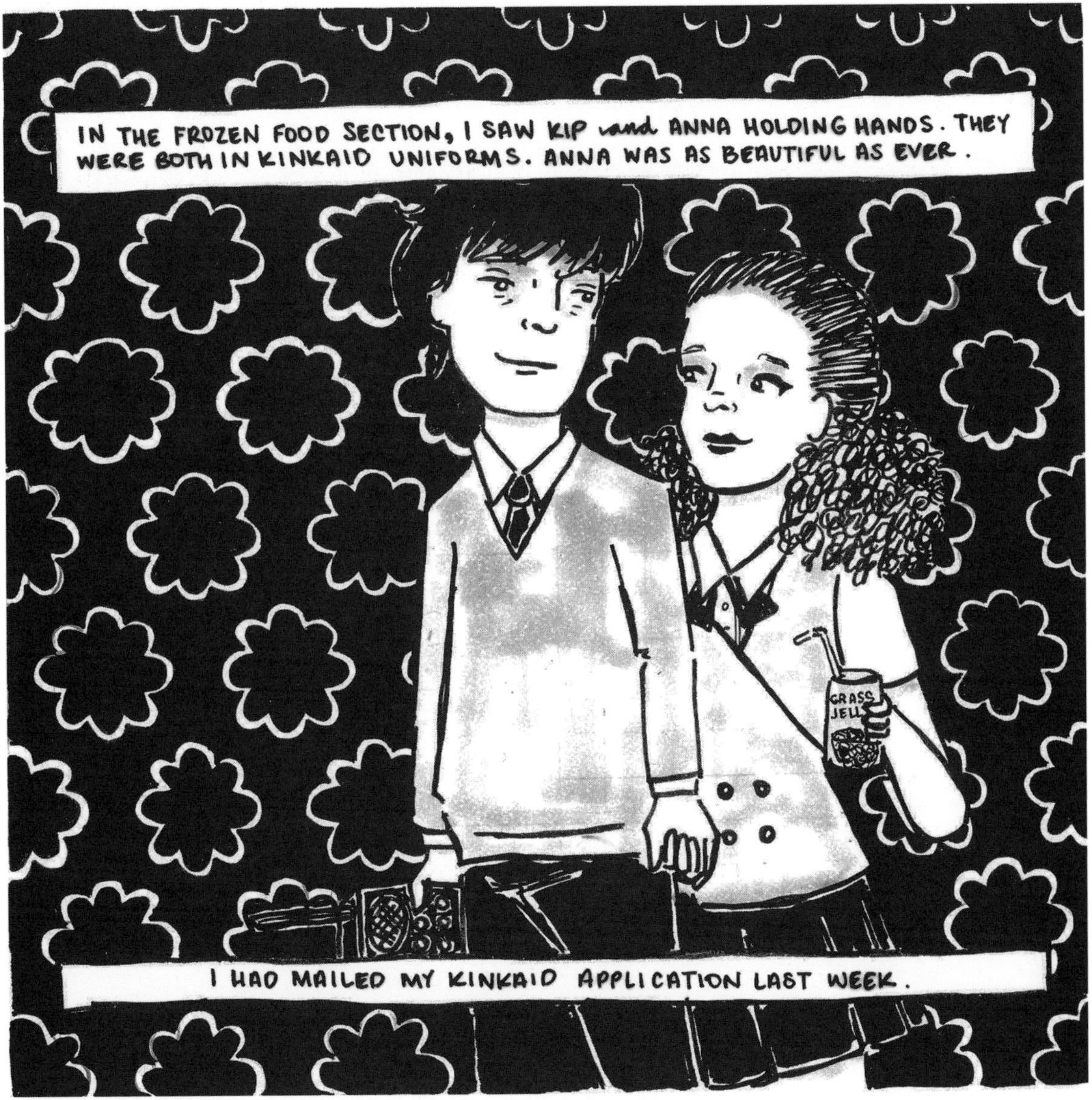
IN THE FROZEN FOOD SECTION, I SAW KIP and ANNA HOLDING HANDS. THEY WERE BOTH IN KINKAID UNIFORMS. ANNA WAS AS BEAUTIFUL AS EVER.
GRASS JELLY
I HAD MAILED MY KINKAID APPLICATION LAST WEEK.

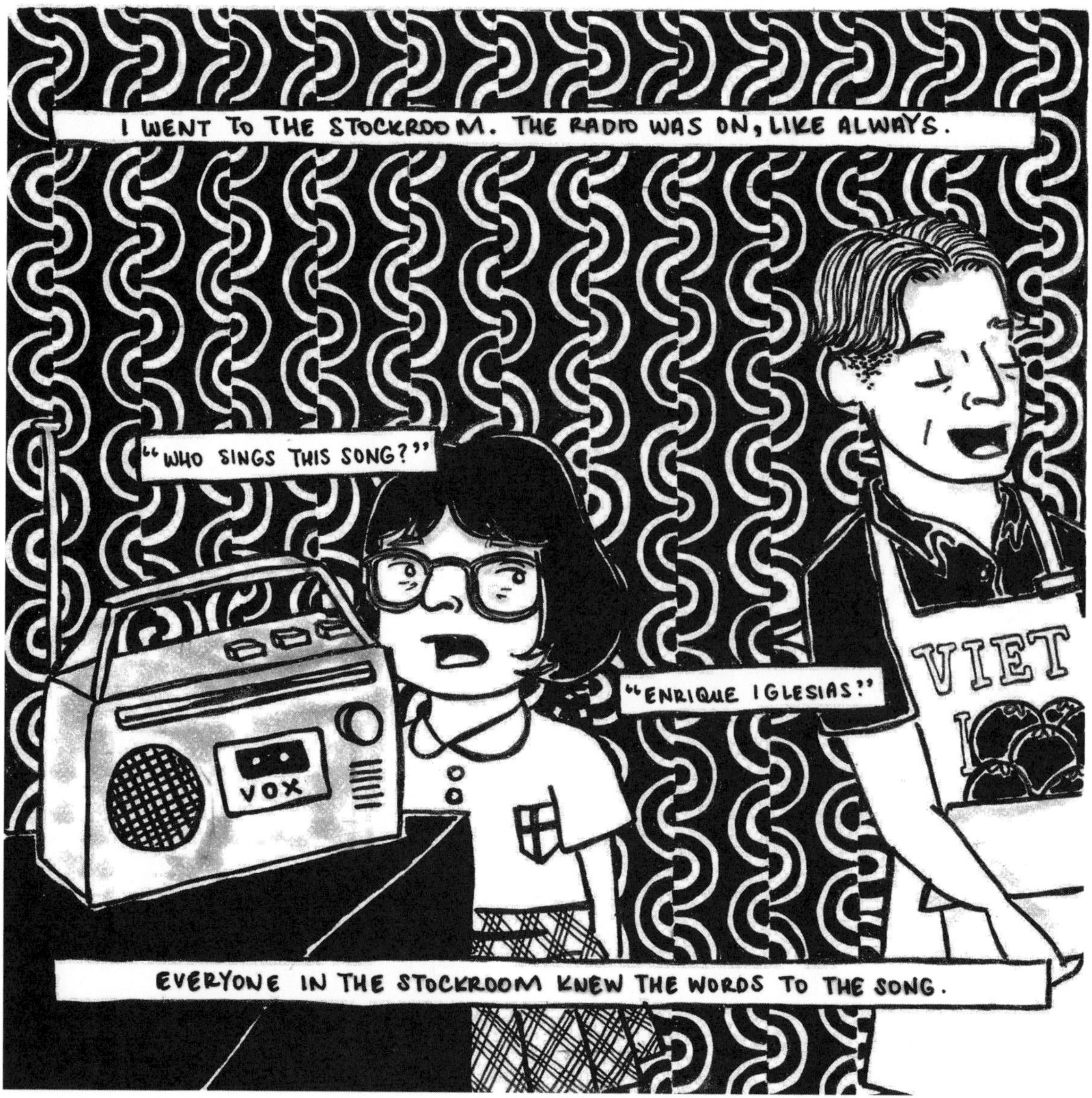
I WENT TO THE STOCKROOM. THE RADIO WAS ON, LIKE ALWAYS.
"WHO SINGS THIS SONG?"
"ENRIQUE IGLESIAS!"
VIET
VOX
EVERYONE IN THE STOCKROOM KNEW THE WORDS TO THE SONG.

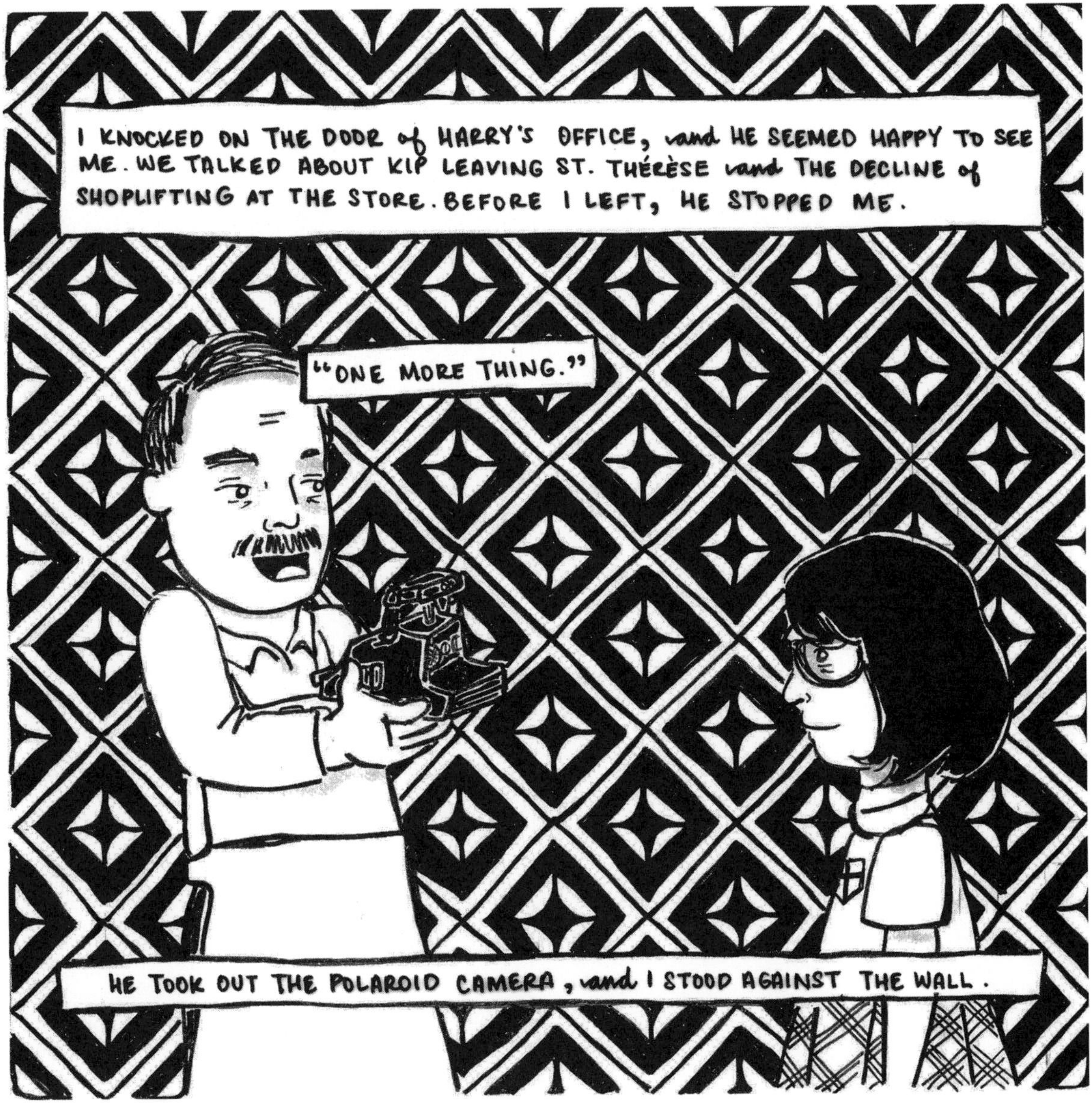
I KNOCKED ON THE DOOR of HARRY'S OFFICE, and HE SEEMED HAPPY TO SEE ME. WE TALKED ABOUT KIP LEAVING ST. THÉRÈSE and THE DECLINE of SHOPLIFTING AT THE STORE. BEFORE I LEFT, HE STOPPED ME.
"ONE MORE THING."
HE TOOK OUT THE POLAROID CAMERA, and I STOOD AGAINST THE WALL.

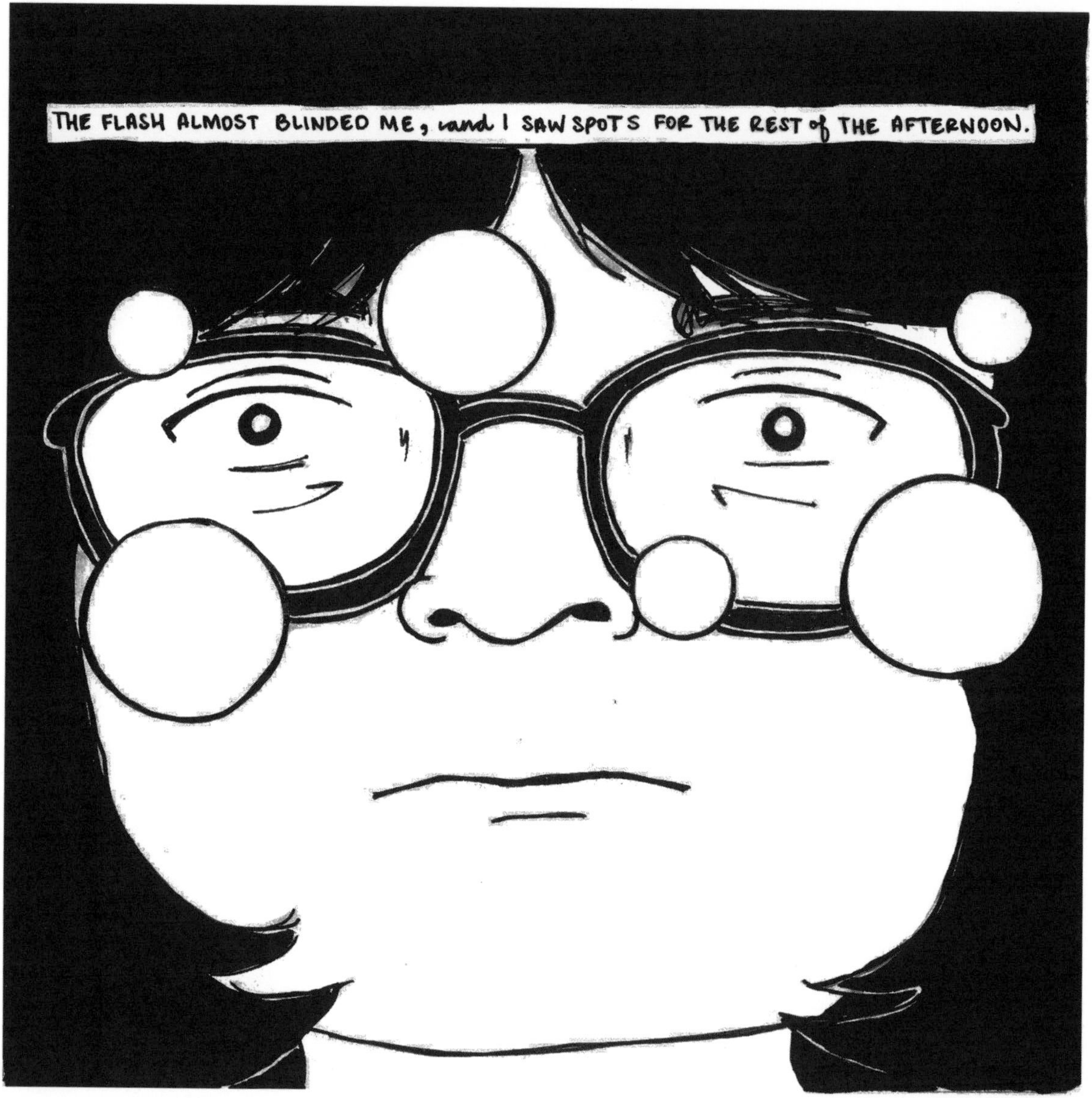
THE FLASH ALMOST BLINDED ME, and I SAW SPOTS FOR THE REST of THE AFTERNOON.

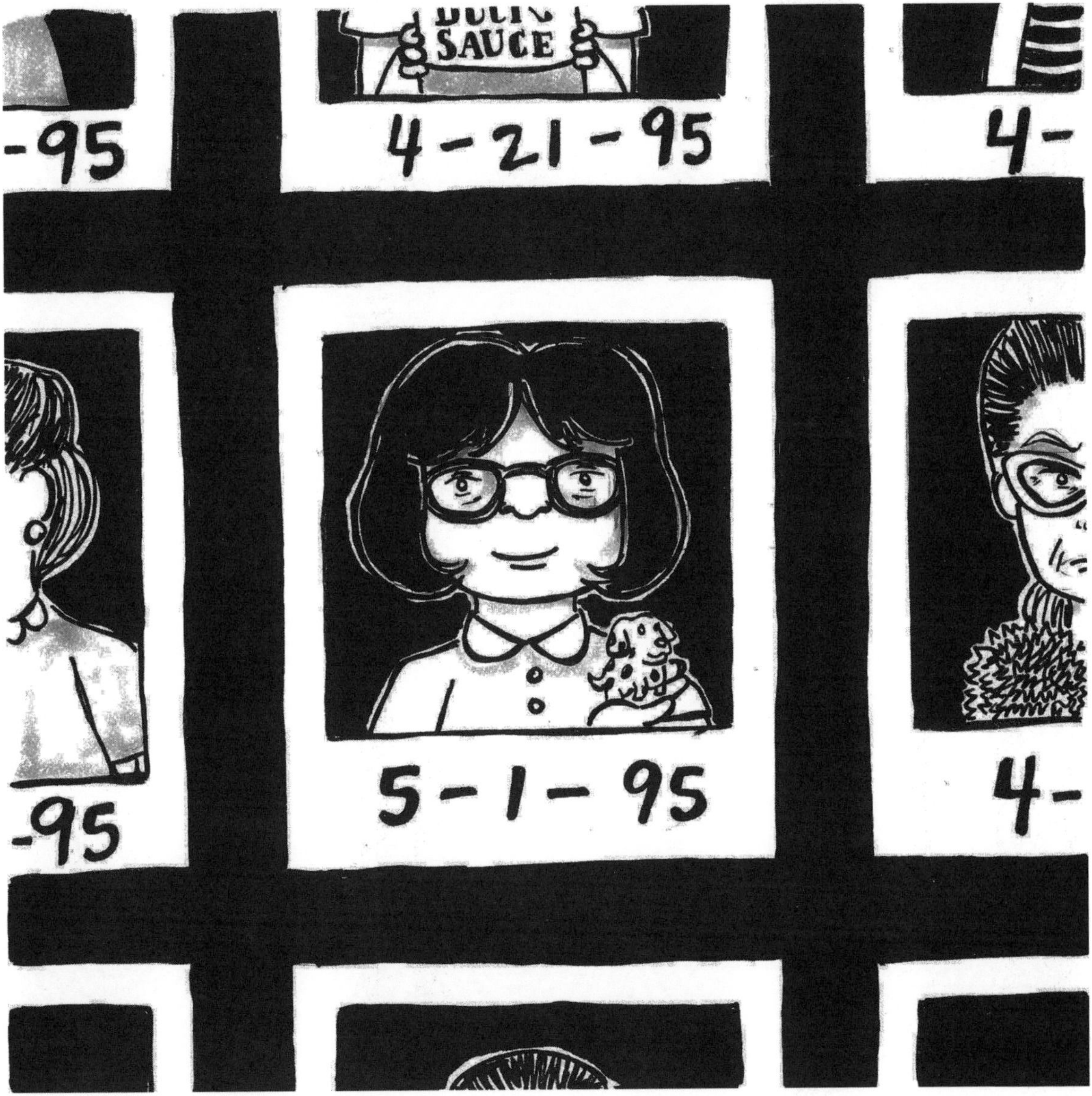
SAUCE
-95
4-21-95
4-
5-1-95
-95
4-

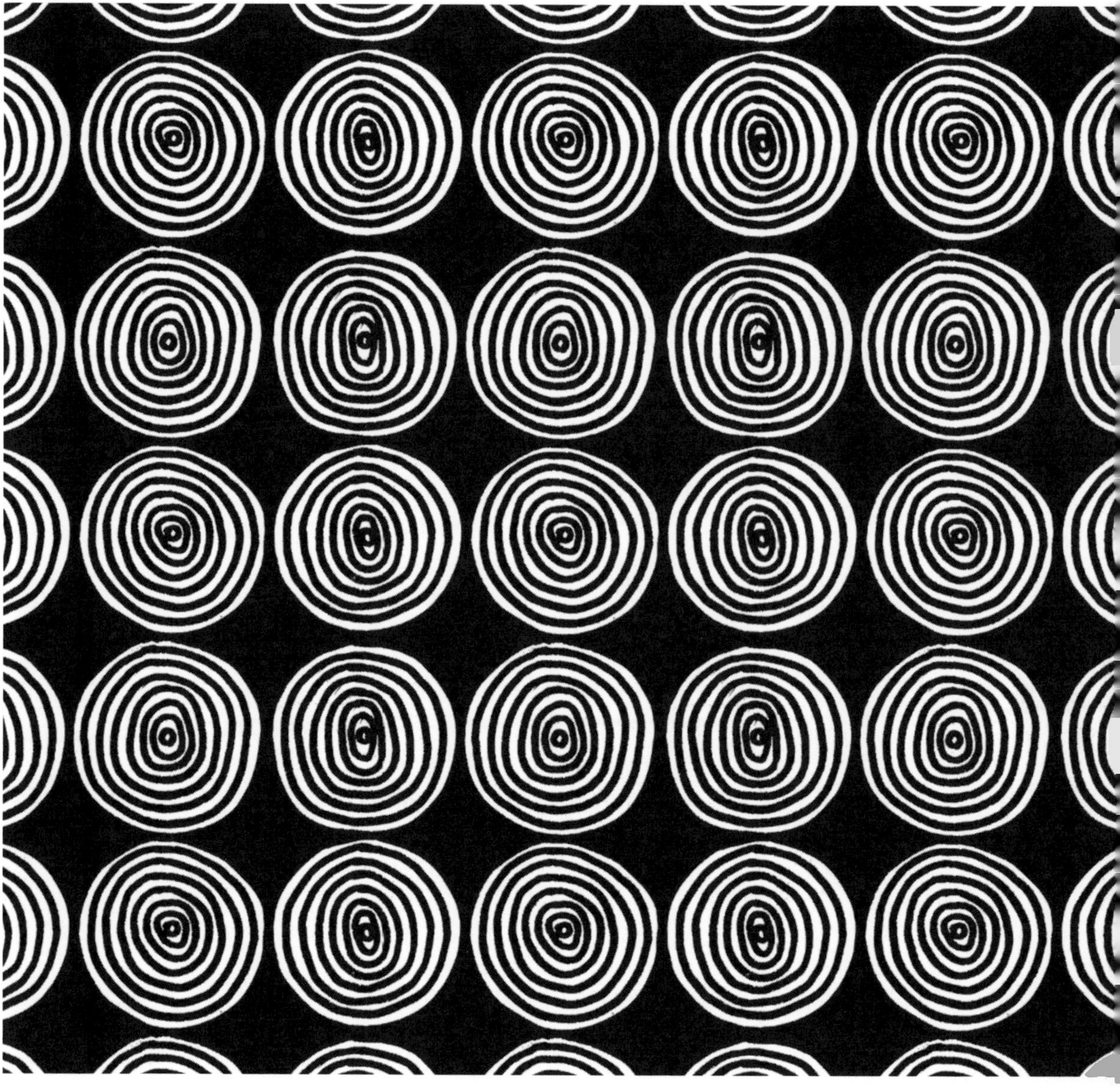

Acknowledgements

Thank you, Kate McKean, Sierra Hahn, and the wonderful team at BOOM! Studios and Archaia, for helping me bring this book to life. Thank you, Nancy Nguyen, Kelly Lin, Thu Doan, and Lauren Rochford, for moral support. Thank you to my professors and classmates in the Pratt Writing Program for reading early drafts of this story. Thank you to my family: Mom, Dad, Christine, and JP. Thank you, Dustin Coates, for being the best. Thank you to Lola and Lolo, for everything.

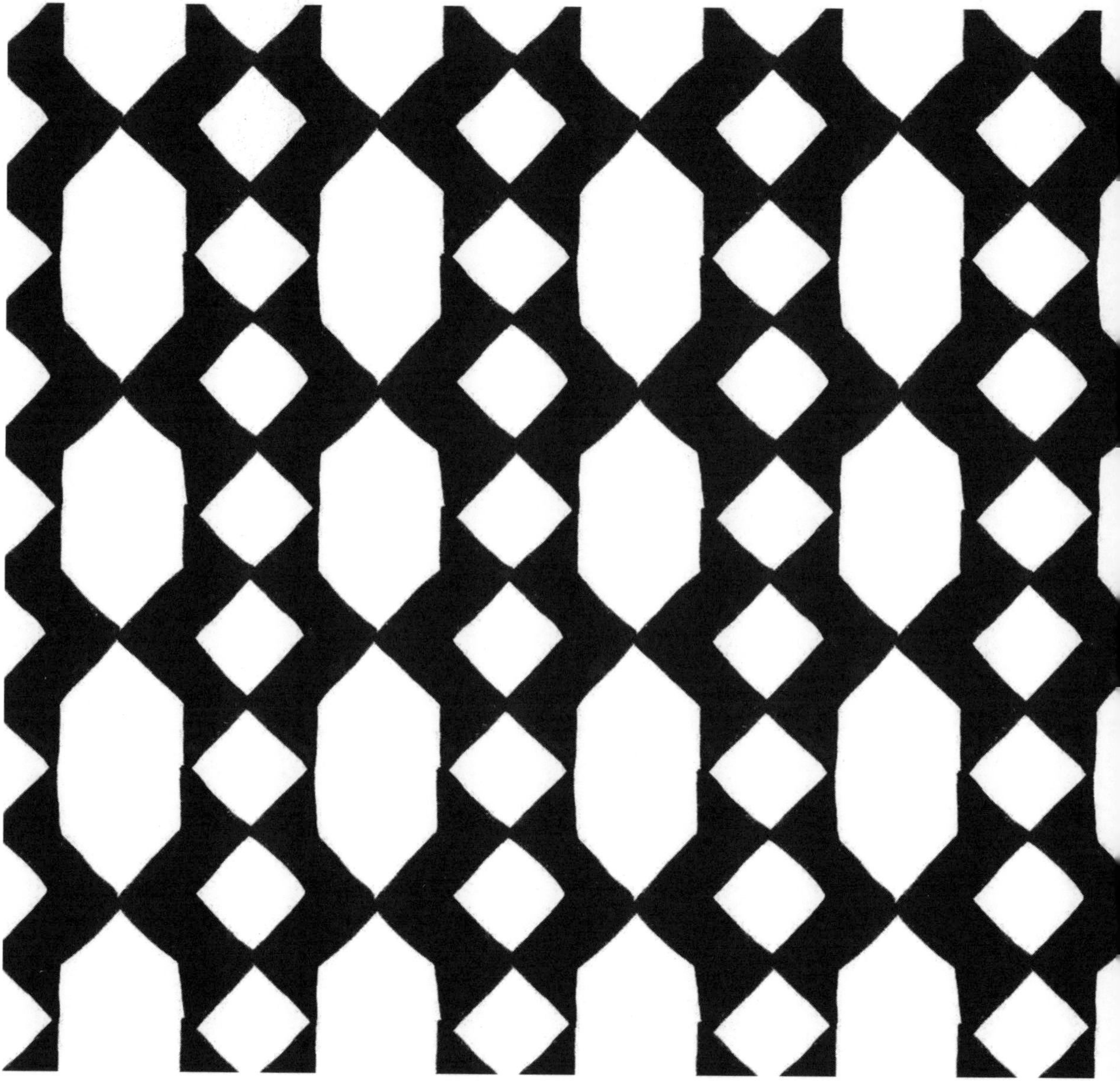

Kate Gavino is a writer and illustrator living in Paris, France. She is the creator of the website, *Last Night's Reading*, which was later published by Penguin Books in 2015. Her work has been featured in BuzzFeed, Lenny Letter, Oprah.com, Rookie, and more.

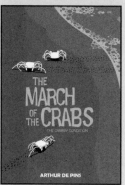

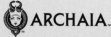

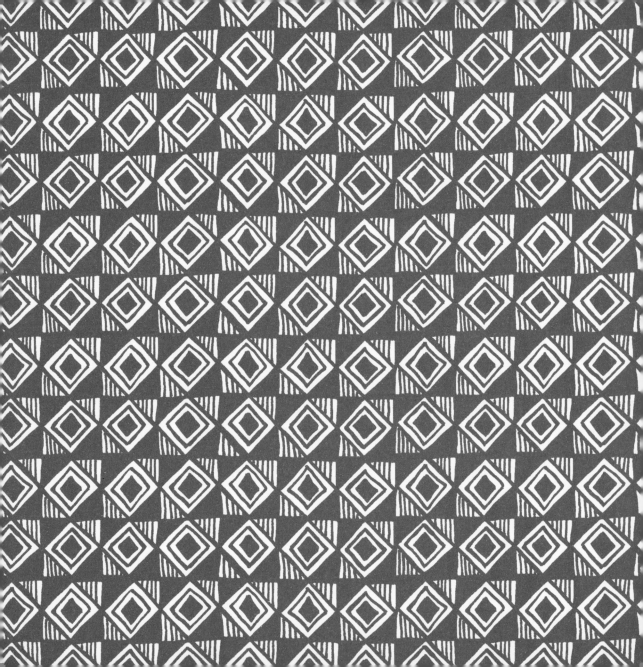